18th Century Records of the German Lutheran Church of Philadelphia,

PENNSYLVANIA
(St. Michael's and Zion)

Volume 2: Baptisms, 1770-1786

Translated by Robert L. Hess, Ph.D.

Edited by F. Edward Wright

HERITAGE BOOKS
2019

HERITAGE BOOKS

AN IMPRINT OF HERITAGE BOOKS, INC.

Books, CDs, and more—Worldwide

For our listing of thousands of titles see our website
at
www.HeritageBooks.com

Published 2019 by
HERITAGE BOOKS, INC.
Publishing Division
5810 Ruatan Street
Berwyn Heights, Md. 20740

International Standard Book Number
Paperbound: 978-1-68034-928-3

18TH-CENTURY RECORDS OF THE GERMAN LUTHERAN CHURCH OF PHILADELPHIA, PENNSYLVANIA
(St. Michael's and Zion)

VOLUME 2: BAPTISMS 1770-1786

CONTENTS

iii

PREFACE

This is the second of a series of volumes, newly translated and transcribed from the original German, of the pastoral records of baptisms, confirmations, marriages, and burials of the German Lutheran congregation at Philadelphia, Pennsylvania (eventually known as *St. Michael's and Zion*) during the Eighteenth Century:

Vol. 1, Baptisms 1745-1769;

Vol. 2, Baptisms 1770-1786;

Vol. 3, Baptisms 1786-1800;

Vol. 4, Marriages 1745-1800 and Confirmations 1745-1769 and 1786;

Vol. 5, Burials 1745-1800.

Acknowledgments

The nine pastors who were appointed to the Philadelphia German Lutheran congregation at one time or another during the 18th Century maintained remarkably consistent and careful records. Frequently they added lagniappes of information describing relationships among the individuals in these records. It seems clear that an assumption by these pastors was that future generations might want to know more about the individuals recorded here. Descendants can be grateful.

Dr. Carl H.A. Schmutzler, pastor of Old Zion Evangelical Lutheran Church, Philadelphia, approved on behalf of that congregation the making and publishing of this translation. (This congregation is the successor to the German Lutheran church at Philadelphia during the 18th Century and as such owns the original register.)

John E. Peterson, archivist of the Lutheran Archives Center at Germantown, Philadelphia, and current custodian of the original register, encouraged the making of this translation, verified need for it, and offered useful suggestions and assistance.

Rebecca J. Hess processed and prepared the five volumes of the transcription here for publication.

INTRODUCTION

Historical Background

Earliest settlers in the area that is now Philadelphia were granted lands there by the colonial goverment of New Sweden in the 1640s, and their religious services were provided by the Swedish state church (Lutheran). The Swedish government continued to support these parishes with ministers and funds even after their colony was taken by the Dutch in 1655, and then in turn taken from the Dutch by England a few years later. The province of Pennsylvania was founded by the English in 1681, and the town of Philadelphia was laid out in 1682 after arranging to relocate the remaining handful of Swedish settlers who had held the site. Freedom of (Christian) worship was a principle on which William Penn founded the new colony. A Swedish Lutheran church that had been constructed in 1669, *Gloria Dei*, was within the limits of the new town of Philadelphia and remained active. Many inhabitants of Philadelphia were English Quakers, who held their religious "meetings" from the beginning. Presbyterian and Baptist congregations were formed in 1695 and met in the same rented building. A Church of England (Episcopalian) church, *Christ Church*, was built at Philadelphia in 1696.

German-speaking people began coming into Pennsylvania in small numbers in 1683, settling first at the village of Germantown eleven miles northwest of Philadelphia (but now within the city limits of Philadelphia). Large numbers of German-speaking immigrants began coming to Philadephia during the 1720s — most of them soon moving on to the frontier, but many remaining in the city.

By 1732 a German-speaking Lutheran congregation existed at Philadelphia, at which time an appeal was made to Europe to provide money and pastors to support it. The Lutherans had no church building there during the 1730s, but in cooperation with the German Reformed congregation they rented a building in which services were held.[1] Itinerant pastor Caspar Stoever (at that time the only Lutheran pastor in all of Pennsylvania) served the German Lutherans at Philadelphia, along with his several other congregations, and in 1733 he started a register for the German Lutherans at Philadelphia listing the names of all the communicants there from 1733 to 1735.[2] The pastor of the Swedish Lutheran Church, John Dylander, then supplied services for the German Lutherans at Philadelphia (and Germantown) until his death in 1741.[1]

In early 1742, arrangements were negotiated for missionaries of the Moravian denomination (who were active among both the Indians and the German-speaking colonists) to provide preaching and the Lutheran sacraments for the Philadelphia German Lutheran congregation. There turned out to be some misgiving concerning the intentions of the Moravians, however, and despite protestations by the Moravians that they now were responsible for the Lutheran

INTRODUCTION

congregation in Philadelphia, they were turned away; thereupon the Moravians built their own church building nearby[1] (but taking with them the Lutheran church book that pastor Stoever had begun earlier).

About this time Lutheran churchmen in Germany, now apparently alarmed over the prospect of losing this and other congregations in Pennsylvania to Moravian missionaries, made preparations to send a fully-qualified Lutheran pastor to Pennsylvania — the Rev. Henry M. Muhlenberg. He arrived at Philadelphia in November 1742 and immediately took steps to take over the Lutheran congregations in and near Philadelphia. Within a year, under his guidance, the Lutherans had erected a church building in Philadelphia; it was called *St. Michael's*.[3]

This congregation subsequently grew very rapidly. By the late 1740s, fifty to sixty baptisms, more than forty marriages, and twenty burials were recorded each year in the churchbook. By the late 1750s there were hundreds of baptisms, marriages, and burials recorded each year. Beginning in 1751, a second pastor was added, and later there were sometimes three pastors. A large schoolhouse was added in 1761, and a number of burial grounds were acquired. The steadily increasing size of the congregation required consruction of a second church building; it was built in 1769, two city blocks from *St. Michael's*; it was called *Zion* church and was one of the largest church buildings in the colonies.[1]

The two churches, *St. Michael's* and *Zion*, were not administered as separate congregations but as a single congregation or parish. The *Zion* church building was sold in 1868, and *St. Michael's* was sold in 1874. (The successor congregation is *Old Zion Evangelical Lutheran Church*, Philadelphia, which in the 21st Century still offers worship services in the German language).

Pastors of the German Lutheran congregation at Philadelphia during the 18th Century were[4]:

1732-1733: Christian Schulz. (There were apparently no German Lutheran records made at Philadelphia during this period.)
1733-1735: J. Caspar Stoever (who listed the communicants of the Philadelphia German Lutheran congregation, in the churchbook later retained by the Philadelphia Moravian congregation[2]).
1737-1741: John Dylander (pastor also of *Gloria Dei* Swedish Lutheran church at Philadelphia, and *St. Michael's* German Lutheran chuch at Germantown). (During this period, any records of German Lutherans at Philadelphia, if they exist, would probably have to have been included in the register of the Swedish Lutheran Church.)
1742: Count N.L. Zinzendorf (a Moravian "Lutheran"), in competition with Valentin Kraft (a self-appointed German Lutheran). (The Moravians

INTRODUCTION

initially claimed responsibility for the register of the German Lutheran congregation at Philadelphia; however, by 1747 it was clear that the Moravian register was that of a separate congregation.[5])

1742-1745: Henry M. Muhlenberg (who recorded the baptisms and marriages of German Lutherans in and around Philadelphia, but the records for these years cannot now be found).

1745-1750: Peter Brunnholtz (initiated the now-surviving register of the German Lutheran congregation at Philadelphia, which subsequent pastors expanded into many books; these are the source for the translation/ transcription here; see below).

1751-1754: Peter Brunnholtz and Matthias Heintzelmann.

1755-1757: Peter Brunnholtz, Matthias Heintzelmann (until 1756), and Frederick Handschu(c)h.

1758-1760: Frederick Handschuch.

1761-1764: Frederick Handschuch and (again) Henry M. Muhlenberg.

1765-1769: Henry M. Muhlenberg and Emanuel Schultze.

1770-1771: Henry M. Muhlenberg, Emanuel Schultze, and John C. Kunze.

1772-1773: Henry M. Muhlenberg and John C. Kunze.

1774-1775: Henry M. Muhlenberg, John C. Kunze, and G. Henry E. Muhlenberg, Jr.

1776-1778: John C. Kunze and G. Henry E. Muhlenberg, Jr.

1779/80-1784: John C. Kunze and Henry Helmuth.

1785-1800+: Henry Helmuth & Frederick Schmidt.

The Original Register

The original register of the German Lutheran congregation at Philadelphia, now kept in the Lutheran Archives at the Lutheran seminary at Germantown, Philadelphia, consists of a series of books.[6] Those containing entries during the period before 1800 are:

Book I: baptisms (1745-1762), marriages (1745-1764), burials (1745-1764), and confirmations (1745-1769) by pastors Brunnholtz, Heintzelman, and Handschuch.

Book II: baptisms (1761-1772), marriages (1761-1772), and burials (1762-1771) by pastors H.M. Muhlenberg, Schultz (pre-1767), and Kunze.

Book III: baptisms (1762-1784), marriages (1771-1784), and burials (1771-1779), by pastors Handschuch, Schultze (after 1767), and Helmuth (in 1779).

Book IV: baptisms (1777-1788), marriages (1777-1792), and burials (1777-1792) by pastors Henry Muhlenberg, Jr., Helmuth (after 1779), and Schmidt.

ix

INTRODUCTION

Book V: baptisms (1789-1799), marriages (1792-1800+), and burials (1792-1800+) by pastor Schmidt; and baptisms (1789-1792) by pastor Helmuth.

Book VI: baptisms (1798-1800+) by pastor Schmidt.

Book VII: baptisms (1793-1800+), marriages (1793-1800+), and burials (1792-1800+) by pastor Helmuth.

Entries in the several volumes of the original register obviously overlapped chronologically. The reason is, that after 1761 the pastors maintained two separate, concurrent lists of pastoral acts. In some years the two separate lists of baptism, marriages, and burials were then entered into the same book, and in other years they were entered into separate books. Even when in the same book, the lists made by different pastors often do not necessarily follow each other chronologically on sequential pages. All this has made it a real challenge, until now, for researchers and translators/transcribers to sort through the original books and pages to find comprehsive lists of baptisms, marriages, or burials for a given year.

Translation, Transcription, and Chronological Structuring

Parts of this register have previously been translated and published. The marriages 1745-1800 were published in the *Pennsylvania Archives*[7] and republished in 1987[8] (but without names of the marriage witnesses, and with the lists for many of the years out of chronological sequence). A transcript of the early baptisms, 1745-1755, was published by the Pennsylvania German Society,[9] then extracted and republished in 1983.[10] Some significant parts of the records between 1762 and 1800 were translated by A.S. Leiby,[11] but this transcript has numerous errors, and the given names in it are artificially anglicized. Extensive pieces of the register are available on the library shelves of the Historical Society of Pennsylvania.[12] The formats of these several volumes, however, are inconsistent; some consist of photocopies of the original German; some are transcripts by Sachse, and others by Leiby. Since the records in these several volumes overlap chronologically, there is no assurance that in total they include all the lists of baptisms, marriages, and burials in the original register.

In planning for this transcript, therefore, it soon became apparent that the most effective way to obtain a comprehensive and chronologically-consistent transcript of the 18th-Century baptisms, confirmations, marriages, and burials was to start by making a fresh translation of all the pre-1800 lists in the above seven books of the original register of the German Lutheran church at Philadelphia[13] — obviously an extensive undertaking. This was done, and each of the resulting lists was annotated with the year, the pastor(s) who made the entries (identified by handwriting, peculiarities in spelling, and associations

X

among lists), and the book of the original register where it had been originally recorded. The annotated lists of baptisms, confirmations, marriages, and burials, were then each compiled in chronological sequence, regardless of the book(s) in which they had been originally recorded, into the five volumes here.

Spelling of Names

Some of the names that appear in this register were those of well-established, widely-known citizens of Philadelphia — not all of them German. (Benjamin Franklin, for example, was recorded as sponsor of a child baptized in December 1749, and of another in December 1753.) Most of the persons named in this register, however, were German, and most were transient residents. Philadephia was the principal debarkation port for German-speaking immigrants pouring into the American colonies, and many of these new immigrants quickly moved onward to the frontiers. Others stayed in the city long enough to perhaps work off indenture bonds, or to marry and have one or two children baptized, before moving on. The pastors of this congregation did have close friends who were members. Even when immigration numbers fell off and the population of the city became relatively stable after the Revolutionary War, however, it seems unlikely that the pastors of this congregation could have had more than passing familiarity with all the many hundreds of individuals whose names were entered in the register there each year.

Consequently, much variation occurred in the spelling of individuals' names in this register. Recall that in the 18th Century, spelling of German surnames was not standardized, either in Europe or America; rather, surnames were spelled phonetically as the respective pastors or scribes thought they should be pronounced in "standard" German. The choice of spelling of an individual's name in the register was up to the pastor who made a given entry, not to the individual, and the several pastors often disagreed among themselves as to the best phonetic spelling of certain surnames.[14] Another factor that affected the phonetic spellings during the 18th Century was that, while the pastors assigned to this urban congregation were highly literate in "standard" German (they all having been university-educated in Germany[5]), the majority of the people of this congregation were of families who had immigrated from places where Palatine-, Swiss-, and other non-"standard" German dialects were spoken; many of the names were thus pronounced with accents different from the "standard" German familiar to the pastors, thus subjecting their phonetic spellings to a pastor's judgment as to how he thought the name should be pronounced in the "standard" German dialect.

Spellings also of the given names in this register were at the pastors' choice. One of the pastors here, for example, consistently spelled out "Margaretha"; a second pastor always spelled this name without the middle "a"; another pastor spelled the same name consistently as "Margarete"; and yet another spelled it "Margreta." Preferences of individual pastors for spelling of names such as Marg(a)ret(h)a(a)(e), "Cat(h)(a)rin(a/e), Elisabet(h)(a)(e), Fri(e)d(e)rich, and He(i)n(e)rich were so consistent that they can be used as a reliable clue for identifying which pastor was responsible for making each list.

It seems obvious that individuals in the 18th Century would not have considered the spelling of their names as they appeared in this (or any other) register to be necessarily "the correct" spelling, nor apparently did they feel any personal obligation to use that spelling subsequently. Family researchers today are advised to keep that in mind. The important point to recognize here is that in this (and other German-language) registers of the 18th Century and before, it was the *pronunciations* of names, not their spellings, that was being documented.

In the transcript here, each name is transcribed exactly as it appeared to be spelled (or abbreviated) in the original of the Philadelphia register. Nine different pastors wrote entries in this register between 1745 and 1800, and the penmanship varied from consistently-legible to moderately difficult (see some examples in the illustration).

Where spelling or dates could not be read unambiguously, either a question mark has been placed here after the name, place, or date, or an alternate reading is given here (in parentheses). In cases where specific letters were illegible, the missing letters are represented here by a blank, __. The translator/transcriber takes responsibility for and regrets any errors of interpretation or transcription. Users of this volume (and of *any* transcript) are urged, if they find entries that are of critical interest to them, to examine them if possible in the original.[16]

For today's readers, certain letters in archaically-spelled names in the original Philadelphia register have been shown in this transcript in parentheses (e.g., the surname *Thiefenbach* in the Philadelphia churchbook is written here as *T(h)iefenbach* (which, without the "h," is how it is pronounced in English, and also how it is spelled now in 20th-Century German). Conversely, a few letters have been <u>added</u> here [in square brackets], again to improve impressions of how a name was/is pronounced (e.g., the surname *Kaz*, in the original Philadelphia churchbook, is transcribed here as Ka[t]z (as it was/is pronounced in English, and is spelled today also in German).

Pastors at Philadelphia in the 18th Century generally used standard feminine endings with the surnames of German females (married and unmarried, with equanimity).[17] Usually this suffix was "-in," (and sometimes was just "-n," particularly after final "r" or "l"). For example, *Schmidtin* was regularly the surname written for a wife of Hans *Schmidt*, and *Müllerin* or *Müllern* was the surname for a wife of Peter *Müller*. These feminine suffixes were usually <u>not</u>

used when writing the surnames of English-speaking females — whose names did constitute a significant percentage of the entries in the Philadelphia register. Use of the feminine endings even with German surnames became optional during the 1790s, and by the year 1800 they are generally absent.

In this translation/transcription, the above suffixes are enclosed in parentheses, because, although these endings were a part of the name as spelled in the original church record, they would not be used in writing the name today (in either German or English).

Personal Titles in the Original Register

The title *Mr.* appears fairly frequently in these Philadelphia church records. It is not known whether this abbreviation was intended to mean the English title "Mister," application of which in English at that time was generally reserved for the gentry; or whether it was intended as the abbreviation for the German word "Meister," which was used to designated master craftsmen; or whether it was intended as the English word "Master," which implied ownership of a slave or an indentured servant. Therefore this title, wherever it appeared in the original, has been transcribed here, in italics, simply as *Mr.* (while the German title "Herr" has been translated here as "Mr." but without italics).

The ministers who made the entries in these Philadelphia church records referred to themselves and to each other sometimes by the title "Pfarrer" (pastor, in English) or sometimes by the title "Prediger" (preacher, in English). Where either of these titles referred to one of the officially-called pastors at the Philadelphia Lutheran Church (see above), both of these titles have been translated here as "pastor" for consistency.

Military titles in the original register appeared sometimes in German but often in English (*e.g.*, either "Hauptmann" or "Captain," either "Soldat" or "soldier"). All the military titles have been transcribed here in the English form.

Titles for women, Frau (Mrs.) or Fraulein (Miss), were not used in the original of the Philadelphia Lutheran register. (In this translation, "Mrs." is sometimes used, but it merely substitutes for the first name of married women in those cases where the first name was not given.) In the original register the word "Frau" or "Ehefrau," when it did appear, consistently meant "wife of" (*e.g.*, "Johannes Schmidt und Frau Anna Maria," or if the wife's name was not known by the pastor, "Johannes Schmidt und Frau").

INTRODUCTION

The Designation "Servant"

Lutheran pastors at Philadelphia used the borrowed English word "servant," rather than the German words "Diener" or "Dienstmädchen," to designate certain individuals. This word "servant" in these German records, had a special meaning; it did not imply a mere occupation, as it does in English today, but identified those persons — men, women, and children — whose services (and behavior) were actually owned by someone else. Wherever this term appeared in the original, therefore, it has been translated here in terms that convey today more accurately what it actually meant at that time, , *i.e.*: "slave" in the case of black "servants," and "bondservant" in the case of the white "servants."

The white bondservants (often referred to now as "indentured servants") were men, women, and children whose services had been sold to a specified master or mistress in compensation for payment of debts they or their parents owed, usually to the master of the ship that had brought them to this country. For whites, the period of bondage stipulated in the contract was typically six or seven years. (For black slaves the period of bondage was in perpetuity.) Owners of "servants" were contractually required to give them food, clothing, and lodging, but these servants were not paid, and they could not quit. On completion of their bondservice, these servants were to be given benefits, depending on their contracts. Husbands and wives who entered servitude were not to be separated except by mutual consent. Those servants bound to serve in Pennsylvania were not to be sold out of the province without their consent. The following is an interesting typical example of such an indenture contract[18]:

"Witnesseth, that Susanna Herbster of her own free will, and consent of her father Laurence Herbster,... hath bound herself servant to ... Christian Schneck [of the Northern Liberties, shoemaker], to serve him ... during the full term of six years, during all of which term she shall serve her master, his executors, administrators, and assigns ... faithfully, and that honestly and obediently in all things as a good and faithful servant ought to do [that is, do whatever the master orders]. And the said Christian Schneck ... shall find and provide for the said servant sufficient meat, drink, apparel, washing, and lodging, and also give her six months' schooling, and ... have her confirmed at the German Lutheran church at Philadelphia,... And at the expiration of her term to have two complete suits of clothes,... also a good bed, bolster, pillows, and blankets worth at least twenty-five dollars...."

Place Names

Some of the places named in this record are no longer found on modern maps of Philadelphia and vicinity: examples are *Point No Point*, on the west bank of

INTRODUCTION

the Delaware River north of Philadelphia, and *Southwark*, which in the early
18th Century was a district in the city of Philadelphia, located just south of the
main part of town. The place called *"the Neck"* which appears fairly often in
these records and is not identifiable; it may have referred to *Penn's Neck*, in
nearby New Jersey.

Some of the places in this record that are identified as being in Philadelphia
County, but outside the city of Philadelphia, are today within the limits of the
city. These include Germantown, the Northern Liberties, Frankford (also spelled
Frankfurt), Kensington, Spring Garden, Lower Dublin, and Byberry as well as
Moyamensing, Passyyunk, Kinsessing, and Upper and Lower Merion Town-
ships. Other places identified in these records as being in Philadelphia County
were in Montgomery County when that county was formed in 1784, including
Whitemarsh, Cheltenham, Abbington, Moreland, Upper Dublin, and Providence
Townships. Many of the men and women named in the register of the
Philadelphia Lutheran church were identified as residents of nearby counties.
Often mentioned were Gloucester County, across the river in what was the
province of West New Jersey; Chester and Bucks Counties in adjoining parts of
Pennsylvania; and more-distant Frederick County in Maryland.

Other German-speaking Churches in (now) Philadelphia

Other German-speaking churches at Philadelphia, where families and
individuals named in this register might also be found, are as follows:

The Moravian church at Philadelphia.
Moravian missionaries were invited in 1742 to provide preachers and a pastor
for the the German Lutheran congregation at Philadelphia (which met at that
time in a rented building). When some of the congregation objected to this
arrangement, the Moravians built their own church building nearby, and several
of the congregation transferred membership there at that time. The Moravians
retained the register that had formerly been used by the German Lutheran
congregation. Marriages and baptisms of the Moravian congregation from 1745
to 1748, are transcribed in the "Church Records of Philadelphia" series, Vol.
Ph1Mr, at the Historical Society of Pennsylvania (also on LDS microfilm
#0020437 Item 7, but catalogued as "St. Michael's Lutheran Church"). The
marriages 1743-1800 were published in the *Pennsylvania Archives*, Ser. 2, Vol.
9, and republished in *Pennsylvania Marriages Prior to 1810*, Vol. 2. (Also on
LDS microfilm #0253247, again on #0823996, and yet again on #0908829).

The (First) Reformed church at Philadelphia.
Reformed and Lutherans at Philadelphia (and elsewhere) often served as baptism
sponsors for each other's children, and they frequently intermarried. Thus,
names of members of both Lutheran and Reformed families are found in each

XV

INTRODUCTION

other's church-books. The Reformed congregation at Philadelphia was in existence by 1725, and they had a church building by 1747.[19] A four-volume transcript was made by W.J. Hinke of the baptisms 1748-1805, confirmations 1768-1831, marriages 1748-1831, and burials 1748-1809 and is at the Evangelical and Reformed Historical Society, Lancaster, PA (and on LDS microfilms #0020352, #0021707, and #1905870). A copy is in the "Church Records of Philadelphia" Ph1R series at the Historical Society of Pennsylvania. Marriages 1748-1802 were published in the *Pennsylvania Archives*, Series 2, Vol. 8 (also on LDS microfilm #0823996 Item 1) and republished in *Pennsylvania Marriages Prior to 1810*, Vol. 1. Records of this congregation were more recently published by F.E Wright in 1997.[20]

The Lutheran church at Germantown (*St. Michael's*).
Germans settled at Germantown before they appeared at Philadelphia. There was a Lutheran congregation at Germantown by 1738; they had a building there soon after.[21] The Lutheran pastors at Germantown and Philadelphia were closely associated, through the *Ministerium* established by Muhlenberg. Names of some individuals and families are found in the registers of both these congregations. Original records of the baptisms 1741-1841, confirmations 1747-1838 (with some gaps), marriages 1751-1841, and burials 1751-1841 are in the Lutheran Archives Center at the Lutheran seminary, Germantown (and on LDS microfilms ##1312443). A transcript of the Germantown records was made in 1896.[22] They were more recently translated by Weiser and Smith and published by Picton Press in 1998.[23]

The Reformed church at Germantown.
A German Reformed congregation existed at Germantown by 1732, and they had a church building by 1739. Between 1746 and 1757 this church operated with the Reformed congregation at Philadelphia, as a single parish.[24] Original records of the Germantown Reformed church, beginning in 1753, are at the Presbyterian Historical Society, Philadelphia (photocopied on LDS microfilm #0503614.) A handwritten transcript made in 1893 is at the Historical Society of Pennsylvania, (and on LDS microfilm #0387867); a typed transcript at at the Evangelical and Reformed Historical Society, Lancaster, PA (and on LDS microfilm #0503614). The records of this congregation were published by F.E. Wright in 1997.[25]

The Swedish Lutheran church at Philadelphia (*Gloria Dei*, or "Old Swedes").
The state church of Sweden (Lutheran) continued to provide religious services for English- and German-speaking people at Philadelphia during much of the 18th Century. From 1737 to 1741 John Dylander, pastor of the Swedish Lutheran church, served concurrently as pastor also of the German Lutheran churches at Philadelphia and Germantown. Baptisms, marriages, and burials at the Swedish Lutheran church beginning in 1750 are on LDS microfilms #034829 to #0384833 and #0511804 to #0511811. Marriages 1750-1810 were published

in *Pennsylvania Archives*, Ser. 2, Vol. 8 (photocopied on LDS microfilms #0874042 and #0823996)..

English-speaking Churches at Philadelphia During the 18th Century

Many of the names found in the baptism, marriage, and burial records here are of English-speaking individuals and families. Some of these names may be found, in addition, in one or more of the following English-speaking churches of Philadelphia:

Christ Church (Church of England/Episcopal) .
A microfilm of the original baptisms, marriages, and burials of Christ Church beginning in 1709 (including the records of *St. Peter's* Church from 1761 to 1832) is in the archives of Old Christ Church, Philadelphia (and also on LDS microfilms #0384707 - #0384708, #1490578 - #1490580, and #1490601). A handwritten transcript made in 1906 is at the Historical Society of Pennsylvania, (and on LDS microfilms #0383276 - #0383283). The marriages 1709-1806 were published in the *Pennsylvania Archives*, Series 2, Vol. 8, and republished in *Pennsylvania Marriages before 1810*, Vol. 1

St. Peter's Church (Church of England/Episcopal).
This church was organized in 1761. The original baptisms, marriages, and burials are included until 1832 in the register of Christ Church, above. A transcript of the *St. Peter's* records is at the Episcopal Diocese, Philadelphia (and photocopied on LDS microfilm #2069126).

St. Paul's Church, Philadelphia (Church of England/Episcopal).
The marriages 1759-1806 were published in the *Pennsylvania Archives*, Series 2, Vol. 9, and republished in *Pennsylvania Marriages before 1810*, Vol. 2. The marriages, baptisms beginning in 1782, and burials beginning in 1790 are on LDS microfilm #1731981.

(*St. George's*) Methodist Episcopal Church, Philadelphia.
Baptisms beginning in 1785, marriages beginning 1789, and burials beginning 1785 are transcribed in the "Church Records of Philadelphia" series, Vol. Ph1M, at the Historical Society of Pennsylvania (also on LDS microfilm #0020437).

First Presbyterian Church, Philadelphia
The marriages 1702-1745 and 1760-1803 were published in the *Pennsylvania Archives*, Series 2, Vol. 9 (also on LDS microfilms #0253247, #0823996 Item 2, and 0908829 Item 1), and republished in *Pennsylvania Marriages before 1810*, Vol. 1. Baptisms 1701-1746 were published in the *Pennsylvania Genealogical Magazine*, Vol. 19, and republished in *Pennsylvania Vital Records*, Genealogical Publishing Co., Vol. 1. (The original baptisms 1701-

1746 and 1760-1806 are photocopied on LDS microfilm #0468374, and the original marriages 1702-1746 and 1760-1803 on LDS microfilm #0505497. A transcript is in the "Church Records of Philadelphia" series, Vol. Ph1P series at the Historical Society of Pennsylvania (also on LDS microfilm #0387873).

Second Presbyterian Church, Philadelphia.
The original baptisms 1745-1870 (with some gaps), marriages 1763-1865 (with gaps), and burials 1782-1833 are at the Presbyterian Historical Socety, Philadelphia (and photocopy on LDS microfilms #0387874). A copy is in the "Church Records of Philadelphia" Ph3P series at the Historical Society of Pennsylvania (also on LDS microfilm #0973460). A transcription of the marriages 1763-1812 was published in *Pennsylvania Archives*, Series 2, Vol. 9 (also on LDS microfilms #0253247, #0823996, and #0908829), and republished in *Pennsylvania Marriages before 1810*, Vol. 2.

Third Presbyterian Church *(Old Pine)*, Philadelphia.
A photocopy of the original records of marriages, baptisms, and communicants beginning in 1768 is at the Presbyterian Historical Socety, Philadelphia (also on LDS microfilms #0901398, #0913134, #0913505, and #0913134). The marriages 1785-1799 were published in the *Pennsylvania Archives*, Series 2, Vol. 9 (also on LDS microfilms #0253247, #0823996, and #0908829), and republished in *Pennsylvania Marriages before 1810*, Vol. 2.

Scots Presbyterian Church (Associate Presbyterians), Philadelphia.
A photocopy and a typescript of the baptisms 1767-1806 and burials 1772-1806 are at the Presbyterian Historical Society, Philadelphia (and on LDS microfilm #0525749); a handwritten transcript of the same records is on LDS microfilm #0505492. Admissions, 1782-1809, are on LDS microfilm #0504372.

First Baptist Church, Philadelphia.
A microfilm of the original records of this congregation is held by the Historical Commission of the Southern Baptist Convention, Nashville; minutes of their meetings began in 1757. The marriage records 1745-1855 and membership registers 1775-1894 are on LDS microfilms #0986474 and #098675. Marriages 1761-1803 were published in the *Pennsylvania Archives*, Series 2, Vol. 8 (and are on LDS microfilms #0874042, Item 1, and #0823996, Item 1).

The Baptist Church, Lower Dublin Township (now part of Philadelphia).
Records beginning in 1689 were published in the *Pennsylvania Magazine of History and Biography*, Vol. 11, and republished in *Pennsylvania Vital Records*, Genealogical Publishing Co., Vol. 1.

INTRODUCTION

Society of Friends (Quaker) Monthly Meetings in Philadelphia.
Original records of monthly meetings at various places in Philadelphia
(including records of births, marriages, deaths, removals, and members) are kept
on microfilm at the Department of Friends' (Quaker's) Records, Philadelphia
(and on LDS microfilms #0020405, #0020418, and #0020465 - #0020478).
These include: the Philadelphia Monthly Meetings, beginning 1677 (limited to
the Middle District after 1773); the Northern District Monthly Meetings,
beginning 1722; the Southern District Monthly Meetings, beginning 1772; and
Green Street Monthly Meetings, beginning 1775. A handwriten transcript of
these original records is at the Historical Society of Pennsylvania (and on LDS
microfilms #0384860 and #038486). The marriages authorized 1682-1756 were
published in the *Pennsylvania Archives*, Series 2, Vol. 9, and republished in
Pennsylvania Marriages before 1810, Vol. 2 (also on LDS microfilms
#0253247, #0823996, and #0908829). The Philadelphia Quaker marriages,
births, and deaths 1682-1800 have been recently republished.[26]

St. Joseph's Catholic Church.
The baptisms beginning in 1758 were published in the Journal of the American
Catholic Historical Society in 1893. The baptisms 1758-1781 were extracted
and republished about 1984 by B. O'Keefe (and are on LDS fisches #6125381,
#61253840, and #6126453). Marriages and baptisms 1771-1786 were extracted
by T.C. Middleton (and are on LDS microfilm #0496869).

END NOTES

1. C.H. Glatfelter, *Pastors and People*, German Lutheran and Reformed
churches in the Pennsylvania field, 1717-1793, Pennsylvania German Society;
Vol. 1, pages 412-413.

2. 1733-1735 list of communicants of the German Lutheran church at Philadelphia, in a section of the register that the Moravians retained when their
members separated from the German Lutherans in 1742; original in Manuscript
Am 7061 in the Historical Society of Pennsylvania (and photocopy on LDS
microfilm #0020437 Item 7).

3. The name *St. Michael's* was given also to the Lutheran church established at
Germantown (now also part of Philadelphia), a fact that has been cause for
confusion among many historians.

4. *Pastors and People*, Vol. I, pages 419-420.

5. Register of the members of the Moravian church at Philadelphia in 1747;
manuscript Am-7085 at the Historical Society of Pennsylvania, Philadelphia.

6. The original register of the German Lutheran church at Philadelphia, consisting of nine books covering the period from 1745 to 1839, is now kept in the Lutheran Archives Center, located at the Lutheran seminary, Germantown, Philadelphia. (Also on microfilm at the Historical Society of Pennsylvania; also on LDS microfilms #1312256 - #1312258).

7. *Pennsylvania Archives*, Series 2, Vol. 9, Marriages of St. Michael's and Zion Lutheran Church, 1745-1800. Also on LDS microfilms #0253247 (filmed in 1961), #0823996 (1971), and #0908829 (1973).

8. *Pennsylvania Marriages prior to 1810*, Genealogical Publishing Co., Baltimore, 1987; Vol 2, Philadelphia Lutheran (St. Michael's and Zion).

9. *Pennsylvania German Society Proceedings*; Vols. 7, 8, and 9. (Also on LDS microfilms #0924110, Item 1, and #0982161, Item 1).

10. *Pennsylvania German Church Records*, Genealogical Publishing Co., Baltimore, 1983; Vol. 1, Philadelphia Lutheran baptisms, 1745-1755.

11. Leiby's translation is at the Evangelical and Reformed Archives, Lancaster, PA: Vol. 1, baptisms, 1762-1784; Vol. 2, baptisms, 1777-1799; Vol. 3, marriages, 1777-1821; Vol. 4, marriages, 1771-1784; and Vol. 5, burials, 1771-1779 and 1777-1834. (Note that these volumes overlap chronologically, and they do not correlate with the Book numbers of the original register.) Leiby's translation is also on LDS microfilms #0940904 and #0940905. Copies of these volumes of Leiby's translation are also included as Volumes 7, 9, 10. and 12 of the Ph2L series at the Historical Society of Pennsylvania; see next endnote.

12. Historical Society of Pennsylvania, Philadelphia; Ph2L series, Records of the German Lutheran Church at Philadelphia before 1800. This Ph2L series consists, specifically, of: Vol. 1, Sachse's transcript of baptisms 1745-1759 (also on LDS microfilm #1035750); Vol II, transcript of baptisms 1751-1771; Vol. 3, photocopy of original baptism entries, 1762-1784; Vol 4, Sachse's transcript of marriages 1745-1764 (also on LDS microfilm #1035750 Item 10); Vol. 5, transcript of lists of burials 1745-1771; Vol. 6, photocopy of marriages 1771-1784 and burials 1771-1779 in German; Vol. 7, Leiby's translation/transcript of baptisms 1762-1784; Vol. 8, transcript of Stover's list of communicants 1733-1735, from the (now) Moravian register; Vol. 9, Leiby's transcript of marriages 1777-1818; Vol. 10, transcript of baptisms 1777-1788; and Vol. 12, transcript of burials 1777-1804 (from Books IV and V of the original).

13. The original register, consisting of nine books covering the period from 1745 to 1839, is now kept in the Lutheran Archives Center, co-located with the Lutheran seminary, Germantown, Philadelphia. It was filmed by the Genealogical Society of Utah in 1946 and filmed again in 1982 (LDS microfilms #1312256 - #1312258).

INTRODUCTION

14. For example, a name like "Meyer" was also correctly spelled, phonetically, as "Mayer," "Meier," or "Maier"; while "Stoh" and "Stoo" were both phonetically correct alternatives for the surname that was later anglicized as "Stow." (Toward the end of the 18th Century many Philadelphia German families, influenced by English practice, began adopting permanent, or "correct," spellings of their family's surnames, but this of course did not change the spellings that had been recorded earlier in the register.)

15. See *Pastors and People*, Vol. I, Part I, "The Pastors."

16. The original register of the German Lutheran church of Philadelphia, in nine books, is archived in the Lutheran Archives Center at the Lutheran Seminary, Germantown, Philadelphia, PA, where it is accessible to researchers. The staff there is very helpful. A photocopy of these original books is on microfilm at the Historical Society of Pennsylvania, Philadelphia (also on LDS microfilms #1312256 - #1312258.)

17. These feminine endings may have constituted a mere "standard-German" formality for the sake of the church records. Final "n's" were unpronounced, for example, in the Pennsylvania and other German dialects spoken by many inhabitants of Philadelphia. On the other hand, some women of this congregation (perhaps those of the more "proper" families?) seem to have preferred the feminine ending with their surnames, both for themselves and their daughters.

18. F. Grubb, *German Immigrant Service Contracts*, register at the port of Philadelphia 1817-1871, published by Genealogy Publishing Co., 1994; pages viii-ix.

19. *Pastors and People*; Vol. I, page 414.

20. F.E. Wright, *Early Church Records of the First Reformed Church of Philadelphia*, 1997: Vol. I, 1748-1780; Vol. 2, 1781-1800.

21. *Pastors and People*; Vol. I, page 408.

22. Series Ph7L of the Records of Churches of Philadelphia before 1800, at the Historical Society of Pennsylvania (also on LDS microfilms #0387895 and #037896.)

23. F.S. Weiser & D.B. Smith, *St. Michael's Evangelical Lutheran Church*, Germantown (now part of Philadelphia), Pennsylvania, 1741-1841, Picton Press, Rockport, ME, 1998.

24. *Pastors and People*, Vol. I, page 410.

25. F.E. Wright, *18th Century Records of the Germantown Reformed Church of Pennsylvania*, taken fom the church register transcribed by W.J. Hinke.

26. A. Miller Watring, *Early Quaker Records of Philadelphia*; in two volumes.

1770, First List
(baptisms by pastors H.M. Muhlenberg and Kunze, all in approximate
chronological sequence, from Book II after the burials)

Joh. Jacob, of Joh. Gerhard Mutzfeld and wife Maria Barbara, b. 29 Dec 1769, bapt. 5 Jan 1770. Sponsors: Jacob Masholder and wife Margretha

Susanna Margretha, of Andreas Hoflinger and wife Margretha, b. 24 Dec 1769, bapt. 7 Jan 1770. Sponsors: Joh. Martin Schnepf and wife Magdalena.

Joh. Jacob, of Andreas Hoflinger and wife Margretha, b. 25 Dec 1769, bapt. 7 Jan 1770. Sponsors not given [same as above?].

Johannes, of Johannes Lepy and wife Elisabeth, b. 8 May 1769, bapt 14 Jan 1770. Sponsors: Johannes Straub and wife Anna Regina.

Sara, of Jeremia Collins and wife Ann, 9 months old on 27 Jan, bapt. 19 Jan 1770. Sponsors: John Gard and wife Elizabeth.

Joseph, of Peter Rose and wife Elisabeth, b. 14 Dec 1769, bapt. 21 Jan 1770. Sponsors: Peter Klein and wife Eva Maria.

Maria Christina, of Michael Schöneck and wife Catharina, b. 6 Jan 1770, bapt. 21 Jan 1770. Sponsors: Adam Hold and wife Maria Catharina.

Barbara, of Johannes Pig and Barbara Diedel(in), b. 24 Dec 1769, bapt. 21 Jan 1770. Sponsors: Daniel (surname obscured) and Barbara Beyer(in).

Anna Maria, of Joh. Georg Lohrmann and wife Anna Justina, b. 15 Jan 1770, bapt. 22 Jan 1770. Sponsors: the parents.

Juliana, of Joh. Bernhard Rebhun and wife Susanna, b. 14 Jan 1770, bapt. 25 Jan 1770. Sponsors: Christian Danecker and wife Juliana.

Christina Margretha, of Caspar Giess and wife Christina, b. 14 Jan 1770, bapt. 28 Jan 1770. Sponsors: Michael Giess and wife Margretha.

Maria Dorothea, of Esther Nesch (a soldier's wife), illegitimate, b. 26 Jan 1770, bapt. 4 Feb 1770. Sponsors: widow Maria Dorothea Schmidt(in)

Christina Elisabeth, of Johannes Garretson and wife Hanna, b. 15 Jan 1770, bapt. 4 Feb 1770. Sponsors: Daniel Häfner and Christin Elisab.

Jacob, of Frederich Werner and wife Maria, b. 13 Jan 1770, bapt. 4 Feb 1770. Sponsors: the parents.

Heinrich, of Anthon Tailer (Catholic) and wife Sybilla Regina, b. 13 Jan 1770, bapt. 11 Feb 1770. Sponsors: Henrich Nagel and wife.

Francis, of Jacob Gottinger and wife Anna Margretha, b. 15 Jan 1770, bapt. 11 Feb 1770. Sponsors: Francis Wolf and wife Anna Margreth.

Johann Georg, of *Mr.* Conrad Abel and wife Margretha, b. 27 Jan 1770. bapt. 11 Feb 1770. Sponsors: Joh. Georg Seitz and wife Elisabeth.

Samuel, of Samuel Printz and wife Anna, b. 7 Feb 1770, bapt. 11 Feb 1770 Sponsors: the father and widow Margretha Huber(in).

Joh. Michael, of Johannes Greiffenstein and wife Maria Dorothea, b. 3 Feb 1770, bapt. 11 Feb 1770. Sponsors: Michael Hotz and wife Catharina.

Pamelia, of Johannes Kehr and wife Sophia (English), b. 9 Feb 1770, bapt. 11 Feb 1770. Sponsors: Amos tailor and Rachel Parmer.

Agnes Henrica, of Daniel Behrens and wife Maria, b. 25 Dec 1769?, bapt, 8 Feb 1770. Sponsor: Agnes Henrica Katz(in).

Anna Philippina, of Mathias Holler and wife Catharina, b. 1? Oct 1769, bapt. 1? Feb 1770. Sponsors: the grandmother Anna Cunig. and her son Jacob?.

Joh. Ernst, of Johannes Mängen and wife Catharina, b. 27 Jan 1770, bapt. 4 Feb 1770. Sponsors: Ernst Mängen and wife.

Joh. Henrich, of Johannes Weiss and wife Maria Margretha, b. 22 Jan 1770, bapt. 18 Feb 1770. Sponsors: Johannes Müller and wife Charlotta.

Maria Elisabeth, of Michael Ginsler and wife Maria Elisabeth, b. 4 Feb 1770, bapt. 18 Feb 1770. Sponsors: Balthas Ginsler and wife Maria Elisabeth.

Ludwig, of Adam Maurer and wife Maria. b. 11 Feb 1770, bapt. 18 Feb 1770. Sponsors: Jacob Reinthaler and wife Maria.

Michael, of Joh. Christoph Senderling and wife Magdalena, b. 16 Jan 1770, bapt. 18 Feb 1770. Sponsors: Michael Leiderle and wife Elisab. (the grandparents).

Hannah, of Jacob Diller (Cath.) and wife Barbara (Luth.), b. 30 Jan 1769, bapt. 18 Feb 1770. Sponsors: Simon Heberle and wife Anna (the grandparents, Lutheran).

Maria Christina, of Adam Ohl and wife Maria Christina, b. 2 Feb 1770, bapt. 18 Feb 1770. Sponsors: David Frischmuth and Barbara (surname obscured), both single.

Christian, of Christian Appel and wife Margreth, b. 22 Feb 1770, bapt. 28 Feb 1770. Sponsors: Christian Kucher and wife Anna Elisabeth.

Joh. Samuel, of Samuel Rondecker and wife Dorothea, b. 12 Feb 1770, bapt. 25 Feb 1770. Sponsors: Joh. Christoph Heinkel and wife Maria.

Anna Catharina, of Peter Biswanger and wife Eva, b. 15 Jan 1770, bapt. 25 Feb 1770. Sponsors: Mr. Johannes Bigler and wife Anna.

Philippina, of Johannes Weng and wife Magdalena, b. 5 Jan 1770, bapt. 4 Mar 1770. Sponsors: Philip Brendle and wife Christina.

James, of Hanna Mallery (a mulatto) and allegedly James McQuiny (illegitimate), b. 8 Nov 1769, bapt. 5 Mar 1770. Sponsor: Mary Jones (a negress).

Adam, of John Amour and wife Mary, b. 25 Oct 1769, bapt. 8 Mar 1770. Sponsors: John Hook and Mary Bambow.

Elisabeth, of John Hook and wife Margretha, b. 22 Feb 1770, bapt. 8 Mar 1770. Sponsors: George Bremmer, Elisabeth Reed, and Cath. Toy.

Rosina, of Philip Lehrer and wife Ursula, b. 22 Sep 1769, bapt. 11 Mar 1770. Sponsors: Melcher Schwerer and wife Rosina.

Maria Magdalena, of Jacob Chress and wife Susanna, b. 13 Feb 1770, bapt. 11 Mar 1770. Sponsors: Johannes Schütz and wife Maria Margretha.

Christina, of Joh. Peter Staut and wife Anna Barbara, b. 31 Dec 1769, bapt. 30 Mar 1770. Sponsors: the parents.

Maria Salome, of Martin Gassner and wife Maria Agnes, b. 3 Feb 1770, bapt. 11 Mar 1770. Sponsors: Henrich Gassner and wife Maria Salome.

Joh. Matthias, of Joh. Paul Dollman and wife Sybilla Catharina, b. 26 Feb 1770, bapt. 11 Mar 1770. Sponsors: Joh. Matthias Dollman and sister Maria Margretha.

Wilhelm, of Andreas Grübel and wife Regina, b. 13 Feb 1770, bapt. 11 Mar 1770. Sponsors: Georg Laib and wife Dorothea.

Johannes, of Christian Minck and wife Anna Catharina, b. 21 Feb 1770, bapt. 18 Mar 1770. Sponsors: Johannes Fritz and wife Anna Catharina.

Catharina, of Henrich Pfiester and wife Barbara, b. 8 Mar 1770, bapt. 18 Mar 1770. Sponsors: Friedrich Ulrich and wife Catharina.
Anna Maria, of Matthias Landeberger and wife Maria Magdalena, b. 6 Mar 1770, bapt. 18 Mar 1770. Sponsors: Thomas Meyer and wife Anna Margretha.
Sophia, of Daniel Burkhard and wife Elisabeth, b. 19 Feb 1770, bapt. 25 Mar 1770. Sponsors: Friedrich Chressler and wife Sophia.
Christopher, of Jacob Penter and wife Dorothea, b. 3 Jan 1770, bapt. 25 Mar 1770. Sponsors: Christoph Behres and wife Dorothea.
Georg Philip, of Georg Türnis and wife Maria Catharina, b. 9 Dec 1769, bapt. 25 Mar 1770. Sponsors: Philip Lader and wife Elisabeth.
Wilhelm, of Henrich Dietz and wife Maria Barbara, b. 9 Mar 1770, bapt. 25 Mar 1770. Sponsors: Wilhelm Engelfried and wife Barbara.
Anna Maria, of Wilhelm Herman and wife Anna Margretha, b. 8 Mar 1770, bapt. 25 Mar 1770. Sponsors: Mr. Wm. Eckard and wife Anna Margretha.
Joh. Michael, of Michael Krebs and wife Catharina, b. 11 Mar 1770, bapt. 25 Mar 1770. Sponsors: Michael Stemler and wife Philippina.
Joh. Jacob, of Christian Persie and wife Maria Magdal., b. 23 Feb 1770, bapt. 25 Mar 1770. Sponsors: Joh. Zacharias Enders and wife Maria Magdalena.
Joh. Georg, of Christoph Kocher and wife Juliana, b. 28 Apr 1769, bapt. 25 Mar 1770. Sponsors: Henrich Henke and wife Maria Elisabeth.
Andreas, of Henrich Steinmetz and wife Barbara, 15 Feb 1770, bapt 25 Mar 1770. Sponsors: Andreas Pärtsch and wife.
Anna Maria, of Philip Setzler and wife Maria, b. 23 Feb 1770, bapt. 25 Mar 1770. Sponsors: Maria Grübel and her brother John Grübel.
Anna Maria, of Philip Schep and wife Maria, b. 28 Jan 1770, bapt. 25 Mar 1770. Sponsors: the parents.
Barbara, of Marcus Doman (Swiss Ref.) and wife Louisa (Luth.), b. 14 Mar 1770, bapt. 1 Apr 1770. Sponsors: Philip Weinemer and wife Barbara.
Susanna, of Henrich Ritter and wife Catharina, b. 6 Jul 1769, bapt. 31 Mar 1770. Sponsors: Michael Burger? and Margreth Ritter.
Julianna, of Jacob Bender and wife Maria, b. 13 Mar 1770, bapt. 1 Apr 1770. Sponsors: Rudolph Banner and wife Ursula.
Maria Eva, of Joh. Martin Sommer and wife Maria, b. 1 Mar 1770, bapt. 1 Apr 1770. Sponsors: Joh. Friedrich Paisch and wife Maria Eva.
Elisabeth, of James? Williams (a negro) and wife __merit, 9 weeks old tomorrow, bapt. 1 Apr 1770. Sponsor: Johannes Tend_rist (a negro).
Christoph, of Adam Grob and wife Elisabeth, b. 4 Apr 1770, bapt. 5 Apr 1770. Sponsors: Sebastian Seibert, and Christoph Robaust and wife Catharina.
Johann Adam, of Johannes Rup and wife Maria Dorothea, b. 19 Mar 1770, bapt. 8 Apr 1770. Sponsors: the parents.
Margretha Catharina, of Mstr. Joh. Philip Truckenmüller and wife Anna Cath., b. 27 Mar 1770, bapt. 8 Apr 1770. Sponsors: Peter Kraft and wife Margretha.
Ann, of David Richardson and wife Ann, b. 1 Apr 1770, bapt. 8 Apr 1770. Sponsors: the parents.
Anna Barbara, of Wygand Specher and wife Regina, b. 28 Dec 1769, bapt. 16 Apr 1770. Sponsors: the mother, and Georg Faseler.

Anna Catharina, of Georg Soeferentz and wife Catharina, b. 25 Mar 1770, bapt. 16 Apr 1770. Sponsors: Ludwig Hess and wife Anna Catharina.

Elisabeth, of Theobald Storck and wife Rosina, b. 1 Apr 1770, bapt. 16 Apr 1770. Sponsors: Elisabeth (surname not given), and Friedrich Schick (single).

Elisabeth, of Peter David Henzel and wife Anna Dorothea, b. 25 Dec 1768, bapt. 16 Apr 1770. Sponsors: the parents.

Joh. Jacob, of Georg Dürr and wife Maria Christina, b. 14 Dec 1769, bapt. 16 Apr 1770. Sponsors: Georg Michael Kraft and wife Johanna Maria.

Conrad, of Johannes Rink and wife Magdalena, b. 2 Oct 1769, bapt. 16 Apr 1770. Sponsors: Conrad Müller and wife Catharina.

Anna Maria, of Michael Anthony and wife Catharina, b. 9 Mar 1770, bapt. 16 Apr 1770. Sponsors: the parents.

Anna Maria [twin?], of Georg Schütz and wife Catharina, birthdate not given, bapt. in Apr 1770. Sponsors: Joh. Philip Klamper and wife Anna Christina.

Joh. Philip [twin?], of Georg Schütz and wife Catharina, b. 25 Dec 1769, bapt. in Apr 1770. Sponsors: same as above.

A child (name not given), of Daniel Bender and wife Sophia Susanna, birth and bapt. dates not given. Sponsors: the parents, and others (names not given).

Elisabeth, of Henrich Kress and wife Anna Maria, b. 16 Apr 1770, bapt. the same day. Sponsors: William Weber and wife Elisabeth.

Anna Maria [twin], of Joh. Jacob Ehrenfeuchter and wife Susanna Margr., b. 21 Apr 1770, bapt. 22 Apr 1770. Sponsors: the parents, and Christiana Kaltmüller(in).

Susanna [twin], of Joh. Jacob Ehrenfeuchter and wife Susanna Margr., b. 21 Apr 1770, bapt. 22 Apr 1770. Sponsors: same as above.

Christina, of Joh. Georg Keuler and wife Barbara, 13 weeks old, bapt. 22 Apr 1770. Sponsors: Joh. Jacob Hentzman (single), and Cath. Müller(in).

Anna Maria, of Joh. Diethrich Riess and wife Rosina Christiana, b. 12 Apr 1770, bapt. 21 Apr 1770. Sponsors: Friedrich Rohr and wife.

Maria Elisabeth, of Conrad Hof and wife Sybilla, b. 9 Apr 1770, bapt. 25 Apr 1770. Sponsors: Joh. Schreiber and wife Elisabeth.

Georg Adam, of Jacob Lintz and wife Anna Maria, b. 13 Apr 1770, bapt. 29 Apr 1770. Sponsors: Georg Adam Bub and wife Catharina.

Peter, of Michael Stauch and wife Anna Margretha, 4 Apr 1770, bapt. 29 Apr 1770. Sponsors: Peter Wagner and wife Dorothea.

George, of Ludewig Brun and wife Sarah, b. 6 Apr 1770, bapt. 29 Apr 1770. Sponsors: George Christein and his mother.

Sarah, of Johannes Fritz and wife Catharina, b. 19 Apr 1770, bapt. 30 Apr 1770. Sponsors: Caspar Geyer and wife Elisabeth.

Matthias, of Andreas Hayer and wife Maria Clara, b. 10 Apr 1770, bapt. 6 May 1770. Sponsors: Matthias Hayer and wife (of New York).

Joh, Georg, of Jacob Schaich and wife Anna Magdalen, b. 2 May 1770, bapt. 27 May 1770. Sponsors: Georg Kiefer and wife.

Maria Elisabeth, of Valentin Hagner and wife Margretha, b. 13 May 1770, bapt. 27 May 1770. Sponsors: Peter Gabel and wife Maria Elisabeth.

Andreas, of Joh. Michael Häntzman and wife Catharina, b. 17 May 1770, bapt. 27 May 1770. Sponsors: Andreas Bauer and wife Barbara.

Johann Christian, of Johann Mauss and wife Anna, b. 12 May 1770, bapt.
27 May 1770. Sponsors: Christian Dürck and wife Maria.

Maria Elisabeth, of Joh. Friedr. Truckenmüller and wife Christina, b. 2 May
1770, bapt. 13 May 1770 at Heidelberg Town [Schaefferstown?]. Sponsors:
Andreas Hefer and wife Eva Elisabeth.

Regina, of Richard Slew and Elisabeth (negroes), b. in Mar 1765, bapt. 20 May
1770 by Mr. Weiser at Heidelberg [Township?] in Berks County. Sponsor:
Maria Catharina Gensemer.

Georg, of Richard Slew and Elisabeth (negroes), b. 17 May 1770, bapt. 20 May
1770 at Heidelberg. Sponsor: Georg Kreb (a negro).

Susannah, of Ernst Christoph Adam and wife Catharina, b. 23 Apr 1770, bapt.
4 Jun 1770. Sponsors: Caspar Gasner and wife Catharina.

Christina Dorothea, of Andreas Beck and wife Margreth, b. 15 May 1770, bapt.
4 Jun 1770. Sponsors: Michael Götz and wife Barbara.

Jacob, of Martin Lantz and wife Juliana, b. 23 May 1770, bapt. 4 Jun 1770.
Sponsors: Jacob Veit and Anna Mog (single).

Joh. Conrad, of Joh. Michael Fuchs and wife Salome, b. 28 Apr 1770, bapt.
4 Jun 1770. Sponsors: Conrad Leibbrand and wife Elisabeth.

Elisabeth, of Conrad Leibbrand and wife Elisabeth, b. 8 Apr 1770, bapt. 4 Jun
1770. Sponsors: Michael Fuchs and wife Salome.

James, of John Jackson and wife Catharine, b. 24 May 1770, bapt. 5 Jun 1770.
Sponsors: Bernhard Rebhun and wife Sophia.

Catharina, of Andreas Stahl and wife Anna Magdal., b. 24 Mar 1770, bapt. 5 Jun
1770. Sponsors: the parents.

Michael, of David Fuchs and wife Margretha, b. 7 Feb 1770, bapt. 10 Jun 1770.
Sponsors: Georg Lange and wife Susanna.

Johann Martin, of Georg Ludwig Barthel and wife Christina, b. 27 Apr 1770,
bapt. 10 Jun 1770. Sponsors: Joh. Martin Wolf and Christina Barthel.

Joh. Peter, of Jacob Wolf and wife Elisabeth, b. 3 Jun 1770, bapt. 10 Jun 1770.
Sponsors: Peter Mierken and wife Catharina.

Anna Catharina, of Johannes Höflein and wife Catharina, b. 7 Jul 1770, bapt.
15 Jul 1770. Sponsors: the parents.

Johannes, of Michael Hotz and wife Catharina, b. 10 Jul 1770, bapt. 15 Jul 1770.
Sponsors: Johannes Greiffenstein and wife Dorothea.

Ottilia, of Johannes Weilenmeyer and wife Anna Maria, b. 12 Jul 1770, bapt.
22 Jul 1770. Sponsors: Michael Böttinger and wife Ottilia.

Joh. Sebastian, of Adam Schmidt and wife Catharina, b. 11 Jul 1770, bapt.
22 Jul 1770. Sponsors: Sebastian Seibert and wife Eva Barbara.

Thomas, of Thomas Englis (an Englishman) and wife Elizabeth, b. 27 Sep 1769,
bapt. 23 Jul 1770. Sponsors: Mrs. Behrns, "etc."

Heinrich, of Mr. Jacob Graess (the mason) and wife Catharina, b. 19 Jul 1770,
bapt. 27 Jul 1770. Sponsors: the mother, and old father Gräss.

Elizabeth, of Jane Stephans (illegitimate), b. 21 Jul 1770, bapt. 22 Jul 1770.
Sponsor: Elisabeth Schreik(in).

Maria, of George Sing and wife Elisabeth, b. 12 Jun 1770, bapt. 29 Jul 1770.
Sponsors: Johannes Schreiber and wife Elisabeth.

Maria Eva, of Johannes Dorn and wife Margreth, 3 weeks old, bapt. 29 Jul 1770.
Sponsor: Maria Eva Rex(in).

Charlotta, of Andreas Orman and wife Albertina, b. 15 Jul 1770, bapt. 29 Jul 1770; the child died. Sponsors: Philip Tauberman and wife Charlotta.

Johannes, of Ernst Henry Dipperger and wife Cathar. Elisab., b. 19 Jul 1770, bapt. 29 Jul 1770. Sponsors: Joh. Henrich Leuthauser and wife Maria Elisabeth.

Johannes, of Peter Swenk and wife Anna Margretha, b. 2 Jul 1770, bapt. 29 Jul 1770. Sponsors: Johannes Greiffenstein and wife Dorothea.

Joh. Samuel, of Michael Hirsch and wife Barbara, b. 17 Jun 1770, bapt. 29 Jul 1770. Sponsors: Samuel Schobert and wife Elisabeth.

Catharina, of Georg Peter Zendler and wife Clara Maria, b. 26 Apr 1770, bapt. 29 Jul 1770. Sponsors: Conrad Müller and wife Catharina.

Fridrich, of Fridrich Lohr and wife Rosina, b. 22 May 1770?, bapt. 30 Jul 1770. Sponsor: the mother.

Christian, of Christian Appel and wife Margreth, b.22 Feb 1770, bapt. 26 Feb 1770. Sponsors: Christian Gruner? and wife Elisabeth.

Catharina Dobelbauer, wife of Friedrich Dobelbauer and dau. of VanOsten?, 25 years old, bapt. 31 Jul 1770. Sponsors: Adam Fuggerod, and Jacob Fuggerod and wife Anna Christina and dau. Anna Catharina.

Maria Catharina, of Friedrich Dobelbauer and wife Catharina (above), 2 years and 10 months old, bapt. 31 Jul 1770. Sponsors: same as above.

Friedrich Jacob, of Friedrich Dobelbauer and wife Catharina (above), 3 months old, bapt. 31 Jul 1770. Sponsors: same as above.

Philippina, of Georg Jung and wife Rosina, b. 10 Jul 1770, bapt. 5 Aug 1770. Sponsors: Jacob Christler and wife Philippina.

Anna Rosina, of Christoph Simon and wife Anna Margretha, b. 21 Jul 1770, bapt. 5 Aug 1770. Sponsors: Ernst Christoph Englert and wife Anna Rosina.

Johann Georg, of Friedrich Dietz and wife Christina, b. 30 Jul 1770, bapt. 5 Aug 1770. Sponsors: *Mr.* Georg Fittler and wife Elisabeth.

Anna, of William Poole (now deceased) and wife Barbara, b. 16 Dec 1765, bapt. 5 Aug 1770. Sponsors: Joh. Fridrich Vogel and Philippine Karst(lin)?, both single.

Samuel, of William Poole and wife Barbara, b. 15 Dec 1768, bapt. 5 Aug 1770. Sponsors: same as above.

Anna Maria, of Adam Harris and wife Christina, b. 5 Jun 1765, bapt. 5 Aug 1770. Sponsor: Barbara Poole?.

Johann Georg, of *Mr.* Johannes Heinmetz and wife Catharina, b. 18 Jul 1770, bapt. 5 Aug 1770. Sponsors: *Mr.* Johannes Keppele and Miss Susanna Keppele.

Anna Margretha, of Nicolaus Jacob and wife Anna Margretha, b. 1 Aug 1770, bapt. 9 Aug 1770. Sponsors: the parents.

Andrew, of Balthas. Böttinger and wife Catharina, b. 15 Jul 1770, bapt. 12 Aug 1770. Sponsors: the parents.

Catharina, of Jacob Ott and wife Catharina, 1½ years old, bapt. 12 Aug 1770. Sponsors: Conrad Müller and wife Catharina.

Catharina, of Michael Pfesterling and wife Elisabeth, birthdate not given, bapt. 12 Aug 1770. Sponsors: the parents.

Elisabeth, of Michael Pfesterling and wife Elisabeth, birthdate not given, bapt. 12 Aug 1770. Sponsors: the parents.

Andreas, of Michael Pfesterling and wife Elisabeth, b. 27 Nov 1769, bapt.
12 Aug 1770. Sponsors: the parents.
Peter William, of William Seit and wife Elisabeth, 6 weeks old last Friday, bapt.
12 Aug 1770. Sponsors: Peter Doerre and Catharina Mans(in), both single.
Joh. Georg, of Joh. Georg Unselt and wife Barbara, b. 3 Aug 1770, bapt. 17 Aug
1770. Sponsors: the parents.
Anna Maria, of Joseph Kaiser and wife Anna Maria, b. 25 Jul 1770, bapt.
19 Aug 1770. Sponsors: Christian Schmidt and wife Anna Maria.
Andreas, of Caspar Buck and wife Anna Margretha, b. 3 Aug 1770, bapt.
19 Aug 1770. Sponsors: Andreas Mertz and wife.
Daniel, of Caspar Chress and wife Catharina Barbara, b. 27 Jul 1770, bapt.
19 Aug 1770. Sponsors: Daniel Jones and wife Barbara.
Stephan, of Stephan Kiegler and wife Elisabeth, b. 5 Aug 1770, bapt. 19 Aug
1770. Sponsors: the parents.
Johann Sebastian, of Sebastian Seibert and wife Barbara, b. 10 Aug 1770, bapt.
19 Aug 1770. Sponsors: Adam Schmidt and wife Catharina.
Anna Barbara, of Johannes Häntzelman and wife Anna, b. 3 Aug 1770, bapt.
19 Aug 1770. Sponsors: Tobias König and wife Anna Barbara.
Joh. Peter, of Georg Wüster and wife Juliana, b. 9 Feb 1770, bapt. 19 Aug 1770.
Sponsors: Bastian Sonnleitner and wife Anna Barbara.
Catharina, of Georg Stoo and wife Barbara, b. 6 Aug 1770, bapt. 19 Aug 1770.
Sponsors: Sebastian Meyer and wife Elisabeth.
Johann Martin, of Martin Sommer and wife Margretha, b. 22 Jul 1770, bapt.
19 Aug 1770. Sponsors: Jacob Braun and Margreth Sommer(in).
Elisabeth, of Bernd Kandler and wife Barbara, b. 29 Jun 1770, bapt. 20 Aug
1770. Sponsors: the mother.
Maria Elisabeth, of Henrich Steller and wife Anna Margreth, b. 12 Aug 1770,
bapt. 20 Aug 1770. Sponsors: Maria Elisabeth Draess(in) and Peter Draess.
Barbara, of Michael Schumacher and wife Susanna, b. 18 Aug 1770, bapt.
24 Aug 1770. Sponsors: the father and Barbara Klingmann(in).
Maria Elisabeth, of Joh. Peter Schwartz and wife Anna Catharina, b. 27 Jul
1770, bapt. 26 Aug 1770. Sponsors: Christian Dierk and wife Maria Rosina.
Joh. Georg, of Joh. Jacob Hauser and wife Catharina, b. 17 Aug 1770, bapt.
26 Aug 1770. Sponsors: Joh. Georg Hauser and wife Sophia.
Anna Maria, of Jacob Seyfried and wife Maria Salome, b. 28 Jul 1770, bapt.
26 Aug 1770. Sponsors: Jacob Seyfried and wife Christina.
Georg, of Johannes Rot(h) and wife Dorothea, b. 15 Aug 1770, bapt. 26 Aug
1770. Sponsors: Joh. Georg Grotz and wife Dorothea.
Anna Catharina, of Joh. Henrich Bless and wife Elisabeth, b. 11 Aug 1770, bapt.
26 Aug 1770. Sponsors: Joh. Jacob Buck and wife Anna Catharina.
Margreth, of Henrich Hofäcker and wife Margreth, b. 25 Dec 1769, bapt.
31 Aug 1770. Sponsors: Mr. Martin Ricas and wife Catharina.
Georg Ludewig, of Mr. Georg Laib and wife Margretha Dorothea, b. 7 Aug
1770, bapt. 2 Sep 1770. Sponsors: Mr. Elias Ludwig Freidel and wife.
Anna Maria, of Johannes Roner and wife Barbara, b. 24 Aug 1770, bapt. 2 Sep
1770. Sponsors: Mr. Peter Dick and wife Anna Maria.

Dorothea Maria, of Andreas Forster and wife Anna Sybilla, b. 24 Aug 1770, bapt. 2 Sep 1770. Sponsors: Dorothea Maria Forster(in) and Peter Schwab, both single.

Catharina, of Friedrich Bantleon and wife Catharina, b. 29 Aug 1770, bapt. 2 Sep 1770. Sponsors: Caspar Haas and wife Catharina.

Johann Peter, of Joh. Wolfgang Gemeinbauer and wife Catharina, b. 11 Aug 1770, bapt. 2 Sep 1770. Sponsors: Wilhelm Herrmann and wife Margreth.

Eva Maria, of Johannes Woller and wife Margretha, b. 11 Aug 1770, bapt. 8 Sep 1770. Sponsors: Johannes Sommer and wife Eva.

Maria Magdalena, of John Mills and wife Elisabeth, b. 2 Sep 1770, bapt. 9 Sep 1770. Sponsors: Joh. Michael Breisch (single) and Maria Magdal. Bad___.

Elisabeth, of Nicolaus Müller and wife Anna Maria, b. 24 Aug 1770, bapt. 9 Sep 1770. Sponsors: Georg Keller and wife Elisab. Barbara.

Catharina, of Christian Schaefer and wife Dorothea, b. 11 Aug 1770, bapt. 9 Sep 1770. Sponsors: Andreas Wacker and wife Catharina.

Anna Maria, of Georg Gebhard and wife Rosina, b. 31 Aug 1770, bapt. 9 Sep 1770. Sponsors: Mr. Johann Bigler and wife Anna Catharina.

Robert, of Martin Perry and wife Mary, b. 16 Aug 1770, bapt. 15 Sep 1770. Sponsors: the parents.

Catharina, of Carl Görtz and wife Catharina, b. 19 Aug 1770, bapt. 16 Sep 1770. Sponsors: the parents.

Anna Catharina, of Andreas Laub and wife Christina, b. 9 Sep 1770, bapt. 16 Sep 1770. Sponsors: Matthias Schmidt and wife Catharina.

Salome, of Georg Hauber and wife Salome, b. 5 Aug 1770, bapt. 16 Sep 1770. Sponsors: Adam Krebs and wife Maria Margreth.

Johannes, of Thomas Eats and wife Barbara, b. 17 Aug 1770, bapt. 16 Sep 1770. Sponsors: Georg Kreis and wife Anna Margreth.

Christina Barbara, of Philip Hofman and wife Anna Maria, b. 10 Jun 1770, bapt. 16 Sep 1770. Sponsors: Tobias Taumüller and wife Barbara.

Peter, of Anna Nagel(in), b. 21 Aug 1770, bapt. 16 Sep 1770. Sponsors: Peter Hauss and Sara Elisabeth Mahn(in).

Georg Thomas, of Josia Shepherd and wife Maria Anna, b. 3 Sep 1770, bapt. 22 Sep 1770. Sponsors: Michael Kuhn and Jacob Waxby.

Magdalena, of Georg Landgraf and wife Magdalena, 10 months old, bapt. 22 Sep 1770. Sponsors: the parents.

Joh. Georg, of Benjamin Comal and wife Charlotte Sophia, b. 8 Sep 1770, bapt. 23 Sep 1770. Sponsors: Joh. Georg Strein and wife Elisab. Henrica.

Catharina, of Christian Stutzman and wife Eva Elisabetha, b. 6 Sep 1770, bapt. 30 Sep 1770. Sponsors: Anna Catharina Diet(h)er and Mich. Meyer.

Jeremias, of Daniel Hofman and wife Margretha, b. 15 Sep 1770, bapt. 27 Sep 1770. Sponsors: Mr. Andreas Burghard and wife.

Conrad, of Andreas Tag and wife Christina, b. 20 Sep 1770, bapt. 30 Sep 1770. Sponsors: Conrad Schmid and wife Anna Maria.

Catharina, of Joh. Peter Hartman and wife Catharina, b. 12 Sep 1770, bapt. 30 Sep 1770. Sponsors: Peter Däse and wife Catharina.

Johann Henrich, of Joh. Adam Swaab and wife Margretha, b. 22 Sep 1770, bapt. 30 Sep 1770. Sponsors: Jacob Swaab and wife Maria.

Philippina, of *Mr.* Georg Seitz and wife Elisabeth, b. 17 Sep 1770, bapt. 30 Sep 1770. Sponsors: *Mr.* Philip Heil and wife Jacobina.

Andreas, of Andreas Leinau and wife Rosina, b. 15 Sep 1770, bapt. 30 Sep 1770. Sponsors: Daniel Hess and wife Catharina.

Catharina, of Christoph Bob and wife Anna Maria, b. 2 Sep 1770, bapt. 30 Sep 1770. Sponsors: Georg Knerr and wife Catharina.

Marcus, of Friedrich Kuhl and wife Susanna, b. 11 Sep 1770, bapt. 5 Oct 1770. Sponsors: the parents.

Sarah, of Martha McKinley (English, illegitimate), b. 3 Feb 1770, bapt. 5 Oct 1770. Sponsors: Margreth Naeve and Kezia Reess.

Theodorus Wilhelm, of Conrad Escher and wife Maria Felicitas, b. 13 Sep 1770, bapt. 7 Oct 1770. Sponsors: Theodorus Wilhelm Wolmer and wife Cathar.

Maria Magdalena, of Christoph Heinkel and wife Maria Eva, b. 19 Sep 1770, bapt. 7 Oct 1770. Sponsors: Peter Steuerwald and wife Maria Magdal.

Joh. Andreas, of Andreas Oberdorf and wife Esther, b. 26 Sep 1770, bapt. 7 Oct 1770. Sponsors: Johannes Öxle and wife Maria.

Catharine, of William Carst and wife Elisabeth, b. 15 Dec 1769, bapt. 7 Oct 1770. Sponsors: Adam Krebs's wife, Susanna Letter, and Cath. Kern(in).

Anna Elisabetha, of Georg Muff and wife Elisabetha, b. 20 Sep 1770, bapt. 7 Oct 1770. Sponsors: Felix Schneider and wife Maria Barbara.

Elizabeth, of John Rice and wife Susanna, b. 12 Sep 1770, bapt. 8 Oct 1770. Sponsors: the parents.

Nicolaus, of Johannes Kaiser and wife Elisabeth, b. 6 Oct 1770, bapt. 8 Oct 1770. Sponsors: Nicolaus Odenwalter (or Odmeralter) and Elisabeth Becker.

Johannes, of Johannes Michael Jobst and wife (name not given) at Kensington (the foster parents?), b. 9 Oct 1770, bapt. 10 Oct 1770. Sponsors: *Mr.* Jacob Beydemann, and Margareth Miltenberger(in) (the child's mother).

Johannes Hevert?, foundling child of (foster mother) Johanna Eleonora Ehrhardt(in), about 5 months old, bapt. 10 Oct 1770. Sponsors: *Mr.* Jacob Beydemann, and Mrs. Ehrhardt(in).

Jacob, of Lorentz Mahn and wife Margretha, b. 29 Sep 1770, bapt. 14 Oct 1770. Sponsors: *Mr.* Michael Schubert and wife Elisabeth.

Johannes, of Josua Metzger and wife Sophia, b. 15 Aug 1770, bapt. 14 Oct 1770. Sponsors: Johannes Goetz and wife Anna Dorothea.

James, of Joh. Lämlin and wife Sarah, birthdate not given, bapt. 19 Oct 1770. Sponsors: Jacob Ritter and his? mother and father Georg.

Johannes, of Wilhelm Weber and wife Elisabeth, b. 8 Oct 1770, bapt. 21 Oct 1770. Sponsors: Johannes Weber and wife Anna Catharina.

Johannes, of Reinhard Uhl and wife Christina, b. 24 Sep 1770, bapt. 21 Oct 1770. Sponsors: Joh. Martin Schahl and wife.

Joh. Christian, of Peter Beck and wife Elisabeth, b. 7 Oct 1770, bapt. 21 Oct 1770. Sponsors: Christian Fidler and wife.

Joh. Heinrich, of Joh. Andreas Rohr and wife Maria Christina, b. 15 Oct 1770, bapt. 21 Oct 1770. Sponsors: Mr. Heinrich Leuthäuser and wife Maria Elisabeth.

Georg, of Andreas Bunter and wife Anna Maria, 8 months old on 25 Oct 1770, bapt. 21 Oct 1770. Sponsors: the mother, and Anna Maria Steinmetz(in).

Catharina of Thomas Wolpert and wife Eva, b. 22 Oct 1770, bapt. the same day?. Sponsor: the father, and Catharina Klemmer(in).

Josua, of Mattheus Volck and wife Catharina, b. 10 Oct 1770, bapt. 23 Oct 1770. Sponsors: Josua Lamparder and wife.

Jacob, of Johannes Kuch and wife Anna Barbara, b. 13 Oct 1770, bapt. 28 Oct 1770. Sponsors: Jacob Burckhardt and wife Barbara.

Catharina, of Johannes Wolf and wife Catharina, b. 26 Oct 1770, bapt. 29 Oct 1770. Sponsors: Mr. Peter Mercken and wife Catharina.

Jacob, of Joh. Wilikens and wife Cathar., b. 9 Oct 1770, bapt. 29 Oct 1770. Sponsors: Jacob Meier (single) and Catharina Fuggerad.

Hantis, of somebody called Miller, b. 4 Jul 1770, bpt. 30 Oct 1770. Sponsors: Marius Weinforth and Catharina Dannele (the stepmother).

Joh. Jacob, of Mr. Jacob Keimle and wife Christina Catharina, b. 21 Oct 1770, bapt. 4 Nov 1770. Sponsors: Mr. Johannes Fritz and wife Catharina.

Jacob, of Andreas Beisch and wife Catharina, b. 23 Sep 1770, bapt. 4 Nov 1770. Sponsors: Johannes Holl and wife Maria.

Margreth, of Paul Hofmann and wife Regina, b. 4 Oct 1770, bapt. 4 Nov 1770. Sponsors: Georg Rosch and wife Margreth.

Caspar, of Caspar Peter and wife Magdalena Maria, b. 18 Oct 1770, bapt. 4 Nov 1770. Sponsors: Caspar Korn and wife Anna Maria.

Eva Maria, of Caspar Wirschum and wife Rosina, b. 28 Sep 1770, bapt. 4 Nov 1770. Sponsors: Georg Kupper *alias* Kiefer and wife Eva Maria.

Johann, of Michael Stricker and wife Margreth, b. 4? Nov 1770, bapt. 6 Nov 1770. Sponsors: the parents.

Salome, of Mr. Wilhelm Goetling and wife Eva Maria, b. 21 Oct 1770, bapt. 10 Nov 1770. Sponsors: the parents.

Johannes, of Mr. Johann Gottfried Ridel and wife Catharina, b. 6 Nov 1770, bapt. 10 Nov 1770. Sponsors: the parents and Andreas Hertzog.

A child (name not given), of Jacob Schmidt and wife Catharina, b. 10 Nov 1770, bapt. date and sponsors not given.

Joh. Georg, of John Bryan and wife Cathrina Dorothea, b. 13 Oct 1770, bapt. 16 Nov 1770. Sponsors: Joh. Georg Brecht and wife.

Georg, of Christina Eschmann (now deceased) and wife (name not given), b. 2 Nov 1770, bapt. 18 Nov 1770. Sponsors: Georg Streper and wife Anna Margreth.

Anna Barbara, of Eva Emmerich(in) and Joh. Fridrich Burgdorf (illegitimate), b. 19 Oct 1770, bapt. 10 Nov 1770. Sponsors: Sebastian Steinmeier and wife Anna Barbara.

Johannes, of Johannes Heimer and wife Mercy, b. 27 Oct 1770, bapt. 10 Nov 1770. Sponsors: Daniel Heimer and Anna Schumann.

Anna Margaretha, of Johann Carst and wife Dorothea, b. in 1768, bapt. 19 Nov 1770. Sponsors: the parents, and Margaretha Burghardt(in) (the grandmother).

Johannes, of Johann Carst and wife Dorothea, b. 13 Nov 1770, bapt. 19 Nov 1770. Sponsors: same as above.

Anna Maria, of Adam Bausch and wife Anna Maria, b. 19 Nov 1770, bapt. 22 Nov 1770. Sponsors: Anna Maria Rei[t]z(in) and Rosina Maria Rauch(in).

Johann Wilhelm, of Wilhelm Shmily and wife Magdalena, b. 26 Oct 1770, bapt. 25 Nov 1770. Sponsors: Johannes Straub and wife Regina.

Johann Georg, of Peter Wildberger and wife Anna Catharina, b. 8 Nov 1770, bapt. 25 Nov 1770. Sponsors: Johann Georg Walker and wife.

Johann Friedrich, of Johann Friedrich Bender and wife Elisab., b. 2 Nov 1770, bapt. 25 Nov 1770. Sponsors: Georg Köller and wife Elisabeth.

Esther, of Jacob Bendler and wife Barbara, b. 27 Jun 1770, bapt. 25 Nov 1770. Sponsors: Joseph Kaiser and wife Anna.

Balthasar, of Peter Wagner and wife Rosina, b. 14 Nov 1770, bapt. 25 Nov 1770. Sponsors: Balthasar Fleischer and wife Catharina.

Martin, of Christian Lu[t]z and wife Susanna, b. 13 Nov 1770, bapt. 26 Nov 1770. Sponsors: the parents, and Martin Lu[t]z (the grandfather?).

Maria Barbara, of Frantz Braunholtz and wife Anna Barbara, b. 7 Nov 1770, bapt. 2 Dec 1770. Sponsors: Joh. Philip Fischer and wife Anna Maria.

Catharina, of Henrich Mithardt and wife Margreth, of 20 Oct 1770, bapt. 1 Dec 1770. Sponsors: the parents.

Catharina, of Johann Georg Pechtel and wife Susanna, b. 22 Nov 1770, bapt. 2 Dec 1770. Sponsors: Jacob Heimisch and wife Catharina.

Elisabetha, of Henrich Pohlentz and wife Anna Sybilla, b. 18 Oct 1770, bapt. 16 Oct 1770. Sponsors: Joh. Wilhelm Klemmer and Anna Elisabeth Kirchner(n).

Elisabeth, of Christoph Zinck and wife Magdalena, b. 18 Nov 1770, bapt. 2 Dec 1770. Sponsors: Christoph Weitbrecht and wife Elisabeth.

Johann Georg, of Johann Jurg Krauss and Anna Catharina, b. 17 Dec 1766, bapt. 3 Dec 1770. Sponsors: the parents.

Joh. Michael, of Johann Jurg Krauss and Anna Catharina, b. 26 Nov 1769, bapt. 3 Dec 1770. Sponsors: the parents.

Barbara, of Joh. Adam (surname not given?) and wife Catharina, b. 17 Nov 1770, bapt. 9 Dec 1770. Sponsors: David Johns and Barbara Schätzlein, both single.

Johann Jacob [twin], of Jacob Dietrich and wife Rosina (of Gloucester County [New Jersey]), b. 1 Sep 1770, bapt. 9 Dec 1770. Sponsors: Christoph Dietrich and wife Elisabeth.

Catharina [twin], of Jacob Dietrich and wife Rosina, b. 1 Sep 1770, bapt. 9 Dec 1770. Sponsors: Andreas Härterich? and wife Elisabeth.

Georg Christoph, of Christoph Dietrich and wife Elisabeth, b. 17 Oct 1770, bapt. 9 Dec 1770. Sponsors: Jacob Dietrich (brother) and wife Rosina.

Johann Ludwig, of Johann Ludewig Gress and wife Anna Christina, b. 26 Sep 1770, bapt 8 Dec 1770. Sponsors: Johann Peter Gress and wife Anna Rosina.

Johann Friedrich, of Johann Benjamin Gasman and wife Anna Maria, b. 1 Dec 1770, bapt. 8 Dec 1770.; Sponsors: Johann Friedrich Bernhold and wife [sic] Maria Bernholdt(in).

John Christian, of Henrich Jonas and wife Catharina, b. 25 Feb 1770, bapt. 8 Dec 1770. Sponsors: John Christian Kruger and wife Anna Catharina.

Margaretha, of Catharina Haerdt(in) and allegedly John Martin? (illegitimate), b. 24 Nov 1770, bapt. 4 Dec 1770. Sponsors: Margartha Haerdt(in) and her husband Henry Haerdt.

Lorentz, of Jacob Zink and wife Catharina, b. 9 Dec 1770, bapt. 16 Dec 1770.
Sponsor: Maria Eva Felds(in)?.

Susanna Magdalena, of Philip Sorg and wife Susanna Magdalena, b. 7 Dec 1770,
bapt. 16 Dec 1770. Sponsors: widow Anna Margretha Mildeberger(in).

Carl, of Carl Bauman and wife Maria, b. 3 Dec 1770, bapt. 16 Dec 1770.
Sponsors: Carl Stoltz?, John Strup, Ra[c]hel Reuth?, and Margr. Stoltz.

Susanna Catharina, of Peter Grim and wife Dorothea Sophia, b. 25 Nov 1770,
bapt. 16 Dec 1770. Sponsors: Johannes Lenckrum? and wife Maria
Catharina.

Maria Margretha, of Martin Schocht and wife Elisabetha, b. 10 Dec 1770, bapt.
16 Dec 1770. Sponsors: Josua Lamparter and wife Maria Catharina.

Christoph Friedrich, of Caspar Haas and wife Catharina, b. 26 Nov 1770, bapt.
16 Dec 1770. Sponsors: Christoph Friedrich Bantleon and wife Catharina.

Johannes, of Adolph Dill and wife Catharina, b. 5 Dec 1770, bapt. 18 Dec 1770.
Sponsors: Johannes Eisser and Maria Elisabeth Zimmer(in).

James, of Joseph Rivers and wife Catharine Eliza beth, b. 10 May 1770, bapt.
17 Dec 1770. Sponsors: James Fairy and wife Eve Elizabeth.

Robert, of George Cook and wife Hannah, b. 7 Oct 1770, bapt. 19 Dec 1770.
Sponsors: *Mr.* Robert Carrier and Jane Johnston.

Jacob, of Geo. Simon Brun and wife Maria? Elisabeth, b. 9 Dec 1770, bapt.
23 Dec 1770. Sponsors: Johann Schneider and wife.

Catharina, of Philip Etter and wife Catharina, b. 11 Oct 1770, bapt. 23 Dec
1770. Sponsors: Georg Rus and wife Margaretha.

Balthasar, of Balthasar Kinzler and wife Elisabetha, b. 4 Dec 1770, bapt. 23 Dec
1770. Sponsors: Wilhelm Engelfried and wife Catharina.

Sibylla Catharina, of Johann Zacharias Schneider and wife Anna Eva Elisabeth,
b. 12 Dec 1770, bapt. 23 Dec 1770. Sponsors: David Dolmann and wife
Sibylla Catharina.

Elisabeth, of Jacob Hoerner and wife Anna, b. 3 Sep 1770, bapt. 23 Dec 1770.
Sponsors: the parents.

Susanna, of Heinrich Poelreb? and wife Magdalena, b. 23 Dec 1770, bapt.
26 Dec 1770. Sponsors: Jacob Gress and wife Susanna.

Johann Adam, of John Buckeli and wife Johannetta (of Kensington, subse-
quentlty married), b. 26 Sep 1770, bapt. 30 Dec 1770. Sponsors: Maria
Elisabeth Habmerich(in)?.

Anna Margaretha, of Johannes Tanhauer and wife Maria, b. 11 Nov 1770, bapt.
30 Dec 1770. Sponsor: Margaretha Mildeberger(in)?.

Christian, of Christian Kneis and wife Christina, b. 18 Dec 1770, bapt. 30 Dec
1770. Sponsors: Wilhelm Engel and wife Catharina.

Margaretha Barbara, of David Uber and wife Anna, b. 26 Dec 1770, bapt.
30 Dec 1770. Sponsors: Lud. Uber and wife Margaretha Barbara.

Henrich, of Henrich Schreiber and wife Margaretha, b. 21 Dec 1770, bapt.
30 Dec 1770. Sponsors: the parents.

1770, Second List
(baptisms by pastors Schultz and Kunze, in chronological sequence, Book III)
Philip, of Joh. Fridrich Linck and wife Margaretha, b. 30 Dec 1769, bapt. 1 Jan
1770. Sponsors: Philip Wegner and wife Catharina.

Elisabeth, of Johann Leonhardt Weber and wife Maria Elisabeth, b. 13 Dec
1769, bapt. 7 Jan 1770. Sponsors: Philip Lader and wife Elisabeth.

Johann, of Johann Philips and wife Christina, b. 9 Dec 1769, bapt. 8 Jan 1770.
Sponsors: the parents.

Maria Elisabeth, of Georg Wentfield and wife, b. 28 Dec 1769, bapt. 15 Jan
1770. Sponsor: Maria Elisabeth Simon(in).

John Wilhelm, of Wilhelm (surname not given), illegitimate, 14 days old, bapt.
15 Jan 1770. Sponsor: Maria Elisabeth Simon(in).

Maria, of Henrich Sommer and wife Catharina, b. 2 Jan 1770, bapt. 21 Jan 1770.
Sponsors: Reinhardt Kammerer and wife Maria.

Georg, of *Mr.* Theodorus Memminger and wife Maria, b. 2 Jan 1770, bapt.
27 Jan 1770. Sponsors: the father, and Rev. Emannuel Shulze and wife
Elisabeth.

Joh. Georg, of Philip Schwartz and wife Christina, b. 28 Jan 1770, bapt. 2 Feb
1770. Sponsors: Rev. Emannuel Shulze and wife Elisabeth.

Philip Jacob, of Jacob Fuggerot(h) and wife Anna Christina, b. 25 Jan 1770,
bapt. 2 Feb 1770. Sponsors: Philip Fuggeroth and wife Maria Barbara.

Jacob, of Bernhardt Kaufmann and wife Anna Margaretha, b. 28 Jan 1770, bapt.
21 Feb 1770. Sponsors: Jacob Meier and wife Anna Maria.

Johann Georg, of Johannes Emmerich and wife Anna Maria, b. 22 Jan 1770,
bapt. 14 Feb 1770. Sponsors: Joh. Georg Sturmfels and wife Anna
Margaretha.

Heinrich (twin), of Henrich Jung and wife Susanna, b. 12 Feb 1770, bapt. 19 Feb
1770. Sponsors: father-in-law Adam Gerih and wife Susanna.

Adam (twin), of Henrich Jung and wife Susanna, b. 12 Feb 1770, bapt. 19 Feb
1770. Sponsors: same as above.

Joh. Fridrich, of Georg Schmidt and wife Barbara, b. 12 Feb 1770, bapt. 22 Feb
1770. Sponsors: Jacob Kloss and wife Sabyna.

Anna Margreth Magdalena., of Jacob Behner and wife Margaretha, b. 16 Feb
1770, bapt. 2 Mar 1770. Sponsor: Joh. Gerling's wife Anna Margreth
Magdalena.

Catharina, of Peter Kraft and wife Margretha, b. 9 Mar 1770, bapt. 18 Mar 1770.
Sponsors: Philip Druckenmiller and wife Catharina.

Ruth, of Rutz Wilson (deceased) and wife Jane, b. 9 Apr 1762, bapt. 25 Mar
1770. Sponsor: Jane Käre (the mother).

Henrich, of William Kare (deceassed) and wife Jane, b. 19 Oct 1769, bapt.
25 Mar 1770. Sponsors: Henrich Grodian and wife Catharina.

(Child's name not given), of William Weidbrecht and Ottilia (surname not
given), illegitimate, b. in 1766, bapt. 17 Mar 1770. Sponsor: William
Gerret's wife.

Philip Jacob, of Alexander Münster and Christina Knop(in), illegitimate, b.
21 Feb 1770, bapt. 26 Mar 1770. Sponsors: Philip Jacob Werner and wife
Anna Magdalene.

Tobias Comins, 51 years of age, and wife Judith, 57 years of age (both free
negroes), bapt. 2 May 1770. Sponsors: Abrahan Schmidt and Lidia
Commens.

Abraham, of Abraham Commens and Ledischie (negroes), 4 months old, bapt.
2 May 1770. Sponsors: Tobias Commens and wife Judy.

(Child's name not given), of Lonnen Month and Helena (negroes), 10 years old, bapt. 2 May 1770. Sponsors: Tobias Commens and wife Judy.

Anna Sybilla, of Johannes Loschet and wife Anna Catharina, b. 29 Apr 1770, bapt. 13 May 1770. Sponsors: the father, and the grandmother, Anna Sybilla Loschet.

Catharina, of Martin Weiss and wife Anna Maria, b. 29 Apr 1770, bapt. 13 May 1770. Sponsors: Anton Billig and Cathrina Haupt(in).

Maria Salome, of George Heidel and wife Maria Salome, b. 6 May 1770, bapt. 13 May 1770. Sponsors: the parents.

Joh. Georg, of Johannes Steinert and wife Elisabeth, b. 5 May 1770, bapt. 14 May 1770. Sponsors: Joh. Georg Steinert and wife Anna Maria.

Joh. Georg, of Christoph Jung and wife Margaret, b. 18 Feb 1770, bapt. 14 May 1770. Sponsors: Joh. Georg Heusel and wife Christina.

Anna Maria, of Jacob Pfingstag and wife Elisabeth, b. 30 Mar 1770, bapt. 17 May 1770. Sponsors: the parents.

Anna Maria, of Fridrich Moch and wife Anna Maria, b. 2 May 1770, bapt. 20 May 1770. Sponsors: Tobias Adam König and wife Anna Barbara.

Simon, of Jacob Heine and wife Anna, b. 3 May 1770, bapt. 30 May 1770. Sponsors: Johannes Salomon and wife.

Barbara, of Johannes Cotig? and wife Barbara, b. 3 May 1770, bapt. 20 May 1770. Sponsors: Andreas (surname not given), and Christiana Essig(in), single.

Maria Catharina, of Joh. Gottfried Hahl and wife Sarah, b. 27 Apr 1770, bapt. 20 May 1770. Sponsors: Maria Catharina Hahl(in), and her parents Philip Hahl and wife Catherina.

Margreth Catharina, of Michael Goenner and wife Christina Elisabeth, b. 5 May 1770, bapt. 24 May 1770. Sponsors: Sigmund Hagelganss and wife Margareth Catharina.

Johannes, of Joh. Henrich Wagner and wife Maria, b. 14 May 1770., bapt. 27 May 1770. Sponsors: Johannes Benedict and Philippine Elisabeth Patt(in).

Elisabetha, of Michael Laut and wife Susanna, b. 15 May 1770, bapt. 27 May 1770. Sponsors: Joh. Georg Bechtel and wife Elisabeth.

Maria Catharina, of Valentin Sorg and wife Anna Maria, b. 23 May 1770, bapt. 3 Jun 1770. Sponsors: Rudolph Lehr and wife Maria Catharina.

Mariana, of Christoph Pfüller and wife Sophia, b. 16 May 1770, bapt. 4 Jun 1770. Sponsors: Martin Fischer and wife Mariana.

Philip, of Martin Sommer and wife Anna Barbara, b. 22 May 1770, bapt. 4 Jun 1770. Sponsors: Philip Sommer and wife Salome.

Rosina, of Joh. David Mauk and wife Elisabeth Catharina, b. 10 May 1770, bapt. 4 Jun 1770. Sponsors: Melchor Lehmann and wife Rosina.

Michael, of Joh. Balthasar Kinsinger and wife Anna Maria, b. 24 Mar 1770, bapt. 7 Jun 1770. Sponsors: Michael Wien and wife Eva.

Catharina, of Joh. Georg Zinck and wife Anna Dorothea, b. 29 Apr 1770, bapt. 10 Jun 1770. Sponsors: Jacob Zinck and wife Catharina.

Anna Margareth, of Philip Pfannekuch and wife Anna Maria, b. 30 May 1770, bapt. 10 Jun 1770. Sponsors: the grandfather Peter Pfannekuch and wife Anna Margareth.

Georg, of Friedrich Dillmann and wife Catharina, b. 4 Jun 1770, bapt. 10 Jun 1770. Sponsors: Georg Daum and wife Elisabeth.

Susanna, of Abraham Fryot and wife Elisabeth, b. 25 Apr 1770, bapt. 10 Jun 1770. Sponsors: Peter Dress and wife Margreth.

Abraham, of William Müller (Ref.) and wife Catharina (Lutheran), b. 17 Dec 1765, bapt. 10 Jun 1770. Sponsors: the parents, and John Cassen and Christina Essig(in), both single.

Christina Elisabeth of William Müller and wife Catharina, b. 30 Mar 1768, bapt. 10 Jun 1770. Sponsors: same as above.

Joh. Wilhelm. of William Müller and wife Catharina, b. 25 Sep 1769, bapt. 10 Jun 1770. Sponsors: same as above.

Samuel, of Conrad Hess and wife Charlotta, b. 11 May 1770, bapt. 11 Jun 1770. Sponsors: Samuel Graaf and widow Elisabeth Maus(in).

Anna Maria of Leonhardt Kessler and wife Anna Maria, b. 9 Jun 1770, bapt. 12 Jun 1770. Sponsors: the parents.

Anna, of Johannes Reinhardt and wife Anna, b. 13 Jun 1770, bapt. 16 Jun 1770. Sponsors: the father, and grandmother Reinhardt(in).

Christina, of Michael Schubart and wife Elisabeth, b. 4 Jun 1770, bapt. 17 Jun 1770. Sponsors: Friederich Heiler and wife Christina.

Susanna, of Andreas Meier and wife Maria Clara, b. 8 May 1770, bapt. 17 Jun 1770. Sponsors: Fridrich Heiler and wife Christina.

Susanna, of Jacob Wisser and wife Susanna Dorothea, b. 27 Feb 1770, bapt. 17 Jun 1770. Sponsors: the parents.

Eva Maria, of John Elworth and wife Catharina, b. 30 Oct 1764, bapt. 17 Jun 1770. Sponsors: Peter Klein and wife Eva Maria.

James, of John Elworth and wife Catharina, b. 8 Dec 1767, bapt. 17 Jun 1770. Sponsors: same as above.

Joh. Fridrich, of Nicolaus Ulrich and wife Eva, b. 16 May 1770, bapt. 24 Jun 1770. Sponsors: Joh. Fridrich Ulrich and wife Anna Catharina.

Joh. Nicolaus, of Joh. Fridrich Ulrich and wife Anna Catharina, b. 18 Jun 1770, bapt. 24 Jun 1770. Sponsors: Nicolaus Baldowek and wife Catharina Schwinger.

Joh. Conrad, of Mr. Andreas Messerschmidt and wife Catharina, b. 18 Jun 1770, bapt. 24 Jun 1770. Sponsors: the parents.

Joh. Peter, of Henrich Mieth and wife Eva Elisabeth, b. 20 May 1770, bapt. 29 Jun 1770. Sponsors: the parents.

William, of William Robinson and wife Maria, b. 20 Jun 1770, bapt. 27 Jun 1770. Sponsors: William McMullin and Elisabeth Cunigur?.

Joh. Martin, of Mr. Martin Rau and wife Barbara, b. 20 Jun 1770, bapt. 30 Jun 1770. Sponsors: the father, and grandmother Christina Ehwald(in).

Anna Margareth, of Jacob Persie and wife Anna Maria, b. 6 May 1770, bapt. 1 Jul 1770. Sponsors: Daniel Hofmann and wife Anna Margareth.

Ernst, of Peter Sommer and wife Catharina, b. 6 May 1770, bapt. 1 Jul 1770. Sponsors: Ernst Maengen and wife Maria.

Anna Maria, of Jacob Loesher and wife Maria, b. 22 Nov 1770 [sic], bapt. 1 Jul 1770. Sponsors: Mr. Johannes Schreiber and wife Anna Catharina.

Jacob, of Casper Oberdorf and wife Margaretha, b. 20 May 1770, bapt. 1 Jul 1770. Sponsors: the parents.

Salome, of Georg Eberhardt and wife Barbara, b. 27 Jun 1770, bapt. 3 Jul 1770. Sponsors: the parents.

Nicolaus, of Niclaus Torberg and wife Anna Rosina, b. 27 Jun 1770, bapt. 7 Jul 1770. Sponsors: the parents.

Elisabeth, of Wilhelm Will and wife Elisabeth, b. 4 May 1770, bapt. 8 Jul 1770. Sponsors: Georg Bender and Margareth Will, both single.

Christian Fridrick, of Theodory Wilhelm Woelmer and wife Catharina, b. 3 Jul 1770, bapt. 8 Jul 1770. Sponsors: the parents.

Johannes, of Joh. Adam Schifferer and wife Dorothea, b. 6 Jul 1770, bapt. 8 Jul 1770. Sponsors: Johannes Weber and wife Margaretha.

Joh. Ludwig, of Joh. Just Veil and wife Maria Magdalena, b. 20 Jun 1770, bapt. 15 Jul 1770. Sponsors: *Mr.* Elias Ludwig Freichel and wife Maria Elisabeth.

Catharina, of Jacob Metzger and wife Catharina, b. 3 Jul 1770, bapt. 15 Jul 1770. Sponsors: Peter Weidmen and wife Catharina.

Joseph, of Joseph Collins and wife Rebecca, b. 25 Jun 1770, bapt. 17 Jul 1770. Sponsors: John Emsen and Mary Mitschel.

Johannes, of Georg Bauer and wife Anna Margaretha, b. 13 Jul 1770, bapt. 17 Jul 1770. Sponsors: Johannes Mäster and Dorothea Gross(in), both single.

Jacob Friedrich, of Jacob Friedrich Escher and wife Ester, birthdate not given, bapt. 19 Jul 1770. Sponsors: the parents.

Sarah, of Jacob Pfeiffer and wife Barbara, b. 27 Feb 1770, bapt. 23 Jul 1770. Sponsors: the parents.

Johann, of George Vetter and wife Maria, b. 25 Jul 1770, bapt. 26 Jul 1770. Sponsors: the parents.

Anna Maria, of Michael Orner and wife Anna Maria, b. 24 Jul 1770, bapt. 23 Jul 1770. Sponsors: the parents.

Joh. Georg, of Georg Rhein and wife Eva, b. 31 Jul 1770, bapt. 5 Aug 1770. Sponsors: Georg Bechtel and wife Elisabeth.

Sybilla, of Hans Georg Harold and wife Regina, from Gloster [Gloucester], b. 25 May 1770, bapt. 5 Aug 1770. Sponsors: Michael Wolf and Margareth Staut(in)?

Christina, of Heinrich Lentz and wife Anna Maria, b. 29 Aug 1770, bapt. 4 Sep 1770. Sponsors: the parents and Matthew Meier's wife Christina.

Johann Christian. of Johannes Fromberger and wife Anna, b. 21 Aug 1770, bapt. 5 Sep 1770. Sponsors: *Mr.* Joh. Nicolaus Weber and wife Christina.

Johann Jacob, of Michael Kuhn and wife Anna Maria, b. 26 Aug 1770, bapt. 9 Sep 1770. Sponsors: Johannes Weiss and Elisabeth Streich(in), both single.

Barbara, of Nathaniel Delapp and wife Anna Maria, b. 22 Feb 1769, bapt. 15 Sep 1770. Sponsors: *Mr.* Jacob Reinthaler and Carl Schaika's wife Barbara.

Magdalena, of John William and wife Dorothea, b. 3 Sep 1770, bapt. 15 Sep 1770. Sponsor: Elisabeth Reinhardt(in).

Elisabeth, of Joh. Georg Herrmann and wife Anna Regina, b. 26 Aug 1770, bapt. 16 Sep 1770. Sponsors: Johann Georg Walcker and wife Dorothea.

Anna Maria, of Jacob Reiser and wife Christina, b. 13 Sep 1770, bapt. 16 Sep 1770. Sponsors: Martin Reiser and wife Catharina.

Christina, of Georg Ganser and wife Salome, b. 22 Aug 1770, bapt. 16 Sep 1770. Sponsors: Henrich Habich and wife Christina.
Elisabeth, of Joh. Gottlieb Schweitzer and wife Elisabeth, b. 30 Jul 1770, bapt. 19 Sep 1770. Sponsors: *Mr.* Dietrich Metzner and wife Elisabeth.
Anna, of Conrad Schindler, from Lancaster Co., b. in 1760, bapt. 19 Sep 1770. Sponsors: the father, and Johann Nicholas Seitz.
Richard, of Richard Cullenz, b. in 1769, bapt. 19 Sep 1770. Sponsor: the father.
Johann Jacob, of Daniel Pohlmann and wife Sophia Catharina, b. 23 Oct 1769, bapt. 4 Nov 1770. Sponsors: Jacob Becker and wife Anna Maria.
Anna Barbara, of Friderich Walther and wife Catharina, b. 21 Oct 1770, bapt. 4 Nov 1770. Sponsors: William Smith and wife Anna.
Maria Catharina, of Christian Diterich and wife Maria Catharina, b. 18 Oct 1770, bapt. 4 Nov 1770. Sponsor: Philipp Hahl's dau., Maria Catharina.
Johannes, of Adam Zinzer and wife Rosina, b. 14 Oct 1769, bapt. 4 Nov 1770. Sponsors: Johannes Lampather and wife Salome.
Johann Conrad, of Philipp Jacob Bechthold and wife Anna Maria, b. 1 Oct 1770, bapt. 4 Nov 1770. Sponsors: Conrad Abel and wife.
Maria Catharine, of Jacob Schmidt and wife Catharina, b. 11 Nov 1770, bapt. 20 Nov 1770. Sponsors: Anna Maria Doer(in) and Catharina Flickinger(in).
Anna Maria, of Wilhelm Heins and wife Maria Cathar., b. 6 Oct 1770, bapt. 18 Nov 1770. Sponsor: the grandmother Anna Maria Grob(in).
Anna Margaretha, of Johann Caust and wife Dorothea, b. in 1768, bapt. 19 Nov 1770. Sponsors: the parents, and the grandmother Margaretha Burghardt(in).
Johannes, of Johann Caust and wife Dorothea, b. 13 Nov 1770, bapt. 19 Nov 1770. Sponsors: same as above..
Jacob, of Conrad Harf and wife Anna, b. 14 Oct 1770, bapt. 10 Dec 1770. Sponsors: Jacob Riess and wife.
Johann Henrich, of Christoph Zimmermann and wife Catherina, b. 3 Nov 1770, bapt. 11 Dec 1770. Sponsors: the parents.

1771, First List
(baptisms by pastors H.M. Muhlenberg and Kunze; all in approximate
chronological sequence, from Book II)
Christina, of Conrad Davis and wife Magdalena Margretha, b. 13 Dec 1770, bapt. 1 Jan 1771. Sponsors: Christian Caster? and Maria Rebecca Reber(in).
Susanna Elisabeth, of *Mr.* Andreas Burckhardt and wife Susanna, b. 15 Dec 1770, bapt. 1 Jan 1771. Sponsors: the parents.
Maria Margaretha, of Henrich Haehns and wife Catharina, b. 15 Dec 1770, bapt. in Jan 1770. Sponsors: Thomas Mayer and wife Margaretha.
Johann Friedrich, of Johann Friedrich Mehl and wife Elisabeth Catharina, b. 27 Dec 1770, bapt. 6 Jan 1771. Sponsors: Johann Friedrich Link? and wife Charlotta.
Joh. Jacob, of Jacob Kiefer? and wife Torothea, b. 27 Oct 1770, bapt. 6 Jan 1771. Sponsors: Joh. Jacob Schmidt and wife Maria Magdalena.
Joh. Dietrich, of Johannes Schweitzer and wife Anna Barbara, b. 10 Dec 1770, bapt. 6 Jan 1771. Sponsors: *Mr.* Joh. Dietrich Metzner and wife Catharina Elisabeth.

Johann Christoph (twin), of Eberhard Diel and wife Catharina, b. 7 Jan 1771, bapt. 13 Jan 1771. Sponsors: Joh. Christoph Hänsman and wife Maria Barbara.

Jacob (twin), of Eberhard Diel and wife Catharina, b. 7 Jan 1771, bapt. 13 Jan 1771. Sponsors: Jacob Bauman and Maria Barbara Mann (in), both single.

David, of *Mr.* Johannes Bigler and wife Anna, b. 29 Dec 1770, bapt. 20 Jan 1771. Sponsors: *Mr.* Georg Walker and wife Anna Dorothea.

Johannes, of Johannes Me[t]z and wife Anna Barbara, b. 9 Jan 1771, 20 Jan 1771. Sponsors: Georg Hauser and wife Sophia.

Anna Margretha, of Anthon Hecht and wife Sophia, b. 29 Jan 1771, bapt. the same day; the child died. Sponsor: Anna Gallys.

Friedrich, of Johannes Graeber and wife Anna Maria, b. 12 Jan 1771, bapt. 3 Feb 1771. Sponsors: Friedrich Abraham Fenstermacher and Barbara Tolneck(in)?.

Ann, of William Shippy and wife Benjamina, b. 5 Jan 1771, bapt. 4 Feb 1771. Sponsors: the parents.

Catharina Salome, of August Salomon and wife Elisabeth, b. 22 Dec 1770, bapt. 16 Feb 1771. Sponsors: Daniel Naumann and Catharina Dolk, both single.

Johann Jacob, of Michael Schäfer and wife Catharian Barbara (recent arrivals), b. 8 Feb 1771, bapt. 17 Feb 1771. Sponsors: Jacob Paulus (single) and Maria Elisab. Laininger(in).

Heinrich, of James Baker and wife Christina, b. 7 Oct 17<u>69</u>, bapt. 15 Feb 1771. Sponsors: Johann Heinr. Urich and wife Anna Barbara.

James, of James Baker and wife Christina, b. 16 Dec 17<u>67</u>, bapt. 15 Feb 1771. Sponsors: same as above.

Johann Georg, of Leonhard Weit and wife Eva Margretha, b. 9 Feb 1771, bapt. 17 Feb 1771. Sponsors: Joh. Georg Schneider (single) and Mary Margr. Baumänn(in).

Mary, of Samuel Moor and wife Mary, b. 22 Feb 1771, bapt. 23 Feb 1771. Sponsors: Patrick Dunn and wife Mary.

Johann Georg, of Caspar Weiss and wife Maria, b. 5 Feb 1771, bapt. 24 Feb 1771. Sponsors: Joh. Georg Forbach and wife Margretha.

Philip, of Wilhelm Seckel and wife (name not given), b.22 Jan 1771, bapt. 24 Feb 1771. Sponsors: *Mr.* Philip Hahl and wife Catharina.

Joh. Georg, of Ernst Mänchen and wife Maria Magdalena, b. 23 Jan 1771, bapt. 24 Feb 1771. Sponsors: Joh. Georg Sommer and wife, and his sister Margreth.

Philip Lewis, of Rudolph Lehr and wife Maria Catharina, b. 11 Feb 1771, bapt. 3 Mar 1771. Sponsors: John Philip Lewis and Susanna Elisabeth Korbmann(in).

John, of Johannes Strenge and wife Catharina Elisabeth, b. 23 Jan 1771, bapt. 3 Mar 1771. Sponsors: the parents.

Wilhelm, of Daniel Frischmuth and wife Barbara, b. 23 Jan 1771, bapt. 3 Mar 1771. Sponsors: the parents.

Anna Catharina, of Johann Lorentz and wife Catharina, b. 23 Feb 1771, bapt. 3 Mar 1771. Sponsors: Christian Pick and wife Christina.

Joh. Georg, of Leonhard Egy and wife Charlotta, b. 27Nov 1769, bapt. in Mar 1771. Sponsors: Carl Sauter and Anna Eva Rissart?.

Ludewig, of *Mr.* Wilhelm Schmidt and wife Anna, b. 25 Feb 1771, bapt. 17 Mar 1771. Sponsors: Ludewig Farmer and wife Anna Maria.

William, of William Vorbah (now deceased) and wife Anna Maria, birthdate not given, bapt. 21 Mar 1771. Sponsors not given.

Benjamin, of William Vorbah (deceased) and wife Anna Maria, 6 weeks old next Sunday, bapt. 21 Mar 1771. Sponsors not given.

James, of William Hederic and wife Rebecca, b. 3 Mar 1771, bapt. 23 Mar 1771. Sponsors: the parents.

William, of Henrich Kress and wife Anna Maria, b. 23 Feb 1771, bapt. 24 Mar 1771. Sponsors: Wilhelm Weber and wife Elisabeth.

Johannes, of Peter Paul and wife Anna Maria, b. 8 Mar 1771, bapt. 24 Mar 1771. Sponsors: Johannes Huber and wife Anna Catharina.

Anna Margaret, of Michael Herman and wife Anna Maria (of Frankford), b. 28 Dec 1770, bapt. 24 Mar 1771. Sponsors: Jacob Herman and Anna Maria Lotz(in).

Maria Elisabet, of Georg Arpengast and wife Maria Magdalena (of Frankford), b. in Sep 1770, bapt. 24 Mar 1771. Sponsors: Leonard Whit? and wife Susanna.

Dorothea, of Johann Nicolaus Wagner and wife Anna Magdalena, b. 25 Jan 1771, bapt. 25 Mar 1771. Sponsors: Jacob Theiss and wife.

Anna Barbara, of Franz Schaeffer and wife Elisabet, b. 20 Mar 1771, bapt. 1 Apr 1771. Sponsors: Anna Barbara Peterson and Peter Pilerry?

George, of James Cuben and wife Anna Barbara, b. 26 Mar 1771, bapt. 29 Mar 1771. Sponsors: *Mr.* George Gimell and Hannah Wall.

Anna Maria, of Christian Rudolph and wife Catharina, b. 16 Jan 1771, bapt. 1 Apr 1771. Sponsors: Henry Lentz and wife Maria.

Barbara, of Michael Diederich and wife Magdalena, b. 22 Mar 1771, bapt. 1 Apr 1771. Sponsors: Peter Krug and Barbara Schaetzl(in).

Christian, of Georg Nagel and wife Elisabetha, b. 20 Mar 1771, bapt. 31 Mar 1771. Sponsors: Christian Galley and wife Margaretha.

Elisabet, of Daniel Losch and wife Dorothea Elisabet, b. 9 Mar 1771, bapt. 31 Mar 1771. Sponsors: Gerhard Hol[t]zkamp and wife Elisabet.

Margaret, of Jacob Graeff and Catharina Margaret (who died), b. 28 Mar 1771, bapt. in Apr 1771. Sponsors: Henrich Mönche and his dau. Margaret Mönch(in).

Friedrich, of Johannes Klein and wife Anna Catharina, b. 15 Jan 1771, bapt. 7 Apr 1771. Sponsors: Friederich Dichang and wife Anna Margaretha.

Eva, of Johannes Gäntner and wife Margaretha, b. in Nov 1770, bapt. 7 Apr 1771. Sponsors: Maria Eva Weisvogel and Johannes Rüb.

Lorenz, of Johann Jacob and wife Maria, b. 15 Mar 1771, bapt. 7 Apr 1771. Sponsors: Lorenz Oppman and wife.

Philip, of Nicolaus Brum and wife Anna Maria, b. 8 Mar 1771, bapt. 7 Apr 1771. Sponsors: the parents.

Rosina Margreth, of Godfred Walter and wife Jane, b. 31 Mar 1771, bapt. 12 Apr 1771. Sponsor: widow Anna Catharina Weidt(in) (the "granny").

Sophia Susanna, of Johannes Henrich Schneider and wife Maria Eliane, b. 25 Mar 1771, bapt. 11 Apr 1771. Sponsors: Daniel Peter and wife Sophia Susanna.

Debora, of Johan Michael Klug and wife Anna, b. 18 Mar 1771, bapt. 14 Apr 1771. Sponsors: the parents.

Philip Jacob, of Zacharias Andres and wife Maria, b. 20 Mar 1771, bapt. 14 Apr 1771. Sponsors: the parents.

Lorentz (twin), of Joh. Friedrich Bast and wife Elisabeth, b. 14 Apr 1771, bapt. 19 Apr 1771. Sponsors: *Mr*. Lorentz Bast and wife.

Johannes (twin), of Joh. Friedrich Bast and wife Elisabeth, b. 14 Apr 1771, bapt. 19 Apr 1771. Sponsors: Johannes Fahns and wife Margreth.

Barbara, of Hinrich Tatz and wife Barbara (from Germantown), b. 9 Jan 1771, bapt. 21 Apr 1771. Sponsors: Philip Later and wife Elisabeth.

Sara Barbara, of Peter Kur[t]z and wife Sara (on the Germantown Road), b. 6 Apr 1771, bapt. 21 Apr 1771. Sponsors: Peter Kur[t]z and Eva Barbara Kur[t]z(in).

Susanna Louisa, of *Mr*. Martin Kreuter and wife Susanna Louisa, b. 1 Apr 1771, bapt. 21 Apr 1771. Sponsors: Susanna Louwisa Gillmann(in) and her father and mother.

Catharina Margretha, of Mstr.Schickele (the barber?) and wife Catharina Margretha, b. 16 Apr 1771, bapt. 21Apr 1771. Sponsors: the parents.

Catharina, of Gottfried Schüsler and wife Anna Elisab., b. 11 Apr 1771, bapt. 28 Apr 1771. Sponsors: Catharina Weid(in) and William Stehn.

Elisabet, of Jacob Veit and wife Anna, b. 28 Mar 1771, bapt. 28 Apr 1771. Sponsors: the parents.

Johann, of Jacob Tauenhauer and wife Maria, b. 1 Mar 1771, bapt. 28 Apr 1771. Sponsors: Nicolaus Wagner and wife Magdalen.

Johann, of Jacob Wagner and wife (name not given), b. in Jan 1771, bapt. 28 Apr 1771. Sponsors: the parents.

Catharine Elisabet, of Georg Way and wife Christina, b. 5 Apr 1771, bapt. in May 1771. Sponsors: the parents.

Anna Elisabetha, of Johan Dieterich Taub and wife Anna Juliana, b. 6 Apr 1771, bapt. 5 May 1771. Sponsors: the parents.

Salome, of JacobRot(h)h and wife Clara, b. 24 Apr 1771, bapt. 5 May 1771. Sponsors: the parents.

Georg Philip, of Georg PhilipWeisman and wife Catharina Salome, b. 6 Apr 1771, bapt. 5 May 1771. Sponsors: Johannes Weidman and wife Margretha Barbara.

Andreas, of Andreas Sengeisen and wife Anna Margaretha, 10 weeks old, bapt. 12 May 1771. Sponsors: Andreas Kirchner and wife Susanna.

William, of William Thomson and wife Mary, b. last Monday, bapt. 12 May 1771. Sponsors: the parents.

Maria, of Andreas Füller and wife Margreth, b. 20 Apr 1771, bapt. 13 May 1771. Sponsors: Joh. Andr. Rohr and wife Maria.

Magdalena, of Georg Gerlinger and wife Maria Christina, b. 3 Apr 1771, bapt. 20 May 1771. Sponsors: Magdalena Stäger and Wm. Bayer.

David, of David (surname and wife's name not given) on the hill, one week old, bapt. 18 May 1771. Sponsors: the parents.

Maria Catharina, of Johannes Slessel and wife Catharina, b. 11 Feb 1771, bapt. 17 May 1771. Sponsors: Conrad Weil and wife Maria Catharina.

Johan Michael, of Samuel Schober and wife Elisabetha, b. 28 Apr 1771, bapt.
18 May 1771. Sponsors: Johan Michael Hirschler and wife.
Michael Johan, of Michael Bettingen and wife Eva, b. 29 Apr 1771, bapt.
19 May 1771. Sponsors: the parents.
Maria Barbara, of Nicolaus Weichhard and wife Susanna, b. 4 Jan 1771, bapt.
19 May 1771. Sponsors: Balthas (surname obscured) and wife Maria Barb.
Margretha, of Johannes Lamparter and wife Salome, b. 29 Apr 1771, bapt.
20 May 1771. Sponsors: the father, and the grandmother Margretha
Lamparter(in).
Rosina Christiana, of Charles Georg and wife Veronica, b. in Feb 1771, bapt.
21 May 1771. Sponsors: Dieterich Rup and wife.
Johann Wilhelm, of Georg Warner and wife Barbara, b. 13 May 1771, bapt.
26 May 1771. Sponsors: Wilhelm Klauer and [wife] Margareta.
Joshua, of William deWeese and wife Hanna, b. 19 Sep 1770, bapt. 26 May
1771. Sponsors: Tobias Adam König and wife Anna Barbara.
Anna Barbara, of Andreas Bauer and wife Anna Barbara, b. in Apr 1771, bapt.
26 May 1771. Sponsors: the parents.
Barbara, of Conrad Zorn and wife Barbara, b. 31 Mar 1771, bapt. 2 Jun 1771.
Sponsors: Henrich Heimmatz and wife Barbara.
Maria Barbara, of Frantz Löscher and wife Maria Barabara, b. 2 Mar 1771, bapt.
9 Jun 1771. Sponsors: Christian Krebs and wife Anna Barbara (the
grandparents).
Johannes Henrich, of Johannes Reinhard and wife Anna Barbara, b. 30 May
1771, bapt. 9 Jun 1771. Sponsors: Johann Henrich Paul and wife Anna
Barbara.
Peter, of John Elwood and wife Catharina, b. 11 Oct 1770, bapt. 9 Jun 1771.
Sponsors: Peter Klein and wife Eva Maria.
Anna Maria, of Peter Chress and wife Rosina, birthdate not given, bapt. 9 Jun
1771. Sponsors: Ludwig Chress and wife Christina.
Johann Matthaeus, of Michael Klein and wife Elisabetha, b. 7 Apr 1771, bapt.
10 Jun 1771. Sponsors: Christian Friedrich Hut(h)man and wife Anna
Catharina.
Catharina Elisabet, of Daniel Ernst and wife Anna Catharina, of Kensington,
b. 20 Jun 1771, bapt. 27 Jun 1771. Sponsor: Catharina Elisabet Bot(h)(in).
Maria Catharina, of Jacob Schaeffer (of Bristol) and wife Juliana, b. 23 Mar
1771, bapt. 14 Jun 1771. Sponsors: the parents.
Wilhelm, of Johan Andreas Rot(h) and wife Barbara, b. 9 Feb 1771, bapt. 16 Jun
1771. Sponsors: Francis Henrich Kämmer and wife Catharina.
Johan Jacob, of Jac. Gottlieb Roll and wife Catharina (40 miles from here in
New Jersey), b.27 Nov 1771, bapt. 16 Jun 1771. Sponsors: Johannes Meister
and wife Dorothea.
Maria, of Christian Spengler and wife Maria Catharina, b. 15 Jun 1771, bapt.
24 Jun 1771. Sponsor: Maria Unger(in).
Maria Eva, of Peter Steyerwald and wife Maria Magdal., b. 19 Jun 1771, bapt.
24 Jun 1771. Sponsors: Christoph Henckel and wife.
Georg, of Christian Nagel and wife Elisabet, b. 26 May 1771, bapt. in Jun 1771.
Sponsors: the parents.

Elisabeth, of Thomas Heiser and wife Barbara, b. 30 Mar 1771, bapt. 26 Jun 1771. Sponsors: the mother, and Catharina Wedels(in)?.
Carl Philip, of Christian Pauli and wife Anna Margreth, b. 19 Jun 1771, bapt. 30 Jun 1771. Sponsors: the parents.
John, of Abel Jones and wife Rosina, b. 21 Mar 1771, bapt. 30 Jun 1771. Sponsors: the parents.
Maria Dorothea, of Wilhelm Hertzog and wife Eva, b. 19 Feb 1771, bapt. 3 Jul 1771. Sponsors: Walther Schwaab and wife Dorothea Maria.
Sophia, of Caspar Lohra and wife Sophia, b. 24 Jun 1771, bapt. 7 Jul 1771. Sponsors: Johannes Hauck and wife Catharina.
Johannes, of Joseph Job and wife Maria Christina, b. 24 Feb 1771, bapt. 7 Jul 1771. Sponsors: Johannes Hohl and wife Maria.
Maria Elisabeth, of Wilhelm Mohr and wife Susanna Maria, b. 22 Apr 1771, bapt. 7 Jul 1771. Sponsors: Nicolaus Lochmann and wife Anna Maria.
Maria Magdalena, of Jacob Schäfer and wife Maria Magdalena, b. 30 Jun 1771, bapt. 7 Jul 1771. Sponsors: Leonhard Albrecht and wife Christina (the grandparents).
Eva Maria, of Peter Klein and wife Catharina Elisabeth, b. 10 Jun 1771, bapt. 7 Jul 1771. Sponsors: John Elwood and wife Catharina, and *Mr.* Preis's wife.
Rebecca [twin], of Joseph Rogers and wife Hanna, b. 6 Mar 1771, bapt. 10 Jul 1771. Sponsors: the parents.
Salome [twin], of Joseph Rogers and wife Hanna, b. 6 Mar 1771, bapt. 10 Jul 1771. Sponsors: the parents.
Jacob, of Daniel Hofman and wife Margreth, of 9 Jul 1771, bapt. 14 Jul 1771. Sponsors: Jacob Pennikof and wife Sibilla.
Maria Margaretha, of Valentin Gesner and wife Maria, b. in May 1771, bapt. 14 Jul 1771. Sponsors: Henrich Gesner and wife Margaretha.
George, of *Mr.* Georg Christoph Reinhold and (English) wife Maria, b. 30 Jun 1771, bapt. 16 Jul 1771. Sponsors: the parents.
Maria Elisabeth, of Jacob Beck and wife Maria Elisabeth, b. 17 Oct 1770, bapt. 18 Jul 1771. Sponsors: the parents.
Michael, of Georg Wunderlich and wife Catharina, b. 13 Jul 1771, bapt. 18 Jul 1771. Sponsors: the parents.
Margaretha, of Johan Schütze and wife Margartha, b. 9 Jul 1771, bapt. 21 Jul 1771. Sponsors: William Welmore? and wife Catharina.
Anna Susanna, of Johan Höltzel and wife Catharina, b. 30 May 1771, bapt. in Jul 1771. Sponsors: Maria St(r)auss(in) and Balthasar St(r)auss.
Ra[c]hel, of Johan Lippy and wife Elisabet, b. 7 Nov 1770, bapt. 21 Jul 1771. Sponsors: Johan Strub and wife Ra[c]hel.
Catharina, of Jacob Rock[e]r and wife Elisabeth, b. 3 Jul 1771, bapt. 21 Jul 1771. Sponsors: Michael Bauer and wife Dorothea.
George, of Friedrich Ties and wife Maria, b. 4 Jul 1771, bapt. 21 Jul 1771. Sponsors: George Unfelt and wife.
Maria, of Jacob Biegler and wife Catharina, b. 5 Jul 1771, bapt. 21 Jul 1771. Sponsors: Conrad Scheller and wife.
Christiana Eleonora, of *Mr.* Christian Pick and wife Christiana Eleonora, b. 6 Jul 1771, bapt. 21 Jul 1771. Sponsors: Philip Jacob Eger and wife Catharina.

Rosina, of Joh David Mautty and wife Elisab. Catharina, b. 30 Jun 1771, bapt. 21 Jul 1771. Sponsors: Melchior Lehman and wife Rosina.
Caspar, of Caspar Kaes and wife Christiana, b. 20 Jul 1771, bapt. 21 Jul 1771. Sponsors: Michael Blocher and Maria Gutmann(in).
Jacob, of Joh. Georg Zinck and wife Anna Dorothea, b. 9 Jun 1771, bapt. 28 Jul 1771. Sponsors: Jacob Zinck and wife Catharina.
Joh. Michael, of Joh. Leonh. Weber and wife Elisabeth, b. 3 Jul 1771, bapt. 28 Jul 1771. Sponsors: Joh. Wolfg. Gemeinbauer and wife Catharina.
Johannes, Georg Ungerer and wife Maria, b. 13 Jul 1771, bapt. 31 Jul 1771. Sponsors: Mr. Johannes Keppele and Mrs. Elisabeth Keppele.
Alexander, of Edward Lasky and [wife] Catharina, b. 10 Jul 1771, bapt. 4 Aug 1771. Sponsors: Conrad Hof and wife.
Johann Heinrich, of Johann Jacob Krämer and wife Ottilia, b. 29 Jun 1771, bapt. 4 Aug 1771. Sponsors: Joh. Henrich Heidel and wife.
Joseph, of James Dorson and wife Christina, b. 31 Dec 1770, bapt. 4 Aug 1771. Sponsors: Joseph Bänks and Catharina
Joseph, of Joseph Smith and wife Abigail, adopted by Mrs. Warner, 2 years and months old, bapt. 5 Aug 1771. Sponsors: godmother Mrs. Warner, and Christoph Meyer and wife.
Elisabeth, of Matthew Bryan and wife Elisabeth, b. 6 Aug 1770, bapt. 6 Aug 1771. Sponsors: Catharine Cocks and Mary Tyderl.
Jesse, of Christian Freund and wife Elisabeth, b. 23 Feb 1771, bapt. 9 Aug 1771. Sponsors: Blasius Bayer and wife.
Maria Catharina, of Johannes Watenmeyer and wife Anna Mar., b. 26 Jul 1771, bapt. 11 Aug 1771. Sponsors: Leonhard Krämer and Maria Cathar. Spiegel(in).
Sara (a former English Quaker), wife of Nicolaus Hogel, 22 years old, bapt. 15 Aug 1771. Sponsors: Ursula Hogel(in) and Barbara Rien.
Margretha Barbara, of Nicolaus Hogal and Sara (above), b. 15 Jun 1771, bapt. 15 Aug 1771. Sponsors: same as above.
Johannes, of Johannes Pänner and wife Anna Catharina, b. 8 Aug 1771, bapt. 18 Aug 1771. Sponsors: Johannes Schade (single), and Anna Elisabeth Bach(in).
Catharina Elisabeth, of Joh. Benedict Schneider and wife Philippina Elisabeth, b. 6 Aug 1771, bapt. 18 Aug 1771. Sponsors: Christopher Hohmüller and wife Catharina Elisabeth.
William, of William Hase and wife Anna Maria, b. 3 Aug 1771, bapt. 19 Aug 1771. Sponsors: Anna Margaretha Mildeberger(in) (representing the Irish sponsors?)
Regina, of John Piercer (an Italian) and wife Henrietta Regina (of Kensington), b. 11 Apr 1768, bapt. 19 Aug 1771. Sponsors: the mother, and Christina Catharina Brand(in).
Rebecca, of John Piercer and wife Henrietta Regina (of Kensington), b. 30 Nov 1771, bapt. 19 Aug 1770?. Sponsors: same as above.
Theodor William, of Gabriel Rambo (of the Neck) and wife, b. 24 Aug 1771, bapt. 26 Aug 1771. Sponsors: Theodor Wilhelm Woelmer and wife Catharina.

Joh. Michael, of Joh. Michael Paetsch and wife Regina Catharina, b. 4 Aug 1771, bapt. 25 Aug 1771. Sponsors: David Paetsch and wife Anna Maria.

Philip Wilhelm, of Johannes Painter and wife Elisabeth, b. 28 Sep 1710, bapt. 25 Aug 1771. Sponsors: Philip Satler and wife Maria.

William, of Wm. Farmer and [wife] Sara, b. 7 Aug 1771, bapt. 25 Aug 1771. Sponsors: Mary McGomery and Mary Pain.

Maria, of Conrad Copia and [wife] Jemima, b. 3 Oct 1770, bapt. 25 Aug 1771. Sponsors: Jacob Löscher and wife Maria.

Elisabet, of Andrew Castel and wife Elisabet, b. 27 Feb 1771, bapt. 29 Aug 1771. Sponsors: the parents.

Salome, of Georg Desohner and wife Catharina, b. 25Apr 171, bapt. 1 Sep 1771. Sponsors: Jacob Bradler and wife Sara Catharina.

John, of David Davis and wife Susanna (a Quaker), b. 27 Sep 1766, bapt. 2 Sep 1771. Sponsors: the parents.

Mary, of David Davis and wife Susanna (a Quaker), b. 17 Jun 1768, bapt. 2 Sep 1771. Sponsors: the parents.

Sarah, of David Davis and wife Susanna (a Quaker), b. 2 Jul 1770, bapt. 2 Sep 1771. Sponsors: the parents.

Anna Margretha, of Adam Ohl and wife Maria Christina, b. 27 Aug 1771, bapt. 4 Sep 1771. Sponsors: the parents.

Elisabet, of Andreas Bechman and wife Catharina, b. 15 Aug 1771, bapt. 8 Sep 1771. Sponsors: Matthaeus Gilbert and wife Elisabet.

Maria, of John Norris (an English Quaker) and wife Maria née Deringer(in), b. 5 Dec 1770, bapt. 13 Sep 1771. Sponsors: the mother, Georg Gasner (single), and Christina Deringer(in).

Catharina, of Johan Freid. Renn and wife Catharina, b. 12 Aug 1771, bapt. 15 Sep 1771. Sponsors: Catharina Wachter(in) and Matthaeus Bechtel.

Adam, of Arnold Becker and wife Elisabet, b. 14 Aug 1771, bapt. 15 Sep 1771. Sponsors: Adam Schatzlein and wife Hanna.

Philip, of Philip Kunsman and wife Maria Cathar., b. 16 Aug 1771, bapt. 15 Sep 1771. Sponsors: the parents.

Dorothea, of Daniel Schaub and wife Catharina, b. 9 Sep 1771, bapt. 16 Sep 1771. Sponsors: Johan Georg Beider and Dorothea Klingeschmidt(in).

Margartha, of Joh. Berh. Rebhuhn and wife Sophia, b. 14 Sep 1771, bapt. 22 Sep 1771. Sponsors: Joh. Mitchell and wife Margaretha.

Jacob, of George Harley (across the river) and wife Margaretha, b. in Jul 1771, bapt. 22 Sep 1771. Sponsors: Christoph Curfess and wife Catharina.

Catharina Elisabet, of Jacob Leiman (22 miles from here across the Skippach) and wife Margretha, b. in May 1771, bapt. 22 Sep 1771. Sponsors: Michael Roehn and wife Elisabet.

Salome, of Mich. Nunnemacher and wife Salome, b. 24 Sep 1771, bapt. 25 Sep 1771. Sponsors: Jacob Kloos and wife Sabina.

Johan Conrad, of Conrad Hof and wife Sibilla, b. 9 Sep 1771, bapt. 28 Sep 1771. Sponsors: Johannes Schreiber and wife Maria Elisabet.

Elisabeth, of Christian Busch and wife Sara, b. 8 Sep1771, bapt. 29 Sep 1771. Sponsor: Elisabeth Criscum_ht(in).

Catharina, of Jacob Wood and wife Maria, b. 16 Sep 1771, bapt. 6 Oct 1771. Sponsors: John Painter and wife Christina.

Salome, of Richard Ludcape and wife Salome, b. 22 Sep 1771, bapt. 6 Oct 1771. Sponsors: Mich. Becker? and wife Anna Maria.

Elisabeth, of Wentzel Fürck and wife Elisabet, b. 21 Sep 1771, bapt. Oct 1771. Sponsor: Elisabeth Frank(in).

Johannes, of Nicolaus Disran and wife Maria, b. 10 Oct 1771, bapt. 19 Oct 1771. Sponsors: Johannes Hinkelman and wife Christina.

Johannes, of Mr. Friedrich Hagner and wife Christina, b. 1 Oct 1771, bapt. 20 Oct 1771. Sponsors: Johan Salomon and wife.

John Saunders, of Philip Merant and wife Martha, 2 months and 4 days old, bapt. 20 Oct 1771. Sponsors: the mother, and Mrs. Walker.

Johannes, of Jacob Schäfer and wife Maria, b. 3 Oct 1771, bapt. 20 Oct 1771. Sponsors: Johannes Cra__ and wife Dorothea.

Phillis, a negress from Maryland, 30 years old, bapt. 17 Oct 1771. Sponsors: Anna Maria Mühlenberg(in) and Margretha Spyker.

Jacob, of Henrich Klein and wife Sophia (near Shamony), b. 6 Feb 1765, bapt. 22 Oct 1771. Sponsors: the mother, and Mr. Jacob Strickler.

Sophia, of Henrich Klein and wife Sophia, b. 1 Jul 1767, bapt. 22 Oct 1771. Sponsors: same as above.

Barbara, of Philip Bender and wife Maria, b. 10 Jul 1771, bapt 25 Oct 1771. Sponsors: the parents.

Johan Adam, of Michael Schoeneck and wife Anna Catharina, b. 5 Oct 1771, bapt. 27 Oct 1771. Sponsors: Johan Adam Hold and wife Anna Maria.

Wilhelmina, of Georg Schmidt (who died 5 weeks ago) and wife Maria Magdalena, b. 7 Oct 1771, bapt. 27 Oct 1771. Sponsors: William Wood, and Conrad Melchen's dau. Wilhelmina.

Joh. Peter, of Joh. Peter Dietz and wife Anna Maria, b. 30 Oct 1771, bapt. 5 Nov 1771. Sponsors: the father, and the midwife Anna.

Jacob, of Cornelius Rabateau and his (German) wife Maria, b. 13 Nov 1770, bapt. 10 Nov 1771. Sponsors: the mother, and Anna Maria Mühlbre__.

Michael, of Christian Lutz and wife Susanna, b. 30 Oct 1771, bapt. 10 Nov 1771. Sponsors: the parents.

Ra[c]hel, of Johan Friedrich Trost and wife Anna Maria, birthdate not given, bapt. 10 Nov 1771. Sponsors: Georg Henr. Gross and [wife] Anna Maria.

Joh. Peter, of Peter Clemens and wife Maria Magdalena, b. 16 Sep 1771, bapt. 10 Nov 1771. Sponsors: Mr. David Schäfer and wife Maria Catharina.

Joh. Gottlieb, of Johan Gottlieb Schweitzer and wife Elisabeth, b. 24 Oct 1771, bapt. 17 Nov 1771. Sponsors: Mr. Christoph Hänsman and wife Barbara.

Anna Maria, of Nicolaus Klein (the blacksmith) and wife Catharina, b. 11 Oct 1771, bapt. 17 Nov 1771. Sponsors: Georg Gräber? and wife Anna Maria.

Rosina, of Jacob Äsch and wife Rosina, b. 20 Oct 1771, bapt. 24 Nov 1771. Sponsors: Michael Hirneisen and wife Rosina.

Joh, Heinrich, of Henrich Pot(h) (of Kensington) and wife Catharina, b. 10 Nov 1771, bapt. 3 Nov 1771. Sponsors: the parents.

Catharina, of Bernhard Kaufmann (of Frankford) and wife Margretha, b. 19 Nov 1771, bapt. 24 Nov 1771. Sponsors: Jaocb Meyer, Jr., and Jacob Fuckerot's dau. Catharina.

Anna Magdalena, of Johannes Kirschner?, of Frankford, and wife Catharina, b. 2 Aug 1771, bapt. 24 Nov 1771. Sponsors: Michael Gross (single) and Anna Magdalena.

Juliana, of Johannes Meister and wife Dorothea, b. 18 Nov 1771, bapt. 24 Nov 1771. Sponsors: Conrad Ring and wife Juliana.

Peter, of Johannes Huber and wife (name not given), b. 29 Oct 1771, bapt. 1 Dec 1771. Sponsors: Peter Paul and wife Anna Maria.

Elisabeth, of Nicolaus Müller and wife Anna Maria, b. 15 Nov 1771, bapt. 1 Dec 1771. Sponsors: Jacob Working and wife Elisabeth.

Wilhelm, of Christop Beuerle and wife Elisabeth, b. 12 Nov 1771, bapt. 1 Dec 1771. Sponsors: Balthas Crämer and wife Elisabeth,

Elisabeth, of Nicolaus Jacob and wife Anna Margretha, b. 24 Nov 1771, bapt. 8 Dec 1771. Sponsors: Joseph Braun and wife Anna Maria.

Maria, of Andreas Weinemer and wife Rosina, b. 12 Nov 1771, bapt. 8 Dec 1771. Sponsors: Bernhard Bug and Maria Ratz(in), both single.

Catharina, of Jacob Weber and wife (name obscured), b. 28 Nov 1771, bapt. 8 Dec 1771. Sponsors: Michael Weber (of Spring Garden) and wife Catharina.

Elisabeth, of Adolph Riel and wife Hanna, b. 26 Dec 1770, bapt. 15 Dec 1771. Sponsors: Georg Sturmfels and wife Anna Margretha.

Elisabeth, of Christian Lauer and wife Elisabeth, b. 8 Dec 1771, bapt. 14 Dec 1771. Sponsors: the parents.

Abraham, of Johannes Schumacher and wife Elisabeth, b. 14 Aug 1770, bapt. 16 Dec 1771. Sponsors: Mr. Abraham Glodin and wife Juliana.

Johann Georg, of Johannes Grübel and wife Christina, b. 11 Dec 1771, bapt. 22 Dec 1771. Sponsors: Georg Laib and wife Dorothea.

Margretha, of Mr. Siegmund Rüle and wife Margartha, b. 13 Nov 1771, bapt. 22 Dec 1771. Sponsors: the parents.

Johannes, of Jacob Pennikof and wife Sybilla, b. 9 Oct 1771, bapt. 22 Dec 1771. Sponsors: Mr. Joh. Nicolaus Weber Horst and wife Maria.

Catharina, of Heinrich Jung and wife Susanna, b. 29 Nov 1771, bapt. 26 Dec 1771. Sponsors: Adam Gerich and wife Susanna.

Maria Margreth, of Peter Karch and wife Elisabeth, b. 24 Nov 1771, bapt. 25 Dec 1771. Sponsors: the parents.

Susanna Elisabeth, of Josua Kasler and wife Magdalena, b. 9 Dec 1771, bapt. 25 Dec 1771. Sponsors: Susanna Elisabeth Schwalbach? and Rudolph Nagel at Mr. Schmid's.

Margreth, of Joseph Mileham and wife Jane, b. 6 May 1771, bapt. 25 Dec 1771. Sponsors: John Rice and wife Susanna.

Johannes, of Johannes Essig and wife Barbara, b. 14 Dec 1771, bapt. 25 Dec 1771. Sponsors: the father and his sister Christiana Essig(in).

Elizabeth, of Johan Fleming (a Scotchman) and wife Margreth, b. 2 Dec 1771, bapt. 29 Dec 1771. Sponsors: the parents.

Balthasar, of Jacob Kestler (a recent arrival) and wife Anna Catharina, b. 8 Dec 1771, bapt. 29 Dec 1771. Sponsors: Balthasar Kuntzler and wife Elisabeth.

Johann Jacob, of Jacob Ehrenfeuchter and wife Susanna Margretha, b. 19 Dec 1771, bapt. 29 Dec 1771. Sponsors: Georg Mauts and wife Dorothea.

1771, Second List
(baptisms by pastors Schultz, Kunze, and a few by H.M. Muhlenberg; all in
approximate chronological sequence, from Book III,)
Catharina, of Nathaniel Pail and wife Mary, b. 17 Oct 1770, bapt. 1 Jan 1771.
   Sponsors: Caspar Christ, Catharina Seng(in), and Catharina Hafner(in).
Joh., of Joh. Fridrich Wagner and wife Margretha, b. 7 Jan 1771, bapt. 9 Jan
   1771. Sponsors: the parents.
Johannes, of Jacob Retzer and wife Susanna, b. 1 Jan 1771, bapt. 20 Jan 1771.
   Sponsors: Johannes Sturg and wife Dorothea.
Johann Michael, of Michael Schoch and wife Margareth, b. 30 Nov 1769, bapt.
   13 Jan 1771. Sponsors: Henrich Schelt and wife Christina.
Catharina, of Balthasar Steinfurth and wife Elisabeth, b. 24 Dec 1770, bapt.
   13 Jan 1771. Sponsors: the parents.
Henrich, of *Mr.* Conrad Boethis and wife Barbara, b. 23 Dec 1770, bapt. 13 Jan
   1771. Sponsors: the schoolteacher *Mr.* Henrich Lentheuser and wife.
Anna Margaretha of Johann Jacob Schubbert and wife Ursula, b. 7 Jan 1771,
   bapt. 13 Jan 1771. Sponsors: Christian Pauli and wife Anna Margaretha.
Andreas, of Andreas Sommer and wife Anna, b. 2 Jan 1771, bapt. 13 Jan 1771.
   Sponsors: Conrad Schlater and wife Christina.
Maria Catharina of Christoph Walpreht and wife Elisabeth, b. 22 Dec 1770,
   bapt. 13 Jan 1771. Sponsors: Christoph Zinck and wife Maria Magdalena.
Thomas, of Ephraim Evans and wife Catharina, b. 15 Nov 1770, bapt. 17 Jan
   1771. Sponsors: the parents.
Maria, of Gerett Hoelsikamb and wife Catharina Elisabeth, b. 11 Jan 1771, bapt.
   18 Jan 1771. Sponsors: Conrad Helster and wife Maria, and Elisabeth
   Heilins?.
Anna Maria, of Joh. Georg Retz and wife Anna Margaretha, b. 28 Nov 1770,
   bapt. 18 Jan 1771. Sponsors: Johannes Harrer and wife Anna Maria.
Maria Margaretha, of William Facundus and wife Dorothea, b. 7 Jan 1771, bapt.
   27 Jan 1771. Sponsors: Michael Goetz and wife Maria.
Johann Georg, of Johann JacobWalker and wife Sophia, b. 13 Jan 1771, bapt.
   27 Jan 1771. Sponsors: Johann Georg Walker (the father's brother) and wife
   Dorothea.
Ra[c]hel, of Johannes Billiger and wife Margaretha, b. 5 Jan 1771, bapt. 27 Jan
   1771. Sponsors: Johannes Grübbel and Barbara Bayer(in).
John, of Robert Mollin (deceased) and wife Catharina, b. 23 Dec 1770, bapt.
   27 Jan 1771. Sponsors: Johannes Fromberg and wife Anna.
Maria, of Adam Schae[t]zlein and wife Hanna, b. 5 Jan 1771, bapt. 3 Feb 1771.
   Sponsors: Nicolaus Banzer and wife Barbara.
Christina, of Jacob Antoni and wife Johanna Jacobina, b. 15 Jan 1771, bapt.
   3 Feb 1771. Sponsors: the parents.
Elisabeth, of Peter Friens and wife Anna Maria, aged 2 years and 2 months old,
   bapt. 6 Feb 1771. Sponsors: Maria Cathar. Schneider(in) and Elisabet
   Hern(in).
Dorothea, of Peter Friens and wife Anna Maria, b. 4 Jul 1770, bapt. 6 Feb 1771.
   Sponsors: Dorothea Meyer(in) and Margaret Lingeisen?.
Jacob, of Jacob Grothauss and wife Catharina Sibella, b. 20 Dec 1770, bapt.
   5 Feb 1771. Sponsors: the parents.

Johann Christoph, of Georg Kinzinger and wife Catharina, b. 26 Jan 1771, bapt. 8 Feb 1771. Sponsors: Johann Christoph Kunze and David Schäffer's dau. Cathariana.

Anna Barbara, of Philipp Werner and wife Anna Magdelena, b. 5 Feb 1771, bapt. 13 Feb 1771. Sponsors: Georg Faesler and wife Anna Barbara.

Johannes, of Georg Adam Fischer? and wife Maria Margaretha, b. 8 Feb 1771, bapt. 24 Feb 1771. Sponsors: Johann Jacob Massholder and wife Maria Magdalena, and Johann Berndt.

Maria, of Adam Folk and wife Catharina, b. 10 Feb 1771, bapt. 3 Mar 1771. Sponsors: the parents.

Maria Elisabeth, of Andreas Schaefer and wife Barbara, b. 22 Jan 1771, bapt. 6 Mar 1771. Sponsors: Maria Elisabeth Schaefer(in).

Maria Barbara, of Heinrich Bekely and wife Margaretha, b. 18 Feb 1771, bapt. 6 Mar 1771. Sponsors: Georg David Seckel and wife Catharina.

Franciscus Wulf, of Georg Penz and wife Hanna, b. 25 Feb 1771, bapt. 10 Mar 1771. Sponsors: Fransciscus Wulf and wife Margaretha.

Rosina, of Adam Hofman and wife Barbara, b. 4 Feb 1771, bapt. 17 Mar 1771. Sponsor: (name not given) and wife Rosina.

Johann Philipp, of Elias Albrecht and wife Catharina, b. 3 Feb 1771, bapt. 16 Mar 1771. Sponsors: Philipp Werner and wife Anna Magdalena.

Lucia, of Christlieb Bahrling and wife Elisabeth, b. 18 Feb 1771, bapt. 23 Mar 1771. Sponsors: the parents.

Catharina, of Matthias Schmid and wife Catharina, b. 5 Mar 1771, bapt. 27 Mar 1771. Sponsors: Andreas Lap and wife Christina Catharina.

Johannes, of Wilhelm Eckard and wife Maria, b. 7 Mar 1771, bapt. 2 Apr 1771. Sponsors: Johannes Rup and wife Maria Dorothea.

Wilhelm, of Jacob Buck and wife Catharina, b. 4 Mar 1771, bapt. 2 Apr 1771. Sponsors: Wilhelm Eckard and wife Maria.

Christoph, of Christoph Heinrich and wife Maria, b. (date not given), bapt. 2 Apr 1771. Sponsors: the grandparents Peter Both and wife Maria Anna.

Johann Philipp, of Christoph Graefel and wife Eva, b. 1 Apr 1771, bapt. 3 Apr 1771. Sponsors: the mother, and Johann Philipp Walter.

Maria Elisabeth, of Johann Adam Witterstein and wife Sophia, b. 25 Mar 1771, bapt. 7 Apr 1771. Sponsors: Andreas Grubel and wife Maria Elisabeth.

Anna Rosina, of Adam Muller and wife Christina, b. 10 Mar 1771, bapt. 11 Apr 1771. Sponsor: Anna Rosina Englert(in).

Joseph, of William Donner and wife, b. 29 Jul 1769, bapt. 23 Apr 1771. Sponsors: Georg Lentz? and wife Elisabeth Baidemann(in).

Sarah, of Caspar Geiger and wife Anna, b. 22 Apr 1771, bapt. 25 Apr 1771. Sponsors: the parents.

Thomas (twin), of Christian Hera and wife Charlotte Louise, b. 13 Apr 1771, bapt. 26 Apr 1771. Sponsors: the parents

Sophia (twin), of Christian Hera and wife Charlotte Louise, b. 13 Apr 1771, bapt. 26 Apr 1771. Sponsors: the parents

Anna Catharina, of John Jacob Huser and wife Cuniganda, (" the father is actually Peter Wiegand"), b. 12 Apr 1771, bapt. 25 Apr 1771. Sponsors: Peter Wiegand and Anna Catharina Folk(?).

Anna Maria, of Johannes Weismann and wife Margaretha Barbara, b. 7 Apr 1771, bapt. 26 Apr 1771. Sponsors: William Hatermann? and wife Susanna Margaretha.

Elisabeth, of Georg Weh and wife Christina, b. 5 Apr 1771, bapt. 5 May 1771. Sponsors: the father, and grandmother Catharina Weh.

Andreus Nicolaus of Andreus Nicolaus Heidenick and wife Elisabeth Margaretha, b. 9 Apr 1771, bapt. 5 May 1771. Sponsors: the mother, and Nicolaus Brun [Brum?].

Jacob, of Andreas Taubert and wife Elisabeth Scheid(in), illegitimate, b. 6 Mar 1771, bapt. 5 May 1771. Sponsors: Catharina Walderick(in) and Jacob Hempelmann.

Johann Georg, of Johann Georg Krauss and wife Catharina, b. 5 Apr 1771, bapt. 1 May 1771. Sponsors: the parents.

Johannes, of Johann Heinr. Schlesmann and wife Catharina, b. 8 May 1771, bapt. 11 May 1771. Sponsors: the parents.

Johann Georg, of Johann Georg Weidemann and wife Maria Eva, b. 12 Apr 1771, bapt. 12 May 1771. Sponsors: the parents, and Maria Magdalena Schuster(in).

Samuel, of Johannes Held and wife Justinia, b. 12 Jun 1768, bapt. 25 May 1771. Sponsors: Nicholaus Reb and wife Christina.

Maria, of Johannes Held and wife Justinia, b. 4 Nov 1770, bapt. 25 May 1771. Sponsor: Catharina Muller(in).

Heinr., of Christoph Getter and wife Anna Margaretha, b. 15 May 1771, bapt, 25 May 1771. Sponsors: the mother, and Heinrich Miet.

Maria Magdalene, of Christoph Getter and wife Anna Margaretha, b. 7 Dec 1766, bapt. 25 May 1771. Sponsor: Barbara Rules?.

Elisabeth, of Christoph Getter and wife Anna Margaretha, b. 16 Mar 1768, bapt., 25 May 1771. Sponsors: Heinrich Miet and Maria Ricker.

Johannes, of Johann Georg Fuhrer and wife Maria, b. in Dec 1770, bapt. 25 May 1771. Sponsors: Johann Heiner. Kühl and wife Sophia.

Anna Maria of Johan Georg Hackinloch and wife Juliana Elisabeth, b. 26 May 1771, bapt. 7 Jun 1771. Sponsors: Philipp Seidelmann and wife Anna Maria.

Margaretha, of Frantz Henrich Caemmer(er) and wife Catharina, b. 29 May 1771, bapt. 15 Jun 1771. Sponsors: Johann Rot(h) and wife Barbara.

Anna Barbara, of Carl Wilhelm Nussack and wife Maria Catharina, b. 2 Jun 1771, bapt. 16 Jun 1771. Sponsors: the parents.

Anna Maria, of Johann Bahrdt and wife Catharina, b. 5 Jun 1771, bapt. 16 Jun 1771. Sponsors: Adam Dietz and wife Anna Maria.

Johann Georg, of Johan Georg Wenzel and wife Nanna Margaretha, b. 7 Jun 1771, bapt. 22 Jun 1771. Sponsors: Johann Georgt Knorr and wife Catharina.

Johann Wilhelm, of Conrad Ring and wife Juliana, b. 22 Jun 1771, bapt. 22 Jun 1771. Sponsors: Johann Joseph Veit and wife Maria Magdalena.

Johann Philip, of Johann Friedr. Lenk and wife Anna Margaretha, b. 27 Jun 1771, bapt. 30 Jun 1771. Sponsors: Johann Philip Wegner and wife Anna Catharina.

Anna Maria, of Johannes Greus and wife Anna Elisabeth, b. 30 Jun 1771, bapt.
7 Jul 1771. Sponsors: Jacob Schell and Anna Maria Koenig(in).
Johannes, of Georg Michael Heil and wife Maria Catharina, b. 30 May 1771,
bapt. 7 Jul 1771. Sponsors: the parents.
Michael, of Martin Heilmann and wife Eva, b. 6 Jun 1771, bapt. 8 Jul 1771.
Sponsors: Alexander Thomson and wife Maria.
Maria, of Georg Lange and wife Susanna, b. 8 Jul 1771, bapt. 14 Jul 1771.
Sponsors: the parents.
Elisabeth, of Jacob Krauss and wife Elisabeth, b. 30 Jun 1771, bapt. 14 Jul 1771.
Sponsors: John Tolmann and wife Elisabeth.
Catharina, of Georg Vetter and wife Catharina, b. 11 Jul 1771, bapt. 17 Jul 1771.
Sponsors: the parents.
Regina, of Jacob Weisert and wife Elisabeth, b. 27 May 1771, bapt. 21 Jul 1771.
Sponsors: Nicolaus Herzebach and wife Regina.
Maria Salome, of Georg Dorn and wife Christina, b. 16 Jul 1771, bapt. 24 Jul
1771. Sponsors: Jacob Haefler and Maria Louisa Muller(in).
Susanna, of Philipp Heil and wife Jacobina, b. 9 Jul 1771, bapt. 25 Jul 1771.
Sponsors: Fried. Schinckel and wife Susanna.
Joseph, of Ruben Allert? and wife Anna, b. 10 Mar 1769, bapt. in Aug 1771.
Sponsors: the parents.
Thomas, of Ruben Allert? and wife Anna, b. 29 Jul 1771, bapt. in Aug 1771.
Sponsors: the parents.
Johannes, of Christian Goht and wife Christina, b. 9 Jul 1771, bapt. 4 Aug 1771.
Sponsors: Johannes Becker and Maria Krebs(in).
Elisabeth, of Peter Weber and wife Maria Catharina, b. 23 Jun 1771, bapt. 9 Aug
1771. Sponsors: Nicolaus Werner and wife Elisabeth.
Catharina, of Daniel Bilger and wife Margaretha, b. 19 Jul 1771, bapt. 11 Aug
1771. Sponsors: Conrad Getbhardt and wife Catharina.
Thomas, of unknown father and Margaretha Nageli, b. in Oct 1770, bapt. 7 Aug
1771. Sponsor: Balthasar Geiger's wife Magdalena.
Catharina, of Michael Wolf and wife Sybilla, b. 6 May 1771, bapt. 7 Aug 1771.
Sponsors: the parents.
Peter, of David Ginnens and wife Margaretha, b. 11 Aug 1771, bapt. 17 Aug
1771. Sponsor: Michael (surname not given).
Maria Magd., of Johannes Henrich and wife Maria, b. 25 Aug 1771, bapt. 1 Sep
1771. Sponsors: Johann Conrad Steinmetz and wife.
Catharina, of Georg Keller and wife Elisabeth, b. 7 Aug 1771, bapt. 1 Sep 1771.
Sponsors: Michael Lots and wife Catharina.
Maria, of Friedr. Ernst Ensminger and wife Catharina, b. 26 Aug 1771, bapt.
1 Sep 1771. Sponsors: Leonard Löscher and wife Maria.
Elisabeth, of Jacob Specht and wife Margaretha, b. 1 May 1771, bapt. 1 Sep
1771. Sponsors: Johannes Specht and Anna Maria Päis(in).
Johannes, of Caspar Jaeger and wife Hanna, b. 13 Aug 1771, bapt. 1 Sep 1771.
Sponsors: Hannah Wolfstein and wife Margaretha.
Jacob, of Michael Haehns and wife Catharina, b. 25 Aug 1771, bapt. 2 Sep
1771. Sponsors: the parents.
Johannes, of Johannes Strohm and wife Eva, b. 22 Jan 1771, bapt. 4 Sep 1771.
Sponsors: the parents.

Johannes, of Louis Lenefaescht and Christina Catharina Schneider(in), illegitimate, b. 23 Aug 1771, bapt. 5 Sep 1771. Sponsor: the mother.

Johannes, of Caspar Schneider and wife Elisabeth, b. 30 Aug 1771, bapt. 8 Sep 1771. Sponsors: John Heller and wife.

Catharina, of Peter Mierkle and wife Catharina, b. 21 Aug 1771, bapt. 5 Sep 1771. Sponsors: David Schaefer and his sister Catharina (single).

Peter, of Melchior Schwerer and wife Rosina, b. 7 Jul 1771, bapt. 14 Sep 1771. Sponsors: Peter Steinme[t]z and wife Margaretha.

Magdalena, of Johann Christian Krebs and wife Elisabeth, b. 21 Aug 1771, bapt. 15 Sep 1771. Sponsors: Georg Hafner and Magdalena Glockner(in).

Adam, of Arnold Becker and wife Elisabeth, b. 14 Aug 1771, bapt. 15 Sep 1771. Sponsors: Adam Schae[t]zlein and wife Hanna.

Simon, of Daniel Sorg and wife Margaretha, b. 13 Sep 1771, bapt. 20 Sep 1771. Sponsors: Simon Heidel and Margaretha Milteberger(in).

Johann Jacob, of Martin Reusser and wife Anna Catharina, b. 10 Sep 1771, bapt. 21 Sep 1771. Sponsors: Johann Carl Schneider and wife Maria.

Anna Margaretha, of Johann Matthaeus Tollmann and wife Anna Catharina, b. 16 Sep 1771, bapt. 29 Sep 1771. Sponsors: Jacob (surname not given) and Anna Catharina.

Margaretha, of Caspar Kiensch and wife Margareth, b. 23 Sep 1771, bapt. 29 Sep 1771. Sponsors: Willhelm Engelfrid and wife Cath. Barbara.

Samuel, of Valentin Welsh and wife Philippina, b. 12 Sep 1771, bapt. 29 Sep 1771. Sponsors: Joh. Graef and wife Maria Magd.

Georg, of Georg Heil and wife Dorothea, b. 11 Sep 1771, bapt. 3 Oct 1771. Sponsors: the parents.

Wilhelm, of Samuel Rosk (an Englishman) and wife Christina Elisabeth, b. 16 Sep 1771, bapt. 8 Oct 1771. Sponsors: Antoni Gilbert and Maria Magdalena Loecher(in).

Anna Magdalena, of Jacob Pfister and wife Magdalena, 3 days old, 1771, bapt. 11 Oct 1771. Sponsor: Anna Magdal. Pfister(in).

Joseph, of Jergan Michael Fox and wife Salome, b. 12 Sep 1771, bapt. 12 Oct 1771. Sponsors: Johann Georg Leibrand and wife Elisabeth.

Carl, of Peter David Hensel and wife Dorothea, b. 27 Dec 1770?, bapt. 13 Oct 1771. Sponsors: the parents.

Johannes, of Johannes Kimmerli and wife Margaretha, b. 4 Oct 1771, bapt. 13 Oct 1771. Sponsors: the parents.

Peter, of John Savoir and wife Elisabeth, b. 5 Sep 1771, bapt. 13 Jul 1771. Sponsor: Peter Cavil? (French).

Johann Philipp, of John Peter Gabel and wife Anna Elisabeth, b. 27 Sep 1771, bapt. 20 Oct 1771. Sponsors: Conrad Wagner and wife Catharina.

Anna Maria, of John Heinr. Katz and wife Rosina, b. 8 Oct 1771, bapt. 20 Oct 1771. Sponsors: Bernhardt Buck and wife Anna Maria Katz(in).

Johann Nicolaus, of William Kemp and wife Anna Sabina, b. 15 Oct 1771, bapt. 20 Oct 1771. Sponsors: Nicolaus Miller and wife Hannah.

Johannes, of Philipp Sommer and wife Salome, b. 15 Dec 1770, bapt. 23 Oct 1771. Sponsors: Johannes Bender and Susanna Riebel(in)?.

Christian, of Johannes Just Schweikardt and wife Elisabeth, b. 7 Sep 1771, bapt. 26 Sep 1771. Sponsor: Christian Krebs and wife.

Eva Catharina, of Georg Borstein? and wife Eva, b. 17 Oct 1771, bapt. 27 Oct 177. Sponsors: Bernhard Bock and Catharina Weis(in).

Amalia, of Georg Grotius and wife Margaretha, b. 13 Aug 1771, bapt. 17 Sep 1771. Sponsors: Georg Stri_y and wife Maria.

Johannes, of Georg Daum and wife Elisabeth, b. 27 Sep 1771, bapt. 27 Oct 1771. Sponsors: the parents.

Anna Margaretha, of Johann Philipp Flor and wife Maria, b. 19 Oct 1771, bapt. 27 Oct 1771. Sponsors: Franz Wolf and wife Anna Margaretha.

Georg, of William Loscher and wife Maria Catharina, b. 4 Sep 1771, bapt. 3 Nov 1771. Sponsors: Georg Loscher and wife Maria.

Martin, of Michael Kintzler and wife Elisabeth, b. 23 Oct 1771, bapt. 3 Nov 1771. Sponsors: Martin Paisch and wife Magdalena.

Elisabetha Catharina, of John Maccaitau and wife Catharina, b. 6 Oct 1771, bapt. 3 Nov 1771. Sponsors: Joh. Friederich Mess (Mehls?) and wife Elisab. Catharina.

Jacob, of Johann Christoph Reinthal and wife Elisabeth, b. 5 Oct 1771, bapt. 3 Nov 1771. Sponsors: The grandparents Joh. Jacob Rheinthaler and wife.

Johannes, of Andreas Meyer and wife Maria Clara, b. 10 Sep 1771, bapt. 3 Nov 1771. Sponsors: Friedrich Heiler and wife Christina.

Anna Catharina, of Joh. Georg Hagenlocher and wife Anna Catharina, b. 28 Dec 1770, bapt. 3 Nov 1771. Sponsors: Andreas Meyer and wife Maria Clara.

Margretha, of Jacob Clauss and wife Margretha, b. 22 Oct 1771, bapt. 17 Nov 1771. Sponsors: the parents.

Anna Margretha, of Carl Birnn and wife Christina Elisabeth, b. 25 Oct 1771, bapt. 17 Nov 1771. Sponsors: Christoph Weidner and wife Margretha.

James Conrad, of James Dennison and Mary, b. 19 May 1771, bapt. 17 Nov 1771. Sponsors: Conrad Ring and wife Juliana.

Matthias, of Johann Palatin Bauer and wife Hanna (who is not yet baptised), from Upper Marion on the Schuylkill, b. 23 Oct 1771, bapt. 22 Nov 1771. Sponsors: the father and his mother Maria Catharina.

Henrich, of Johann Jacob Gress and wife Susanna, b. 30 Aug 1771, bapt. 22 Nov 1771. Sponsors: Henrich Volkel and wife Magdalena.

Johannes, of Carl Schneider and wife Anna Maria, b. 18 Nov 1771, bapt. 24 Nov 1771. Sponsors: Johannes Schneider and wife Anna Maria Reiser(in).

Maria Elisabeth, of Jacob Dehner and wife Margaretha, b. 16 Nov 1771, bapt. 24 Nov 1771. Sponsors: the father and his sister Anna Margar. Magdalena Gahling.

Christian, of Johann Kinzli and wife Margaretha, b. 8 Nov 1771, bapt. 24 Nov 1771. Sponsors: Christian Kinzli and wife Margaretha.

Georg, of Grieffich Grieffich and wife Sarah, b. 9 Jun 1771, bapt. 24 Nov 1771. Sponsors: Michael Orner and wife Anna Maria.

Mary, of David Rondels and wife Barbara, b. 11 Nov 1771, bapt. 24 Nov 1771. Sponsors: Michael Orner and wife Mary.

William, of Martin Fiess and Dorothea, not yet married, b. 25 Jul 1771, bapt. 24 Nov 1771. Sponsors: Thomas Bohr and Rebecca Callins.

John, of Simon Davis and wife Fronica, b. 1 Sep 1771, bapt. 10 Oct 1771. Sponsors: the mother, and Elisabeth Seibel.

Anna Catharine, of Johann Daniel and wife Anna Catharina, b. 21 Aug 1769, bapt. 22 Nov 1771. Sponsors: the mother, and Johann Henr. Rot(h)?.

Anna Maria, of Johann Kling and wife Anna, b. 3 Dec 1771, bapt. 5 Dec 1771. Sponsors: Ludew. Merner and wife Anna Maria.

Maria Elisabeth, of Peter Jung and wife Maria Magdalena, b. 5 Nov 1771, bapt. 5 Dec 1771. Sponsors: Conrad Schelier and wife Maria Elisabeth.

Philipp, of Friedrich Müller and wife Catharina, 14 days old, bapt. 8 Dec 1771. Sponsors: Philipp Läder and wife Elisabeth.

Salome, of Michael Müller and wife Christina, b. 2 Dec 1771, bapt. 8 Dec 1771. Sponsors: the parents.

Johann William (twin), of Francisc. Janthus and wife Anna Magdalena (who died giving birth), b. 7 Dec 1771, bapt. the same day. Sponsors: the father, and Sophia Margaretha Geret(in).

Franciscus (twin), of Francisc. Jant(h)us and wife Anna Magdalena, b. 7 Dec 1771, bapt. 17 Dec 1771. Sponsors: same as above.

Johannes, of Moses Hammer and wife Christina, b. 28 Nov 1771, bapt. 8 Dec 1771. Sponsors: Jacob Diegel and wife Hanna.

Henrich, of Friedr. Paul and wife Elisabeth, b. 1 Dec 1771, bapt. 13 Dec 1771. Sponsors: Christoph Kunze, and Henr. Cotus' wife Catharina, .

Peter, of Philipp Pfankuchen and wife Anna Maria, b. 8 Dec 1771, bapt. 18 Dec 1771. Sponsors: Peter Pfankuchen and wife Anna Margaretha.

Anna Margretha, of Anthony Hecht and wife Sophia, b. 15 Dec 1771, bapt. 29 Dec 1771. Sponsors: Christian Gally and wife Anna Margretha.

John Adam, of Philip Lehrer and wife Ursula, b. 22 May 1771, bapt. 29 Dec 1771. Sponsors: Johann Adam Diederle, single, and his sister Catharina.

Joh. Heinrich of Joh. Heinrich Bauer and wife Barbara, b. 21 Dec 1771, bapt. 26 Dec 1771. Sponsors: the father, and mother-in-law Fagner(in).

1772, First List
(baptisms by pastors Muhlenberg and Kunze; all in approximate chronological sequence, from Book II)

Salome, of John Facy and wife Christina, b. 21 Dec 1771, bapt. 1 Jan 1772. Sponsors: Joh. Philip Weisman and wife Salome.

Johan Henrich, of Friedrich Nebel and wife Margaret, 19 Jan 1772, bapt. 30 Apr 1772. Sponsors: Johan Thomas Bach and wife Cathar.

Johannes, of Johannes Gries and wife Barbara, b. 15 Apr? 1772, bapt. 3 May 1772. Sponsors: Elisab. Pertsch and Christine Pertsch.

Anna, of Mr. Melchior Lüben and wife Hannah, b. in Apr 1772, bapt. in May 1772. Sponsors: Michael Bottinger and wife.

1772, Second List
(baptisms by pastor Kunze, from Book III)

John Georg, of John George Tollman and wife Anna Mary, b. 16 Nov 1771, bapt. 1 Jan 1772. Sponsor: the father.

Margaretha, of Michael Beyer and wife Elisabeth, b. 5 Nov 1771, bapt. 1 Jan 1772. Sponsors: the father, and Heinrich Schneider's wife Margaretha.

Christian, of Christopher Jung and wife Margretha, b. 6 Dec 1771, bapt. 5 Jan 1772. Sponsors: Christian Jung and wife Carolina.

Johannes, of Johannes Christopher and wife Elisabeth, b. 4 Dec 1771, bapt. 5 Jan 1772. Sponsors: the child's grandmother Cress(in), and great-grandfather Johannes Cress..

Hanna, of Johann Conrad Schlatter and wife Christina, b. 30 Dec 1771, bapt. 5 Jan 1772. Sponsors: Andreas Sommer and wife Hanna.

Margaretha, of Valentin Sorg and wife Anna Maria, b. 30 Dec 1771, bapt. 7 Jan 1772. Sponsors: Adolph Lehr and wife Margaretha.

Georg, of Michael Strecker and wife Anna Margaretha, b. 7 Jan 1772, bapt. the same day. Sponsors: the parents and their dau. Cathar. Burghardt(in).

Michael, of Jacob Wolf and wife Anna Catharina, b. 4 Jan 1772, bapt. 11 Jan 1772. Sponsors: Michael Wolf and wife Sybilla.

Jacob, of Friedrich Dietz and wife Christina, b. 4 Jan 1772, bapt. 11 Jan 1772. Sponsors: Jacob Fidler and his mother Elisabeth (*Mr.* George Fidler's wife).

Georg Gottfried, of Benjamin Friedrich Wolpert and wife Anna Barbara, b. 28 Dec 1771, bapt. 12 Jan 1772. Sponsors: *Mr.* Georg Gottfried Wolpert and wife Anna Margretha.

Maria, of *Mr.* George Wirth and wife Maria, b. 18 Dec 1771, bapt. 12 Jan 1772. Sponsors: *Mr.* Georg Esterle and wife Maria.

Catharina, of Carl Müller and wife Anna Magdalena, b. 1 Jan 1772, bapt. 12 Jan 1772. Sponsors: Jacob Kless and wife Sabina.

Georg, of John Jackson and wife Martha, b. 3 Nov 1771, bapt. 13 Jan 1772. Sponsors: Georg Hirt and wife Margaretha.

Anna, of William Clifford, (a soldier) and wife Jane, b. 12 Jan 1772, bapt. 15 Jan 1772. Sponsors: the father "and two more."

Catharina, of Christian Apfel and wife Margaretha, b. 13 Jan 1772, bapt. 15 Jan 1772. Sponsors: Adam Tile and wife Catharina.

Johann Henrich, of Johann Benniford and wife Susanna, b. 29 Dec 1771, bapt. 17 Jan 1772. Sponsors: Henrich Phillipp and Elisabeth Julie, single.

Salome, of *Mr.* Josua Lampater and wife Catharina, b. 28 Dec 1771, bapt. 18 Jan 1772. Sponsors: Laurence Mahn and wife Margretha.

Jacob, of Jacob Bender and wife Maria, b. 12 Jan 1772, bapt. 18 Jan 1772. Sponsors: the father, and mother-in-law Eva Elisabeth Weisbach(in).

Catharina, of Philip Mietmann and wife Euphronia, b. 5 Jan 1772, bapt. 19 Jan 1772. Sponsors: Philip Dick and wife Catharina.

Catharina, of Joh. Peter Wolpert and wife, b. 9 Dec 1771, bapt. 26 Jan 1772. Sponsors: the father, and Catharina Corb(in).

Johannes, of Henrich Meisinger and wife Juliana, b. 10 Jan 1772, bapt. 26 Jan 1772. Sponsors: Johann Foggerod and wife Christina.

Joh. Fransciscus, of Frantz Braunholtz and wife Anna Barbara, b. 22 Nov 1771, bapt. 26 Jan 1772. Sponsors: Johann Daniel Schmid and Anna Schuster(in), both single.

Joh. Georg, of Joh. Georg Schreck and wife Margretha, b. 29 Nov 1771, bapt. 26 Jan 1772. Sponsors: Conrad Kiemle and wife Maria Sophia.

Johann Peter, of Georg Adam Schmidt and wife Anna Christina, b. 12 Jan 1772, bapt. 26 Jan 1772. Sponsors: Joh. Peter Mährlin and wife Maria Dorothea.

Hiskia, of Joseph Warner (deceased) and wife Hanna, b. 16 Jan 1768, bapt. 26 Jan 1772. Sponsors: Johannes Mutschidler and wife Margretha.

Maria Margretha, of Lorentz Opmann and wife Anna Maria, b. 18 Jan 1772.,
    bapt. 26 Jan 1772. Sponsors: Johannes Jacobs and wife Maria Margretha.
David, of Henrich Lentz and wife Anna Maria, b. 30 Nov 1771, bapt. 26 Jan
    1772. Sponsors: the parents.
Elizabeth, of Thomas Search and wife Catharina, b. 16 Sep 1771, bapt. 26 Jan
    1772. Sponsor: widow Anna Barbara Spitzer(in),.
Maria, of Johann Gottfriedt Riedel and wife Magdalena Catharina, b. 27 Jan
    1772, bapt. 2 Feb 1772. Sponsors: ___ Schof and wife.
Sara, of Melchior Weissinger and wife Maria, b. 15 Jan 1772, bapt. 2 Feb 1772.
    Sponsors: Balthasar Stauss and wife.
Heinrich Alexander, of Henrich Mayer (a sugar-boiler) and wife Catharina, b.
    21 Jan 1772, bapt. 2 Feb 1772. Sponsors: the parents?
James, of James Nelson and wife Margretha (bondservants in the Bettering's
    house?), 3 months old, bapt. 2 Feb 1772. Sponsors: "several evidences."
Johannes, of Georg Hof and wife Maria Margaretha, b. 19 Aug 1771, bapt.
    3 Feb 1772. Sponsors: the parents.
Maria, of Christian Friedrich Stuber and wife Elisabeth, b. 3 Jan 1772, bapt.
    4 Feb 1772. Sponsors: *Mr.* Johannes Weber and wife Maria.
James, of James Fellon and Francisca Schweitzer(in), 2 months old, bapt. 6 Feb
    1772. Sponsors: the mother, and Elisabeth Wright.
Maria Magdal., of Georg Jacob Hausmann and wife Maria (Ref.), b. 21 Jan
    1772, bapt. 5 Feb 1772. Sponsors: Henrich Miet and wife Elisabeth.
Joh. Georg, of Henrich Moses and wife Susanna, b. 24 Jan 1772, bapt. 9 Feb
    1772. Sponsors: Georg Bluhm and wife Hanna.
Joh. Martin, of Andreas Lap and wife Christina, b. 8 Feb 1772, bapt. 16 Feb
    1772. Sponsors: Joh. Martin Schmidt and wife Agnes Catharina.
Margretha, of Wilhelm Klauer and wife Margretha, b. 27 Jan 1772, bapt. 16 Feb
    1772. Sponsors: Georg Warner and wife Barbara.
Christina, of Sebastian Mully and wife Elisabeth Catharina, b. 9 Feb 1772, bapt.
    16 Feb 1772. Sponsors: Joh. Georg Ackerman and wife Christine.
Jacob, of Jacob Lesher, of Frankford, and wife Anna Maria, b. 9 Jan 1772, bapt.
    16 Feb 1772. Sponsors: Michael Hermann and wife Anna Maria.
Elisabeth, of Isaac Sutton, of Frankford, and wife Anna, 7 years old last Jul,
    bapt. 16 Feb 1772. Sponsors: John Sutton and wife Sarah.
Ludwig, of Theodorus Memminger and wife Maria, b. 31 Jan 1772, bapt. 29 Feb
    1772. Sponsors: the parents.
Christian, of Caspar Christ and wife Catharina, b. 14 Feb 1772, bapt. 1 Mar
    1772. Sponsors: Christian Gally and wife.
Johannes, of Joh. Adam Bausch and wife Anna Maria, b. 6 Feb 1772, bapt.
    1 Mar 1772. Sponsors: Joh. Georg Wentzel and wife Anna Margaretha.
John Michael, of Michael Penny and wife Rosina, b. 5 Feb 1772, bapt. 1 Mar
    1772. Sponsors: John Bauer and wife Barbara.
Johann Jacob, of William North and Catharina Brechel(in), b. 5 Feb 1772, bapt.
    25 Feb 1772. Sponsors: Joh. Jacob Scheppach and wife Maria Ursula.
Maria Dorothea, of Georg Jung and wife Rosina, b. 9 Feb 1772, bapt. 8 Mar
    1772. Sponsors: *Mr.* Georg Walker and wife Maria Dorothea.
Charlotta Elisabeth, of Carl Truckenmüller and wife Susanna, b. 15 Feb 1772,
    bapt. 8 Mar 1772. Sponsors: Michael Gönner and wife Charlotta Elisabeth.

Joh. Christopher, of Christian Heinrich and wife Anna Christina, b. 18 Jan 1772, bapt. 8 Mar 1772. Sponsors: Johannes Christoph and wife Elisabeth.

Elisabeth, of Johannes Geiser and wife Elisabeth, b. 7 Jan 1772, bapt. 8 Mar 1772. Sponsors: the parents.

Peter, of Anthon Armbrüster and wife Maria Catharina (2nd. wife), b. 6 Feb 1772, bapt. 12 Mar 1772. Sponsors: Peter Schuttehelm and wife Elisabeth.

Anna Catharine, of Georg Mildeberger and wife Catharina, b. 15 Feb 1772, bapt. 15 Mar 1772. Sponsors: the grandparents Michael Mildeberger and wife Christina.

Johannes, of Christian Kientzel and wife Anna Margaretha, b. 28 Feb 1772, bapt. 15 Mar 1772. Sponsors: Johannes Greiffenstein and wife Dorothea.

Johannes, of Johannes Michael and wife, on Germantown Street, b. 22 Feb 1772, bapt. 15 Mar 1772. Sponsors: Peter Wagner and wife.

Maria Margaretha, of George Heidel and wife Maria Salome, b. 2, Mar 772, bapt. 15 Mar 1772. Sponsors: the parents, and grandmother Dorn(in)..

Gottfried, of Michael Schleihof and wife Anna Barbara, b. 3 Jan 1772, bapt. 18 Mar 1772. Sponsors: Philip Lehrer and wife Ursula.

A child (name not given), of Michael Schubbart and wife, (birth date not given), bapt. 16 Mar 1772. Sponsors: Friedr. Heiler and wife.

Carl Ludewig (twin), of Henrich Darser and wife Margareta, b. 22 Dec 1771, bapt. 18 Mar 1772. Sponsors: the parents, and Paul Daser.

Georg (twin), of Henrich Darser and wife Margareta, b. 22 Dec 1771, bapt. 18 Mar 1772. Sponsors: the parents.

Johann Jacob, of Nicolaus Herzebach and wife Regina, (birth date not given), bapt. 19 Mar 1772. Sponsors: Johann Jacob Weissert and wife Elisabeth.

Rosina, of Samnuel Prinz and wife Anna, b. 7 Mar 1772, bapt. 22 Mar 1772. Sponsors: Michael Hirneisen and wife Rosina.

Maria Elisabeth, of Georg Laib and wife Margretha Dorothea, b. 22 Feb 1772, bapt. 22 Mar 1772. Sponsors: Mr. Elias Ludewig Treickel and wife Elisabeth.

Maria, of Henrich Moore, from Maryland, and wife Catharina, b. 25 Dec 1771, bapt. 18 Mar 1772. Sponsors: the mother, and grandmother Eva Schluster(in).

Johann Peter, of Michael Hotz and wife Catharina, b. 9 Mar 1772, bapt. 22 Mar 1772. Sponsors: Mr. Peter Dick and wife Maria.

Anna Maria, of Adam Knoblauch and wife Anna Barbara, b. 20 Mar 1772, bapt. 22 Mar 1772. Sponsors: Mr. Joh. Philip Fischer and wife Anna Maria.

Sarah, of Samuel Kreu[t]z and wife Elisabeth, b. 7 Nov 1771, bapt. 20 Mar 1772. Sponsors: Georg Mildeberger and wife.

Abraham, of Christian Rush and wife Sarah, b. 11 Oct 1771, bapt. 22 Mar 1772. Sponsors: Abraham B_dybaker and Septima Farmer.

Johann Adam, of Philip Riess and wife Agnes, b. 12 Mar 1772, bapt. 29 Mar 1772. Sponsors: Joh. Adam Sauer, single, and Philippina Münch(in).

Johannes, of William Weber and wife Elisabeth, b. 17 Mar 1772, bapt. 29 Mar 1772. Sponsors: Johannes Mutschittler, and the grandmother Anna Catharina.

Dorothea, of Matth. Starter (or Harter) and wife Dorothea, b. 6 Mar 1772, bapt. 29 Mar 1772. Sponsors: Friedr. Lenk and wife Charlotta.

Jacob, of Daniel Knodel and wife Anna Maria, b. 15 Mar 1772, bapt. 29 Mar 1772. Sponsors: Jacob Kiefer, single, and Jacobina Reusch(in).

Johann Peter, of Nicolaus Reb and wife Christina, b. 24 Mar 1772, bapt. 29 Mar 1772. Sponsors: Peter Klein and wife.

Johann Leonhard, of Francis Sauer and wife Apollonia, b. 2 Jan 1772, bapt. 29 Mar 1772. Sponsors: Joh. Leonhard Weber and wife Elisabeth.

James, of Robert Clunie (soldier) and wife Mary, b. 22 Mar 1772, bapt. 30 Mar 1772. Sponsors: the father and other witnesses.

Sebastian, of Johann Adam Grob and wife Elisabeth, b. 3 Apr 1772, bapt. 5 Apr 1772. Sponsors: Sebastian Seibert and wife Barbara.

Matthias, of Peter Rose and wife Sara Elisabeth, b. 1 Mar 1772, bapt. 15 Apr 1772. Sponsors: Peter Klein and wife Eva Maria.

Barbara, of Nicolaus Wagner and wife Anna Magdalena, b. 6 Feb 1772, bapt. 5 Apr 1772. Sponsors: Jacob Burghardt and wife Barbara.

Johannes, of Michael Schumacher and wife Susanna, b. 23 Mar 1772, bapt. 5 Apr 1772. Sponsors: Christian Gally and wife Margretha.

Maria, of Caspar Haas and wife Catharina, b. 25 Mar 1772, bapt. 5 Apr 1772. Sponsors: George Fetter and wife Maria.

Johann Philip, of Johann Peter Bill and Anna Margaretha Bill(in), b. 24 Feb 1772, bapt. 5 Apr 1772. Sponsors: Johannes Eberhardt and Catharina Mauss(in).

Maria Elisabeth, of Peter Dechert, from Tulpehocken, and wife Gertrude, b. 22 Mar 1772, bapt. 6 Apr 1772. Sponsors: the mother, and Anna Klein(in).

Catharina Magdalena, of Joseph Rivers and wife Catharina, b. 12 Feb 1772, bapt. 12 Apr 1772. Sponsors: Joh. Heckert and wife Anna Maria.

Jacob, of Johannes Wagner and wife Elisabeth, b. 25 Feb 1772, bapt. 12 Apr 1772. Sponsors: Jacob Stöss and wife Salome.

Johannes, of Johannes Vogel and wife Mary, b. 14 Mar 1772, bapt. 5 Apr 1772. Sponsors: Johannes Unangst and wife Cathar. Margareth.

Johannes, of Philip Springer and wife Eva, newly arrived, b. 15 Oct 1771, bapt. 12 Apr 1772. Sponsors: Johannes Jacobs and wife Maria.

Samuel, of William Carl Evans and wife Eva, b. 21 Mar 1772, bapt. 14 Apr 1772. Sponsors: John Buckinham and wife.

William, of Christian Lehmann, the notary, 20 years old, bapt. 16 Apr 1772. Sponsors: Rev. Kuntze and Rev. Heinrich Mühlenberg.

Georg, of Georg Hoch and wife Dorothea, b. 7 Apr 1772, bapt. 9 Apr 1772. Sponsors: Peter Rieb and wife Catharina.

Margretha, of Melchior Horner of [New] Jersey, and wife Elisabeth, b. 15 Dec 1771, bapt. 19 Apr 1772. Sponsors: Dr. Podo Otto and wife Margretha.

Johann Georg, of Michael Wolf and wife Margretha, b. 2 Nov 1771, bapt. 19 Apr 1772. Sponsors: David Uber and wife Anna.

Eva Catharina, of Georg Forbach and wife Anna Margareta, b. 19 Mar 1772, bapt. 19 Apr 1772. Sponsors: Christoph Meier and wife Eva Catharina.

Johannes, of Gottfried Weltel of Maryland and wife Christina, b. 6 May 1763, bapt. 22 Apr 1772. Sponsors: the parents, and Wilhelm Friedrich Wirth (or Wörth), from Wilmington..

Wilhelm, of Gottfried Weltel and wife Christina, b. 13 Apr 1772, bapt. 22 Apr 1772. Sponsors: same as above.

Johannes, of Johann Barent and wife Barbara, b. 21 Apr 1772, bapt. 26 Apr 1772. Sponsors: Johann Messerschmidt and wife Barbara.

Georg, of Philip Bechtold and wife Anna Maria, b. 6 Mar 1772, bapt. 26 Apr 1772. Sponsors: Georg Seitz and wife Elisabeth.

Regina, of Robert Chews (Quaker) and wife Elisabeth (Lutheran), b. 1 Jan 1772, bapt. 26 Apr 1772. Sponsor: the maternal grandmother Maria Magdal. (Kress?).

Johannes, of Philipp Hawkins and wife Catharina, b. 6 Mar 1772, bapt. 2 May 1772. Sponsors: Henrich Corte and his sister Margaretha.

John Philipp, of Fried. Ernst and wife Maria Clara, b. 20 Apr 1772, bapt. 3 May 1772. Sponsors: Joh. Phil. Alberti and wife Anna Barbara.

Catharina, of Andreas Gressel and wife Dorothea Sophia, b. 12 Mar 1772, bapt. 3 May 1772. Sponsors: Cathar. Gressel(in) and Johannes Gressel.

Johann Henrich, of Friedrich Nebel and wife Margaret, b. 19 Jan 1770?, bapt. 30 May 1772. Sponsors: Johann Thomas Bach and wife Cathar.

Johannes, of Johannes Griess and wife Barbara, b. 15 Apr 1772, bapt. 31 May 1772. Sponsors: Elisabet and Christina Perssel.

Johannes, of Johann Heinrich Dietz and wife Anna Barbara, b. 25 Mar 1772, bapt. 10 May 1772. Sponsors: Johannes Wilhelm Engelfried and wife Catharina.

Esther, of Daniel Pender and wife Sophia Susanna, b. 27 Apr 1772, bapt. 10 May 1772. Sponsors: Johann Weinkauf and Esther Ott(in).

Anna, of Melchior Lüben and wife Hannah, b. 17 Apr 1772, bapt. 10 May 1772. Sponsors: Michael Bedinger and wife Eva.

William, of William Wollington and wife Susanna, b. 14 Apr 1772, bapt. 11 May 1772. Sponsors: John Wollington, and Will Seitz's widow Elisabeth.

Maria Elisabet, of Johann Christopher Senterling and wife Maria, b. 17 Apr 1772, bapt. in May 1772. Sponsors: Michael Dieter and wife Maria Elisabeth.

Ernst, of Nicolaus Ulrich and wife Eva, b. 24 Feb 1772, bapt. 27 May 1772. Sponsors: Friedrich Ulrich and Maria Magdalena.

Anna Sophia, of Christoph Simon and wife Anna Margareta, b. 12 Mar 1772, bapt. 24 May 1772. Sponsors: Ernst Christoph Engler and wife Rosina.

Georg Adam, of Ehrhardt Giebelhaus and wife Maria Barbara, b. 18 May 1772, bapt. 24 May 1772. Sponsors: Georg Adam Schmidt and wife Anna Juliana.

Adam, of Johannes Klein and wife Catharina, b. 3 Mar 1772, bapt. 24 May 1772. Sponsors: Adam Lehr and Maria Witmann(in).

Catharina, of Johannes Naevi and wife Elisabeth, b. 3 Apr 1772, bapt. 24 May 1772. Sponsors: Christoph Haensmann and his dau. Catharina.

Elisabet, of Martin Summer and wife Barbara, b. 9 Apr 1772, bapt. 24 May 1772. Sponsors: Nicolaus Rotenwald and wife Elisabet.

Maria Elisabet, of Wilhelm Heins and wife Catharina, b. 29 Dec 1771, bapt. 24 May 1772. Sponsor: Maria Margareta Rose(lin).

Rachel, of James (Jonas?) Kleinsy and wife Elisabeth, b. 28 Feb 1772, bapt. 24 May 1772. Sponsors: the parents.

(Child's name not given), of Caspar Graess and wife Catharina, b. 1 Apr 1772, bapt. 24 May 1772. Sponsors: the father, and the maternal grandmother Hafner(in).

Johan Martin, of Johan Georg Gettling and wife Maria Christina, b. 23 May
1772, bapt. 28 May 1772. Sponsor: Johan Martin Rapp and wife.
Susanna Regina, of Christian Stützer and wife Christina, b. 23 Dec 1770, bapt.
28 May 1772. Sponsors: Charles Hofmann and wife Susanna Regina.
Sara, of Johannes Müller and wife Maria, b. 2 May 1771, bapt. 30 May 1772.
Sponsors: the father, and Dorothea Caput.
Susanna, of Johannes Feldenberger and wife Susanna, b. 20 May 1772, bapt.
31 May 1772. Sponsors: Susanna Swalbach and Rudolph Nagel.
Philippina, of Johann Fromberger and wife Anna, b. 17 May 1772, bapt.
30 May 1772. Sponsors: Nicol. Weber and wife Christina.
Michael, of Jac. Riess and wife Magdalena, b. 5 May 1772, bapt. 30 May 1772.
Sponsors: Michael Kamper and wife Elisabeth.
Elisabeth, of Johann Nicolaus Rot(h)ewalter and wife Elisabeth, b. 28 May
1772, bapt. 30 May 1772. Sponsors: Johannes Kaiser and wife Elisabeth.
Elisabeth, of Jacob Steinmeier and wife Anna Catharina, b. 3 May 1772, bapt.
30 May 1772. Sponsors: the parents.
Johannes, of Georg Wüster and wife Juliana, b. 1 Feb 1772, bapt. 31 May 1772.
Sponsors: Sebastian Sonleitner and wife Margretha.
Johannes, of Caspar Wirschum and wife Rosina, b. 19 May 1772, bapt. 31 May
1772. Sponsors: Joh. Georg Kieser and wife Eva Maria.
Regina, of Matthaeus Landenberger (wife's name not given), b. 19 May 1772,
bapt. 7 Jun 1772. Sponsors: Thomas Meier and wife Margareta.
Ludwig, of Ludwig Braun and wife Sarah, b. 10 Nov 1771, bapt. 7 Jun 1772.
Sponsors: the parents.
Catherina, of Martin Walter and wife Barbara, b. 28 Feb 1772, bapt. 7 Jun 1772.
Sponsors: Georg Russ and wife Margaretha.
Joh. Adam, of Adam Schmidt and wife Catharina, b. 26 May 1772, bapt. 7 Jun
1772. Sponsors: Sebastian Seibert and wife Anna Barbara.
Elisabeth, of Jacob Diethrich and wife Augustina, b. 24 Jan 1772, bapt. 7 Jun
1772. Sponsor: Peter Clemens' wife Maria.
Jacob, of Jacob Kochler and wife Catharina, 13 months old, bapt. 7 Jun 1772.
Sponsors: Matthais Sommer and wife Elisabeth.
Johannes, of Johannes Grind and Magdalena Denninger, illegitimate, b. 25 May
1772, bapt. 7 Jun 1772. Sponsors: Johan Jacob Danninger and wife Barbara.
Jacob, of Georg Kerman and wife Elisabeth, at Frankford, b. 25 Aug 1766, bapt.
4 May 1772. Sponsors: Jacob Meier and wife Anna Maria.
Conrad, of Georg Peter Zindler and wife Anna Maria, at Frankford, b. 20 Oct
1771, bapt. 7 Jun 1772. Sponsors: Henrich Meier and Margaret Matzman.
George, of George Lehman (bondservant of Mr. Bath__) and Anna Emit
(English, from the Great Valley), b. 1 Apr 1772, bapt. 9 Jun 1772. Sponsors:
various witnesses.
Susanna, of William Kuhli and wife Elisabeth, from Maryland, b. 22 Oct 1771,
bapt. 10 Jun 1772. Sponsor: Susanna Retzel.
Maria, of Theodorus Wilhelm Wölmer and wife Catharine, b. 30 May 1772,
bapt. 10 Jun 1772. Sponsors: John Conrad Eschart and wife Maria.
Maria, of Niclaus Diel and wife Maria, b. 17 Oct 1771, bapt. 13 Jun 1772.
Sponsors: Maria Gerier(in) and husband Adam Geier.

Johann Christian ,of Joh. Georg Moser and wife Anna Dorothea, b. 17 Apr 1772, bapt. 14 Jun 1772. Sponsors: John Christian Rot(h) and wife Anna Catharine.

Maria, of Mr. Conrad Abel and wife Margretha, b. 3 Jun 1772, bapt. 14 Jun 1772. Sponsors: Philip Jacob Bechtold and wife Anna Maria.

Maria Margretha, of Mr. Joh. Wilhelm Trautwein and wife Anna Maria, b. 21 Dec 1771, bapt. 14 Jun 1772. Sponsors: the parents.

Maria, of Daniel Kirschner and wife Philippina, b. 4 Apr 1772, bapt. 14 Jun 1772. Sponsors: Georg Oesterli and wife Maria.

Joh. Heinrich, of Peter Arnold and wife Maria, b. 26 May 1772, bapt. 14 Jun 1772. Sponsors: the grandpaaretns Joh. Heinrich Gilbert and wife Catharina.

Christina Barbara, of Jacob Becker and wife Regina, b. 28 Sep 1771, bapt. 14 Jun 1772. Sponsors: the mother, and the grandmother Christina Barbara Foliker(in)?.

Catharina, of Jacob Keimle and wife Catharina, b. 14 Jun 1772, bapt. 19 Jun 1772. Sponsors: Johannes Fri[t]z and wife Catharina.

Maria, of Owen Kirchen and wife Margareta, b. 13 May 1772, bapt. 29 Jun 1772. Sponsors: Georg Krauskopf and wife Margareta.

Johannes, of Georg Turner and wife Maria Catharina, b. 3 May 1772, bapt. 19 Jun 1772. Sponsors: the parents.

Anna Maria, of Cornelius Braun and wife Maria Magdalena, b. 15 Mar 1772, bapt. 21 Jun 1772. Sponsors: Daniel Knodel and wife Anna Maria.

Margaretha Anna, of Georg Landgraf and wife Magdalena, b. 29 Apr 1772, bapt. 21 Jun 1772. Sponsor: Anna Margretha Spat(in).

Abel, of Abel Lippincot and wife Catharina, b. 9 Jun 1772, bapt. 21 Jun 1772. Sponsor: Elisabeth Ringsbach?.

William, of William Hamilton and wife Rosina, b. 9 Mar 1772, bapt. 28 Jun 1772. {This entry was interposed later, and was in English.}

Philip Wilhelm, of Robert Vernon and wife Philippina, b. 31 Jan 1772, bapt. 21 Jun 1772. Sponsors: the mother, and the grandmother Catharina Hertzbach(in).

Georg, of Sebastian Heiler and wife Elisabeth, b. 12 Jun 1772, bapt. 28 Jun 1772. Sponsors: Georg Russ and wife Margaretha.

Anna Elisabeth, of Johannes Höflein and wife Anna Cathar., b. 15 Jun 1772, bapt. 28 Jun 1772. Sponsors: the parents.

Maria Elisabeth, of Philip Stock and wife Catharina, b. 28 May 1772, bapt. 28 Jun 1772. Sponsors: Michael Diederle and wife Maria Elisabeth.

Peter, of John Toy and wife Catharina, b. 27 May 1772, bapt. 28 Jun 1772. Sponsors: Peter Wagner and wife Rosina.

Charlotte, of Leonard Eger and wife Charlotte, b. in Jun 1772, bapt. 30 Jun 1772. Sponsors: the mother, and the grandmother Anna Eva Kifsort(in)?.

Isaac, of Isaac Dewherst and wife Elizabeth, b. 21 Feb 1772, bapt. 2 Jul 1772. Sponsors: the parents.

Maria Regina, of Wilhelm Will and wife Elisabeth, b. 4 May 1772, bapt. 2 Jul 1772. Sponsors: Ludwig Penter and Rachel Hahn(in).

Maria, of Christoph Weidner and wife Margaretha, b. 16 Jan 1772, bapt. 5 Jul 1772. Sponsor: Michael Weber's dau. Maria Weber(in).

Maria Eva, of Martin Wagner and wife Margaretha, b. 11 Feb 1772, bapt. 5 Jul 1772. Sponsors: Valentin Griech and Maria Dietz(in), single.

Maria Margaretha, of Johann Christ. Pfiller and wife Sophia, b. 13 Jun 1772, bapt. 5 Jul 1772. Sponsors: John Rohr and wife Maria.

Adam Walter, of Joh. Walter Schwab and wife Anna Margretha, 11 months old, bapt. 5 Jul 1772. Sponsors: Joh. Adam Schiesser and wife Dorothea.

Margaretha, of Johann Hoch and wife Barbara, b. 12 Apr 1772, bapt. 5 Jul 1772. Sponsors: Leonard Hoch and his sister Margaretha.

Elisabeth Dorothea, of Josua Metzger and wife Sophia, b. in Mar 1772, bapt. 5 Jul 1772. Sponsors: Johannes Gätz and wife Anna Dorothea.

Susanna Elisabeth, of William Fairle and wife Elisabeth, b. 23 Jun 1772, bapt. 5 Jul 1772. Sponsors: William Love (English) and Elisabeth Gilbert(in).

Juliana, of Abraham Glodin (Ref.) and wife Juliana (Luth.), b. 2 Jul 1772, bapt. 6 Jul 1772. Sponsor: the parents.

George, of Rebecca Donnel, 7 months old, bapt. 9 Jul 1772. Sponsors: Barbara Schütz(in) and Elisabeth Thomas.

Daniel, of William Bechtel and wife Elisabeth, b. 31 Mar 1772, bapt. 8 Jul 1772. Sponsors: Daniel Gasner and [whose?] sister Elisabeth.

Heinrich, of Philip May and wife Anna Maria, b. 19 Jun 1772, bapt. 12 Jul 1772. Sponsors: Henrich Rathschlag and wife Margar. Elisabeth.

Johannes, of Peter Mattheus Abel and wife Maria Philippina, b. 25 Jun 1772, bapt. 12 Jul 1772. Sponsors: Johannes Hager and wife Anna Cath.

Charles, of Christopher Lang and wife Margaret, b. 11 Oct 1769, bapt. 12 Jul 1772. Sponsors: David Jones and wife Barbara.

Maria Magdalena, of Paulus Michael Beck and wife Maria Magdalena, b. 11 Jul 1772, bapt. 19 Jul 1772. Sponsors: the parents.

Joseph, of Anna Nagel(in) and Peter Hauss, illegitimate, b. 27 Jun 1772, bapt. 19 Jul 1772. Sponsors: Sara Mahn(in), and Georg Harrison's wife Catharina.

Mary, of Thomas Heid and wife Anna, b. 30 Jun 1772, bapt. 20 Jul 1772. Sponsors: the mother and Mary Shaw.

Johannes, of Ludewig Mader and wife Elisabeth, b. 10 Jul 1772, bapt. 23 Jul 1772. Sponsors: Johannes Gerlach and wife Anna Maria.

Rosina, of Philipp Georg Knecht and wife Anna Maria, b. 18 Jul 1772, bapt. 25 Jul 1772. Sponsors: Peter Gress and wife Rosina.

Maria Elisabeth, of Wilhelm Dietz and wife Maria Catharina, b. 10 Jul 1772, bapt. 26 Jul 1772. Sponsors: *Mr.* Georg Seitz and wife Maria Elisabeth.

Catharina, of Joh. Michael Jobst and wife Margretha, b. 19 Mar 1772, bapt. 26 Jul 1772. Sponsors: Michael Weber and wife Catharina.

Anna Maria, of Nicolaus Lochman and wife Johanna Maria, b. 10 Jul 1772, bapt. 26 Jul 1772. Sponsors: Georg Russ and wife Maria Margretha.

Catharina, of Ferdinand Mayenmoder (a Frenchman) and wife Catharina, b. 22 Jul 1772, bapt. 28 Jul 1772. Sponsor: Anna Klem(in).

Jacob, of Joh. Friedr. Moels and wife Cathar. Elisabeth, b. 13 Jul 1772, bapt. 26 Jul 1772. Sponsors: Jacob Graef and wife Catharina.

Dorothea Magdalena, of Joh. Martin Paisch and wife Magdalena, b. 18 Jul 1772, bapt. 26 Jul 1772. Sponsors: Martin Paisch's brother (name not given), and Dorothea Caput.

Catharina, of Jacob Bäsley and wife Magdalena, b. 1 Aug 1772, bapt. the same day. Sponsors: Daniel Hofman and wife Anna Margaretha.

George, of Adam Rudolph (a widower) and Elisabeth Bold(in), illegitimate, b. 1 Jan 1772, bapt. 1 Aug 1772. Sponsors: Georg Wunderlich and wife Catharina.

Regina, of Johannes Bauer and wife Catharina, b. 22 Jan 1772, bapt. 2 Aug 1772. Sponsors: Johannes Mass and Catharina Meier(in)..

Henry, of Johan Gottfr. Hall and wife Sarah, b. 17 Jul 1772, bapt. 2 Aug 1772. Sponsors: Philip Hall and his dau. Catharina.

William, of John Night and wife Elisabeth, b. 1 Aug 1772, bapt. 2 Aug 1772. Sponsors: the parents and George Cook.

Sarah, of John Lawton and wife Ann, about 6 years old, bapt. 2 Aug 1772. Sponsors: John Night, George Cook, and Elizabeth Night.

Job, of John Lawton and wife Ann, last Jan 3 years old, bapt. 2 Aug 1772. Sponsors: same as above.

Jesse, of John Lawton and wife Ann, 1½ years old, bapt. 2 Aug 1772. Sponsors: same as above.

Maria Margretha, of Christian Keller and wife Maria Susanna, b. 26 Dec 1771, bapt. 3 Aug 1772. Sponsors: the mother and Juliana Schül(in).

Martha Rebecca, of Joh. Georg Lohrmann and wife Anna Justina, b. 27 Jul 1772, bapt. 3 Aug 1772. Sponsors: the parents.

Philipp (twin), of Christoph Graefly and wife Eva, b. 22 Jul 1772, bapt. 4 Aug 1772. Sponsors: the parents.

Joh. Georg (twin), of Christoph Graefly and wife Eva, b. 22 Jul 1772, bapt. 4 Aug 1772. Sponsors: the parents and Joh. Georg Graefly.

Catharina, of Henrich Ritter and wife Catharina, b. 21 Jan 1772, bapt. 3 Jul 1772. Sponsors: Georg Pob and wife Cathar.

Margaretha, of Peter Ritter and wife Penelope, b. 10 Jul 1772, bapt. 5 Aug 1772. Sponsors: Georg Ritter and wife Marg.

Maria, of John Colly and wife Maria, b. 30 Jul 1772, bapt. 6 Aug 1772. Sponsors: the parents.

Catharina, of Fried. Enzmunger and wife Catharina, b. 2 Aug 1772, bapt. 7 Aug 1772. Sponsors: Joh. Georg Horne and wife.

Johann Caspar, of Peter Derry and wife Elisabeth, b. 25 Jul 1772, bapt. 9 Aug 1772. Sponsors: Johann Caspar Wahl and wife Elisabeth.

Anna Maria, of Philipp Werner and wife Magdalena, b. 15 Jul 1772, bapt. 9 Aug 1772. Sponsors: Henrich Schneider and wife Anna Maria.

Johann Michael, of Jacob Schmidt and wife Maria Magdalena, b. 21 Jul 1772, bapt. 9 Aug 1772. Sponsors: Michael Schreiber and Elisabeth Hausmann(in).

Catharina, of Michael Omensetter and wife Catharina, b. 9 Aug 1772, bapt. 9 Aug 1772. Sponsors: the parents.

Eva Catharina, of Georg Wunderlich and wife Catharina, b. 6 Jul 1772, bapt. 10 Aug 1772. Sponsors: Ludwig Stür[t]z and wife Eva Catharina.

John, of John Hill and wife Anna, b. 25 Apr 1772, bapt. 10 Aug 1772. Sponsor: the mother.

Margretha, of George Heiler and wife Ann, b. 3 Aug 1772, bapt. 12 Aug 1772. Sponsors: the mother and Mary Chappel.

Edward, of *Mr.* Cotbus (birth and baptism dates and sponsors not given.)

John Jacob, of *Mr.* Georg Michael Kraft and wife Johanna Maria, b. 11 Aug 1772, bapt. 16 Aug 1772. Sponsors: Jacob Weber and wife Elisabetha.

John Ludwig, of Michael Kuhn and wife Maria, b. 27 Jul 1772, bapt. 16 Aug 1772. Sponsors: John Ludwig Pannakuche and Maria Magdalena Weiss(in).

Wilhelm, of Friederich Warner and wife Maria, b. 3 Aug 1772, bapt. 16 Aug 1772. Sponsors: the parents.

Johannes, of Jacob Seyfried and wife Maria Salome, b. 26 Jul 1772, bapt. 16 Aug 1772. Sponsors: the grandparents Jacob Seyfried and wife Christina.

Johannes, of Jacob Unbehend and wife Anna Maria, b. 23 Jul 1772, bapt. 16 Aug 1772. Sponsors: Johannes Löser and Catharina Unbehend.

Georg, of George Hummel and wife Elisabet, b. 1 Jul 1772, bapt. 18 Aug 1772. Sponsors: Georg Klein and wife Barbara.

Philippina, a Negro child, slave of Christoph Curfess and Catharina, 5 years old, 1772, bapt. 18 Mar 1772. Sponsors: the master and mistress [unnamed, unless they were Christoph and Catharina Curfess].

Christina, of Wilh. Miller and wife Catharina, b. 8 Oct 1771, bapt. 18 Aug 1772. Sponsors: the father and Christina Essig(in).

Joh. Phil., of Anna Maria Lu(t)z(in), (the father is a bondservant), b. 29 Jul 1772, bapt. 17 Aug 1772. Sponsors: Joh. Skimpf and Apollonia Schmidt(in).

John, of Peter Ritter and wife Catharina, b. 6 Aug 1772, bapt. 21 Aug 1772. Sponsors: Mary Welch and Mary Mühlenberg.

Johann Carl, of Siegmund Hagelgans and wife Margaretha, b. 14 Aug 1772, bapt. 23 Aug 1772. Sponsors: Michael Gönner and wife Charlotta.

Johann Friedr., of Johan Schaefer and wife Marg., b. 15 Aug 1772, bapt. 22 Aug 1772. Sponsors: the father and the grandmother.

Catharina, of Adam Schaetzlein and wife Hanna, b. 15 Aug 1772, bapt. 22 Aug 1772. Sponsor: the grandparents Cath. and Bartholomaes Schae[t]zlein.

Joseph, of Georg Stauss and wife Esther, b. 16 Aug 1772, bapt. 30 Aug 1772. Sponsors: Paul Cover and wife.

Johan Michael, of Johan Wolf Gemeinbauer and wife Catharina, b. 10 Aug 1772, bapt. 30 Aug 1772. Sponsors: Johan Weber and wife Elisabeth.

Johan, of Henrich Hesse and wife Sarah, b. 7 Aug 1772, bapt. 30 Aug 1772. Sponsors: Johannes Clear and wife Catharina.

Johan Heinrich, of Johan Garrison and wife Hannah, b. in Apr 1772, bapt. 30 Aug 1772. Sponsors: Johan Heinrich Schmidt and his dau. Anna Maria Wilk(in).

Mary, of William Finley and wife Susanna, b. 11 Aug 1772, bapt. 30 Aug 1772. Sponsor: Mary Gisson.

Ruldop, of Philip Klein and wife Elisabeth, b. 24 Aug 1772, bapt. 6 Sep 1772. Sponsors: Rudolph Lehr and wife Catharina.

Henrich, of Friedrich Bantleon and wife Catharina, b. 21 Aug 1772, bapt. 6 Sep 1772. Sponsors: Henrich Weber and widow Hanna Schreiber?.

Maria Elisabeth, of Joh. Henrich Pless and wife Elisabeth, b. 23 Aug 1772, bapt. 6 Sep 1772. Sponsors: Heinrich Sommer and wife Maria Catharina.

Margretha, of Joh. Adam Wilhelm (Ref.) and wife Dorothea, b. 27 Jul 1772, bapt. 6 Sep 1772. Sponsors: Wilhelm Staut and wife Margretha.

Elisabeth, of Daniel Frischmut and wife Barbara, b. 21 Sep 1772, bapt. 9 Sep 1772. Sponsors: the parents.

Isaac, of Joh. Andreas Dewald and his English wife Hanna, b. 9 Jun 1764, bapt. 9 Sep 1772. Sponsors: the father, and Alexander Greenwood, and old Mr. Soefferens' wife Sara Elisabeth.

Sara, of Joh. Andreas Dewald and wife Hanna, b. 21 Apr 1769, bapt. 9 Sep 1772. Sponsors: same as above.

Margretha Elisabeth, of Joh. Andreas Dewald and wife Hanna, b. 5 May 1772, bapt. 9 Sep 1772. Sponsors: same as above.

Charles, of Georg Wans (Englishman) and wife Sara, b. 2 Mar 1769, bapt. 9 Sep 1772. Sponsors: the parents, and Joh. Andreas Dewald.

John, of Georg Wans and wife Sara, b. 1 Mar 1771, bapt. 9 Sep 1772. Sponsors: same as above.

Adam, of Johannes Heil and wife Maria, b. 27 Aug 1772, bapt. 13 Sep 1772. Sponsors: Adam Stricker and wife Rebecca Elisabeth.

Michael, of Elias Frey and wife Maria, b. 24 Aug 1772., bapt. 13 Sep 1772. Sponsors: Michael Riem and wife Elisabeth.

Elisabeth, of Peter Willerich and wife Elisabeth, b. 22 Aug 1772, bapt. 13 Sep 1772. Sponsors: Ludewig Starck, single, and Elisabeth (surname not given).

Elisabeth, of Christian Schäfer and wife Dorothea, b. 11 Aug 1772, bapt. 13 Sep 1772. Sponsors: David Eberhard and wife Elisabeth.

Johann Heinrich, of Thomas Hervy and wife Maria Margaretha, at Cricket Billet, b. 27 Jun 1772, bapt. 3 Sep 1772. Sponsors: Joh. Heinrich Sauer (Pauer?) and wife Anna Barbara.

Georg Jacob, of Daniel Hofmann and wife Margareta, b. 8 Sep 1772, bapt. 16 Sep 1772. Sponsors: Georg Jacob Oesterle and wife Maria.

Friedrich, of Henr. Friedrich Kühl and wife Susanna, b. 4 Sep 1772, bapt. 17 Sep 1772. Sponsors: the parents.

Anton, of Jacob Frieborn and wife Dorothea, b. 15 Aug 1772, bapt. 19 Sep 1772. Sponsors: Johann Steigel and wife Catha.

Maria Eva, of Philip Dietz and wife Cathar. b. 3 Sep 1772, bapt. 20 Sep 1772. Sponsors: Maria Eva Dietz(in), single, and Valentin (surname not given).

Johann Georg, of John Rup and wife Maria, b. 8 Sep 1772, bapt. 20 Sep 1772. Sponsors: Wilhelm Eckardt and wife Maria.

Jacob, of Georg Bauer and wife Margaretha, b. 13 Sep 1772, bapt. 27 Sep 1772. Sponsors: Jacob Senger and wife Elisabeth.

Johannes, of Jacob Kiebler and wife Catharina, b. 29 Sep 1772, bapt. 27 Sep 1772. Sponsors: Andreas Tag and wife Christina.

Maria Magdalena, of Christoph Zimmermann and wife Catharina, b. 10 Sep 1772, bapt. 20 Sep 1772. Sponsors: the father and Jacob Sheik's wife Anna Magdal.

Elisabeth, of Conrad Paethis and wife Barbara, b. 10 Sep 1772, bapt. 27 Sep 1772. Sponsors: Henrich Leuthauser and wife Elisabeth.

Anna Barbara, of Johan Martin Sommer and wife Margaretha, b. 3 Sep 1772, bapt. 27 Sep 1772. Sponsors: Georg Sommer and Anna Neischwanger(in), both single.

Hanna, of Christian Zink and wife Margaretha, b. 25 Sep 1771, bapt. 27 Sep 1772. Sponsors: the parents.

Jacob, of Georg Hauber and wife Salome, b. 18 Aug 1772, bapt. 27 Sep 1772. Sponsors: Adam Krebs and wife Maria.

Johan Pater, of Gottfried Crumbach and wife Barbara, b. 18 Sep 1772, bapt. 27 Sep 1772. Sponsors: the parents.

Erhard, of Jacob Wolf and wife Elisabet, b. 25 Mar 1772, bapt. 31 Oct 1772. Sponsors: the mother, and widow Anna Ursula Müller(in).

Johannes, of Georg Gebhard and wife Rosina, b. 17 Sep 1772, bapt. 4 Oct 1772. Sponsors: Johannes Biegler and wife Anna.

Georg, of Georg Schneider and wife Maria, b. 20 Sep 1772, bapt. 4 Oct 1772. Sponsors: the parents.

Cathar., of Adam Mincer and wife Rosina, b. in Aug 1772, bapt. 4 Oct 1772. Sponsors: the father, and widow Cathar. Wedelson.

John Ludwig, of Wilhelm Ludwig Truckenmüller and wife Rachel, b. 10 Aug 1772, bapt. 5 Oct 1772. Sponsors: the grandfather and grandmother Truckenmüller.

Thomas, of Philipp Heil and wife Jacobina b. 12 Sep 1772, bapt. 5 Oct 1772. Sponsors: the parents.

Joh. Nicol. of Jacob Pister and wife Margaretha, b. 8 Sep 1772, bapt. 10 Oct 1772. Sponsor: Joh. Nic. Doebler.

An. Barb., of Jacob Bettinger and wife Anna Maria, b. 10 Aug 1772, bapt. 10 Oct 1772. Sponsors: Jacob Rüber and wife An. Barbara.

Maria Barbara, of Peter Kraft and wife Margaretha, b. 23 Sep 1772, bapt. 11 Oct 1772. Sponsors: the father and Maria Barbara Keimsli(n)?.

Joh., of Caspar Bock and wife Anna Marg., b. 9 Sep 1772, bapt. 11 Oct 1772. Sponsors: Joh. Krüger and wife Anna Catharina.

Andreas, of Andrew Geier and wife Barbara, b. 8 Sep 1772, bapt. 11 Oct 1772. Sponsors: And. Bosshart and wife Mar. Barbara/

Anna Maria, of Johann Fischer and wife Eva Catharina, b. 3 Oct 1772, bapt. 11 Oct 1772. Sponsors: Henry Nutter (Englishman) and wife Anna Maria.

Johann Peter, of Valentin Hagner and wife Margaretha, b. 1 Oct 1772, bapt. 11 Oct 1772. Sponsors: Johan Peter Gabel and wife Elisabeth.

Salomon, of Friedrich Thielman and wife Catharina, b. 25 Sep 1772, bapt. 11 Oct 1772. Sponsors: Friedrich Dietz and wife Catharina.

Richard, of David Munzer and wife Jemima, b. 30 Aug 1772, bapt. 10 Oct 1772. (The child was near death.)

Anna Maria, of Theobald Stork and wife Rosina, b. 24 Sep 1772, bapt. 11 Oct 1772. Sponsors: Friedrich Schi__ and Maria Zink(in).

Elisabeth, of Philip Schep and wife Anna Maria, b. 27 Apr 1772, bapt. 11 Oct 1772. Sponsor: Andreas Tanger's wife Catherina.

Hanna, of Georg Weller and wife Dorothea, at Reading, b. 4 Oct 1772, bapt. 13 Oct 1772. (Sponsors not given.)

Maria, of Philipp Waeger and wife Maria, b. 26 Sep 1772, bapt. 10 Oct 1772. Sponsors: Christoph Keller and wife Maria.

Christina, of Heinrich Philipp and wife Clara, near Reading, b. 7 Jun 1772, bapt. 2 Oct 1772. Sponsors: Valentin Mogel and Christian Phillips(in).

Margareta, of Caspar Wolf and wife Juliana, b. 10 Sep 1772, bapt. 4 Oct 1772. Sponsors: Jacob Seyfriedt and wife Elisabeth.

Maria Christina, of Georg Schneider and wife Hanna, at Reading, (birth date not given), bapt. 1 Oct 1772. Sponsors: Conrad Beck and Maria Doroth. Wealsch?.

Jacob, of Georg Krausskopf and wife Margretha , b. 26 Aug 1772, bapt. 12 Oct 1772. Sponsors: the parents.

Christina, of Georg Krausskopf and wife Margreth, b. 4 Nov 1771, bapt. 12 Oct 1772. Sponsors: the parents.

Margaretha, of Johannes Waeger and wife Sara, b. 31 Jul 1770, bapt. 15 Oct 1772. Sponsors: Philip Stein and wife Margretha.

Johannes, of Johannes Waeger and wife Sara, b. 23 Sep 1772, bapt. 15 Oct 1772. Sponsors: Joh. Frank and wife Margretha.

Jacob, of Jacob Ammon and wife Catherina, b. 19 Aug 1772, bapt. 17 Oct 1772. Sponsors: Jac. Büdinger and wife Anna Maria.

Andreas, of Johann Georg Honold and wife Regina, b. 19 Aug 1772, bapt. 18 Oct 1772. Sponsors: Michael Wolf and Margretha Stauch(in).

Barbara, of Georg Hergesheimer and wife Rosina, b. 22 Aug 1772, bapt. 18 Oct 1772. Sponsors: Franciscus Heinecke and wife Barbara.

Maria Regina, of Johannes Loschet and wife Anna Catharina, b. 23 Sep 1772, bapt. 18 Oct 1772. Sponsors: Andreas Weh and Maria Regina Fischer(in).

Joh. Jacob, of Leonhard Kesler and wife Anna Maria, b. 4 Oct 1772, bapt. 18 Oct 1772. Sponsors: Jacob Carl and wife Barbara.

Anna Catharina, of Adam Witterstein and wife Sophia, b. 28 Sep 1772, bapt. 18 Oct 1772. Sponsors: John Witterstein and wife Anna Elisabeth.

Catharina, of Joseph Hiller and wife Elisabeth, at Reading, b. 22 Jun 1772, bapt. 4 Oct 1772. Sponsors: Adam Wickmann and wife Catharina.

Elisabeth, of Caspar Oberdorf and wife Margaretha, in Jersey, b. 16 Sep 1772, bapt. 18 Oct 1772. Sponsors: the parents.

Christina, of Henrich Fällkle and wife Maria, 2 months old, bapt. 18 Oct 1772. Sponsors: Joh. Georg Hafner and wife Christina, at [Penn's] Neck.

Jacob, of Joh. Heinrich Karling and wife Margaretha Magdalena, b. 30 Sep 1772, bapt. 20 Oct 1772. Sponsors: *Mr.* Jacob Benson (a Dane) and Mrs. Catharina Edwards.

Theobald, of Theobald Closs and wife Susanna, b. 22 Oct 1772, bapt. 25 Oct 1772. Sponsors: Theobald Storck and wife Rosina.

Jacob, of Joh. Nicolaus Hinckel and wife Susanna, b. 11 Apr 1772, bapt. 25 Oct 1772. Sponsors: Pancratius Nitzel and wife.

Christina, of Philipp Jung and wife Christina, b. 3 Oct 1772, bapt. 29 Oct 1772. Sponsors: Conrad Schelles and wife Maria Elisabeth.

William, of William Wood and wife Elisabeth, b. 6 Sep 1772, bapt. 25 Oct 1772. Sponsors: William Bulgean and Hanna Fisher.

Georg, of William Ashton and wife Catharina, b. 14 Dec 1769, bapt. 24 Oct 1772. Sponsors: Georg Oesterle and wife Maria.

Catharina, of William Ashton and wife Catharina, b. 12 Oct 1770, bapt. 24 Oct 1772. Sponsors: same as above.

Jacob, of John Koch and wife Barbara, b. 6 Oct 1772, bapt. 25 Oct 1772. Sponsors: Jacob Barckardt and wife Barbara.

John Jacob, of Valentin Schneider and wife Rosina Magdalena, b. 30 Oct 1772, bapt. 25 Oct 1772. Sponsors: Joh. Jac. Kochendoerfer and [whose?] mother Anna Kochendoerfer(in).

Philipp, of Christoph Muller and wife Elisabeth, b. 2 Oct 1772, bapt. 9 Oct 1772. Sponsors: Philipp Eger and wife Elisabeth.

Anna Maria, of Henrich Tatz and wife Margretha, b. 1 Oct 1772, bapt. 1 Nov 1772. Sponsors: the grandparents Adam Tatz and wife Anna Maria.
Maria Juliana, of John Jacob Meier and wife Maria Juliana, b. 10 Oct 1772, bapt. 1 Nov 1772. Sponsors: Philipp Alberti and wife Anna Barbara.
Catharina, of Adam Derr and wife Catharina née Tolmann(in), b. 25 Oct 1772, bapt. 1 Nov 1772. Sponsors: the parents.
Catharina, of Christian Lutz and wife Susanna, b. 26 Sep 1772, bapt. 1 Nov 1772. Sponsors: George Christin and wife Jemima.
Catharina, of Jacob Nägele and wife Susanna, b. 26 Sep 1772, bapt. 1 Nov 1772. Sponsors: Daniel Greiner and wife Catharina.
Georg, of Michael Guterman and wife Agnes, b. 16 Oct 1772, bapt. 1 Nov 1772. Sponsors: Georg Österlin and wife Maria.
Philip, of Jacob Trockenrod and wife Anna Christina, at Frankford, b. 2 Sep 1772, bapt. 1 Nov 1772. Sponsors: Philip Focherod and wife Maria Barbara.
Leonhard, of Michael Herman and wife Anna Maria, b. 15 Aug 1772, bapt. 1 Nov 1772. Sponsors: Leonhard Hoh, single, and Margaretha Notz(in).
Anna, of Henrich Bach and wife Catharina, 20 months old, bapt. 2 Nov 1772. Sponsors: the mother and Barbara Klein(in).
Anna Margareta, of Philipp Sörg and wife Susanna Magdalena, b. 21 Oct 1772, bapt. 8 Nov 1772. Sponsors: the father and Anna Margareta Mildeberger.
Elisabet, of Johannes Emrich and wife Maria, b. 27 Oct 1772, bapt. 8 Nov 1772. Sponsors: Johan Jacob Bumm and wife Elisabeth.
Johan Philip, of Christian Jost and wife Christina, b. 6 Oct 1772, bapt. 8 Nov 1772. Sponsors: Johan Philip Krebs and his sister Anna Maria.
Joh. Martin, of Joh. Martin Sommer and wife Maria, b. 4 Oct 1772, bapt. 8 Nov 1772. Sponsors: the parents.
Maria Barbara, of Johan Mills (Englishman) and wife Maria, b. 22 Oct 1772, bapt. 8 Nov 1772. Sponsors: Johann Essig and wife Maria Barbara.
Barbara, of Johannes Gressel and wife Catharina, b. 14 Jun 1772, bapt. 8 Nov 1772. Sponsors: Daniel Killmann and paternal grandmother Barbara Gressl(in).
Sarah, of Johannes Graef and wife Maria Magdalena, b. 8 Nov 1772, bapt. the same day. Sponsors: Caspar Graef and wife Catharina.
Maria, of Georg Dorn and wife Christina, b. 23 Oct 1772, bapt. 8 Nov 1772. Sponsor: the grandmother Maria Dorn(in).
Johannes, of William Carst and wife Elisabeth, from Willmington, b. 26 Nov 1771, bapt. 11 Nov 1772. Sponsors: the parents and Mary Tailor.
Maria Catharina, of Friedrich Schmidt and wife Catharina, from Valley Forge, b. 7 Sep 1772, bapt. 12 Nov 1772. Sponsor: Mr. Philip Hall and wife Maria Catharina Susanna.
Elisabeth, of Michael Klingmann and wife Anna Elisabeth, b. 21 Mar 1757, bapt. 12 Nov 1772. Sponsors: the parents, the grandmother widow Elisabeth Müller(in) (a widow), and Peter Treuer.
Regina, of Michael Klingmann and wife Anna Elisabeth, b. 19 Apr 1759, bapt. 12 Nov 1772. Sponsors: same as above.
Barbara, of Michael Klingmann and wife Anna Elisabeth, b. 16 Jun 1761, bapt. 12 Nov 1772. Sponsors: same as above.

Catharina, of Michael Klingmann and wife Anna Elisabeth, b. 27 Jun 1763, bapt. 12 Nov 1772. Sponsors: same as above.

Michael, of Michael Klingmann and wife Anna Elisabeth, b. 7 Feb 1765, bapt. 12 Nov 1772. Sponsors: same as above.

Anna Elisab., of Michael Klingmann and wife Anna Elisabeth, b. 27 Sep 1766, bapt. 12 Nov 1772. Sponsors: same as above.

Jacob, of Michael Klingmann and wife Anna Elisabeth, b. 9 Jun 1768, bapt. 12 Nov 1772. Sponsors: same as above.

Hanna, of Michael Klingmann and wife Anna Elisabeth, b. 22 Feb 1770, bapt. 12 Nov 1772. Sponsors: same as above.

Georg Philip, of Michael Klingmann and wife Anna Elisabeth, b. 25 Dec 1771, bapt. 12 Nov 1772. Sponsors: same as above.

Joh. Philipp, of Johann Fleeman and wife Elisabeth, b. 2 Jun 1772, bapt. 10 Nov 1772. Sponsors: Joh. Philipp Alberti and wife Barbara.

Jacob, of Joh. Diestmann and wife Anna Maria, b. Palm Sunday 1768, bapt. 12 Nov 1772. Sponsors: Jacob Schaefer and wife Maria.

Elisabeth, of Joh. Diestmann and wife Anna Maria, b. 3 Nov 1772, bapt. 12 Nov 1772. Sponsor: Elisabeth Christ.

Joh. Georg, of Martin Row and wife Barbara, b. 6 Nov 1772, bapt. 13 Nov 1772. Sponsors: the father, and the maternal grandmother Justina Elisabeth Ehwald(in).

Joh. Georg, of Joseph Kaiser and wife Anna, b. 28 Sep 1772, bapt. 15 Nov 1772. Sponsors: John Georg Kieffer and wife Eva.

Heinrich Peter, of Peter Kurtz and wife Sara, b. 30 Oct 1772, bapt. 5 Nov 772. Sponsors: Heinrich Kurtz and widow Eva Barbara Kurtz (the grandmother).

Anna Maria, of the schoolmaster Jacob Franck and wife Barbara, b. 4 Nov 1772, bapt. 11 Nov 1772. Sponsors: Heinrich Mühlenberg and wife Anna Maria.

Johanna Sophia, of Deder Grimm and wife Sophia Dorothea, b. 25 Oct 1772, bapt. 15 Nov 1772. Sponsors: Siegesmund Copia and wife Magdalena Sophia.

Jacob, of Adam Schisterer and wife Dorothea, b. 5 Nov 1772, bapt. 15 Nov 1772. Sponsors: Jacob Schisterer and Margretha Sommer(in).

Anna Catharina, of Peter Klein and wife Rehanna, b. 2 Nov 1772, bapt. 15 Nov 1772. Sponsors: Johannes Klein and wife Anna Catharina.

Elisabeth, of Joh. Becker (soldier in the barracks) and wife Maria, b. 12 Jul 1772, bapt. 18 Nov 1772. Sponsors: James Sabing and wife Hesther.

Rosina, of Georg Windfield and wife Rosina, from New York, b. 18 Oct 1772, bapt. 18 Nov 1772. Sponsors: the mother and Hesther Sabing.

Magdalena, 15-year-old dau. of Anton Gilbert and wife Sophia, b. 9 Sep 1756, bapt. 19 Nov 1772. Sponsors: Samuel Rosk and Elisabeth Barbara Keller(in).

Carl, of Heinrich Klepper and wife Christina, b. 22 Apr 1770, bapt. 20 Nov 1772. Sponsors: the parents.

Samuel, of Johan Helsel? and wife Cathar., b. in Oct 1772, bapt. 21 Nov 1772. Sponsors: the mother's parents Hans and wife Maria (surname not given).

Nicolaus, of Nicolaus Brom and wife Anna Maria, b. 8 Oct 1772, bapt. 21 Nov 1772. Sponsors: the parents.

Johan Heinrich, of Jacob Retzer and wife Susanna, b. 4 Nov 1772, bapt. 21 Nov 1772. Sponsors: Henrich Tepperwein and Margareth Mönch(in)'s daughter.

Elisabet, of Elisabet Suton (an English lady from the West Indies; the father is a so-called gentleman), illegitimate, 7 weeks old, bapt. 21 Nov 1772. Sponsor: Jacob Dey. The child died.

Anna Margaretha, of Johann Gotlieb Steinbeck and wife Maria Cath. (both newly-arrived bondservants), b. 16 Oct 1772, bapt. 21 Nov 1772. Sponsors: the parents.

Susanna, of Johannes Renk and wife Magdalena, b. 2 Nov 1772, bapt. 21 Nov 1772. Sponsors: Conrad Müller and wife Cathar. (the mother's sister).

Ludewig, of Ludewig Falkenstein and wife Maria, b. 7 Nov 1772, bapt. 27 Nov 1772. Sponsors: the parents.

Christina Regina, of Henrich Hornberger and wife Magdalena, from Maryland, b. 10 Nov 1772, bapt. 27 Nov 1772. Sponsors: the parents.

Johannes, of Joh. Thomas Gon and wife Catharina Elisabeth, b. 2 Nov 1772, bapt. 29 Nov 1772. Sponsors: Johannes Gans and wife Anna Schutz(in).

Johan David, of Johan David Uber and wife Anna, b. 9 Nov 1772, bapt. 26 Nov 1772. Sponsors: Ludwig Uber and wife Margaretha.

Elisabeth, of Georg Hackinbach and wife Elisabeth, b. 17 Nov 1772, bapt. 29 Nov 1772. Sponsors: Philipp Seidelmann and wife Elisabeth.

Philippina Elisabeta, of Georg Wilhelm Mohr and wife Susanna Elisabeth, b. 14 Nov 1772, bapt. 29 Nov 1772. Sponsors: Benedict Schneider and wife Philippina Elisab.

Anna, wife of Jacob Dreass, bapt. 30 Nov 1772. Sponsors: Jacob Draess, his mother, and Henrich Steller's wife.

Georg, of Jacob Philips and wife Christina, b. 14 Nov 1772, bapt. 31 Dec 1772. Sponsors: the parents.

Georg David, of Wilh. Goetling and wife Eva Maria, b. 12 Nov 1772, bapt. 4 Dec 1772. Sponsors: the parents.

Cathar., of Wilhelm Herman and wife Anna Margaretha, b. 8 Nov 1772, bapt. 6 Dec 1772. Sponsors: Wolf Bauer and wife Cathar.

Anna Maria, of Henrich Gress and wife Maria, b. 16 Nov 1772, bapt. 6 Dec 1772. Sponsors: Jacob Schwab and wife Anna Maria.

Cathar. Dorothea, of John Georg Förer and wife Catharina, b. 20 Nov 1772, bapt. 6 Dec 1772. Sponsors: Johan Fürch and wife Dorothea.

Adam, of Mattheaus Fuchs and wife Anna Maria, b. 25 Nov 1772, bapt. 6 Dec 1772. Sponsors: Adam Molidor and wife Margaretha Winkl(in).

Cathar. Barbara, of Francis Kruger and wife Eleonore, b. in Jan 1772 , bapt. 5 Dec 1772. Sponsors: Johan Peter Staut and wife Anna Barbara.

Keppele, of Johannes Odenheimer and wife Maria, b. 2 Nov 1772, bapt. 8 Dec 1772. Sponsors: Henrich Keppele, Sr., and wife Catharina.

Elisabet, of John Hower [Howard?] and wife Margaret, b. 9 Oct 1769, bapt. 9 Dec 1772. Sponsors: the parents.

Johannes, of Peter Mann and wife Maria, b. 10 Dec 1772, bapt. 13 Dec 1772. Sponsors: Johannes Löhr and wife Elisabeth.

Maria Catharina, of Jac. Reasser and wife Eva Catharina, b. 2 Dec 1772, bapt. 13 Dec 1772. Sponsors: Martin Reasser and wife Maria Cathar.

Christina Elisabeth, of Joh. Gottfried Meyer and wife Catharina, b. 4 Dec 1772, bapt. 13 Dec 1772. Sponsors: the maternal grandparents Joh. Michael Rihm and wife Elisabeth.

Jacob, of Andreas Tag and wife Christina, b. 3 Dec 1772, bapt. 13 Dec 1772. Sponsors: Jacob Kubler and wife Catharina, who live 22 miles from here.

Johan Georg, of Johann Georg Muff and wife Elisabeth, b. 26 Aug 1772, bapt. 13 Dec 1772. Sponsors: the parents.

Georg, of Philip Jacobs and wife Margaretha, b. 5 Mar 1770, bapt. 15 Dec 1772. Sponsors: Georg Fidler and wife Elisabet.

Mary, of Samuel Leviston [Livingston] and wife Eva, 5 months old, bapt. 17 Dec 1772. Sponsor: Jacob Henck's dau. Anna Gertraut Henck(in), single

Jacob, of Joh. Georg Peschel? and wife Susanna, b. 5 Dec 1772, bapt. 20 Dec 1772. Sponsors: Jacob Heimisch and wife Catharina.

Jacob, of Benjamin Meier and wife Regina, b. 11 Nov 1772, bapt. 20 Dec 1772. Sponsors: Johannes Emmerich and wife Maria Elisabeth.

Johann Peter, of Peter Dietz and wife Anna Maria, b. 14 Dec 1772, bapt. 20 Dec 1772. Sponsors: Sebastian Seibert and wife Eva Barbara.

Mary, of John Hall and wife Mary, b. 5 Nov 1772, bapt. 20 Dec 1772. Sponsors: Gottfried Fürk and wife Catharina.

Johannes, of Mr. Henrich Böckle and wife Margretha, b. 15 Nov 1772, bapt. 20 Dec 1772. Sponsors: Mr. Lorentz Bast and wife.

Daniel, of Christlieb Barthling and wife Elisabeth, b. 18 Nov 1772, bapt. 21 Dec 1772. Sponsors: the father and Christina Friedling.

Elisabet (twin), of Georg Martin and wife Maria, b. 22 Dec 1772, bapt. 23 Dec 1772. Sponsors: Michael Roehm and wife Elisabet

Cath. Barbara (twin), of Georg Martin and wife Maria, b. 22 Dec 1772, bapt. 23 Dec 1772. Sponsors: ___ Engelfried and wife Cath. Barbara.

Matthaeus, of Martin Schnep and wife Anna Maria, b. 7 Nov 1772, bapt. 25 Dec 1772. Sponsors: Matthaeus Hohl and wife Maria Magdalena.

Henrich, of Henrich Hains and wife Catharina, b. 27 Nov 1772, bapt. 25 Dec 1772. Sponsors: the parents.

Anna Maria, of Johan Kling and wife Anna Cathar., b. 19 Nov 1772, bapt. 25 Dec 1772. Sponsors: Ludwig Farmer and wife Anna Maria.

Henrich, of Henrich Stebber and wife Anna Marg., b. 7 Dec 1772, bapt. 25 Dec 1772. Sponsors: Peter Draess and his sister Elisabet.

Maria Cathar., of Peter Marling and wife Maria Dorothea, b. 18 Dec 1772, bapt. 27 Dec 1772. Sponsors: Friedr. Frolich, single, and Cathar. Friebel(in).

Margareta, of Johannes Kimmerle and wife Maria, b. 21 Dec 772, bapt. 27 Dec 1772. Sponsors: Lorenz Oppmann and wife Margareta.

Friedrich, of Wilh. Schmidt and wife Anna, b. 28 Nov 1772, bapt. 24 Dec 1772. Sponsors: Ludewig Agricola (alias Farmer) and wife. Anna.

Johann Henrich, of Johann Heinrich Boht and wife Cath. Elisab., at Kensington, b. 18 Dec 1772, bapt. 29 Dec 1772. Sponsors: Andreas Hains and wife Elisabeth.

Georg, of Zacharias Reis and wife Maria, at Pikeland, b. in Dec 1772, bapt. 20 Dec 1772. Sponsors: Georg Diery and wife Maria.

Jacob, of Peter Caput and wife Dorothea, b. 27 Jul 1763, bapt. 7 Aug 1763. Sponsors: James Lyon and wife Dorothea.

Dorothea Marg., of Peter Caput and wife Dorothea, b. 27Aug 1765, bapt. 31Aug 1765. Sponsors: James Lyon and wife Dorothea.
Petrus Jeremias, of Peter Caput and wife Dorothea, b. 14Apr 1767, bapt. 19Apr 1767. Sponsors: Jeremias Bodewein and wife Elisabeth.
Casper Petrus, of Peter Caput and wife Dorothea, b. 22Mar 1769, bapt. 26Mar 1760. Sponsors: Caspar Heily? and wife Elisabeth.
Anna, of Peter Caput and wife Dorothea, b. 10Sep 1772, bapt. 16Sep 1772. Sponsors: ___ Laniard and wife Anna.

1773
(baptisms by pastors Muhlenberg, Jr. and Sr., and Kunze;
all in chronological sequence, from Book III)
Georg, of Christian Persie and wife Maria, b. 3Feb 1772, bapt. 1Jan 1773. Sponsors: the parents.
Elisabet, of Jacob Bandel and wife Regina Barbara, b. 5Jan 1772, bapt. 1Jan 1773. Sponsors:the parents.
Margareta Dorothea, of Martin Weiss and wife Anna Martha, b. 8Dec 1772, bapt. 3Jan 1773. Sponsors: Jacob Dietrich and wife Dorothea.
William, of Thomas Goucher and wife Hannah, b. 3Sep 1772, bapt. 3Jan 1773. Sponsors: Charles Harton and wife.
Philipp, of John Jacob Scheig and wife Anna Magdalena, b. 21Dec 1772, bapt. 3Jan 1773. Sponsors: Philipp Hahl and wife Susanna.
Christian, of Johannes Greiffenstein and wife Dorothea, b. 20Dec 1772, bapt. 3Jan 1773. Sponsors: Christian Kiensli and wife Anna Margretha.
Daniel, of Christoph Adam and wife Margar., b. 30Oct 1772, bapt. 7Jan 1773. Sponsors: Daniel Gesner and his sister Elisabete.
Philip, of Catharina Stuz(in) and Joseph Watson (bondservant with Mr. Gibson), 2weeks less 2 days old, bapt. 4Jan 1773. Sponsors: Philipp Schinkler and Margretha Stutz(in), both single.
Susanna Christina, of Johannes Weisman and wife Margaretha, b. 30Dec 1772, bapt. 10Jan 1773. Sponsors: Jacob Roht and wife Susanna.
Georg Drecher, a turner and son of an Englishman, bapt. 8Jan 1773. He soon died.
Elisabeth, of Johannes Unangst and wife Catharina, 4 weeks old, bapt. 10Jan 1773. Sponsor: Barbara Brechel.
Elisabeth, of Johannes Freiburg and wife Susanna, b. 27Nov 1772, bapt. 10Jan 1773. Sponsors: Johannes Gummy and Elisabeth Becker(in).
Elisabeth, of Vincents Kuhn and wife Elisabeth, b. 5Jan 1773, bapt. 10Jan 1773. Sponsors: the parents.
James, of James Cuben and wife Barbara, b. 9Jan 1773, bapt. 11Jan 1773. Sponsors: the father and Anna Barbara Wenkleiner?.
Anna Maria, of Daniel Knodel and wife Anna Maria, b. 11Jan 1773, bapt. 11Jan 1773. Sponsors: the parents.
Elisabet, of John Jarson and wife Catharine, b. 14Dec 1772, bapt. 11Jan 1773. Sponsors: Christoph Schleich and wife Elisabet.
Elisabeth, of Jacob Graeff (master miller) and wife Maria Catharina, b. 9 Jan 1773, bapt. 16 Jan 1773. Sponsors: the parents.

Hanna Maria, of Adolph Rühl and wife Hanna, b. 24 Oct 1772, bapt. 17 Jan 1773. Sponsors: the parents.

Regina Margar., of Georg Michael Hock and wife Catharina, b. 3 Jan 1773, bapt. 17 Jan 1773. Sponsors: Michael Gutman and wife Regina Marg.

Adam (twin), of Christoph Stimmel and wife Maria Eva, b. 10 Jan 1773, bapt. 17 Jan 1773. Sponsors: Peter Steyerwald and wife, Maria Magdalena and their dau. Dorothea.

Eva (twin), of Christoph Stimmel and wife Maria Eva, b. 10 Jan 1773, bapt. 17 Jan 1773. Sponsors: same as above.

Maria Elisabeth, of Joh. Andr. Rohr and wife Maria Christina, b. 8 Jan 1773, bapt. 17 Jan 1773. Sponsors: Henrich Leithauser and wife Maria Elisabeth.

Jacob, of David Jennings and wife Marg., b. 6 Jan 1773, bapt. 17 Jan 1773. Sponsors: Jacob Oeringer (also known as Orange) and wife Hanna.

Christina, of John Martin Meier and wife Dorothea, 18 weeks old, bapt. 18 Jan 1773. Sponsors: Conrad Steiger and wife Christina (the mother's sister)..

Margareta, of Johann Georg Zeissinger and wife Maria Margar., b. 20 Jan 1773, bapt. 20 Jan 1773. Sponsors: the parents and Margareta Burghardt(in). The child died.

George, of Johannes Pentor and wife Susanna, b. 7 Jan 1773, bapt. 24 Jan 1773. Sponsors: the maternal grandparents Nicolaus Ribbel and wife Susanna.

Johannes, of Jacob Riel and wife Rachel (an English woman), b. 7 Jan 1773, bapt. 24 Jan 1773. Sponsors: the parents.

Anna Maria, of Andreas Sommer and wife Anna, b. 2 Jan 1773, bapt. 24 Jan 1773. Sponsors: Jacob Rheintaler and wife Anna Maria.

Johann Georg, of Joh. Michael Hähns and wife Anna Catharine, b. 8 Jan 1773, bapt. 24 Jan 1773. Sponsors: Joh. Georg Schreier and wife.

Ann, of William Oldfield and wife Cathar., b. in Dec 1771, bapt. 25 Jan 1773. Sponsor: the mother.

Thomas, of Rosina Pä[t]z(in) and Samuel Legui?, illegitimate, b. 23 Dec 1772, bapt. 24 Jan 1773. Sponsors: Rosina's mother Pä[t]z(in) and sister.

Sophia Dorothea, of Jacob Reif and wife Dorothea, b. 13 Jan 1773, bapt. 31 Jan 1773. Sponsors: John Eihenpraeger and Margar. Lampater(in), both single.

Georg, of Peter Grof (Gros?) and wife Catharina, b. 23 Dec 1772, bapt. 31 Jan 1773. Sponsors: Georg Hofsäs, and Anna Honck, both single.

Susanna, of Christoph Hansel and wife Elisabeth, b. 5 Jan 1773, bapt. 2 Feb 1773. Sponsors: the parents.

John Adam, of Adam Spiegelmeier and wife Catharina, b. 13 Jan 1773, bapt. 29 Jan 1773. Sponsors: the parents and Elisab. Ros.

Wilhelm, of Dieterich Ries and wife Christiana, b. 10 Jan 1773, bapt. 31 Jan 1773. Sponsors: Wilhelm Eockard and wife Maria.

Elisabet, of John Moore (an English man) and wife Sara, b. 12 Mar 1771, bapt. 31 Jan 1773. Sponsors: Georg Bauer and Mary Hollowel.

Cathar., of Johan Schumacher and wife Agnes, b. in Oct 1772, bapt. 31 Jan 1773. Sponsors: Georg Kur[t]z and wife Cathar. Zinck.

Anna Maria, of Joh. Georg Herman (the barber) and wife Anna Regina, b. 5 Jan 1773, bapt. 1 Feb 1773. Sponsors: mstr. Georg Walker and wife Anna Dorothea.

Maria Catharina, of Robert Wilson and wife Sara, b. 14 Nov 1773, bapt. 1 Feb 1773. Sponsor: John Schweitzer's wife Maria Catharina..

Matthias, of Michael Schuch and wife Margareta, b. 18 Dec 1772, bapt. 6 Feb 1773. Sponsors: Johannes Houck and wife Catharina.

Caspar, of Caspar Schneider and wife Elisabeth, b. 18 Jan 1773, bapt. 6 Feb 1773. Sponsors: the parents.

Johanna Elisabetha, of Philip Jacob Weiss and wife Sybilla Magdalena, b. 4 Jan 1773, bapt. 7 Feb 1773. Sponsors: Johann Georg Klein and Elisabeth Klein(in).

Johannes, of Friedrich Paul and wife Elisabeth, b. 28 Jan 1773, bapt. 7 Feb 1773. Sponsors: John Thomas and wife Barbara.

Johann Michael, of Georg Reinhard and wife Maria Magdalena, b. 23 Jan 1773, bapt. 7 Feb 1773. Sponsors: the parents.

Johannes Caspar, of Georg Rehn and wife Eva, b. 28 Jan 1773, bapt. 7 Feb 1773. Sponsors: Caspar Wahl and wife Catharina.

Margretha Charlotta, of Michael Gönner and wife Charlotta, b. 17 Jan 1773, bapt. 17 Feb 1773. Sponsors: Siegmund Hagelgans and wife Margretha.

Georg Andreas, of Georg Way and wife Christina (who died), b. 11 Jan 1773, bapt. 17 Feb 1773. Sponsors: Andreas Way and Rahel Fischer.

Elisabeth, of Caspar Jager and wife Hanna, b. in Jan 1773, bapt. 7 Feb 1773. (Sponsors not given.)

Catharina, of Johan Adam Swab and wife Margareta, b. 25 Jan 1773, bapt. 7 Feb 1773. Sponsors: his brother Jacob Bernard Swab and wife Anna Maria.

Henrich, of Henrich Schreiber and wife Margaretha, b. 28 Jan 1773, bapt. 11 Feb 1773. Sponsors: the grandparents Mr. George Walker and wife Anna Dorothea.

Johannes, of Johannes Weiss and wife Elisabeth, b. 5 Feb 1773, bapt. 12 Feb 1773. Sponsors: the grandparents Johannes Weiss and wife Maria Magdalena.

John, of Johannes Weiss, Sr., adopted, the son of a bondservant of Mary Job, b. 3 Mar 1769, bapt. 12 Feb 1773. Sponsors: the master and mistress Johannes Weiss Sr. and wife Maria Magdal.

Maria Cathar., of Johann Dan. Ernst and wife Catharina, b. 24 May 1772, bapt. 14 Feb 1773. Sponsors: Jacob Reintaler and wife Anna Maria.

Maria Margar., of Johannes Metz and wife Anna Barbara, b. 27 Jan 1773, bapt. 14 Feb 1773. Sponsors: Sch. Sonnenleuchter and wife Maria Marg.

Joh. Peter, of Joh. Peter Beck and wife Elisabeth, b. 22 Jan 1773, bapt. 14 Feb 1773. Sponsors: the parents and grandparents.

Johan Friedr., of Friedrich Moch and wife Anna Maria, b. 25 Feb 1773, bapt. 25 Feb 1773. Sponsors: Adam Koenig and wife Anna Barbar.

Maria, of Georg Christein and wife Maria Marianna, b. 11 Feb 1773, bapt. 24 Feb 1773. Sponsors: Georg Kiefer and Eva Maria.

Johannes, of Georg Kreper and wife Anna Maria, b. 5 Feb 1773, bapt. 24 Feb 1773. Sponsors: Joh. Nicolaus Wagner and wife Magdalena.

Elisabeth, of Adam Foulck and wife Catharina, b. 1 Feb 1773, bapt. 14? Feb 1773. Sponsors: Dieterich Ries and wife Christina.

Catharina Elisabeth, of Joh. Leonhard Weber and wife Elisabeth, b. 6 Feb 1773, bapt. 22 Feb 1773. Sponsors: Wolfgang Gemeinbauer and wife Catharina.

Johann Heinrich, of Valentin Gesner and wife Maria Agnes, b. 18 Dec 1772, bapt. 22 Feb 1773. Sponsors: Heinrich Gesner and wife Margretha.

Elisabet, of Paul Daser and wife Maria, b. 16 Sep 1772, bapt. 22 Feb 1773. Sponsors: the parents.

Johan Georg, of John Backwik? and wife Margaret, b. 30 Jan 1773, bapt. 14 Feb 1773. Sponsors: Georg Hauss and Regina Meier(in), both single..

Sara, of Johan Georg Weil and wife Elisabeth, b. 20 Dec 1772, bapt. 2 Feb 1773. Sponsors: the parents and Catharina Weil(in).

Ann, of James Jefferies and wife Anna, 7 months old, bapt. 23 Feb 1773. Sponsors: Jacob Becker and wife Christina.

Johannes, of Johannes Müller and wife Elisabeth, b. 18 Feb 1773, bapt. 22 Feb 1773. Sponsors: Christian Lauer and wife Elisabeth.

Georg Jacob, of Peter Jung and wife Magdalena, b. 10 Feb 1773, bapt. 26 Feb 1773. Sponsors: Georg Jung and wife Rosina.

Henrich, of Henrich Benner and wife Catharina Elisabeth, b. 22 Feb 1773, bapt. 28 Feb 1773. Sponsors: Jacob Veit, single, and his sister Anna Cathar.

Johannes, of Christian Danecker and wife Juliana, b. 16 Feb 1773, bapt. 28 Feb 1773. Sponsors: John Georg Stähly and wife Christina.

Catharina, of Andreas Pfiller and wife Margaretha, b. 30 Jan 1773, bapt. 28 Feb 1773. Sponsors: George Way and his widowed mother Catharina Way.

Georg, of Jacob Schaefer and wife Maria, b. 22 Feb 1773, Feb 28, 1773. Sponsors: Joh. Georg Kramp and wife Dorothea.

Anna Maria, of Wilhelm Stotz and wife Ursula, b. 13 Feb 1773, bapt. 28 Feb 1773. Sponsors: Jacob Maurer and wife Maria.

Johan Philip, of Joh. Philip Jacob (deceased) and wife Margar., b. 2 Feb 1773, bapt. 21 Mar 1773. Sponsors: *Mr.* Georg Fidler and wife Elisabeth.

Mary, of James Moore (a Negro) and Elisabeth, 2 years old, bapt. 2 Mar 1773. Sponsor: William Gibbins.

Jane Catharina, of Richard Cruise (a Negro), and wife Hagar, 2 years old, bapt. 2 Mar 1773. Sponsor: William Gibbins.

Wilhelm, of John Jones and *Mr.* Mart. Ries's dau. Anna Maria, illegitimate, b. 2 Feb 1773, bapt. 5 Mar 1773. Sponsors: the grandparents Martin Ries and wife Cathar.

Elisab., of John Ludewig and wife Elisabeth, b. 31 Dec 1772, bapt. 7 Mar 1773. Sponsors: Frid. Sebast. Marker and Elisab. Bohl(in).

Joh. Wilhelm, of Joh. Ludewig and wife Elisabeth, b. 19 Nov 1771, bapt. 7 Mar 1773, an adopted orphan child. Sponsor: Marg. Haus.

Michael, of Michael Ross and wife Elisabeth, from Jersey, b. 4 Feb 1770, bapt. 17 Mar 1773. Sponsors: Georg Ross and wife Elisabeth.

Jacob, of Michael Ross and wife Elisabeth, from Jersey, b. 17 Jul 1772, bapt. 17 Mar 1773. Sponsors: Georg Ross and wife Elisabeth.

Hanna Maria, of Theobald Scheibel and wife Agnes, b. 4 Mar 1773, bapt. 8 Mar 1773. Sponsors: Johann Heller and Anna Maria Ehwald(in).

Christoph, of John Wilh. Rediger and wife Catharina Christina, b. 8 Mar 1773, bapt. 12 Mar 1773. Sponsors: Christoph Kunze and wife Margareta.

Emanuel, of Peter Fiess and wife Anna Maria, b. 10 Mar 1773, bapt.13 Mar 1773. Sponsors: Anna Kaiser(in) and Anna Maria Henrich(in).

Johannes, of Georg Ungere and wife Anna Maria, b. 11 Feb 1773, bapt. 13 Mar
1773. Sponsors: Johannes Keppele and Miss Elisabeth Keppele.

Isaac, of Salomon Abel and wife Margretha, b. 27 Jan 1773, bapt. 14 Mar 1773.
Sponsors:the parents.

Lorenz, of Martin Hermstadter and wife Anna, b. 2 Jan 1773, bapt. 17 Mar
1773. Sponsors: Lorenz Lapp and wife Dorothea.

Catharina, of Friedrich Ulrich and wife Catharina, b. 10 Mar 1773, bapt. 15 Mar
1773, Sponsors: the mother and grandmother Anna Maria Ulrich.

Rosina Barbara, of Jacob Horr and wife Maria Magdalena, an adopted child, b.
2 Jan 1773, bapt. 21 Mar 1773. Sponsors: *Mr.* Philip Alberly and wife
Barbara.

Andreas, of Johannes Rot(h) and wife Dorothea, b. 6 Mar 1773, bapt. 21 Mar
1773. Sponsors: *Mr.* Georg Grotz and wife Dorothea.

Christoph Henrich, of Jacob Vister and wife Anna Maria, b. 27 Feb 1773, bapt.
28 Mar 1773. Sponsors: Christoph Henr. Leiman and Miss Sara Doroth.
Kühn.

Margaret, of Wendel Becker and wife Maria, b. in Dec 1770, bapt. 28 Mar 1773.
Sponsors: the parents.

Johannes, of Henrich Court and wife Regina, b. 20 Mar 1773, bapt. 20 Mar
1773. Sponsors: the parents.

Maria, of Henrich Court and wife Regina, b. 21 Sep 1770, bapt. 30 Mar 1773.
Sponsors: the parents.

Eleonora Catharina, of Christian Kunckel and wife Catharina, b. 28 Mar 1773,
bapt. 30 Mar 1773. Sponsors: Conrad Hensler and Miss Eleonor
Kunckel(in).

Peter Valentin, of Valentin Sorg and wife Anna Maria, b. 2 Apr 1773, bapt.
4 Apr 1773. Sponsors: Peter Becker and wife Maria Magdalena.

Anna Margretha, of Thomas Lehman and wife Catharina, b. 9 Feb 1773, bapt.
4 Apr 1773. Sponsors: the parents, and Caspar Stroebel and wife Catharina.

Catharina, of Jacob Rim and wife Catharina, b. 16 Mar 1773, bapt. 4 Apr 1773.
Sponsors: Arnold Krämer and wife Catharina.

Mary, of John Macclaine and wife, b. 13 Mar 1773, bapt. 29 Mar 1773.
Sponsors: the parents.

Christian, of Johann Gottlieb Schweizer and wife Elisabeth, b. 14 Feb 1773,
bapt. 3 Apr 1773. Sponsors: Christoph Haensmann and wife Barbara.

Johan, of Christian Rosch (also known as Rush) and wife Sarah, b. 11 Feb 1773,
bapt. 4 Apr 1773. Sponsors: Johan Koch and wife Barbara.

Eleonora, of Johannes Weiss and wife Maria Margaretha, 9 months old, bapt.
4 Apr 1773. Sponsor: Eleonora Mühller(in).

Bartholomæus, of Johannes Adam and wife Catharina, b. 15 Mar 1773, bapt.
12 Apr 1773. Sponsors: Bartholomæus Schatzlein and wife Catharina.

Elias, of Johan Jost Veit and wife Maria Magdalena, b. 24 Mar 1773, bapt.
8 Apr 1773. Sponsors: Elias Ludwig Treichel and wife Maria Elisabeth.

Johannes, of Salomon Sell and wife Cathar. (birth date not given), bapt. 8 Apr
1773. Sponsors: John Jost Veit and wife Maria Elisabeth.

Joh. Adam, of Johan Lambarter and wife Sarah, b. 9 Apr 1773, bapt. the same
day. Sponsors: the parents.

Matthias, of Henr. Polenz and wife Sibilia, b. 19 Feb 1773, bapt. 11 Apr 1773. Sponsors: Matthias Gilbert and wife Elisabeth.

Johann Lorenz, of Friedr. Reinhold and wife Anna Cath., who live across the river 10 miles away, b. 1 Oct 1770, bapt. 12 Apr 1773. Sponsors: Lorenz Schonau and wife Marg.

Maria Margareta, of Henrich Sommer and wife Catharina, b. 20 Mar 1773, bapt. 12 Apr 1773. Sponsors: Ludew. Starck and Anna Marga. Lampader(in), single.

Wilhelmine, of Jacob Henrichel and wife Catharina, b. 5 Apr 1773, bapt. 12 Apr 1773. Sponsors: Baltus Henrichel and Peter Klein's dau. Wilhelmine, both single.

Elisabeth Catharina, of Heinrich Emig and wife Margretha, b. 10 Mar 1773, bapt. 11 Apr 1773. Sponsors: Catharina Süss(in), single, and Jacob Murken.

Joh. Philipp, of Johannes Rieb and wife Susanna, b. 21 Mar 1773, bapt. 11 Apr 1773. Sponsors: Michael Schneider and wife Anna Barbara.

Anna Margaretha, of Joh. Georg Kreiss and wife Catharina, b. 7 Mar 1773, bapt. 11 Apr 1773. Sponsors: Georg Kreiss and wife Anna Margaretha.

Catharina, of John Richard and wife Elisabeth, b. 14 Jan 1773, bapt. 11 Apr 1773. Sponsors: the parents.

Anna Margretha, of Peter Sommer and wife Maria Catharina, b. 8 Mar 1773, bapt. 12 Apr 1773. Sponsors: Matthias Sommer and wife Margretha Mänch(in).

Maria Elisabeth, of Franciscus Jandus and wife Maria Elisabeth, b. 1 Feb 1773, bapt. 13 Apr 1773. Sponsors: the parents.

Joh. Matthias, of Johann Andreas Schmidt and wife Catharina, b. 20 Mar 1773, bapt. 17 Apr 1773. Sponsors: the parents.

Daniel, of Johan Georg Saslian? and wife Maria Eva, b. 6 Apr 1773, bapt. 18 Apr 1773. Sponsors: Daniel Burghardt and wife Catharina.

Michael, of Johannes Bauer and wife Anna Barbara, b. 6 Apr 1773, bapt. 18 Apr 1773. Sponsors: Michael Chennick and wife Catharina.

Sara, of Georg Schneck and wife Barbara, b. 2 Mar 1773, bapt. 14 Apr 1773. Sponsors: Georg Knorr and wife Catharina, and Elisabet Schubbart.

Elisabet, of Andreas Bauer and wife Barbara, b. 4 Apr 1773, bapt. 18 Apr 1773. Sponsors: Valentin Klager and wife Elisabeth.

Friedrich, of Joh. Friedr. Schmidt (the Lutheran preacher at Germantown) and wife Anna Barbara, b. 1 Mar 1773, bapt. 10 Apr 1773. Sponsors: the parents.

Joseph, of Joseph Winn and wife Elisabeth, b. 1 Sep 1771, bapt. 19 Apr 1773. Sponsor: Johann Gilbert.

Johannes, of John Fischer and wife Anna Maria, b. 1 Apr 1773, bapt. 14 Apr 1773. Sponsors: Johannes Schneider and wife Eva.

Joseph, of Felix Rein and wife Cathar., b. 31 Mar 1773, bapt. 19 Apr 1773. Sponsors: the parents.

Anna Margar., of Georg Unselt and wife Anna Marg., b. 4 Apr 1773, bapt. 25 Apr 1773. Sponsors: Friedrich Wolpert and wife Anna Margar.

Margar., of Georg Knerr and wife Catharina, b. 11 Apr 1773, bapt. 25 Apr 1773. Sponsors: Lorenz Opman and wife Margar.

Elisabeth, of Joh. Lorenz and wife Catharina, b. 7 Apr 1773, bapt. 25 Apr 1773.
Sponsors: Christian Bick and wife Christina.
Johannes, of Andreas Erdman Leinau and wife Rosina, b. in Apr 1773, bapt.
25 Apr 1773. Sponsors: Daniel Hess and wife Gertraudt.
Elisabet, of Henrich Jung and wife Susanna, b. 15 Apr 1773, bapt. 29 May 1773.
Sponsors: Adam Gerich and wife Susanna.
Maria Christina, of Joh. Jacob Heine and wife Anna, b. 16 Mar 1773, bapt.
8 May 1773. Sponsors: the parents.
Georg, of Jacob Bender and wife Maria, b. 27 Mar 1773, bapt. 2 May 1773.
Sponsors: Wendel Weh and his sister Opportuna.
Dorothea, of Johann Friedr. Bender and wife Elisabeth, b. 14 Mar 1773, bapt.
2 May 1773. Sponsor: the mother.
Salome, of Jacob Omensetter and wife Elisabeth, b. 14 Mar 1773, bapt. 2 May
1773. Sponsors: Georg Leib and wife Dorothea.
Maria Magdalena, of John Jacob Hausser and wife Elisabeth, b. 17 Apr 1773,
bapt. 2 May 1773. Sponsors: the parents.
Jacob, of Johannes Leix and wife Catharina, b. 19 Mar 1768, bapt. 2 May 1773.
Sponsors: Jacob Danehauer and wife Maria.
Nancy, of Johannes Leix and wife Catharina, b. in Dec 1769, bapt. 2 May 1773.
Sponsors: Heinrich May and wife Elisabeth.
Daniel, of Johannes Leix and wife Catharina, b. 3 Jan 1772, bapt. 2 May 1773.
Sponsors: Daniel Burghard and wife Catharina.
Heinrich, of Johannes Berrick and Maria Mog, illegitimate, b. in Jan 1773, bapt.
2 May 1773. Sponsors: Heinrich Mog and his sister.
Johannes, of *Mr.* Eberhard Diel and Catharina, b. 20 Apr 1773, bapt. 9 May
1773. Sponsors: Johannes Figel? and wife Anna Marg.
Joseph, of Elisabeth Galloway and John Parrot, b. 21 Mar 1771, bapt. 3 May
1773. Sponsor: [in English] "the mother and another woman."
James, of Elisabeth Galloway and John Parrot, b. 1 Jan 1771, bapt. 3 May 1773.
Sponsors: same as above.
Georg, of Samuel Schober and wife Elisabeth, b. 1 May 1773, bapt. 6 May 1773.
Sponsors: Georg Schee and wife Barbara.
Rudolph, of Rudolph Lohr and wife Anna Maria, b. 18 Apr 1773, bapt. 26 May
1773. Sponsors: Philipp Klein and wife Susanna Elisabet.
Anna Barbara, of Christoph Schleich and wife Elisabeth, b. 25 Apr 1773, bapt.
9 May 1773. Sponsors: Hans Gürg Scher and wife Anna Barbara.
Catharina, of Henrich Jonas and wife Marg., b. 9 Apr 1770, bapt. 26 May 1773.
Sponsors: Christoph Schmidt and Cathar. Forny?, both single.
Sophia, of Henrich Jonas and wife Marg., b. 7 Jan 1773, bapt. 8 May 1773.
Sponsors: Georg Wunderlich and wife Catharina.
Johan, of Patrick Deibelin and widow Magdalena Schneeberg(in), illegitimate, b.
31 Mar 1773, bapt. 11 May 1773. Sponsor: the mother.
Rebecca, of David Richardson and wife Ann, b. 9 May 1773, bapt. 12 May
1773. Sponsors: the parents.
Margaret, of O'Brian Dachedy and wife Jemina, b. 8 Apr 1772, bapt. 13 May
1773. Sponsors: the parents.
Maria Elisabeth, of Wilhelm Löscher and wife Mar. Cath, b. 13 Apr 1773, bapt.
16 May 1773. Sponsors: Georg Löscher and wife Maria.

Catharina, of Joh. Peter Steinmetz and wife Maria, b. 7 Apr 1773, bapt. 15 May 1773. Sponsors: Melchior Schwerer and wife Rosina.

Joh. Henrich, of Christian Haag and wife Anna, b. 3 May 1773, bapt. 16 May 1773. Sponsors: Johan Rebhun and wife Sophia.

Anna Catharina, of Georg Soefferens and wife Catharina, b. 24 Apr 1773, bapt. 16 May 1773. Sponsors: Ludewig Hess and wife Catharina.

Maria Dorothea, of Conrad Ring and wife Juliana, b. 25 Apr 1773, bapt. 16 May 1773. Sponsors: Johannes Meister and wife Maria Dorothea.

Wilhelm, of Wilhelm Eckard and wife Maria, b. 15 Mar 1773, bapt. 15 May 1773. Sponsors: the father, and the mother's sister Catherina.

Maria Susanna, of Georg Geiler and wife Barbara, b. 28 Jan 1773, bapt. 16 May 1773. Sponsors: Jacob Rheisling and wife Maria Catharina.

Benjamin, of Ephrem Evans and wife Catharina, b. 18 Jul 1772, bapt. 17 May 1773. Sponsors: the parents.

Adam (twin), of Sebastian Seibert and wife Barbara, b. 17 May 1773, bapt. 22 May 1773. Sponsors: Adam Schmidt and wife Cathar.

Joh. Sebastian (twin), of Sebastian Seibert and wife Barbara, b. 17 May 1773, bapt. 22 May 1773. Sponsor: the father.

Johannes, of Joh. Michael Fuchs and wife Salome, b. 3 May 1773, bapt. 23 May 1773. Sponsors: Johannes Straub and wife Regina.

Johann Casper, of Johannes Öxlein and wife Magdalena, b. 8 May 1773, bapt. 23 May 1773. Sponsors: Caspar Schiessler and wife Regina.

Anna Barbara, of Georg Ludew. Barthel and wife Christina, b. 3 May 1773, bapt. 23 May 1773. Sponsors: Tobias König and wife Barbara.

Johann Matthias (twin), of Joh. Michael Preusch and wife Anna Maria, b. 25 May 1773, bapt. 28 May 1773. Sponsors: Friedr. Ernst and wife.

Johan Friedrich (twin), of Joh. Michael Preusch and wife Anna Maria, b. 25 May 1773, bapt. 28 May 1773. Sponsors: Joh. Matthias Scheulemann and wife.

Maria, of Jacob Sulger and wife, b. 26 May 1773, bapt. 27 May 1773. The mother Dorothea was baptized, but died. Sponsors: the grandparents Maria Ursula Scheppach(in) and husband Jacob.

Andreas, of Daniel Metz and wife Susanna, b. 28 Aug 1772, bapt. 28 Nov 1773. Sponsors: Andreas Mertz and wife Anna Marg.

Cath. Elisab., of Henrich Dietz and wife Anna Barbara, b. 20 May 1773, bapt. 30 May 1773. Sponsors: John Wilh. Engelfried and wife Catharina Barbara.

Adam, of Jacob Pfeiffer and wife Barbara, b. 22 Feb 1772, bapt. 29 May 1773. Sponsors: the parents.

Philipp, of Leonhard Kraemer and wife Anna Maria, b. 13 May 1773, bapt. 29 May 1773. Sponsors: Philipp Klein and wife Elisabeth.

Henry, of Nicol. Koehler and wife Maria, from Chester, b. 21 May 1773, bapt. 29 May 1773. Sponsors: the parents.

Anna Marg., of Henrich Moses and wife Catharina, b. 2 May 1773, bapt. 30 May 1773. Sponsors: Georg Bluhm and wife Philippina.

Johannes, of Jacob Herman and wife Catharina, b. 29 Oct 1772, bapt. 30 May 1773. Sponsors: the parents and Christian Hermann(in) and wife.

Hanna, of Johannes Held and wife Christina, b. 10 Jan 1772, bapt. 31 May 1773. Sponsors: Jacob Henrichel and wife Catharina.

Catharina, of Joh. Friedr. Linck and wife Anna Margaretha, b. 9 Apr 1773, bapt.
31 May 1773. Sponsors: Joh. Philipp Wagner and wife Anna Catharina.
Maria, of Jacob Müller and wife Margareta, b. 22 May 1773, bapt. 31 May
1773. Sponsors: Nicolaus Schram and wife Anna Maria.
Margareta Elisabet, of Christoph Reinhold and wife Maria, b. 30 Apr 1773, bapt.
31 May 1773. Sponsor: Maria Elisabeth née Reinhold(in).
Elisabet, of Georg Gerling and wife Maria Christina, b. 26 Feb 1773, bapt.
31 May 1773. Sponsors: Christoph Wilpert and Rosina Schütz(in), both
single.
Friedrich, of Jacob Becker and wife Christina, b. 24 May 1772, bapt. 31 May
1773. Sponsors: Wilhelm Wenger, single, and Elisabet Christ.
Aemilia, of Georg Death and wife Margaretha, b. 2 May 1772, bapt. 31 May
1773. Sponsors: the parents.
Thomas, of Georg Köln (Köle?) and wife Euphronica, b. 11 Feb 1770, bapt.
31 May 1773. Sponsors: Johannes Heckert and wife Anna Catharina.
Joh. Georg, of George Köln (Köle?) and wife Euphronica, b. 11 May 1773, bapt.
31 May 1773. Sponsors: Joseph Rivers and wife Catharina.
Maria Catharina, of Christian Spengler and wife Maria Catharina, b. 3 Apr 1773,
bapt. 3 Jun 1773. Sponsors: the parents and grandmother Maria Ungar(in).
Jacob, of Johannes Huber and wife Catharina, b. 8 May 1773, bapt. 6 Jun 1773.
Sponsors: Peter Paul and wife Mary.
Caleb, apprentice of Johannes Straub, 11 years old on 6 Jun, bapt. 6 May 1773.
Sponsors: Mr. Straub and wife Regina.
Johannes, of Ludwig Degen and wife Eva, b. 11 Jan 1773, bapt. 6 Jun 1773.
Sponsors: Johannes Straub and wife Regina.
Philipp Jacob, of Johann Jacob Walker and wife Sophia, b. 1 May 1773, bapt.
6 Jun 1773. Sponsors: Georg Walker and wife Dorothea.
Cathar. Maria, of Mich. Mankeson and wife Appolonia, b. 5 Jun 1773, bapt.
6 Jun 1773. Sponsors: Dan. Heuman and wife Cath., and Joh. and Cath.
Mankeson.
Catharina, of Georg Wüster and wife Juliana, 6-7 months old, bapt. 6 Jun 1773.
Sponsors: Sebast. Sonleitner and wife Maria Marg.
Johan, of Jacob Leiman and wife Marg., b. 5 Mar 1773, bapt. 6 Jun 1773.
Sponsors: Michael Rehm and wife Elisabeth.
Johan, of Benjamin Morgan and wife Hesther, b. 14 Nov 1772, bapt. 6 Jun 1773.
Sponsors: Johan Landeberger and his mother Magdalena.
Georg, of Georg Stoo and wife Barbara, b. 27 May 1773, bapt. 6 Jun 1773.
Sponsors: the parents.
Friedrich, of Jacob Heimar and wife Martha, b. 30 Dec 1772, bapt. 6 Jun 1773.
Sponsor: grandfather Friedrich Heimar and wife Catharina.
Adam, of Israel Eberle and wife Christina, b. 6 Nov 1772, bapt. 8 Jun 1773.
Sponsors: Adam May and wife Anna.
Elisabet, of John Potts and wife Mary, b. 26 Sep 1772, bapt. 9 Jun 1773.
Sponsors: the father and James Maccarnie.
Anna Barbara, of Conrad Davis and wife Ann Magdalen, b. 3 May 1773, bapt.
13 Jun 1773. Sponsors: Christian Unger and wife Anna Barbara.
Johann Jacob, of Gottlieb Roll and wife Catharina, b. 21 May 1773, bapt. 13 Jun
1773. Sponsors: Jacob Gross and wife Catharina.

Anna Cath., of Jacob Becker and wife Anna Maria, b. 11 Jun 1773, bapt. 16 Jun 1773. Sponsors: Michael Scheneck and wife Anna Catha.

Michael, of Jacob Löscher and wife Anna Maria, b. 28 Mar 1773, bapt. 12 Jun 1773. Sponsors: the parents.

Franz, of Franz Schaefer and wife Elisabet, b. 17 May 1773, bapt. 12 Jun 1773. Sponsors: the parents.

Wilhelm, of Wilh. Nick and wife Maria Eva, b. 11 Jun 1773, bapt. 17 Jun 1773. Sponsor: the mother.

Anna Elisabet, of Theobald Schram and wife Catharina née Buskirk, bapt. 17 Jun 1773. Sponsors: Pancratius Nitzel and wife Anna Elisabeth.

Martha, of John Leacock and wife Martha, b. 8 Jan 1771, bapt. 17 Jun 1773. Sponsors: Isaac Streth? and Sara Whitebread.

Salome, of Jacob Antony and wife Jacobea, b. 5 Jan 1773, bapt. 20 Jun 1773. Sponsors: Nicolaus Jacob and wife Maria Marg.

Johannes, of Carl Bauman and wife Maria, b. 7 Jun 1773, bapt. 20 Jun 1773. Sponsors: Johan Strup and wife Rachel.

Ernst, of Ernst Mänchen and wife Maria, b. 10 Jun 1773, bapt. 20 Jun 1773. Sponsor: Johannes Mänchen.

Catharine, of Johann Mänchen and wife Catharina, b. 6 Jun 1773, bapt. 20 Jun 1773. Sponsors: Adolph Gillman and wife Catharine.

Maria, of Bernhard Burk and wife Maria, 8 days old, bapt. 19 Jun 1773. Sponsors: the parents.

Adam, of Martin Fiess and wife Dorothea, b. 16 May 1773, bapt. 19 Jun 1773. Sponsors: Adam Klampfort, and Martin Kreuter's dau. Catharina.

Valentin, of Valentin Krug and wife Maria Eva, b. 5 Jun 1773, bapt. 20 Jun 1773. Sponsors: Valentin Hofman and Barbara Merg(in).

Magdalena, of Jacob Kraus and wife Elisabeth, b. 5 Jun 1773, bapt. 20 Jun 1773. Sponsors: Henrich Rahn and wife Magdalena.

Catharina, of Georg Michael Heil and wife Maria Catharina, b. 12 May 1773, bapt. 20 Jun 1773. Sponsors: the parents.

Johannes, of Johann Conrad Hess and wife Charlotte, b. 1 Jun 1773, bapt. 21 Jun 1773. Sponsors: Johann Eberhardt and wife Catharina.

Maria, of William Aesten and wife Maria Catharina, b. 1 May 1773, bapt. 21 Jun 1773. Sponsors: Georg Oesterling and wife Maria.

Margaret, of Peter Schwar[t]z and wife Anna Catharina, b. 17 Jun 1773, bapt. 22 Jun 1773. Sponsors: Georg Adam Pfister and wife Margareta.

Margretha, of Alex. McClain and wife Anna Maria, 3 years old, bapt. 22 Jun 1773. Sponsors: Sybilla Raxer(in) and Maria Muhlenberg(in).

Maria, of John Jackson and wife Martha, b. 14 Jun 1773, bapt. 22 Jun 1773. Sponsors: Maria Weber and Anna Maria ___.

Johannes, of Johannes Curas or Carres (an English man), the mother's name is not known, b. 1 May 1773, bapt. 23 Jun 1773. Sponsors: Jac. Ehrhard's wife Eleonora, Margareta Kunz, and the Rev. Muhlenberg's dau. Maria..

Anna, of John King and wife, (English people), 8 days old, bapt. 25 Jun 1773. Sponsors: the parents and grandmother King, a widow.

Joh. Georg, of Michael Müller and wife Christina, b. 25 May 1773, bapt. 27 Jun 1773. Sponsors: *Mr.* Georg Seitz and wife Margretha.

Joh. Georg, of Andreas Matter and wife Anna Maria, b. 21 Jun 1773, bapt. 27 Jun 1773. Sponsors: Joh. Georg Steinfals and wife Anna Margaretha.

Georg Friedrich, of Georg Schneider, b. 6 May 1773, bapt. 28 Jun 1773. Sponsors: Georg Friedr. Wolpert and wife Maria Margaretha.

Elisabeth, of Jacob Weisert and wife Elisabeth, b. 7 Sep 1772, bapt. 30 Jun 1773. Sponsors: the mother and Regina Hertzbach(in).

Joh. Caspar, of Abraham Bachman and wife Maria Philippina, b. 30 Jun 1773, bapt. 30 Jun 1773. Sponsors: the grandparents Caspar Graef and wife Catharina.

William, of Johannes Weiss and wife Susanna, b. 30 Jun 1773, bapt. 30 Jun 1773. Sponsors: the father and Salome Ganzer(in).

William, of Thomas Williams and wife Hanna, b. 4 Jan 1772, bapt. 2 Jul 1773. Sponsors: the parents, and Philip Lader and wife Elisabeth.

Henrich Philipp, of Elisabeth Gallus(in) and reportedly Henry Philips (a coach driver), b. 2 Jul 1773, bapt. 2 Jul 1773. Sponsors: Philip Lader and wife Elisabeth.

Johann Heinrich, of Peter Schneider and wife Anna Elisabeth, b. 4 Jun 1773, bapt. 4 Jul 1773. Sponsors: Christoph Heidtel and wife Anna Maria.

Catharina, of Christian Lauer and wife Christina, b. 23 Jun 1773, bapt. 4 Jul 1773. Sponsors: Mr. Balthasar Fleischer and wife Catharina.

Maria Barbara, of Conrad Escher and wife Maria Felice, b. 29 Mar 1773, bapt. 4 Jul 1773. Sponsors: Jacob Ulrich Sinzel and Maria Barbara Esher(in), both single.

Johannes, of Michael Patsche and wife Regina Margretha, b. 10 Jun 1773, bapt. 4 Jul 1773. Sponsors: David Paetsch and wife Anna Maria.

Johann Georg, of Joh. Nicolaus Müller and wife Anna Maria, b. 25 Jun 1773, bapt. 11 Jul 1773. Sponsors: the grandfather Joh. Georg Schmid and Juliana Wildberger(in) and her father Peter Wildberger.

Maria Dorothea, of Johannes Grübel and wife Christina, b. 10 Jun 1773, bapt. 11 Jul 1773. Sponsors: Mr. Georg Laib and wife Dorothea.

Christoph., of Michael Schoemacher and wife Susanna Maria, b. 11 Jun 1773, bapt. 11 Jul 1773. Sponsors: Christopher Rau and wife.

Johannes, of Johann Laemmel and wife Sarah, (Quakers), b. 20 Feb 1773, bapt. 11 Jul 1773. Sponsors: Jacob Bauer and wife Maria Clara.

Johan Heinrich, of Friedrich Tobias Blauer? and wife Catharina, b. 3 May 1772, bapt. 17 Jul 1773. Sponsors: Joh. Adolph Gilman and wife.

Johann Conrad, of Joh. Jacob Schneider and wife Anna, b. 13 Jun, 13 years old, bapt. 17 Jul 1773. Sponsors: the parents and their son Joh. Georg.

Anna Maria, of John Jacob Schneider and wife Anna, 11 years old, bapt. 17 Jul 1773. Sponsors: same as above.

Johannes, of John Jacob Schneider and wife Anna, 9 years old, bapt. 17 Jul 1773. Sponsors: same as above..

Joh. Georg, of Johannes Dern and wife Marg., b. 29 Jun 1773, bapt. 18 Jul 1773. Sponsors: Joh. Georg Dern and wife Christine.

Maria Elisabet, of Philip Spielman and wife Anna Maria, b. 18 Mar 1773, bapt. 22 Jul 1773. Sponsors: Johannes Spiegel and wife Anna Elisabet.

338   PHILADELPHIA GERMAN LUTHERAN CHURCH

Richard, son of unknown parents, apprentice of Philip Spielman, b. 10 Apr 17__,
bapt. 22 Jul 1773. Sponsors: Christoph Adam and wife, in place of his
parents.
Joh. Henrich, of Joh. Melch. Gebhard and wife Anna Catharina, b. 1 Jun 1773,
bapt. 23 Jul 1773. Sponsors: the parents.
Anna Maria, of Friederica Regina (illegitimate), b. 21 Jul 1773, bapt. 25 Jul
1773. Sponsors: Bernhard Beck and wife Maria.
Joh. Peter, of Johannes Mos and wife Catharina, b. 16 Jul 1773, bapt. 23 Jul
1773. Sponsors: John Peter Bek and wife Marg.
Joh. Wilhelm, of Jacob Klauss and wife Marg., b. 8 Jul 1773, bapt. 25 Jul 1773.
Sponsors: Sigmund Copia and wife Sophia.
Johan Adam, of Nicolaus Panzer and wife Elisabeth, b. 16 Jul 1773, bapt. 25 Jul
1773. Sponsors: Johan Adam Schatzlein and wife Hanna.
Johannes, of Valentin Welsch and wife Philippina, b. 9 Jul 1773, bapt. 25 Jul
1773. Sponsors: Johannes Graef and wife Magdalena.
Elisabeth, of Johann Zerter (Xerter?) and wife Catharina, b. 26 Jul 1773, bapt.
1 Aug 1773. Sponsors: Johan Surger and Cath. Gut(hin) (or Gutheim).
Hanna Rosina, of Jacob Biegler and wife Dorothea Catharina, b. 7 Jul 1773,
bapt. 1 Aug 1773. Sponsors: Jacob Rebele and wife Rosina.
Chloe, of Francis Löscher and wife Barbara, b. 25 May 1773, bapt. 1 Aug 1773.
Sponsors: Jacob Bauer and wife Chloe.
Johannes, of Johannes Eberhard and wife Catharina, b. 3 Jul 1773, bapt. 1 Aug
1773. Sponsors: the parents.
Maria Cath., of Joh. Balthas. Geier and wife Maria Magd.., b. 2 Mar 1773, bapt.
3 Aug 1773. Sponsors: the parents.
William, of Thomas Watson and wife Elisabeth, b. 11 Apr 1773, bapt. 26 Jul
1773. Sponsors: the parents.
Joh. Mathias, of William Farley and wife Elisabeth, b. 28 Jun 1773, bapt. 1, Aug
1773. Sponsors: Math. Schackson and Henrietta Cath. Dick(in).
Joh. Georg, of Richard Sorger and wife Sibylla, b. 17 Jun 1773, bapt. 1 Aug
1773 Sponsors: Joh. Georg Bauman and wife Elisabeth.
Sophia Susanna, of Caspar Wirschum and wife Rosina, b. 27 Jul 1773, bapt.
3 Aug 1773. Sponsors: Daniel Bender and wife Sophia Susanna.
Rosina, of Johann Conrad Schlatter and wife Christina, b. 18 Jul 1773, bapt.
3 Aug 1773. Sponsor: Rosina Gottschuld(in).
Anna Catharina, of Phil. Jacob Bechtold and wife Anna Maria, b. 14 Jul 1773,
bapt. 18 Aug 1773. Sponsors: Georg Sei[t]z and wife Elisabeth.
Philip, of Johannes Biegler and wife Anna, b. 13 Jul 1773, bapt. 8 Aug 1773.
Sponsors: Georg Walker and wife Anna Dorothea.
Johann Martin, of John Martin Wolf and wife Diana, b. 19 Nov 1772, bapt.
8 Aug 1773. Sponsors: Charles Brotheneck? and wife.
Matthias (twin), of Jacob Ehrenfeuchter and wife Susanna, 6 weeks old, bapt.
8 Aug 1773. Sponsors: Matthaeus Schagar, and [whose?] mother Elisabeth.
Susanna (twin), of Jacob Ehren Seuchter and wife Susanna, 6 weeks old, bapt.
8 Aug 1773. Sponsors: Joh. Friedr. Foln and wife Margareta.
Margar., of Caspar Christ and wife Catharina, b. 31 Aug 1773, bapt. 9 Aug
1773. Sponsors: Christian Gally and wife Marg.

Wilhelm Friedrich, of David Fuchs and wife Margareta, b. 3 May 1773, bapt.
11 Aug 1773. Sponsors: the mother and Georg Lange.
Johannes, of Johann Graeber and wife Elisabeth, b. in Feb 1773, bapt. 11 Aug
1773. Sponsors: Georg Farly and wife Marg.
Johannes, of Paul Hofmann and wife Regina, b. 24 Jul 1773, bapt. 14 Aug 1773.
Sponsors: Johannes Hinckel and wife Christina.
Georg, of Nicolaus Jacob and wife Margareta, b. 3 Jul 1773, bapt. 14 Aug 1773.
Sponsors: Joseph Rab (Ram?) and wife Maria.
Maria Barbara, of Jacob Moo[t]z and wife Maria Barbara, b. 30 Jul 1773, bapt.
14 Aug 1773. Sponsors: Peter Armbruster and Joh. Bullmann's single
daughter Mar. Eleon.
Georg, of Johann Elwood and wife Catharina, b. 22 Oct 1772, bapt. 18 Aug
1773. Sponsors: Peter Klein and wife Eva Maria.
Sophia, of Georg Reier? and wife Anna Margaret, b. 26 Jan 1773, bapt. 15 Aug
1773. Sponsors: Henrich Deppenwein and wife Elisabeth Julia?, and John
Kobut? and wife.
Catharina, of Peter Schelleberger and wife Dorothea, b. 11 Jun 1773, bapt.
15 Aug 1773. Sponsors: the parents.
Maria (twin), of Hartmann Lauer and wife Elisabeth, b. 10 Aug 1773, bapt.
15 Aug 1773. Sponsors: the parents and Anna Maria Wilkson.
Elisabeth (twin), of Hartmann Lauer and wife Elisabeth, b. 10 Aug 1773, bapt.
15 Aug 1773. Sponsors: the parents and Martha Lauer(in).
Catharina, of Sebastian Heil and wife Elisabeth, b. 13 Aug 1773, bapt. 16 Aug
1773. Sponsors: the father and Henr. Grotler's wife Catharina. .
Henrich, of Henrich Caemmerer and wife Catharina, b. 18 Jul 1773, bapt.
18 Aug 1773. Sponsors: the parents and the mother's sister Catharina
Schu[t]z(in).
Jacob, of Daniel Baerens and wife Maria, b. 25 Jul 1773, bapt. 22 Aug 1773.
Sponsors: Jacob Teiss and wife Dorothea.
Christina, of Michael Stauch and wife Margaretha, b. 12 Aug 1773, bapt. 22 Aug
1773. Sponsors: the parents and Georg Mildeberg and wife Catharina.
Jacob, of *Mr.* Henrich Dipperger and wife Catharina Elisabeth, b. 11 Aug 1773,
bapt. 22 Aug 1773. Sponsors: the father and Sarah Mahn(in).
Maria, of pastor Johann Christoph Kunze and wife Henrietta Margareta, b.
17 Aug 1773, bapt. 22 Aug 1773. Sponsors: the maternal grandparents Rev.
Henr. Melchior Muhlenberg, Sr., and wife Maria and dau. Maria Cathar.
Muhlenberg.
Elisabeth, of Friedrich Wilt and wife Anna Elisabeth, b. 25 Dec 1770, bapt.
22 Aug 1773. Sponsors: the parents.
Christina Barbara, of Johann Georg Zinck and wife Dorothea, b. 6 Jan 1773,
bapt. 22 Aug 1773. Sponsors: David Kreb? and wife Christina Barbara.
Mary, of George Tallman and wife Mary, b. 17 Aug 1773, bapt. 23 Aug 1773.
Sponsors: the mother and Maria Deringer(in).
James, of Malachy Davis and wife Mary, 1 year old, bapt. 23 Aug 1773.
Sponsors: the parents, and Anna Cook and Maria Deoringer(in).
Anna Maria, of Thomas Heiser and wife Barbara, b. 27 Jul 1773, bapt. 24 Aug
1773. Sponsors: the grandmother Barbara Heiser(in), and Thomas Heiser.

Catharina Elisabeth, of Adam Ohl and wife Maria Christina, b. 15 Aug 1773, bapt. 29 Aug 1773. Sponsors: Joh. Georg Ohl and wife Cath. Elisabeth, who live in Germany (the parents stood in for them)..

Elisabet, of Adolph Dill and wife Catharina, b. 4 Aug 1773, bapt. 28 Aug 1773. Sponsors: Andreas Heitrich and wife Elisabeth.

Cath. Elisab., of Joh. Stuckert Becker and wife Elisabeth, b. 24 Aug 1773, bapt. 28 Aug 1773. Sponsors: the parents.

Ernst, of Ernst Forster and wife Mary, b. 21 Aug 1773, bapt. 29 Aug 1773. Sponsors: Ernst Heuser and wife Magdalena.

Jacob, of Joseph Wright and wife Catharine, b. 28 Jul 1773, bapt. 29 Aug 1773. Sponsors: the parents and Peter? Jacob Warner.

Joh. Henrich, of Friedr. Hütner and Maria, b. 12 Aug 1773, bapt. 30 Aug 1773. Sponsors: the parents.

Catharina, of Michael Steinhauer and wife Barbara, b. 25 Aug 1773, bapt. 29 Aug 1773. Sponsor: the maternal grandmother Catharina Blower?.

Anna Catherina, of Philipp Lehrer and wife Ursula, b. 8 Sep 1772, bapt. 4 Aug 1773. Sponsors: Johannes Hauck and wife Anna Catharina.

Maria, of Johannes Kehl and wife Margretha, b. 25 Aug 1773, bapt. 5 Sep 1773. Sponsors: Johannes Scheppach and wife Maria.

Joh. Heinrich, of Philip Sommer and wife Salome, b. 8 Aug 1773, bapt. 5 Sep 1773. Sponsors: Heinrich Sommer and wife Catharina.

Joh. Peter, of Zacharias Lösch and wife Maria, b. 29 Aug 1773, bapt. 5 Sep 1773. Sponsors: Joh. Peter Kraft and wife Margaretha.

Wilhelm, of Georg Knodel and wife Elisabeth, b. 20 Aug 1773, bapt. 5 Sep 1773. Sponsors: Wilhelm Bat(h)o and wife Elisabeth.

Andreas Samuel, of Andreas Burckhardt (former deacon) and wife, b. 26 Aug 1773, bapt. 5 Sep 1773. Sponsors: the parents.

Simon, of Jacob Dauenhauer and wife Maria, b. 20 Aug 1773, bapt. 5 Sep 1773. Sponsors: Johannes Wagner and wife Maria.

Sara Elisabeth, of William Wyard and wife Elisabeth, 5 years old next 13 Feb, bapt. 5 Sep 1773. Sponsors: Nicolaus Ribel and wife Sara.

John Sanders, of William Wyard and wife Elisabeth, 4 years old next 22 Feb, bapt. 5 Sep 1773. Sponsors: John Penter and wife Susanna.

Joseph, of Henrich Hill and wife Sara, b. 24 Apr 1773, bapt. 5 Sep 1773. Sponsors: Henrich Hill (grandfather) and Catharina Müller(in).

Wilhelm, of Johann Michael Klug and wife Anna, b. 14 Aug 1773, bapt. 5 Sep 1773. Sponsors: the parents.

Wilhelm, of Samuel Ross and wife Christina, b. 10 Jun 1773, bapt. 9 Sep 1773. Sponsor: Anthon Gilbert (the grandfather).

William, of Joseph George and wife Agnes, foster parents, b. 9 Mar 1773, bapt. 10 Sep 1773. Sponsor: Rosa George.

Michael, of Michael Schubarth and wife Elisabeth, Elder, of the Cong., b. 27 Aug 1773, bapt. 12 Sep 1773. Sponsors: Friedr. Heiler and wife Christina.

Maria, of Carl Truckenmuller and wife Susanna, b. 14 Aug 1773, bapt. 12 Sep 1773. Sponsors: Michael Goenner and wife Charlotte.

Johannes, of Georg Henry and wife Hanna, b. 30 Aug 1773, bapt. 12 Sep 1773. Sponsors: John Fasy and wife Christina.

Catharina Elisabeth, of Jacob Meyer and wife Anna Maria, b. 11 Aug 1773, bapt. 12 Sep 1773. Sponsors: Joh. Henrich Pot(h) and wife Catharina Elisab.

Andreas, of Christoph Gilbert and wife Sophia, b. 2 Sep 1773, bapt. 12 Sep 1773. Sponsors: Andreas Forster and his dau. Sophia Dorothea.

Cornelia, of Johannes Fri[t]z and wife Catharina, b. 22 Aug 1773, bapt. 16 Sep 1773. Sponsors: Casper Geiger and wife Elisabeth.

Maria Magdalena, of Leonhard Fichlin and wife Elisabeth, b. 7 Apr 1773, bapt. 16 Sep 1773. Sponsors: Zacharias Endres and wife Magdalena Jauch(in).

Catharina, of Gabriel Rambow and wife Mary, b. 25 Aug 1773, bapt. 19 Sep 1773. Sponsors: Johannes Krauss and wife Catharina.

Joh. Nicolaus, of Johannes Meister and wife Dorothea, b. 11 Sep 1773, bapt. 19 Sep 1773. Sponsors: Nicolaus Walter and Rosina Beron(in), single.

Georg Philipp, of Georg Sei[t]z and wife Elisabeth, b. 7 Sep 1773, bapt. 19 Sep 1773. Sponsors: Philip Jacob Bechthold and wife Anna Maria.

Henrietta, of Gottlieb Sternbeck and wife Roethshield?, b. 29 Jul 1773, bapt. 19 Sep 1773. Sponsor: Henrich Sternbeck.

Georg Valentin, of Johannes Reinhard and wife Anna Barbara, b. 15 Sep 1773, bapt. 16 Sep 1773. Sponsors: Christopher Kurtz and wife Margretha.

Maria, of Jacob Güntner and wife Catharina, b. 2 Sep 1773, bapt. 19 Sep 1773. Sponsors: Carl Müller and wife Maria.

Johannes, of schoolmaster Joh. Adam Molidor and wife Margretha, b. 14 Sep 1773, bapt. 19 Sep 1773. Sponsors: Johannes Klein and wife.

Johannes, of Johann Ronser? and wife Barbara, b. 13 Sep 1773, bapt. 19 Sep 1773. Sponsors: the parents.

Elisabeth, of Dieterich Bairle and wife Sophia, b. 15 May 1773, bapt. 21 Sep 1773. Sponsors: Martin Ries and Johannes Baumann.

Catharina, of Henrich Hofecker and wife Margareta, b. 6 Oct 1772, bapt. 20 Sep 1773. Sponsors: Martin Ries and wife Catharina.

Maria, of Christoph Reinthaler and wife Elisabeth, b. 26 Aug 1773, bapt. 23 Sep 1773. Sponsors: Jacob Reinthaler and wife Maria.

Anna Maria, of Joh. Georg Haerling and wife Margareta, b. 14 Sep 1773, bapt. 26 Sep 1773. Sponsors: Jacob Schwab and wife Anna Maria.

Johannes, of Philipp Springer and wife Eva, b. 18 Sep 1773, bapt. 26 Sep 1773. Sponsors: the parents.

Maria Magdalena, of Matthias Schleigmann and wife Maria, b. 16 Sep 1773, bapt. 28 Sep 1773. Sponsors: Johannes Schu[t]z and wife Maria Margretha.

Mathaeus, of Lorenz Oppmann and wife Anna Margareta, b. 22 Aug 1773, bapt. 26 Sep 1773. Sponsors: Martin Schmidt and wife Anna Catharina.

Anna Christina, of Georg Adam Schmidt and wife Anna Christina, b. 18 Jul 1773, bapt. 26 Sep 1773. Sponsors: the parents.

Maria Margreth, of Joh. Benjamin Gasman and wife Anna Maria, b. 25 Aug 1773, bapt. 26 Sep 1773. Sponsors: Joh. Ludewig Starck and wife Maria Margaretha.

Friedrich Jacob, of Friedrich Jacob Walker and wife Jane, b. 29 Aug 1773, bapt. 29 Sep 1773. Sponsors: the parents.

Samuel, of Friedrich Dietz and wife Christina, b. 22 Sep 1773, bapt. 9 Oct 1773. Sponsors: *Mr.* Georg Fidler and wife Elisabeth.

Friedrich, of Anthon Hecht and wife Sophia, b. 22 Sep 1773, bapt. 3 Oct 1773.
Sponsors: Friedrich Shick and wife Barbara.

Catharina Elisabeth, of Henrich Jonas and wife Anna Catharina, b. 10 Sep 1773,
bapt. 3 Oct 1773. Sponsors: Daniel Grub and wife [Mrs.] Grup(in).

Daniel, of Michael Graf and wife Margreth, b. 28 Aug 1773, bapt. 3 Oct 1773.
Sponsors: Daniel Draess and [whose?] sister Catharina.

Hanna Wacker(in), a friend of Esy More at Germantown, bapt. after profession
of faith, 7 Oct 1773. Sponsors: Philip Hay and wife, and several friends.

Margareta, of Georg Kidd and wife Margareta, b. 26 Sep 1773, bapt. 11 Oct
1773. Sponsors: Michael Stauch and wife Margareta.

Joh. Georg, of Georg Klein and wife Louisa, b. 10 Sep 1773, Oct 10, 1773.
Sponsors: Andreas Tag and wife Christina.

William, of Martin Perry and wife Maria, b. 13 Jun 1773, bapt. 12 Oct 1773.
Sponsors: the parents and the grandfather.

Barbara, of Johannes Eders and wife Christina, b. 20 Aug 1773, bapt. 17 Oct
1773. Sponsor: the grandmother Barbara Fort(in).

Jacob, of Joh. Christoph Senderling and wife Anna Maria, b. 18 Jul 1773, bapt.
17 Oct 1773. Sponsors: Jacob Beck and wife Maria Elisabeth.

Elisabeth, of Michael Schnöneck and wife Anna Catharina, b. 23 Sep 1773, bapt.
17 Oct 1773. Sponsors: Adam Hold and wife Maria Christina.

Henrich, of Conrad Zorn and wife Barbara, b. 31 Aug 1773, bapt. 17 Oct 1773.
Sponsors: Henrich Steinmetz and wife Barbara.

Samuel, of John Willis and wife Christina, b. in Mar 1773?, bapt. 17 Oct 1773.
Sponsors: Johann Leckrum and wife.

Elisabeth, of Adam Metz and wife Barbara, b. 27 Sep 1773, bapt. 17 Oct 1773.
Sponsors: Peter Swob and Elisabeth Strupp(in), both single.

Joh. Jacob, of Andreas Meyer and wife Maria Clara, b. 14 Mar 1773, bapt.
18 Oct 1773. Sponsors: the mother and her brother John Jacob Maurer.

Maria, of Johann Kohl and wife Elisabetha, b. 15 Oct 1773, bapt. 20 Oct 1773.
Sponsor: the father.

Maria Charlotte, of Friedrich Ermentraud and wife Catharina, b. 22 Jun 1772,
bapt. 29 Oct 1773. Sponsors: Heinr. Weinkauf and Miss Maria Ehwald(in).

Elisabeth, of Friedrich Ties and wife Maria, b. 17 Oct 1773, bapt. 31 Oct 1773.
Sponsors: Johannes Stuckhardt and wife Elisabeth.

Maria Margretha, of Joh. Georg Hafner and wife Magdalena, b. 3 Oct 1773,
bapt. 31 Oct 1773. Sponsors: Jacob Schwäbel and wife Maria Margretha.

Elisabeth (twin), of Peter Kress and wife Rosina, b. 13 Oct 1773, bapt. 31 Oct
1773. Sponsors: Martin Holder and wife Elisabeth.

Salome (twin), of Peter Kress and wife Rosina, b. 13 Oct 1773, bapt. 31 Oct
1773. Sponsors: same as above.

Anna Maria, of Joh. Nicolaus Rot(h)enwalter and wife Elisabetha, b. 29 Oct
1773, bapt. 31 Oct 1773. Sponsors: Joh. Martin Sommer and wife Anna
Barbara.

Johannes, of Peter Biswanger and wife Eva, b. 27 Sep 1773, bapt. 31 Oct 1773.
Sponsors: Johannes Heller and wife Christina.

Catharina, of Nicolaus Müller and wife Anna Maria, b. 13 Oct 1773, bapt.
31 Oct 1773. Sponsors: Christian Gänsel and wife Catharina.

Johannes, of Wendel Tierk and wife Elisabeth, b. 28 Sep 1773, bapt. 31 Oct 1773. Sponsors: Johannes Bach and wife Elisabeth.

Anna Margretha, of Adam Pausch and wife Anna Maria, b. 27 Oct 1773, bapt. 7 Nov 1773. Sponsors: Georg Wentzel and wife Anna Margretha.

Joh. Peter, of Georg Weidman and wife Maria Eva, b. 27 Sep 1773, bapt. 6 Nov 1773. Sponsors: Henrich Kress and wife Anna Maria.

Elisabeth, of Heinrich Kurtz and wife Rosina, b. 29 Oct 1773, bapt. 7 Nov 1773. Sponsors: Bernhard Buck and wife Maria.

Jacob, of William Smeily and wife Maria, b. 18 Oct 1773, bapt. 7 Nov 1773. Sponsors: Christopher Young and wife Margreth.

Martin Friedrich, of Martin Noll and wife Elisabeth, b. 21 Oct 1773, bapt. 7 Nov 1773. Sponsors: Frederich Mehl and wife Magdalena.

Anna Maria, of Henrich Lentz and wife Anna Maria, b. 17 Oct 1773, bapt. 7 Nov 1773. Sponsors: the parents.

William, of Peter Derry and wife Elisabeth, b. 7 Nov 1773, bapt. 7 Nov 1773. Sponsors: Caspar Wahl and wife Elisabeth.

Elisabeth, of Joh. Jacob Elgert and wife Elisabeth, b. 1 Oct 1773, aboard ship, bapt. 7 Nov 1773. Sponsors: the parents, and Peter Gabriel and Anna Elisabeth Thomas.

Anna Maria, of Michael Walker and wife Barbara, b. 8 Aug 1773, bapt. 10 Nov 1773. Sponsors: the parents, who live in Bucks County.

Joh. Philip, of Peter Weber and wife Anna Magdalena, b. 23 Oct 1773, bapt. 14 Nov 1773. Sponsors: Nicolaus Warner and wife Elisabetha.

Anna Maria, of Georg Staus and wife Esther, b. 27 Oct 1773, bapt. 14 Nov 1773. Sponsors: *Mr.* Paul Kober and wife Anna Barbara.

Margretha, of Friedrich Wolpert and wife Margretha, b. 28 Oct 1773, bapt. 14 Nov 1773. Sponsors: *Mr.* Georg Wolpert and wife Margretha.

Eva Maria, of Peter Klein and wife Eva Maria, b. 24 Oct 1773, bapt. 14 Nov 1773. Sponsors: Matthias Preiss, and wife Elisabeth and their son Peter.

Georg Heinrich, of Heinrich Keppele and wife Catharina, b. 12 Sep 1773, bapt. 14 Nov 1773. Sponsors: Heinrich Keppele, Sr., and wife Catharina.

Anna Maria, of Edward Lasky and wife Catharina, b. 2 Nov 1773, bapt. 16 Nov 1773. Sponsors: *Mr.* Martin Riess and wife Catharina.

Johannes, of Johannes Beck and wife Anna Maria, who live at Pottsgrove, b. 7 Feb 1773, bapt. 16 Nov 1773. Sponsors: Edward Lasky and wife Catharina.

Mary, of John McLawsen? and wife Catharina, b. 21 Feb 1773, bapt. 18 Nov 1773. Sponsors: the parents and Mary Marshal.

Joh. Jacob, of *Mr.* Jacob Graef and wife Elisabeth, b. 6 Nov 1773, bapt. 19 Nov 1773. Sponsors: *Mr.* Caspar Graeff and wife Catharina.

Michael, of Johannes Lutz and wife Magdalena, b. 2 Nov 1773, bapt. 21 Nov 1773. Sponsors: Michael Regenbogen and wife Catharina.

Georg, of David Steinmeier and wife Catharina, b. 30 Oct 1773, bapt. 21 Nov 1773. Sponsors: Georg Gro[t]z and wife Dorothea.

Georg Thomas, of John Scheeles and Anna Tresure (illegitimate), b. 20 Jul 1773, bapt. 21 Nov 1773. Sponsors: Georg Bauer (in camp) and wife Anna Margareta.

Johann Heinrich, of Adam Zansinger and wife Susanna, b. 31 Oct 1773, bapt. 21 Nov 1773. Sponsors: Joh. Heinrich Keppele Sr., and wife Catharina.

Johann Leonhard, of Leonhard Roht and wife Charlotta, b. 16 Oct 1773, bapt. 24 Nov 1773. Sponsors: Samuel Groff and wife Christiana Friderica.

Margareta Henrietta, of Georg Leib and wife Margaretha Dorothea, b. 28 Oct 1773, bapt. 1 Nov 1773. Sponsors: Rev. Muhlenberg, Sr., and Johann Christ. Kunze and wife Margareta Henrietta.

Charlotte, of Christian Schul[t]z and wife Maria, b. 22 Oct 1773, bapt. 29 Oct 1773. Sponsors: Henrich Haertel and wife Margareta.

Johannes, of Christoph Henrich and wife Anna Maria, b. 18 Nov 1773, bapt. 23 Nov 1773. Sponsors: the parents.

Peter, of Peter Timbrook and wife Margreth, from Jersey, b. 15 Nov 1773, bapt. 26 Nov 1773. Sponsors: the mother and Peter Smick.

Catharina, of Georg Jung and wife Rosina, b. 28 Oct 1773, bapt. 28 Nov 1773. Sponsors: *Mr.* Georg Walker and wife Dorothea.

Jacob, of Wilhelm Kämpf and wife Anna Sabina, b. 21 Nov 1773, bapt. 28 Nov 1773. Sponsors: Jacob Weber and wife Elisabeth.

Joh. Friedrich, of Heinrich Meyer and wife Catharina, b. 23 Nov 1773, bapt. 28 Nov 1773. Sponsors: Joh. Friedrich Kosting and Christina Tolneck(in).

Joh. Henrich, of Henrich Hafner and wife Anna Elisabeth, b. 26 Oct 1773, bapt. 28 Nov 1773. Sponsors: Joh. Henrich Müller and Maria Hafner(in).

Anna Maria, of Jacob Wolf and wife Anna Catharina, b. 8 Nov 1773, bapt. 28 Nov 1773. Sponsors: Leonard Kræmer and wife Anna Maria.

Carl Preuss, of Johann Zacharias Schneider and wife, b. 21 Nov 1773, bapt. 26 Nov 1773. Sponsors: Carl Preuss and wife Maria Magdalena.

Elisabeth, of Georg Mildeberger and wife Catharina, b. 30 Oct 1773, bapt. 28 Nov 1773. Sponsors: the grandparents Michael Mildeberger and wife Catharina.

John Bernhard, of Jacob Schreck and wife Maria, b. 14 Oct 1773, bapt. 28 Nov 1773. Sponsors: Joh. Bernhard Scheib and wife Catharina Bub(in).

Margretha, of Joh. Martin Paysch and wife Magdalena, b. 9 Oct 1773, bapt. 28 Nov 1773. Sponsors: *Mr.* Georg Grotz and wife Margretha.

Magdalena, of Daniel Frid. Schmidt and wife Barbara, b. 30 Oct 1773, bapt. 28 Nov 1773. Sponsors the father, and mother-in-law Magdalena Graff.

Peter, of James Tresure and his German wife Juliana, b. 4 Nov 1773, bapt. 28 Nov 1773. Sponsor: the grandmother, and Barbara Kochendoerfer.

Anna Maria, of Georg Kurtz and wife Dorothea, b. 11 Nov 1773, bapt. 5 Dec 1773. Sponsors: Johannes Preiss and Maria Elisabeth Schall(in).

Anna Susanna, of Joh. Michael Rieb and wife Martha, b. 11 Aug 1773, bapt. 4 Dec 1773. Sponsors: Johannes Rieb and wife Anna Susanna.

Elisabeth Catharina, of Nicolaus Klein and wife Catharina, b. 7 Nov 1773, bapt. 5 Dec 1773. Sponsors: Henrich Wagner and wife Else Catharina.

Maria Magdalena, of Jacob Mezger and wife Apollonia Cathar., b. 16 Nov 1773, bapt. 5 Dec 1773. Sponsor: the mother and Maria Magdalena Suter(in).

Cath. Elisab., of John Pater Belier and wife An. Marg., b. 17 Oct 1773, bapt. 5 Dec 1773. Sponsors: Joh. Christ. Müller and wife Cathar. Elisab.

Johann Jacob, of Benedict Schneider and wife Philippina Elisabeth, b. 30 Oct 1773, bapt. 5 Dec 1773. Sponsors: Joh. Jacob Homüller and Elisab. Schwinn(in).

Michael, of Jacob Beck and wife Maria Elisabeth, b. 5 Aug 1773, bapt. 5 Dec 1773. Sponsors: Michael Regenboge and wife Catharina.

Susan Marg., of Peter Klein and wife Maria, b. 16 Oct 1773, bapt. 5 Dec 1773. Sponsors: Phil. Klein and Susan Reiss.

Regina, of Bernh. Kaufman and wife An. Marg., b. 1 Dec 1773, bapt. 9 Dec 1773. Sponsors: Joh. Kaufman and Reg. Meyer(in).

Sarah, of John Bevering and wife Sara, b. 1 Oct 1773, bapt. 11 Dec 1773. Sponsors: the parents.

Cath., of Jacob Baideman and wife An. Elisabeth, b. 9 Nov 1773, bapt. 12 Dec 1773. Sponsors: Geo. Wilpert and wife Marg.

John Charles, of John Shrack and wife Marg., b. 11 Sep 1773, bapt. 11 Dec 1773. Sponsors: William Farby and wife Elisabeth.

Eva Barbara, of George Seibert and wife Margareta, b. 27 Sep 1773, bapt. 18 Dec 1773. Sponsors: Johann Michael Goe[t]z and wife Eva Barbara.

Henrich, of Henr. Kuns? and wife Maria Juliana, b. 9 Dec 1773, bapt. 19 Dec 1773. Sponsors: Henrich Hencke and wife Elisabeth.

Susanna Maria, of Friedr. Carls and wife Elisabeth, b. 22 Nov 1773, bapt. 19 Dec 1773. Sponsors: Jacob Bauer and wife Maria.

Barbara, of Daniel Water and wife Elisabeth, b. 6 Dec 1773, bapt. 19 Dec 1773. Sponsors: Johannes Hofmann and wife Barbara.

Wilhelm, of Johannes Warner and wife Rahel, b. 27 Nov 1773, bapt. 19 Dec 1773. Sponsors: Wilhelm Hoek? and wife Catharina.

Regina, of Johannes Clauss and wife Christina Catharina, b. 17 Aug 1773, bapt. 20 Dec 1773. Sponsors: the parents.

Jacob Schrack [aged 23], son of Simon John Schrack and wife Elisabeth, b. 1 Mar 1750, bapt. 21 Dec 1773. Sponsors: the parents.

Mary, wife of John Schrack and dau. of Henry Cherry, b. 10 Mar 1744, bapt. 21 Dec 1773. Sponsors: "relatives" (not named).

Christina Margareta, of Jacob Ehrhardt and wife Johanetta, b. 22 Dec 1773, bapt. 23 Dec 1773. Sponsors: Michael Hermann and wife Christina Marg.

Anna Maria, of Michael Poes and wife Maria, b. 11 Dec 1773, bapt. 26 Dec 1773. Sponsors: the father and Catharina Weber(in).

Valentin, of Nicolaus Ulrich and wife Eva, b. 20 Nov 1773, bapt. 26 Dec 1773. Sponsors: Valentin Hofmann and Fronica Hartmann(in).

Peter, of Sigmund Copia and wife Sophia Magdalena, b. 10 Dec 1773, bapt. 26 Dec 1773. Sponsors: Peter Dick and wife Maria.

Elisabeth, of Caspar Wist and wife Eva Maria, b. 9 Dec 1773, bapt. 25 Dec 1773. Sponsors: the father and Eva Forbach(in).

Johann Jacob, of Johann Henrich Conrad and wife Anna Maria, b. 11 Dec 1773, bapt. 26 Dec 1773. Sponsors: John Jacob Kreis and wife Susanna Catharina.

Johan Georg, of Johann Christian Fleisch and wife Rosina Dorothea, b. 15 Dec 1773, bapt. 26 Dec 1773. Sponsors: Johannes Ostertag and wife Regina Catharina, and Johann Georg Schneck.

Joseph, of Wilhelm Ludewig Truckenmüller and wife Rahel, b. 22 Nov 1773, bapt. 31 Dec 1773. Sponsors: the mother and Joseph Baling.

1774

(baptisms by pastors Muhlenberg, Sr. and Jr., and Kunze;
all in chronological sequence from Book III)

Christoph, of Georg Zimmermann and wife Margareta Catarina, b. 15 Dec 1773, bapt. 1 Jan 1774. Sponsors: Christoph Haensmann and wife Hanna Margareta.

Johannes, of Jacob Specht and wife Margareta, b. 9 Nov 1773, bapt. 2 Jan 1774. Sponsors: Johann Specht and Christina. Dres(in).

Eva Maria, of Martin Schreiner and wife Anna Rosina, b. 20 Dec 1773, bapt. 2 Jan 1774. Sponsors: Peter Klein and wife Eva Maria.

Johann Georg, of Elias Landvess and wife Catharina, b. 17 Dec 1773, bapt. 2 Jan 1774. Sponsors: Johannes Schneider and wife Catharina.

Sara, of Lorentz Mahn and wife Anna Margaretha, b. 30 Dec 1773, bapt. 7 Jan 1774. Sponsors: Johannes Lamparter and wife Sarah.

Johannes, of Georg Bob and wife Maria, aged 4 days, bapt. 7 Jan 1774. Sponsors: the parents and grandparents.

Joseph, of Peter Paul and wife Anna Maria, b. 20 Dec 1773, bapt. 9 Jan 1774. Sponsors: the parents.

Johannes, of Johann Geiser and wife Maria Elisabeth, b. 25 Dec 1773, bapt. 13 Jan 1774. Sponsors: the parents.

Johann Jacob, of Johann Jacob Seger and wife Barbara, b. 7 Jan 1774, bapt. 14 Jan 1774. Sponsors: Jacob Kiemle and wife Margaret.

Susanna, of Melchior Weissinger and wife Maria, b. 8 Dec 1773, bapt. 15 Jan 1774. Sponsors: Balthasar Stauss and wife Maria.

Joh. Peter, of Johann Peter Weygand and wife Cunigunda, b. 3 Jan 1774, bapt. 14 Jan 1774. Sponsors: Adolph Dill and wife Catharina.

Maria Elisabeth, of Johannes Haas and wife Salome, b. 9 Jan 1774, bapt. 16 Jan 1774. Sponsors: Henrich Bitterson and wife Maria Elisabeth.

Joh. David, of David Schäffer and wife Elisabeth, b. 11 Jan 1774, bapt. 16 Jan 1774. Sponsors: the grandparents Joh. David Schaeffer (trustee) and wife Maria Catharina.

Margreth, of Arnold Becker and wife Elisabeth, b. 14 Dec 1773, bapt. 16 Jan 1774. Sponsors: *Mr.* Johannes Biegler and wife Anna.

Margareta, of Joseph Denros and Abigail Wiley, illegitimate, b. in Dec 1773, bapt. 16 Jan 1774. Sponsors: Rosina Margareta Geret(in).

Ludewig, of Ludew. Wirt and wife Anna Margareta, b. 3 Mar 1771, bapt. 17 Jan 1774. Sponsors: the parents.

Salome, of Ludew. Wirt and wife Anna Margareta, b. 2 dec 1773, bapt. 17 Jan 1774. Sponsors: the parents.

Elisabeth, of Christian Persie and wife Maria, b. 25 Jul 1773, bapt. 22 Jan 1774. Sponsors: the parents.

Joh. Jacob, of Joh. Jacob Becker and wife Regina, b. 1 Jan 1774, bapt. 23 Jan 1774. Sponsors: Jacob Pafhausser? and wife Susanna.

Elisabeth, of Philip Werner and wife Anna Magd., b. 4 Jan 1774, bapt. 23 Jan 1774. Sponsors: Johannes Bauman and wife Elisabeth.

Maria Euphronica, of Henrich Rohn and wife Magdalena, b. 2 Jan 1774, bapt. 23 Jan 1774. Sponsors: Henrich Fahns and wife.

Johann Georg, of Jacob Keimle and wife Margareta, b. 27 Jan 1774, bapt. 30 Jan 1774. Sponsor: Johannes Fri[t]z and wife Anna Catherina.

Thomas, of Johannes Heil and wife Maria, b. 17 Jan 1774, bapt. 1 Feb 1774. Sponsors: the parents.

Georg, of Lorentz Sandmann and wife Maria Magdel., b. in Apr 1773, bapt. 2 Feb 1774. Sponsors: Georg Knerr and wife Catharina.

Anna Margretha, of Andreas Bachman and wife Catharina, b. 10 Jan 1774, bapt. 3 Feb 1774. Sponsors: Ludewig Grauer and Margaretha Gilbert(in), both single.

Catharina, of Philip Pankuch and wife Maria, b. 28 Jan 1774, bapt. 6 Feb 1774. Sponsors: Johannes Starck and Catharina Pankuch(in).

Susanna Barbara, of Georg Wirt and wife Maria, b. 11 Jan 1774, bapt. 6 Feb 1774. Sponsors: Georg Honig and wife Barbara.

Johann Christian, of Joh. Adam Witterstein and wife Sophia, b. 23 Jan 1774, bapt. 6 Feb 1774. Sponsors: the parents.

Mary, of Joseph Frankenberger and wife Maria, b. 2 Nov 1773, bapt. 6 Feb 1774. Sponsors: the parents, and the grandmother, widow Wes(in).

Philippina (known as Phoeby) Carbet, from Maxatawny (a bondservant of Mr. Ludewig Dowig), 16 years old, bapt. 10 Feb 1774. Sponsors: Mr. Dowig's wife and Polly Muhlenberg.

Johann Daniel, of Daniel Burghardt and wife Catharina, b. 9 Jan 1774, bapt. 13 Feb 1774. Sponsors: Johann Ka_ket and wife Elisabeth.

Catharina Elisabeth, of Jacob Kessler and wife Catharina, b. 30 Jan 1774, bapt. 13 Feb 1774. Sponsors: Michael Schafer and wife Catharina Elisabeth.

Catharina, of Christian Kinzel and wife Margareta, b. 25 Jan 1774, bapt. 13 Feb 1774. Sponsors: Martin Wo[t]zer and wife Catharina.

Johann Friedrich, of David Uber and wife Anna, b. 27 Jan 1774, bapt. 13 Feb 1774. Sponsor: Johann Friedr. Woelpert.

Sophia, of Christian Dick and wife Christiana, b. 26 Jan 1774, bapt. 13 Feb 1774. Sponsors: Johann Lorenz and wife Catharina.

Joh. Henrich, of Joh. Friedrich Schick and wife Barbara, b. 27 Jan 1774, bapt. 13 Feb 1774. Sponsors: the parents and grandparents.

Gertraut, of Philip Meyerle and wife Anna Esther, b. 13 Feb 1774, bapt. 20 Feb 1774. Sponsors: Michael Kuhns and wife Gertraut.

Henrich, of Andreas Foerster and wife Hanna, b. 18 Feb 1774, bapt. 27 Feb 1774. Sponsors: Henrich Meier and wife Catharina.

Dorothea, of Friedr. Orn and wife Elisabeth, b. 14 Feb 1774, bapt. 27 Feb 1774. Sponsors: Matthaeus Stats and wife Dorothea.

Johannes, of Johannes Pless and wife Elisabeth, b. 9 Feb 1774, bapt. 27 Feb 1774. Sponsors: Johannes Metz and wife Barbara.

Johann Peter, of Joh. Henrich Pot(h) and wife Catharina Elisab., b. 19 Feb 1774, bapt. 27 Feb 1774. Sponsors: The grandparents Peter Rot(h) and Anna Maria.

Elisabeth, of Johannes Jacob and wife Anna Maria, b. 4 Nov 1773, bapt. 27 Feb 1774. Sponsors: Lorentz Opman and wife Elisabeth.

Joh. Georg, of Jacob Schmid and wife Anna Maria, b. 27 Feb 1774, bapt. 27 Feb 1774. Sponsors: Joh. Georg Backos and wife Salome.

348   PHILADELPHIA GERMAN LUTHERAN CHURCH

Johann Heinrich, of Rudolp Nagel and wife Susanna, b. 19 Feb 1774, bapt.
27 Feb 1774. Sponsors: The grandparents Heinrich Schwalbach and wife
Catharina.
Johannes, of John Buss (Bub?) and wife Anna, b. 21 Dec 1773, bapt. 28 Feb
1774. Sponsors: the grandparents and Johann Ellwood.
Johannes, of Conrad Buetkis and wife Anna Barbara, b. 15 Feb 1774, bapt.
3 Mar 1774. Sponsors: the parents.
Joh. Samuel, of Eberhard Lankep and wife Catharina, b. 5 Feb 1774, bapt. 6 Mar
1774. Sponsors: the grandmother Maria Magdalena Willer(in) and Joh.
Deter.
Johann Georg, of Johann Georg Goettle and wife Anna, b. 14 Feb 1774, bapt.
6 Mar 1774. Sponsors: Johann Georg Seifferheld and wife Christina.
Heinrich, of Adam Knoblauch and wife Barbara, b. 2 Mar 1774, bapt. 6 Mar
1774. Sponsors: Heinrich Oxsfel?, single and Christina Sartorius.
Samuel, of Conrad Leibbrand and wife Elisabeth (who died), b. 11 Feb 1774,
bapt. 6 Mar 1774. Sponsors: Michael Fuchs and wife Salome.
Johannes, of Joh. Jacob Schwaab and wife Margretha, b. 30 Jan 1774, bapt.
6 Mar 1774. Sponsors: Johann Adam Schwaab and wife Margretha.
Anna Margreth, of Johannes Klein and wife Anna Catharina, b. 21 Jan 1774,
bapt. 10 Mar 1774. Sponsors: Friedrich Dischan and wife Anna Margaretha.
Georg Michael, of Gottfried Grumbach and wife Barbara, b. 15 Jan 1774, bapt.
10 Mar 1774. Sponsors: the parents.
Catharina Margareta, of Melchior Schwerer and wife Lovina [sic], b. 19 Dec
1773, bapt. 13 Mar 1774. Sponsors: Rudolf Lehr and wife Catharina.
Henrich, of Joh. Wilhelm Weber and wife Elisabeth, b. 23 Feb 1774, bapt.
13 Mar 1774. Sponsors: Henrich Kress and wife Maria.
Maria Rosina Catharina, of Anthon Armbruster and wife Christina Maria, b.
8 Sep 1773, bapt. 12 Mar 1774. Sponsors: Maria Rosina Catharina and her
husband Martin Abitsch?.
Johannes, of Martin Dietz and wife Margretha, b. 2 Mar 1774, bapt. 13 Mar
1774. Sponsors: Joh. Balthasar Klein and Maria Eva Hamber(in).
Maria Margaretha, of Philip Etter and wife Catharina, b. 10 Jan 1774, bapt.
13 Mar 1774. Sponsors: the parents and Sara Elisab. Mahn(in).
Elisabet, of Johan Graesel and wife Magdalene, b. 13 Mar 1774, bapt. 20 Mar
1774. Sponsors: N. Spiegel and wife Elisabet, from Penns Neck.
Sebastian, of Sebastian Schweicker and wife Agnesia Maria, b. 16 Feb 1774,
bapt. 20 Mar 1774. Sponsors: Sebastian Seiffert and wife Barbara.
Johan Georg, of Fridr. Heineman and wife Catharine, b. 13 Feb 1774, bapt.
20 Mar 1774. Sponsors: Georg Klein and wife Elisabet.
Catharine, of Jacob Buck and wife Cath., b. 2 Mar 1774, bapt. 21 Mar 1774.
Sponsors: Wilhelm Ewert and wife Margaret.
Georg, of Georg Vorbach (also known as Forepaugh) and wife Anna Marg., b.
4 Mar 1774, bapt. 20 Mar 1774. Sponsors: Caspar West and wife Eva.
Susanna Margret, of Johannes Bach and wife Elisabetha, b. 23 Feb 1774, bapt.
20 Mar 1774. Sponsors: the father and Susanna Margretha Bach(in).
Gottlieb, of Jacob Zink and wife Magdalena, b. 21 Jan 1774, bapt. 20 Mar 1774.
Sponsors: Gottlieb Zinck and wife Catharina.

Christian Philip, of Christian Jost and wife Christina Barb., b. 5 Mar 1774, bapt. 20 Mar 1774. Sponsors: Joh. Philip Krebs and [wife] Barbara Krebs(in).

Magdalene, of Daniel Knodel and wife Anna Maria, b. 5 Mar 1774, bapt. 20 Mar 1774. Sponsors: Franz Wilh. Hetmansperger and Magdalena Losch(in).

Joh. Andreas, of Joh. Georg Vetter and wife Hanna, b. 22 Feb 1774, bapt. 20 Mar 1774. Sponsors: the parents.

Johannes, of Barbara Sachs(in)? (a bondservant of Mr. Wm. Hofmann) and "an American" [Neuländer]," 6 months old, bapt. 20 Mar 1774. Sponsors: Johannes Elgert and wife Anna Margaretha.

Johannes, of Johann Jacob Gress and wife Susanna, b. 5 Mar 1774, bapt. 27 Mar 1774. Sponsors: Johannes Shu[t]z and wife Margareta.

Johannes, of Samuel Prinz and wife Anna, b. 2 Mar 1774, bapt. 27 Mar 1774. Sponsors: the father and Rosina __reis(in).

Joh. Peter, of Joh. Peter Steuerwald and wife Maria Magdalena, b. 3 Mar 1774, bapt. 27 Mar 1774. Sponsors: Christoph Hinkel and wife Maria Eva.

Conrad, of Georg Turnis and wife Maria Christina, b. 4 Feb 1774, bapt. 27 Mar 1774. Sponsors: Conrad Becker and wife Maria Catharina.

Elisabeth Barb., of Friedrich Vogel and wife Barbara, b. 8 Mar 1774, bapt. 27 Mar 1774. Sponsors: Johann Martin Wieland and wife Elisabeth Barbara.

Christian, of Christian Nagel and wife Elisabeth, b. 10 Mar 1774, bapt. 27 Mar 1774. Sponsors: the father and his sister Maria Ruth(sin).

Joh. Georg, of Johannes Fisher and wife Catharina, b. 21 Mar 1774, bapt. 28 Mar 1774. Sponsors: Joh. Georg Seitz and wife Elisabeth.

Anna Margar., of Joh. Gerhard Mutzheld and wife Barbara, b. 22 Mar 1774, bapt. 31 Mar 1774. Sponsors: Jacob Masholder and wife Anna Margareta.

Johann Michael, of Martin Reusser and wife Catharina, b. 22 Mar 1774, bapt. 2 Apr 1774. Sponsors: Jacob Reusser and wife Eva.

Johannes, of Jacob Schifferer and wife Maria Juliana, b. 1 Jan 1774, bapt. 2 Apr 1774. Sponsors: Joh. Adam Schifferer and wife Dorothea, and Francis Roberts and wife Anna.

Salome, of Anna Maria Zett(in) (a bondservant with Mr. Stretch), illegitimate, b. 15 Feb 1774, bapt. 3 Apr 1774. Sponsors: Salome Adams, single, and Henrich Ernst.

Andreas, of Andreas Weh and wife Regina, b. 28 Feb 1774, bapt. 3 Apr 1774. Sponsors: the parents.

Georg, of Georg Heydel and wife Salome, b. 6 Mar 1774, bapt. 3 Apr 1774. Sponsors: the parents.

Johannes, of Joh. Philip Mitman and wife Euphronica, (birth date not given), bapt. 3 Apr 1774. Sponsor: Michael Zinser.

Johannes, of Johannes Schäfer and wife Sophia Maria, b. 21 Mar 1774, bapt. 3 Apr 1774. Sponsors: Mr. Johannes Keppele and Miss Elisabeth Keppel(in).

Maria Susanna, of Georg Lange and wife Susanna, b. 2 Apr 1774, bapt. 4 Apr 1774. Sponsors: Friedr. Ernst and wife Maria Clara.

Anna, of ___ Aertius (deceased) and now widow Anna Kuntz(in), confirmed in 1774 (age not given), bapt. 9 Mar 1774.

Georg, of Johann Nicolaus Wagner, b. 16 Feb 1774, bapt. 4 Apr 1774.
Sponsors: Georg Schmidt and wife Anna Margareta.

Anna Elisabeth, of Peter Mierken and wife Catharina, b. 28 Dec 1773, bapt.
4 Apr 1774. Sponsors: the parents.

Johann Andreas, of Christoph Zinck and wife Magdalena, b. 6 Mar 1774, bapt.
4 Apr 1774. Sponsors: the parents.

Johann Georg, of Peter Arnold and wife Maria, b. 15 Jan 1774, bapt. 4 Apr
1774. Sponsor: Johann Andreas Beckmann and wife Catharina.

Joh. Matthias, of Johannes Leix and wife Catharina, b. 26 Sep 1773, bapt. 4 Apr
1774. Sponsors: Adam Grof and wife Catharina.

Peter, of Christoph Dietrich and wife Elisabeth, b. 15 Sep 1773, bapt. 7 Apr
1774. Sponsors: Adolf Dill and wife Catharina.

Benedict, of Wilhelm Mohr and wife Susanna, b. 25 Mar 1774, bapt. 6 Apr
1774. Sponsors: Benedict Schneider and wife Philippina Elisabeth.

Johann Joseph, of Joh. Georg Hoss and wife Margretha, b. 7 Feb 1774, bapt.
6 Apr 1774. Sponsors: the parents.

Jacob, of Georg Stump and wife Maria, b. 17 Feb 1774, bapt. 10 Apr 1774.
Sponsors: Jacob Kieffer and Elisabeth Halt(in), both single.

Johannes, of Michael Klingmann and wife Anna Elisabeth, b. 5 Feb 1774, bapt.
8 Apr 1774. Sponsors: *Mr.* Johann Jacob Müller and wife Elisabeth, from
Potts Mill.

Peter, of Christoph Hirt and wife Susanna, b. 1 Feb 1774, bapt. 10 Apr 1774.
Sponsors: Peter Eisenbrey and wife Dorothea.

Joh. Heinrich, of Christian Heinrich Habig and wife Anna Christina, b. 24 Mar
1774, bapt. 10 Apr 1774. Sponsors: Georg Realling and wife Maria.

Joh.. Wilhelm, of Johannes Kinsle and wife Margreth, b. 25 Mar 1774, bapt.
10 Apr 1774. Sponsors: Johannes Greiffenstein and wife Dorothea.

Margretha, of Daniel Pillegar and wife Margretha, b. 20 Jan 1774, bapt. 10 Apr
1774. Sponsors: Johannes Pillegar and wife Margretha.

Henrich, of Johannes Fischer and wife Catharina, b. 8 Jan 1774, bapt. 10 Apr
1774. Sponsors: Henrich Lentz and wife Anna Maria.

Joh. Peter, of Christoph Gihl and wife Elisabeth, b. 16 Dec 1773, bapt. 10 Apr
1774. Sponsors: Peter Laub and wife Margretha.

Anna Rosina, of Jacob Diet(h)rich and wife Anna Rosina, b. 22 Nov 1773, bapt.
10 Apr 1774. Sponsors: Daniel Schaab and wife Catharina.

Heinrich, of Christoph Bryer and wife Apollonia, b. 18 Mar 1774, bapt. 11 Apr
1774. Sponsors: Heinrich Keppele, Jr., and wife Catharina.

Susanna, of Daniel Hofmann and wife Margaretha, b. 11 Apr 1774, bapt. 11 Apr
1774. Sponsors: the father and Mrs. Pennikof stood in for Andr. Burkhardt
and wife Susanna.

John, of William Groves (a soldier in the barracks) and wife Dorothea, b. 7 Dec
1773, bapt. 12 Apr 1774. Sponsors: the mother and Henrich Jonas' wife.

William, of William Groves and wife Dorothea, 3 years old, bapt. 12 Apr 1774,
Sponsors: same as above.

Johannes, of Gottfried Henrich and wife Catharina, b. 22 Feb 1774, bapt. 17 Apr
1774. Sponsors: Johannes Kaufmann and Elisabeth Vockerod.

Jacob, of Peter Karch and wife Elisabeth, b. 20 Dec 1773, bapt. 16 Apr 1774.
Sponsors: the father and his mother Barbara Karch(in).

Catharina, of Johannes Freiburger and wife Susanna, b. 27 Mar 1774, bapt.
17 Apr 1774. Sponsors: Philipp Ohler and wife Catharina.
Justina Maria, of Johann Matthias Tollmann and wife Anna Catharina, b. 27 Mar
1774, bapt. 17 Apr 1774. Sponsors: Jacob Solliger and wife Anna
Margareta.
Elisabeth, of Joh. Friedrich Mehl and wife Elisabeth, b. 25 Mar 1774, bapt.
17 Apr 1774. Sponsors: Jacob Brandt and wife Elisabeth.
Anna Catharina, of Johannes Odenheimer and wife Maria, b. 15 Apr 1774, bapt.
17 Apr 1774. Sponsors: the grandparents Heinrich Keppele, Sr. and wife
Anna Catharina.
Philip, of Friedrich Lindemann and Sara Dorothea, b. 13 Apr 1774, bapt. 19 Apr
1774. Sponsors: Mr. Philip Alberty and wife.
Gideon, of Gideon Babcock (deceased) and his widow Margretha, from Egg
Harbor, b. 22 Nov 1773, bapt. 20 Apr 1774. Sponsors: Daniel Frischmuth
and wife Barbara.
Valentin, of Johann Peter Gabel and wife Anna Elisabeth, b. 13 Apr 1774, bapt.
6 May 1774. Sponsors: Valentin Hagner and wife Margareta.
Georg, of Michael Miller and wife Christina, b. 17 Apr 1774, bapt. 7 May 1774.
Sponsors: Georg Seitz and wife.
Johannes, of Johannes Gummy and wife Catharina, b. 9 Jan 1774, bapt. 8 May
1774. Sponsors: Carl Müller (bondservant with Matt. Meyer), and Gertraut
Schad(in).
Elisabeth, of Friedrich Ernst and wife Maria Clara, b. 10 May 1774, bapt.
15 May 1774. Sponsors: Wilhelm Lehmann and Elisabeth Fiedler.
Maria Magdalena, of Jacob Ries and wife Magdalena, b. 29 Apr 1774, bapt.
15 May 1774. Sponsors: Conrad Schmidt and wife Maria Magdalena.
Georg, of Michael Bauer and wife Catharina, b. 24 Sep 1773, bapt. 15 May
1774. Sponsors: Georg Christein and wife Jemina.
Anna Elisabeth, of Georg Häusel and wife Catharina, b. 5 Apr 1774, bapt.
15 May 1774. Sponsors: the grandparents Johannes Phaü and wife Anna
Elisabeth.
Anna Maria Rosina, of Catharina Graef(in), illegitimate, b. 2 May 1774, bapt.
17 May 1774. Sponsors: Matthias Graef and wife Elisabeth, who live at
[Penns] Neck.
Philip Jacob, of Wilhelm Schmidt and wife Anna, b. 1 May 1774, bapt. 17 May
1774. Sponsors: the parents.
Maria, of Thomas Lehman and wife Catharina, b. 24 Mar 1774, bapt. 22 May
1774. Sponsors: Caspar Strobele and wife Catharina.
Johan Georg, of Johannes Friedr. Bast and (wife's name not given), b. 25 Dec
1773, bapt. 23 May 1774. Sponsors: Georg Budo and wife Elisabeth.
Johann Jacob, of Michael Wolf and wife Margareta, b. 7 Jan 1774, bapt. 22 May
1774. Sponsors: David Huber and wife Hanna.
Maria Margretha, of Wilhelm Barkhard and wife Catharina, b. 27 Apr 1774,
bapt. 22 May 1774. Sponsors: Mr. Adam Pfister and wife Maria Margretha.
Anna Maria, of Conrad Harf and wife Anna, b. 18 Feb 1774, bapt. 22 May 1774.
Sponsors: Nicolaus Müller and wife Anna Maria.
Caspar, of Friedrick Wild and wife Anna, b. in Apr 1774, bapt. 23 May 1774.
Sponsors: Caspar Dehn and wife Margareta.

Rahel, of Jacob Losher and wife Anna Maria, b. 30 Mar 1774, bapt. 23 May 1774. Sponsors: the parents, at Frankford.

Anna Barbara, of Georg Metzger and wife Elisabeth, b. 7 May 1774, bapt. 23 May 1774. Sponsors: the grandparents Conrad Hof and wife Sibilla.

Adam, of Johannes Barnhold? and wife Maria, 3 months old, bapt. 23 May 1774. Sponsors: Adam Alberger and wife Maria Elisabeth.

Jacob, of Melchior Hörner and wife Elisabeth, b. 16 Apr 1773, bapt. 24 May 1774. Sponsors: the parents.

Georg, of Georg Christein and wife Jemima, b. 22 May 1774, bapt. 29 May 1774. Sponsors: Georg Kiefer and wife Eva Maria.

Maria Barbara, of Fiedr. Mog and wife Maria, b. 13 May 1774, bapt. 29 May 1774. Sponsors: Adam Koenig and wife Anna Barbara.

Peter, of Gottfried Hager and wife Catharina, b. 16 May 1774, bapt. 24 May 1774. Sponsor: the father.

Anna Margretha, of William Wood and wife Susanna Margretha, b. 5 Mar 1774, bapt. 29 May 1774. Sponsors: Jacob Schwäbel and wife Anna Margretha.

David, of Thomas and wife Rosina (Mr. Graef's negroes), b. 8 May 1774, bapt. 29 May 1774. Sponsors: Devonshire and Susanna ("Christians").

Joh. Georg, of Michael Jost and wife Margaretha, b. 26 Feb 1774, bapt. 29 May 1774. Sponsors: the father and his mother, Rosina Rösle.

Benjamin Jacob, of Michael Dewald and wife Elisabeth, b. 28 Feb 1774, bapt. 29 May 1774. Sponsor: the mother and Jacob Müller.

Josua, of George Lamparter and wife Sophia, b. 7 May 1774, bapt. 29 May 1774. Sponsors: the parents.

Hanna, of Henrich Poekele and wife Margareta, b. 5 Feb 1774, Sponsors: Jun 2, 1774. Sponsors: David Schneider and wife Nancy.

Andreas, of Johannes Lindfelder and wife Eva, b. 14 Jun 1772, bapt. 3 Jun 1774. Sponsors: Joh.. Melchior Matzinger and Joh. Michael Matzinger.

Maria Catharina, of Johannes Lindfelder and wife Eva, b. 14 Feb 1774, bapt. 3 Jun 1774. Sponsors: Catharine Dorothea Rummel(in) and Anna Catharina Koch(in).

Samuel, of Christian Dannecker and wife Juliana, b. 24 Mar 1774, bapt. 25 May 1774. Sponsors: Georg Staehle and wife Christina.

Catharina, of Michael Ho[t]z and wife Catharina, b. 12 May 1774, bapt. 5 Jun 1774. Sponsors: Peter Dick and wife Anna Maria.

Johann Georg, of Johann Jacob Kraemer and wife Otillia, b. 26 Mar 1774, bapt. 25 Jun 1774. Sponsors: Johan Christoph Heitel and wife Anna Maria.

Barbara, of Gabriel Steinbach and wife Anna Christina, b. 12 Feb 17__, bapt. 5 Jun 1774. Sponsors: Joh. Adam Beck and Miser(in)

Catharina, of Gabriel Steinbach and wife Anna Christina, b. 12 Dec 1771, bapt. 5 Jun 1774. Sponsors: Adolph Dill and wife Catharina.

Johann Adam, of Gabriel Steinbach and wife Anna Christina, b. 2 Feb 1774, bapt. 5 Jun 1774. Sponsor: Barbara Biler?

Elizabeth, of Nicolaus Diel and wife Anna Maria, b. 7 May 1774, bapt. 7 Jun 1774. Sponsors: the parents.

Elisabeth, of John Cartwright and wife Margreth, b. 3 Jun 1774, bapt. 9 Jun 1774. Sponsors: the parents, and Joh. Philips' wife (the grandmother)..

Georg, of Johan Benner and wife Catharina, of New Jersey, b. 1 Jun 1774, bapt.
9 Jun 1774. Sponsors: Georg Merckel and Elisabeth Pechtold(in).
Maria, of Jacob Pennikop and wife Sybilla, b. 5 May 1774, bapt. 12 Jun 1774.
Sponsors: Johannes Weber and wife Maria.
Eleonor, of William Dewese and wife Hanna, b. 13 Sep 1772, bapt. 12 Jun 1774.
Sponsors: Tobias König and wife Barbara.
Johannes, of Andreas Weimar and wife Rosina, b. 15 May 1774, bapt. 12 Jun
1774. Sponsors: Johannes Schweitzer and wife Catharina.
Catharina, of Philip Klein and wife Elisabeth, b. 5 Jun 1774, bapt. 19 Jun 1774.
Sponsors: Rudolph Lehr and wife Catharina.
Jacob, of Johannes Penter and wife Susanna, b. 27 May 1774, bapt. 19 Jun 1774.
Sponsors: Jacob Penter and wife Dorothea.
Magdalena, of Wandel Wendling and wife Albertine, b. 19 Apr 1774, bapt. in
Jun 1774. Sponsors: Nicolaus Mumbauer and wife Magdalena.
Samuel, of Johannes Kassen and wife Eleonore, 4 months old, bapt. 19 Jun
1774. Sponsors: the parents.
Catharina Maria, of Gotthard David Flickwir and wife Anna Sophia, b. 1 May
1774, bapt. 19 Jun 1774. Sponsors: the parents and Catharina Maria
Warner(in).
Margretha, of Friedrich Dampfel and wife Maria Eva, b. 23 Jun 1774, bapt.
26 Jun 1774. Sponsors: Balthasar Kinzler and wife Margretha.
Maria, of Carl Schaefer and wife Agnes, b. 5 Jun 1774, bapt. 26 Jun 1774.
Sponsors: the parents.
Margaret, of Georg Betsch and wife Catharine, b. 8 Jun 1774, bapt. 26 Jun 1774.
Sponsors: Philip Steiner and wife Margreth.
Johan Wilhelm, of Michael Kuhn and wife Anna Maria, b. 19 May 1774, bapt.
26 Jun 1774. Sponsors: the parents.
Christian, of Christian Jung and wife Caroline, b. 12 Jun 1774, bapt. 1 Jul 1774.
Sponsors: the parents.
Maria Elisabeth, of Peter Schneider and wife Elisabeth, b. 25 Jun 1774, bapt.
3 Jul 1774. Sponsors: Johann Christoph Heibel and wife Anna Maria.
Jacob Friedrich, of Joh. Jacob Swain and wife Maria, b. 14 Jun 1774, bapt. 3 Jul
1774. Sponsors: Georg Friedrich Bayer and Elisabet Margarete.
Henrich, of Wilhelm Klett? and wife Margareta, b. 10 Jun 1774, bapt. 3 Jul
1774. Sponsors: Henrich Otto and Margareta Schmal[t]z(in)?.
Johann Adam, of Joseph Baneker and Catharina, b. 22 May 1774, bapt. 3 Jul
1774. Sponsor: Johann Adam Halberger.
Wilhelm Georg, of Georg Heil and wife Dorothea, b. 19 Jun 1774, bapt. 4 Jul
1774. Sponsors: the parents.
Jacob, of Thomas Kan and wife Elisab. Cath., b. 14 Jun 1774, bapt. 7 Jul 1774.
Sponsors: Jacob Baum and wife Elisabeth.
Georg Philip, of Elias Albrecht and wife Maria Cath., b. 18 Jul 1773, bapt. 8 Jul
1774. Sponsors: Philip Werner and wife Anna Magdalena.
Maria, of Joseph Geiser and wife Anna Maria, b. 26 Jun 1774, bapt. 13 Jul 1774.
Sponsors: Stephan Kraus and wife Margareta.
Johannes, of Joh. Pillger and wife Margaretha, b. 13 Jun 1774, bapt. 5 Jul 1774.
Sponsors: Joh. Fuchs and wife Maria.

Elisabet, of James Schammel and wife Elisabet, b. 26 Jun 1774, bapt. 14 Jul 1774. Sponsor: widow Elisabet Graaf(in).

Maria Catharina, of Johannes Haelsch and wife Catharina, b. 5 Jun 1774, bapt. 17 Jul 1774. Sponsors: Balthasar Straus? and wife Maria.

Maria, of Peter Grof and wife Cath., b. 10 May 1774, bapt. 17 Jul 1774. Sponsors: the father and widow Gräss(in).

Daniel, of Samuel Lephingston [Livingston] and wife Eva, b. 4 May 1774, bapt. 17 Jul 1774. Sponsors: Abraham Grenadier and Christine? Gräss(in).

Johannes, of Joh. Herman and wife Catharina, b. 1 Jul 1774, bapt. 21 Jul 1774. Sponsors: the parents.

Maria Elisabeth, of Mr. John Steinmetz and wife Catharina, b. 17 Jul 1774, bapt. 27 Jul 1774. Sponsors: Heinrich Keppele and widow Elisab. Steinmetz(in).

Joh. Georg, of Joh. Jost Schweighard and wife Hanna, at [Penns] Neck, b. 14 Oct 1773, bapt. 13 Jul 1774. Sponsors: the parents.

Salome, of Gerard Holtzcamp and wife Catharina Elisabeth, b. 1 Feb 1774, bapt. 12 Jul 1774. Sponsors: Joh. Kohl? and wife Maria Esther

Jonathan Wilhelm, of Andreas Beck and wife Margretha, b. 15 Jun 1773, bapt. 10 Jul 1774. Sponsors: the mother, and Joh. Beck and wife Barbara.

Sarah, of Matthias Landenberger and wife Maria, b. 4 Jun 1774, bapt. 24 Jul 1774. Sponsors: Thomas Meier and wife Margareta.

Johann Philip, of Johann Jacob Pop and wife Elisabetha, b. 27 Nov 1772, bapt. 22 Jul 1774. Sponsors: the parents.

Rebecca, of Peter Habkison and wife Maria, b. 31 May 1774, bapt. 21 Jul 1774. Sponsors: the parents, and Margareta Kunz(in) and Dan. Lehmann.

Maria Rosina, of widow Esther Epstein (illegitimate), b. 31 May 1774, bapt. 26 Jul 1774. Sponsors: Barbara Berend and Maria Rosina Meyer.

Anna Elisabeth, of Thomas Betton and Maria Margar. Libert(in) (an unmarried bondservant), b. 9 Jul 1774, bapt. 30 Jul 1774. Sponsors: Johannes Scheib? and wife Anna Elisabetha.

David, of Georg Eberhard and wife Barbara, b. 19 Jul 1774, bapt. 29 Jul 1774. Sponsors: the parents.

Catharine Elisabet, of Joseph Rivers (English) and wife Cath. Elis. , b. 26 Jul 1774, bapt. 29 Jul 1774. Sponsors: Jacob Kriegemeier and Cath. Magd. Kehl(in).

Ludwig, of Ferdinand Marmuton and wife Maria Catharina, b. 12 May 1774, bapt. 31 Jul 1774. Sponsors: Joh. Ludwig Stark and wife Maria Margareta.

Sophia, of Wilhelm Trat(h)wein and wife Maria, b. 16 Apr 1774, bapt. 1 Aug 1774. Sponsors: the mother and Rosina Walter(in).

Maria Magdalena, of Nicolaus Braun and wife Anna Maria, b. 16 Jun 1774, bapt. 1 Aug 1774. Sponsors: the mother and John Wagner's wife Catharina.

Maria, of Adam Hoffman and wife Barbara, b. 22 May 1774, bapt. 6 Aug 1774. Sponsors: Henrich Kur[t]z and wife Rosina.

Dorothea Margareta, of Wilhelm Will and wife Elisabeth, b. 3 May 1774, bapt. 6 Aug 1774. Sponsors: Jacob Dieter and wife Dorothea.

Elisabeth, of Jacob Penter and wife Mary (English people), b. 14 May 1773, bapt. 6 Aug 1774. Sponsors: Wilh. Will and wife Elisabeth.

Jacob, of Carl Müller and wife Marg., b. 23 Jul 1774, bapt. 7 Aug 1774. Sponsors: Jacob Gönter and wife Catharina.

Elisabet, of John Oar and wife Sarah, b. 29 Jul 1773, bapt. 7 Aug 1774.
Sponsors: the mother and Joh. Tauber.
Regina Dorothea, of Johannes Grabel, b. 22 Jul 1774, bapt. 7 Aug 1774.
Sponsor: the grandmother Regina Dorothea Grabel(in).
Bernhard, of William Aschton and wife, b. 10 Jul 1774, bapt. 8 Aug 1774.
Sponsors: Zacharias Enders and wife Anna Maria.
Joh. Thomas, of Joh. Lamparder and wife Sarah, b. 6 Aug 1774, bapt. 10 Aug
1774. Sponsors: Joh. Thom. Bishart and Barb. Menzer(in).
James, of John MacClaine and wife, b. 12 Aug 1774, bapt. 12 Aug 1774.
Sponsors: the parents.
Joh., of Joh. Kreisel and wife Cath., b. 1 May 1774, bapt. 12 Aug 1774.
Sponsors: the parents.
Catharina, of Georg Knerr and wife Catharina, b. 29 Jul 1774, bapt. 14 Aug
1774. Sponsors: Urban Fribeli and wife Barbara.
Maria Elis., of Wilh. Woelmer (deceased) and wife Catharina, b. 29 Jul 1774,
bapt. 14 Aug 1774. Sponsors: the mother, and Joh. Conrad Stecher and wife
Maria Felicia.
Peter, of Joh. Feltenberger and wife Susanna, b. 8 Aug 1774, bapt. 14 Aug 1774.
Sponsors: Peter Craemer and wife Susanna.
Maria Salome, of Jacob Seyfried and wife, b. 17 Jul 1774, bapt. 14 Aug 1774.
Sponsors: Johann Jacob Seyfried and wife Christina.
Catharina, of Philip Heit and wife Elisabeth, b. in Jul 1774, bapt. 14 Aug 1774.
Sponsors: Martin Knoblauch and wife Maria Agnes.
Maria, of Wilhelm Schaef and wife Barbara, b. 23 Jul 1774, bapt. 14 Aug 1774.
Sponsors: Georg David Seckel and wife Maria.
Philip, of Johannes Kress and wife Anne Elis., b. 28 Jul 1774, bapt. 14 Aug
1774. Sponsors: Philip Naas and wife Anne Elisabeth.
Maria Catharina, of Christoph Kucher and wife Anna Maria, b. 23 Jul 1774,
bapt. 15 Aug 1774. Sponsors: David Schaefer and wife Maria Catharina.
Samuel, of Samuel Kile and wife, b. 11 Mar 1774, bapt. 15 Aug 1774. Sponsor:
Jane Fife.
Abel, of Abel Jones and wife Rosina, b. 8 Apr 1774, bapt. 15 Aug 1774 at
Pikestown at the laying of the corner stone. Sponsors: the parents, and
grandmother Rosina Barbara Koppenhaver?.
Johann Henrich, of Johann Gottlieb Eberle and wife Louisa, b. 19 Nov 1773,
bapt. 15 Aug 1774. Sponsor: Heinrich Heilmann, single.
Elisabeth, of Michael Heilmann and wife Susanna, b. 23 May 1774, bapt.
15 Aug 1774. Sponsors: the grandparents Adam Heilmann and wife Elisab.,
and Elisab. Küfer(in).
Johannes, of Johann Wilhelm Coop and wife Catharina, b. 30 Jan 1769, bapt.
17 Aug 1774. Sponsor: Jacob Walter (Waller?).
Margareta, of Johann Wilhelm Coop and wife Catharina, b. 28 Apr 1770, bapt.
17 Aug 1774. Sponsor: same as above.
Carl Philip, of Johann Wilhelm Coop and wife Catherina, b. 26 May 1773, bapt.
17 Aug 1774. Sponsor: same as above.
Johannes, of Joh. Jacob Wisser and wife Susanna, b. 18 Jun 1774, bapt. 20 Aug
1774. Sponsors: Joh. Wilhelm Kiet and wife Maria Marg.

Maria Sophia, of Simon Eberle and wife Maria Sophia, who live 11 miles from Lancaster, b. 12 May 1774, bapt. 21 Aug 1774. Sponsors: Mr. Georg Seitz and wife Mar. Elisabet.

Andreas, of Henrich Schlessman and wife Catharina, b. 3 Aug 1774, bapt. 23 Aug 1774. Sponsors: the parents.

Catharina, of Abraham Cloding and wife Juliana, b. 17 Aug 1774, bapt. 23 Aug 1774. Sponsors: the parents.

Maria, of Andreas Kirck and wife Maria Elisabeth, b. 21 Aug 1774, bapt. 25 Aug 1774. Sponsors: Georg _rnes and wife Maria.

Sophia, of Benjamin Commat (English) and wife Charlotte, b. 6 Aug 1774, bapt. 24 Aug 1774. Sponsors: Gottfried Menat and Frederica Sophia Horing(in).

Salome, of John How? and wife Eva Barbara, b. 18 Aug 1774, bapt. 28 Aug 1774. Sponsors: Alexander Greenwood and wife Salome.

Maria Esther, of Petrus Muhlenberg, preacher in Dunmore County, Virginia, and wife Hanna, b. 22 Aug 1774, bapt. 28 Aug 1774. Sponsors: Heinrich Muhlenberg, (pastor of Zions and Michaels in Philadelphia) and wife Anna Maria, and P. Matthias Moller.

Johannes Balthasar, of Johannes Emmerich and wife Maria , b. 14 Aug 1774, bapt. 28 Aug 1774. Sponsors: Johannes Balthasar Emmerich and Magdalena Steinme[t]z(in).

Georg, of Anton Billig and wife Catharina, b. 6 Aug 1774, bapt. 27 Aug 1774. Sponsors: Georg Christein and wife Jemina.

Maria, of Christian Schaefer and wife Dorothea, b. 5 Aug 1774, bapt. 28 Aug 1774. Sponsors: brother-in-law Andreas Wa[l]ker and paternal grandmother Maria Schaefer(in).

Susanna Catharina, of Carl Seng and Magdalena Graef(in), b. 31 Aug 1774, bapt. 31 Aug 1774. Sponsors: Mr. Friedr. Schinkel's wife Susanna, and Jac. Graef's wife Catharina.

Catharina, of Johann Ehrhardt Eisenbry and wife Catharina, b. 27 Aug 1774, bapt. 31 Aug 1774. Sponsors: the parents.

Elisabeth, of Johannes Griess and wife Barbara, b. 18 Aug 1774, bapt. 3 Sep 1774. Sponsors: Jacob Weissman and wife Elisabet.

Anna Maria, of Conrad Lindner and wife Elisabeth, b. 21 Aug 1774, bapt. 2 Sep 1774. Sponsors: Zacharias Enders and wife Maria.

Wilhelm, of Henrich Jung and wife Susanna, b. 9, Aug 774, bapt. 4 Sep 1774. Sponsors: Adam Gerich, widower, and Cath. Weil(in).

Elisabet, of Michael Steinhauer and wife Barbara, b. 18 Aug 1774, bapt. 4 Sep 1774. Sponsors: the parents.

Johannes, of Adam Wagner and wife Catharina, b. 20 Aug 1774, bapt. 4 Sep 1774. Sponsors: Johannes Wuckerer and Catharina Rish(in).

Maria Elis., of Joh. Dietr. Fischer and wife Maria, b. 22 Aug 1774, bapt. 11 Sep 1774. Sponsors: Marie Elis. Kab(in) and Joh. Friedr. Vogel, both single.

Anna Dorothea, of Peter Wildberger and wife Anna Catharina, b. 30 Aug 1774, bapt. 10 Sep 1774. Sponsors: Georg Walker and wife Anna Dorothea.

Johannes, of Wenzel Becker and wife Anna Maria, b. 7 Sep 1774, bapt. 10 Sep 1774. Sponsors: th eparents.

Johanna Catharina, of Johann Ludw. Weber and wife Elisabeth, b. 1 Sep 1774, bapt. 11 Sep 1774. Sponsors: Johannes Klees and wife Johanna Catharina.

Maria, of Georg Schneider and wife Maria, b. 20 Aug 1774, bapt. 11 Sep 1774. Sponsors: the father and [whose?] sister Maria Schneider(in).

Jacob, of Georg Dorn and wife Christina, b. 25 Aug 1774, bapt. 11 Sep 1774. Sponsors: Jacob Steinme[t]z and wife Dorothea.

Johannes, of Peter Fiestenthal and wife Marg., b. 3 Sep 1774, bapt. 17 Sep 1774. Sponsors: the parents.

Georg, of Jacob Kath (deceased) and wife Maria, b. 20 Nov 1772, bapt. 16 Sep 1774. Sponsors: Georg Butler and Magdalene Danniger(in).

Johannes, of William Love and wife Elisabet, b. 7 Jun 1774, bapt. 17 Sep 1774. Sponsors: Anton Gilbert and Magdalene Gilbert(in).

Philip, of Philip Sorg and wife Susanna Magd., b. 14 Sep 1774, bapt. 17 Sep 1774. Sponsors: the father and Anna Marg. Mildeberger(in).

Jacob, of Georg Hummel and wife Elisabeth, b. 8 Aug 1774, bapt. 17 Sep 1774. Sponsors: Jacob Gantus and Elisabet Baitemann(in), single.

Johann Adam, of Daniel Heumann and wife Catharina, b. 10 Sep 1774, bapt. 17 Sep 1774. Sponsors: Johann Adam Heimbach and wife Hanna.

Henrich, of Anton Gilbert and wife Sophia, b. 25 Jul 1760, bapt. 17 Sep 1774. (Sponsors not given.)

Anna Maria, of Adam Schiffer and wife Dorothea, b. 9 Sep 1774, bapt. 18 Sep 1774. Sponsors: Daniel Sommer and wife Maria.

Georg, of Joh. Henr. Appel and wife Anna Magd., b. 7 Sep 1774, bapt. 18 Sep 1774. Sponsors: Joh. Georg Vogel and Anna Magdel. Bastian(in), both single.

Margar. Barbara, of Andreas Uhler and wife Regina, b. 5 Aug 1774, bapt. 15 Sep 1774. Sponsors: Johannes Weisman and wife Marg. Barbara.

Margareta Elisabeth, of Simon Reuss and wife Barbara, b. 11 Jul 1773, bapt. 18 Sep 1774. Sponsor: Elisabeth Greon.

Wilhelm, of Wilhelm Hains and wife Catharine, b. 11 Aug 1774, bapt. 25 Sep 1774. Sponsors: Friedr. Hains and wife Elisabet.

Catharine Elisabet, of Jacob Antoni and wife Jacobea, b. 10 Sep 1774, bapt. 10 Sep 1774. Sponsors: the parents.

Peter, of Jacob Reif and wife Dorothea, b. 10 Sep 1774, bapt. 25 Sep 1774. Sponsors: Peter Eisenbrey and wife Dorothea.

Christian, of Henrich Bits and wife Barbara, b. 7 Sep 1774, bapt. 4 Oct 1774. Sponsors: Conrad Bits and Christine Neiswander(in), her sister.

Elisabet, of Bernhard Buck and wife Maria, b. 2 Sep 1774, bapt. 25 Sep 1774. Sponsors: Michael Katz and Elisabeth Franks.

Maria Elisab., of Martin Sommer and wife Marg., b. 14 Sep 1774, bapt. 25 Sep 1774. Sponsors: Joh. Sommer and Maria Bertsch(in).

Marg. Magdalena, of Joh. Jacob Kot(h) and wife Catharina, who live 14 miles from Lancaster, b. 15 May 1773, bapt. 25 Sep 1774. Sponsors: Ernst. Mänchen and wife Marg. Magd.

Caspar, of David Jennings and wife Anna Maria, b. 12 Sep 1774, bapt. 25 Sep 1774. Sponsors: Caspar Keithe and wife Charlotte.

Dorothea, of Joh. Georg. Dürr and wife Christine, b. 31 Aug 1774, bapt. 24 Sep 1774. Sponsors: Math. Staats and wife Dorothea.

Hannah, of Johannes Hinckle and wife Christina, b. 26 Aug 1774, bapt. 3 Oct 1774. Sponsors: the parents.

Jacob, of Johannes Fries and wife Anna, b. 30 Aug 1774, bapt. 4 Oct 1774.
Sponsors: Jacob Fries and wife Margaretha.
Sophia, of Georg Hüber? and wife Maria Salome, b. 21 Sep 1774, bapt. 4 Sep
1774. Sponsors: Adam Krebs and wife Anna Maria.
Elisabet, of Georg Schu[t]z and wife Catharina, b. 21 Jul 1774, bapt. 6 Oct 1774.
Sponsors: Philipp Clumberg and wife Christine.
Elisabeth, of Martin Waker and wife Barbara, b. 9 Sep 1774, bapt. 1 Oct 1774.
Sponsors: Joh. Wendelmor and Bastian Mehr's wife Ester.
Elisabeth, of Martin Cox and wife Catharina, b. 13 May 1772, bapt. 4 Oct 1774.
Sponsors: the parents.
Wilhelm, of Martin Cox and wife Catharina, b. 17 Apr 1774, bapt. 4 Oct 1774.
Sponsors: William Wieking and wife Marg.
Hanna, of Valentin Bauer and wife Hanna, b. 17 Aug 1774, bapt. 5 Oct 1774.
Sponsors: the parents.
Friedrich, of Friedr. Ulrich and wife Catharina, b. 13 Sep 1774, bapt. 9 Oct
1774. Sponsors: Nicolaus Ulrich and his mother Maria Madg.
Sara, of Peter Kraft and wife Margareta, b. 1 Oct 1774, bapt. 9 Oct 1774.
Sponsors: Georg Daum and wife Sara.
Jacob, of Johann Braun and wife Anna Catharina, b. 11 Aug 1774, bapt. 9 Oct
1774. Sponsors: Jacob Kiefer and wife.
Elisabet, of Friedr. Doppelbauer and wife Catharina, b. 28 Sep 1774, bapt. 9 Oct
1774. Sponsors: Johan Heiler and Elisabet Lohra(in).
Johannes, of Johannes Preis and wife Maria Magd., b. 3 Aug 1774, bapt. 9 Oct
1774. Sponsors: Johannes Kaiser and Anna Maur(in).
Dorothea (twin), of Adam Weisbart and wife Barbara, b. 30 Sep 1774, bapt.
9 Oct 1774. Sponsors: Dorothea Götz(in) and her dau. Elisabet Baker?
Anna Maria (twin), of Adam Weisbart and wife Barbara, b. 30 Sep 1774, bapt.
9 Oct 1774. Sponsors: same as above.
Anna Margareta, of Jacob Plocher and wife Elisabeth, b. 21 Sep 1774, bapt.
4 Oct 1774. Sponsors: Michael Bauer and wife Dorothea.
Catharina, of Christoph Muller and wife Elisabeth, b. 30 Sep 1774, bapt. 9 Oct
1774. Sponsors: Johannes Becker and wife Catharina.
Michael, of Michael Schleihoff and wife Anna Maria, b. 2 Sep 1774, bapt. 8 Oct
1774. Sponsors: Michael Herrman and wife Anna Maria.
Henrich, of Barbara Schleihoff and Henrich Boecle, illegitimate, b. 31 May
1774, bapt. 8 Oct 1774. Sponsors: Michael Schleihoff and wife Anna Maria.
Georg, of Johannes Waker and wife Catharina, b. 22 Sep 1774, bapt. 9 Oct
1774. Sponsor: Georg Hert.
Henrich, of Martin Sommer and wife Anna Barbara, b. 29 Apr 1774, bapt. 9 Oct
1774. Sponsors: Henrich Sommer and wife Cath.
Magdalena, of Michael Schumacher and wife Susanna, b. 21 Sep 1774, bapt.
9 Oct 1774. Sponsors: the parents.
Eva Maria, of Jacob Bets (Bris_?) and wife Barbara, b. 22 May 1774, bapt.
9 Oct 1774. Sponsors: Peter Klein and wife Eva Maria.
Elisabet, of Mathaeus Schmidt and wife Catharina, b. 29 Sep 1774, bapt. 12 Oct
1774. Sponsors: the parents.
Johannes, of Elias Frei and wife Maria, b. 25 Sep 1774, bapt. 16 Oct 1774.
Sponsors: Michael Roem and wife Elisabeth.

Johannes Matthius, of Michael Schog and wife Margaretha, b. 4 Sep 1774, bapt. 8 Oct 1774. Sponsors: Johannes Hauck and wife Catharina.

Michael, of Michael Kiesler and wife Elis., b. 1 Oct 1774, bapt. 8 Oct 1774. Sponsors: Michael Bastian and Maria Kinsler(in).

Anna Maria, of Philip May and wife Anna, b. 24 Oct 1772, bapt. 6 Oct 1774. Sponsors: the parents.

Anna Maria, of Johna Wilh. Negele and wife Sophia, b. 11 Oct 1774, bapt. 16 Oct 1774. Sponsors: Adam Krebs and wife Anna Maria.

Susanna, of Leonhard Kesler and wife Maria Susanna, b. 29 Sep 1774, bapt. 16 Oct 1774. Sponsor: Georg Ki[t]z and wife Apollonia.

Anna Barbara, of Patrick Quin and wife Anna Catharine, b. 18 Sep 1774, bapt. 16 Oct 1774. Sponsors: Jacob Burghard and wife Anna Barbara.

Catharina, of Andreas Bauer and wife Barbara, b. 22 Sep 1774, bapt. 16 Oct 1774. Sponsors: Michael Haehns and wife Catharina.

Anna Margaretha, of Christoph Schaefer and wife Anna, b. 16 Oct 1774, bapt. 18 Oct 1774. Sponsors: Johannes Kehl and wife Anna Marg.

Georg, of Johann Gottlieb Schweizer and wife Elisabetha, b. 22 Oct 1774, bapt. 23 Oct 1774. Sponsors: Georg Zimmermann and wife Catharina.

Johannes, of Johannes Mast and wife Anna Eva, b. 23 Sep 1774, bapt. 23 Oct 1774. Sponsors: Johannes Schuster and Catharina Dresler(in).

Maria Christina, of Johann Meier and wife Maria Catharina, b. 6 Oct 1774, bapt. 23 Oct 1774. Sponsors: Johann Michael Roem and wife Elisabeth.

Jacob, of Eberhardt Leatenberger and wife Elisabetha Dorothea, b. 9 Oct 1774, bapt. 23 Oct 1774. Sponsors: Jacob Sohn and Juliana Kaemmerli(n).

Martin, of Christian Lu[t]z and wife Susanna, b. 23 Sep 1774, bapt. 23 Oct 1774. Sponsors: Martin Lu[t]z and wife Catharina.

Catharina, of Casper Haas and wife Anna Cathar., b. 10 Oct 1774, bapt. 23 Oct 1774. Sponsors: the parents.

Anna Maria, of Lud. Braun and wife Maria Sarah, b. 16 Sep 1774, bapt. 23 Oct 1774. Sponsors: Matthias Miller and (name obscured).

Elisabet, of Christoph Jung and wife Margaretha, b. 4 Oct 1774, bapt. 30 Oct 1774. Sponsors: Christian Jung and wife Catharina.

Johan, of Johan David Knies (Nees) and wife Anna Clara Doroth., b. 13 Oct 1774, bapt. 30 Oct 1774. Sponsors: Joh. Michael Strecker and wife Maria Marg., and Marg. Seidel(in).

Adam, of Adam Münster and wife Rosina, b. 14 Oct 1774, bapt. 30 Oct 1774. Sponsors: Johann Egy and Barb. Klein(in).

Elisabeth, of Rudolph Lehr and wife Catharina, b. 30 Oct 1774, bapt. 30 Oct 1774. Sponsors: Phil. Klein and wife Elisabeth.

Elisabet, of Georg Hirkisheimer and wife Rosina, b. 5 Oct 1774, bapt. 30 Oct 1774. Sponsors: Michael Keppler and Barbara Münzer(in).

Anna Maria, of Johann Wolf. Gemeinbauer and wife Anna Catharina, b. 9 Oct 1774, bapt. 30 Oct 1774. Sponsors: the parents and Anna Maria Schiffer(in)?.

Elisabet, of Christ. Fuchs and wife Dorothea, b. 20 Oct 1774, bapt. 30 Oct 1774. Sponsors: the parents.

Maria, of Andreas Geier and wife Barbara, b. 11 Oct 1774, bapt. 30 Oct 1774. Sponsors: Andreas Bossard and Barb. Ramminger(in)?.

Elisabeth, of Georg Schu[t]z and wife Catharina, b. 21 Jul 1774, bapt. 24 Oct 1774. Sponsors: Philip Clamberg and wife Christina.

Elisabeth, of Martin Walter and wife Barbara, b. 9 Sep 1774, bapt. 1 Nov 1774. Sponsor: Johann Wendelmor and wife Barb.

Wilhelm, of Andreas Boettinger and wife Catharina, b. 12? Oct 1774, bapt. 6 Nov 1774. Sponsors: Wilhelm Die[t]z and wife Cath.

Mathaeus, of Adam Heimbach and wife Hanna, b. 8 Oct 1774, bapt. 6 Nov 1774. Sponsors: Mathaeus Sommer and wife Regina.

Michael, of Georg Martin and wife Maria, b. 22 Oct 1774, bapt. 6 Nov 1774. Sponsors: Michael Roemer and wife.

Carl Bernhard, of Christian Stützer and wife Christine, b. 24 Jul 1774, bapt. 6 Nov 1774. Sponsors: Carl Bernhard Hofman and wife Sus. Regina.

Johann Fridrich, of Johannes Gahn and wife Margaret, b. 6 Nov 1774, bapt. 7 Nov 1774. Sponsors: Wilh. Heins and wife Cathar.

Philip, of Johan Kling and wife Anna Marg., b. 7 Oct 1774, bapt. 13 Nov 1774. Sponsors: Philip Hall and wife Susanna.

Peter, of Peter Mährling and wife Maria Dorothea, b. 21 Oct 1774, bapt. 13 Nov 1774. Sponsors: the parents.

Maria Margaretha, of Christoph Henrich and wife Anna Maria, b. 6 Nov 1774, bapt. 13 Nov 1774. Sponsors: Peter Both and wife Anna Maria.

Philip, of Philip Dietz and wife Catharina, b. 20 Oct 1774, bapt. 13 Nov 1774. Sponsors: the parents.

Johan Gerhard, of Christian Obersteg and wife Margaretha, b. 31 Oct 1774, bapt. 15 Nov 1774. Sponsors: Johan Fohr and wife Maria Cath.

Anna Catharina, of Johannes Simion and wife Catharina, b. 3 Oct 1774, bapt. 20 Nov 1774. Sponsors: Georg Birckenbeil and Anna Margar. Bruger(in)?.

Jacob, of Peter Kur[t]z and wife Sara, b. 3 Nov 1774, bapt. 21 Nov 1774. Sponsors: Jacob (illegible) and wife.

Johann Georg, of Jacob Boettinger and wife Anna Maria, b. 27 Oct 1774, bapt. 20 Nov 1774. Sponsors: Georg Stackel and wife Christina.

Anna Maria, of Jacob Reusser and wife Christina, b. 15 Nov 1774, bapt. 20 Nov 1774. Sponsors: Martin Reusser and wife Anna Catharina.

Johannes, of Theodorus Memminger and wife Maria, b. 23 Oct 1774, bapt. 21 Nov 1774. Sponsor: the father.

Joseph, of Wilhelm Kerrel and wife Elisabeth, b. 8 Sep 1774, bapt. 23 Nov 1774. Sponsors: the mother and Catharine Philip.

Johann Andreas, of Johan Georg Lohrmann and wife Anna Justinia, b. 27 Oct 1774, bapt. 25 Nov 1774. Sponsors: the parents.

Barbara, of Jacob Aesch and wife Rosina, b. 6 Nov 1774, bapt. 27 Nov 1774. Sponsors: Michael Ka[t]z and Rosina Veih(in)?.

Jacob Henrich, of Nicolaus Reb and wife Christina, b. 1 Nov 1774, bapt. 27 Nov 1774. Sponsors: Jacob Henrich and wife Catherine.

Jacob, of Jacob Motz and wife Maria Barbara, b. 17 Nov 1774, bapt. 27 Nov 1774. Sponsors: Jacob Pennihof and wife Sarah.

Sophia Dorothea, of Josua Mezger and wife Sophia, bapt. 27 Nov 1774. Sponsor: Dorothea Jaegerdorf(in).

Mary, of William Karft and wife Elisabeth, b. 28 Dec 1773, bapt. 30 Nov 1774. Sponsors: the parents.

Esther, of Joh. Kohl and wife Esther, b. 21 Sep 1774, bapt. 2 Dec 1774.
Sponsors: Garett Holzcomb and wife Elisabet.
Peter, of John Miles and wife Elisabeth, b. 12 Nov 1774, bapt. 4 Dec 1774.
Sponsors: Peter Mahn and wife Anna Maria.
Joh. Georg, of Joh. Georg Honold and wife Regina, b. 12 Oct 1774, bapt. 4 Dec
1774. Sponsors: Michael Stauch and wife Margaret.
Anna Maria, of Michael Herman and wife Anna Maria, b. 30 Aug 1774, bapt.
4 Dec 1774. Sponsors: Baltus Schneider and wife Margar.
Maria Magdalena, of Karl Friedrich Voelker and Susanna Spun(in), illegitimate,
b. 25 Nov 1774, bapt. 10 Dec 1774. Sponsors: Michael Bastian and wife M.
Magdalena.
Johannes, of Joh. Michael Preusch and wife Maria, b. 23 Nov 1774, bapt.
11 Dec 1774. Sponsors: Joh. Preusch and Maria Cath. Lambader(in).
Andreas, of Joh. Weidenmeyer and wife Maria, b. 13 Oct 1774, bapt. 11 Dec
1774. Sponsors: Andreas Förster and wife Anna Sybila.
Elisabet, of Maria Bock(in) and Georg Benderi, illegitimate, b. 31 Aug 1774,
bapt. 12 Dec 1774. Sponsors: Jacob Brant and wife Elisabet.
Henrich, of Henrich Polenz and wife Anna Sybila, b. 15 Dec 1774, bapt. 15 Dec
1774. Sponsors: the parents.
Daniel, of Martin Roh and wife, b. 11 Dec 1774, bapt. 11 Dec 1774. Sponsors:
the father, and grandmother Elisabeth Ehr__.
Sophia Magd., of Peter Grimm and wife Doroth. Soph., b. 27 Nov 1774, bapt.
18 Dec 1774. Sponsors: Sigemund Copia and wife Sophia Magd.
Margareta, of Anton Hecht and wife Sophia, b. 13 Dec 1774, bapt. 18 Dec 1774.
Sponsors: Christian Galler and wife.
Anna Catharina, of Goerg Kur[t]z and wife Margareta, b. 30 Nov 1774, bapt.
18 Dec 1774. Sponsors: Johann Biegler and wife Anna Cath..
Christine, of Caspar Würschum and wife Rosina, b. 26 Nov 1774, bapt. 18 Dec
1774. Sponsors: Carl Wolpert and Christine Rosch(in).
Jacob, of Christian Haag and wife Anna, b. 23 Nov 1774, bapt. 18 Dec 1774.
Sponsors: Jacob Andr. Sützel and wife Barbara.
Elisabeth, of Christlieb Baehrdling and wife Elisabet, b. 19 Oct 1774, bapt.
18 Dec 1774. Sponsors: the parents.
Johann Christoph, of Samuel Rondiger and wife Dorothea, b. 13 Dec 1774, bapt.
25 Dec 1774. Sponsors: Christoph Henkel and wife Eva.
Maria Eva, of Joh. Friedr. Kehn and wife Catherine, b. 2 Dec 1774, bapt. 20 Dec
1774. Sponsors: Joh. Martin Schuster and wife Maria Elis.
Georg, of Johann Georg Bechtel and wife Susanna, b. 30 Nov 1774, bapt.
25 Dec 1774. Sponsors: Johan Georg Ki[t]z and wife Apollonia.
Georg, of Robert Samuel and wife Deborah, b. 28 Jan 1771, bapt. 26 Dec 1774.
Sponsors: Johann Robertson and Elisabeth Hunt.
Elisabeth, of Robert Samuel and wife Deborah, b. 1 Sep 1774, bapt. 26 Dec
1774. Sponsors: John Schaefer and Elisabeth Vegler?.
Maria Magdal., of Georg Hafner and wife Magdalena, b. 30 Nov 1774, bapt.
26 Dec 1774. Sponsors: Jacob Schwebel and wife Maria Magdalena.
Henrich, of Henrich Meyer and wife Anna Ursula, b. 9 Dec 1774, bapt. 26 Dec
1774. Sponsors: the parents.

John, of Owen Clansy and wife Elisabet, b. 30 Sep 1774, bapt. 25 Dec 1774. Sponsors: John Handering and Mary McCanny.

Georg Jacob, of Georg Jacob Hausmann and wife Mar. Apollonia, b. 24 Nov 1774, bapt. 26 Dec 1774. Sponsor: schoolmaster Jacob Franck.

Georg, of Georg Gebhard and wife Rosina, b. 11 Dec 1774, bapt. 26 Dec 1774. Sponsors: the parents.

Robert, an adopted child, of Robert Brit and wife Sara, b. 12 Jan 1773, bapt. 24 Dec 1774. Sponsors: John Wilkes and Elisabeth Rosseler.

Michael, of Andreas Lapp and wife, (birth date not given) bapt. 28 Dec 1774. Sponsors: the mother and Michael Lapp.

Maria Catharina, of Johann Christoph Kunz (a preacher) and wife Margareta Henrietta, b. 22 Dec 1774, bapt. 28 Dec 1774. Sponsors: Rev. Henr. Muhlenberg, Jr., pastor here, and wife Maria Catharina.

Salome, of Peter Jung and wife Magdalena, b. 15 Dec 1774, bapt. 31 Dec 1774. Sponsors: Conrad Scheller and wife Elisabet.

1775
(baptisms by pastors Kunze and G.H.E. Muhlenberg, Jr.;
in chronological seauence, from Book III)

Andreas, of Andreas Tag and Christina, b. 14 Dec 1774, bapt. 1 Jan 1775. Sponsors: Georg Klein and wife Elisabet.

Johann Gottfried, of Cord Cordes and Margarete, b. 30 Dec 1774, bapt. 1 Jan 1775. Sponsors: Johann Gottfried Schesing? and Philippina. Kochendoerfer(in).

Johann Christian, of Philip Heger and Catharine, b. 21 Dec 1774, bapt. 1 Jan 1775. Sponsors: Johann Christian Klohr and wife Anna Catharina.

Johannes, of John Ronn and Barbara, b. 24 Dec 1774, bapt. 1 Jan 1775. Sponsors: Johannes Greifenstein and wife Dorothea.

Johann Georg, of Georg Cancer and Salome, b. 25 Dec 1774, bapt. 1 Jan 1775. Sponsors: Georg Zeissinger and Margareta Wolfgang(in).

Joh. David, of David Behler and Anna Maria, b. 6 Apr 1772, bapt. 1 Jan 1775. Sponsors: the parents.

William, of Andrew Filler and Margaret, b. 10 Dec 1774, bapt. 2 Jan 1775. Sponsors: Susanna Derry and William Hensly.

Johannes, of Joh. Adam Hoch and Barbara, b. 31 Mar 1774, bapt. 2 Jan 1775. Sponsors: the grandparents Joh. Hoch and wife Marg.

Margareta, of Georg Zinck and Johanna, b. 24 Nov 1774, bapt. 3 Jan 1775. Sponsors: the mother and Margareta Uber(in).

Susanna, of Franz Braunholtz and Barbara, b. 9 Dec 1774, bapt. 6 Jan 1775. Sponsors: the parents.

Maria Magd., of Stephan Rügener and Elisabet, b. 11 Dec 1774, bapt. 8 Jan 1775. Sponsors: Peter Dischan and wife Susanna.

Anna, of Valentin Hagner and M. Barbara, b. 20 Dec 1774, bapt. 8 Jan 1775. Sponsors: Peter Gabel and wife Elisabet.

Elisabet, of Martin Nole and Elisab., b. 5 Jan 1775, bapt. 8 Jan 1775. Sponsor: Elisabeth Hotz(in).

Joh. Wilhelm, of Philip Schindler and Marg., b. 5 Dec 1774, bapt. 8 Jan 1775. Sponsors: Joh. Wilh. Stutz and Ursula.

Johan (twin), of Johann Kihl and Anna Marg., b. 5 Jan 1775, bapt. 9 Jan 1775. Sponsors: John King and wife wife Magdalene.

Barbara (twin), of Johann Kihl and Anna Marg., b. 5 Jan 1775, bapt. 9 Jan 1775. Sponsors: Joh. Georg Sachs and Barbara.

John, of Isaac Kelly and Elisabet, b. in Jul 1774, bapt. 10 Jan 1775. Sponsors: the parents.

Catharina, of Abraham Bachmann and Philippina, b. 31 Dec 1774, bapt. 12 Jan 1775. Sponsors: Caspar Graef and wife Catharina.

Heinrich, of Caspar Schneider and Elisabeth, b. 29 Dec 1774, bapt. 15 Jan 1775. Sponsors: Heinr. Dul and Elis. Freuheim(in)?.

Wilhelm, of Christoph Adam and Catharina, b. 2 Nov 1774, bapt. 15 Jan 1775. Sponsors: the father, and Cath. Gasner(in)

Maria, of William Fairly and Elis., b. 9 Jan 1775, bapt. 15 Jan 1775. Sponsor: Elis. Ehrenfeucht.

Valentinus, of Benjamin Greenaway and Anna, b. 9 Nov 1774, bapt. 15 Jan 1775. Sponsors: Valentinus Bartholome and Margareta Paulson.

Christina Cathar., of Christian Kunckel and Catharina, b. 8 Jan 1775, bapt. 15 Jan 1775. Sponsors: Johannes and Christina Kunckel (the father's brother and sister).

Anna Marg., of Joh. Nicol. Hinckel and Anna Susanna, b. 11 May 1774, bapt. 20 Jan 1775. Sponsors: Christian Gally and wife Anna Marg.

Sarah, of Adam Schätzlein and Hanna, b. 18 Dec 1774, bapt. 22 Jan 1775. Sponsors: Johan Schneider and Sara Schätzlein.

Elisabet, of Jacob Hauser and Elisabet, b. 1 Jan 1775, bapt. 22 Jan 1775. Sponsors: the parents.

Christiana, of Will. Stoll and Christiana, b. 8 Jan 1775, bapt. 22 Jan 1775. Sponsors: the parents.

Samuel, of Samuel Moor and Elisabeth, b. 6 Jan 1775, bapt. 22 Jan 1775. Sponsors: George Green and Susanna Jetter(in).

Maria Magdal., of Wencesl. Türk and Anna Elisabeth, b. 10 Dec 1774, bapt. 22 Jan 1775. Sponsors: Johannes Sauder and wife Maria Magdal.

Johann Jacob, of Christoph Zimmermann and Catharina, b. 18 Jan 1775, bapt. 22 Jan 1775, Sponsors: Jacob Scheig and wife Anna Magdal.

Catharine, of Jacob Hauser and Maria, b. 17 Jan 1775, bapt. 22 Jan 1775. Sponsors: Ludwig Stotz and wife Catharina.

Martha, of Elisabet Matmakel? and James Cromlich, illegitimate, b. 9 Oct 1774, bapt. 2 Jan 1775. Sponsor: Catherine Wilcocks.

Joh. Ludwig, of Henrich Felten and Maria Dorothea, b. 6 Jan 1775, bapt. 28 Jan 1775. Sponsors: Johann Linn and wife Catharina.

Henrich, of Georg Hagenloch and Elisabet, b. 15 Jan 1775, bapt. 29 Jan 1775. Sponsors: Henrich Kur[t]z and wife Rosina.

Johannes, of Henrich Hains and Catharina, b. 6 Jan 1775, bapt. 29 Jan 1775. Sponsors: the parents.

Joh. Adam, of Johannes Ostertag and Eva Catharina, b. 21 Jan 1775, bapt. 29 Jan 1775. Sponsors: Adam Graef and wife.

Maria Martha, of Ehrhard Giebelhaus and Maria Barbara, b. 20 Jan 1775, bapt. 29 Jan 1775. Sponsors: the parents.

Anna Marg., of Adam Molidor and Anna Marg., b. 21 Dec 1774, bapt. 29 Jan 1775. Sponsors: Joh. Klein and wife Anna Cath.

William, of Margar. Meier(in), of Frankford, and Wilh. Bertsch, illegitimate, b. 16 Jan 1775, bapt. 3 Feb 1775. Sponsors: Bernhard Kaufmann and wife.

Dorothea, of Jacob Sulger and Margar., b. 30 Jan 1775, bapt. 5 Feb 1775. Sponsors: the father and widow Doroth. Schmidt.

Maria Marg., of Jacob Van Lahn and Johanna Maria, b. 29 Jan 1775, bapt. 5 Feb 1775. Sponsors: Friedr. Wolpert and wife Maria Marg.

Joh. Nicolaus, of Joh. Leon. Gettman and Anna Marg., b. 27 Jan 1775, bapt. 5 Feb 1775. Sponsors: Joh. Nicol. Walter and wife Rosina.

Maria Salome, of Joh. Christoph Philler and Sophia, b. 17 Jan 1775, bapt. 5 Feb 1775. Sponsors: Mich. Rehm and wife Maria Elis..

Sophia, of Friedr. Greiner and Elisabet, b. 29 Jan bapt. 8 Feb 1775. Sponsors: Joh. Fuchs and wife Sophia.

Maria, of Johannes Höflein and Catharina, b. 2 Feb 1775, bapt. 12 Feb 1775. Sponsors: the parents.

Cath. Salome, of Georg Bastian and Maria Eva, b. 3 Feb 1775, bapt. 11 Feb 1775. (Sponsors not given.)

Catharina, of Jacob Unbehend and Anna Maria, b. 18 Jan 1775, bapt. 12 Feb 1775. Sponsors: Catharina Unbehend(in) and Joh. Sander, both single.

Johan Georg, of Joh. Metz and wife Anna Barbara, b. 4 Feb 1775, bapt. 12 Feb 1775. Sponsors: Joh. Georg Hauser and wife Sophia.

Wilhelm, of Joh. Georg Sorg and Magdalene, b. 18 Oct 1774, bapt. 12 Feb 1775. Sponsors: Will. Losche and wife Maria Catharine.

Georg Michael, of Michael Kraft and Jwife oh. Maria, b. 3 Feb 1775, bapt. 12 Feb 1775. Sponsors: Jacob Weber and wife Elisabeth.

Maria, of Joh. Willis and Christina, b. 1 Jan 1775, bapt. 5 Feb 1775. Sponsors: Joh. Leckerum and wife Catharina.

Daniel, of Henrich Brosius and Catharine, b. 30 May 1774, bapt. 16 Feb 1775. Sponsor: the mother.

Catharine, of Henrich Depruin and Anna Margaretha, b. 11 Jan 1775, bapt. 19 Feb 1775. Sponsors: Peter Sommer and wife Catharine.

Maria, of William Seckel and Maria, b. 16 Jan 1775, bapt. 19 Feb 1775. Sponsors: the parents.

Elisabeth, of Joh. Weiss and Elisabeth, b. 20 Jan 1775, bapt. 20 Feb 1775. Sponsors: the parents.

John Leithaüs, of John Thomson and Elisabet, b. 21 Nov 1774, bapt. 23 Feb 1775. Sponsors: Mr. Metzner and wife Cath. Elisabet.

Johann Georg, of Jacob Riegel and Catharina, b. 5 Feb 1775, bapt. 24 Feb 1775. Sponsors: Georg Steever? and wife Anna Marg.

Johann Georg, of Adam Bausch and Anna Maria, b. 28 Feb 1775, bapt. 26 Feb 1775. Sponsor: Johan Georg Wendel?.

Johannes, of Philipp Heil and Jacobina, b. 7 Feb 1775, bapt. 26 Feb 1775. Sponsors: Johannes Heil and wife Maria.

Matheaus, of Mathaeus Schütz and Barbara, b. 16 Feb 1775, bapt. 26 Feb 1775. Sponsors: Nicol. Stat and Cath. Schütz(in).

Johannes Bachman, a youth from [New] Jersey, bapt. 3 Mar 1775.

Dorothea, of Georg Bauer and Margareta, b. 17 Feb 1775, bapt. 5 Mar 1775. Sponsors: Jacob Diess and wife Dorothea.

Joh. Jacob, of Sebastian Heiler and Elisabet, b. 6 Feb 1775, bapt. 5 Mar 1775. Sponsors: the parents.

Conrad, of Benja. Harrison and Marg., b. 21 Jan 1775, bapt. 5 Mar 1775. Sponsors: Conrad Müller and wife Catharine.

Wilhelm, of Carl Georg and Euphemia Sus.,b. 17 Aug 1774, bapt. 5 Mar 1775. Sponsor: Anna Maria Kohr(in).

Elisabet, of Friedr. Lauterbrun and Margaret, b. 21 Feb 1775, bapt. 7 Mar 1775. Sponsors: Jacob Schroder and wife.

Eva, of Matthias Witmar and Catharina Eva, b. 28 Feb 1775, bapt. 12 Mar 1775. Sponsors: Christian Lu[t]z and wife Susanna.

Anna Marg., of Wilh. Facundus and Dorothea, b. 20 Feb 1775, bapt. in Mar 1775. Sponsors: Michael Götz and wife Anna.

Elisabet, of Adam Grob and Elisabet, b. 9 Mar 1775, bapt. 12 Mar 1775. Sponsors: Adam Schmidt and wife Cath.

Elisabet, of Henrich Koch and Anna Maria, b. 19 Feb 1775, bapt. 12 Mar 1775. Sponsors: Wilhelm Weber and wife Elisabet.

Susanna, of Michael Gutermann and Susanna, b. 29 Feb 1775, bapt. 13 Mar 1775. Sponsors: Valentin Hofmann and wife Susanna.

Anna Cath., of Casp. Oberdorf and Anna Cath., b. 6 Oct 1774, bapt. 14 Mar 1775. Sponsors: Joh. Starke and Anna Cath. Pannekuch(in).

Margar., of Christoph Gräfly and Eva, b. 20 Mar 1774, bapt. 13 Mar 1775. Sponsors: the parents.

William, of William Rees and Elis., b. 1 Feb 1771, bapt. 14 Mar 1775. Sponsors: the parents.

Joseph, of William Rees and Elis., b. 18 Sep 1773, bapt. 14 Mar 1775. Sponsors: the parents.

Catharine, of Adam Zanzinger and Susanna, b. 25 Feb 1775, bapt. 19 Mar 1775. Sponsors: Mrs. Cathar. Keppele and Mr. Henry Keppele, Sr.

Hannah, of Joh. Michael Fuchs and Salome, b. 16 Feb 1775, bapt. 21 Mar 1775. Sponsors: Conrad Seibrandt and wife Hannah.

Maria, of Friedr. Werner and Maria, b. 7 Mar 1775, bapt. 22 Mar 1775. Sponsors: the parents.

Friedr. Wilhelm, of Henrich Wilh. Hafner and Elisabeth, b. 22 Jan 1775, bapt. 24 Mar 1775. Sponsors: Friedr. Wilh. Hafner and wife Catharina.

Anna, of Georg Krause and Anna Catharina, b. 2 Feb 1775, bapt. 13 Feb 1775. Sponsors: the parents.

Johann Friedr., of Michael Schubart and Elisabet, b. 5 Mar 1775, bapt. 26 Mar 1775. Sponsors: Friedr. Heiler and wife Christina.

Charlotte, of Georg Stra_ and Elisabeth, b. 10 Feb 1775, bapt. 26 Mar 1775. Sponsors: Christ. Kalkbrenner and wife Charlotta.

Anna Cath., of Mr. Carl Nushang and Anna Cath., b. 3 Mar 1775, bapt. 26 Mar 1775. Sponsors: Joh. Biegler and wife Anna Cath.

Maria, of Joh. Zensfelder and Jacobine, b. 24 Jan 1775, bapt. 26 Mar 1775. Sponsors: Peter Kraft and wife Maria.

Caspar, of Peter Dörry and Elisabet, b. 4 Mar 1775, bapt. 26 Mar 1775. Sponsors: Caspar Wahl and wife Elisabet.

Rebecca, of Georg Retzer and Marg., b. 7 Mar 1775, bapt. 26 Mar 1775. Sponsors: Georg Retzer and wife Sophia.

Margaret Catharine [adopted?], of Gottfried Derick and Catharine, soon to be 5 years old, bapt. 26 Mar 1775. Sponsors: Henrich Muhlenberg and wife Catharine.

Maria, of Georg Christoph Reinhold and Maria, b. 17 Feb 1775, bapt. 31 Mar 1775. Sponsors: the mother and Heinr. Weinkauf.

Child (name not given), of Joh. Adam Schwab and Anna Margaretha, b. 22 Mar 1775, bapt. 31 Mar 1775. Sponsors: Elisabet Lorenz, and Jacob Schwab and wife.

Elisabeth, of Jacob Nessler and Anna Margretha, b. 13 Mar 1775, bapt. 31 Mar 1775. Sponsors: Henrich Jonas and wife Elisabeth.

Johann Philip, of Jacob Eckfeld and Elisabeth, b. 22 Mar 1775, bapt. 2 Apr 1775. Sponsors: Philipp Zep and wife Maria Margareta.

Maria Magdalena, of Johann Escher and Anna, b. 19 Mar 1775, bapt. 2 Apr 1775. Sponsors: Peter Schreiber and wife Maria.

Joh. Caspar, of Johannes Stinchman and Anna Maria, b. 2 Mar 1775, bapt. 9 Apr 1775. Sponsors: Caspar Schüster and wife Regina.

Christine, of Peter Wellrich? and Elisabet, b. 9 Feb 1775, bapt. 9 Apr 1775. Sponsors: Christine Laub(in) and Phil. Hartman.

Catharine, of Andreas Sommer and Anna, b. 16 Feb 1775, bapt. 9 Apr 1775. Sponsors: the father, and Rosina Witner and Joh. Scheldian?.

Juliana Henrietta Kur[t]z(in), b. 13 Dec 1759, bapt. and confirmed 13 Apr 1775.

Elisabet Becker, b. 15 May 1757, bapt. and confirmed 13 Apr 1775.

Friedrich, of Peter Gräf and Elisabet, b. 4 Apr 1775, bapt. 16 Apr 1775. Sponsors: Joh. Friedr. Burstel and Maria Kuhn(in), both single.

Christian Fried. Ludewig, of Zach. Endres and Anna Maria, b. 12 Mar 1775, bapt. 17 Apr 1775. Sponsors: Christian Jauch and wife Maria.

Anna Doro., of Friedrich Springer and Mariane, b. 23 Mar 1775, bapt. 17 Apr 1775. Sponsors: John Georg Schaal and Elisabet Hofmann(in)

Michael, of Dietrich Bayerle and Sabina, b. 15 Nov 1774, bapt. 17 Apr 1775. Sponsors: Michael Abb and wife Anna Maria.

Jacob, of Jacob Rezer and Susanna, b. 4 Mar 1775, bapt. 17 Apr 1775. Sponsors: Georg Rezer and wife Sophia.

Jacob, of Johannes Derk (now deceased) and Elenora Strohbanck(in), b. 28 Mar 1767, bapt. 21 Apr 1775. Sponsor: Christina Cathar. Brentler(in).

Georg David, of Georg Jung and Rosina, b. 24 Feb 1775, bapt. 23 Apr 1775. Sponsors: Georg Walker and wife Dorothea.

Elisabeth, of Leonhard Weid and Eva Margareth, b. 24 Mar 1775, bapt. 23 Apr 1775. Sponsors: Michael Dressler and Elisabeth Weid(in).

Johann Georg, of Valentin Heid and Barbara, b. 18 Apr 1775, bapt. 27 Apr 1775. Sponsors: Georg Bastian and wife Maria Eva.

Johann Michael, of Jacob Kiefer and Elisabeth, b. 19 Apr 1775, bapt. 30 Apr 1775. Sponsors: Michael Staemler and wife Elisabeth.

Johann Georg, of Johann Michael Kraft and Dorothea, b. 19 Apr 1775, bapt. 30 Apr 1775. Sponsors: Conrad Hoff and wife Maria Sybila.

Michael, of Bernhard Seip? and Johanna, b. 14 Apr 1775, bapt. 30 Apr 1775. Sponsors: Michael Frick and wife Margareta.

Mar. Elisabeth, of Michael Pfeiffer and Regina, b. 24 Apr 1775, bapt. 3 May
1775. Sponsors: Nicolaus Eisenmenger and Hanna Pfeiffer.
Regina, of Simon Fairley and Catharina, b. 17 Jun 1769, bapt. 3 May 1775.
Sponsors: Michael Pfeiffer and wife Regina.
David, of Johann Philipps and Christina, b. 17 Apr 1775, bapt. 4 May 1775.
Sponsors: the parents.
Hanna, of Joh. Friedr. Müller and Sophia Dorothea, b. 1 Dec 1774, bapt. 7 May
1775. Sponsors: the mother, and Anna Barbara Adams.
Johannes, of Daniel Burghard and Catharina, b. 27 Mar 1775, bapt. 7 May 1775.
Sponsors: Johann Cappel and wife Elisabeth.
Anna Maria, of Jacob Freeborn and Dorothea, b. 29 Aug 1774, bapt. 7 May
1775. Sponsors: Henrich Lenz and wife Anna Maria.
Joh. Gottfried, of Franz Janthus and Elisabeth, b. 5 May 1775, bapt. 14 May
1775. Sponsors: Joh. Adam Teutschenbach and wife Anna Barbara.
Friedr., of Peter Munseas and Catharina, b. 5 May 1775, bapt. 14 May 1775.
Sponsor: Joh. Friedr. Albrecht.
Joh. Hartman, of Hartman Lauer and wife Elis., b. 8 Mar 1775, bapt. 14 May
1775. Sponsors: Joh. Heinr. Kayser and wife Anna Maria.
Johannes, of Johannes Wagner and Elisabeth, b. 2 Feb 1775, bapt. 7 May 1775.
Sponsors: the grandparents Johannes Stoss and wife Salome.
Anna Maria Catharina, of Heinrich Keppele, Jr., and Catharina, b. 19 Apr 1775,
bapt. 7 May 1775. Sponsors: Henrich Keppele and Anna Elisabeth
Gross(in).
Thomas Fitzgerland (son of Patrick Fitzgerland), b. 6 Mar 1755, bapt. and
confirmed 15 Apr 1775.
Catharina, of Peter Wagner and Rosina, b. 2 May 1775, bapt. 7 May 1775.
Sponsors: the parents, and Catharina Robaust(in).
Michael, of Matthias Fuchs and Elisabeth, b. 16 Apr 1775, bapt. 8 May 1775.
Sponsors: Michael Preiss and wife Anna Maria.
Christina Catharina, of Conrad Henzler and Eleonora, b. 2 May 1775, bapt.
8 May 1775. Sponsors: Johannes Kunkel and wife Christina.
Catharina Dorothea, of Jacob Müller and Margaretha, b. 7 May 1775, bapt.
14 May 1775. Sponsors: Peter Hartman and wife Dorothea.
Joh. Heinrich, of Johannes Schumacher and Agnes, b. 9 Mar 1775, bapt. 14 May
1775. Sponsors: Joh. Heinrich Diel and wife Anna Sophia.
Joh. Peter, of Andreas Heiderich and Elisabeth, b. 10 Sep 1774, bapt. 15 May
1775. Sponsors: Peter Becker and wife Maria Magdalena.
Daniel, of Joh. Georg Zeisinger and Anna Maria, b. 9 May 1775, bapt. 17 May
1775 Sponsors: the parents and Mrs. Dorothea Casch.
Joh. Adam, of Heinrich Fenzel and Maria Dorothea, b. 20 Mar 1775, bapt.
18 May 1775. Sponsors: Adam Widderstin and wife Sophia Charlotte.
Joh[anna] Maria, of Joh. Conr. Esser and Maria, b. 30 Apr 1775, bapt. 21 May
1775. Sponsors: Michael Kraft and wife Joh. Maria.
Joh. Gottlieb, of Nicol. Panzer and Elisabeth, b. 15 May 1775, bapt. 21 May
1775. Sponsors: the father, and grandmother Elisabet Bohne.
Jacob, of Joh. Geiser, b. 5 May 1775, bapt. 22 May 1775. Sponsors: the father,
and Anna Susanna Zimmermann(in).

Elisabeth, of Jacob Marker and Elisabeth, b. 21 Apr 1775, bapt. 20 May 1775. Sponsors: Johann Klingmann and wife Elisabeth.

Dorothea, of Johann Wilh. Sternkorb and Sybilla, b. 12 May 1775, bapt. 26 May 1775. Sponsors: the parents.

Philippina Rosina, of Philipp Weiss and Sybilla, b. 19 May 1775, bapt. 28 May 1775. Sponsors: the parents.

Elisabeth, of Peter Dietz and Margareta, b. 17 May 1775, bapt. 28 May 1775. Sponsors: Sebastian Seubert and wife Eva Barbara.

Anna Catharine, of Johann Leppi and Elisabeth, b. 16 May 1775, bapt. 28 May 1775. Sponsors: Jacob Kesler and wife Anna Catharina.

Maria Magdalena, of Peter Armbruster and Eleonora, b. 16 May 1775, bapt. 28 May 1775. Sponsors: Francisc. Wilh. Hetmansperger and wife Mar. Magdalena.

Susanna, of Theophilus Hawkin, and Hanna Giebel(in) illegitimate, b. 14 May 1775, bapt. 28 May 1775. Sponsors: Adam Rau and wife Susanna.

Juliana, of Wilhelm Steward and Juliana, b. 1 May 1775, bapt. 28 May 1775. Sponsors: Philipp Fischer and wife Anna Maria.

Maria Elisab., of Joh. Jacob Fe[t]zer and Magdalena, b. 11 May 1775, bapt. 28 May 1775. Sponsors: Johann Jac. Bayerle and Elisabeth Hess(in).

Christina, of Johann Gottlieb Steinbecher and Christina, b. 28 May 1775, bapt. 28 May 1775. Sponsors: Georg Fuggeroth and dau. Christina.

Wilhelm, of Joseph Likey and Catharina, b. 13 May 1775, bapt. 28 May 1775. Sponsors: Mattheus Schekhorn? and wife Cathar.

Elisabeth, of Joh. Felix and Catharina, b. 3 Apr 1775, bapt. 29 May 1775. Sponsors: Lorenz Wenz and wife Elisabeth.

Elisabeth, of Henrich Groh and Catharina, b. 21 May 1775, bapt. 4 Jun 1775. Sponsors: Sebastian Heiler and wife Catharina.

An. Catharina, of Michael Schoe_ich and An. Catharina, b. 22 May 1775, bapt. 4 Jun 1775. Sponsors: Adam Holt and wife Mar. Christina.

Marg., of Jacob Klauss and Marg., b. 6 May 1775, bapt. 4 Jun 1775. Sponsors: Daniel Schwanfelder and Margar. Dress(in).

Wilhelm, of Christian Persie and Maria, b. 8 Mar 1775, bapt. 4 Jun 1775. Sponsors: the parents.

Joh. Georg, of Jacob Bender and Barb, b. 27 Apr 1774, bapt. 4 Jun 1775. Sponsors: the parents.

Philip, of Phil. Springer and Eva, b. 21 Nov 1774, bapt. 4 Jun 1775. Sponsors: the parents.

Maria Cath., of Georg Gerling and Christina, b. 7 Feb 1775, bapt. 5 Jun 1775. Sponsors: Ludwig Gerling and Mar. Cathr. Chriss.

Georg, of Wilhelm Schmidt and Anna, b. 25 May 1775, bapt. 11 Jun 1775. Sponsors: Ludwig Farmer and wife Maria.

Joh. Nicol., of Joh. Christoph Senderling and Maria, b. 15 Apr 1775, bapt. 11 Jun 1775. Sponsors: Joh. Nicol. Senterling and Barbara Stutzman, both single.

Eva Maria, of Joh. Nicol. Herzbach and Regina, b. 30 May 1775, bapt. 11 Jun 1775. Sponsors: Joh. Georg Kiefer and wife Eva Marg.

Anna Cathar., of Peter Sommer and Catharina, b. 10 May 1775, bapt. 11 Jun 1775. Sponsors: Henr. Sommer and wife Anna Cathar.

Andreas, of Andr. Barrenstecher and Maria, b. 9 Jan 1775, bapt. 11 Jun 1775. Sponsor: the parents, and grandmother Barb. Haus(in).

Valentin, of Anna Maria Keppele, illegitimate, bapt. 12 Jun 1775.

Joh. Georg, of Andreas Mattern and Anna Maria, b. 15 Jun 1775, bapt. 18 Jun 1775. Sponsors: Joh. Georg Sturmfels and wife Anna Marg.

Elisabet, of Michael Rup and Anna Marg., b. 9 Jun 1775, bapt. 18 Jun 1775. Sponsors: Georg Bechtel and wife Elisabet.

Martha, of William Wyet and Elisabet, b. 25 Dec 1774, bapt. 18 Jun 1775. Sponsors: the parents.

Maria Marg., of Christian Fleisch and Rosina Dorothea, b. 10 Feb 1775, bapt. 10 Jun 1775. Sponsors: Friedr. Schroder and Maria Marg. Korn.

Thomas, of Thomas Dickinson and Marg., b. in Apr 1775, bapt. 14 Jun 1775. Sponsors: the parents.

Daniel, of Daniel Schab and Catherine, b. 8 Jun 1775, bapt. 22 Jun 1775. Sponsors: the parents.

Elisabeth, of Henrich Schreiber and Margareta, b. 31 May 1775, bapt. 25 Jun 1775. Sponsor: Sara Elisabeth Mahn(in).

Friedrich, of Christoph Wolpert and Margaretha, b. 30 Jan 1775, bapt. 25 Jun 1775. Sponsors: Friedr. Wolpert and Margar. Woelpert.

Susanna, of Jacob Shepherd and Maria, b. 13 Jun 1775, bapt. 25 Jun 1775. Sponsors: Joh. Bander and wife Margar. ___.

Wilhelm, of Conrad Baethis and Barbara, b. 15 Jun 1775, bapt. 26 Jun 1775. Sponsors: the parents.

Maria Cathar., of Rudolph Nagel and Susanna, b. 16 Jun 1775, bapt. 25 Jun 1775. Sponsors: the grandparents Henr. Schwalbach and wife Catharina.

Ludwig, of Ludwig Evans and Sybilla Rosina Schneider(in) illegitimate, b. 18 Jun 1775, Jun 25, 1775. Sponsors: Jacob Claus and wife (name not given).

Sarah, of Jacob Herman and Catharine, b. 8 Apr 1775, bapt. 3 Jul 1775. Sponsors: the parents.

Elisabeth, of Henrich Daser and Margar., b. 2 May 1775, bapt. 4 Jul 1775. Sponsors: David Eberhart and wife Elis.

Anna Doroth., of Christoph Heinckel and Eva, b. 21 Jun 1775, 8 Jul 1775. Sponsors: Joh. Georg Geiger and Anna Doroth. Steierwald.

Regina Marg., of Georg Reinhard and Maria Magd., b. 17 Jun 1775, bapt. 2 Jul 1775. Sponsors: Michael Gutman and wife Regina Marg.

Joh. Georg, of Joh. Omensetter and (name not given), b. 16 May 1775, bapt. 6 Jul 1775. Sponsors: Georg Laib and wife Dorothea.

Barbara, of Christian Spengler and Catharina, b. 27 Jun 1775, bapt. 6 Jul 1775. Sponsors: James Cuban and wife Anna Barbara.

Joseph, of Joseph Penrose and Maria Sabina Minck illegitimate, b. 8 Mar 1775, bapt. in Jul 1775. Sponsors: Christian Mink and wife Cath.

An. Cath., of Phil. Georg Knecht and Anna Maria, b. 15 Jun 1775, bapt. 9 Jul 1775. Sponsors: Bastian Redinger and his sister Anna Redinger.

Wilhelm, of Mr. Joh. Lorenz Worst and Catharine, b. 25 Jun 1775, bapt. 9 Jul 1775. Sponsors: Christian Pick and wife Christine.

Joh. Peter, of Joh. Mills (deceased) and Elisabeth, b. 1 Oct 1774, bapt. 9 Jul 1775. Sponsors: Peter Math. Aren and wife Maria Philippine.

Adam, of Adam Geyer and Maria, b. 2 Feb 1775, bapt. 11 Jul 1775. Sponsors: the parents.

Esther, of Joh. Adams (deceased) and Cath., b. 22 Jun 1775, bapt. 12 Jul 1775. Sponsors: the mother, and widow Kochendörfer.

Sabina Marg., of Adolph Dill and Catharina, b. 6 Jul 1775, bapt. 18 Jul 1775. Sponsors: Adam Seibert and Sab. Marg. Reitebach(in).

Jacob Benjam., of John Whitaker (English) and Maria, b. 14 Mar 1774, bapt. 15 Jul 1775. Sponsors: the parents.

John, of Philip Hirsch and Rebecca Scuffel, illegitimate, b. 8 Jun 1775, bapt. 17 Jul 1775. Sponsors: John Fan and Veronica Tortel.

Samuel, of Thomas Watson and Mary, b. 22 Jun 1775, bapt. 17 Jul 1775. Sponsors: the parents.

Joh. Jacob, of Peter Weber and Anna, b. 14 Jul 1775, bapt. 23 Jul 1775. Sponsors: John Eckfeld and wife Elisabeth.

Elisabeth, of Johann Gottfried Riedel and Magdalena, b. 14 Jul 1775, bapt. 23 Jul 1775. (Sponsors not given.)

Debora, of Georg Falmann? and Maria, b. 9 Sep 1774, bapt. 13 Jul 1775. Sponsor: Maria Trafinger(in).

Mar. Magdalena, of Georg Seifferheld and Christina Elisabeth, b. 19 Jul 1775, bapt. 30 Jul 1775. Sponsors: Henrich Emet and Mar. Magdalena Seifferheld(in).

Melchior, of Adam Dieter and Catharina, b. 5 Jul 1775, bapt. 30 Jul 1775. Sponsors: Melchior Schwerer and wife Rosina.

_____ Krebs (child's name, birthdate and bapt. date not given). Sponsor: (first name not given) Kunz.

Johannes, of Johann Adam Pontius and Elisabeth, b. 18 Jul 1775, bapt. 20 Jul 1775. Sponsors: Johann Weidmann and Charlotte Kalkbrenner(in).

Mar. Magdalena, of Martin Baisch and Mar. Magdalena, b. 13 Jul 1775, bapt. 30 Jul 1775. Sponsors: Georg Job and wife Doroth,

Georg, of Theobald Scheibele and Agnes, b. 24 Jul 1775, bapt. 30 Jul 1775. Sponsors: Georg Seitz and wife (name not given).

Anna Maria, of Jacob Schreiber and Cath., b. 23 Jul 1774, bapt. 24 Jul 1775. Sponsor: the mother.

Maria, of Christoph Weidner and Margareta, b. 8 Jul 1775, bapt. 27 Jul 1775. Sponsors: Michael Muller and Cath. Weber(in).

Mathias, of James Frazer and Juliana, b. 24 Jun 1775, bapt. 30 Jul 1775. Sponsor: Sus. Rose.

Maria Magdalena, of Salomon Seller and Catharine, b. 28 May 1775, bapt. 4 Aug 1775. Sponsors: Johan Jost Veit and wife Maria Magd.

Margareta, of Jacob Masholder and Margareta, b. 19 Jul 1775, bapt. 6 Aug 1775. Sponsors: Adam Pfisterer and wife Anna Margareta.

Joh. Gottfriedt, of Friedr. Lindemann and Sara Dorothea, b. 17 Jul 1775, bapt. 6 Aug 1775. Sponsors: Joh. Gottfr. Turck and wife Cathar.

Maria Barbara, of Zachar. Loesch and Maria Barbara, b. 27 Jul 1775, bapt. 6 Aug 1775. Sponsor: Barbara Keimle.

Wilh. Friedr., of Benedict Schneider and Philippina Elis., b. 8 Jul 1775, bapt. 6 Aug 1775. Sponsors: Wilh. Friedr. Walter and Joh[hanna] Maria Lochmann(in).

Ann, of Joseph Wildham and Jane, b. 1 Jan 1774, bapt. 7 Aug 1775. Sponsor: Susanna Rice.

Lorenz, of Thomas Yaust and Ursula, b. in Mar 1767, bapt. 8 Aug 1775. Sponsors: the mother, and Mar. Mühlenberg and Elis. Wehn(in).

David, of Thomas Yaust and Ursula, b. 13 Sep 1769, bapt. 8 Aug 1775. Sponsors: same as above.

Ursula, of Thomas Yaust and Ursula, b. 31 Mar 1775, bapt. 8 Aug 1775. Sponsors: same as above.

Johan Daniel, of Joh. Friedr. Dietz and Christina, b. 29 Jul 1775, bapt. 8 Aug 1775. Sponsors: Georg Fidler and wife Elis.

Christian Friedrich, of Friedrich Henzel and Anna Margareta, b. 1 Aug 1775, bapt. 13 Aug 1775. Sponsors: Christina Henzel, and the grandmother Maria Dorothea.

Barbara, of Andreas Beck and Barbara, b. 29 Jul 1775, bapt. 13 Aug 1775. Sponsors: Jacob Seger and wife Barbara.

Johannes, of Michael Bauer and Catharine, b. 2 Apr 1775, bapt. 13 Aug 1775. Sponsors: Georg Christein and wife Jemina.

Joh. Andreas, of Christoph Zink and Magdal., b. 15 Jun 1775, bapt. 13 Aug 1775. Sponsors: Christoph Weit and wife Mar. Magd.

Henrich, of Daniel Peter Neumann and Catharina (who died), b. 3 Aug 1775, bapt. 13 Aug 1775. Sponsors: Mr. Friedr. Kuhl and wife (name not given).

John, of Jacob Thomas and Mary, b. 13 Nov 1774, bapt. 13 Aug 1775. Sponsor: Thomas Morgan.

Catharina, of Heinrich Depperwin and Margareta, b. 11 Jul 1775, bapt. 13 Aug 1775. Sponsor: Christine Draess.

Johannes, of John Heil and Maria, b. 26 Jul 1775, bapt. 16 Aug 1775. Sponsors: Johannes Maret and wife Barbara.

Johannes, of John Cartwright and Catharine, b. 11 Aug 1775, bapt. 17 Aug 1775. Sponsors: Joh. Boyd and wife (name not given).

Catharina, of Friedr. Paul and Elisabeth, b. 11 Aug 1775, bapt. 17 Aug 1775. Sponsors: the parents and Friedrich Kehler.

Georg Friedrich, of Georg Conrad Haas and Maria Magdalena, b. 10 Aug 1775, bapt. 20 Aug 1775. Sponsors: Friedrich Kehl and wife Maria Magdalena.

Susanna, of Caspar Kindisch and Anna Margareta, b. 20 Jul 1775, bapt. 10 Aug 1775. Sponsors: Jacob Riger and wife Susanna.

Elisabeth, of Andreas Burghardt and Susanna, b. 6 Aug 1775, bapt. 20 Aug 1775. Sponsors: the parents.

Barbara, of Adam Metz and Barbara, b. 10 Aug 1775, bapt. 20 Aug 1775. Sponsors: Caspar Wahl and wife Elisabeth.

Wilhelm, of Jacob Negele and Anna, b. 21 Sep 1773, bapt. 22 Aug 1775. Sponsors: the parents.

Polly, of Henrich Berg and Hanna, 5 months old, bapt. 24 Aug 1775. Sponsors: Jacob Grace and wife Margar. The child soon died.

Anna Margareta, of Jacob Walker and Sophia, b. 17 Aug 1775, bapt. 25 Aug 1775. Sponsors: Georg Walker and wife Dorothea.

Maria, of Valentin Hofmann and Susanna, b. 7 Aug 1775, bapt. 25 Aug 1775. Sponsor: Maria Shippy.

Georg, of Jacob Kitz and Elisabet, b. 25 Aug 1775, bapt. 27 Aug 1775. Sponsors: Georg Kitz and wife Appol.

Joh. Georg, of Joh. Clear and Anna Cath., b. 22 Aug 1775, bapt. 27 Aug 1775. Sponsors: Joh. Georg Seitz and wife Elis.

Sophia, of Magdalena Kohl(in) and reportedly Christian Lauer (illegitimate), b. 28 Jul 1775, bapt. 27 Aug 1775. Sponsors: Anna Sophia Omensetter(in) and Georg Vogel.

Maria, of Wilhelm Nolt and Christine, b. 10 Aug 1775, bapt. 27 Aug 1775. Sponsors: Peter Dräss and wife Maria.

Anna Catharine, of Johanna Wesler(in), single, and reportedly Thomas Wilkins, illegitimate, b. 8 Jul 1775, bapt. 30 Aug 1775. Sponsors: Casp. Federer and wife Catharina.

Philip, of Jacob Lautenschlager and Catharina, b. 27 Aug 1775, bapt. 1 Sep 1775. Sponsors: the parents.

Johannes Gerhard, of Johannes Birkenbeiler and Anna Maria, b. 20 Aug 1775, bapt. 3 Sep 1775. Sponsors: Georg Stehler and wife Christina.

Christopher, of Johannes Moos and Catharina, b. 10 May 1775, bapt. 3 Sep 1775. Sponsors: Joh. Phil. Muller and wife Elisabeth.

Joh. Philipp, of Jacob Graef (the tailor) and Elisabeth, b. 27 Aug 1775, bapt. 5 Sep 1775. Sponsors: Philipp Dick and wife Catharina.

Theobold, of Benjamin Gasman and Maria, b. 31 Jul 1775, bapt. 3 Sep 1775. Sponsors: Theobold Stork and wife Rosina.

Thomas, of John Eastie and Sarah, b. 31 Jul 1775, bapt. 7 Sep 1775. Sponsors: the mother, and Cath. Leacock.

Maria, of Henr. Dietz and Barbara, b. 25 Aug 1775, bapt. 9 Sep 1775. Sponsors: Wilh. Engelfried and wife Maria Cathar.

Philip, of Valentin Krieg and Cath., b. 20 Aug 1775, bapt. 10 Sep 1775. Sponsors: Philipp Weiss and Sybilla.

Peter, of Georg Merkel and Anne, b. 27 Aug 1775, bapt. 10 Sep 1775. Sponsors: the parents.

Wilhelm, of Georg Kehn and Eva, b. 3 Sep 1775, bapt. 10 Sep 1775. Sponsors: Wilhelm Kehn and Margar. Wall (the mother's sister).

Anna, of Caspar Wittebach and Anna Gertraud, b. 7 Sep 1775, bapt. 10 Sep 1775. Sponsors: the parents.

Friedrich, of Jacob Graef (the mason) and Maria, b. 27 Aug 1775, bapt. 10 Sep 1775. Sponsors: Friedrich Schenkel and wife Susanna.

Joh. Georg, of Phil. Warner and Anna Magd., b. 6 Aug 1775, bapt. 10 Sep 1775. Sponsors: Joh. Baumann and wife Elisabeth.

Dorothea, of Joh. Rot(h) and Dorothea, b. 23 Aug 1775, bapt. 10 Sep 1775. Sponsors: Georg Gro[t]z and wife Dorothea.

Anna Maria, of Peter Heimbach and Elisabeth, b. 23 Aug 1775, bapt. 17 Sep 1775. Sponsors: Joh. Bickenbeiler and wife Anna Maria.

Georg, of Thomas Wieler and Elisab., b. 6 Sep 1775, bapt. 12 Sep 1775. Sponsors: the parents.

Johannes, of Joh. Wendelmor and Barbara, b. 23 Aug 1775, bapt. 13 Sep 1775. Sponsors: the parents.

Bernard, of Andreas Schoch and Cath., b. 28 Aug 1775, bapt. 17 Sep 1775. Sponsors: Bernard Kaufman and wife Marg.

Philip, of Franz Wilh. Helmansberger and Anna Maria, b. 12 Sep 1775, bapt. 17 Sep 1775. Sponsors: Philip Klein and Elisabeth Fiss.

Elisabet, of Georg Bachhol[t]z and Veronica, b. 29 Aug 1775, bapt. 16 Sep 1775. Sponsors: the parents.

Joh. Georg, of Jacob Egy and Margaret, 7 months old, bapt. 19 Sep 1775. Sponsors: Wilhelm Facundus and wife Lorreth?.

Joh. Philip, of Joh. Phil. Spielman and Anna Maria, aged 25 years, bapt. 21 Sep 1775. Sponsors: Joh. Remig Spiegel and wife Elis.

Maria Dorothea, of Jacob Keimle and Christina Cathar., b. 7 Sep 1775, bapt. 24 Sep 1775. Sponsors: Johannes Rup and wife Maria Dorothea.

Georg, of Georg Mich. Heil and Maria Catharina, b. 2 Sep 1775, bapt. 24 Sep 1775. Sponsors: the parents.

Susanna Cath., of Christoph Becker and Catharina, b. 15 Sep 1775, bapt. 24 Sep 1775. Sponsors: Johannes Hilarius Becker and wife Cathar.

Catharine, of Henr. Moser and Susanna, b. 29 Aug 1775, bapt. 24 Sep 1775. Sponsors: Georg Blum and wife Catharine.

Anna Elisab., of Peter Walker and Anthonieta, b. 29 Aug 1775, bapt. 21 Sep 1775. Sponsors: the father and Anna Klemmer.

Matthias, of Friedrich Ahl and Elisabeth, b. 15 Sep 1775, bapt. 26 Sep 1775. Sponsors: the father, and the grandmother Dorothea Startz(in).

Georg Caspar, of Joh. Joseph Happel and Ann. Marg., b. 10 Sep 1775, bapt. 1 Oct 1775. Sponsors: Georg Caspar Strecker, Georg Casp. Seifferheld, and Cath. Col__.

Johannes, of Wilh. Kerls and Anna Cathar., bapt. Aug, b. 11 Sep 1775, bapt. 1 Oct 1775. Sponsors: Johannes Schätzler and Barbara Huber(in).

Cath. Barbara, of Valentin Schneider and Rosina, b. 18 Sep 1775, bapt. 1 Oct 1775. Sponsors: Joh. Wilh. Engelfried and wife Cathar. Barbara.

Johannes, of Joh. Grubel and Christina, b. 17 Sep 1775, bapt. 1 Oct 1775. Sponsors: the parents.

Maria Magd., of Ludwig Pannkuchen and Maria, b. 6 Sep 1775, bapt. 1 Oct 1775. Sponsors: the parents.

Elisabeth, of Franz Schaefer and Elis., b. 9 Aug 1775, bapt. 2 Oct 1775. Sponsors: the parents.

Johannes, of Valentin Sorg and An. Maria, b. 24 Sep 1775, bapt. 2 Oct 1775. Sponsors: Joh. Gerlach and wife An. Maria.

Joh. Martin, of Joh. Balthasar Emmerich and Anna Maria, b. 22 Sep 1775, bapt. 8 Oct 1775. Sponsors: Martin Ries and wife (name not given).

Laban, of Christian Kosch [or Rosch] and Sarah, b. 27 Jul 1775, bapt. 8 Oct 1775. Sponsors: Wilh. Powel and Barbara Teusch? .

Joh. Jacob, of Georg Daum and Sarah, b. 25 Sep 1775, bapt. 8 Oct 1775. Sponsors: Joh. Jacob Bitter and wife Juliana.

Regina Elisabeth, of Conrad Ring and Juliana, b. 29 Mar 1775, bapt. 8 Oct 1775. Sponsors: the parents.

Peter, of Wilh. Bathos and Elisabeth, b. 4 Oct 1775, bapt. 4 Oct 1775. Sponsors: Adam Rex and Marg. Dress(in).

Joh. Bernhardt, of Henr. Kurtz and Rosina, b. 4 Oct 1775, bapt. 15 Oct 1775. Sponsors: Joh. Bernhardt Bock and wife Maria.

Maria Magd., of Joh. Nic. Rot(h)enwalder and Elisabet, b. 6 Oct 1775, bapt. 15 Oct 1775. Sponsors: Joh. Martin Schweitzer and wife Maria Magd.
Mar. Magd., of Friedr. Shick and Barbara, b. 2 Oct 1775, bapt. 15 Oct 1775. Sponsors: the parents.
Sophia, of Daniel Kiermann and Elisabeth, b. 1 Oct 1775, bapt. 15 Oct 1775. Sponsors: Johann Lorentz and his dau. Sophia.
An. Maria, of Henr. Conrad Shultz and Anna Mar., b. 7 Oct 1775, bapt. 14 Oct 1775. Sponsors: the parents.
Georg, of Friedr. Vogel and Elisabeth, b. 9 Oct 1775, bapt. 21 Oct 1775. Sponsors: Georg Oesterle and wife Maria, and Johannes Schneider's wife Eva.
Johannes, of Friedr. Vogel and Elisabeth, b. 9 Oct 1775, bapt. 21 Oct 1775. Sponsors: same as above.
Anna Catharina, of Melcher Weissinger and Maria, b. 23 Sep 1775, bapt. 21 Oct 1775. Sponsors: Balthasar Staus and wife Maria.
Georg Heinr., of Joh. Georg Kien and Maria Marg., b. 27 Aug 1775, bapt. 15 Oct 1775. Sponsors: Henrich Nagel and wife (name not given).
Agnes Maria, of Friedrich Bricks and Anna Magd., b. 24 Sep 1775, bapt. 22 Oct 1775. Sponsors: Sebast. Schweiger and wife Agnes Maria.
Catharina, of Martin Fies and Dorothea, b. 4 Oct 1775, bapt. 29 Oct 1775. Sponsors: the mother, and Jacob Fies.
Emos, of Andreas Lock and Catharine, b. in Nov 1773, bapt. 29 Oct 1775. Sponsors: Lorenz Schwab and wife Marg.
Michael, of Jacob Stauch and Sara (who died), b. 1 Jan 1775, bapt. 26 Oct 1775. Sponsor: the father.
Daniel, of Daniel Frischmuth and Barbara, b. 29 Sep 1775, bapt. 29 Oct 1775. Sponsors: Henr. Stiller and wife Margareta.
Susanna, of Michael Lutz and Susanna, b. 28 Sep 1775, bapt. 5 Nov 1775. Sponsors: Martin Lutz and wife Cathar.
Samuel, of Samuel Fromberger and Anna, b. 21 Oct 1775, bapt. 6 Nov 1775. Sponsors: Nicol. Weber and wife (name not given).
Dorothea, of Joh. Koch and Barbara, b. 12 Oct 1775, bapt. 5 Nov 1775. Sponsors: Jacob Teiss and wife Dorothea.
Anna Elisabeth, of Johannes Freiberg and Susanna, b. 24 Oct 1775, bapt. 5 Nov 1775. Sponsors: Johannes Gummi and wife Catharina.
Alex. Henry, of Alexan. Adamson and Maria, b. 13 Sep 1775, bapt. 5 Nov 1775. Sponsors: James Persy and wife Henrietta.
Johannes, of Johannes Wacker and Catharina, b. 14 Oct 1775, bapt. 5 Nov 1775. Sponsors: Georg Hirt and his dau. Anna Magd. Davis.
Conr. Wilhelm, of Henrich Kaemmerer and Catharina, b. 13 Oct 1775, bapt. 12 Nov 1775. Sponsors: Conrad Baethis and wife Barbara.
Anna Dor., of Joh. Eberhard and (name not given), b. 13 Oct 1775, bapt. 12 Nov 1775. Sponsors: Mr. Georg Wa[l]ker and wife Dorothea.
Philip, of Georg Hofman and Magd., b. 11 Sep 1775, bapt. 15 Nov 1775. Sponsor: Philip Blot.
Christine, of Peter Biswanger and Eva, b. 21 Oct 1775, bapt. 15 Nov 1775. Sponsors: Joh. Heller and wife Christine.

An. Marg., of Andr. Weh and Regina, b. 31 Oct 1775, bapt. 12 Nov 1775.
Sponsors: David Morgan and Anna Marg. Kunkel(in).
Maria Elis., of Georg Death and Mary., b. in Oct 1775, bapt. 12 Nov 1775.
Sponsors: the parents, and Elis. Grist(in).
William, of James Cartwright and Barbara, b. 1 April, 1775, bapt. 15 Nov 1775.
Sponsors: William Bitts and Barbara Hood.
Ambros, of Andreas Graeter and Ann, b. 1 April, 1775, bapt. 17 Nov 1775.
Sponsors: the parents.
Joh. Wilh., of Caspar Cress and Cathar., b. 26 Oct 1775, bapt. 19 Nov 1775.
Sponsors: Christian Gally and wife Margar.
Maria, of Henr. Jonas and Cath., b. 24 Oct 1775, bapt. 19 Nov 1775. Sponsors:
Joh. Kaiser and wife Maria.
Georg, of Jac. Dietrich and Augustina, b. 31 Oct 1775, bapt. 19 Nov 1775.
Sponsors: Georg Knerr and wife Cath.
An. Dorothea, of Peter Shelleberger and Dorothea, b. 22 Oct 1775, bapt. 26 Nov
1775. Sponsors: Math. Schackar and Dor. Steyerwald(in).
Doroth., of Peter Gress and Rosina, b. 10 Nov 1775, bapt. 26 Nov 1775.
Sponsors: Jacob Theiss and wife Doroth..
Christian, of Nicol. Müller and Anna Maria, b. 31 Oct 1775, bapt. 26 Nov 1775.
Sponsors: Christian Genzel and wife Cath.
Jul. Cathar., of James Cunningham and Eleonor, b. 20 Mar 1775, bapt. 30 Nov
1775. Sponsors: the parents.
An. Maria, of Wilh. Mohr and Susanna Maria, b. 30 Oct 1775, bapt. 3 Dec 1775.
Sponsors: Nicol. Lochman and wife Anna Maria.
An. Maria, of Jac. Ehrenfeuchter? and Susanna Marg., b. 12 Oct 1775, bapt.
3 Dec 1775. Sponsors: Peter Pauer and wife Anna Maria.
An. Justina, of Joh. Jac. Wolf and Maria Catharina, b. 22 Nov 1775, bapt. 3 Dec
1775. Sponsor: the grandmother Anna Justina.
Elis., of Andr. Beck and Eva Marg., b. 15 Oct 1775, bapt. 2 Nov 1775.
Sponsors: Joh. Kiffert and wife Elisabet.
Maria Elis., of David Schaefer, Jr., and Elis., b. 16 Oct 1775, bapt. 30 Nov 1775.
Sponsors: David Schaefer, Sr., and wife (name not given).
Daniel Henr., of Daniel Suttcliff? (deceased) and Cath. Has [who has re-
married?], b. 31 Mar 1774, bapt. 12 Nov 1775. In the presence of Henr.
Muhlenberg and wife Cath.
Joh. Jacob, of Joh. Weisman and Marg. Barb., b. 4 Nov 1775, bapt. 3 Dec 1775.
Sponsors: the parents.
Eva, of (father's first name not given) Loescher and Catharina, b. 27 Nov 1775,
bapt. 5 Dec 1775. Sponsors: Georg Fries and wife Catharina.
An. Cath., of Jacob Werner and Salome, b. 21 Nov 1775, bapt. 10 Dec 1775.
Sponsors: Georg Göttle and wife Hanna.
Jac. Martin, of Georg Muff and Elisabet, b. 13 Nov 1775, bapt. 10 Dec 1775.
Sponsors: the father, and Clara Danninger(in).
Rachel, of Richard Thomas and Sarah, b. 20 Nov 1775, bapt. 14 Dec 1775.
Sponsor: Sarah Hall.
Elisabet, of Dietr. Wilh. Bicking and Elisabet, b. 12 Nov 1775, bapt. 13 Dec
1775. Sponsors: the father, and Cath. Rass(in)?.

Maria Magd., of Wilhelm Löscher and Maria Cath., b. 19 Oct 1775, bapt. 17 Dec 1775. Sponsors: Georg Löscher and his sister Maria Magd. Loesher(in).

Christine, of Joh. Westenberger and Barbara, b. 29 Aug 1775, bapt. 17 Dec 1775. Sponsors: Henr. Sched and wife Christine.

Maria Elisab., of Wilhelm Hermann and Susanna Marg., b. 13 Nov 1775, bapt. 17 Dec 1775. Sponsors: Johann Christian Glaubfluger and Maria Elisab. Gemeinbauer(in).

Carl, of Martin Die[t]z and Sabina Margar., b. 9 Dec 1775, bapt. 17 Dec 1775. Sponsors: Carl Herzenberger and Sabina Jauch

Cathar. Elisab., of Johannes Meister and Dorothea, b. 10 Dec 1775, bapt. 17 Dec 1775. Sponsors: Gottlieb Roll and wife Anna Cath.

Margareta, of Peter Klein and Eva Maria, b. 27 Nov 1775, bapt. 17 Dec 1775. Sponsors: Matth. Price and wife Elisabeth.

Maria Cath., of Jacob Weitman and Elisabet, b. 27 Nov 1775, bapt. 18 Dec 1775. Sponsor: Cath. Muhlenberg(in).

Joh. Friedr., of Joh. Klein (deceased) and Hanna, b. 1 Jul 1775, bapt. 18 Dec 1775. Sponsors: Friedr. Duschant and wife (name not given).

Mar. Sabina, of Peter Kuhn and Elisabeth, b. 18 Dec 1775, bapt. 19 Dec 1775. Sponsors: Henrich Keppele, Sr., and Mrs. Jac. Kuhn(in).

Anna Marg., of Nicol. Klein and Cath., b. 13 Dec 1775, bapt. 24 Dec 1775. Sponsors: Joh. Elcher and wife Anna Marg.

Maria, of John Starke and Anna Cath., b. 11 Dec 1775, bapt. 24 Dec 1775. Sponsors: Phil. Pannkuchen and wife Maria.

Carl, of Jacob Gontner and Catharina, b. 10 Dec 1775, bapt. 24 Dec 1775. Sponsors: the parents.

Veronica, of Jacob Kaufman and Maria Barb., b. 7 Dec 1775, bapt. 24 Dec 1775. Sponsors: Phil. Mietman and wife Veronica.

Anna Marg., of Ludwig Kehl and Elisabet, b. 8 Dec 1775, bapt. 25 Dec 1775. Sponsors: Georg Krugemeier and wife Anna Marg.

Peter, of Joh. Peter Sonleutner and Elisabet, b. 6 Sep 1775, bapt. 25 Dec 1775. Sponsors: the parents.

Joh. Jacob, of Christian Lauer and Elisabet, b. 3 Dec 1775, bapt. 25 Dec 1775. Sponsor: Jacob Ratz.

Joh. Georg, of Joh. Georg Staus and Esther, b. 11 Dec 1775, bapt. 25 Dec 1775. Sponsors: Paul Cober and wife (name not given).

Elis. Cath., of Friedr. Lutz and Catharina, b. 14 Dec 1775, bapt. 26 Dec 1775. Sponsors: Bastian Wully and wife Elis. Cath.

Maria Magd., of Phil. Meyerle and Anna Esther, b. 15 Dec 1775, bapt. 31 Dec 1775. Sponsors: Michael Kuns and wife Cath.

Nicol., of Nicol. Hermstad and Cath., birthdate not given, bapt. 25 Dec 1775. (Sponsors not given.)

1776
(baptisms by pastors Kunze and G.H.E. Muhlenberg, Jr., in chronological sequence from Book III)

Elisabeth, of Johannes Schaefer and Susanna, b. 12 Dec 1775, bapt. 7 Jan 1776. Sponsors: Johannes Schut and wife Margareta.

Joh. Jacob, of Christian Jost and Christina, b. 21 Dec 1775, bapt. 7 Jan 1776.
Sponsors: Joh. Jac. Bauer and wife Maria Clara.
Peter, of Wilhelm Warner and Wilhelmine, b. 18 Dec 1775, bapt. 7 Jan 1776.
Sponsors: Peter Klein and wife Maria.
Anna Christina, of Jacob Haine and Anna, b. 7 Dec 1775, bapt. 7 Jan 1776.
Sponsors: Joh. Andr. Rohr and wife Mar. Christina.
Abraham, of Gotfried Walter and Jane, b. 16 Dec 1775, bapt. 7 Jan 1776.
Sponsors: the parents, and widow White.
Mary Magd. Rosina, of Jacob Pfister (deceased) and Maria, b. 5 Nov 1775, bapt.
7 Jan 1776. Sponsors: Maria Magd. Pfister(in) and Rosina Hergesheim(in).
Anna Margar., of Jacob Kessler and Catharina, b. 31 Dec 1775, bapt. 14 Jan
1776. Sponsors: Joh. Martin Hertle and wife Anna Marg.
Georg, of Georg Christein and Jemina, b. 30 Dec 1775, bapt. 14 Jan 1776.
Sponsors: Joh. Georg Kiefer and wife Eva Maria.
An. Margareta, of Nicolaus Muller and Anna Maria, b. 28 Dec 1775, bapt.
14 Jan 1776. Sponsors: Michael Stricker? and wife An. Marg.
Joh. Georg, of Johannes Linnenberg and Anna Margareta, b. 5 Jan 1776, bapt.
14 Jan 1776. Sponsors: Georg Sei[t]z and wife Elisabeth.
Georg, of Friedr. Wolpert and Margaretha, b. 3 Dec 1775, bapt. 14 Jan 1776.
Sponsors: Georg Wolpert and wife Marg.
Cathar., of Edward Glasgow and Catharine, 5 weeks old, bapt. 14 Jan 1776.
Sponsors: Joh. Balth. Emmerich and wife Maria.
Joh. Martin, of Friedr. Vogel and Cath. Barb., b. 31 Dec 1775, bapt. 14 Jan
1776. Sponsors: Joh. Mart. Wieland and Elis. Stegner(in).
Anna Mar., of Joh. Mich. Häns and Cathar., b. 3 Jan 1776, bapt. 14 Jan 1776.
Sponsors: Andr. Bauer and wife Anna Maria.
Elisabet, of Peter Schwimmer and Martha, b. 4 Jul 1773, bapt. 16 Jan 1776.
Sponsors: the mother, and "Mr." Phil. Hales.
Susanna, of Peter Schwimmer and Martha, b. 19 Dec 1775, bapt. 16 Jan 1776.
Sponsors: the mother and "Mr." Phil. Hales.
Canoth, of Canoth McConnet and Susanna, b. 6 Jan 1776, bapt. 16 Jan 1776.
Sponsors: the mother, and "Mr." Phil. Hales.
Elisabet, of Jacob Buck and Catharine, b. 31 Dec 1775, bapt. 21 Jan 1776.
Sponsors: Joh Weiss and wife Elisabet.
John, of William Burkert and Sara, b. 2 Jan 1776, bapt. 22 Jan 1776. Sponsors:
the parents.
Johannes, of Conrad Deweter and Catharina, b. 29 Dec 1775, bapt. 21 Jan 1776.
Sponsors: Johannes Jaiser and wife Mar. Elisab.
Charles, of Martin Derry and Maria, b. 17 Jun 1775, bapt. 25 Jan 1776.
Sponsors: the parents.
Maria Magd., of Mich. Schweitzer and Elisabeth, b. 8 Jan 1776, bapt. 28 Jan
1776. Sponsors: Martin Schweitzer and wife Maria.
Joh. Georg, of Phil. Pannekuche and Maria, b. 14 Jan 1776, bapt. 28 Jan 1776.
Sponsors: Joh. Georg Schneider and wife Anna Maria.
Joh. Georg, of Johannes Lamperter and Sara, b. 16 Dec 1775, bapt. 28 Jan 1776.
Sponsors: Georg Kunz, and Marc. Munzer and his sister Sara.

378   PHILADELPHIA GERMAN LUTHERAN CHURCH

Anna Margaret, of Wilhelm Lehmann and Elisabeth, b. 18 Jan 1776, bapt. 28 Jan 1776. Sponsors: the father, and the grandparents Christian Fiedler and wife (name not given).
Christoph, of Heinr. Engelfried and Catharina, b. 16 Jan 1776, bapt. 28 Jan 1776. Sponsors: Christoph Knies and Cathar. Rebestock(in).
Georg Ernst, of Johannes Fritz and Catharina, b. 3 Jan 1776, bapt. 29 Jan 1776. Sponsors: Caspar Geier and wife Elisabeth.
Georg, of Andr. Förster and An. Sybilla, b. 28 Jan 1776, bapt. 4 Feb 1776. Sponsors: Joh. Georg Senft and Charl[otte] Graf(in).
Michael, of Mich. Stauch and Margar., b. 3 Jan 1776, bapt. 4 Feb 1776. Sponsors: Sebast. Seibert and wife (name not given).
Susanna, of Jac. Bademan and (name not given), b. 13 Nov 1776, bapt. 2 Feb 1776. Sponsors: Mich. Kampfer and wife Susanna.
Henrich, of Dan. Pohlman and (name not given), birthdate not given, bapt. 2 Feb 1776. Sponsor: Jacob Baileman.
Cathar., of Henr. Sommer and Catharina, b. 14 Jan 1776, bapt. 4 Feb 1776. Sponsors: Peter Sommer and wife Cath.
Johannes, of Daniel Knodel and Anna Maria, b. 7 Jan 1776, bapt. 4 Feb 1776. Sponsors: Joh.. Frickhöfer and Marg. Stucker(in).
Child (name not given), of Joh. Braun and Maria, b. 17 Jan 1776, bapt. 4 Feb 1776. Sponsors: the parents.
Joh. Ehrhard, of Johann Ehrhard Eissenberk and Catharina, b. 23 Jan 1776, bapt. 4 Feb 1776. Sponsors: the parents.
Joh. Christian, of Joh. Peter Meier and Anna Maria, b. 30 Jan 1776, bapt. 11 Feb 1776. Sponsors: Christ. Schaefer and wife Dorothea.
Catharina, of Wilhelm Weber and Elisabeth, b. 29 Jan 1776, bapt. 11 Feb 1776. Sponsors: Joh. Motschutter, and the grandmother Anna Cathar. Weber(in).
An. Margaretha, of Joh. Conrad Schlatter and Christine, b. 5 Jan 1776, bapt. 11 Feb 1776. Sponsor: Marg. Reif(in).
Wilh., of Christoph Reintaler and Elisabet, b. 15 Jul 1775, bapt. 11 Feb 1776. Sponsors: the parents.
Caspar, of Phil. Seidelman and Anna Maria, b. 31 Jan 1776, bapt. 11 Feb 1776. Sponsors: Caspar Geier and wife Elis.
Cathar. Dorothea, of Jacob Seger and Barbara, b. 2 Feb 1776, bapt. 18 Feb 1776. Sponsors: Jacob Keinle and wife Cath. Dorothea.
Wilhelm, of Ludew. Barthel and Christina, b. 2 Feb 1776, bapt. 17 Feb 1776. Sponsors: the father, and Mich. Naegele and Sophia.
Elisabet, of Friedr. Stuber and Elisabeth, b. 6 Jan 1776, bapt. 15 Feb 1776. Sponsors: Joh. Weber and wife Maria.
Anna Maria, of Joh. Jac. Ehrhard {Gerret (= Gerhard?) in the burials} and Johanetta Eleonor, b. 14 Jan 1776, bapt. 18 Feb 1776. Sponsors: the parents.
Margar., of Abr. Cloding and Juliana, b. 4 Feb 1776, bapt. 19 Feb 1776. Sponsors: the parents.
Joh. Conrad, of Martin Braun and Maria, b. 14 Feb 1776, bapt. 25 Feb 1776. Sponsors: Conrad Seifart and Elisabeth Jung(in).
Joh. Carl, of Carl Schneider and Maria, b. 10 Feb 1776, bapt. 25 Feb 1776. Sponsors: Johannes Messerschmidt and sister Anna Barbara.

Catharine, of Daniel Bastian and Johanna, b. 15 Feb 1776, bapt. 25 Feb 1776.
Sponsors: Nicol. Walter and [wife] Rosina.
Maria Magdal., of Mich. Schweitzer and Elisabeth, b. 8 Jan 1776, bapt. 28 Jan
1776. Sponsors: Martin Schweitzer and wife Maria Magd.
John, of Benj. Commat and Charlotte, b. 8 Feb 1776, bapt. 25 Feb 1776.
Sponsors: Joh. Krampf Dorck and [wife] Doroth.
Jacob, of Will. Fairley and Elisabet, b. 21 Feb 1776, bapt. 25 Feb 1776.
Sponsors: Jac. Ehrenfeuchter and [wife] Susanna.
Joh. Henrich, of Joh. Henr. Both and Cath. Elis., b. 20 Feb 1776, bapt. 1 Mar
1776. Sponsors: the father, and Cath. Heim(sin).
Anna, of Francis Löscher and Barbara, b. 16 Jul 1775, bapt. 25 Feb 1776.
Sponsor: Ann Facus.
Elisabet, of Jean Bourgal and Margar., b. 16 Feb 1776, bapt. 25 Feb 1776.
Sponsors: Elis. Heftrig(in) and Anton Gerard.
Isaac, of Georg Heitel and Salome, b. 5 Feb 1776, bapt. 25 Feb 1776. Sponsors:
the parents.
Anna Maria Barbara, of Andreas Tag and Christina, b. 15 Feb 1776, bapt. 3 Mar
1776. Sponsors: Adam Teutschenbach and wife Barbara.
Carl Philip (twin), of Friedr. Jeremias and Magdal., b. 22 Feb 1776, bapt. 3 Mar
1776. Sponsor: Carl Philip Ebert. and Clara Denninger.
Clara, (twin), of Friedr. Jeremias and Magdal., b. 22 Feb 1776, bapt. 3 Mar
1776. Sponsor: Clara Denninger.
Margar. (twin), of Georg Vetter and Hanna, b. 22 Feb 1776, bapt. 2 Mar 1776.
Sponsors: the parents.
Henrich, (twin), of Georg Vetter and Hanna, b. 22 Feb 1776, bapt. 2 Mar 1776.
Sponsors: the parents.
Anna Maria, of Conrad Hess and Charlotte, b. 19 Jan 1776, bapt. 4 Mar 1776.
Sponsors: Michael Kraft and wife Anna Maria.
Mary, of John Leppard and Mary, b. 8 Feb 1776, bapt. 7 Mar 1776. Sponsors:
the mother, and John Kunze.
Johannes, of David Behler and Maria, b. 18 Jan 1776, bapt. 8 Mar 1776.
Sponsors: Mattheus Kalbfleisch and his sister Maria Kalbfleisch.
Elisab. Charlotte, of Michael Kinzler and Elisabeth, b. 29 Feb 1776, bapt.
10 Mar 1776. Sponsors: Friedr. Marder and wife Mar. Elisabeth.
Sybilla, of Daniel Billiger and Margareta, b. 19 Feb 1776, bapt. 10 Mar 1776.
Sponsors: Johann Billiger and wife Margareta.
Maria, of ___ Heinholt (the father in prison for making [counterfeiting?] money)
and wife Cath., b. 15 Feb 1776, bapt. 10 Mar 1776. Sponsors: Friedr.
Ensminger and Maria Hofmann(in).
Peter (twin), of George Strein and Esther, b. 23 Feb 1776, bapt. 10 Mar 1776.
Sponsors: Peter Sonleutner and wife (not named), and Eva Barbara Götz(in).
Jacob, (twin), of George Strein and Esther, b. 23 Feb 1776, bapt. 10 Mar 1776.
Sponsors: Jac. Bast and Marg. Unger(in).
Maria Hanna, of Joh. Low and Eva, b. 20 Nov 1775, bapt. 10 Mar 1776.
Sponsors: Henry Emig and Magd. Seifferheld.
Margar., of Jacob Schroeder and Juliana, b. 18 Jan 1776, bapt. 10 Mar 1776.
Sponsors: Christian Lederborn and wife Marg.

Christian, of Christian Kinzler and Anna Marg., b. 29 Feb 1776, bapt. 10 Mar 1776. Sponsors: the parents.

Barbara, of Georg Pop and Maria, b. 3 Feb 1776, bapt. 10 Mar 1776. Sponsors: Henr. Schreiber and wife Margareta.

Joh. Michael, of Johann Michael Jobst and Marg., b. 25 Jan 1776, bapt. 10 Mar 1776. Sponsors: the father, and the grandmother Ann. Marg. Mildeberger(in).

Mar. Philippina, of Lorenz Seckel and Barbara, b. 10 Feb 1776, bapt. 10 Mar 1776. Sponsors: grandfather Georg Dav. Seckel, and maternal grandmother Mar. Philippina Chrisler(in).

Joseph, of John Helzet and Cath., b. 7 Feb 1776, bapt. 17 Mar 1776. Sponsors: Balt. Staus and wife Maria.

Anna Maria, of Thom. Fischer and Roxy (Rony?), b. 1 Sep 1775, bapt. 17 Mar 1776. Sponsors: Phil. Fischer and wife Anna Maria.

Susanna, of Conrad Leibbrand and Susanna, b. 25 Dec 1775, bapt. 17 Mar 1776. Sponsors: Mich. Fuchs and wife Salome.

Benjamin, of Anton Rühl and Philippina, b. 14 Oct 1775, bapt. 20 Mar 1776. Sponsors: the mother, and Johann Wilhelm Maller.

James, of James Carpenter and Maria, b. 20 Feb 1776, bapt. 20 Mar 1776. Sponsor: Anna Margareta Dress(in).

Georg, of Wilhelm Wolf? and Christina, b. in Nov 1774, bapt. 20 Mar 1776. Sponsors: John Fasy and Ann. Mar. Lips.

Elisab., of Georg Schenck and Elisabeth, b. 4 Mar 1776, bapt. 24 Mar 1776. Sponsors: the parents.

Wilh., of Wilhelm Kempf and Sabina, b. 2 Mar 1776, bapt. 24 Mar 1776. Sponsors: the parents.

Jacob, of Joh. Math. Dollman and Ann. Cath., b. 3 Mar 1776, bapt. 24 Mar 1776. Sponsors: Jacob Sulger and wife An. Marg.

Sara, of Mich. Steinhauer and Barbara, b. 28 Feb 1776, bapt. 24 Mar 1776. Sponsors: Jacob Seibert and wife Sara..

Christine, of Christian Paschetow and Christine, b. 10 Mar 1776, bapt. 24 Mar 1776. Sponsors: Christine Dress(in) and Adam Hendel.

Joh. Friedr., of Joh. Friedr. Mehl and Cath., b. 10 Mar 1776, bapt. 24 Mar 1776. Sponsors: Joh. Friedr. Link and wife Charlotte.

Margar., of Andr. Philler and Margaretha, b. 15 Mar 1776, bapt. 24 Mar 1776. Sponsors: the parents.

Philipp [twin], of Nicolaus Essling and Mar. Zimmermann(in), illegitimate, b. 9 Mar 1776, bapt. 21 Mar 1776. Sponsors: Philipp Helder and wife Eva.

Anna Catharina [twin], of Nicolaus Essling and Mar. Zimmermann(in), illegitimate, b. 9 Mar 1776, bapt. 21 Mar 1776. Sponsors: Valentin Reis and Cathar. Zimmermann.

Catharina Regina, of Anthony Armbruster and Mar. Christina, b. 26 Feb 1776, bapt. 26 Mar 1776. Sponsors: Joh. Dan. Waltenberg and wife Catharina.

Ann, of Thomas Goucher and Hanna, 11 months old, bapt. 28 Mar 1776. Sponsor: Peter de Haven.

Ann. Cath. [twin], of Joh. Leon. Heil and Anna Maria, b. 18 Dec 1775, bapt. 31 Mar 1776. Sponsors: Joh. Mos and [wife] Susanna.

Susanna (twin), of Joh. Leon. Heil and Anna Maria, b. 18 Dec 1775, bapt. 31 Mar 1776. Sponsor: Anna Cath. Fritz.

Johannes, of Johannes Conrad Bererung and Margar., b. 16 Jan 1776, bapt. 31 Mar 1776. Sponsors: Johannes Goe[t]z and wife Dorothea.

Maria, of Georg Pater and Margaretha, b. 23 Mar 1776, bapt. 3 Apr 1776. Sponsors: Maria Klein(in) and Susanna Reiss(in).

Adam, of Leon. Kraemer and An. Maria, b. 12 Mar 1776, bapt. 31 Mar 1776. Sponsors: Ad. Stricker and wife (name not given).

Matthias, of Philipp Stocker? and Salome, b. 30 Oct 1775, bapt. 5 Apr 1776. Sponsors: Matthias Sommer and wife Rahel.

Anna, of Michael Wolf and Margaretha, b. 25 Jan 1776, bapt. 7 Apr 1776. Sponsors: David Huber and wife Anna.

Anna Margareta, of Joseph Stauch and Eva Rosina, b. 24 Sep 1775, bapt. 8 Apr 1776. Sponsors: Michael Stauch and wife Margar.

Johannes, of Ernst Maengen and Mar. Magdalena, b. 6 Mar 1776, bapt. 8 Apr 1776. Sponsors: Johannes Maengen and wife Cathar.

Johannes, of Johann Nicolaus Wagner and Magdalena, b. 17 May 1775, bapt. 8 Apr 1776. Sponsors: Georg Streper and wife (name not given).

Joh. Henrich, of Johann Georg Schinck and Elisabeth Sophia, b. 2 Apr 1776, bapt. 14 Apr 1776. Sponsor: Johann Henr. Ruhl.

Michael, of Michael Klingmann and Anna Elisabeth, b. 24 Sep 1775, bapt. 13 Apr 1776. Sponsors: Jacob Merckel and wife Elisab..

Philipp, of Philipp Miser and Elisabeth, b. 19 Oct 1775, bapt. 13 Apr 1776. Sponsor: the grandmother Elisab. Klingmann(in).

Anna Christina, of Georg Adam Schmidt and Anna Christina, b. 4 Feb 1776, bapt. 14 Apr 1776. Sponsors: the parents.

Jacob, of Jacob Henriegel and Catharine, b. 9 Apr 1776, bapt. 14 Apr 1776. Sponsors: Nicolaus Reb and wife Christina.

Charlotta Eleonora, of Jacob Meier and Anna Maria, b. 11 Mar 1776, bapt. 28 Apr 1776. Sponsors: Johannes Miller and Charlotta Eleonora.

Gottfried, of Jacob Tauenhauer and Maria, b. 5 Mar 1776, bapt. 12 Apr 1776. Sponsors: Joh. Hauk and wife Catharina.

Catharina, of Johannes Specht and Catharina, b. 3 Apr 1776, bapt. 15 Apr 1776. Sponsors: the parents.

Maria Elisabeth, of Georg Wirt and Maria, b. 9 Apr 1776, bapt. 15 Apr 1776. Sponsors: Daniel Neuman and wife Marg.

Joh. Jacob, of Peter Bell and Anna Marg., b. 12 Mar 1776, bapt. in Apr 1776. Sponsors: Joh. Jac. Rotter and wife Cath.

Peter, of Georg Turnis and Maria Cath., b. 4 Apr 1776, bapt. 14 Apr 1776. Sponsors: Joh. Surfar? and Maria Ham___.

Elisabeth, of Peter Grof and Catharina, b. 17 Jan 1776, bapt. 21 Apr 1776. Sponsors: the father, and Catharina Kuhl(in).

Maria, of Adam Zanzinger and Susanna, b. 26 May 1775, bapt. 20 Apr 1776. Sponsors: grandfather Henr. Keppele, Sr., Mrs. Cathar. Keppele, and the wife (name not given) of Henry Keppele, Jr.

Adam, of Henr. Meyer and Anna Ursula, b. 13 Apr 1776, bapt. 28 Apr 1776. Sponsors: the parents.

Cathar., of Friedr. Borstel and Catharina, b. 14 Apr 1776, bapt. 28 Apr 1776. Sponsors: Christoph Fort and wife Cath.

Elisabet, of Christoph Ziegler and Susanna, b. in Mar 1772, bapt. 28 Apr 1776. Sponsors: the parents.

Christoph, of Christoph Ziegler and Susanna, b. 21 Mar 1774, bapt. 28 Apr 1776. Sponsors: the parents.

Joh. Michael, of Joh. Schaefer and Maria, birthdate not given, bapt. 30 Apr 1776. Sponsor: Joh. Mich. Stotz.

Georg [twin], of Adam Folk and Catharina, b. 23 Apr 1776, bapt. 30 Apr 1776. Sponsors: Georg Waker and wife Dorothea.

Dorothea Susanna [twin], of Adam Folk and Catharina, b. 23 Apr 1776, bapt. 30 Apr 1776. Sponsor: Elisabet Keates.

Elisab., of Frid. Mühlenberg (preacher at New York) and Catharina, b. 26 Apr 1776, bapt. 1 May 1776. Sponsors: Elis. Barge, Elis. Schul[t]z and Elis. Schaeffer.

Sarah Elisab., of Peter Mann and Anna Maria, b. 14 Apr 1776, bapt. 5 May 1776. Sponsors: the father, and Elisabet Peterson.

Joh. Henr., of Martin Schreier and Anna Rosina, b. 22 Apr 1776, bapt. 5 May 1776. Sponsors: Peter Klein and wife Maria.

Joh. Henrich, of Joh. Ried and Susanna, b. 18 Apr 1776, bapt. 5 May 1776. Sponsors: Henr. Lentz and wife (name not given).

Henrich, of Henr. Meier and Cathar., b. 6 Apr 1775, bapt. 6 May 1776. Sponsors: the father and his sister Marg. Meier.

Catharine, of Adam Hellerman and Charlotte (English, still not baptized), b. 22 Mar 1776, bapt. 13 May 1776. Sponsor: the father.

Adam Hellerman's wife was bapt. 13 May 1776 [see above].

Cath., of Georg Hof and An. Marg., b. 11 Mar 1776, bapt. 13 May 1776. Sponsors: the parents.

Barbara, of Philip Mietman and Euphronica, b. 16 Apr 1776, bapt. 5 May 1776. Sponsors: Georg Honig and wife Barbara.

Georg, of Georg Bodick and Sophia (unbaptized), b. 11 Apr 1776, bapt. 3 May 1776. Sponsor(s): Christian Rot(h)'s step-daughter [and?] widow Dress(in).

Michael, of Gottfried Krumbach and Barbara, b. 1 Apr 1776, bapt. 3 May 1776. Sponsors: the parents.

Carl Joseph, of Georg Schneider and (name not given), birthdate not given, bapt. 16 May 1776. Sponsor: Carl Joseph Wolpert.

Wilhelm, of Christoph Kucher and An. Mar., b. 11 May 1776, bapt. 16 May 1776. Sponsors: Dav. Schaefer, Jr., and wife (name not given).

Anna Sophia, of Joh. Melchior Schwerer and Rosina, b. 1 Mar 1776, bapt. 19 May 1776. Sponsors: Adam Engert and Cath. Schwerer(in).

Christine Susan., of Peter Lavenstein and Cathar., b. 27 Oct 1775, bapt. 19 May 1776. Sponsor: Anna Christ. Seinericht.

Georg Adam, of Phil. Jac. Bechtold and Anna Maria, b. 12 Apr 1776, bapt. 19 May 1776. Sponsors: Georg Seitz and wife Catharina.

An. Maria, of Georg Wunderlich and Catharine, b. 25 Dec 1775, bapt. 19 May 1776. Sponsors: the parents.

Andr., of Joh. Reis and Sus., b. 18 Aug 1775, bapt. the same day. Sponsors: the parents.

Margar., of Jacob Schreck and Maria, b. 4 May 1776, bapt. 19 May 1776.
Sponsor: Marg. Syng.
Maria Ros., of Christian Derick and Maria Rosina, b. 17 May 1776, bapt.
19 May 1776. Sponsors: the parents.
Elisabet, of Christoph Schleich and Elisabeth, b. 1 May 1776, bapt. 26 May
1776. Sponsors: Georg Scherer and Elis. Kraus(in).
Joh. Jacob, of Jacob Beck and Elisabeth, b. 18 Feb 1776, bapt. 26 May 1776.
Sponsors: Mich. Regenbog and wife Catharina.
Johannes, of Henrich Meyer and Catharina, b. 19 May 1776, bapt. 26 May 1776.
Sponsors: the parents.
Michael, of Joh. Leon. Weber and Elisabet, b. 6 May 1776, bapt. 26 May 1776.
Sponsors: Wolfg. Gemeinbauer and [wife] Catharina.
Anton, of Gottfr. Sorgübel and Catharine, b. 6 Apr 1776, bapt. 27 May 1776.
Sponsors: Anton Birkenbeiler and wife (name not given).
Matthias, of Math. Shleigman and Mary, b. 2 Apr 1776, bapt. 8 May 1776.
Sponsor: the mother.
Mark, of Mark Thomson and Sarah, b. 30 Apr 1776, bapt. 15 May 1776.
Sponsors: the parents.
Joh. Mathias, of Michael Klein and Elisabeth, b. 6 Sep 1775, bapt. 26 May
1776. Sponsors: Math. Kalbfleisch and sister Maria Kalbfleisch(in).
Magdal., of Christoph Homüller and An. Maria, b. 1 Jan 1776, bapt. 28 May
1776. Sponsors: Ernst Heiser and wife Magdal.
Thomas, of Caspar Cox and Elisabeth, b. 8 Apr 1775, bapt. 29 May 1776.
Sponsors: Henry Muller and wife Ann.
Maria Elis., of Friedr. Kirls and Elisabeth, b. 26 Apr 1776, bapt. 2 Jun 1776.
Sponsors: Jacob Bauer and wife Maria Clara.
Maria Juliana, of Jacob Jung and Elisabet, b. 20 May 1776, bapt. 2 Jun 1776.
Sponsors: Jacob Jung and wife Maria Juliana.
Peter, of Christoph Hirt and Susanna, b. 8 Mar 1776, bapt. 2 Jun 1776.
Sponsors: Peter Hoy and wife Amalia.
Anna Maria, of Joseph Kaiser and Anna Maria, b. 4 May 1776, bapt. 2 Jun 1776.
Sponsors: Georg Burdenheim and his dau. Anna Maria.
Sarah, of Math. Schmidt and Agnes Cathr., b. 6 May 1776, bapt. 5 Jun 1776.
Sponsors: the parents.
Jacob, of Georg Moser and Ann. Doroth., b. 30 May 1776, bapt. 7 Jun 1776.
Sponsors: the parents.
Hans Georg, of Mich. Schoch and Magd., b. 27 Apr 1776, bapt. 9 Jun 1776.
Sponsors: Joh. Hauk and wife Cath.
Cath., of Gottfried Grimm and Rosina, b. 23 May 1776, bapt. 9 Jun 1776.
Sponsors: Jacob Keimle and wife Cath.
Elis. Marg., of Adam Knoblauch and Barbara, b. 27 May 1776, bapt. 9 Jun
1776. Sponsors: Friedr. Beyerle and Elisabet Barkin.
Sara, of Jacob Motz and Barbara, b. 27 May 1776, bapt. 9 Jun 1776. Sponsors:
Jacob Pennihof and wife Sara.
Johannes, of Adam Rau and Susana, birthdate not given, bapt. 9 Jun 1776.
Sponsors: Joh. Heiser and wife Agnes.
Anna, of Joh. Huber and Catharina, b. 30 Apr 1776, bapt. 9 Jun 1776. Sponsors:
Peter Paul Deringer and wife Maria.

Barbara, of James Pegnam (English) and Maria, b. 17 Apr 1776, bapt. 11 Jun 1776. Sponsors: Andr. Bauer and wife Barbara.

Johannes, of Bernhard Kaufman and Anna Marg., b. 12 May 1776, bapt. 13 Jun 1776. Sponsors: Joh. Müller and wife Maria.

Maria, of Joh. Müller and Maria, b. 19 Aug 1775, bapt. 13 Jun 1776. Sponsors: Joh. Haubinsac and sister Barb.

Georg, of Georg Kinzinger and Catharina, b. 6 Jun 1776, bapt. 14 Jun 1776. Sponsors: the parents.

Juliana, of Gabriel Steinbach and Christina, b. 24 Apr 1776, bapt. 10 Jun 1776. Sponsors: Mich. Fischer and Julianna Dill(in).

Wilhelm, of Georg Lange and Susanna, b. 7 Jun 1776, bapt. 16 Jun 1776. Sponsors: Wilh. Lehman and wife Elis.

Maria Doroth., of Joh. Gresel and Cathar., b. 27 Mar 1776, bapt. 16 Jun 1776. Sponsors: the father, and Elisabet Weil(in).

Thomas, of Nicol. Diel and Maria, 10 miles from here, b. 20 Apr 1776, bapt. 16 Jun 1776. Sponsors: the parents.

Cathar., of Wilh. Burkhart and Cathar., b. 9 May 1776, bapt. 20 Jun 1776. Sponsors: Adam Pfister and wife Cath.

Magdal., of Joh. Hahn and Anna Magdalena, b. 15 Jun 1776, bapt. 26 Jun 1776. Sponsors: Maria Magd. Wenz(in) and Gabriel Kern (a tailor).

Elisabet, of Elisabet Wilt and reportedly Andr. Kennedy, b. 24 Feb 1774, bapt. 27 Jun 1776. Sponsor: Maria Wilt(in).

Johann Jacob, of Martin Hertel and Margareta, b. 21 Jun 1776, bapt. 30 Jun 1776. Sponsors: Jacob Scheppach and wife Ursula.

Barbara, of Adam Schmidt and Catharina, b. 10 Jun 1776, bapt. 30 Jun 1776. Sponsors: Jacob Seier and wife Mar. Barbara.

Salome Elis., of Georg Phil. Weisman and Catharina, b. 7 Jun 1776, bapt. 30 Jun 1776. Sponsors: Georg Bechtel and wife Elis.

Wilhelm, of Peter Arnold and Maria, b. 24 Apr 1776, bapt. 30 Jun 1776. Sponsors: the father, and the grandmother Cath. Buller?.

Elisabeth, of Will. Pontey (English) and Anna, b. 5 Jun 1776, bapt. 5 Jul 1776. Sponsors: the parents.

Elisabet, of Joh. Banes and Catharina (both bakers?), b. 30 May 1776, bapt. 6 Jul 1776. Sponsors: the parents.

Maria Whitaker, John Whitaker's wife, bapt. 4 Jul 1776.

An. Marg., of Friedr. Wilt and Anna, b. 1 Feb 1776, bapt. 7 Jul 1776. Sponsors: Joh. Weidman and [wife] Anna Marg.

Maria Esther, of Daniel Wiehal and Johanna, b. 8 Jul 1775, bapt. 7 Jul 1776. Sponsors: Johannes Rohr and wife Mar. Christina.

Joh. Georg, of Jacob Kriesemeier and Magdalena, b. 1 Jul 1776, bapt. 12 Jul 1776. Sponsors: the grandfather Georg Kriesemeier and wife Anna Margareta.

Elisabeth, of Michael Albrecht and Juliana, bapt. 14 Jul 1776. Sponsors: Joh. Haas and wife Elisabeth.

Hanna, of Abel Jones and Rosina, b. 12 Apr 1776, bapt. 14 Jul 1776. Sponsors: the parents.

William, of William Turner and Susanna, b. 14 Dec 1775, bapt. 18 Jul 1776. Sponsor: Sara Bakeoven.

Adam, of Adam Molitor and Anna Margareta, b. 8 Jul 1776, bapt. 18 Jul 1776. Sponsors: the parents.

Anna Marg., of Georg Milteberger and Anna Catharina, b. 28 Apr 1776, bapt. 17 Jul 1776. Sponsors: the father and mother.

Cathar., of Michael Hotz and Catharina, b. 8 Jul 1776, bapt. 21 Jul 1776. Sponsors: Martin Kiensle and wife Maria, and Peter Dick's wife (name not given).

Maria, of Georg Feitenberger and Elisabeth, b. 20 Jul 1776, bapt. 20 Jul 1776. Sponsors: the mothe,r and Juliana Dick(in).

Joh. Friedrich, of Mich. Omensetter and Catharina, b. 28 Jun 1776, bapt. 21 Jul 1776. Sponsors: Cath. Reich(in) and Joh. Friedr. Vogel.

Ludwig, of Ludw. Degen and Eva, b. 30 Jan 1776, bapt. 21 Jul 1776. Sponsors: the parents.

An. Maria, of Joh. Fischer and Anna Maria, b. 30 Jun 1776, bapt. 21 Jul 1776. Sponsors: the parents.

Joh. Jacob, of Jacob Specht and Margar., b. 15 May 1776, bapt. 21 Jul 1776. Sponsors: Georg Specht and wife Anna Marg.

Johannes, of Jacob Ries and Magdalene, b. 10 Jul 1776, bapt. 22 Jul 1776. Sponsors: the parents.

Regina, of David Kübler and Margar., b. 27 Mar 1775, bapt. 22 Jul 1776. Sponsors: the parents.

Jacob, of Joh. Harvay and Anna Marg., b. in Sep 1775, bapt. 25 Jul 1776. Sponsors: the parents.

Georg, of Gottfried Henrich and Catharina, b. 29 Jun 1776, bapt. 27 Jul 1776. Sponsors: Georg Volker and wife Barbara.

Jacob, of Jacob Biegler and Catharina, b. 16 Jul 1776, bapt. 28 Jul 1776. Sponsors: Henr. Sackman and wife Christ. Marg.

Joh. Jac., of Joh. Wudeling and Anna Clara, b. in Apr 1776, bapt. 26 Jul 1776. Sponsors: Joh. Martin Ricker and Ann. Cathr. Schlatter(in).

Johannes, of Joh. Fügel. Schulm and Margareta, b. 22 Jul 1776, bapt. 28 Jul 1776. Sponsors: Joh. Wucherer and Elis. Roht(in), both single.

Adam, of Adolph Dill and Catharine, b. 29 Jun 1776, bapt. 28 Jul 1776. Sponsors: Adam Seibert and Sabina Keitebach(in).

Johann Ludwig, of Johann David Huber and Anna, b. 25 Jul 1776, bapt. 28 Jul 1776. Sponsors: the father and grandmother Margareta Huber(in).

Jonathan, of John Lamle and Sarah, b. 13 Feb 1776, bapt. 29 Jul 1776. Sponsor: Eva Laemle.

Elisabeth, of Henr. Hovocks (alias Hawrich) and Christina, b. 13 Jul 1776, bapt. 29 Jul 1776. Sponsors: John Firelock (or Tirelock) and wife Elisabeth (Dicklauch).

Mary, of Neamian Dunlap and Elisabeth, b. 9 Sep 1770, bapt. 26 Jul 1776. Sponsor: the mother.

Sarah, of Georg Molitor and Sarah, b. 17 May 1775, bapt. 30 Jul 1776. Sponsors: Johannes Hold and wife Mar.

Michael, of Peter Dress and Maria, b. 20 Jul 1776, bapt. 30 Jul 1776. Sponsor: the father.

Nicolaus, of Wendel Wendelin and Henrietta, b. 3 Jul 1776, bapt. 1 Aug 1776. Sponsors: Nicol. Mombauer and wife Magdalena.

Nicolaus, of Nicolaus Ulrich and Eva, b. 10 Mar 1776, bapt. 3 Aug 1776.
Sponsors: the mother, and Catharina Lang(in).

Elisab. Sabele?, of Martin Weiss and Maria, b. 11 Feb 1776, bapt. 4 Aug 1776.
Sponsor: Felix Schneider and wife (name illegible).

Johannes, of Christian Piercy (alias Piersin) and Maria, b. 21 Jul 1776, bapt.
5 Aug 1776. Sponsor: Johannes (illegible).

Sara, of Thomas Schmidt and Dorothea, b. 30 Jun 1776, bapt. 5 Aug 1776.
Sponsors: Melchior Naef and wife Magd.

Johannes, of Georg Baetsch and Catharina, b. 29 Jul 1776, bapt. 7 Aug 1776.
Sponsor: the mother.

Johann David, of William Thomas Husher and Eva Elisabeth, b. 29 Jul 1776,
bapt. 8 Aug 1776. Sponsor: Anna Elisab. Hohlwager(in).

Johannes, of Paulus Bahrdt and Regina, b. 17 Jul 1776, bapt. 9 Aug 1776.
Sponsor: Dor. Götz(in).

Georg, of Georg Bastian and Maria Eva, b. 12 Jul 1776, bapt. 10 Aug 1776.
Sponsors: Casp. Daniel Burkhard and Catharina.

Christina, of Jacob Seyfried and Mar. Salome, b. 12 Jul 1776, bapt. 11 Aug
1776. Sponsors: Joh. Jac. Seyfried and wife Christ.

Joh. Georg, of Michael Kraft and Joh[hanna] Maria, b. 15 Jul 1776, bapt.
11 Aug 1776. Sponsors: Joh. Georg Esterly and Maria Sybille.

Joh. Jacob, of Will. Aschton and Catharina, b. 16 May 1776, bapt. 4 Aug 1776.
Sponsors: Joh. Jacob Hafner and wife Barbara.

Friedrich, of Friedr. Schmidt (from the valley) and Catharine, b. 12 Mar 1776,
bapt. 10 Aug 1776. Sponsors: the parents.

Maria, of Martin Heilemann and Eva Christina, b. 4 Dec 1774, bapt. 16 Aug
1776. Sponsors: the mother, and the grandparents Michael Hermann and
wife Margareta.

Christian, of Martin Heilmann and Eva Christina, b. 14 Mar 1776, bapt. 16 Aug
1776. Sponsors: same as above..

Peter, of Peter Kraft and Margareta, b. 5 Aug 1776, bapt. 18 Aug 1776.
Sponsors: the father, and Ursula Kiemle.

Susanna, of Dietrich Schmonker and Catharina, b. 8 Aug 1776, bapt. 18 Aug
1776. Sponsors: Paul Caspar Breton and wife Susanna.

Anna Maria, of Andr. Lepp and Maria Magd., b. 13 Aug 1776, bapt. 18 Aug
1776. Sponsors: Maria Engel(in) and Henrich Wagerhorst.

Salome, of Philip Meger and Salome, b. 1 Aug 1776, bapt. 18 Aug 1776.
Sponsors: Joh. Motz and Barb. Fehm(in).

Dorothea, of Jacob Steinmeier and Cath., b. 25 Jul 1776, bapt. 18 Aug 1776.
Sponsors: the parents.

Johannes, of Joh. Bender and Susanna, b. 27 Jul 1776, bapt. 18 Aug 1776.
Sponsors: Jac. Omensetter and Elisabeth.

Johannes, of Joh. Friedr. Ulrich and Catharina, b. 14 Jul 1776, bapt. 19 Aug
1776. Sponsor: the mother, and the grandmother An. Mar. Ulrich.

Susanna, of Georg Hafner and Maria Magdalena, b. 28 Jul 1776, bapt. 21 Aug
1776. Sponsors: grandfather Joh. Georg Hafner, and maternal grandmother
Susanna Loscher(in).

Maria Barbara, of Andr. Barrenstecher and Maria, b. 16 Jul 1776, bapt. 25 Aug
1776. Sponsors: Andreas Beck and wife Maria Barbara.

Catharina, of Conr. Horf and Anna, b. 7 Jul 1776, bapt. 25 Aug 1776. Sponsors: the parents.

Johannes, of Sebastian Heiler and Elisabeth, b. 30 Jul 1776, bapt. 25 Aug 1776. Sponsors: the parents.

Elis. Cathar., of Jacob Marker and Elisabeth, b. 19 Jul 1776, bapt. 25 Aug 1776. Sponsors: Cath. Stutz(in), Elis. Tarlock, and Friedr. Stutz.

Anna Catharina, of Wilhelm Schaeff and Barbara, b. 10 Aug 1776, bapt. 10 Aug 1776. Sponsor: the grandmother Catharina Schaeff..

Joh. Jacob, of Friedr. Springer and Maria, b. 10 Aug 1776, bapt. 26 Aug 1776. Sponsors: Joh. Haaf and Barb. Schutzman(in).

Joseph, of Georg Geier and Maria, b. 4 Mar 1776, bapt. 27 Aug 1776. Sponsors: Georg Meter and wife Maria.

Doroth. Margar., of William Will and Elisabet, b. 23 Mar 1776, bapt. 31 Aug 1776. Sponsors: Joh. Bender and Margar. Kubel (or Rubel?).

Susanna Barbara, of Jacob Pennighof and Sibylla, b. 16 Jun 1776, bapt. 1 Sep 1776. Sponsors: Jacob Motz and wife Sus. Barb.

Elisabet, of Christian Obersteg and Margar., b. 27 Jul 1776, bapt. 1 Sep 1776. Sponsors: Joh. Müller and wife Elis.

Elis. Charlotta, of Conr. King and Juliana, b. 24 Jul 1776, bapt. 1 Sep 1776. Sponsors: Mich. Kenner and wife Charlotte.

Maria Cath., of Theobald Klein and Margar. (nee Falkner(in)), b. 18 Feb 1776, bapt. 1 Sep 1776. Sponsors: Georg Gertlinger and Maria Cath. Christ(in).

Joh. Ludwig, of James Baker and Christine, b. 15 Nov 1775, bapt. 1 Sep 1776. Sponsors: Ludwig Gerlinger and wife Marg. Cath. Christ(in).

Mary, of John Hook and Margar., b. 17 Nov 1771, bapt. 5 Sep 1776. Sponsors: the parents.

John, of John Hook and Margar. b. 30 Oct 1773, 1776, bapt. 5 Sep 1776. Sponsors: the parents.

Esther, of John Hook and Margar., b. 3 Aug 1775, bapt. 5 Sep 1776. Sponsors: the parents.

Jacob, of Conrad Lindner and Elisabeth, b. 25 Jul 1776, bapt. 5 Sep 1776. Sponsors: Zacharias Endres and wife Anna Maria.

Maria Elis., of Johannes Braun and Catharine, b. 15 Jun 1776, bapt. 8 Sep 1776. Sponsors: Carl Jung and sister Maria Elis. Jung(in).

An. Elis., of Philip Sorg and An. Magd., b. 26 Aug 1776, bapt. 8 Sep 1776. Sponsors: John Michael Milteberger and An. Elis. Schmidt(in).

Charlotte, of Jacob Philips and Christine, b. 6 Aug 1776, bapt. 11 Sep 1776. Sponsors: the parents.

An. Maria, of Georg Ruth (deceased) and An. Maria, b. 17 Apr 1776, bapt. 12 Sep 1776. Sponsor: the mother.

Joh. Baltz., of Sebast. Fr[anz?] Marker and Elis. Charlotte, b. 31 Aug 1776, bapt. 15 Sep 1776. Sponsors: Joh. Balt. Kiensle and wife Elis.

Catharina, of Andreas Geier and Barbara, b. 29 Aug 1776, bapt. 15 Sep 1776. Sponsors: Andr. Bosard and wife Catharina.

Samuel, of Christian Jung and Caroline, b. 27 Jul 1776, bapt. 15 Sep 1776. Sponsors: the parents.

Maria Catharine, of Henrich Mühlenberg, Jr., (preacher here) and Catharine, b. 2 Sep 1776, bapt. 15 Sep 1776. Sponsors: the grandparents Philip Hall and wife Susanna Cathar., and Henr. Muhlenberg, Sr. and [wife] Maria.

Jacob, of Jacob Schwab and Maria, b. 28 Aug 1776, bapt. 15 Sep 1776. Sponsors: the parents.

Elisabet, of Christian Schaefer and Dorothea, b. 12 Jun 1776, bapt. 15 Sep 1776. Sponsors: David Eberhard and wife Elisabeth.

Elisab., of Christoph Wilpert and Marg., b. 4 Aug 1776, bapt. 15 Sep 1776. Sponsors: Jacob Schoch and Elis. Warner.

Christoph, of Johann Georg Fink and Dorothea, b. 9 Aug 1776, bapt. 15 Sep 1776. Sponsor: Christoph Haensmann and wife Barbara.

Albertina Philippina, of Paul Hofmann and Regina, b. 28 Aug 1776, bapt. 15 Sep 1776. Sponsor: Albertina Philippina Kochen__.

Johannes, of Christian Nagel and Elisabeth, b. 16 Sep 1776, bapt. 18 Sep 1776. Sponsors: the parents.

Heinrich, of Georg Christoph Reinhold and Maria, b. 16 Jun 1776, bapt. 22 Sep 1776. Sponsors: Henr. Weinkauf and wife Elisab.

Daniel, of John Henerton and Hanna, b. 14 May 1776, bapt. 21 Sep 1776. Sponsors: Conrad Ring and wife Juliana.

Joh. Adam, of Friedr. Mock and Maria, b. 18 Jul 1776, bapt. 22 Sep 1776. Sponsors: Tobias Koenig and wife Barbara.

A child (name not given), of Nicolaus Hinkel and Susan., b. 8 Mar 1776, bapt. 22 Sep 1776. Sponsors: Christian Gally and wife Margar.

Michael, of Joh. Kensel and Marg., b. 11 Sep 1776, bapt. 22 Sep 1776. Sponsors: Michael Stricker and wife Marg.

Cornelia, of Christlieb Baerdling and Elisabeth, b. 18 Aug 1776, bapt. 22 Sep 1776. Sponsors: the parents.

Georg Friedr., of Joh. Jac. Schwer? and Maria, b. 16 Aug 1776, bapt. 22 Sep 1776. Sponsors: Georg Friedrich Boier and wife Elisab. Margaret.

Cath., of Henr. Apfel and Christine, b. 9 Sep 1776, bapt. 22 Sep 1776. Sponsors: Cath. Knoblauch(in) and Adam Knoblauch.

Child (name not given), of Joh. Fries (mother's name and child's birthdate not given). Sponsors: Thomas Meier and wife Margar.

Jacob, of Abr. Bachmann and Philippina, b. 17 Sep 1776, bapt. 24 Sep 1776. Sponsors: Caspar Graf and wife (name not given).

Henrich, of Philip Reibold and Veronica, b. 20 Sep 1776, bapt. 28 Sep 1776. Sponsors: Henr. Fauns and wife Veronica.

Mar. Elisab., of Christoph Zimmerman and Catharina, b. 16 Sep 1776, bapt. 29 Sep 1776. Sponsors: Henrich Lies and wife Anna Maria.

Elisabet, of Ludw. Bender and Margaretha, b. 31 Aug 1776, bapt. 28 Sep 1776. Sponsors: Jacob Bender and wife Dorothea.

Anna, of Jacob Petrie (deceased) and Rosina, b. 1 Sep 1776, bapt. 29 Sep 1776. Sponsors: Samuel Fromberger and wife Anna.

Catharina, of Caspar Schneider and Elisabeth, b. 7 Sep 1776, bapt. 29 Sep 1776. Sponsors: Adolph Dill and wife Catharina.

Elisabeth, of Peter Wagner and Rosina, b. 10 Sep 1776, bapt. 29 Sep 1776. Sponsors: Isaac Stahl and Elisabeth Fleisch(in).

Elisabeth, of Anthony Billig and Catharina, b. 27 Aug 1776, bapt. 29 Sep 1776. Sponsors: Georg Sei[t]z and wife Elisabeth.

Johanna, of Adam Widderstein and Sophia, b. 8 Sep 1776, bapt. 29 Sep 1776. Sponsors: John Widderstein and wife Anna Elis.

Jacob, of Johann Georg Hesler and Hanna, b. 28 Sep 1776, bapt. 3 Oct 1776. Sponsors: Jacob Seger and wife Barbara.

Christian Georg, of Georg Simon Brun and Elisabeth, b. 2 Oct 1776, bapt. 6 Oct 1776. Sponsors: Christian Kalkbrenner and (illegible).

Jacob, of Samuel Prenz and Anna, b. 20 Sep 1776, bapt. 6 Oct 1776. Sponsor: the parents, and Sophia Hirneisen.

Samuel, of Michael Kuhn and Anna Maria, b. 7 Sep 1776, Oct 6, 1776. Sponsors: the parents.

Jacob, of Arnold Becker and Elisabeth, b. 21 Aug 1776, bapt. 6 Oct 1776. Sponsors: Johannes Biegler and wife Anna Cathar.

Elisabeth, of Johannes Grabel and Christine, b. 14 Sep 1776, bapt. 6 Oct 1776. Sponsors: Mich. Kaerner and wife Anna Maria.

Dorothea Elisabeth, of Henrich Denzel and Maria, b. 20 Jun 1776, bapt. 6 Oct 1776. Sponsors: Adam Widderstein and wife Sophia Charlotte.

Joh. Georg, of Eberhard Diel and Catharine, b. 2 Oct 1776, bapt. 8 Oct 1776. Sponsors: the parents.

Esther, of Andreas Keppele and Maria, b. 16 Sep 1776, bapt. 10 Oct 1776. Sponsors: the father, and the grandmother Esther Meier(in).

Anton, of Martin Noll and Elisab. Barbara, b. 24 Aug 1776, bapt. 11 Oct 1776. Sponsors: Michael Campfer and wife Susannae

Catharine, of Joh. Jacob and Anna Maria, b. 18 Aug 1776, bapt. in Oct 1776. Sponsors: Jacob Walter and wife Catharine.

Catharina Elisabeth, of Joh. Christoph Kun[t]z (preacher here) and Margareta Henrietta, b. 4 Oct 1776, bapt. 13 Oct 1776. Sponsors: Henrich Muhlenberg, Sr., Eva Elisabeth Schul[t]z(in), and Mar. Cathar. Muhlenberg.

Joh. David, of Joh. Bast and Elisabeth, b. 29 Jun 1776, bapt. 14 Oct 1776. Sponsors: David Uber and wife Anna.

Maria, of Joh. Rusk and Cathar., b. 29 May 1776, bapt. 14 Oct 1776. Sponsors: Jacob Wolf and Maria Strehl(in).

Mar. Sabina, of Georg Gutel, b. 7 Oct 1776, bapt. 14 Oct 1776. Sponsors: Martin Rab and [wife] Sabina.

Johann Jacob, of Philipp Trucker and Catharina, b. 4 Oct 1776, bapt. 19 Oct 1776. Sponsors: Johann Jacob Schwefel and wife Elisab.

Valentin, of Valent. Bartholomais and Margar., b. 10 Sep 1776, bapt. 19 Oct 1776. Sponsors: Christian Letter? and wife Cath.

Georg, of J. Bauer and Barbara, b. 6 Oct 1776, bapt. 20 Oct 1776. Sponsors: Mich. Scheneck and wife Catharine.

Christine, of Wilh. Ritter and Catharine, b. 10 Aug 1776, bapt. 14 Sep 1776. Sponsors: Wilh. Rediger and wife Christine.

Margar., of Wilhelm Ritter and Catharina, b. 1 May 1774, bapt. 14 Sep 1776. Sponsor: Margar. Schwanseler(in).

Sara Elis., of Joh. Hinkel and Christine, b. 1 Sep 1776, bapt. 29 Sep 1776. Sponsors: the parents.

Johannes, of Daniel Naumann and Maria, b. 14 Oct 1776, bapt. 20 Oct 1776. Sponsors: Johannes Liebricht and wife Catharina.

Maria, of Lorenz Schwab and Margareta, b. 2 Oct 1776, bapt. 20 Oct 1776. Sponsors: Christoph Ra[t]z and wife Margareta.

Maria, of Martin Hermstadt and Nancy, b. 23 Jan 1776, bapt. 20 Oct 1776. Sponsors: the father, and Maria Barb. Hermstadt.

Maria, of Georg Heil and Dorothea, b. 23 Oct 1776, bapt. 23 Oct 1776. Sponsors: Johannes Heil and wife Maria.

Mar. Barbara, of Peter Mehrling and Mar. Dorothea, b. 10 Oct 1776, bapt. 20 Oct 1776. Sponsors: Vobar Friebly and wife Mar. Barbara.

Joh. Christian, of Valent Gasner and Maria, b. 9 Aug 1774, bapt. 21 Oct 1776. Sponsor: the grandmother Maria Rein(in).

Joh. Michael, of Joh. Fischer (deceased) and Regina, b. 12 Oct 1776, bapt. 20 Oct 1776. Sponsors: Mich. Götz and wife Maria.

Jacob, of Georg Schenck and Barbara, b. 10 Sep 1776, bapt. 21 Oct 1776. Sponsors: Georg Knerr and wife Barb.

Joseph, of Joseph Todd and Elisabet, b. 20 Jan 1775, bapt. 21 Oct 1776. Sponsors: the parents.

Anna Mar., of Joh. Weger and Sarah, b. 4 Aug 1776, bapt. 24 Oct 1776. Sponsors: Philip Weger and wife Anna Maria.

Ann. Marg., of Peter Gabel and Elisabet, b. 20 Sep 1776, bapt. 27 Oct 1776. Sponsors: Valentin Hagner and wife Ann. Marg.

Jacob, of Georg Henr. Meier and Eva Christ., b. 23 Sep 1776, bapt. 27 Oct 1776. Sponsors: Jacob Meier and wife Maria.

Samuel, of Abel Lippencot (deceased) and Catharina, b. 20 Jul 1776, bapt. 26 Oct 1776. Sponsors: the mother, and Sophia Wister.

Elisabeth, of Andr. Erdmanleiner and Rosina, b. 2 Oct 1776, bapt. 27 Oct 1776. Sponsors: Johannes Wacker and [wife] Elisab. Rosina.

Elisab., of Joh. Bach and Elisabeth, b. 21 Sep 1776, bapt. 27 Oct 1776. Sponsors: the parents.

Elisabet, of Joh. Gott. Steinbacher and Maria Cath., b. 29 Aug 1776, bapt. 27 Oct 1776. Sponsors: Georg Fuggerod and wife Elisabet.

Ann, of Thom. Jones and Mary, b. 10 Oct 1776, bapt. 27 Oct 1776. Sponsors: the parents.

Regina, of John Baker and Regina, b. 26 Oct 1776, bapt. 28 Oct 1776. Sponsor: the grandmother (name not given).

Gottfried, of Steph. Sulger and Johanna, b. 26 Oct 1776, bapt. 1 Nov 1776. Sponsors: the parents, and Anna Maria Brecht(in).

Carl, of Carl Bauman and Maria, b. 21 Oct 1776, bapt. 9 Nov 1776. Sponsor: Joh. Strup and wife Rahel.

Regina, of Casp. Grubel and Sara, b. 2 Sep 1776, bapt. 2 Nov 1776. Sponsors: Adam Widderstein and wife Sophia Charlotte.

Mar. Marg., of Valent. Hofman and Susan., b. 27 Oct 1776, bapt. 3 Nov 1776. Sponsors: Mich. Zinger and wife Mar. Marg.

Eva Maria, of Peter Geiger and An. Maria, b. 22 Oct 1776, bapt. 3 Nov 1776. Sponsors: Maria Magd. Abel(in) and Jacob Kuhn.

Elisabet, of Jacob Duffene and Maria, b. 22 Oct 1776, bapt. 3 Nov 1776. Sponsors: Andr. Klein and wife Elis.

Margar., of Ad. Scheffer and Doroth., b. 15 Oct 1776, bapt. 3 Nov 1776.
Sponsors: the parents.
Elisab., of Joh. Peter Schull and Elisabeth Marg., b. 28 Oct 1776, bapt. 3 Nov
1776. Sponsors: Elisabet Schneider(in) and Maria Felix.
Elisabet, of Joh. Chapman and Veronica, b. 4 Jul 1776, bapt. 3 Nov 1776.
Sponsors: the father, and Ros. Marg. Gerrick(in).
Joh. Michael, of Georg Weideman and wife Eva, b. 8 Oct 1776, bapt. 3 Nov
1776. Sponsors: Joh. Michael Hocher and Gottfried Hager.
Georg, of William Stewart and Juliana, b. 8 Oct 1776, bapt. 3 Nov 1776.
Sponsors: William Stewart and Margaret Sonleitner.
Cath. Margar., of Daniel Coller and Margaretha, b. 4 Mar 1776, bapt. 4 Nov
1776. Sponsors: Carl Baumann and wife Maria.
Anthony, of John Pierce and Mary, b. 29 Oct 1776, bapt. 4 Nov 1776.
Sponsors: Anthony Gilbert and wife Elisabet.
Johannes, of Henr. Schlesmann and Cathar., b. 21 Sep 1776, bapt. 7 Nov 1776.
Sponsors: the parents.
Peter Ervin, of Peter Hopkins and Mary, b. 7 Jul 1776, bapt. 7 Nov 1776.
Sponsors: the parents.
Joseph Henr., of Georg Jac. Jung and Rosina, b. 3 Sep 1776, bapt. 10 Nov 1776.
Sponsors: Henr. Mock and wife Sara.
Christine, of Lorenz Mohr and An. Maria, b. 31 Aug 1776, bapt. 10 Nov 1776.
Sponsors: Caspar Strupel and Catharine Strubel.
Philipp, of Philip Heger and An. Cath., birthdate not given, bapt. 10 Nov 1776.
Sponsors: Philipp Reibold and wife Veronica.
Christ. Mar., of James Wharton and Christine, b. 17 Jun 1776, bapt. 10 Nov
1776. Sponsor: Mrs. Seiba__cht(in).
Mar. Elisab., of Casp. Graef and Susanne, b. 20 Oct 1776, bapt. 10 Nov 1776.
Sponsors: Joh. Graef and Maria Elisab. Mauss(in).
Maria, of Jacob Jung and Margar., b. 15 Oct 1776, bapt. 10 Nov 1776.
Sponsors: Jacob Schmidt and sister Maria.
Cathar., of Joh. Harrison and Margar., b. 24 Oct 1776, bapt. 10 Nov 1776.
Sponsors: Conrad Miller and wife Cath.
Catharine, of Johan Bernhold and Maria, b. 6 Nov 1776, bapt. 12 Nov 1776.
Sponsor: Cath. Altberger.
Elisabeth, of Elias Albrecht and Cathar., b. 30 Dec 1775, bapt. 13 Nov 1776.
Sponsors: the parents, and Elis. Risch(in).
Barbara, of Johann Kehl and Margareta, b. 11 Nov 1776, bapt. 13 Nov 1776.
Sponsors: Joh. Georg Leuter and wife Barbara.
Elisabeth, of Michael Albrecht and Juliana, b. 31 Dec 1775, bapt. 6 Nov 1776.
Sponsors: Johannes Haas and wife Elisabeth.
Michael, of Mich. Frey and Maria, b. 2 Nov 1776, bapt. 17 Nov 1776.
Sponsors: Mich. Rehm and wife Eva.
Maria, of Peter Werner and Eva, b. 12 Oct 1776, bapt. 17 Nov 1776. (Sponsors
not given.)
Elisabet, of Michael Grof and Marg., b. 19 Oct 1776, bapt. 7 Nov 1776.
Sponsors: Elisabet Bartho[w] and husband Wilhelm.
An. Barbara, of Joh. Hartman and Maria, b. 30 Oct 1776, bapt. 17 Nov 1776.
Sponsors: Will. Beil and wife Anna Barb.

Michael, of Anton Hecht and Sophia, b. 13 Nov 1776, bapt. 17 Nov 1776.
Sponsors: Friedr. Schick and wife Eva Barb.

Catharine, of "Mr." Sigm[und] Kühle and Margar., b. 25 Oct 1776, bapt. 17 Nov
1776. Sponsors: the parents, and Cath. Schaef (single).

Salome, of John Witcraft and Hanna, b. 18 Mar 1776, bapt. 17 Nov 1776.
Sponsors: Johann Georg Haaser? and wife Sophia.

Conrad, of Andr. Rath and An. Maria, b. 19 Oct 1776, bapt. 17 Nov 1776.
Sponsors: the parents.

Maria, of Joh. Aesch and Margareta, b. 2 Nov 1776, bapt. 17 Nov 1776.
Sponsors: Jac. Aesch and wife Lovina.

Joh. Jacob, of Joh. Nic. Wendeling and Cath., b. 27 Aug 1776, bapt. 19 Nov
1776. Sponsors: Joh. Jac. Grauan and [wife] Anna Albertine.

Joh. Friedr., of Martin Menold and Rosina, b. 17 Oct 1776, bapt. 21 Nov 1776.
Sponsors: the parents.

Mar. Magd., of Peter Jung and Mar. Magd., b. 2 Nov 1776, bapt. 24 Nov 1776.
Sponsors: Conr. Scheller and wife Elis.

Jacob, of Joh. Georg Reininger and Catharina, b. 22 Nov 1776, bapt. 24 Nov
1776. Sponsors: Jacob Merker and wife Elisabeth.

Johan, of Jacob Klauss and Margar., b. 24 Nov 1776, bapt. 25 Nov 1776.
Sponsors: the parents.

Margaret, of Georg Mallo and Elisabet, b. 9 Oct 1776, bapt. 29 Nov 1776.
Sponsors: the father, and Maria Cath. Wein(in).

Margar., of Henr. Dasbe? and Regina, b. 25 Nov 1776, bapt. 30 Nov 1776.
Sponsor: Marg. Das(in)?.

Andreas, of Paul Fügner and Rebecca, b. 15 Nov 1776, bapt. 1 Dec 1776.
Sponsors: Andreas Fügner, Sr., and wife Sophia Agatha.

An. Eva, of Joh. Bauman and Elisabeth, b. 19 Nov 1776, bapt. 1 Dec 1776.
Sponsors: Christoph. Meier and Anna Eva.

Philip, of Christian Haag and Anna, b. 30 Nov 1776, bapt. 1 Dec 1776.
Sponsors: the parents, and Elis. Grabel.

Elisabeth, of Wilhelm Eckard and Maria, b. 5 Nov 1776, bapt. 4 Dec 1776
Sponsors: the parents.

Margar., of Christ. Fuchs and Dorothea, b. 24 Nov 1776, bapt. 4 Dec 1776.
Sponsors: the parents.

Phil. Jacob, of Michael Immel and Cath., b. 8 Nov 1776, bapt. 4 Dec 1776.
Sponsors: Phil. Jacob Marsteller and wife (name not given).

Mary Elis., of Joseph Benk and Catharine, b. 10 Nov 1776, bapt. 8 Dec 1776.
Sponsor: Elis. Gerlach.

Georg, of Joh. Fischer and Catharine, b. 23 Jul 1776, bapt. 8 Dec 1776.
Sponsors: the parents.

Susanna [twin], of Sebastian Schweckard and Agnes Maria, b. 7 Dec 1776, bapt.
10 Dec 1776. Sponsors: Conrad Rosch and wife Susanna.

Anna [twin], of Sebastian Schweckard and Agnes Maria, b. 7 Dec 1776, bapt.
10 Dec 1776. Sponsors: the father, and Anna Schaber(in).

John, of John Guse and Catharine, b. 1 Dec 1776, bapt. 11 Dec 1776. Sponsors:
the parents.

Johannes, of Jacob Pechtel and Susanna, b. 29 Nov 1776, bapt. 11 Dec 1776.
Sponsor: the mother.

Johannes, of Conrad Schaefer and Agatha, b. 29 Oct 1776, bapt. 11 Dec 1776. Sponsor: the grandmother Anna Maria Schaefer.

Margareta, of Emanuel Meisterzim and Ann. Margaret, b. 21 Sep 1776, bapt. 11 Dec 1776. Sponsors: the mother, and David Ott.

Joseph, of William Worther? and Jane, b. 16 Nov 1776, bapt. 12 Dec 1776. Sponsors: the mother, the pastor, and Mr. Dav. Ott.

Mary, of Robert Humphreys and Ann, b. 10 Apr 1776, bapt. 12 Dec 1776. Sponsors: the mother, and Margareta S___ (the pastor's sister).

Anna Susanna, of Johannes Kling and Anna Margaret, b. 11 Nov 1776, bapt. 13 Dec 1776. Sponsors: the parents.

Christoph, of Joh. Georg Seifferheld and Christina, b. 8 Dec 1776, bapt. 15 Dec 1776. Sponsors: Christoph Weidner and wife Maria.

Catharina, of Johann Steinme[t]z and Maria, b. 8 Sep 1776, bapt. 15 Dec 1776. Sponsors: the parents.

Maria, of Samuel Bryan and Barbara, b. 20 Jul 1776, bapt. 15 Dec 1776. Sponsor: the mother, and Johannes Lampe.

Maria, of Georg Zindler and Clara Maria, b. 12 Oct 1774, bapt. 17 Dec 1776. Sponsors: David Ott (the pastor), and Phil. Fischer.

Elisabeth, of Christoph Jung and Margareta, b. 28 Nov 1776, bapt. 22 Dec 1776. Sponsors: Christian Jung and wife Carolina.

Johann Peter, of Leonard Eltlin and Elisabeth, b. 16 Dec 1776, bapt. 22 Dec 1776. Sponsors: Peter Hahn and wife Cathar.

Elisabeth, of Georg Klein and Elisabeth, b. 17 Dec 1776, bapt. 22 Dec 1776. Sponsor: widow Eva Maria Klein(in).

Joh. Andreas, of Joh. Andreas Rohr and Maria Christina, b. 7 Dec 1776, bapt. 29 Dec 1776. Sponsors: the parents.

Sophia, of Andreas Baider and Barbara, b. 16 Dec 1776, bapt. 29 Dec 1776. Sponsors: the parents.

Simon, of Joh. Greifenstein and Dorothea, b. 16 Dec 1776, bapt. 29 Dec 1776. Sponsors: Simon Heitel and Barbara Roner(in)..

Johann, of Johann Mills and Elisabeth, b. 24 Dec 1776, bapt. 28 Dec 1776. Sponsors: Peter Mahn and wife Maria.

Daniel, of Daniel Ernst and Catharine, b. 20 Sep 1774, bapt. 29 Dec 1776. Sponsors: Andr. Sommer and Anna.

Elisabet, of Daniel Ernst and Catharine, b. 17 Oct 1776, bapt. 29 Dec 1776. Sponsors: same as above.

Sara, of Andr. Sommer and Anna, b. 30 Nov 1776, bapt. 29 Dec 1776. Sponsors: Conr. Schlatter and wife Christina.

Francis, of James Bowizer and Rosanna, b. 22 Jan 1776, bapt. 29 Dec 1776. Sponsors: the parents.

Maria, of David Knies and Clara, b. 6 Dec 1776, bapt. 31 Dec 1776. Sponsors: the parents.

1777, First List
(baptisms by pastor Kunze, from Book III)
Beginning this year, pastor Muhlenberg, Jr., made his baptism and other entries separately in Book IV, while pastor Kunze continued to use Book III. For the first four months of 1777, however, Muhlenberg's baptisms from Book IV were

copied also into Book III (along with Kunze's). The following list consists of all the baptisms in 1777 from Book III. {The entries that were duplicated in Book IV are marked here by asterisks: in some cases Muhlenberg's entries in Book IV differed slightly in detail from the "duplicates" in Book III; such differences are indicated here in curly brackets.}

*Jacob, of Hartman Lauer and Elisabet, b. 14 Nov 1776, bapt. 6 Jan 1777. Sponsor: Anna Mauer(in).

Johannes, of Doct[or] Thorn Bond (deceased) and Maria Roner(in), b. 3 Jan 1777, bapt. 6 Jan 1777. Sponsor: Barbara Roner(in).

Joh. Jacob, of Jacob Eckfeld and Elisabeth, b. 2 Jan 1777, bapt. 7 Jan 1777. Sponsors: the parents.

Joh. Jacob, of Jacob Ki[t]z and Elisabeth, b. 27 Dec 1776, bapt. 7 Jan 1777. Sponsors: the father, and the grandmother Apoll[onia] Ki[t]z(in).

Regina, of Gottfried Rap and Elisabeth, b. 10 Dec 1776, bapt. 7 Jan 1777. Sponsors: Melchior Naef and wife Margareta.

*Mathaeus, of Jacob Ruhl {Rühl} and Catharine, b. 6 Dec 1776, bapt. 7 Jan 1777. Sponsor: Mathaeus Kraemer.

*Georg Lorenz, of Joh. Jaeger and Maria, b. 22 Dec 1776, bapt. 12 Jan 1777. Sponsors: Georg Lor. Gasner and Susan. Fidler(in).

*Georg, of Georg Bachhol[t]z and Veronica, b. 5 Dec 1776, bapt. 3 Jan 1777. Sponsors: Joh. Unangst and wife Cath{ar}.

*Joh. Henr{ich}, of A{dam} Bauer and Anna Maria, b. in Dec 1776, bapt. 12 Jan 1777. Sponsors: the parents, and Elis. Wenz.

*Catharine, of Joh. Breakfield and Anna Maria, b. 4 Jan 1777, bapt. 12 Jan 1777. Sponsors: Math. Volking and wife (not named).

Elisabeth, of Thomas Hall and Hanna, b. 20 Oct 1776, bapt. 19 Jan 1777. Sponsors: Joh. Braun and the mother's sister Elisab. Jung(in).

Maria Anna, of Johann Jac. Hauser and Elisabeth, b. 28 Dec 1776, bapt. 29 Jan 1777. Sponsors: Phil. Kunzmann and Maria Ann Bender(in).

Charles, of John Cartright and Catharine, b. 6 Jan 1777, bapt. 19 Jan 1777. Sponsors: Charles Grier and wife (name not given).

Johannes, of Joh. Felteberger and Magdalene, b. 19 Jan 1777, bapt. 19 Jan 1777. Sponsors: Anton Otman and wife (name not given).

Maria, of Samuel Humphreys and Nancy, b. 16 Feb 1776, bapt. 19 Jan 1777. Sponsor: Christian Kuns.

*Peter, of Math. Ros and Susanne, b. 21 Jan 1777, bapt. 26 Jan 1777. Sponsors: Math. Müller and G{ertr}. Whit(in).

*Philipp, of Joh. Griess and Barbara, b. 6 Jan 1776, bapt. 26 Jan 1777. Sponsors: Phil{ip} Wurm and wife Maria.

Adam, of Adam Stork and Elisabeth, b. 7 Jan 1777, bapt. 2 Feb 1777. Sponsors: the father, and the grandmother Catharina Stork(in).

Johann Jacob, of Michael Schoeneck and Anna Catharina, birthdate not given, bapt. 2 Feb 1777. Sponsors: Adam Holt and wife Mar. Christina.

Jacob, of Jacob Sulger and Margarete, b. 22 Jan 1777, bapt. 2 Feb 1777. Sponsors: the parents.

Christian Carl, of Ehrhard Giebelhaus and Maria Barbara, b. 29 Jan 1777, bapt. 2 Feb 1777. Sponsors: Christian Carl Jung and wife Maria Dor.

Anna Elisabeth, of Michael Goe[t]z and Maria, b. 16 Dec 1776, bapt. 2 Feb 1777. Sponsors: the father, and Cath. Weber(in).
Maria Magdalene, of Carl Muller and Catharina Magd., b. 12 Jan 1777, bapt. 3 Feb 1777. Sponsors: the parents.
*Elisabet, of Philip Schmidt and Elisabeth, b. 11 Jan 1777, bapt. 3 Feb 1777. Sponsors: the parents.
*Elisabet, of Eberh{ard} Leitenberger and Elisabet, b. 27 Nov 1776, bapt. 3 Feb 1777. Sponsors: the parents.
Joh. Friedrich, of Jacob Keimle and Christina Catharina, b. 17 Jan 1777, bapt. 5 Feb 1777. Sponsors: the father, and Ursula Barbara Keimle.
Margareta Lydia, of Georg Leib and Dorothea, b. 15 Jan 1777, bapt. 6 Feb 1777. Sponsors: Johann Chr. Kunze and wife Henr. Margar.
*Joh. Georg, of Martin Reisser and Catharine, b. 29 Jan 1777, bapt. 9 Feb 1777. Sponsors: Joh. Berend and wife Barbara.
Elisabeth, of Henrich Steller and Anna Margaret, b. 21 Jan 1777, bapt. 9 Feb 1777. Sponsors: Wilh. Beatho and wife Elisa.
Johannes, of Christian Kuhn and Mar., b. 20 Jan 1777, bapt. 9 Feb 1777. Sponsors: Johann Boecle and wife Margareta.
*Benjamin, of Michael Schumacher and Susanna, b. 22 Jan 1777, bapt. 9 Feb 1777. Sponsors: the parents.
Flora Rosina, of Henr. Michael Demer and Maria Jacobina, b. 1 Feb 1777, bapt. 9 Feb 1777. Sponsors: Christian Woelke and Rosina Schumacher(in).
*Doroth{ea} Elis., of Carl Friedr. Henschel and Anna Doroth., b. 4 Feb 1777, bapt. 12 Feb 1777. Sponsors: Christian Hero and wife Charlotte Louise.
*Catharine, of Andreas Bettinger and Catharine, b. 27 Jan 1777, bapt. 16 Feb 1777. Sponsors: Gott{lieb} Spannagel and wife Catharina.
*Marg. Dorothea, of Joh. Carl Preis and Magdalene, b. 16 Dec 1776, bapt. 16 Feb 1777. Sponsors: Georg Streper and wife Dorothea.
*Samuel, of Thomas Truck and Mary, b. 15 Dec 1776, bapt. 16 Feb 1777. Sponsors: the parents.
Catharina, of Philipp Steuber (deceased) and Margareta, b. 4 Apr 1767, bapt. 16 Feb 1777. Sponsors: Michael Steuber, Valent. Ulrich?, and Ant. Lechber.
Philipp, of Philipp Steuber (deceased) and Margareta, b. in 1770, bapt. 16 Feb 1777. Sponsor: Michael Steuber.
Christina, of Philipp Steuber (deceased) and Margareta, b. in 1773, bapt. 16 Feb 1777. Sponsor: Michael Steuber.
Barbara, of Mich. Steuber (son of the deceased Philipp Steuber, above) and Magdalena, b. in 1777, bapt. 16 Feb 1777.
*Elisab., of Friedr. Greiner and Elisabet, b. 15 Feb 1777, bapt. 16 Feb 1777. Sponsors: the parents.
*Wilhelm, of Henr. Fuhr and An. Elis., b. 30 Jan 1777, bapt. 23 Feb 1777. Sponsors: Wilh. Friedrich and wife Cath.
*Sus. Cath{ar}., of Dieter Bicking {Picking} and {Elisab.}, {b. 8 Jan 1777, bapt. 30 Jan 1777}. Sponsors: Phil{ip} Hall and wife {Sus. Cath.}.
*Christoph, of Joh. Flory (Catholic) and Elisab., b. 28 Jan 1777, bapt. 23 Feb 1777. Sponsors: the mother, and Adam Rockenberger.
*Mar{ia} Barbara, of Adam Mentzer {Menser} and Rosine, b. 22 Jan 1777, bapt. 22 Feb 1777. Sponsors: the father, and Barb. Rein(in).

*Philip, of Philip Benn and Rosine, b. 13 Sep 1776, bapt. 23 Feb 1777.
Sponsors: Gottlieb Rohl {Roll} and wife (not named).

Mar. Rosina, of Henrich Conrad and Maria, b. 29 Jan 1777, bapt. 23 Feb 1777.
Sponsors: Peter Gress and wife Mar. Rosina.

Johannes, of John Willis (unbaptised) and Christina, b. in 1776, bapt. 23 Feb
1777. Sponsors: Johann Leckrum and wife Catharina.

Johannes, of Jacob Re[t]zer and Susanna, b. 25 Jan 1777, bapt. 28 Feb 1777.
Sponsors: Johannes Foerrich and wife Dorothea.

*Maria Magdalena, of Joh. Strohbank (deceased) and Maria, b. 9 Sep 1776,
bapt. 2 Mar 1777. Sponsor: the mother.

*Hanna, of John Wa[l]ker and Catharina, b. 2 {24} Jan 1777, bapt. 2 Mar 1777.
Sponsors: Jacob Gress and wife Margar.

*Joh. Henr., of Jacob Antony and Jacobine, {b. about Ascher [Ash Wednesday?]
1777}, bapt. 2 {25} Mar} 1777. Sponsors: Henr. Steinmetz and wife
Barbara.

*Margar., of Georg Dorn and Christine, b. 16 Feb 1777, bapt. 2 Mar {24 Mar}
1777. Sponsors: Marg{ar}. Dorn(in) and Adam Kemminger.

Joh. Georg, of Johann Scha[t]zler and Barbara, b. 24 Jan 1777, bapt. 5 Mar
1777. Sponsors: Joh. Georg Krauss and wife Catharina.

*Eva Cath{arine}, of Joh. Mart{in} Sommer and Maria Eva, b. 1 Feb 1777,
bapt. 6 Mar 1777. Sponsor: the mother.

*Wilhelmine Elis., of Phil{ip} Pfleger and Wilhelmina, b. 4 Feb 1777, bapt.
6 Mar 1777. Sponsors: Jacob Bleibtren and Elisabet Panzer(in)?

*Elisa, of Elis[h]a Truby and Margareta, b. 17 Jan 1777, bapt. 22 Feb 1777.
Sponsors: the parents.

*Joh[anna] Maria, of Georg Dürr and Maria Christine (who died), b. 6 Mar
1777, bapt. 7 Mar 1777. Sponsors: Mich{ael} Kraft and wife (not named).

Jacob, of Nicolaus Disserong and Maria, b. 26 Feb 1777, bapt. 8 Mar 1777.
Sponsors: Jacob Miller and wife Anna Margareta.

*Susanne, of Christian Lutz and Susanne, b. 23 Jan 1777, bapt. 9 Mar 1777.
Sponsors: Georg Christein and wife Jemima.

Isaac Warner (a married man), son of Isaac Warner (30 years deceased) and
Veronica (7 years deceased), b. 4 Aug 1735, bapt. 9 Mar 1777. Witnesses
were the communicants in Zion Church last Sunday.

*Marg{aret} Elis{ab}., of Mr. Mich{ael} Müller {now deceased} and Christine,
b. 28 Feb 1777, bapt. 9 Mar 1777. Sponsors: Georg Seitz and wife
Marg{ar}. Elis.

Johannes, of Christoph Müller and Elisabeth, b. 8 Feb 1777, bapt. 11 Mar 1777.
Sponsors: Johannes Becker and wife Catharina.

{Samuel, of Daniel Hofman and wife Margar., b. 11 Dec 1776, bapt. 12 Mar
1777. Sponsors: the parents.}

*Johan, of Henrich Emmert {Emert} and Maria, b. 28 Feb 1777, bapt. 16 Mar
1777. Sponsors: Joh{annes} Kaufman and wife Maria.

*Joh{an} Jacob, of Theob{ald} Storch {Stork} and Rosine, b. 23 Feb 1777,
bapt. 15 Mar 1777. Sponsors: Jac{ob} Swefel {Schwefel} and wife Maria
Magd.

Catharina, of Martin Sommer and Anna Barbara, b. 23 Feb 1777, bapt. 15 Mar
1777. Sponsors: Peter Sommer and wife Catharina.

Catharina, of Balthasar Emmerich and Maria, b. 4 Mar 1777, bapt. 15 Mar 1777.
Sponsors: Martin Ries and wife Catharina.
*An{na} Cath{arina}, of Georg Zeisiger and An{na} Maria, b. 25 Feb 1777,
bapt. 15 Mar 1777. Sponsors: the parents.
*Joh{an} Friedrich, of Friedr{ich} Lauterbrun and Margareta, b. 4 Mar 1777,
bapt. 18 Mar 1777. Sponsors: Joh. Schute {Schütz} and wife Margar.
*Philip{pine} Elisab., of Bened{ict} Schneider and wife (not named), b. 25 Jan
1777, bapt. 19 Mar 1777. Sponsors: the parents.
*Philip, of Joh{an} Höflein and Cath{arine}., b. 10 Mar 1777, bapt. 21 Mar
1777. Sponsors: the parents.
*Joseph, of Peter Weber and An{na} Magd{al}., b. 10 Feb 1777, bapt. 23 Mar
1777. Sponsors: the parents, and Joseph Walker and wife Margar. (who are
English).
*Sara Elis{abet}, of Georg Kur[t]z and Sara Elis{ab}., b. 2 Jan 1777, bapt.
23 Mar 1777. Sponsors: the parents.
Johann, of Joh. Breckle and Anna, b. 2 Mar 1777, bapt. 23 Mar 1777. Sponsors:
Jacob Sülzel and wife Maria Barbara.
*Elisabet, of Henr{ich} Lenz and An. Maria, b. 15 Dec 1776, bapt. 23 Mar
1777. Sponsors: the parents.
*Johannes Georg, of Friedr{ich} Reifle and An. Marg., b. {17} Dec 1776, bapt.
23 {24} Mar 1777. Sponsors: Georg Hafner and Maria Cath. Mänmeier?.
Esther, of Michael Schubert and Elisabeth, b. 4 Mar 1777, bapt. 30 Mar 1777.
Sponsors: Friedr. Hailer and wife Christina,
Johannes [twin], of Gerhard Hol[t]zcamp and Elisabeth, b. 25 Feb 1777, bapt.
14 Mar 1777. Sponsors: Conrad Alster and wife Anna Maria.
Margaret [twin], of Gerhard Hol[t]zcamp and Elisabeth, b. 25 Feb 1777, bapt.
14 Mar 1777. Sponsors: same as above.
*Joh{an} Friedr{ich}, of Philip Heit and Elisabet, b. 31 Jan 1777, bapt. 30 Mar
1777. Sponsors: {Joh.} Friedr. Kücherer and wife Esther? Elis.
Joshua Archir, of Georg Koch and Catharina, birthdate not given, bapt. 30 Mar
1777. Sponsor: Joshua Archur.
*An{na} Maria, of Philip Kolb and Cathar., b. 10 Dec 1776, bapt. 31 Mar 1777.
Sponsors: Jac{ob} Nagel and Maria Gros(in).
*Maria Cath., of Joh. Friedr{ich} Meier and Maria, b. 3 Jul 1776, bapt. 31 Mar
1777. Sponsors: Maria Elis. Rohn(in)?.
Wilhelm, of Jacob Graef and Elisabeth, b. 27 Mar 1777, bapt. 2 Apr 1777.
Sponsors: Phil. Dick and wife Catharina.
*Joh{an} Georg, of Martin Sommer and Margar., b. 10 Jan 1777, bapt. 3 Apr
1777. Sponsors: Joh{annes} Mänchen and wife Cathar.
Mar. Elisabeth, of Joh. Joseph Graf and Dorothea, b. 27 Mat 1777, bapt. 6 Apr
1777. Sponsors: Joh. Nic. Grimm and wife Mar.? Magdal.
Johannes, of Johannes Freyburg and Susann, b. 24 Mar 1777, bapt. 6 Apr 1777.
Sponsors: Joh. Gummi and wife An. Cathar.
*Henrich, of Rudolph Nagel and Susanna, b. 26 Mar 1777, bapt. 6 Apr 1777.
Sponsors: Henr{ich} Schwalbach and wife Cath.
*An{na} Martha, of Joh{an} Adam Schwab and Anne Martha, b. 30 Mar
{10 Mar} 1777, bapt. 7 Apr 1777. Sponsors: the parents.

*Margar{et}, of Andr{eas} Philler and Margar., b. 25 Mar {26 Mar} 1777, bapt. 6 Apr 1777. Sponsors: the parents.
*Margar{et}, of Georg Fries and Cathar{ine}, b. 10 Aug 1776, bapt. 6 Apr 1777. Sponsors: Georg Wölperd {Wölper} and wife Marg{ar}.
*An{na} Maria, of Georg Kehl and Veronica, b. 28 Feb 1775, bapt. 7 Apr 1777. Sponsors: Jac{ob} Kreinmeier {Kreismeier} and wife An{ne} Maria.
*Georg, of William Tennis and Rachel, b. 11 Jan 1777, bapt. 10 Apr 1777. Sponsors: Georg Streper and wife An. Maria {Dorothea}.
Margareta, of Jacob Pfister and Margareta, b. 1 Mar 1777, bapt. 15 Apr 1777. Sponsors: the parents.
Maria, of John Green and Elisabeth Hera at Joseph Stiler's place, b. 11 Mar 1777, bapt. 15 Apr 1777. Sponsors: Leonhard Kesler and Maria Jung.
Anna Barbara, of Peter Grimm and Dorothea, b. 19 Mar 1777, bapt. 13 Apr 1777. Sponsors: the parents.
Friedrich, of Caspar Haas and Catharina, b. 27 Mar 1777, bapt. 14 Apr 1777. Sponsors: the parents.
Philip, of Joh. Stark and Cathar., b. 25 Mar 1777, bapt. 15 Apr 1777. Sponsors: Phil. Pannekuche and wife Cathar.
John Willis (an Englishman, married), son of Johann Willis and Diana, b. 6 Jul 1747, bapt. 15 Apr 1777. He died 16 Sep 1777.
Regina Catharina, of Lorenz Lass and Dorothea, b. 15 Apr 1777, bapt. 18 Apr 1777. Sponsors: Caspar Schüster and wife Regina.
Andreas, of Andreas Kirck and Maria Elisab., b. 6 Apr 1777, bapt. 14 Apr 1777. Sponsors: the parents.
*Joh{an} Friedr{ich}, of Joh. Christian Whitvogel and Anna, b. 25 Aug 1775, bapt. 17 Apr 1777. Sponsors: the parents.
Abraham, of Joseph Pennrose and Abigail Whyle David Pennrose), b. in 1774, bapt. 17 Apr 1777. Sponsors: Catharina Weid(in) and her dau. Rosina Marg. Geick(in).
*Elisab{et}, of Joh{annes} Engel and Susanne, b. 4 Apr 1777, bapt. 20 Apr 1777. Sponsors: Mich. Rehm and Anna Elisab. Rehm(in).
*Joh{an}. Peter, of Jacob Kraemer and Ottilia, b. 15 May 1776, bapt. 21 Apr 1777. Sponsors: Joh{an} Christoph Heitel and wife Anna Maria.
Johannes, of Jacob Hauser and Magdalena, b. 30 Mar 1777, bapt. 20 Apr 1777. Sponsors: Johan Schaefer and wife Soph. Maria.
*Elisabet, of Jacob Reisser and Eva, b. 11 Apr 1777, bapt. 27 Apr 1777. Sponsors: Martin Reisser and wife Catharina {Maria}.
Elisabeth, of Gotthelf David Flickwir and Sophia, b. 8 Apr 1777, bapt. 27 Apr 1777. Sponsors: Henrich Weinkauf and wife Elisabeth.
Joh. Friedr., of Friedr. Meier and Sarah Elisabeth, b. 11 Apr 1777, bapt. 27 Apr 1777. Sponsors: the father, and Sarah Mahn(in).
Peter, of Joh. Christoph Senderling and Maria, b. 8 Feb 1777, bapt. 27 Apr 1777. Sponsors: Peter Operer? and wife Barbara.
Jacob, of Jacob Loescher and Maria, b. 15 Jan 1777, bapt. 27 Apr 1777. Sponsors: Jacob Leivensetter and Christina Hermann(in).
Susanna, of Henrich Herbst and Susanna, b. 12 Aug 1776, bapt. 7 May 1777. Sponsors: Johannes Schaefer and [wife] Susanna.

Rachel, of Jonas Abraham and Sarah, b. 7 May 1777, bapt. the same day .
Sponsors: the father, and Marg. Folling.
Heinr. Leopold, of Heinrich Leopold (baron vonArndt) and Susanna, b. 2 May
1777, bapt. 9 May 1777. Sponsors: Dr. Friedrich Feil and wife Maria....
Sarah, of Georg Kanzer and Elisabeth, birthdate not given, bapt. 11 May 1777.
Sponsors: Adam Grabel and wife Elisabeth.
Cathar. Elisab., of Johann Blaes (now deceased) and Elisabeth, b. 7 Oct 1776,
bapt. 11 May 1777. Sponsors: Ferdinand Malmiton and wife Elisab.
A child (name not given), of Jacob Sailer and Aemelia, birthdate not given, bapt.
14 May 1777. (Sponsors not given.)
Apollonia, of Leonard Kesler and Maria, b. 4 May 1777, bapt. 18 May 1777.
Sponsors: Georg Ki[t]z and wife Apollonia.
Georg, of Georg Haerly and Barbara, b. 20 Oct 1776, bapt. 29 May 1777.
Sponsors: Martin Schmidt and wife Cath.
Hanna, of Conrad VonHold and Elisabeth, b. 26 Feb 1777, bapt. 21 May 1777.
Sponsors: Henrich Freytag and Elisabeth Far_laender(in).
Anna Maria, of Jacob Bittinger and Anna Maria, b. 20 Feb 1777, bapt. 25 May
1777. Sponsors: Leonard Loescher and wife Anna Maria.
Christian Bastian, of Philipp Gross and Margareta, b. 18 May 1777, bapt. 1 Jun
1777. Sponsors: Christian Jost and wife Christ. Barbara.
Johann Georg, of Joh. Death and Mary, b. 3 Mar 1777, bapt. 5 Jun 1777.
Sponsor: Anna Marg. Milteberger(in).
Michael, of Henr. Me[t]z and Amelia, b. 3 Feb 1776, bapt. 5 Jun 1777.
Sponsors: the grandfather Peter Hay and grandmother (name not given).
Wilhelm, of Valentin Bauer and Anna, b. 9 Nov 1776, bapt. 18 Jun 1777.
Sponsor: widow Elisab. Blaes.
Margareta, of Georg Daum and Sarah, b. 6 Jun 1777, bapt. 21 Jun 1777.
Sponsors: Peter Kraft and wife Margareta.
Anna Maria, of Rev. Heinrich Moeller (the preacher) and Esther, b. 21 Jun 1777,
bapt. 29 Jun 1777. Sponsor: Anna Maria Ott(in).
Regina, of Jacob Kaufmann and Maria Barbara, b. 18 Jun 1777, bapt. 29 Jun
1777. Sponsors: the parents.
Elisabeth, of Jacob Wagner and Grace, (birth and baptism dates not given).
Sponsors: Nicolaus Wagner and wife Magdalena.
Jacob, of Jacob Wagner and Grace, (birth and baptism dates not given).
Sponsors: sane as above.
Maria, of Jacob Wagner and Grace, (birth and baptism dates not given).
Sponsors: same as above.
Anna Cathar., of Johann Georg Escher? and Anna Catharina, b. 13 Jul 1777,
bapt. 19 Jul 1777. Sponsor: Anna Elisabeth Van [sic].
An. Maria, of Leonard Kettmann and Anna Margareta, b. 7 Jul 1777, bapt.
20 Jul 1777. Sponsors: Leonard Kraemer and wife Anna Maria.
Mar. Magdalena, of Benjamin Gasner and Maria Magdalena, b. 24 Jun 1777,
bapt. 29 Jul 1777. Sponsors: Georg Lauer (or Sauer) and [wife] Mar.
Magdalena.
Maria Dorothea, of Peter Schneider and Elisabeth, b. 1 Jul 1777, bapt. 20 Jul
1777. Sponsors: Johannes Griffenstein and wife Maria Dorothea.

Johannes, of Johann Adam Goebler and Susanna, b. 24 Jul 1777, bapt. 24 Jul 1777. Sponsors: Joh. Adam Goebler and Cath. Barbara Engelbrecht(in)?.

Elisabeth, of Jacob Stauch and Rosina, b. 26 Jan 1777, bapt. 2 Jul 1777. Sponsors: the parents.

Thomas, of Johann Fromberg and Anna, b. 23 May 1777, bapt. 26 Jul 1777. Sponsors: Nicolaus Weber and wife Sophia.

Jacob, of Johannes Heil and Maria, b. 10 Jul 1777, bapt. 26 Jul 1777. Sponsors: Jacob Graef and wife Maria.

Johannes, of Andreas Mattern and Anna Maria, b. 18 Jul 1777, bapt. 20 Jul 1777. Sponsors: the grandparents Joh. Kunckel and wife Maria Christina.

Johann Friedrich, of Christoph Friedrich Dobelbauer and Catharina, b. 18 May 1777, bapt. 1 Aug 1777. Sponsors: the parents.

Johanna Elisabetha, of Anton Eberhard and Philippina, b. 12 Jul 1777, bapt. 3 Aug 1777. Sponsors: Joh. Balthas. Klein and Elisabeth.

Matthaeus, of Leon. Egy and Charlotte, b. 13 Jun 1777, bapt. 5 Aug 1777. Sponsors: Math. Kiffert and wife Maria.

Sarah, of Leon. Egy and Charlotte, b. in Apr 1774, bapt. 5 Aug 1777. Sponsors: Georg __ackose and wife Sara.

Rebecca, of Valentin Sorg and Anna, b. 20 Jul 1777, bapt. 10 Aug 1777. Sponsors: the father, and Anna Maria Gerlach(in).

Joh. Jacob, of Gottfried Strechleger? and Nancy, b. 1 May 1777, bapt. 10 Aug 1777. Sponsors: Jacob Salser and wife Anna Barb.

Elisabeth, of Georg Molitor and Sarah, b. 26 Jun 1777, bapt. 14 Aug 1777. Sponsors: Jacob Hold and wife Elisabeth.

Christina Maria, of William Shippy (mother's name not given; the child's sponsors are foster parents), illegitimate, b. 8 May 1775, bapt. 11 Aug 1777. Sponsors: Joh. Andr. Rot(h) and wife Barbara.

Joh. Georg, of Peter Schranck and Sophia, b. 16 Jul 1777, bapt. 17 Aug 1777. Sponsors: Georg Schranck and wife Cathar.

Sophia, of Georg Henrich and Anna, b. 31 Jul 1777, bapt. 17 Aug 1777. Sponsors: the parents.

Elisabeth, of Andreas Weikeman and Rosina, b. 17 Jul 1777, bapt. 17 Aug 1777. Sponsors: the father and Catharina Schweizer(in).

Elisabeth, of Peter Kur[t]z and Sarah, b. 15 Aug 1777, bapt. 21 Aug 1777. Sponsors: the parents, and the grandmother (name not given).

Georg, of Michael Lu[t]z and Susanna, b. 26 Jul 1777, bapt. 23 Aug 1777. Sponsors: the mother, and Mrs. Christina Geret(in).

Nicolaus, of Nicolaus Panzer and Elisabeth, b. 17 Aug 1777, bapt. 24 Aug 1777. Sponsors: the parents.

Joh. Georg, of Joh. Georg Denzel and Sarah, b. 28 Jul 1776, bapt. 24 Aug 1777. Sponsors: Joh. Georg Herold and wife Regina.

William, of John Hill and Anna Nancy Williams, b. and bapt., near death, 30 Aug 1777.

Johannes, of Conrad Haas and Magdalena, b. 12 Aug 1777, bapt. 31 Aug 1777. Sponsors: Joh. Schneider and wife Eva.

Maria, of Bernhardt Buck and Maria, b. 12 Aug 1777, bapt. 30 Aug 1777. Sponsors: the parents

Mar.. Magdal., of Georg Reinhardt and Mar. Magdalena, b. 15 Aug 1777, bapt. 31 Aug 1777. Sponsors: Michael Gutmann and wife Regina Margaretha..

Daniel, of Daniel Schaut and Catharina, b. 22 Aug 1777, bapt. 31 Aug 1777. Sponsors: Tobias Koenig and wife Barbara.

Margareta, of Georg Merckel and Nancy, b. 29 Jul 1777, bapt. 31 Aug 1777. Sponsors: the parents.

Zacharias, of Zachar. Loesch and Maria, b. 7 Sep 1777, bapt. 14 Sep 1777. Sponsors: the father, and Barbara Kiemle.

Georg, of Georg Schenck and Sophia, b. in Dec 1775, bapt. 14 Sep 1777. Sponsors: Georg Bauer and wife Margareta.

Hanna, of John Billeiersler? and Hanna, b. in Dec 1775, bapt. 14 Sep 1777. Sponsor: the mother.

Ludwig, of Henr. Curt and Regina, b. 15 Sep 1777, bapt. 15 Sep 1777. Sponsors: the parents.

Margareta, of He(name not given), wifeser and Margareta, b. 23 Jul 1777, bapt. 15 Sep 1777. Sponsors: the parents, and Henr. Aec__.

Dorothea, of Martin Peisch and Maria Magd., b. 26 Aug 1777, bapt. 14 Sep 1777. Sponsors: Georg Gro[t]z and wife Dorothea.

Georg (a foundling), about 6 months old, bapt. 13 Sep 1777. Sponsors: Peter Weil and wife Catharina (the foster parents).

Margareta, of Wilhelm Patto and Elisab., b. 1 Sep 1777, bapt. 14 Sep 1777. Sponsors: the father, and Margaret Dres(in).

Maria Margar., of Carl Wolpert and Catharina, b. 14 Sep 1777, bapt. 21 Sep 1777. Sponsors: the grandparents Friedr. Wolpert and wife Maria Margareta.

Valentine, of Valentin Hagner and Margarete, b. 2 Sep 1777, bapt. 21 Sep 1777. Sponsors: Peter Gabel and wife Elisabeth.

Michael, of Jacob Seger and Barbara, b. 20 Sep 1777, bapt. 21 Sep 1777. Sponsors: Michael Stricker and wife Margareta.

Mar. Cathar., of Georg Michael Heil and Maria Catharine, b. 29 Aug 1777, bapt. 21 Sep 1777. Sponsors: the parents.

Jacob, of Johannes Fri[t]z and Catharina, b. 8 Sep 1777, bapt. 21 Sep 1777. Sponsors: Caspar Geier and wife Elisabeth.

Wilhelm, of Joh. Geisser and Elisabeth, b. 21 Aug 1777, bapt. 21 Sep 1777. Sponsors: the parents.

Hanna, of Ludewig Wirt and Anna Margaret, b. 5 Dec 1776, bapt. 21 Sep 1777. Sponsors: the parents.

Anna Barbara, of Ludewig Wirt and Anna Margaret, b. 23 May 1774, bapt. 21 Sep 1777. Sponsors: the parents.

Georg, of Georg Hofmann and Magdalena, b. 22 Sep 1777, bapt. 29 Sep 1777. Sponsors: the parents.

Elisabeth, of Benj. Trotter? and Mar. Elisabeth, b. 19 Sep 1777, bapt. 4 Oct 1777. Sponsor(s): Georg (illegible).

Catharina, of James Cartwright and Barbara, b. 29 Sep 1777, bapt. the same day. Sponsor: Cathar. (illegible).

Jacob Ulrich, of Johann Georg Aescher and Maria Regina, b. 20 Sep 1777, bapt. 5 Oct 1777. Sponsors: Jacob Sülzer and wife Barbara.

Christian, of Andreas Foerster? and Hanna, b. 2 Oct 1777, bapt. 5 Oct 1777. Sponsor(s): Christian (illegible).

Margar. Catharine, of Anna Elisabeth Evinger and Isaac Koch (illegitimate), b. 20 Jun 1777, bapt. 6 Oct 1777. Sponsor: the [grand?] mother Anna Margareta Evinger.

Henrich, of Henrich Otto and Anna Maria, b. 10 Sep 1777, bapt. 7 Oct 1777. Sponsors: the parents.

Philipp, of Johann Wilhelm Stirnkorb and Sibylle, b. 9 Oct 1777, bapt. 12 Oct 1777. Sponsors: the parents.

Matthaeus, of Henrich Boot(h) and Anna Catharina, b. 9 Oct 1777, bapt. 12 Oct 1777. Sponsors: Matthaeus Boot(h) and wife [sic] Cath. Holzkamp(in).

Joh[anna] Margareta, of Stephan Sulliger and Anna Eleonora, b. 3 Oct 1777, bapt. 12 Oct 1777. Sponsors: Jacob Sulliger and wife Margareta.

Joh. Christian, of Friedrich S___ and Barbara, b. 4 Oct 1777, bapt. 12 Oct 1777. Sponsors: the parents.

Peter, of Joh. Ehrhard Eissenbren and Catharina, b. 10 Oct 1777, bapt. 19 Oct 1777. Sponsors: the grandparents Peter Eisenbrey and wife Joh. Dorothea.

Anna Maria, of Johann Strub and Regina, b. 18 Oct 1777, bapt. 29 Oct 1777. Sponsors: Michael Fuchs and wife Salome.

Anna Maria, of Nicolaus Shiller? and Anna Maria, b. 4 Oct 1777, bapt. 26 Oct 1777. Sponsors: Wilhelm Kaempf and wife Anna Maria.

Andreas, of Philipp Schmidt and Susanna, b. 27 Sep 1777, bapt. 31 Oct 1777. Sponsors: Andreas Schmidt and Christina Cath. Brand(in)?.

Joh. Adam, of Philipp Reibold and Veronica, b. 10 Oct 1777, bapt. 2 Nov 1777. Sponsors: the parents.

Heinr. Adam, of Carl Miller and Anna Barbara, b. 9 Oct 1777, bapt. 3 Nov 1777. Sponsors: Henr. Adam Ma_einer and wife Maria.

Maria Ursula, of Johann Martin Haertel and wife Maria, b. 1 Nov 1777, bapt. 9 Nov 1777. Sponsors: Jacob Scheppach and Mar. Ursula.

Jacob, of Henrich Haaks and Catharina, b. 10 Oct bapt. 9 Nov 1777. Sponsors: the parents.

Catharina, of Georg Jacob Stuzel and Catharina, b. 23 May 1777, bapt. 9 Nov 1777. Sponsors: the parents.

Maria Magd., of Johann Peter Walter and Antoinette, b. 29 Oct 1777, bapt. 10 Nov 1777. Sponsor: Catharina Stemper(in).

Elisabeth, of Wilhelm Lehmann and Elisabeth, b. 30 Oct 1777, bapt. 13 Nov 1777. Sponsors: the father, and the grandmother Elisab. Lehmann,

Catharine, of John Hurley and Ann, b. 3 Nov 1777, bapt. 13 Nov 1777. Sponsor: Catharina Graemer?.

Barbara, of Henrich Meier and Anna Ursula, b. 30 Oct 1777, bapt. 16 Nov 1777. Sponsors: the parents.

Catharine Elisabeth, of Friedrich Maerker and Charlotte Elisabeth, b. 30 Oct 1777, bapt. 16 Nov 1777. Sponsors: Johann Balthasar and wife Maria Elisabeth.

Catharina, of Georg Barren and Margaret, b. 26 Oct 1777, bapt. 16 Nov 1777. Sponsors: Charles Jones and wife Anna Catharina.

Joh. Hilarius, of Johann Christoph Becker and Catharina, b. 29 Oct 1777, bapt. 15 Nov 1777. Sponsors: the father's brother Joh. Hilarius, the grandfather Joh. Hilarius, and Maria Kreuder(in).

William, of Charles Chreer and Catharine, b. 30 Oct 1777, bapt. 16 Nov 1777.
Sponsors: Charles Chreer and Polly Meckes?.
Anna, of Georg Kehl and Veronica, b. 21 Sep 1777, bapt. 20 Nov 1777.
Sponsors: Matthias Graemer and Anna Bok(in).
Peter, of Christian Haag and Anna, b. 7 Nov 1777, bapt. 23 Nov 1777.
Sponsors: Peter Hahn and wife Cathar.
Anna Maria, of Johann Lepp and Elisabeth, b. 22 Oct 1777, bapt. 23 Nov 1777.
Sponsors: Jacob Kesler and wife Catharina.
Georg, of Daniel Knodel and Anna Maria, b. 15 Oct 1777, bapt. 23 Nov 1777.
Sponsors: Georg Paetsch and wife Catharina.
Georg Nicholaus, of Martin Die[t]z and Maria Margaret, b. 8 Nov 1777, bapt.
26 Nov 1777. Sponsors: Nicolaus Miller and wife Mar.
Catharina, of Peter Heimbach and Elisabeth, b. 28 Sep 1777, bapt. 30 Nov 1777.
Sponsors: John Birckenbeiler and wife Catharina.
David, of Adam Schae[t]zlein and Hanna, b. 9 Oct 1777, bapt. 30 Nov 1777.
Sponsors: the parents.
Susanna, of Wilhelm Mohr and Susanna, b. 2 Oct 1777, bapt. 30 Nov 1777.
Sponsors: the parents.
Catharina?, of Georg Haehnley and Catharina, b. 20 Nov 1777, bapt. 30 Nov
1777. Sponsors: the father, and Elisabeth Jeorg(in).
John, of John Linch and Marg., b. 13 Nov 1777, bapt. 30 Nov 1777. Sponsor:
Anna Schaber(in).
Jeane, of Peter Rohn and Susanna, b. 2 Nov 1777, bapt. 2 Dec 1777. Sponsor:
the mother.
Henrich, of Henrich Graef and Anna Maria, b. 10 Sep 1777, bapt. 2 Dec 1777.
Sponsors: the parents
Samuel, of Samuel Osborne and Hesther, b. 4 Nov 1777, bapt. 3 Dec 1777.
Sponsor: Anna Margareta Rucken____.
Elisabeth, of Johannes Schaefer and Susanna, b. 30 Nov 1777, bapt. 5 Dec 1777.
Sponsors: Johann Heinrich Herbst and wife Elisabeth.
Eva Maria, of Wilhelm Warner and Wilhelmina, b. 5 Dec 1777, bapt. 7 Dec
1777. Sponsor: Eva Mar. Klein(in).
Johannes, of Johannes Graef (Casp. Graef's son), and Catharina Fasten, b.
24 Sep 1777, bapt. 5 Dec 1777. Sponsors: Joh. Henr. Herbst and wife
Elisabeth.
Cathar. Barbara, of Friedrich Vogel and Catharina, b. 17 Nov 1777, bapt. 7 Dec
1777. Sponsors: Jonathan Dressler? And Elisabeth Hay.
Johannes, of Johannes David Jones and Susanna Elisabeth, b. 19 Sep 1777,
bapt. 10 Dec 1777. Sponsors: Johannes Heger and sister Catharina
Hege(lin).
Catharina, of Wilhelm Loescher and Catharina, b. 23 Nov 1777, bapt. 14 Dec
1777. Sponsors: Johann Georg Loescher and Barbara Unger(in).
Andreas Philipp, of Franz Wilhelm Hetmansperger and Maria Magdalena, b.
4 Nov 1777, bapt. 14 Dec 1777. Sponsors: Philipp Klein and wife Elisabeth.
Elisabeth, of Mordechai Baire? and Mary, b. 6 Dec 1777, bapt. 18 Dec 1777.
Sponsor: the mother.
Johann, of Johann Hicks and Catharine b. 15 Nov 1777, bapt. 18 Dec 1777.
Sponsors: John Story, Thomas Lin, and Maria Hamm?.

Gottlieb, of Conrad Bernhardt and Catharina, b. 11 Dec 1777, bapt. 21 Dec 1777. Sponsors: Gottlieb Zinck and wife Catharina.

Georg, of Georg Feuchtenberg and Elisabeth, b. 18 Dec 1777, bapt. 21 Dec 1777. Sponsors: the parents.

Anna Barbara, of Joh. Georg Dering and Anna Barbara, b. 8 Dec 1777, bapt. 22 Dec 1777. Sponsors: the parents.

Wilhelm, of Johannes Bures and Sarah, b. 22 Nov 1777, bapt. 25 Dec 1777. Sponsors: Georg Brunner and wife Anna Maria.

Maria Eva, of Friedrich Vogel and Elisabeth, b. 6 Nov 1777, bapt. 25 Dec 1777. Sponsors: Johannes Schneider and wife Mar. Eva.

Simeon, of John Connaly and Barbara, b. 21 Dec 1777, bapt. 26 Dec 1777. Sponsors: Philipp Thomas and wife Elisabeth.

Jacob Friederich, of Andreas Beck and Barbara, b. 19 Dec 1777, bapt. 28 Dec 1777. Sponsors: Jacob Segler and wife Barbara.

Bernhard, of James Flori and Catharina, b. 23 Dec 1777, bapt. 31 Dec 1777. Sponsors: Henrich Storr and wife Eleonora.

Maria, of Johann Carl Freis? and Magdalene, b. 17 Dec 1777, bapt. 29 Dec 1777. Sponsors: Georg Striby and wife Dorothea.

1777, Second List
(baptisms by pastor G.H.E. Muhlenberg, Jr., from Book IV)
Note: in the original churchbook, the first 53 entries in 1777 recorded by G.H.E. Muhlenberg, in Book IV, were duplicated by pastor Kunze in the latter's 1777 list (inBook III), above. Those duplicate entries are not transcribed here, as the information in them is essentially the same as in the entries marked by asterisks in the 1777 First List, above. Entries by pastor Muhlenberg that were recorded uniquely in Book IV then begin as follows:
William, of Thomas Hampton and wife Agnes, b. 1 Apr 1777, bapt. 11 Apr 1777. Sponsor: the mother.

Susanne Margar., of Georg Keimle (whose wife left him [died?]) and widow An. Maria Kendel, b. 20 Jun 1776, bapt. 11 Apr 1777. Sponsors: Peter Kraft and Ursula Keimle.

In the original churchbook, four more baptisms appeared here that were duplicated into Kunze's 1777 list; see the 1777 First List. The entries by pastor Muhlenberg that are found only Book IV then resume, as follows:
John, of William Oliver and wife Maria, b. 5 Oct 1776, bapt. 3 May 1777. Sponsors: the parents.

Johannes, of Johannes Emmerich and wife Maria, b. 19 Apr 1777, bapt. 4 May 1777. Sponsors: Balthasar Emmerich and wife Maria.

Samuel, of Michael Müller and wife Barbara, b. 9 Apr 1777, bapt. 4 May 1777. Sponsors: Barth. Schaetzlein and wife Cath.

Susanne, of Johan Fahl and wife Cath., b. 4 Mar 1777, bapt. 4 May 1777. Sponsors: Adam Kemminger and wife Susanne.

Joh. Peter, of Henr. Debruin? and wife Margar., b. 12 Mar 1777, bapt. 4 May 1777. Sponsors: Peter Sommer and wife Catharine.

Michael, of Jacob Herman and wife Cathar., b. 10 Jan 1777, bapt. 4 May 1777. Sponsors: the parents.

Elisabet, of Isaac Kelly and wife Elisabet,b. 5 Jan 1777, bapt. 6 May 1777.
    Sponsor: the mother.
Anna Dorothea, of John Moor and Sarah, b. 8 Apr 1777, bapt. 11 May 1777.
    Sponsors: Jaocb Deis and wife Doroth.
David, of Joh. Helzel and wife Cathar., b. 10 Apr 1777, bapt. 11 May 1777.
    Sponsors: Balt. Staus and wife Maria.
Johan, of Joh. Freimuth and wife Mar. Elis., b. 21 Apr 1777, bapt. 11 May 1777.
    Sponsors: Joh. Braun and wife Cathar.
Anna Barb., of Joh. David Pontius and An. Elis., b. 23 Apr 1777, bapt. 11 May
    1777. Sponsors: Christian Kalckbrenner and Anna Barb. Paesch(in), single.
Friedrich, of Georg Gebhard and Rosina, b. 7 Apr 1777, bapt. 11 May 1777.
    Sponsors: Joh. Biegler and wife Anna.
Wilhelm, of Martin Walter and wife Barbara, b. 9 Dec 1776, bapt. 18 May 1777.
    Sponsors: the parents.
Joh. Georg, of Joh. Georg Pauer and An. Marg. b. 14 Apr 1777, bapt. 18 May
    1777. Sponsors: Joh. Jac. Deis and wife Dorothea.
Eva Maria, of Elisab. vanUpstraat? and a soldier in camp, b. 11 May 1777, bapt.
    18 May 1777. Sponsor: widow Maria Klein(in).
Joh. Jacob, of Mich. Herman (deceased) and Maria, b. 2 Apr 1777, bapt. 18 May
    1777. Sponsors: Joh. Jac. Leibensieder and Christine Hermann(in).
Mary, of Paul Kingston and Mary, b. 2 Feb 1777, bapt. 18 May 1777. Sponsors:
    Joh. Mer[t]z and Mary Johnson.
Sara, of Peter Mierken and Cathar., b. in Jan 1777, bapt. 19 May 1777.
    Sponsors: the parents.
Robert, of Wilh. Kerl and Elisabet, b. 5 Feb 1777, bapt. 20 May 1777. Sponsor:
    the mother.
Maria, of Georg Sohnleutner and Cath. b. 13 Apr 1777, bapt. 14 May 1777.
    Sponsors: Philip Fischer and Anna Maria.
Jacob, of Michael Bauer and wife Cath., b. 30 Nov 1776, bapt. 26 May 1777.
    Sponsors: the father, and Jemima Christein(in).
Joseph, of Henr. Brosius and wife Cathar., b. 29 Jun 1776, bapt. 26 May 1777.
    Sponsor: the mother.
William, of Will. Carter and wife Elis., b. 12 Oct 1775, bapt. 26 May 1777.
    Sponsors: Thomas Harper and wife (name not given), Samuel Fischer, and
    Georg Taylor.
Anna Maria, of Joh. Weiss and wife Elisabet, b. 5 May 1777, bapt. 1 Jun 1777.
    Sponsors: Wilhelm Eckert and wife Anna Maria.
Johannes, of Joh. Görger and wife An. Maria, b. 8 May 1777, bapt. 1 Jun 1777.
    Sponsors: the parents.
Jacob, of Peter Kress and Rosina, b. 10 May 1777, bapt. 8 Jun 1777. Sponsors:
    Jacob Deis and wife Doroth.
Johannes, of Joh. Wolfg. Gemeinbauer and wife Anna Cath., b. 31 May 1777,
    bapt. 15 Jun 1777. Sponsors: the parents, and mother-in-law Anna Maria
    Jeiffer(in)?.
Maria, of Phil. Springer and wife Eva, b. 8 Jan 1777, bapt. 15 Jun 1777.
    Sponsors: the parents.
Elisabet, of Math. Rus? and wife Ann, b. 5 Nov 1773, bapt. 1 Jun 1777.
    Sponsors: Dietr. Wilh. Bicking and wife Elis.

Elisabet, of Peter Eichler (deceased) and Marg., b. 1 May 1777, bapt. 22 Jun 1777. Sponsor: the mother.
Anna Margar., of Nicol. Klein and wife Cath., b. 15 Jun 1777, bapt. 29 Jun 1777. Sponsors: Joh. Elgert and wife Anna Marg.
Anna Barbara, of Georg Hummel and wife Elisab., b. 19 Dep 1776, bapt. 29 Jun 1777. Sponsors: Henr. Urich and wife Anna Barbara.
Wilhelm, of Conrad Paethis and Barbara, b. 14 Jun 1777, bapt. 29 Jun 1777. Sponsors: the parents.
Johan David, of Ludwig Schneider and Cathar., b. 23 Jun 1777, bapt. 6 Jul 1777. Sponsors: David Uber and wife Anna.
Samuel, of Joh. Mich. Fuchs and Salome, b. 24 Jun 1777, bapt. 6 Jul 1777. Sponsors: Joh. Strup and wife Regina. (The child died.)
Susanne, of Henr. Andr. Meier and Cathar., b. 6 Jul 1777, bapt 13 Jul 1777. Sponsors: Joh. Henr. Hol[t]z and wife Susanne.
Georg, of Georg Haginloch and wife Elisab., b. 2 Jul 1777, bapt. 15 Jul 1777. Sponsors: Henr. Kur[t]z and wife Ros.
Peter, of Martin Fies and Dorothea, b. 1 Jul 1777, bapt. 20 Jul 1777. Sponsors: Peter Mierken and wife Cath.
Susanne, of Math. Landeberger and Maria, b. 23 May 1777, bapt. 21 Jul 1777. Sponsors: Thomas Meier and wife Margar.
Georg, of Daniel Huber and wife Eva, b. 25 May 777, bapt. 21 Jul 1777. Sponsors: the parents.
Susanne, of Cath. McCloy and Richard Butler (illegitimate), b. 18 Jul 177, bapt. 21 Jul 1777. Sponsor: Susan Armitage.
Anna Cathar., of Christopher Bilger [Bigler?] and Anna Soph., b. 28 Jun 1777, bapt. 27 Jul 1777. Sponsors: the parents.
Charlotte, of John Bambridge and Priscilla, b. 19 Jun 1777, bapt. 27 Jul 1777. Sponsors: the parents.
Johan, of Conr. Dewiter and wife Cathar., b. 16 Jun 1777, bapt. 27 Jul 1777. Sponsors: the mother, and Wilhelm Lehman.
Anna Maria, of Philip May and Anna Maria, b. 17 Jul 1777, bapt. 27 Jul 1777. Sponsors: the parents.
Catharine, of Joh. Straub and Margar., b. 19 Jul 1777, bapt. 29 Jul 1777. Sponsors: the parents.
Joh. Georg, of Philip Knapp and wife Cath., b. 29 Jul 1777, bapt. 30 Jul 1777. Sponsors: Joh. Georg Schrank and wife Catharine.
Anna Cath., of Fridr. Mock and wife An. Maria, b. 21 Jul 1777, bapt. 3 Aug 1777. Sponsors: Tobias Koenig and wife Barbara.
Daniel, of Christian Schütz and Marg., b. 28 Jun 1777, bapt. 3 Aug 1777. Sponsor: Daniel Kosch.
Ludwig, of Georg Gerlinger and wife Christ., b. during Easter month 1777, bapt. 3 Aug 1777. Sponsor: Ludwig Gerlinger.
Rebecca, of Daniel Schittel and Elisabet, b. 15 Sep 1775, bapt. 5 Aug 1777. Sponsor: Rebecca Evans.
Johannes, of Joh. Loschet and Catharine, b. 18 Jul 1777, bapt. 2 Aug 1777. Sponsors: the parents.
Edward, of Edward Fife and Jean, b. 1 Dec 1776, bapt. 7 Aug 1777. Sponsor: the mother.

Sara, of Joh. Mänchen and Catharine, b. 1 Aug 1777, bapt. 10 Aug 1777. Sponsors: Ernst Mänchen and dau. Sara.
Elisabet, of Math. Schelhorn and Cathar. b. 19 Jul 1777, bapt. 10 Aug 1777. Sponsors: Conrad Vorster and Elis. Fischer(in) (single).
Melchior, of Henriette Dick(in) and Melchior Ross? (illegitimate), b. 18 Jul 1777, bapt. 11 Aug 1777. Sponsor: gran. [sic} Helzel(in).
Anna Catharine, of Andr. Tag and wife Christine, b. 8 Aug 1777, bapt. 17 Aug 1777. Sponsors: Mich. Schenerer and wife Cath.
Joh. David, of Joh. Ostertag and Eva Cathar., b. 3 Aug 1777, bapt. 17 Aug 1777. Sponsors: Joh. Phil. David Ott (the schoolmaster) and Christina Barb. Danner(in).
Philip, of Georg Schneider and wife Maria, b. 25 Jul 1777, bapt. 17 Aug 1777. Sponsors: Philip Pankuchen and wife Maria.
Maria, of Peter Gräf and Elisabet, b. 3 Aug 1777, bapt. 17 Aug 1777. Sponsors: the father, and Maria Kuhn(in).
Elisabet, of Peter Witterich and Elisabet, b. 14 Mar 1777, bapt.20 Aug 1777. Sponsors: Christophel Gie and wife Elis.
Elisabet, of Joh. Hepp and wife Catharine, b. 30 Jul 1777, bapt. 24 Aug 1777. Sponsor: widow Holder(in).
Georg, of Daniel Frischmut and Barbara, b. 22 Jul 1777, bapt. 28 Aug 1777. Sponsors: the parents.
Elisabet, of Joh. Hervey and Margar., b. 19 Jul 1777, bapt. 31 Aug 1777. Sponsors: the parents.
Elisabet, of George Peary? and Ann, b. 6 Aug 1777, bapt. 31 Aug 1777. Sponsor: Christine Rol(in).
Mary, of Thomas Watson and Mary, b. 5 Aug 1777, bapt. 31 Aug 1777. Sponsors: the parents.
Baltasar, of Michael Kinsler and Elisab., b. 10 Aug 1777, bapt. 31 Aug 1777. Sponsors: Balth. Kinsler and wife Elis.
Johanna, of Henr. Deitz and Maria Barb., b. 4 Jul 1777, bapt. 7 Sep. 1777. Sponsors: Wilh. Engelfrid and wife Cath. Barbara.
Elisabet, of Jacob Ewald and Jane, b. 31 Aug 1777, bapt. 6 Sep 1777. Sponsors: Jacob Ewald and wife (name not given).
Jacob, of Samuel Gilbert and Cathar., b. 26 Aug 1777, bapt. 14 Sep 1777. Sponsors: Jacob Brand and wife Elis.
Note: Pastor G.H.E. Muhlenberg, Jr.,resided outside the lines of British troops occupying Philadelphia, from Sep 1777 to Jul 1778.

1778, First List
(baptisms by pastor Kunze, from Book III)
Joh. Georg, of Georg Zimmermann and Anna Margareta, b. 19 Dec 1777, bapt. 1 Jan 1778. Sponsors: Christoph Haensmann and wife Mar. Barb.
Christina Barbara, of Christian Jost and Christina Barbara, b. 27 Nov 1777, bapt. 1 Jan 1778. Sponsors: th eparents.
Johann Jacob, of Gottfried Grimm and Rosina Magdalena, b. 27 Dec 1777, bapt. 4 Jan 1778. Sponsors: Jacob Kiemle and wife Christina Catharina.
Maria Margaret, of Adam Me[t]z and Barbara, b. 5 Dec 1777, bapt. 4 Jan 1778. Sponsors: Johannes Me[t]z and wife Anna Barbara.

PHILADELPHIA GERMAN LUTHERAN CHURCH

Elisabeth, of John Mercy and Anna, b. 29 Dec 1777, bapt. 4 Jan 1778. Sponsor: "Mr." Daniel Schroeter.
Laetitia Mary, of William Hill and Sarah, b. 19 Dec 1777, bapt. 4 Jan 1778. Sponsors: John Humphreys, William Sowerspy, Margareth Wilkins, and Laetitia Growl..
Martin, of Abraham Hargus and Maria, b. 10 Dec 1777, bapt. 11 Jan 1778. Sponsors: the mother, and Martin Roh and wife (name not given).
Johann Martin, of Michael Schweizer and Elisabeth, b. 24 Dec 1777, bapt. 11 Jan 1778. Sponsors: Martin Schweizer and wife Magdalena.
Johann Frederich, of Johann Nicolaus Cur[t]z and Catharina, b. 15 Dec 1777, bapt. 11 Jan 1778. Sponsors: Johann Hartmann and Catharina Strek__.
Ann, of Charles Dorn and Ann, b. 3 Jan 1778, bapt. 11 Jan 1778. Sponsors: Patrick Simon, Abigail Hilary, and Anna Barb. La_d.
Catharine, of Johannes Krüger and Catharina, b. 12 Jan 1778, bapt. 18 Jan 1778. Sponsors: Andreas (illegible) and wife Catharina.
Johann Adam, of Henrich Meier and Catharina, b. 11 Jan 1778, bapt. 18 Jan 1778. Sponsors: Johann Adam Rot(h) and Elisabeth Kaemmer(in).
Elisabeth, of Georg Miller and Charlotte, b. 9 Jan 1778, bapt. 18 Jan 1778. Sponsors: the parents.
Anna Cathar., of Georg Bartak and Charlotta, b. 4 Jan 1778, bapt. 18 Jan 1778. Sponsors: the parents.
Conrad, of Johann Conrad and Anna Maria, b. 18 Oct 1777, bapt. 18 Jan 1778. Sponsors: the parents.
Thomas, of Tenes Buckley and Catharina, b. 13 Jan 1778, bapt. 18 Jan 1778. Sponsors: the parents.
Johann Jacob, of Johann Friedr. Fischer and Anna Maria, b. 3 Dec 1777, bapt. 25 Jan 1778. Sponsors: Joh. Jacob Obersley, and Adam Faber and wife Cathar.
Wilhelm, of Wilhelm Weber and Elisabeth, b. 15 Jan 1778, bapt. 25 Jan 1778. Sponsors: Johann Motschutting and the grandmother Cathar. Weber(in).
A child, (name not given), of Johannes Kerl and Maria Elisabeth, b. 8 Jan 1778, bapt. 25 Jan 1778. Sponsors: Conrad Fromm, and Henr. Pfeiffer's wife (name not given).
Christopher, of Philipp Meierle and Anna Esther, b. 24 Jan 1778, bapt. 25 Jan 1778. Sponsors: the parents.
Elisabeth, of Jacob Gress and Elisabeth, b. 22 Dec 1777, bapt. 25 Jan 1778. Sponsors: Elisabeth Stowey(in) and Johann Leihmann.
Johann Jacob, of Georg Strein and Esther, b. 19 Dec 1777, bapt. 25 Jan 1778. Sponsor: Joh. Jac. (surname not given).
Margareta, of Walter Welsh and Marg., b. 8 Jan 1778, bapt. 25 Jan 1778. Sponsors: John Ward, Henr. Wesbrick and Marg. Robertson.
Georg, of Andreas Weh and Regina, b. 10 Nov 1777, bapt. 25 Jan 1778. (Sponsors not given.)
Jacob, of Jacob Riel and Catharina, b. 14 Jan 1778, bapt. 1 Feb 1778. Sponsors: Johan Georg Kraemer and wife Catharina.
Magdalena, of Leonard Kramer and Ann. Margareta, b. 13 Jan 1778, bapt. 29 Jan 1778. Sponsors: the father, and Sarah Mahn(in).

Anna Maria, of John Meels and Elisabeth, b. 4 Jan 1778, bapt. 3 Feb 1778.
Sponsors: the mother, and Peter Mahn.
Elisabeth, of Joseph Milan and Jemina, b. 19 Mar 1777, bapt. 3 Feb 1778.
(Sponsors not given.)
Elisabeth, of Adam Fieder and Catharina, b. 16 Dec 1777, bapt. 6 Feb 1778.
Sponsor: Rosina Scherer(in).
Johannes, of Johann Lamparder and Sarah, b. 14 Jan 1778, bapt. 8 Feb 1778.
Sponsors: the parents.
Catharina, of Mattheus Schu[t]z and Dorothea, b. 15 Aug 1776, bapt. 8 Feb
1778. Sponsors: Marcus Ring and Cathar. Schu[t]z(in).
Georg, of William Kug and Catharina, b. 1 Feb 1778, bapt. 8 Feb 1778.
Sponsors: John Fisher, and John West and wife Margaretha.
James, of Daniel Burgelt? and Margaret, b. 1 Jan 1778, bapt. 8 Feb 1778.
Sponsors: the parents, and Elisab. Willman.
Catharina, of Johannes Moos and Catharina, b. 11 Dec 1777, bapt. 14 Feb 1778.
Sponsors: Johann Friedr. Ulrich and wife Catharina.
Henrich, of Martin Roh and Barbara, b. 3 Feb 1778, bapt. 6 Feb 1778.
Sponsors: the parents (but the father was not present).
Joh. Nicolaus, of Nicolaus Rep and Christina, b. 6 Feb 1778, bapt. 15 Feb 1778.
Sponsors: Jacob Henriegel and wife Catharina.
Michael, of Joseph Kaiser and Anna, b. 1 Sunday in Advent 1777, bapt. 15 Feb
1778. Sponsors: Michael Stimeler and wife Elisabeth.
Anna Catharina, of Georg Moser and Anna Dorothea, b. 25 Jan 1778, bapt.
15 Feb 1778. Sponsors: the father, and Cathar. Forster(in)
Ann, of Samuel Winly and Marg., b. 8 Feb 1778, bapt. 15 Feb 1778. Sponsors:
William Turrington, Wm. Butler, Marg. Stovel and Susanna Me_.
Maria Elisabeth, of Matthaus Schlatter and Elisabeth, b. 6 Feb 1778, bapt.
15 Feb 1778. Sponsor: Maria Schlatter(n).
Andreas, of Martin Kolman and Mary, b. 1 Feb 1778, bapt. 15 Feb 1778.
Sponsor: Sara Town(in).
Mary, of William Hickcox and Martha, b. 4 Feb 1778, bapt. 15 Feb 1778.
Sponsor: Ann Kinsey.
Mary [twin], of Peter Tower and Mary, b. 15 Dec 1777, bapt. 15 Feb 1778.
Sponsor: Daniel Grant.
Sarah twin], of Peter Tower and Mary, b. 15 Dec 1777, bapt. 15 Feb 1778.
Sponsors: John Chapmann and Cathar. St.Gowan?.
Charlotte, of Johannes Wackerer and Elisabeth, b. 20 Jan 1778, bapt. 16 Feb
1778. Sponsors: the parents.
David, of Johann Klag and Maria Magdalena, b. 9 Feb 1778, bapt. 16 Feb 1778.
Sponsors: the parents.
Benjamin, of Thomas Whitaker and Elisabeth, b. 10 Feb 1778, bapt. 16 Feb
1778. Sponsors: the mother, and Isaia Sitten?.
Peter, of Jacob Miller and Margaret, b. 3 Feb 1778, bapt. 18 Feb 1778.
Sponsors: Peter Miller and Elisab. Bartsch(in).
Johann Jacob, of Jacob Buck and Catharina, b. 2 Feb 1778, bapt. 22 Feb 1778.
Sponsors: the parents.
Joh. Michael, of Joh. Michael Kerls and Charlotta, b. 26 Jan 1778, bapt. 22 Feb
1778. Sponsor: Margareta Cathar. Trutland(in)?.

410   PHILADELPHIA GERMAN LUTHERAN CHURCH

Maria Christina, of Joh. Georg Me[t]zinger and Francisca, b. 12 Feb 1778, bapt.
23 Feb 1778. Sponsors: Joh. Melchior Me[t]zinger and wife Christina.
Magdalena, of Friedr. Aron and Elisabeth, b. 25 Jan 1778, bapt. 24 Feb 1778.
Sponsor: Dorothea Stats(in).
Paul Caspar, of Jacob Omensetter and Elisabetha, birthdate not given, bapt.
26 Feb 1778. Sponsors: Paul Briton and wife Susanna.
William, of William McBarriel and Mrs. Christina Rendsheimer(in), illegitimate,
b. 6 Jan 1778, bapt. 27 Feb 1778. Sponsor: Maria Rendsheimer(in).
Philippina, of Johannes Linneberger and Anna Margareta, b. 18 Jan 1778, bapt.
1 Mar 1778. Sponsors: Georg Sei[t]z and wife Elisab.
Carl Joseph, of Henrich Engelfried and Catharina, b. 2 Feb 1778, bapt. 1 Mar
1778. Sponsors: Carl Joseph Wolpert and wife Catharina.
Johann Georg, of Georg Hafner and Magdalena, b. 28 Dec 1777, bapt. 3 Mar
1778. Sponsors: Johann Georg Klettner and Sara Klettner(in).
Johannes, of Friedrich Ulrich and Catharina, b. 23 Dec 1777, bapt. 6 Mar 1778.
Sponsors: Johannes Moos and wife Anna Catharina.
Jacob, of Conrad Flescher? and Maria, b. 7 Feb 1778, bapt. 7 Mar 1778.
Sponsors: Jacob Sager and wife Susanna Barbara.
Friedrich, of Philipp Werner and Maria Magd., b. 9 Feb 1778, bapt. 8 Mar 1778.
Sponsors: Friedr. Gross and Elisab. Steinmetz.
Maria, of Georg Low and Nancy, b. Mar 11, 1778, bapt. 11 Mar 1778.
Sponsor: John Vi(t)zgerald.
Carl Joseph, of John Conner and Rachel, b. 31 Dec 1777, bapt. 9 Mar 1778.
Sponsors: Carl Joseph Wolpert and wife Catharina.
Johann, of Eberhard Lutenberger and Anna Doroth. Elisab., b. 12 Jan 1778,
bapt. 12 Mar 1778. Sponsors: the parents.
Johann Michael [twin], of Johann Meier and Catharina (who died), b. 26 Jan
1778, bapt. 13 Mar 1778. Sponsors: Johann Michael Rehm and wife
Elisabeth.
Catharina, [twin], of Johann Meier and Catharina (who died), b. 26 Jan 1778,
bapt. 13 Mar 1778. Sponsors: same as above.
Anna, of Friedrich Werner and Maria, bapt. 15 Mar 1778. Sponsors: Johann
Blackrose and wife Anna.
Elisabeth, of Friedr. Hainemann and Catharina, b. 1 Feb 1778, bapt. 14 Mar
1778. Sponsors: Georg Klein and wife Elisabetha.
Wilhelm, of Johann Huber and Catharina, b. 14 Jan 1778, bapt. 14 Mar 1778.
Sponsors: Peter Paul and wife Maria.
Wilhelm, of Wilhelm Burghard and Sarah, b. 24 Aug 1777, bapt. 17 Mar 1778.
Sponsors: the parents.
Joseph, of Andreas Beusch and Catharina, b. 17 Feb 1773, bapt. 18 Mar 1778.
Sponsors: the parents.
Thomas, of Andreas Beusch and Catharina, b. 4 Oct 1775, bapt. 18 Mar 1778.
Sponsors: the parents.
Georg., of Andreas Beusch and Catharina, b. 11 Jul 1777, bapt. 18 Mar 1778.
Sponsors: the parents.
Anna Margareta, of Michael Jobst and Margareta, b. 18 Feb 1778, bapt. 18 Mar
1778. Sponsors: the mothr, and Anna Marg. Mildeberger(in).

Jacob, of Nicolaus Wagner and Magdalena, b. 13 Nov 1777, bapt. 19 Mar 1778.
Sponsors: the parents.
Susanna Cathar., of Michael Pfeifer and Regina, b. 8 Mar 1778, bapt. 22 Mar
1778. Sponsors: Michael Pfeifer and wife Susanna.
Joh. Georg, of Carl Lorche and Johanna, b. 2 Mar 1778, bapt. 22 Mar 1778.
Sponsors: Capt. Georg Krug and L[ieut.] Joh. Engelhardt.
Eva, of Christian Lauer and Elisabeth, b. 1 Mar 1778, bapt. 22 Mar 1778.
Sponsors: Jacob Reise and wife Eva.
Sophia, of Robert Gerret and Elisabeth, b. 17 Dec 1777, bapt. 22 Mar 1778.
Sponsors: Adam Muller and Catharina Springer(in).
Barbara, of Georg Vetter and Anna, b. 1 Mar 1778, bapt. 22 Mar 1778.
Sponsors: the parents.
Joh. Wilhelm, of Johannes Grubel and Christina, b. 9 Mar 1778, bapt. 22 Mar
1778. Sponsors: the parents.
Juliana, of John Gartner and Appolonia Wolf(in), illegitimate, b. 21 Mar 1778,
bapt. 29 Mar 1778. Sponsor: Juliana Weiker(in).
Johannes, of Caspar Christ and Catharina, b. 3 Mar 1778, bapt. 29 Mar 1778.
Sponsors: Johannes Veldenberger and Regina Ott___.
Elisabeth, of Christian Wilke and Rosina, b. 19 Mar 1778, bapt. 31 Mar 1778.
Sponsors: the father, and Susanna Schumacher(in).
Simon, of Johann Georg Linck and Elisabeth, b. 27 Feb 1778, bapt. 1 Apr 1778.
Sponsors: the parents and Simon Linck.
Susanna Maria, of Johann Conrad Gebhard and Anna Maria, b. 24 Mar 1778,
bapt. 2 Apr 1778. Sponsors: Peter S_olt___ and wife Susanna.
Johann Jacob, of Georg Genser and Catharina, b. 28 Dec 1777, bapt. 2 Apr
1778. Sponsors: Peter Both and wife Susanna.
Elisabeth, of Henrich Reis and Hanna, b. 2 Mar 1778, bapt. 5 Apr 1778.
Sponsors: Philipp Burg and wife Elisabeth.
Georg David, of Johann David Seckel and Maria, b. 22 Mar 1778, bapt. 5 Apr
1778. Sponsors: Adam Geier and wife (name not given).
Eleonor, of Ambros Allen and Margaretha, b. 1 Apr 1778, bapt. 5 Apr 1778.
(Sponsor not given.)
Joseph, of Joseph Lehmann and Elisabeth, b. 25 Dec 1777, bapt. 5 Apr 1778.
Sponsors: Johann Phil. Gerber and [wife] Eva Maria.
Anna Margareta, of Christoph Kiel and Elisabeth, b. 2 Apr 1778, bapt. 7 Apr
1778. Sponsors: Georg Kriechenmeier and wife Anna Margareta.
Wilhelm, of Matthaeus Schmidt and Catharine, b. 4 Mar 1778, bapt. 6 Apr 1778.
Sponsors: the parents.
Catharina, of Christian Langbecht and Elisabeth, b. 28 Dec 1777, bapt. 8 Apr
1778. Sponsors: Andreas Jung, Wilhelm Reinhardt Reyfeldscher?, Christina
Keppel(in), and Catharina Pfister(in).
Jacob, of Christian Lu[t]z and Susanna, b. 20 Mar 1778, bapt. 9 Apr 1778.
Sponsors: Jacob Ernst Kling (sergeant with the "Auss. Jägren") and Maria?
Christina.
Rosina, of Johannes Krauss and Catharina, b. 5 Apr 1778, bapt. 9 Apr 1778.
Sponsors: Martin Menold and wife Rosina.
Jacob, of Jacob Hesch and Rosina, b. 15 Mar 1778, bapt. 12 Apr 1778.
Sponsors: the parents.

Anna, of Christian Lehmann (deceased) and Elisabeth, b. in Nov 1777?, bapt. 16 Apr 1778. Sponsors: all the confirmands in 1778.

Johannes, of Henrich Jonas and [wife] Catharina, b. 26 Mar 1778, bapt. 19 Apr 1778. Sponsors: John Moore and wife Sarah.

Henrich, of Friedrich Lu[t]z and Catharina, b. 11 Apr 1778, bapt. 22 Apr 1778. Sponsors: Henrich Huber and Maria Suss(in)?.

Georg Jacob, of Georg Kur[t]z and Margareta, b. 8 Apr 1778, bapt. 21 Apr 1778. Sponsors: Jacob Sutzel and wife Barbara.

Elisab. Barbara, of Adam Knoblauch and Elisab. Barbara, b. 10 Jan 1778, bapt. 17 Apr 1778. Sponsors: the parents.

Johann Carl, of Martin Braun and Anna Maria, b. 5 Dec 1777, bapt. 26 Apr 1778. Sponsors: Carl Jung and Elisabetha Klepper(in).

Margareta Dorothea, of Georg Schneck and Elisabeth, b. 9 Apr 1778, bapt. 26 Apr 1778. Sponsors: Georg Gro[t]z and wife Marg. Doroth.

Johan Daniel, of Martin Krieg and Maria Eva, b. 18 Apr 1778, bapt. 26 Apr 1778. Sponsors: Johann Daniel Quendel? and Catharina Bratler(in).

Jacob, of Anton Haehn and Catharina, b. 10 Oct 1777, bapt. 27 Apr 1778, Sponsors: Martin Rap and wife Mar. Salome.

Rosina, of Joseph Stauch and Rosina, b. 12 Nov 1777, bapt. 27 Apr 1778. Sponsors: Martin Rap and wife Mar. Salome.

Elisabeth, of Capt. James King and Maria, b. 21 Mar 1778, bapt. 1 May 1778. Sponsors: Waker Dason Fauiet? and wife [sic] Mar. Marg. Turner.

Maria, of Joh. Nicol. Miller and Anna Maria, b. 18 Apr 1778, bapt. 3 May 1778. Sponsors: Nicol. Weber and dau. Maria.

Elisabeth, of Christian Pashet y and Christina, b. 22 Mar 1778, bapt. 3 May 1778. Sponsors: Wilh. Niclosin and wife Hanna.

Jeane, of Georg Gibbons and Theresia, b. 25 Jan 1778, bapt. 8 May 1778. Sponsor: Anna Maria Dor(in).

Johannes, of Andreas Geier and Barbara, b. 19 Apr 1778, bapt. 10 May 1778. Sponsors: Andreas Posard and Barbara Ramminger(in).

William, of William Pew and Barbara, b. 10 Nov 1777, bapt. 12 May 1778. Sponsors: Joh. David Nies and wife Dorothea.

Johann Wilhelm, of Georg Philipp Weismann and Cathar. Elisabeth, b. 7 May 1778, bapt. 15 May 1778. Sponsors: the parents and Sara Mohn(in).

Johann Jacob, of James Gallacher and Maria, b. 28 Apr 1778, bapt. 17 May 1778. Sponsors: Johann Jacob Kesler and wife Anna Cathar.

Maria Catharina, of Johannes Preusch and Maria Cathar., b. 27 Apr 1778, bapt. 17 May 1778. Sponsors: Joh. Michael Preusch and Maria Cathar. Preusch(in).

Johann Henrich, of Henrich Sommer and Catharina, b. 18 Apr 1778, bapt. 17 May 1778. Sponsors: the parents.

Anna, of Joseph Linden and Anna, b. 2 May 1778, bapt. 17 May 1778. Sponsors: Alexander Jonson and Patrick McEw___.

Maria Magdalene, of Anton Hecht and Sophia, b. 25 Apr 1778, bapt. 17 Apr 1778. (Sponsors not given.)

Esther, of Georg Staus and Esther Dorothea, b. 14 May 1778, bapt. 24 May 1778. Sponsors: Paul Kober and wife Barbara.

Christina, of Jacob Schroeder and Christina Juliana, b. 10 Mar 1778, bapt. 24 May 1778. Sponsors: Christian Lang and wife Chrisina.

Richard, of Richard Roper and Anna, b. 5 Apr 1778, bapt. 24 May 1778. Sponsors: John Rice and Wm. Ben__.

Johann Andreas, of Johann Henrich Tierkop and Anna Maria, b. 25 Apr 1778, bapt. 26 May 1778. Sponsors: Johann Andreas Nesselstraw and wife Anna Maria, and Magdalena Thomsdun?.

Anna Maria, of Adam Pausch and Anna Maria, b. 17 May 1778, bapt. 29 May 1778. Sponsors: the parents.

Anthony, of Ephraim Evans and Catharina, b. 22 Dec 1777, bapt. 2 Jun 1778. Sponsor: the mother.

John, of Ephraim Evans and Catharina, b. 20 Oct 1772, bapt. 2 Jun 1778. Sponsosr: the mother.

Joseph, of Ephraim Evans and Catharina, b. 18 Dec 1775, bapt. 2 Jun 1778. Sponsor: the mother.

Elisabeth, of Jacob Razer and Susanna, b. 9 May 1778, bapt. 6 Jun 1778. Sponsors: Georg Razer and Dorothea Furch(in).

Michael, of Johann Braun and Anna Catharina, b. 28 May 1778, bapt. 9 Jun 1778. Sponsors: Carl Jung and Maria Elisabeth Jung(in).

Johann Gottfried, of Gottfried Zürchubel and Catharina, b. 1 May 1778, bapt. 8 Jun 1778. Sponsor: Johann Manscher and wife Cath.

Carl, of Carl Wilhelm Nushag and Catharina, b. 24 May 1778, bapt. 14 Jun 1778. Sponsors: the parents.

Elisabeth, of Sigmund Copia and Sophia Magdalena, b. 31 May 1778, bapt. 14 Jun 1778. Sponsors: Peter Grimm and wife Dorothea.

Margareta, of Henrich Beckely and Elisabeth, b. 12 Mar 1778, bapt. 14 Jun 1778. Sponsors: the grandparents Henrich Bec_ and (not named).

Joh. Michael, of Georg Kehrlmann? and Elisabeth, b. 24 Dec 1777, bapt. 20 Jun 1778. Sponsors: Georg Keiler and wife Barbara.

Samuel, of Jacob Klaus and Margareta, b. 4 May 1778, bapt. 29 Jun 1778. Sponsors: the parents.

Margaret, of William Varley and Elizabeth, b. 8 Nov 1777, bapt. 24 Jun 1778. Sponsors: the father, and Rosina Margar. Geret(in).

Georg, of Johann Chargeau and Catharina, b. in Sep 1777, bapt. 26 Jun 1778. Sponsors: Georg Fischer and wife [sic] Maria Messinger.

Martin, of Joh. Jacob Kessler and Anna Catharine, b. 28 Jun 1778, bapt. 1 Jul 1778. Sponsors: Martin Haertle and wife Margareta.

Samuel, of Johannes Kessler and Maria Magdalena, b. 17 Apr 1778, bapt. 2 Jul 1778. Sponsors: Samuel Neidlinger and wife Maria Elisabeth.

Johannes, of Michael Schreihof and Anna Maria, b. 4 Apr 1778, bapt. 6 Jul 1778. Sponsors: Johann Urlein and Anna Maria.

Jacob, of David Dieterich and Christina, b. 21 Jun 1778, bapt. 5 Jul 1778. Sponsors: Jacob Dietrich and wife Margareta.

Anna Maria, of Caspar Oberdorf and Margareta, b. 18 Sep 1777, bapt. 12 Jul 1778. Sponsors: Leonhard Buck and wife Maria.

Maria, of Philip Pannekuch and Maria, b. 2 Dec 1777, bapt. 12 Jul 1778. Sponsors: Leonhard Buck and wife Maria.

Sarah, of Joh. Jost Schweighardt and Hanna, (bapt. by Rev. Muhlenberg Sr.), b. 18 Jun 1777, bapt. 18 Jul 1778. Sponsors: the parents.

Sarah, of Michael Wolf and Margareta, b. 4 Jan 1778, bapt. 18 Jul 1778. Sponsors: David Wer and wife Anna.

Christoph, of Johann Georg Schneider and Anna Margareta, b. 18 Mar 1778, bapt. 18 Jul 1778. Sponsors: Christoph No[t]z and wife (name not legible).

Georg Jacob, of Philipp Heger and Anna Cathar., b. 29 Jan 1778, bapt. 19 Jul 1778. Sponsors: Johannes Heger and wife Anna Catharina.

Heinrich, of Henrich Kur[t]z and Rosina, b. 28 Mar 1778, bapt. 19 Jul 778. Sponsors: Bernhard Buck and wife (name not legible).

Maria Margreth, of Georg Vogel and Elisabeth, b. 19 Jun 1778, bapt. 19 Jul 1778. Sponsors: Friedrich Vogel and Marg. Stan___.

Elisabeth, of Peter Kaig and Elisabeth, b. 4 Jun 1778, bapt. 19 Jul 1778. Sponsors: the parents.

Regina, of Joh. Edelmann and Sarah, b. 29 Jul 1777, bapt. 20 Jul 1778. Sponsors: Jacob Haine and wife Esther.

Margretha, of Andr. Uhler and Regina, b. 8 Jul 1778, bapt. 26 Jul 1778. Sponsors: Wm. Herman and wife Margar.

Elisabeth, of Edward Laiky and Cathar., b. 26 Jul 1778, bapt. 26 Jul 1778. Sponsors: Joh. Peck and Elisab. Cook.

Jacob, of Euphronia (a slave of Georg Jung), b. 2 May 1778, bapt. 26 Jul 1778. Sponsor: H. Muhlenberg.

Margareta, of Johannes Conning and Christine, b. 6 Jan 1777, bapt. 31 Jul 1778. Sponsor: the mother's sister Catharina Border(in).

Carl, of Marcus Mantelius and Christine, b. 24 Jul 1778, bapt. 1 Aug 1778. Sponsors: the parents.

Nicolaus, of Philipp Werner and Anna Magdalena, b. 8 Jun 1778, bapt. 2 Aug 1778. Sponsors: Nicolaus Panzer and wife Elisabeth.

Marg., of John Williams and Marg., b. 6 Jun 1777, bapt. 2 Aug 1778. Sponsor: Franc. Menz's wife? Elizabeth.

Elisabeth, of Conrad Harf and Anna, b. 9 Apr 1778, bapt. 7 Aug 1778. Sponsors: the mother, and Nicol. Miller's wife.

Anna Maria, of Wilhelm Joh. Neu and Elisabeth, b. 27 Aug 1777, bapt. 9 Aug 1778. Sponsors: Andreas Heng and wife Anna Maria.

Jacob, of John Preis and Anna, b. 25 Mar 1778, bapt. 9 Aug 1778. Sponsors: Johann Jacob Kellor and wife Elisabeth.

Maria Margareta, of Johannes Weitenmeier and Maria, b. 15 May 1778, bapt. 9 Aug 1778. Sponsor: Maria Margar. Grommel(in).

Johann, of Wilhelm Kaempf and Anna Maria, b. 11 Aug 1778, bapt. 12 Aug 1778. Sponsors: Johannes Christian Kaempf and wife Maria.

Christoph, of Christoph Schlug and Elisabeth, b. 11 Aug 1778, bapt. 16 Aug 1778. Sponsors: the parents.

Johann Joseph, of Valentin Gosner and Maria Agnes, b. 27 Jul 1778, bapt. 20 Aug 1778. Sponsors: the parents.

Anna Elisabeth, of Joseph Mansfild and Anna Magdalena, b. 6 Aug 1778, bapt. 20 Aug 1778. Sponsors: Johannes Abel and sister Elisabeth.

Maria, of Johannes Feil and Philippina, b. 6 Aug 1778, bapt. 23 Aug 1778. Sponsor: the grandmother Philippina Christler.

Hannah, of Wilhelm Stur[t]z and Regina, b. 7 Jun 1778, bapt. 23 Aug 1778. Sponsors: Georg Stur[t]z and Anna Graes(lin).
Philippina, of Jacob Bechthold and Anna Maria, b. 6 Mar 1778, bapt. 25 Aug 1778. Sponsors: Georg Ri[t]z and wife Maria Elisabeth.
Johann Peter, of Philipp Sommer and Salome, b. 14 Sep 1777, bapt. 29 Aug 1778. Sponsors: the parents.
Christoph, of Christoph Mohr and Catharina, b. 19 Aug 1778, bapt. 29 Aug 1778. Sponsors: the parents.
Joseph Martin, of Martin Boref and Catharina, b. 14 Aug 1778, bapt. 31 Aug 1778. Sponsors: Peter Mahn and wife Anna Maria.
Catharina, of Daniel Frischmuth and Barbara, b. 29 Jul 1778, bapt. 6 Sep 1778. Sponsors: Michael Ho[t]z and wife Catharina.
Michael, of Jacob Seger and Barbara, b. 18 Aug 1778, bapt. 6 Sep 1778. Sponsors: Michael Stricker and wife Margareta.
Carolina Susanna, of Christian Stüzer and Christina, b. 18 Aug 1778, bapt. 6 Sep 1778. Sponsors: Carl Hofmann and wife Susanna Regina.
Hester, of Henr. Dipperger and Cathar. Elisab., b. 25 Aug 1778, bapt. 6 Sep 1778. Sponsors: Col. Ludwig Farmer and wife Anna Maria.
Adam, of Jacob Graeker? and Susanna, b. 21 Aug 1778, bapt. 6 Sep 1778. Sponsors: Adam Schaefer and Maria Heil(in).
Jacob [twin?], of Jacob Bender and Catharina, birthdate not given, bapt. 16 Sep 1778. Sponsors: the grandparents Jacob Bender and wife Dorothea.
Elisabeth, [twin?], of Jacob Bender and Catharina, birthdate not given, bapt. 16 Sep 1778. Sponsors: same as above.
Maria, of Bernhard Buck and Maria, b. 31 Aug 1778, bapt. 20 Sep 1778. Sponsors: the father, and Elisabeth Franck.
Joh. Jacob, of Eberhard Diel and Catharina, b. 20 Aug 1778, bapt. 20 Sep 1778. Sponsors: Jacob Kaufman and An. Maria.
Maria Eva, of Georg Bastian and Maria Eva, b. 6 Sep 1778, bapt. 23 Sep 1778. Sponsors: Gabriel Kern and wife Magdalena.
Catharina, of Leonhard Fischer and Susanna, b. 31 Aug 1778, bapt. 27 Sep 1778. Sponsors: Jacob Kiemle and wife Cathar. Christina.
William, of Nathaniel Richard and Hannah, b. in 1774, bapt. 28 Sep 1778. Sponsors: Nicolaus Jacobs and Cathar. Berthhold.
Joseph, of Henr. Kaemmerer and Catharina, b. 7 Dec 1777, bapt. 8 Oct 1778. Sponsors: Conrad Baethis and wife Barbara.
Charlotte Susanna, of Conrad Hess and Charlotte, b. 3 Oct 1778, bapt. 10 Oct 1778. Sponsor: Susanna Graes(in).
Georg, of Matthaeus Gilbert and Christina, b. 16 Sep 1778, bapt. 11 Oct 1778. Sponsors: Georg Fuggerod and wife Barbara.
Margareta, of Georg Bub and Maria, b. 8 Oct 1778, bapt. 14 Oct 1778. Sponsors: Henrich Schruber and wife Margareta.
Joh. Wilhelm, of Peter Paul and Anna Maria, b. 4 Sep 1778, bapt. 15 Oct 1778. Sponsors: Parents.
Rudolf, of Johann Burghard Fischer and Catharina, b. 27 Sep 1778, bapt. 10 Oct 1778. Sponsors: Rudolf Lehr and wife Catharina.
Johan Georg, of Jacob Ulrich Sutzel and Barbara, b. 17 Oct 1778, bapt. 17 Oct 1778. Sponsors: Johann Georg Kur[t]z and wife (not named).

Maria Aletta, of Adolf Christian Hederich and Nancy, b. 28 Sep 1778, bapt. 28 Sep 1778. Sponsor: Col. Lutherlow and Maria Haso___.
Elisabeth, of Georg Rehn? and Catharina, b. 3 Oct 1778, bapt. 30 Oct 1778. Sponsors: Caspar Wahl and wife Elisab..
Joseph Reed, of Andreas Berkhardt and Susanna, b. 15 Oct 1778, bapt. 1 Nov 1778. Sponsors: the parents.
Samuel, of Johannes Brugges and Catharina, b. 20 Jun 1778, bapt. 1 Nov 1778. Sponsor: Christian Danneck.
Margareta Barbara, of Jacob Kiemle and Christina Catharina, b. 27 Oct 1778, bapt. 8 Nov 1778. Sponsors: the father, and Ursula Barbara Kiemli(n).
Samuel, of Johann Rohner and Barbara, b. 1 Nov 1778, bapt. 15 Nov 1778. Sponsors: Johann Grieffenstein and wife Dorothea.
Elisabeth, of Jacob Ki[t]z and Elisabeth, b. 25 Oct 1778, bapt. 28 Nov 1778. Sponsors: Matthius Scheuer___ and wife Barbara.
Apollonia, of Georg Ki[t]z and Margareta, b. 6 Nov 1778, bapt. 28 Nov 1778. Sponsors: Georg Ki[t]z and wife Apollonia.
Philipp Jacob, of Georg Kinzinger and Catharina, b. 13 Nov 1778, bapt. 29 Nov 1778. Sponsors: Philipp Jacob Weiss and wife Catharina.
Elisabeth, of Jacob Buss and Barbara, b. 23 Jan 1777, bapt. 3 Dec 1778. Sponsor: Eva Maria Klein(in).
Johann Philipp, of Johannes Hoetzel and Catharina, b. 24 Oct 1778, bapt. 6 Dec 1778. Sponsors: Balthasar Staus and wife Maria.
Anna Elisabeth, of Rudolph Nagel and Susanna, b. 31 Nov 1778, bapt. 15 Dec 1778. Sponsors: Henrich Schwa_bach and wife Cathar.
Johannes, of Georg Razer and Catharina, b. 11 Dec 1778, bapt. 16 Dec 1778. Sponsors: Georg Razer and Sophia.
Adam Simon, of Peter Kuhn and Elisabeth, b. 19 Nov 1778, bapt. 19 Dec 1778. Sponsors: the parents.
Joh. Gottfried, of Gottfried Grumbach and Barbara, b. 12 Sep 1778, bapt. 21 Dec 1778. Sponsors: the parents.
Catharina Barbara, of Nicolaus Hauler (of Frankford [Pennsylvania]) and Anna Maria, b. 24 Sep 1778, bapt. 21 Dec 1778. Sponsors: Carl Joseph Wolpert and wife Catharina.
Elisabeth Fortun, (a foundling, parents unknown), b. 27 Dec 1777, bapt. 21 Dec 1778. Sponsors: Jacob Kiemle and Elisabeth Schweizer(in).
Dorothea Regina, of Ludwig Bender and Margareta, b. 14 Oct 1778, bapt. 23 Dec 1778. Sponsors: Christian Schaefer and wife Dorothea.
Maria Magdalena, of Georg Gro[t]z and Margareta Dorothea, b. 15 Dec 1778, bapt. 25 Dec 1778. Sponsors: John Martin Teum? and wife Maria Magdal.
Elisabeth, of Johannes Rieb and Susanna, b. 9 Dec 1778, bapt. 28 Dec 1778. Sponsors: Leonard Rieb and wife Elisabeth.

1778, Second List
(baptisms by pastor G.H.E. Muhlenberg, Jr., from Book IV)
(Note; he resided outside British-occupied Philadelphia until Jul 1778.)
William Godfrey, of Richard Thomas and wife Sara, b. 11 Nov 1777, bapt. 6 Jul
1778. Sponsors: the parents.
Christoph, of Christoph Brannon and wife Ann, b. in May 1776, bapt. 22 Jul
1778. Sponsor: Margar. Burghart(in).
Catharine, of Friedr. Link and wife Cath. Barb., b. 3 Jul 1778, bapt. 26 Jul 1778.
Sponsors: the parents.
Susanne, of Adam Kemminger and Susanne, b. 8 Jul 1778, bapt. 26 Jul 1778.
Sponsors: the parents.
Johannes, of Johannes Haas and wife Elisab., b. 4 Jun 1778, bapt. 26 Jul 1778.
Sponsors: Joh. Haas and wife Elis.
Wilhelm, of (parents names not given), b. 4 Jun 1778, bapt. 26 Jul 1778.
Sponsors: Christoph Senterling and wife Anna Mar.
David, of Johannes Fischer and wife Cath.,b. 6 May 1778, bapt. 26 Jul 1778.
Sponsors: the parents.
Maria, of Andreas Leinau and wife Rosine, b. 3 Jul 1778, bapt. 26 Jul 1778.
Sponsors: Daniel Hess and wife Anna Gertraut.
Anna Maria, of Caspar Kindisch and wife Marg., b. 3 Jul 1778, bapt. 2 Aug
1778. Sponsors: Jacob Ritzer? and wife Susanne.
Jacob, of Michael Mays? and Abby, b. 1 Jun 1778, bapt. 2 Aug 1778. Sponsors:
Jacob Heimar and wife Mercy.
Johan Michael, of Michael Gilbert and Anna, b. 25 Jan 1778, bapt. 10 Aug
1778. Sponsors: the parents.
Johanna, of Nicolaus Hinkel and wife Anna, b. 16 Dec 1777, bapt. 16 Aug 1778.
Sponsors: Johannes Bender and wife Catharine.
Elisabet, of Jacob Rohn and wife Lydia, b. 15 Jul 1778, bapt. 16 Aug 1778.
Sponsors: Math. Both and Christine Rohn.
Anna Maria Catharina, of Rev. Johan Christoph Kunze (preacher here) and wife
Margar. Henrietta, b. 20 Aug 1778, bapt. the same day. Sponsors: brother-in-
law Franciscus Swaine? and wife Maria Cathar.
Anna, of Philip Jacob Burg and wife Elisab., b. 8 Aug 1778, bapt. 23 Aug 1778.
Sponsors: Henr. Reis and wife Anna.
Jacob, of Joh. Jacob Wolf and wife Cathar., b.7 Aug 1778, bapt. 23 Aug 1778.
Sponsors: the parents.
Johan, of Isaac Stahl and wife Elis., b. 7 Aug 1778, bapt. 23 Aug 1778.
Sponsors: brother-in-law Balth. Fleischer and wife Cathar.
Edward, of Daniel Dress and wife Mary, b. 25 Jul 1778, bapt. 23 Aug 1778.
Sponsors: the parents.
Margaret, of Thomas Garwick and wife Christina, b. in Feb 1778, bapt. 23 Aug
1778. Sponsors: Johannes Krauter and wife Margar.
Christiana Maria, of Henr. Drei_elter and wife Margar., b. 21 Aug 1778, bapt.
25 Aug 1778. Sponsors: the grandparents Salomon.
Elisabet Margar., of Ludwig Kehl and wife Elisab., b. 21 Aug 1778, bapt. 2 Sep
1778. Sponsors: Jeremia Kehl and widow Elis. Fary.
Jacob Ferdinand, of Jacob Wilhelm Facundus and wife Dorothea, b. 22 Aug
1778, bapt. 28 Aug 1778. Sponsors: the father, mother, and Maria Kitz(in).

Isaac, of Gottfried Walter and wife Jean (now deceased), b. in Mar 1778, bapt. 28 Aug 1778. Sponsor: widow Anna Cath. White(in).

Rebecca, of Melchior Weissirger and wife Maria, b. 18 Dec 1777, bapt. 30 Aug 1778. Sponsors: Balth. Staus and wife Maria.

Anna, of Conrad Kohrman and wife Elis., b. 1 Aug 1778, bapt. 29 Aug 1778. Sponsors: the mother, and Anna Kotter(in).

Henrietta, of Mr. Henrich Keppele and wife Catharine, b. 6 Aug 1778, bapt. 30 Aug 1778. Sponsors: the parents, and Mrs. Susanne Zanzinger.

Maria Elisabet, of Johan Eberhard and Catharine, b. 1 Sep 1778, bapt. 12 Sep 1778. Sponsors: Georg Walker and wife Anna Dorothea.

Maria, of Michael Müller and wife Barb., b. 19 Aug 1778, bapt. 13 Sep 1778. Sponsors: the maternal grandparents Barthol. Schaetzlein and wife Cath.

Jacob, of Jacob Werner and wife Sarah, b. 12 Aug 1778, bapt. 13 Sep 1778. Sponsors: Georg Goettle and wife Hanna.

Mary, of Bartholom Glyn and Elisabet, b. 12 Jul 1778, bapt. 17 Sep 1778. Sponsors: Cath. Dörr and Margar. Price.

Johan Jacob, of Isaac Anderson and wife Elisabet, b. 2 May 1778, bapt. 20 Sep 1778. Sponsors: Joh. Jacob Eiterich and Juliana Dill(in).

Maria, of William Alexander and Rebecca, b. 21 Aug 1778, bapt. 20 Sep 1778. Sponsor: Maria Alexander.

Maria Elis., of Philip Gerber and wife Maria, b. 30 Aug 1778, bapt. 20 Sep 1778. Sponsors: Joh Kohm and wife Mar. Cath.

Friedrich, of Leonard Heil and wife Anna Maria, b. 16 Jun 1778, bapt. 20 Sep 1778. Sponsors: the parents.

Rosina Magdalene, of Alexander Lintsch and wife Ros. Magd., b. 1 Sep 1778, bapt. 27 Sep 1778. Sponsors: Henr. Dietz and wife Maria Barbara.

Catherine, of Martin Kühnhauer and wife Elisab., b. 8 Sep 1778, bapt. 4 Oct 1778. Sponsors: Johannes Kraus and wife Catharine.

Johan Georg, of Georg Sohnleutner and wife Cathar., b. 3 Sep 1778, bapt. 4 Oct 1778. Sponsors: Philip Fischer and wife Anna Maria.

Georg, of William Kohrt and wife Cathar., b. 18 Sep 1778, bapt. 4 Oct 1778. (Sponsors not given.)

Jacob, of Johannes Pilliger and Margaret, b. 10 Aug 1778, bapt. 4 Oct 1778. Sponsors: Isaac Brant and wife Elisabet.

Johan Simon, of Georg Knerr and wife Catharine, b. 28 Aug 1778, bapt. 4 Oct 1778. Sponsors: Urban Friebel and wife Maria Barbara.

Philip, of Joh. Weger and wife Sarah, b. 7 Oct 1778, bapt. 14 Oct 1778. Sponsors: Philip Weger and wife Maria.

Joh. Jacob, of Joh. Jacob Unbehend and wife Maria, b. 30 Sep 1778, bapt. 16 Oct 1778. Sponsors: the father, and Cath. Spigel(in) (single).

Regina, of Caspar Wurschun and wife Rosina, b. 2 Oct 1778, bapt. 18 Oct 1778. Sponsors: Henr. Kayser and wife [sic] Christina Nagel(in)

Joh., of Adam Schaefer and wife Dorothea, b. 23 Sep 1778, bapt. 18 Oct 1778. Sponsors: the parents.

Joh. Henrich, of Joh. Wagner and wife Elisab., b. 15 Oct 1777, bapt. 18 Oct 1778. Sponsors: Joh. Henr. Mänchen and wife (name not given).

Elisabet, of Joh. Birkenbeiler and wife Cath., birthdate not given, bapt. 18 Oct 1778. Sponsors: Peter Heimbach and wife Elis.

Henry, of Thomas Richmond and wife Cath., b. 28 Sep 1778, bapt. 18 Oct 1778.
Sponsors: Henry Vinemer and Elisabet Hess(in).
Rebecca, of William Stewart and wife Juliana, b. 23 Sep 1778, bapt 18 Oct
1778. Sponsors: Philip Fischer and wife Maria.
Sus. Christine, of Joh. Kennedy and Susanna, 9 months old, bapt. 18 Oct 1778.
Sponsors: the father, and widow Simon(in).
Jacob, of Peter Birwanger and wife Eva., b. 31 Aug 1778, bapt. 4 Oct 1778.
Sponsors: Joh. Biegler and wife Anna Cath.
George, of Caspar Cox and wife Martha, b. 23 Sep 1777, bapt. 20 Oct 1778.
Sponsors: Christoph Meyer and Sara.
John, of Jost Humphreys and wife Margaret, b. in Oct 1777, bapt. 23 Oct 1778.
Sponsor: Hugh McDowel.
Archibald, of James Frazer and wife Juliana, b. 2 Feb 1778, bapt. 25 Oct 1778.
Sponsors: Math. Müller and Maria Hall(in).
Daniel, of Daniel Pilger and wife Marg., b. 19 Jun 1778, bapt. 25 Oct 1778.
Sponsors: Johan Pilger and wife Margar.
Maria [twin], of Christian Ruth and wife Sara, b. 16 Aug 1778, bapt. 31 Oct
1778. Sponsors: Carl Preis and wife Anna Maria.
Sara [twin], of Christian Ruth and wife Sara, b. 16 Aug 1778, bapt. 31 Oct 1778.
Sponsors: the parents.
Maria, of Jacob Pennighoff and wife Sybilla, b. 15? Sep 1778, bapt. 4 Oct 1778.
Sponsors: the parents.
Elisabet, of Georg Stephens and wife Mary, b. 4 Oct 1778, bapt. 1 Nov 1778.
Sponsors: Joh. Penter and wife Susanne
Georg, of Peter Sohnleutner and wife Elis., b. 10 Jul 1778, bapt. 1 Nov 1778.
Sponsors: the parents.
John, of Ellis Livingston and wife Mary, b. 1 Oct 1778, bapt. 4 Nov 1778.
Sponsor: Martha Thomson.
David, of Christian Schaefer and wife Doroth., b. 1 Nov 1778, bapt. 6 Nov 1778.
Sponsors: David Eberhard and wife Elisabet.
Joh. Friedr., of Caspar Whitbach and wife Anna, b. 11 Jun 1778, bapt. 8 Nov
1778. Sponsors: Friedr. Vogel and wife Cathar.
Jacob, of Joh. Schaefer and wife Maria, b. 25 Oct 1778, bapt. 8 Nov 1778.
Sponsors: Jacob Winey and wife Sus. Margar.
Joh. Henrich, of Thomas McClean and Elisab., b. 8 Nov 1778, baapt. 12 Nov
1778. Sponsor: Elis. Boehm(in).
Joseph, of Valentin Wenhold and wife Anna, b. in Jun 1766, bapt. 14 Nov 1778.
Sponsors: the parents.
Valentin, of Valentin Wenhold and wife Anna, b. 24 Jan 1771, bapt. 14 Nov
1778. Sponsors: the parents.
Johannes, of Valentin Wenhold and wife Anna, b. 20 Oct 1778, bapt. 14 Nov
1778. Sponsors: the parents.
Henrich, of Henr. Moses and wife Susanne b. 6 Nov 1778, bapt. 22 Nov 1778.
Sponsors: Georg Blum and wife Christine.
Daniel, of Balthas. Emmerich and wife Maria, b. 11 Nov 1778, bapt. 22 Nov
1778. Sponsors: Joh. Emmerich and wife Maria.
Maria Regina, of Joh. Bach and wife Elisabet, b. 11 Nov 1778, bapt. 22 Nov
1778. Sponsors: Math. Sommer and wife Maria Reg.

Philip William, of John Brea[k]field and Mary, b. 22 Oct 1778, bapt. 22 Nov 1778. Sponsors: Philip Wilh. Cohlman and wife Mary.

Barbara, of Daniel Gilbert and wife Cath., b. 2 Nov 1778, bapt. 29 Nov 1778. Sponsors: Anton Birkenbeiler and wife Barbara.

Joh. Benjamin, of Benjamin Quadt and wife Charlotte, b. 20 Nov 1778, bapt. 29 Nov 1778. Sponsors: Joh. Kramp and wife Dorothea.

Philippine (twin), of Peter Ritter and wife Prunella, b. 18 Aug 1778, bapt. 29 Nov 1778. Sponsors: the mother, and John Fulton.

Catharine, (twin), of Peter Ritter and wife Prunella, b. 18 Aug 1778, bapt. 29 Nov 1778. Sponsors: James Fulton and wife (name not given).

Sarah, of Michael Bayer and wife Elis., b. 29 Sep 1778, bapt. 29 Nov 1778. . Sponsors: Peter Ritter and wife Brunella.

Joh. Friedrich, of Joh. Bernhold and wife Dorothea, b. 23 Nov 1778, bapt. 6 Dec 1778. Sponsors: Friedrich Wölpert and wife Margar.

Magdalene, of Valentin Hofman and wife Susanne, b. 26 Nov 1778, bapt. 6 Dec 1778. Sponsors: Andr. Lexter and wife Magdalene.

Johannes, of Abraham Bachman and wife Philippine, b. 26 Nov 1778, bapt. 3 Dec 1778. Sponsors: Caspar Gräf and wife Maria.

Michael, of Conrad Leibbrand and wife Hanna, b. 7 May 1778, bapt. 6 Dec 1778, Sponsors: Peter Süs and wife Cathar.

Elisabeth, of George England and Cathar., b. 2 Dec 1778, bapt. 6 Dec 1778. Sponsors: Will. Brown, Elis. Stewart, and Elis. Fagan.

Anna Catharine, of Georg Kehl and wife Veronica, b. 29 Nov 1778, bapt. 13 Dec 1778. Sponsors: Friedr. Lendorf and Cath. Geiler(in).

Maria, of Johan Unangst and wife Cath., b. 22 Nov 1778, bapt. 13 Dec 1778. Sponsors: Georg Bachhol[t]z and wife Maria.

Christine, of Wilhelm Hays and wife Maria?, b. 16? Dec 1778, bapt. 17 Dec 1778. Sponsor: Christine Wals(in).

Esther, of Thomas Day and wife Mary, b. 27 Oct 1778, bapt. 17 Dec 1778. Sponsor: the mother.

Christine Doroth., of David Uber and wife Anna, b. 7 Dec 1778, bapt. 20 Dec 1778. Sponsors: Adam Schuster and wife Christine Dorothea.

Adam, of Johannes Koch and wife Anna, b. 6 Dec 1778, bapt. 20 Dec 1778. Sponsors: Adam Krebs and wife Anna Maria.

Regina, of Adam Witterstein and wife Sophia, b. 2 Dec 1778, bapt. 20 Dec 1778. Sponsors: Andr. Grübel and wife Regina.

Regina Barbara, of Carl Preis and wife Maria Magd., b. 6 Nov 1778, bapt. 25 Dec 1778. Sponsors: Caspar Schüster and wife Regina.

Mary of Godfrey Hamlet and Barbara, b. 19 Sep 1778, bapt. 25 Dec 1778. Sponsors: James McGinny and wife Mary.

Sarah, of Robert Cunningham and Lucinda, b. 14 Dec 1778, bapt. 25 Dec 1778. Sponsors: Thomas Sullivan and Christiana McCormick.

Joh. Wilhelm of Michael Steinhauer and wife Barbara, b. 4 Dec 1778, bapt. 26 Dec 1778. Sponsors: the parents.

Elisabet, of Charles Jones and wife Catharine, b. 28 Nov 1778, bapt. 27 Dec 1778. Sponsors: Georg Fritz and wife Elisabet.

Catharina, of Andr. Lobstein and wife Elisab., b. 28 Dec 1778, bapt. 30 Dec 1778. Sponsors: Jacob Graf and Cath. Saner(in)?.

Maria, of Elisha Truby and Margar., b. 23 Nov 1778, bapt. 30 Dec 1778. Sponsors: Gabriel Kern and wife Magdalene.

Magdalene Gaffert, almost 22 years old, was baptized on her sickbed, 31 Dec 1778.

Rachel, of Georg Miltenberger and wife Cathar., b. 25 Nov 1778, bapt. 31 Dec 1778. (Sponsors not given.)

1779, First List
(baptisms by pastor Kunze and Helmuth; all in approximate chronological sequence, from Book III)

Martin [twin], of Henrich Koch and Margareta Schneider (illegitimate), b. 1 Jan 1779, bapt. 3 Jan 1779. Sponsors: Martin Schneider and wife Magdalena.

Henrich, [twin], of Henrich Koch and Margareta Schneider (illegitimate), b. 1 Jan 1779, bapt. 3 Jan 1779. Sponsors: Friedrich Schütz and wife Barbara.

Elisabeth Margareta, of Major Pellford (*aide-de-camp* to Gen. Howe) and Catharina Grob(in) (illegitimate), b. 12 Dec 1778, bapt. 3 Jan 1779. Sponsors: (first name not given) Kaise__ and wife Elisabeth Marg.

Adam, of Michael Hay and Maria, b. 7 Jan 1779, bapt. 9 Jan 1779. Sponsor: Eva Lob(in)?.

Catharina, of Joseph Cully and Catharina, b. 4 Jan 1779, bapt. 10 Jan 1779. Sponsors: Mich. Omensetter and wife Catharina.

Gottfried, of William Wooster and Anna, b. 6 Jan 1779, bapt. 11 Jan 1779. Sponsors: Anna Margareta and Dorothea Claus(in)?.

Peter, of Peter Kur[t]z and Sarah, b. 30 Dec 1778, bapt. 13 Jan 1779. Sponsors: the parents.

David, of Adam Schuster and Christina Dorothea, b. 8 Jan 1779, bapt. 8 Jan 1779. Sponsors: David Wu__ and wife Anna.

Maria Margareta, of Jacob Ries and Mar. Magdalena, b. 31 Dec 1778, bapt. 16 Jan 1779. Sponsors: Philipp Zetter? and wife Barbara?.

Jacob, of Jacob Specht and Margareta, b. 28 Apr 1778, bapt. 18 Jan 1779. Sponsors: Georg Specht and wife Margareta.

Henrich, of John Philipps and Christina, b. 15 Dec 1778, bapt. 18 Jan 1779. Sponsors: the parents.

Jacob, of Peter Mehrelin and Maria, b. 16 Jan 1779, bapt. 31 Jan 1779. Sponsors: Joh. Henr. (illegible) and wife Catharina.

Johann Jacob, of Johann Stephan Sulliger and Johanna, b. 28 Jan 1779, bapt. 7 Feb 1779. Sponsors: Johan Jacob Sulliger and wife An. Marg.

Georg Heinrich, of Henrich Herbst and Elisabeth, b. 10 Feb 1779, bapt. 14 Feb 1779. Sponsors: Georg Kitz and wife Appolonia.

Maria Charlotte, of Michael Kraft and Johanna Maria, b. 27 Jan 1779, bapt. 14 Feb 1779. Sponsors: Conrad Hess and wife Charlotte Christina.

Georg, of Georg? Spynck and Magdalena, b. 2 Feb 1779, bapt. 20 Feb 1779. Sponsors: Georg Bastian and wife Magd.

Georg, of Friedr. Gesch and Catharina, b. 13 Feb 1779, bapt. 21 Feb 1779. Sponsors: Georg Ki[t]z, Jr., and wife Margareta.

Maria, of Christian Kühn and Maria, b. 4 Feb 1779, bapt. 21 Feb 1779. Sponsors: Mich. Blanchorn and wife Maria.

Joh. Jacob, of Johannes Freiberg and Susanna, b. 1 Feb 1779, bapt. 21 Feb 1779. Sponsors: the father, and Mar. Magdalena Santor(in)?.

Rudolph, of Johannes Veltenberger and Magdalena, b. 7 Feb 1779, bapt. 21 Feb 1779. Sponsors: Rudolph Nagel and wife Susanna.

Maria Catharina, of Jacob Pfister and Margareta, b. 2 Feb 1779, bapt. 21 Feb 1779. Sponsors: Philipp Kunzmann and wife Maria Cathar.

Johann Friedrich, of Henrich Apfel and Christina, b. 16 Jan 1779, bapt. 21 Feb 1779. Sponsors: Friedrich Brodbeck and wife Margareta.

Johannes, of Philipp Krebs and Margareta, b. 6, Feb 779, bapt. 28 Feb 1779. Sponsors: Johannes Kunckel and wife Maria Cla_.

Salome, of Emanuel Meisterzeim and Margareta, b. 11 Jan 1779, bapt. 7 Mar 1779. Sponsors: Georg Schätzlein and sister Salome Schätzlein(in).

Philipp, of Philipp Mietmann and Veronica, b. 13 Feb 1779, bapt. 7 Mar 1779. Sponsors: Philipp Dick and wife Cath.

Jacob, of Peter Kraft and Margareta, b. 2 Mar 1779, bapt. 21 Mar 1779. Sponsors: Jacob Kiemle and wife Catharina.

Jacob, of Melchior Ki[t]z and Margareta, b. 10 Mar 1779, bapt. 20 Mar 1779. Sponsors: Jacob Ki[t]z and wife Elisabeth.

Elisabeth, of Andreas Rot(h) and Anna Maria, b. 17 Dec 1778, bapt. 21 Mar 1779. Sponsors: Balthas. Schoennel and Catharina Rot(hin), single.

Margareta, of Heinrich Huber and Agnes, b. 1 Mar 1779, bapt. 21 Mar 1779. Sponsors: Sebastian Wulle and wife An. Barb.

Jacob, of Peter Gress and Rosina, b. 21 Mar 1779, bapt. 5, Apr 779. Sponsors: Jacob Teis and wife Dorothea.

Jonathan, of Lorenz Schüster and Maria, b. 7 Apr 1774, bapt. 25 Apr 1779. Sponsors: Adam Schüster and wife Christina Dorothea.

Mercy, of Lorenz Schüster and Maria, b. 6 Mar 1776, bapt. 25 Apr 1779. Sponsors: same as above.

Dorothea, of Lorenz Schüster and Maria, b. 30 Nov 1778, bapt. 25 Apr 1779. Sponsors: same as above.

Georg Michael, of Jacob Eckfeld and Anna Elisabeth, b. 18 Mar 1779, bapt. 6 Apr 1779. Sponsors: Michael Gutmann and wife Margaret.

Georg, of Georg Kelly and Catharina, b. 18 Mar 1776, bapt. 7 Apr 1779. Sponsor: Peter Kinst?.

Maria, of Henrich Eppele and Barbara, b. 11 Mar 1779, bapt. 8 Apr 1779. Sponsors: Andreas Eppele and wife Maria.

Elisabeth, of Jacob Meier and Margaret, b. 26 Mar 1779, bapt. 11 Apr 1779. Sponsors: Caspar Vetterer and Elisabeth Hart.

Susanna, of Henrich Conrad and Maria, b. 15 Mar 1779, bapt. 11 Apr 1779. Sponsors: Joh. Schaefer and wife Susanna Dorothea.

Wilhelm, of Peter Graf and Catharina, b. 19 Mar 1779, bapt. 11 Apr 1779. Sponsors: Wilh. Battean and wife Elisabeth.

Maria, of Johann Friedr. Kochler and Maria, b. 18 Mar 1779, bapt. 11 Apr 1779. Sponsors: John Georg Kochler and wife Maria Elisabeth.

Catharina, of Conrad Baethis and Barbara, b. 18 Mar 1779, bapt. 16 Apr 1779. Sponsors: Henr. Kaemmerer and wife Catharina.

Maria Margareta, of Johann Joseph Gra[t]z and Maria Dorothea, b. 5 Apr 1779, bapt. 17 Apr 1779. Sponsors: Johann Friedr. Woelpert and wife Margareta.

Matthaeus, of Christoph Ziegler and Susanna, b. 2 Mar 1779, bapt. 27 Apr 1779. Sponsors: the parents.

Johannes, of Michael Lap and Margareta, b. 25 Apr 1779, bapt. 28 Apr 1779. Sponsors: Johannes Shü[t]z and wife Margareta.

Sarah, of Georg Daum and Sarah, b. 19 Apr 1779, bapt. 2 May 1779. Sponsors: Jacob Bitter and wife Juliana.

Cath. Elis., of Conrad Divetter and Cath. Elis., b. 9 Apr 1779, bapt. 2 May 1779. Sponsors: John Benner and wife Cath.

Georg Jacob, of Carl Schneider and Anna Maria, b. 14 Apr 1779, bapt. 2 May 1779. Sponsors: Johannes Messerschmidt and sister Barbara.

Elisabeth, of Georg Michael Heil and Maria Catharina, b. 10 Apr 1779, bapt. 2 May 1779. Sponsors: the parents.

Jacob, of Johannes Morst and Anna Eva, b. 22 Aug 1778, bapt. 5 May 1779. Sponsors: the parents.

Joh. Wilhelm, of Johann William Hockel and Susanna, b. 22 Apr 1779, bapt. 9 May 1779. Sponsors: Reinhard Uhl and wife Christiana.

Elisabeth, of Johannes Hesch and Margareta, b. 27 Apr 1779, bapt. 9 May 1779. Sponsors: Thomas Fischer and Elisab. Hott__.

Mary, of James Butler and Mary Burckerd (illegitimate), b. 1 May 1779, bapt. 2 May 1779. Sponsors: John Elfried and wife Cathar..

Christina Elisabeth, of Johannes Georg Goetling and Henriette, b. 18 Apr 1779, bapt. 9 May 1779. Sponsors: Joh. Georg Seifferheld and wife Christina Elisabeth.

Georg, of Christian Jung and Carolina Juliana, b. 24 Apr 1779, bapt. 10 May 1779. Sponsors: Georg Daum and wife Sarah.

Philipp, of Daniel Jones and Sophia Elisabeth, b. 3 May 1779, bapt. 11 May 1779. Sponsors: Philipp Heger and wife Catharina.

Johannes, of Johannes Flauer and Elisabeth, b. 22 Apr 1779, bapt. 13 May 1779. Sponsors: the parents.

Johannes, of Elisabeth Bahrd(in), b. 1 May 1779, bapt. 13 May 1779. Sponsors: Johannes Goe[t]z and Dorothea [this may be the same child as above].

Elisabeth, of Henrich Meier and Catharina, b. 28 Apr 1779, bapt. 16 May 1779. Sponsors: Wilhelm Benno and wife Maria Elisab.

Joh. Georg, of Johannes Hunter and Anna Maria, b. 12 Mar 1779, bapt. 17 May 1779. Sponsors: Georg Bechtold and wife Elisabeth.

Elisabeth, of Richard Bleu and Ann, b. 3 Dec 1778, bapt. 16 May 1779. Sponsors: the mother, and John Simpson.

Maria Barbara, of Johannes Brechle and Anna, b. 10 Dec 1778, bapt. 18 May 1779. Sponsors: Jacob Sultzel and wife Maria Barb.

Maria Catharina, of Michael Theobald and Elisabeth, b. 28 Sep 1776, bapt. 23 May 1779. Sponsors: Philipp Knapp and wife Catharina.

Elisabeth Esther, of Michael Theobald and Elisabeth, b. 28 Apr 1779, bapt. 23 May 1779. Sponsors: Philipp Knapp and wife Catharina.

Maria, of Henr. deForrest and Magdalena, b. 6 May 1779, bapt. 23 May 1779. Sponsors: Peter Osious and wife Maria.

Henrich, of Henrich Gress and Anna Maria, b. 29 Apr 1779, bapt. 25 May 1779. Sponsors: the father, and the grandmother Ann. Mar. Heilmann(in)an.

Johann Nicolaus, of Georg Schreider and Maria, b. 8 May 1779, bapt. 28 May 1779. Sponsors: the parents.
Georg Christoph, of Wilhelm Sarninghausen, M.D., and Elisabeth, b. 16 May 1779, bapt. 27 May 1779. Sponsors: Georg Christoph Dold? and Charlotte Kalkbrenner(in).
Maria Elisabeth, of Peter Armbruster and Margareta, b. 24 May 1779, bapt. 30 May 1779. Sponsors: Johannes Paul? and wife Mar. Elisabeth.
Henrich, of Henrich Nagel and Barbara, b. 9 May 1779, bapt. 30 May 1779. Sponsors: Henrich Nagel and wife (name not given).
Christian, of Christian Kensel and Margaretha, b. 14 May 1779, bapt. 30 May 1779. Sponsors: the parents.
Conrad, of Wilhelm Mohr and Susanna, b. 27 Oct 1778, bapt. 30 May 1779. Sponsors: Conrad Schneider and Anna Mar. Lochmann(in).
Johannes, of Johannes Weber and Veronica, b. 27 Oct 1778, bapt. 30 May 1779. Sponsors: the parents.
Christina Margareta [twin], of Peter Greb and Elisabeth, b. 29 May 1779, bapt. 2 Jun 1779. Sponsors: the parents, and Christina Margareta Huber(in)
Anna Magdalena [twin], of Peter Greb and Elisabeth, b. 29 May 1779, bapt. 2 Jun 1779. Sponsors: same as above.
Salome, of Joh. Nicol. Wagner and Magdalena, b. 28 May 1779, bapt. 3 Jun 1779. Sponsors: the parents.
Johannes, of Johannes Schae[t]zlein and Barbara, b. 29 Apr 1779, bapt. 7 Jun 1779. Sponsors: Johannes Krauss and wife Catharina.
Catharina, of Johannes Lorenz and Catharina, b. 2 Jun 1779, bapt. 7 Jun 1779. Sponsors: Friedr. Froelicher? and wife Catharina.
Joseph, of John Moore and Sarah (birth date not given), bapt. 7 Jun 1779. Sponsors: Jacob Teis and wife.
Johann Friedrich, of Friedrich Ermantraud (of Kent County, Maryland) and Catharina, b. 20 Jan 1779, bapt. 4 Jun 1779. Sponsors: Johann Heller and wife Christina.
Jacob, of Henrich Fuhr and Elisabeth, b. 15 May 1779, bapt. 4 Jun 1779. Sponsors: Jacob Esler and Margareta Schumacher(in).
Jacob [twin], of Michael Albrecht and Juliana, b. 16 Jun 1779, bapt. 18 Jun 1779. Sponsor: Anna Sto[c]k(in).
Anna Magdalena [twin], of Michael Albrecht and Juliana, b. 16 Jun 1779, bapt. 18 Jun 1779. Sponsor: same as above.
Nicolaus, of Philipp Mäyer and Salome, b. 31 May 1779, bapt. 20 Jun 1779. Sponsors: Nicolaus Miller and wife Maria.
Johannes, of Michael Albrecht and Juliana, b. 12 Mar 1777, bapt. 18 Jun 1779. Sponsors: Jacob Inck and Anna Stock(in)..
Maria Margareta, of Georg Haber and Salome, b. 17 May 1779, bapt. 20 Jun 1779. Sponsors: Adam Krebs and wife Maria.
Rebecca, of Georg Gebhard and Rosina, b. 14 May 1779, bapt. 20 Jun 1779. Sponsors: Johannes Biegler and wife Anna.
Elisabeth, of Johannes Rosk and Catharine, b. 19 Jan 1778, bapt. 21 Jun 1779. Sponsors: Jacob Holl and sister Elisabeth.
Johann William, of Joh. Wilh. Burghard and Sarah, b. 19 Apr 1779, bapt. 22 Jun 1779. Sponsors: the parents.

Elisabeth, of Heinrich Both and Elisabeth, b. 5 Jan 1779, bapt. 22 Jun 1779.
Sponsors: Matthius Stommel and wife Christina.
Elisabeth, of Adam Zanzinger and Susanna, b. 21 May 1779, bapt. 23 Jun 1779.
Sponsors: Henrich Keppele, Sr., and Elisab. Gross(in).
Johan Jacob, of Martin Sommer and Margareta, b. 8 Jun 1779, bapt. 27 Jun
1779. Sponsors: Johannes Schoeneker? and Catharina.
Georg, of Ludwig Rohner and Maria, b. 8 Jun 1779, bapt. 27 Jun 1779.
Sponsors: Georg Bender and wife Rosina Margar.
Leonhard, of Leonhard Weid and Eva, b. 18 Jun 1779, bapt. 27 Jun 1779.
Sponsors: the father, and Elisab. Vogel(in).
Georg Michael, of Johannes Jaeger, b. 10 Jun 1779, bapt. 27 Jun 1779.
Sponsors: Michael Fischer and wife Maria Hermann.
Johann Friedrich [twin], of Johann Friedrich Meier and Margareta, b. 29 Jun
1779, bapt. 29 Jun 1779. Sponsors: the father, and Cathar. Lamparder.
Catharina [twin], of Johann Friedrich Meier and Margareta Catharina, b. 29 Jun
1779, bapt. 29 Jun 1779. Sponsors: same as above.
Johan Peter [twin], of Philipp Truckenmiller and Mar. Catharina, b. 26 Jun 1779,
bapt. 29 Jun 1779. Sponsors: the mother, and Peter Walter and wife Barb.
Maria Cathar. [twin], of Philipp Truckenmiller and Mar. Catharina, b. 26 Jun
1779, bapt. 29 Jun 1779. Sponsors: same as above.
Jacob Ulrich, of Georg Kur[t]z and Margareta, b. 27 Jun 1779, bapt. 3 Jul 1779.
Sponsors: Jacob Ulrich Sultzel and wife Barbara.
Henry, of William Mason and Mary, b. 5 Jun 1779, bapt. 5 Jul 1779. Sponsors:
the parents.
Maria Margareta., of Johann Georg Senft and Charlotte, b. 26 Jun 1779, bapt.
6 Jul 1779. Sponsors: Wilhelm Rehn and Maria Margareta Gross(in).
Elisabeth, of Philipp Heil and Jacobina, b. 26 Jun 1779, bapt. 10 Jul 1779.
Sponsors: Georg Sei[t]z and wife Elisabeth.
Valentin, of Johannes Asmus and Catharina, b. 13 Jun 1779, bapt. 10 Jul 1779.
Sponsors: Valentin Hofmann and wife Susanna.
Susanna, of Daniel Rosch and Susanna, b. 12 Mar 1779, bapt. 12 Jul 1779.
Sponsors: the grandparents Conrad Rosch and wife Susanna.
Johannes, of Anton Kern and Catharina, b. 4 Jul 1779, bapt. 21 Jul 1779.
Sponsors: Johannes Weng and wife Magd.
Sarah, of Adam Folk and Catharina, b. 20 Jun 1779, bapt. 4 Jul 1779. Sponsors:
Georg Waker and wife Dorothea.
Eva, of Conrad Haas and Magdalene, b. 8 Jul 1779, bapt. 17 Jul 1779.
Sponsors: Johannes Schneider and wife Eva.
Joh. Friedrich, of David Schaefer and Elisabeth, b. 1 Jul 1779, bapt. 18 Jul 1779.
Sponsors: Friedrich Muhlenberg and wife Catharina.
Jacobina, of Jacob Schaefer and Catharina, b. 22 Jun 1779, bapt. 18 Jul 1779.
Sponsors: the parents, and the grandmother Jacobina Schaefer.
Jacob, of Jacob Graff and Elisabeth, b. 12 Jun 1779, bapt. 5 Jul 1779. Sponsors:
Caspar Graff and dau. Elisabeth.
Cath. Elisabeth, of Leonhard Craemer and Anna Maria, b. 22 Jun 1779, bapt.
8 Jul 1779. Sponsors: Cath. Elisabeth Fischer and Gottlieb Mezger.
Esther, of Johann Hook and Margareta, b. 5 Mar 1777, bapt. 11 Jun 1779.
Sponsors: the parents.

Anna, of Johann Hook and Margareta, b. 17 Jan 1779, bapt. 11 Jun 1779.
Sponsors: the parents.
Andreas, of Friedrich Paul and Elisabeth, b. 2 Jul 1779, bapt. 12 Jul 1779.
Sponsors: Balthasar Clymer and wife Elisabeth.
Christina Barbara, of Joh. Adam Schwab and Anna Martha, b. 16 Jul 1779, bapt.
21 Jul 1779. Sponsors: the parents.
Elisabeth, of Valentin Beck and Margareta (English woman), b. 18 Sep 1778,
bapt. 24 Jul 1779. Sponsors: the mother, and Jacob Beck.
Adam, of Michael Uber and Maria, b. 21 Jul 1779, bapt. 25 Jul 1779. Sponsors:
Joh. Adam Schumacher and wife Christina.
Georg, of Martin Wal[t]z and Maria (English woman), birthdate not given, bapt.
26 Jul 1779, Sponsor: the grandfather Mart. Wal[t]z.
Jacob, of Philipp Neuheuer and Juliana, b. 27 Jul 1779, bapt. 26 Jul 1779.
Sponsor: the grandmother Cath. Connor.
Johannes, of Mich. Cath. Wartman and Sarah, b. 27 Jul 1779, bapt. 27 Jul 1779.
Sponsor: Elisab. Cath. Wolt___.
Louis, of William Thorn and Catharine, b. 7 May 1779, bapt. 30 Jul 1779.
Sponsor: Anna Maria Faster(in).
Maria Dorothea, of Johann Georg Fenzel and Salome, b. 23 Jul 1779, bapt.
8 Aug 1779. Sponsors: Johann Greiffenstein and wife Mar. Dorothea.
Johan David, of Johann Friedr. Woelpert and Margaret, b. 27 Jul 1779, bapt.
8 Aug 1779. Sponsors: David Uber and wife Anna Maria.
Joseph, of Joseph Kemmel and Elisabeth, b. 2 Aug 1779, bapt. 9 Aug 1779.
Sponsors: Jacob Schwab and the grandmother Mrs. Ried(in).
Rosina Elisabeth, of Thomas Jones and Barbara, b. 1 Jul 1779, bapt. 12 Aug
1779. Sponsors: the mother, and Barbara Dominick.
Maria Magdal., of Jacob Schnell and Elisabeth, b. 22 Jul 1779, bapt. 13 Aug
1779. Sponsors: Friedr. Weis and wife Mar. Magdalena.
*Note: in the original register, 11 baptisms by pastor Helmuth appear here; see
the Second List II, below. Baptisms by pastor Kunze then continue, as
follows:*
Georg, of Johannes Wucherer and Elisabeth, b. 10 Aug 1779, bapt. 16 Aug
1779. Sponsors: the parents.
Georg, of Georg Suss and Anna Margareta, b. 15 Aug 1779, bapt. 19 Aug 1779.
Sponsors: the parents.
Jacob, of Christian Fuchs and Dorothea, b. 13 Aug 1779, bapt. 22 Aug 1779.
Sponsors: Jacob Ulrich Su[t]zel and wife An. Barb.
Elisabeth, of John Canada and Susanna, b. 7 Aug 1779, bapt. 24 Aug 1779.
Sponsors: the father, and Anna Christina Seineruh(in).
Heinrich, of Jacob Miller and Barbara, b. 29 Jul 1779, bapt. 22 Aug 1779.
Sponsors: Heinr. Schmidt and wife Magdalena.
Elisabeth, of Christoph Mohr and Catharina, b. 25 Aug 1779, bapt. 29 Aug
1779. Sponsors: Elisabeth Fuhrer and Ludw. Fuhrer.
Thomas, of Heinrich Meiers and Catharina, b. 8 Aug 1779, bapt. 29 Aug 1779.
Sponsors: Thomas Meier and wife Margareta.
Christina, of Andreas Tag and Christina, b. 25 Aug 1779, bapt. 29 Aug 1779.
Sponsors: the parents.

Maria, of Wilhelm Kirn and Catharina, b. 1 Aug 1779, bapt. 29 Aug 1779.
Sponsors: Conrad Rosch and wife Susanna.
Moses, of Thomas Watson and Mary, b. 15 Aug 1779, bapt. 29 Aug 1779.
Sponsors: the parents.
William, of Samuel King and Sarah, b. 4 Jun 1779, bapt. 29 Aug 1779.
(Sponsors not given.)
Maria, of Johannes Waker and Catharina, b. 28 Jul 1779, bapt. 30 Aug 1779.
Sponsors: Johannes Hert and wife Margareta.
A child (name not given), of Christina Bu[t]z(in) (illegitimate, the father an
apprentice), b. 30 Aug 1779, bapt. 31 Aug 1779. Sponsors: Friedr. Vogel
and wife Cath.
Friedrich, of Johannes Butler and Susanna, b. 14 Aug 1779, bapt. 4 Sep 1779.
Sponsors: Friedr. Vogel and wife Elisabeth.
Cathar. Barbara, of Carl Joseph Wolpert and Catharina, b. 29 Aug 1779, bapt.
5 Sep 1779. Sponsors: Wilhelm Engelfried and wife Catharina.
Peter, of Johannes Geiger? and Anna Maria, b. 16 Aug 1779, bapt. 5 Sep 1779.
Sponsors: the mother, and Peter Walter.
Hanna Christiana, of Johann Christoph (pastor here at Philiadelphia) and
Margareta Henriette, b. 29 Aug 1779, bapt. 5 Sep 1779. Sponsors: Mr.
Heinr. Keppele, Sr., Gen. Peter Muhlenberg's wife Anna, and Christian
Wiebeck's wife Christina.
Heinrich, of Andreas Beck and Margareta, b. 29 Sep 1778, bapt. 15 Sep 1779.
Sponsors: Andreas Beck and wife Barbara.
Catharina, of Friedrich Arn and Elisabeth, b. 2 Sep 1779, bapt. 12 Sep 1779.
Sponsors: Johannes Gummi and wife Catharina.
Heinrich, of Matthaeus Bolt and Veronica, b. 1 Aug 1779, bapt. 13 Sep 1779.
Sponsors: Henr. Schmidt and wife Anna Catharina.
Sophia, of Christlieb Baehrdling and Elisabeth, b. 6 Sep 1779, bapt. 19 Sep
1779. Sponsors: the parents.
Jacob, of Jacob Kaufmann and Margareta, b. 20 Aug 1779, bapt. 19 Sep 1779.
Sponsors: the parents.
Georg, of Johannes Greus and Barbara, b. 2 Sep 1779, bapt. 19 Sep 1779.
Sponsors: Georg Rehn and wife Eva.
Christian, of Daniel Knodel and Anna Maria, b. 14 Sep 1779, bapt. 19 Sep 1779.
Sponsors: Christian Diem and wife Magdalena.
Johannes, of David Ott and Catharina, b. 30 Aug 1779, bapt. 19 Sep 1779.
Sponsor: Wilhelm Raedinger and wife (name not given).
Jacob, of Christian Obersteg and Margareta, b. 13 Sep 1779, bapt. 19 Sep 1779.
Sponsors: Jacob Ruhl and wife Cathar. in place of Mrs. Anna Metaberger(in).
Georg, of Adam Münzer and Lovina, b. 11 Aug 1779, bapt. 20 Sep 1779.
Sponsors: Thomas Fischer and wife Elisabetha.
Philippina, of Benedict Schneider and Philippina, b. 29 Jul 1779, bapt. 20 Sep
1779. Sponsors: the parents.
Wilhelm, of Wilhelm Lehman and Elisabeth, b. 14 Sep 1779, bapt. 29 Sep 1779.
Sponsors: the parents.
Elisabeth, of Zacharias Loesch and Maria, b. 23 Sep 1779, bapt. 28 Sep 1779.
Sponsors: Ursula Barbara Kiemle and Leonh. Kiemle.

Catharina, of Johann Glasser and Christina, b. 16 Sep 1779, bapt. 3 Oct 1779.
Sponsors: the parents.
Henrich, of Jacob Strumbeck and Maria, b. 11 Sep 1779, bapt. 5 Oct 1779.
Sponsors: Jacob Anthony and Barbara Steinme[t]z.
Salome Elisa, of Peter Heimbach and Elisabeth, b. 11 Aug 1779, bapt. 20 Sep
1779. Sponsors: John Birkenbeiter and wife Catharina.
Maria Elisabeth, of Georg Besch and Catharina, b. 26 Sep 1779, bapt. 3 Oct
1779. Sponsors: Wilh. Benno and wife Maria Elisab.
John, of William Harrison and Mary, b. 20 Jan 1777, bapt. 3 Oct 1779.
Sponsors: the parents.
Carl, of Jacob Graef, Jr., and Maria, b. 17 Sep 1779, bapt. 10 Oct 1779.
Sponsors: Carl Sing and wife Margareta.
Joh. Georg, of Martin Peusch (alias Baush) and Maria Magdal., b. 23 Sep 1779,
bapt. 10 Oct 1779. Sponsors: Georg Gro[t]z and wife Dorothia.
Maria Margar., of Conrad Hensler and Eleonora Cathar., b. 2 Oct 1779, bapt.
10 Oct 1779. Sponsors: Georg Sturmfels and wife Mar. Margareta.
George, of Daniel Burial and Margareta, b. 24 Sep 1779, bapt. 10 Oct 1779.
Sponsors: Georg Broenning and wife Elisabeth.
Catharina, of Jacob Schwab and Margareta, b. 4 Oct 1779, bapt. 17 Oct 1779.
Sponsors: Johannes Feil and wife Catharina.
Daniel, of Michael Stotz and Catharina, b. 3 Oct 1779, bapt. 17 Oct 1779.
Sponsors: Daniel Frischmuth and wife Barbara
Elisabeth, of Matthaeus Riemer and Salome, b. 16 Jul 1779, bapt. 19 Oct 1779.
Sponsors: Adolph Riel and wife Hannah.
Hanna, of Adolph Riel and Hanna, b. in 1775, bapt. 19 Oct 1779. Sponsor: the
mother.
Thomas, of Adolph Riel and Hanna, b. in 1778, bapt. 19 Oct 1779. Sponsors:
the parents.
Margareta, of Rudolf Forrester (of Chester County) and Anna Catharina, b.
5 Aug 1779, bapt. 23 Oct 1779. Sponsors: the mother, and Margaret
Kunz(in).
Maria Magdalena, of Georg Erlinger and Christina, b. 28 Aug 1779, bapt.
24 Oct 1779. Sponsors: Carl Preis and wife Maria Magdalena.
Anna Maria, of Johann Michael Mo[t]z and Barbara, b. 12 Oct 1779, bapt.
24 Oct 1779. Sponsors: Philip Meger and Maria Miller.
Juliana, of Leonhard Jacobi and Margareta, b. 14 Oct 1779, bapt. 24 Oct 1779.
Sponsors: Georg Heppele and wife Juliana.
Margareta, of Henrich Schreiber and Margareta, b. 16 Oct 1779, bapt. 28 Oct
1779. Sponsors: the parents.
Henrich, of Caspar Schneider and Elisabeth, b. 27 Oct 1779, bapt. 1 Nov 1779.
Sponsors: Henr. Diel and Mrs. Kiemle.
Henrich, of Peter Lex and Elisabeth, b. 4 Oct 1779, bapt. 4 Nov 1779.
Sponsors: Henrich Ruth and wife Elisabeth.
(In the original, 17 more baptisms by pastor Helmuth appear her.) Baptisms by
pastor Kunze begin again, as follows:
Johannes, of Peter Schell and Margareta, b. 3 Sep 1779, bapt. 8 Nov 1779.
Sponsor: Johannes Fuchs.

Anna Maria, of Christian Kunckel and Catharina, b. 29 Oct 1779, bapt. 6 Nov
1779. Sponsors: Andreas Mattern and wife Anna Maria.
Andreas, of Joseph Canada and Magdalene, b. 22 Sep 1779, bapt. 6 Nov 1779.
Sponsors: Andreas Beck and wife Barbara.
Joh. Jacob, of Jacob Bühler and Dorothea Cathar., b. 21 Oct 1779, bapt. 7 Nov
1779. Sponsors: Heinr. Beckmeier? and wife Catharina Marg.
Anna, of Johannes Gressel and Catharina, b. 23 Jul 1779, bapt. 7 Nov 1779.
Sponsors: Georg Frey and wife Anna Weit.
Georg, of Balthasar Grof and Catharina, b. 1 Oct 1779, bapt. 7 Nov 1779.
Sponsors: Peter Hartmann and wife Catharina.
Elisabeth, of Friedrich Kirls and Elisabeth, b. 12 Sep 1779, bapt. 8 Nov 1779.
Sponsors: Johannes Daum and wife Maria.
Johannes, of Johann Schaefer and Susanna, b. 25 Oct 1779, bapt. 9 Nov 1779.
Sponsors: Johann Schü[t]z and wife Margaretha.
Anna Catharina, of William Pew and Barbara, b. 5 Nov 1779, bapt. 14 Nov
1779. Sponsors: Jacob Gross and wife Cathar.
Jacob, of Michael Schleihof and Maria, b. 9 Aug 1779, bapt. 21 Nov 1779.
Sponsors: Philipp Lehr and wife Dorothea.
Joh. Georg, of Joh. Georg Schmidt and Eva, b. 22 Nov 1779, bapt. 28 Nov 1779.
Sponsors: Joh. Georg Hof and wife Dorothea.
Ann, of William Bondy and Ann, b. 12 Oct 1779, bapt. 28 Nov 1779. Sponsors:
Philipp Lehr and wife Anna.
Christian, of John Albert and Hanna Maria, b. 10 Nov 1779, bapt. 28 Nov 1779.
Sponsors: Christian Uhl and wife Elisabeth.
Anna Sophia, of Peter Walter and Antonette, b. 9 Nov 1779, bapt. 28 Nov 1779.
Sponsors: David Flickwier and wife Anna Sophia.
Margareta, of Wilhelm Picking and Elisabeth, b. 6 Nov 1779, bapt. 29 Nov
1779. Sponsors: Gottfried Schwing and wife Margareta.
Carl Friederich, of Peter Muhlenberg, Jr., and Hanna, b. 16 Nov 1779, bapt.
30 Nov 1779. Sponsors: Friedrich August Conrad Muhlenberg, and Andreas
Keppele and wife Maria.
Christoph Carl, of Michael Kinzler and Maria Elisabeth, b. 24 Nov 1779, bapt.
6 Dec 1779. Sponsors: Christoph Carl Beringer and wife Margareta.
Anna Margar., of Daniel Gerhard and Elisabeth, b. 26 Nov 1779, bapt. 5 Dec
1779. Sponsors: Valentin Unbehend and wife Sophia..
Georg Friederich, of Georg Schneck and Elisabeth, b. 24 Nov 1779, bapt. 3 Dec
1779. Sponsors: Friederich Dresler and wife Sophia.
Anna Magdalena, of Zacharias Endres and Maria, b. 17 Nov 1779, bapt. 5 Dec
1779. Sponsors: Johannes Wagner and wife Anna Magd.
Paul Caspar, of Michael Boule and Christina, b. 27 Nov 1779, bapt. 27 Nov
1779. Sponsors: Paul Caspar Briton and wife Susanna.
Susanna, of Johannes Hepp and Catharina, b. 29 Nov 1779, bapt. 6 Dec 1779.
Sponsors: the parents.
Johannes, of Johann Heinrich Meier and Catharina, b. 3 Dec 1779, bapt. 10 Dec
1779. Sponsors: the father, and Mar. Cathar. Truckenmüller.
Anna Maria, of Johann Koch and Rosina Dorothea, b. 26 Nov 1779, bapt.
12 Dec 1779. Sponsors: Joh. Eberhard Geis and wife Cathar.

Ludewig, of Georg Bareleck and Catharina, b. 29 Nov 1779, bapt. 12 Dec 1779.
Sponsors: Ludewig Forres and wife Elis.
Johann Adam, of Johann Adam Wagner and Catharina, b. 24 Nov 1779, bapt.
12 Dec 1779. Sponsors: Joh. Reifschneider and wife Anna Maria.
Christoph Joseph, of Friedrich Walter and Martha, b. 10 Oct 1779, bapt. 12 Dec
1779. Sponsors: Georg Hafner and wife. (name not given).
Catharina Friedricka, of Friedrich Seger and Juliana, b. 22 Nov 1779, bapt.
12 Dec 1779, Sponsors: the parents.
Johann Heinrich, of Johannes Heims and Elisabeth, b. 17 Nov 1779, bapt.
12 Dec 1779. Sponsors: Johann Heinr. Bott_ and wife Elisabeth.
Elisabeth, of Jacob Anthony and Jacobaea, b. 6 Dec 1779, bapt. 19 Dec 1779.
Sponsors: Georg Schleuter? and wife Elisab.
Hanna, of Adam Schae[t]zlein and Hanna, b. 9 Nov 1779, bapt. 19 Dec 1779.
Sponsors: Barthol Schaetzlein and wife Cathar.
Hanna Catharina, of Georg Ludewig Bräcking and Elisabeth, b. 27 Nov 1779,
bapt. 20 Dec 1779. Sponsor: Catharina Eckard(in).
John, of Stephan Gordon and Mary, b. 7 Jan 1777, bapt. 26 Dec 1779.
Sponsors: Georg Sei[t]z and wife Elisab.
Johann Georg, of Michael Schubert and Elisabeth, b. 10 Dec 1779, bapt. 26 Dec
1779. Sponsors: Friedrich Heiler and wife (illegible).
Catharina, of Conrad Daum and Susanna, b. 10 Dec 1779, bapt. 26 Dec 1779.
Sponsors: Andreas Riegler and wife Cathar.
Anna Catharina, of Henrich Herberger and Susanna, b. 6 Dec 1779, bapt. 26 Dec
1779. (Sponsors not given.)

1779, Second List
(baptisms begun by G.H.E. Muhlenberg, Jr., in Book IV; then continued by
pastor Helmuth, in Book III)
In the original register, this list begins with baptisms by pastor G.H.E. Muhlen-
berg, Jr., at the beginning of Book IV, as follows:
Johan, of Johan Bender and wife Marg., b. 9 Dec 1778, bapt. 7 Jan 1779.
Sponsors: Henr. Fahns and wife Veronica.
Elisabet, of Georg Schad and wife Susanne, b. 26 Dec 1778, bapt. 10 Jan 1779.
Sponsors: Conrad King, and wife Hanna, and son Johannes.
Susanne, of Joh. Kraus and wife Ann, b. 5 Jan 1779, bapt. 10 Jan 1779.
(Sponsors not given.)
Hanna, of Joh. Andr. Annick and wife Anna Barbara, b. 5 Jan 1779, bapt. 10 Jan
1779. Sponsors: Henrich Reis and wife Hanna.
Eva Maria, of Nicol. Herzbach and wife Regina, b. 26 Oct 1778, bapt. 10 Jan
1779. Sponsors: Jacob Reisser and wife Eva Maria.
Joh[anna] Cath. Eleonora, of Benjamin Armbrüster and wife Barbara, b. 1 Jan
1779, bapt. 10 Jan 1779. Sponsors: Anton Armbrüster and Joh[anna] Cathar.
Eleonora Schlemer(in).
Anna Catharine, of Jacob Beck and wife Maria Elis., b. 23 Nov 1778, bapt.
10 Jan 1779. Sponsors: Michael Regenberger and wife Cath.
Henrich, of Henrich Müller and wife Maria, b. 6 Dec 1778, bapt. 11 Jan 1779.
Sponsors: the parents.

Georg Leonard, of Joseph Warner (deceased) and wife Maria, b. 26 Mar 1775, bapt. 14 Jan 1777 [*sic*]. Sponsors: Georg Leonard Huber and Louisa Huber(in).

Joh. Peter [twin], of Joh.Peter Merk and wife Sarah, b. 9 Dec 1778, bapt. 17 Jan 1779. Sponsors: Eve Brant and her sister Elis. Kapp(in).

Ann [twin], of Joh. Peter Merk and wife Sarah, b. 9 Dec 1778, bapt. 17 Jan 1779. Sponsors: same as above.

Catharine, of William Atkinson and wife Elis., b. 19 Dec 1778, bapt. 17 Jan 1779. Sponsors: Joh. Schenk and wife Catharine.

Abigail, of Philip Burkert and wife Jean, b. 1 Jun 1778, bapt. 17 Jan 1779. Sponsors: the parents.

Leonard, of Johannes Günsel and wife Margar., b. 28 Dec 1778, bapt. 24 Jan 1779. Sponsors: Leonard Kraemer and wife Maria.

Joh. Georg, of Joh. Bender and wife Susanne, b. 1 Jan 1779, bapt. 24 Jan 1779. Sponsors: Joh. Georg Kuhn and wife Anna Maria.

Joh. Georg, of Joh. Conr. Denkfelder and wife Elis., b. 13 Dec 1778, bapt. 24 Jan 1779. Sponsors Joh. Georg Rummel and Mrs. Friedrich(in).

Elisab., of Elias Frey and wife Maria, b. 17 Jan 1779, bapt. 24 Jan 1779 Sponsors Michael Rehm and wife Elis.

Daniel, of Sebastian Heiler and wife Elisabet, b. 19 Dec 1778, bapt. 24 Jan 1779. Sponsors: the parents.

Johannes, of Leonard Rieb and wife Elisabet, b. 1 Jan 1779, bapt. 24 Jan 1779. Sponsors: Joh. Fritz and Cathar. (illegible).

Henrich, of Christian Retten and wife Cathar., b. 28 Jan 1779, bapt. 31 Jan 1779. Sponsors: the parents.

Cath., of Math. Dollman and wife Cath., b. 18 Jan 1779, bapt. 2 Feb 1779. Sponsors: Jacob Rutter? and wife Cath.

Joh. Peter, of Joh. Steinmetz and wife Maria, b. 30 Nov 1778, bapt. 7 Feb 1779. Sponsors: Joh. Martin Vorster and Marg. Dürr(in), single.

Wilhelm, of Wilh. Groly and wife Anna Maria, b. 3 Jan 1779, bapt. 7 Feb 1779. Sponsors: Wilh. Schmidt and Barb. Groff(in).

Nicolaus, of Jacob Schaefer and wife Magdal., b. 17 Jan 1779, bapt. 7 Feb 1779. Sponsors: Nicol. Rübel and wife Salome.

Johannes [twin], of John Cartwright and wife Cath., b. 8 Feb 1779, bapt. 7 Feb 1779. Sponsors: Joh. Biegler and wife Anna Cathar.

Joh. Christian [twin], of John Cartwright and wife Cath., b. 8 Feb 1779, bapt. 7 Feb 1779. Sponsors: Joh.. Chr. Frölich and wife Elis.

Catharina, of Jacob Nesle and wife Margar., b. 10 Jan 1778, bapt., 7 Feb 1779. Sponsor: the mother.

Sophia, of Johan. Tart and wife Cath. Esther, b. 6 Feb 179, bapt. 11 Feb 1779. Sponsors: Johan Bruderson and Sophia Elis. Erbsoder(in).

Isabel, of Thomas Hampton and wife Ann, b. 10 Feb 1779, bapt. 11 Feb 1779. Sponsors: John Simson and Hugh McCondre?

Philippine Margar., of Friedrich Rehn and wife Cath., b. 20 Jan 1779, bapt. 14 Feb 1779. Sponsors Johannes Schneider and wife Margar.

Henrich, of Anrdr. Heg and wife Maria, b. in Dec 1778, bapt. 14 Feb 1779. Sponsors: Henrich Flick and wife Maria Cath.

Johan, of David Thomson and wife Marg., b. 4 Feb 1779, ' ·· . 14 Feb 1779.
Sponsors: Joh. Kaiser and wife Elisabet.
William, of Isaac Kelly and wife Elis., b. 15 Nov 177, bapt. 14 Feb 1779.
Sponsors: William Powel and wife Barbara.
Andreas, of Andr. Eppele and wife Maria birthdate not given, bapt. 14 Feb 1779.
Sponsors: the grandparents Mr. Georg Eppele and wife Maria.
Jacob, of Francis Löscher and wife Barba., 5 Jan 1778, 16 Feb 1779. Sponsors:
Christine Jost(in) and Christian Jost.
Joh. Georg, of Susan. Doroth. Leib(in) and an English soldier named Fulton, b.
16 Jan 1779, bapt. 16 Feb 1779. Sponsors: Georg Schall and Maria Christine
Schall(in).
Maria Barbara, of Joh. Little and wife Cathar, b. 10 Jan 1779, bapt. 16 Feb
1779. Sponsor: Maria Barb. Koenig(in).
Joh. Georg, of Daniel Ernst and Cath.,b. 4 Feb 1779, bapt. 20 Feb 1779.
Sponsors: Joh. Georg Krauch.
Friedrich, of Georg Klein and wife Elis., b. 20 Jan 1779, bapt. 21 Feb 1779.
Sponsors: Friedrich Heineman and wife Cath.
Joh. Michael Jacob, of Jacob Gut (deceased) and wife Marg., b. 25 Feb 1776,
bapt. 21 Feb 1779. Sponsors: Joh. Michael Jacob and wife Maria Susanne.
Maria Susanne, of Jacob Gut (deceased) and wife Marg., b. 4 Jun 1778, bapt.
21 Feb 1779. Sponsors: same as above.
Catharine, of Friedrich Vogel and wife Cath., b. 2 Feb 1779, bapt. 21Feb 1779.
Sponsors: Jacob Keimel and [wife] Elisab.
Maria Elisab., of Georg Weideman and wife Maria, b. 31 Jan 1779, bapt. 21 Feb
1779. Sponsors: Leonard Roht and Maria Hauk(in)?.
Nicolaus, of Michael Schoch and wife Margar., b. 13 Jan 1779, bapt. 23 Feb
1779. Sponsors: the parents.
Susanne, of Samuel Prinz and wife Anna Susanne, b. 18 Jan 1779, bapt. 25 Feb
1779. Sponsors: Georg Fidler and wife Susanne.
Catharine, of Jac. Steinmeier and wife Cath., b. 19 Feb 1779, bapt. 20 Feb 1779.
Sponsors: Caspar Wahl and wife Elisabet.
Joh. Jacob, of Joh. Michael Jobst and wife Marg., b. 18 Feb 1779, bapt. 20 Feb
1779. Sponsors: Joh. Jacob Grut and wife Cathar.
Catharine, of Peter Wagner and wife Rosina, b. 24? Jan 1779, bapt. 28 Feb
1779. Sponsors: the father, and Mrs. Brobanst(in)?.
Georg, of William Collin and wife Susanne, b. 6 Feb 1779, bapt. 3 Mar 1779.
Sponsors: the parents.
Anna Barb., of Georg Adam Schmidt and wife Christine, b. 18 Feb 1779, bapt.
14 Mar 1779. Sponsors: the parents.
Elisabet, of Georg Tirnis? and wife Maria Cath., b. 26 Dec 1778, bapt. 14 Mar
1779. Sponsors: Philip Laders and widow Elisabet.
Hanna, of Thomas Feal? and Cath., b. 9 Feb 1779, bapt. 15 Mar 1779.
Sponsors: Conrad Ring and wife Juliana.
Daniel, of Philip Sorg and wife Sus. Magdalena, b. 8 Mar 1779, bapt. 20 Mar
1779. Sponsors: Daniel Sorg and wife (first name obscured) Marg.
Elisabet, of Jonathan Stanton and wife Jemima, b. 15 Mar 1779, bapt. 21 Mar
1779. Sponsors: Michael Katz and Elisabet Schop?.

Maria Margaret, of Peter Meiers and wife Anna Maria, b. 18 Ma 1779, bapt. 21 Mar 1779. Sponsors: Ludwig Winkler and wife Margar.

Anna Maria, of Joh. Emmerich and wife Maria, b. 17 Mar 1779, bapt. 21 Mar 1779. Sponsors: Henr. Lenz and wife Anna Maria.

Georg Heinrich, of the Rev. Henrich Müller [Jr.] and wife Esther, b. 15 Mar 1779, bapt. 21 Mar 1779. Sponsors: Georg Kitz and wife Appollonia.

Johannes, of Elisabet Volk(in) and Joh. Schneider (illegitimate), b. in Jan 1779, bapt. 23 Mar 1779. Sponsors: Adam Schaefer and wife Doroth.

Sophia, of Philip Pfleger and wife Wilhelmina, b. 1 Mar 1779, bapt. 26 Mar 1779. Sponsors: Joh. Fries and wife Sophia.

Rosina [twin], of Jacob Stans and wife Rosina, b. 8 Feb 1779, bapt. 28 Mar 1779. Sponsor: the father (the mother has not yet been confirmed.)

Cathar. [twin], of Jacob Stans and wife Rosina, b. 8 Feb 1779, bapt. 28 Mar 1779. Sponsor: same as above.

Elisabet, of Jacob Reisser and wife Eva Christine, b. 11 Mar 1779, bapt. 28 Mar 1779. Sponsors: Reisser and wife Cath.

Johan, of Joh. Starke and wife Catharine, b. 17 Feb 1779, bapt. 28 Mar 1779. Sponsors: Ludw. Pankuchen and wife Magdalena.

Anna Cath., of Joh. Weis and wife Eliabet, b. 25 Feb 1779, bapt. 28 Mar 1779. Sponsors: Jac. Bock and wife Cath.

Anna, of Andr. Sommer and wife Anna, b. 31 Jan 1779, bapt 28 Mar 1779. Sponsors: the father, and Maria Maur(in).

Margar., of Michael Eberle and wife Maria Cath., b. in Feb 1779, bapt. 31 Mar 1779. Sponsor: Margar. Fulton.

Philip, of Jacob Herman and wife Cathar., b. 12 Mar 1779, bapt. 4 Apr 1779. Sponsors: Joh. Hüber and Jacob Löscher.

Martin, of Martin Heileman and wife Eva, b. 20 Apr 1778, bapt. 4 Apr 1779. Sponsor: Jacob Leibensieder.

Margar., of Joh. Friedr. Spatz and wife Elisabet, b. 9 Mar 1779, bapt. 5 Apr 1779. Sponsors: the father, and grandmother Margar.

Anna Margar., of Christoph Wolpert and wife Margar., b. 15 Feb 1779, bapt. 5 Apr 1779. Sponsors: Georg Sturnsfels? and wife Anna Margretha.

Maria Margar., of Peter Meiers and wife Anna Maria, b. 18 Mar 1779, bapt. 20 Mar 1779. Sponsors: Ludwig Winkler and wife Margar.

Jacob, of Joh. Kohl and wife Esther, b. 4 Mar 1779, bapt. 4 Apr 1779. Sponsors: the father and his sister Doroth. Farra_.

Elisabet, of Phil. Pannekuchen and wife Maria, b. 23 Mar 1779, bapt. 18 Apr 1779. Sponsors: Jac. Bock and wife Cathar.

Maria, of Lorenz Schwab and wife Margar., b. 1 Apr 1779, bapt. 18 Apr 1779. Sponsors: Phil. Jac. Bechtold and wife Maria.

Susanne, of Conrad Seibert and wife Maria Christiana, b. 23 Mar 1779, bapt. 18 Apr 1779. Sponsors: Casp. Seibert and Sus. Seibert(in).

Ann, of John Bayer (deceased) and wife Sara, b. 7 Dec 1778, bapt. 22 Apr 1779. Sponsors: Philip Reiter and Eva Schlatter.

Henrich, of Eberhard Leitenberg and wife Elis., b. 6 Apr 1779, bapt. 25 Apr 1779. Sponsors: Henr. Urie and wife Anna Barb.

Marcus, of Joh. Lambarter and wife Salome, b. 18 Apr 1779, bap. 2 Apr 1779. Sponsors: Marc. Menzer and wife Salome.

Regina, of Georg Milteberger and wife Cath., b. 25 Oct 1778, bapt. 27 Apr 1779. Sponsor: the child's grandmother (name not given).

Sara, of Jacob Hainy and wife Anna Margar., b. 4 Mar 1779, bapt. 27 Apr 1779. Sponsors: Joh. Hainy and Cath. Schaefer(in).

Joseph Lehman was bapt. on Maundy Thursday, 1779, in the presence of all the confirmands.

Elisabet Kur[t]z(in) was bapt. on Maundy Thursday in the presence of all the confirmands.

Catharina, of David Nichs and wife Dorothea, b. 30 Apr 1779, bapt. 13 May 1779. Sponsors: the parents.

Wilhelm, of Wilhelm Stoh? and wife Christine, b. 7 May 1779, bapt. 13 May 1779. Sponsors: Wilh. Batho and wife Elisabet.

Pastor Muhlenberg, Jr., was transferred from the Philadelphia church in 1779. The baptisms of this list were continued by new pastor Helmuth; rather than continuing them in Book IV, they were inserted among pastor Kunze's baptisms in Book III, following 126 of Kunze's baptisms in 1779, as follows:

Daniel, of John Steinme[t]z and Catharina, b. 29 Oct 1776, bapt. 18 Jul 1779. Sponsors: John Steinme[t]z and Barbara Helmuth.

Samuel, of Johann Getter and Anna Maria, b. 9 Feb 1779, bapt. 18 Jul 1779. Sponsors: Joh. Medschiller? and wife Anna Margareta.

Magdalena, of Johann Sullivan and Rebecca, b. 23 Apr 1778, bapt. 20 Jul 1779. Sponsors: Adam Weber and wife Magdalena.

Georg Michael, of Georg Michael Heck and Anna Catharine, b. 12 Jul 1779, bapt. 25 Jul 1779. Sponsors: Georg Michael Gutmann and wife Regina Margareta.

Elisabeth, of Marcus Montelius and Christina, b. 18 Jul 1779, bapt. 1 Aug 1779. Sponsors: the parents.

Maria Elisab., of Wilhelm Kempf and Anna Sabina, b. 30 Jul 1779, bapt. 1 Aug 1779. Sponsors: Jacob Weber and wife Maria Elisabeth.

Elisabeth, of Carl Enoch Schebach and Hanna, b. 17 Jul 1779, bapt. 1 Aug 1779. Sponsors: Heinrich Polinz and wife Eva Elisabeth.

Catharina Maria, of Nicolaus Johnson and Margareta, b. 9 Jul 1779, bapt. 1 Aug 1779. Sponsors: Isaac Werner and wife Cath. Maria.

Georg David, of Wilhelm Sheaff and Maria Barbara, b. 5 Jul 1779, bapt. 9 Aug 1779. Sponsors: Georg David Seckel and wife Maria Cathar.

Anna Maria, of Adam Rein and Christina Susanna, b. 20 Jul 1779, bapt. 15 Aug 1779. Sponsors: Johann Miller and Polly Evan.

Elisabeth, of Johann Kribbel and Christina, b. 2 Aug 1779, bapt. 14 Aug 1779. Sponsors: the parents.

(Note: in the original, 51 more baptisms of the First List appear here.) Pastor Helmuth's baptisms continue, as follows:

Johann, of Jacob Becker and Margareta, b. 16 Aug 1779, bapt. 22 Aug 1779. Sponsors: Johann Kunz? and wife Catharina.

Wilhelm, of Wilhelm Kiesler and Charlotta, b. 2 Aug 1779, bapt. 22 Aug 1779. Sponsors: Johan Balthasar Kinsler and wife Maria Elisabeth.

Elisabeth, of Wilhelm Kotsch? and Elisabeth, b. 17 Aug 1779, bapt. 24 Aug 1779. Sponsors: the parents.

Philip, of Heinrich Emmert and Maria Magdalene, b. 17 Aug 1779, bapt. 29 Aug 1779. Sponsors: Phil. Zepp and wife Margar.

Thomas, of William Tobys and Hanna, b. 10 Oct 1773, bapt. 29 Aug 1779. Sponsors: Tobias Adam Koenig and wife Anna Barbara.

Hilarius, of Georg Adam Becker and Catharina, b. 30 Aug 1779, bapt. 31 Aug 1779. Sponsors: Hilarius Becker and wife Cath.

Joh. Daniel, of Johann Daniel Stuber and Eva, b. 2 Feb 1779, bapt. 1 Sep 1779. Sponsors: the parents.

Helena, of Georg Leib and Margareta Doroth., b. 13 Aug 1779, bapt. 3 Sep 1779. Sponsors: the parents.

Johann Jacob, of Johann Adam Dill and Catharina, b. 24 Feb 1779, bapt. 9 Sep 1779. Sponsors: Andreas Heidrich and wife Elisabeth.

(In the original, 28 more baptisms of the First List appear here.) Baptisms by pastor Helmuth continue again, as follows:

Margareta, of Andreas Bauer and Barbara, b. 15 Aug 1779, bapt. 5 Sep 1779. Sponsors: Phil. Alberger and wife (illegible).

Margareta, of John Graff and Susanna, b. 16 Oct 1779, bapt. 5 Sep 1779. Sponsors: Margareta Graff(in) and Phil. Fox.

Anna Marga., of John Mich. Haehns and Anna Cathar., b. 8 Aug 1779, bapt. 5 Sep 1779. Sponsors: the father, and Anna Marg. Sterl(in).

Maria Barb., of Georg Escher and Eva, b. 28 Aug 1779, bapt. 8 Sep 1779. Sponsors: Christoph Henzmann and wife Maria Barbara.

Maria Elis., of John Neu and Elisabeth, b. 2 Sep 1779, bapt. 9 Sep 1779. Sponsors: Lud. Neu and wife Mar. El. An..

Jacob, of Christian Oberstech and Margareta, b. 13 Sep 1779, bapt. 19 Sep 1779. Sponsors: Jacob Rehl and wife Cath.

Margareta, of Daniel Hoffmann and Margareta, b. 23 Sep 1779, bapt. 23 Sep 1779. Sponsor: Johanna Burkhart(in).

Christina, of Johan Freihefer and Anna Maria, b. 29 Aug 1779, bapt. 26 Sep 1779. Sponsors: Albert Craemer and wife Christina.

Elisabeth, of Joh. Wenzel and Christina, b. 17 Sep 1779, bapt. 26 Sep 1779. Sponsors: Jacob Demand and wife Elisa.

Joh. Joseph, of Martin Reiser and Catharina, b. 16 Sep 1779, bapt. 26 Sep 1779. Sponsors: Jacob Reiser and wife Eva.

Elisab., of Adam Hess and Elisabeth, b. 20 Jul 1779, bapt. 27 Sep 1779. Sponsor: Susanna Kerch(in).

Isaac, of Isaac Kobler and Barbara, b. 22 Jan 1777, bapt. 9 Sep 1779. Sponsors: the mother.

Carl, of Carl Schaeffer and Agata, b. 16 Sep 1779, bapt. 19 Sep 1779. Sponsor: Anna Maria Schaeffer.

Sa(h)ra Susanna, of Adam Kidler and Elisabeth, b. 22 Nov 1778, bapt. 26 Sep 1779. Sponsors: Mich. Sharp and wife Susanna.

Andreas, of Jacob Braun and Catharina, b. 13 Aug 1779, bapt. 14 Oct 1779. Sponsors: Andr. Baer[en]stecher, and Ruth Hirschhorn.

Cath., of Johann Schneider and Margareta, b. 11 Sep 1779, bapt. 3 Oct 1779. Sponsors: Geo. Scheible and wife Cath.

Johann, of Franz Wil. Hetmonsberger? and Maria Magdalena, b. 22 Sep 1779, bapt. 2 Oct 1779. Sponsors: Joh. Henckel and wife Christina.

Marg. Barbara, of Joh. Bryan and Catharina, b. 12 Jul 1778, bapt. 8 Oct 1779.
Sponsor: Marg. Barb. Brechtl(in)?.
Maria, of Peter Dress and Maria, b. 29 Sep 1779, bapt. 10 Oct 1779. Sponsors:
the parents.
Christian, of Jacob Heinrich and Catharina, b. 9 Oct 1779, bapt. 16 Oct 1779.
Sponsors: Christ. Heinrich and wife Magdal.
Johann, of Johann Braun and Maria, b. 4 Oct 1779, bapt. 17 Oct 1779.
Sponsors: the parents.
Elisabeth, of Nicolaus Panzer and Elisa., b. 16 Oct 1779, bapt. 24 Oct 1779.
Sponsors: the parents.
Elisabeth, of Andreas Fäller and Margareta, b. 30 Sep 1779, bapt. 24 Oct 1779.
Sponsors: the parents.
Susanna, of Leonh. Rusk and Maria Magd., b. 14 Oct 1779, bapt. 24 Oct 1779.
Sponsors: the father, and Maria Eva Weit(in).
A child (name not given), of Daniel Braeutigam (no other information given).
Conrad, of Joh. Jacob and Anna Maria, b. 12 Sep 1779, bapt. 5 Nov 1779.
Sponsors: the parents.
Heinr. Emannuel, of Conrad Leser and Christina, b. 12 Oct 1773, bapt. 6 Nov
1779. Sponsors: Frid. Jeremias and wife Magdalena.
Joseph, of Conrad Leser and Christina, b. 12 Oct 1778, bapt. 6 Nov 1779.
Sponsor: the mother.
Adam, of Joh. Frid. Ulrich and Catharina, b. 10 Aug 1779, bapt. 16 Nov 1779.
Sponsor: Anna Maria Ulrich.
Andreas, of Andr. Forster and Anna, b. 13 Oct 1779, bapt. 21 Nov 1779.
Sponsors: the parents.
Peter, of Nicolaus Doeble and Margareta, b. 7 Nov 1779, bapt. 21 Nov 1779.
Sponsors: Peter Hey and wife Mar.
Michael, of Jacob Ruehl and Catharina, b. 17 Nov 1779, bapt. 12 Dec 1779.
Sponsors: Michael App and wife Anna Maria.
Jacob, of Jacob Leiberzetter and Christina, b. 5 Jun 1779, bapt. 12 Dec 1779.
Sponsor: James Wallace and wife.
Maria Magd., of Mattheus Schü[t]z and Barbara, b. 9 Oct 1779, bapt. 21 Dec
1779. Sponsor: Hanna Forst(in).
Heinrich, of Nicol. Hirt and Magdalena, b. 17 Aug 1779, bapt. 24 Dec 1779.
Sponsors: Joh. Henr. Hirt and wife Maria Margareta.
Joh. Dav., of Gottlieb Spannagel and Elisabeth, b. 27 Nov 1779, bapt. 26 Dec
1779. Sponsors: Joh. Kling and Cath. Weimann.
Maria, of William Elvanson and Sarah, b. 12 Dec 1779, bapt. 27 Dec 1779.
Sponsors: the father, and Hetty Wilson.

1780, First List
(baptisms by pastor Kunze, from Book III)
Maria Magdalena, of Christoph Friedrich Wegmann and Margareta, b. 11 Dec
1779, bapt. 1 Jan 1780. Sponsors: Philip Weger and Magdalena
Happasher(in).
Johannes, of Daniel Harrer and Lydia, b. 31 Oct 1779, bapt. 1 Jan 1780.
Sponsors: Johannes Harrer and wife Marianna.

Catharina, of Dietrich Montsu and Catharina, b. 22 Dec 1779, bapt. 9 Jan 1780.
Sponsors: John Henrich Mein and wife Cathar.
Philipp, of Jacob Buck and Catharina, b. 5 Jan 1780, bapt. 11 Jan 1780.
Sponsors: Philipp Pfankuchen and wife Maria.
Clark, of James Spencer and Ann, b. 3 Oct 1779, bapt. 12 Jan 1780. Sponsors:
Georg Buckhol[t]z and wife Veronica.
Maria Louisa, of Christoph Becker and Catharina, b. 9 Jan 1780, bapt. 16 Jan
1780. Sponsors: Paul Casper Breton and wife Susanna, and dau. Maria
Kraender(in).
Georg David, of Gottfried Grimm and Rosina, b. 30 Dec 1779, bapt. 18 Jan
1780. Sponsors: Jacob Kiemle and wife Christina Catharina.
Johann Philipp, of Benjamin Gasmonn and Anna Maria, b. 27 Dec 1779, bapt.
16 Jan 1780. Sponsors: Philipp Reibold and wife Elisabeth.
Joseph, of Edward Rivert and Eva, b. 6 Dec 1779, bapt. 17 Jan 1780. Sponsor:
Maria Da[t]z(in).
Anna Maria, of Johann Tromberg and Anna, b. 9 Dec 1779, bapt. 24 Jan 1780.
Sponsors: Nicolaus Weber and wife Christina.
Johann Georg, of Christoph Miller and Elisabeth, b. 18 Jan 1780, bapt. 24 Jan
1780. Sponsors: Georg Birckenbiel and Elisabeth Poerk__.
Christian, of Christian Wilke and Rosina, b. 11 Jan 1780, bapt. 24 Jan 1780.
Sponsors: Christian Letter and wife Catharina.
Margareta, of Carl Miller and Magdalena, b. 13 Dec 1779, bapt. 25 Jan 1780.
Sponsors: Jacob Goentner and wife Catharina.
Veronica, of Philipp Reibold and Elisabeth, b. 17 Jan 1780, bapt. 30 Jan 1780.
Sponsors: Johannes Reibold and wife Veronica, Henr. Jahns's dau.
Catharina Elisabeth, of Andreas Heim and Sabina, b. 18 Jan 1780, bapt. 30 Jan
1780. Sponsors: Johann Henrich Bot(h) and wife Catharina Elisab.
Johann Stephan, of Jacob Sulliger and Margareta, b. 31 Jan 1780, bapt. 6 Feb
1780. Sponsors: Stephan Sulliger and wife Johanna.
Johann Henrich, of Jacob Meier and Anna Maria, b. 28 Jan 1780, bapt. 6 Feb
1780. Sponsors: Johann Henrich Bot(h) and wife Catharina Elisabeth.
Elisabeth, of John Rusk and Catharina, b. 13 Jan 1780, bapt. 10 Feb 1780.
Sponsors: Thomas Fischer and wife Elisabeth.
Johanna, of Michael Stauch and Margareta, b. 9 Jan 1780, bapt. 20 Feb 1780.
Sponsors: Johannes Fromberger and wife Johanna.
Henrich, of Georg Bob and Maria, b. 22 Jan 1780, bapt. 20 Feb 1780. Sponsors:
Henrich Strub and wife Susanna.
Michael, of Michael Miller and Christina, b. 30 Jan 1780, bapt. 20 Feb 1780.
Sponsors: Georg Sei[t]z and wife Elisabeth.
Carl, of Friedrich and Catharina Beck, b. 7, Feb 1780, bapt. 27 Feb 1780.
Sponsors: Carl Schilbach and wife Hanna.
(In the original, 14 baptisms of the Second List appear here.) Baptisms by
pastor Kunze continue, as follows:
Elisabeth, of Joh. Wolff and Anna Maria, b. 8 Jan 1780, bapt. 26 Feb 1780.
Sponsors: the parents.
Fridrich, of Joh. Fischer and Anna Maria, b. 5 Feb 1780, bapt. 27 Feb 1780.
Sponsor: the father.

Johann, of Martin Ludwig and Elisabeth, b. 21 Jan 1780, bapt. 8 Feb 1780.
Sponsors: Joh. Strupp and Peggy Walck.
Catharina, of Phil. Werner and Magdalena, b. 26 Jan 1780, bapt. 13 Feb 1780.
Sponsors: the parents.
Cath. Marg., of Georg Phil. Weissmann and Cath. Margar., b. 21 Jan 1780, bapt.
13 Feb 1780. Sponsors: the parents.
Balthasar, of Isaac Koch and Eva, b. 10 Dec 1779, bapt. 23 Feb 1780.
Sponsors: Balthasar Steinforth and wife Elisabeth.
Wilhelm, of Wilhelm Weber and Elisabeth, b. 2 Feb 1780, bapt. 20 Feb 1780.
Sponsors: Joh. Mudschidler and Anna Cath. Weber(in).
Elisabeth, of Jacob Weitmann and Elisabeth, b. 26 Dec 1779, bapt. 20 Feb 1780.
Sponsors: Christian Rot(h) and Elisabeth Weitmann.
Nicolaus, of Heinr. Reiss and Hanna, b. 5 Feb 1780, bapt. 27 Feb 1780.
Sponsors: Nicol. Weber and wife Christina.
Jacob, of Joh. Strauch and Margareta, b. 22 Feb 1780, bapt. 27 Feb 1780.
Sponsors: the parents.
Joseph, of Georg Lorenz Gassner and Christina, b. 16 Feb 1780, bapt. 5 Mar
1780. Sponsors: the father, and Daniel Waker's wife Elisabeth (sister).
Wilhelm, of Wilhelm Batteau and Elisabeth, b. 19 Feb 1780, bapt. 5 Mar 1780.
Sponsors: the parents.
Anna Margareta, of Robert Marks and Elisabeth, b. 13 Feb 1780, bapt. 5 Mar
1780. Sponsors: Georg Bauer and wife Anna Margareta.
Magdalena, of Johannes Nicholaus Die[t]z and Catharina, b. 23 Feb 1780, bapt.
8 Mar 1780. Sponsors: the parents.
Maria Salome, of Johan Georg Feissinger and Anna Maria Margareta, b. 7 Feb
1780, bapt. 12 Mar 1780. Sponsors: Georg Cancer and wife Maria. Salome.
Samuel, of Michael Fuchs and Salome, b. 22 Feb 1780, bapt. 19 Mar 1780.
Sponsors: Conrad Leibbrand and wife Hanna.
Peter, of Peter Bingemann and Catharina, b. 3 Mar 1780, bapt. 19 Mar 1780.
Sponsors: Peter Schwar[t]z and wife Catharina.
Johann, of Jacob Miller and Margareta, b. 19 Mar 1780, bapt. 24 Mar 1780.
Sponsors: Johann Miller and wife Elisab.
Anna Maria, of ___ Cassel and (name not given), b. in 1762, bapt. and
confirmed 28 Mar 1780.
William, of John Mackenight and Margareta, b. 1 Feb 1780, bapt. 23 Mar 1780.
Sponsors: Barnaby Scully and Mary Cunningham.
Charles, of Thomas McKindley and Eva, b. 3 Oct 1779, bapt. 24 Mar 1780.
Sponsor: the mother.
Martin, of Leonard Schmidt and Barbara, b. 8 Jan 1780, bapt. 27 Mar 1780.
Sponsors: Martin Schmidt and wife Catharina.
Sophia, of Wilhelm Schoenneck and Catharina, b. 7 Feb 1780, bapt. 27 Mar
1780. Sponsors: Adam Hoh and wife Mar. Christina.
Peter, of Johann Mells and Elisabeth, b. 19 Mar 1780, bapt. 20 Mar 1780.
Sponsors: Peter Mahn and wife An. Mar.
Elisabet, of Johannes Freeman and Elisabet, b. in Feb 1780, bapt. 26 Mar 1780.
Sponsor: Elisabet Mells.

Johann Georg, of Wolfgang Gemeinbauer and Anna Cathar., b. 7 Mar 1780,
   bapt. 27 Mar 1780. Sponsors: Johan Georg Steinmann and wife Anna Margareta.
Georg, of John Brooks and Catharina, b. 4 Mar 1780, bapt. 27 Mar 1780.
   Sponsors: Christian Danecker and wife Juliana.
A child (name not given), of Jacob Haine and Margareta, b. 16 Mar 1780, bapt.
   27 Mar 1780. Sponsors: Johann Friedr. Haine and wife Salome.
Anna Maria, of Philip Jacob Burk and Elisabeth, b. 10 Dec 1779, bapt. 27 Mar
   1780. Sponsors: Johannes Reifschneider and wife Anna Maria.
Heinrich, of Johann Eberhard Eissenbren? and Catharina, b. 24 Mar 1780, bapt.
   2 Apr 1780. Sponsors: Henr. Rathschlag and wife Elisabeth.
Salome, of Michael Miller and Barbara, b. 1 Mar 1780, bapt. 9 Apr 1780.
   Sponsors: Bartholomaius Schae[t]zlein and wife Catharina.
Catharina, of Henrich Meier and Anna Ursula, b. 30 Mar 1780, bapt. 9 Apr
   1780. Sponsors: the parents.
Elisabet, of Henrich Boecle and Elisabet, b. 3 Feb 1780, bapt. 9 Apr 1780.
   Sponsors: Daniel Boecle and sister Elisabet.
*(In the original, 21 more baptisms from the Second List appear here.) Baptisms
   by pastor Kunze then continue again, as follows:*
Henry [twin], of John Helm and Debora, b. 7 Apr 1780, bapt. 10 Apr 1780.
   Sponsors: Johann Motschitler and wife Anna Margareta.
John Bethel [twin], of John Helm and Debora, b. 7 Apr 1780, bapt. 10 Apr 1780.
   Sponsors: same as above.
Jacob, of Johann Freimuth and Elisabeth, b. 12 Apr 1780, bapt. 16 Apr 1780.
   Sponsors: Jacob Meier and wife Juliana.
Elisabeth, of Henrich Schrubb and Eva, b. 7, Apr 780, bapt. 16 Apr 1780.
   Sponsor: the grandmother Barbara Leibert(in).
Maria, of Johann Christoph Senderling and Maria, b. 21 Jan 1780, bapt. 16 Apr
   1780. Sponsors: the father, and Maria Bauer(in).
Michael, of Johannes Angel and Anna Maria, b. 28 Feb 1780, bapt. 18 Apr
   1780. Sponsors: Michael Pfeister and [wife] Ra[c]hel.
Johann Friedr. [twin], of Johann Ma[t]z and Anna Barbara, b. 16 Apr 1780, bapt.
   the same day. Sponsors: Johann Friedr. Linck and wife Charlotte.
Elisabet [twin], of Johann Ma[t]z and Anna Barbara, b. 16 Apr 1780, bapt. the
   same day. Sponsors: Johann Georg Hausser (widower) and Elisabet Weh
   (single).
Philipp, of Adam Stork (or Stock) and Elisabet, b. 28 Mar 1780, bapt. 26 Apr
   1780. Sponsors: Johann Philipp and wife Cathar.
Maria Christina, of Andreas Mattern and Anna Maria, b. 15 Apr 1780, bapt.
   30 Apr 1780. Sponsors: Johannes Kunckel and wife Maria Christina.
Friedrich, of David Dieterich and Christina, b. 28 Apr 1780, bapt. 14 May 1780.
   Sponsors: Friedrich Weckerley and wife Elisab.
Jacob, of Adam Schmidt and Catharina, b. 4 May 1780, bapt. 14 May 1780.
   Sponsors: Jacob Seier and wife Maria Barbara.
Margareta, of Michael Preusch and Maria, b. 22 Apr 1780, bapt. 14 May 1780.
   Sponsors: Gottfried Schwing and wife Margar.
Charles, of John Godfrew and Margareta, b. 11 Apr 1780, bapt. 14 May 1780.
   Sponsors: the mother, and Sebastian Wulle.

Elisabeth, of Eman. Jacob Alborn and Elisabeth, b. 1 May 1780, bapt. 14 May
1780. Sponsors: Johannes Schlechter and wife Elisab.

Johannes, of Johannes Bergs and Salome, b. 7 Jan 1779, bapt. 15 May 1780.
Sponsor: Johannes Vetterle.

Elisabeth, of Friedrich Linck and Barbara, b. 11 May 1780, bapt. 20 May 1780.
Sponsors: the parents.

Andreas, of Isaac Anderson and Elisabeth, b. 25 Feb 1780, bapt. 20 May 1780.
Sponsors: Andreas Heiderich and wife Elisabeth.

Anna, of Friedrich Stuber and Elisabet, b. 3 Apr 1780, bapt. 20 May 1780.
Sponsors: Johannes Weber and wife Maria.

Henrich Philipp, of Conrad Verglass and Anna Maria, b. 20 May 1780, bapt.
25 May 1780. Sponsors: the parents.

Anna Barbara, of Christian Haag and Anna, b. 26 Aug 1780, bapt. 27 May 1780.
Sponsors: Jacob Sulzel and wife Barbara.

Elisabet, of Georg Reinhard and Magdalena, b. 5 May 1780, bapt. 27 May 1780.
Sponsors: Nicolaus Hess and wife Wilhelmina.

Maria, of Johann Nicolaus Wendeling and Catharina, b. 28 Nov 1779, bapt.
29 May 1780. Sponsors: Wendel Wendeling and wife Maria.

Matthias, of Matthias Landenberger and Maria, b. 1 May 1780, bapt. 2 Jun 1780.
Sponsors: the parents.

Andreas, of Georg Vogel and Elisabeth, b. 23 May 1780, bapt. 11 Jun 1780.
Sponsors: Andreas Burckard and wife Susanna.

Margareta Henrietta, of Johannes Rug__ and Elisabeth, b. 21 May 1780, bapt.
11 Jun 1780. Sponsors: Joh. Christoph Kunze (preacher here) and wife Henr.
Margareta.

Friederich, of Henrich Kaemmerer and Catharina, b. 18 May 1780, bapt. 15 Jun
1780. Sponsors: Conrad Baetis and wife Barbara.

Benjamin, of Benjamin Telemaster? and Anna Magd., b. 17 Mar 1780, bapt.
18 Jun 1780. Sponsors: Georg Sorrel and [wife] Maria Magd.

Maria Magdalena, of Michael Seps and Catharina, b. 8 Jun 1780, bapt. 18 Jun
1780. Sponsors: Martin Schweizer and wife Mar. Magdal.

Michael, of Melchior Weissinger and Maria, b. 31 Jan 1780, bapt. 20 Jun 1780.
Sponsor: Balthas. Staus.

Matthaeus, of Martin Sommer and Barbara, b. 11 Jun 1780, bapt. 26 Jun 1780.
Sponsors: Matthaeus Sommer and wife Rahel.

Johann Adam, of Adam Dieter and Catharina, b. 10 Apr 1780, bapt. 26 Jun
1780. Sponsors: the parents.

Henrich, of Michael Gilbert and Hanna, b. 9 Jun 1780, bapt. 26 Jun 1780.
Sponsors: Henrich Schrub and wife Eva.

Joseph, of Johann Friedrich Kochler and Maria, b. 17 Jun 1780, bapt. 26 Jun
1780. Sponsors: Johannes Krausner? and wife Anna.

Edward, of Edward Lasky and Catharina, b. 9 May 1780, bapt. 26 Jun 1780.
Sponsors: Conrad Hof and wife Sibylla.

Magdalene, of Caspar Christ and Catharina, b. 13 Jun 1780, bapt. 2 Jul 1780.
Sponsors: Johannes Veldeberger and wife Magdalene.

Maria Christina, of Christoph Filler and Sophia, b. 26 Jun 1780, bapt. 9 Jul
1780. Sponsors: Johann Andreas Rohr and wife Maria Christina.

Georg, of Georg Merckel and Anna, b. 11 Jun 1780, bapt. 9 Jul 1780. Sponsors: the parents.

Capt. Adolf Christian Hederick's wife Anna, nee Naegel(in), Jul 12, 1780. Sponsors: from the church council Mich. Schubart, G. Sei[t]z, J. Daum, ___ Dress...; the two pastors were present.

Susanna, of Matthius Schmidt and Catharina, b. 12 Jun 1780, bapt. 12 Jul 1780. Sponsors: the parents.

Philipp, of Philipp Klein and Elisabet, b. 13 Jun 1780, bapt. 14 Jul 1780. Sponsors: Rudolf Lehr and wife Catharina.

Daniel, of Daniel Jones and Sophia Elisab., b. 15 May 1780, bapt. 15 Jul 1780. Sponsors: Phil. Heger and wife Catharina.

Catharina, of Johannes Reimel and Elisabet, b. 21 Jun 1780, bapt. 15 Jul 1780. Sponsors: Friedrich Vogel and wife Catharina.

Maria Barbara, of Joseph Hüler and Barbara, b. 13 May 1780, bapt. 23 Jul 1780. Sponsors: Georg Sachs and wife Barbara.

Maria Margareta, of Johann Bender and Margareta, b. 13 Jun 1780, bapt. 23 Jul 1780. Sponsors: the father, Maria Kür[t]z, and Dorothea Bender(in).

Daniel, of Georg Christoph Reinhold and Maria, b. 27 Sep 1779, bapt. 23 Jul 1780. Sponsors: Henr. Weinkauf and wife (name not given).

Susanna, of Balthasar Emmerich and Maria, b. 16 Jul 1780, bapt. 23 Jul 1780. Sponsors: Valentine Ries and wife Susanna.

Catharina Friederica, of Johannes Fugel and Margareta, b. 9 Jul 1780, bapt. 30 Jul 1780. Sponsors: Georg Shaf and wife Catharina.

Johannes, of Georg Heidel and Salome, b. 7 Jul 1780, bapt. 1 Aug 1780. Sponsors: the parents.

Philipp Conrad, of Johannes Kunckel and Maria Clara, b. 30 Jul 1780, bapt. 7 Aug 1780. Sponsors: Philipp Conrad Kunckel and wife Eleanora.

Maria, of Johann Schumann and Elisabet, b. 31 Jul 1780, bapt. 7 Aug 1780. Sponsors: the parents and Maria Gutton?.

Johann Wilhelm, of Wilhelm Warner and Wilhelmine, b. 25 Jul 1780, bapt. 7 Aug 1780. Sponsors: Johann Peter Litsch and wife Eva Maria.

Eva Christine, of Henrich Schlatter and Anna Maria, b. 28 Dec 1779, bapt. 10 Aug 1780. Sponsors: the father, and Eva Christina Dieter(in).

Catharina, of Georg Stephens and Margareta, b. 4 Aug 1780, bapt. 11 Aug 1780. Sponsors: Joh. Bened. Schneider and wife Philippina Elisab.

Magdalena Elisabet, of Johannes Nagel and Elisabet, b. 8 Aug 1780, bapt. 13 Aug 1780. Sponsors: Remigius Spiegel and wife Maria Elisab.

Maria Margareta, of Jacob Geiger and Catharina, b. 6 Aug 1780, bapt. 13 Aug 1780. Sponsors: the grandfather Andreaus Burghard and Cath. __sha_ler.

Susanna, of Georg Dehn and Eleonor, b. 7 Aug 1780, bapt. 20 Aug 1780. Sponsors: Caspar Paul and wife Dor. Susanna.

Johannes, of Johan Brevill and Mary, b. 16 Aug 1780, bapt. 20 Aug 1780. Sponsors: Johann Hinckel and wife Christina.

Elisabeth, of Gotfried Schwing and Margar., b. 17 Aug 1780, bapt. 20 Aug 1780. Sponsors: Wilhelm Lehman and wife Elisabeth.

Esther, of Jacob Ki[t]z and Elisabet, b. 14 Aug 1780, bapt. 25 Aug 1780. Sponsors: the grandparents Georg and Apollonia Ki[t]z.

Elisabet, of Adam Pausch and Anna Maria, b. 13 Aug 1780, bapt. 27 Aug 1780. Sponsors: Jacob Demant and wife Elisab.
Elisabeth, of Johann Krauss and Anna, b. 18 Aug 1780, bapt. 10 Sep 1780. Sponsors: Johann Benno and wife Maria Elisabeth.
Johannes, of Daniel Frischmuth and Barbara, b. 2 Aug 1780, bapt. 10 Sep 1780. Sponsors: the parents.
Joh. Daniel, of Georg Stauss and Esther, b. 29 Aug 1780, bapt. 10 Sep 1780. Sponsors: Paul Kober and wife Barbara.
Catharina, of Georg Heart and Barbara, b. 21 Mar 1780, bapt. 10 Sep 1780. Sponsors: Martin Schmid and wife Catharina.
Maria, of Andreas Burghardt and Susanna, b. 25 Aug 1780, bapt. 10 Sep 1780. Sponsors: the parents.
Georg Keppele, of Heinrich Helmut (pastor here) and Barbara, b. 29 Aug 1780, bapt. 11 Sep 1780. Sponsors: Mr. Heinrich Keppele Sr., and wife Catharina Steinme[t]z(in).
Catharina, of Georg Sohnleitner and Catharina, b. 3 Sep 1780, bapt. 14 Sep 1780. Sponsors: the father, and Maria Unbehend(in).
Henrich, of Carl Rosen and Alice, b. 6 Sep 1780, bapt. 17 Sep 1780. Sponsors: Heinrich Parry, and Alexander Parry and wife Jeaney.
Anna Maria, of Johann Nicolaus Wagner and Magdalena, b. 11 Sep 1780, bapt. 17 Sep 1780. Sponsors: Zacharias Endres and wife Anna Maria.
Philipp, of John Cartwright and Catharina, b. 3 Sep 1780, bapt. 17 Sep 1780. Sponsors: Philipp Reibold and wife Elisabeth.
Ann, of Georg Bickham and Christina, b. 29 Aug 1780, bapt. 17 Sep 1780 Sponsors: the parents.
Johann David, of David Uber and Anna, b. 14 Sep 1780, bapt. 24 Sep 1780. Sponsors: the parents.
Margareta, of Peter Jung and Magdalena, b. 27 Sep 1780, bapt. 10 Oct 1780. Sponsors: Jacob Witmann and wife Margareta (the sister).
William, of Joseph Gates and Maria, b. 13 Dec 1780, bapt. 10 Oct 1780. Sponsors: Valentin Hofmann and wife Susanna.
Friedrich, of Anton Hecht and Sophia, b. 21 Sep 1780, bapt. 10 Oct 1780. Sponsors: Friedrich Schick and wife Eva Barbara.
Maria Magdalena, of Johannes Kriger and Catharina, b. 17 Sep 1780, bapt. 10 Oct 1780. Sponsors: Andreas Riegler and wife Catharina.
Regina, of Heinrich Kur[t]z and Regina, b. 25 Aug 1780, bapt. 1 Oct 1780. Sponsors: the parents.
Elisabeth, of Johannes Kling and Elisab., b. 12 Dec 1779, bapt. 2 Oct 1780. Sponsors: the parents.
Maria Magdalena, of Adam Schuster and Dorothea, b. 26 Sep 1780, bapt. 8 Oct 1780. Sponsors: Michael Uber and wife Mar. Magdalena.
Eva Maria, of Joseph Lehmann and Elisabet, b. 20 Sep 1780, bapt. 8 Oct 1780. Sponsors: Philipp Dackery? and wife Eva Maria.
Johannes, of Caspar Betzeler and (name not given), b. 6 Mar 1779, bapt. 11 Oct 1780. Sponsors: Johannes Rup and wife.
Georg, of Johann Dieterich and (name not given), b. 10 May 1778, bapt. 11 Oct 1780. Sponsors: Georg Haerle and wife (name not given).

Johannes, of Martin Heins and (name not given), b. 9 Aug 1778, bapt. 11 Oct 1780. Sponsors: the parents.
A child (name not given), of Martin Heims and (name not given), b. 6 Mar 1776, bapt. 11 Oct 1780. Sponsors: the parents.
Wilhelm, of Heinrich Diemant and Elisabet, b. 13 May 1775, bapt. 11 Oct 1780. Sponsors: the parents.
Elisabet, of Heinrich Diemant and Elisabet, b. 3 Jul 1773, bapt. 11 Oct 1780. Sponsors: the parents.
Anna Elisab., of Heinrich Diemant and Elisabet, b. 13 May 1777, bapt. 11 Oct 1780. Sponsors: the parents.
Adam, of Conrad Adam Dickfelder and Elisabet, b. 3 Sep 1780, bapt. 13 Oct 1780. Sponsors: the parents.
Elisabet, of Wilhelm Braun and Dorothea, b. 12 Sep 1780, bapt. 18 Oct 1780. Sponsors: Joh. Haens and wife Elisabet.
Caspar, of Georg Rehn and Eva, b. 9 Oct 1780, bapt. 17 Oct 1780. Sponsors: Caspar Wahl and wife Catharina.
Henrich, of Georg Bastian and Eva, b. 9 Oct 1780, bapt. 19 Oct 1780. Sponsors: Henr. Bastian and wife Cathar.
Catharina, of William Roberts and Catharina, b. 1 Oct 1780, bapt. 19 Oct 1780. Sponsors: Rudolf Ahrn? and wife Cath.
Johann Philipp, of Johann Georg Diebold and Eva, b. 16 Mar 1778, bapt. 21 Oct 1780. Sponsors: the parents.
Carl, of Johann Georg Diebold and Eva, b. 24 Mar 1780, bapt. 21 Oct 1780. Sponsors: the parents.
Maria, of Carl Preis and Maria Magdalena, b. 23 Oct 1780, bapt. 24 Oct 1780. Sponsors: Georg Striby and wife Dorothea.
Anna Maria, of Christian Kinzel and Margareta, b. 27 Sep 1780, bapt. 23 Oct 1780. Sponsors: Johann Reifenschneider and wife Anna Maria.
Elisabet, of Peter Klein and Maria, b. 24 Oct 1780, bapt. 25 Oct 1780. Sponsors: Johannes Reite and Elis. Schneider.
Maria Magdalena, of Friedrich Sent and Eva Barbara, b. 15 Oct 1780, bapt. 29 Oct 1780. Sponsors: the parents.
Johann Adam, of Georg Ganzer and Salome, b. 18 Oct 1780, Sponsors: 29 Oct 1780. Sponsors: Adam Grob and wife Elisabet.
Johann Jacob, of Michael Ka[t]z and Elisabet, b. 23 Oct 1780, bapt. 29 Oct 1780. Sponsors: Johann Bernhard Buck and wife Maria.
Catharina, of Daniel Sharp and Catharina, b. 19 Oct 1780, bapt. 30 Oct 1780. Sponsors: Tobias Koenig and wife Barbara.
Johann Georg, of Conrad Harf (who lives in New Jersey) and Anna, b. 22 Jul 1780, bapt. 8 Nov 1780. Sponsors: the parents.
Johann Michael, of Georg Feuchtenberger and Elisabeth, b. 5 Nov 1780, bapt. 12 Nov 1780. Sponsors: Michael Reut? and wife Catharina.
Anna Barbara, of Friedrich Lu[t]z and Catharina, b. 29 Oct 1780, bapt. 12 Nov 1780. Sponsors: Jacob Suss and wife Elisabeth.
Rosina Amalia, of Gottfried Rapp and Elisabet, b. 15 Oct 1780, bapt. 19 Nov 1780. Sponsors: Nicolaus Senderling and Rosina Jacob(in).
Margareta, of Peregriene Jones and Charlotte, b. 29 Sep 1780, bapt. 19 Nov 1780. Sponsors: Willhelm and Margareta Diel.

Peter, of Conrad Seyfart and Maria Christiana, b. 7 Nov 1780, bapt. 19 Nov
1780. Sponsors: Adam Seibert and wife Sabina.
Helena, of Leonhard Jacobi and Margareta, b. 1 Nov 1780, bapt. 19 Nov 1780.
Sponsors: the parents.
Susanna, of Valentin Hofmann and Susanna, b. 3 Nov 1780, bapt. 26 Nov 1780.
Sponsors: Johann Henzelman and wife Anna Mar.
Johann Peter, of Jacob Kiemle and Christina, b. 14 Nov 1780, bapt. 3 Dec 1780.
Sponsors: Johann Peter Kraft and wife Margareta.
Georg, of Johann Georg Senft and Charlotta, b. 16 Nov 1780, bapt. 3 Dec 1780.
Sponsors: Georg Feuchtenberger and wife Elisabeth.
Johannes, of Balthasar Schenck and Maria Catharina, b. 27 Oct 1780, bapt.
3 Dec 1780. Sponsors: Johannes Weiss and wife [sic] Magdalena Burghard.
Peter, of Andreas Keppele and Maria, b. 15 Nov 1780, bapt. 3 Dec 1780.
Sponsors: the parents, and Peter Muhlenberg and wife Anna.
Elisabeth, of William Livingston and Ann, b. 10 Aug 1780, bapt. 3 Dec 1780.
Sponsors: Juliana deZedwi[t]z and Ann Boucher.
Maria Magar., of Wilhelm Gaab and Maria, b. 12 Nov 1780, bapt. 9 Dec 1780.
Sponsors: the parents.
Maria Christina, of Friedrich Heinsmann and Catharina, b. 20 Nov 1780, bapt.
10 Dec 1780. Sponsors: Johannes Rohr and wife Maria Christina.
Elisabeth, of Caspar Schneider and Elisabeth, b. 9 Dec 1780, bapt. 10 Dec 1780.
Sponsors: the parents, and Barbara Weit.
Johannes Peter, of Peter Benzel and Christina, b. 27 Nov 1780, bapt. 16 Dec
1780. Sponsor: the grandmother Anna Margareta Gand(in).
Philipp Jacob, of Lorenz Schwab and Margareta, b. 1 Dec 1780, bapt. 17 Dec
1780. Sponsors: Phil. Jacob Bechtold and wife Maria.
Elisabeth, of Andreas Lobstein and Elisabeth, b. 18 Dec 1780, bapt. 24 Dec
1780. Sponsors: Johann Leibinger and wife Catharina.
Johannes, of Andreas Rot(h) and Anna Maria, b. 1 Nov 1780, bapt. 24 Dec
1780. Sponsors: Peter Schell and wife Margareta.
*(Note: in the original, 116 more baptisms from the end of the Second List were
entered here; they are included below.)*

1780, Second List
(baptisms by pastor Helmuth, from Book III)
*In the original register, these baptisms by Helmuth are introduced after
23 baptisms of the 1780 First List, as follows:*
Magdalena, of Johann Yayser and Elisabeth, b. 17 Dec 1779, bapt. 8 Jan 1780.
Sponsors: the parents.
Anna Margareta, of Henrich Die[t]z and Anna Barbara, b. 3, Dec 779, bapt.
8 Jan 1780. Sponsors: Wilhelm Engelfried and Margar. Anna Wack(in)?.
Louis, of Frid. Tobelbauer and Catharina, b. 8 Oct 1779, bapt. 14 Jan 1780.
Sponsors: the parents.
Anna Catharina, of Isaac Stahl and Elisabeth, b. 21 Dec 1779, bapt. 16 Jan 1780.
Sponsors: Balthasar Fleischer and wife Anna Cath.

Cathar. Doroth., of Wilhelm Facundus and Dorothea, b. 4 Dec 1779, bapt. 17 Jan 1780. Sponsors: Michael Ki[t]z and wife Maria.

Sarah, of Heinrich Brosius and Catharina, b. 11 May 1778, bapt. 20 Jan 1780. Sponsor: the mother.

Catharina, of Henrich Lenz and Anna Maria, b. 8, Sep 779, bapt. 18 Jan 1780. Sponsors: the parents.

Christian, of Christian Lu[t]z and Susanna, b. 12 Dec 1779, bapt. 18 Jan 1780. Sponsors: Heinr. Kramle and Sophia Isserts?.

Andreas, of Andr. Lapp and Christina, b. 7 Jan 1780, bapt. 14 Jan 1780. Sponsors: the parents.

Jacob, of Georg Hafner and Magdalena, b. 21 Nov 1779, bapt. 23 Jan 1780, Sponsors: Jacob Schwebel and wife Margareta.

Regina Dorothea, of Heinrich Denzel and Maria Dorothea, b. 5 Jan 1780, bapt. 23 Jan 1780. Sponsors: Andr. Kribbel and wife Anna Regina.

Peter, of Daniel Dress and Maria, b. 2 Jan 1780, bapt. 25 Jan 1780. Sponsors: the parents.

Joh. Jonas, of Heinr. Mich. Demmer and Maria Jacobina, b. 22 Jan 1780, bapt. 27 Jan 1780. Sponsors: Jonas Heberstreit and wife Barbara.

Anna Rosina, of Frid. Linck and Elisabeth, b. 19 Jan 1780, bapt. 27 Jan 1780. Sponsors: Nicol. Walter and wife Anna Rosina.

(In the original, 33 baptisms of the First List appear here.) The baptisms by pastor Helmuth continue as follows:

Elisabeth, of Jacob Hackenmüller and Polly, b. 31 Jan 1780, bapt. 6 Mar 1780. Sponsors: the parents.

Nancy, of Adam Me[t]z and Barbara, b. 4 Feb 1780, bapt. 6 Mar 1780. Sponsors: Elisab. Krabbel(in) and Matthias Krabbel.

Samuel, of Samuel Yehic and Leah, b. 6 Dec 1779, bapt. 5 Mar 1780. Sponsors: Peter Preffontain and wife Leah.

Catharina, of Abraham Hargys and Marg., b. 21 Oct 1779, bapt. 10 Mar 1780. Sponsors: Benjamin Brooks and wife Marg. Cath.

Elisabeth, of Andreas Way and Regina, b. 12 Feb 1780, bapt. 12 Mar 1780. Sponsors: the mother, and Georg Way.

Andreas, of Jacob Duffene and Maria, b. 20 Feb 1780, bapt. 22 Mar 1780. Sponsors: Andreas Klein and Elisabeth.

Maria Christina, of Joh. Andr. Rohr and Maria Christina, b. 10 Mar 1780, bapt. 19 Mar 1780. Sponsors: the parents.

Georg Conrad, of Phil. Mayerle and Esther, b. 13 Mar 1780, bapt. 21 Mar 1780. Sponsors: Conrad Mayerle and wife Cathar.

Anna Cath., of Peter Gabel and Elisabeth, b. 2 Nov 1779, bapt. 27 Mar 1780. Sponsors: the parents.

Anna, of Joh. Bowmann and Elisabeth, b. 13 Mar 1780, bapt. 27 Mar 1780. Sponsors: Phil. Werner and wife Anna.

Elisabeth, of Thomas Haal and Hanna, b. 3 Feb 1780, bapt. 28 Mar 1780. Sponsors: Johann Miller and wife Catharina

Jacob, of Daniel Huber and Anna Maria, b. 16 Mar 1780, bapt. 29 Mar 1780. Sponsors: Jacob Schieber and wife Magdalena.

Johann, of Joh. Lager and Margareta, b. 16 Feb 1780, bapt. 20 Mar 1780. Sponsors: the parents.

Maria Elisab., of Frid. Sebast. Malter and Elisab. Charlotta, b. 25 Mar 1780, bapt. 2 Apr 1780. Sponsors: Balthasar Kinzler and wife Maria Elis..

Johann, of Michael Hay and Maria, b. 27 Mar 1780, bapt. 2 Apr 1780. Sponsors: Peter Hay and wife Maria.

Johann, of Joh. Weitmann and Magdalena, b. 17 Dec 1779, bapt. 2 Apr 1780. Sponsors: Johann Weitmann and Marg. Pflur___.

Michael, of Thomas Johnson and Margareta, b. 16 Dec 1779, bapt. 5 Apr 1780. Sponsors: the parents and Louis Horne.

Maria, of Christian Gesner and Magdalena, b. 5 Mar 1780, bapt. 8 Apr 1780. Sponsors: Johann Kopp? and wife Maria.

Michael, of Johann Engel and Susanna Cathar., b. 17 Mar 1780, bapt. 8 Apr 1780. Sponsors: Michael Riehm and wife Maria Elisab.

Joanna Charlotta, of Conrad Hess and Charlotta, b. 9 Mar 1780, bapt. 9 Apr 1780. Sponsors: Michael Krafft and wife Johanna Maria.

Maria Anna, of Joseph Schepperd and Maria, b. 7 Mar 1780, bapt. 9 Apr 1780. Sponsors: Robert Francys Grant and Susanna Millenberger.

(In the original, 121 more baptisms of the First List appear here.) The baptisms by pastor Helmuth then resume, as follows:

Johann, of Elisabeth Schneider(in) and reportedly Johann Turner, b. 10 Dec 1778, bapt. 10 Apr 1780. Sponsor: Adam Schaefer's wife Margareta Dorothea,

Anna Margar., of Joh. Weger and Sahra, b. 10 Mar 1780, bapt. 14 Apr 1780. Sponsors: Anna Marg. Franck(in) and Phil. Weger.

Lorenz, of Lorenz Reinhard and Johanna Elisab., b. 19 Feb 1780, bapt. 16 Apr 1780. Sponsors: Friedr. Kaltoven and Elis. Sensfelder(in).

Johann, of Johann Spa[t]z and Elisabeth, b. 20 Mar 1780, bapt. 16 Apr 1780. Sponsor: Johann Kopia and Peggy Burkhard.

Elisabeth, of Joh. Leonhard Weber and Elisabeth, b. 6 Nov 1780, bapt. 16 Apr 1780. Sponsors: Michael Stricker and wife Maria Magareta.

Georg, of Andreas Barenstecher and Maria, b. 26 Mar 1780, bapt. 16 Apr 1780. Sponsors: Georg Kieffer and wife Eva Maria.

Johann, of Christoph Reinthaler and Elisabeth, b. 14 Feb 1780, bapt. 20 Apr 1780. Sponsors: Johann Schmidt and wife Margareta.

Wilhelm, of Georg Forbach and Margareta, b. 8 Apr 1780, bapt. 20 Apr 1780. Sponsors: Andreas Meyer and Maria Forbach.

Valentin, of Valentin Bereiff? and Catharina, b. 15 Apr 1780, bapt. 30 Apr 1780. Sponsors: Valentin Riess and wife Susanna.

Georg, of Jacob Stauch and Rosina, b. 15 Mar 1780, bapt. 7 May 1780. Sponsors: the parents.

Nicolaus, of Leonhard Walter and Philippina, b. 24 Apr 1780, bapt. 6 May 1780. Sponsors: Nicolaus Walter and wife Rosina.

Sara Elisab., of Philip Werner and Anna Magdalene, b. 26 Apr 1780, bapt. 14 May 1780. Sponsors: the parents.

Cathar. Magdalena, of Joh. Conrad Gebhard and Anna Maria, b. 9 Mar 1780, bapt. 14 May 1780. Sponsors: Joh. Conrad Gebhard and wife Cath., and sister-in-law Anna Maria Got(in).

Wilhelm, of Andreas Geyer and Barbara, b. 13 May 1780, bapt. 18 May 1780. Sponsors: Andreas Boshard and wife Barbara.

Johann Gottlieb, of Fredrich Jeremias and Maria Magdalena, b. 5 Apr 1780, bapt. 20 May 1780. Sponsors: the parents.

Wilhelm, of Johann Christoph Witvogel and Anna, b. 22 Mar 1780, bapt. 30 May 1780. Sponsor: the father.

Cath. Margar., of Michael Schuch and Margareta, b. 10 Apr 1780, bapt. 4 Jun 1780. Sponsors: Johann Hauck and wife Cath.

Joh. Georg, of Joh. Emmerich and Elisabeth, b. 7 May 1780, bapt. 4 Jun 1780. Sponsors: Joh. Georg Seyfferheld and wife Christina Elisab.

Susanna Maria, of Joh. Dienstmann and Anna Maria, b. 6 May 1780, bapt. 5 Jun 1780. Sponsor: widow Susanna Maria Busch(in).

Johann, of Nicolaus Brumm and Anna Maria, b. 14 Mar 1767, bapt. 11 Jun 1780. Sponsors: the parents.

Georg, of Nicolaus Brumm and Anna Maria, b. 8 Dec 1774, bapt. 11 Jun 1780. Sponsors: the parents.

Margareta, of Nicolaus Brumm and Anna Maria, b. 15 Oct 1779, bapt. 11 Jun 1780. Sponsors: the parents.

Catharina, of Peter Auner and Margareta, b. 28 May 1780, bapt. 18 Jun 1780. Sponsors: Wilhelm Jones and wife Eva Livy.

Rebecca Doroth., of Peter Mercker and Catharina, b. 20 Jun 1780, bapt. 21 Jun 1780. Sponsor: the father, and Doroth. Fiss(in).

Catharina, of Georg Thorn and Christina, b. 14 Apr 1780, bapt. 17 May 1780. Sponsors: the parents.

Maria, of Joh. Wagner and Elisabeth, b. 27 Jan 1780, bapt. 22 Jun 1780. Sponsors: the parents.

Anna Cath., of Benjamin Armbrüster and Barbara, b. 10 Jun 1780, bapt. 25 Jun 1780. Sponsors: Jacob Nenni? and wife Anna Cath.

Maria, of Johann Phile and Philippina, b. 18 May 1780, bapt. 26 Jun 1780. Sponsors: the father, and grandmother Phil[ippina] C__st(in).

Charlotta, of Jacob Diderich and Rosina, b. 3 May 1777, bapt. 27 Jun 1780. Sponsor: Margareta Sauter(in).

Christina, of Jacob Diderich and Rosina, b. 22 Aug 1779, bapt. 27 Jun 1780. Sponsor: same as above.

Johann Phil., of Christoph Diderich and Elisabeth, b. 18 Nov 1779, bapt. 27 Jun 1780. Sponsors: Andreas Heiderich? and wife Elisabeth.

Samuel, of Conrad Leibrandt and Hanna, b. 10 May 1780, bapt. 2 Jul 1780. Sponsors: Michael Fuchs and wife Salome.

Maria Cath., of Johann David Seckel and Maria, b. 7 Jun 1780, bapt. 2 Jul 1780. Sponsors: Georg David Seckel and wife Maria Cath.

Elisabeth, of Jacob Pearsy and Maria, b. 1 Sep 1780, bapt. 2 Jul 1780. Sponsors: Sophia Leidy and John McCord.

Peter, of Peter Kuhn and Elisabeth, b. 6 Jun 1780, bapt. 3 Jul 1780. Sponsors: the parents.

Margareta, of Theobald Klein and Margareta, b. 10 Nov 1779, bapt. 13 Jul 1780. Sponsors: the parents.

Johann, of Thimothy Donnehew and Anna, b. 6 Dec 1779, bapt. 24 Jul 1780. Sponsor: Rody Barn.

Catharina, of Jacob Crüger and Maria, b. 8 Jul 1780, bapt. 27 Jul 1780. Sponsor: the mother.

Wilhelm, of Andreas Uhler and Rahel, b. 9 Jun 1780, bapt. 30 Jul 1780.
Sponsors: Wilhelm Hermann and wife Margareta.
Christina, of Christian Lachtleben and Catharina, b. 5 Aug 1780, bapt. 6 Aug
1780. Sponsors: Michael Miller and wife Christina.
Isaac, of Johann Edelmann and Sahra, b. 26 Sep 1780. bapt. 12 Aug 1780.
Sponsors: the mother, and David Rischong.
Joh. Jacob, of Johann Weiss and Elisabeth, b. 24 Jul 1780, bapt. 13 Aug 1780.
Sponsors: the parents.
Anna Margar [twin], of Georg Bauer and Anna Margareta, b. 7 Aug 1780, bapt.
12 Aug 1780. Sponsors: Jacob Theis and wife Doroth.
Sophia Elisab. [twin], of Georg Bauer and Anna Margareta, b. 7 Aug 1780, bapt.
12 Aug 1780. Sponsors: Georg Schrenck and wife Soph. Elis.
Jacob, of Jacob Ehwald and Jeany, b. 25 Dec 1779, bapt. 13 Aug 1780.
Sponsors: the parents.
Margareta, of Heinrich Depperwill and Margareta, b. 1 Aug 1780, bapt. 27 Aug
1780. Sponsors: the parents.
Georg Conrad, of Conrad Lindner and Elisabeth, b. 17 Jul 1780, bapt. 20 Aug
1780. Sponsors: Georg Pachtel and wife Elisabeth.
Margareta, of Georg Habecher and Maria, b. 15 Aug 1780, bapt. 27 Aug 1780.
Sponsors: Phil. Weger and Marg. Frank(in).
Johann, of Fridrich Thui (or Thai) and Elisabeth, b. 3 Aug 1780, bapt. 27 Aug
1780. Sponsors: the parents.
Elisabeth, of Jacob Diderich and Margareta, b. 17 Aug 1780, bapt. 29 Aug 1780.
Sponsors: the parents.
Leonhard, of Conrad Rohrmann and Elisabeth, b. 31 Aug 1780, bapt. 10 Sep
1780. Sponsors: Leonhard Craemer and wife (name not given).
Elisabeth, of Johann Geyer and Christina, b. 25 Aug 1780, bapt. 17 Sep 1780.
Sponsors: Balthasar Clymer and Elisabeth.
Catharina, of Franck Weimann and Catharina, b. 16 Aug 1780, bapt. 16 Sep
1780. Sponsor: the mother.
Johann, of Johann Moos and Catharina, b. 16 Jul 1780, bapt. 16 Sep 1780.
Sponsor: the mother.
Elisabeth, of Jacob Schroeder and Juliana, b. 10 Jul 1780, bapt. 17 Sep 1780.
Sponsors: Michael Miller and wife Catharina.
Elisabeth, of Edward Feise and Jeany, b. 24 May 1779, bapt. 18 Sep 1780.
Sponsor: the mother.
Elisabeth, of Johann Pears and Maria, b. 6 Feb 1779, bapt. 20 Sep 1780.
Sponsors: Martin Noll and wife Barbara.
Christian, of Phil. Dennest and Maria, b. 18 Sep 1780, bapt. 24 Oct 1780.
Sponsors: Christian Spillenberg and wife Catharina.
Elisabeth, of Wilhelm Stuart and Juliana, b. 14 Jul 1780, bapt. 25 Sep 1780.
Sponsors: Thomas Fischer and wife Elisabeth.
Maria Susanna, of Edward Sawton and Catharina, b. 17 Aug 1780, bapt. 26 Sep
1780. Sponsor: Maria Susanna Scharp(in).
Elisabeth, of Heinrich Krummel and Sophia, b. 24 Sep 1780, bapt. 1 Oct 1780.
Sponsors: the parents.
Henrich, of Christian Pearsy and Maria, b. 24 Sep 1780, bapt. 2 Oct 1780.
Sponsors: the parents.

Anna Magd., of Johann Walcker and Catharina, b. 6 Aug 1780, bapt. 3 Oct 1780. Sponsor: Anna Magdalena Hirt(in).
Maria, of Jacob Kraemer and Susanna, b. 24 Sep 1780, bapt. 7 Oct 1780. Sponsors: Caspar Strubel and Maria Schlieps.
Philip, of Johann Wester and Christina, b. 12 Sep 1780, bapt. 8 Oct 1780. Sponsor: the mother.
Rahel, of Dennys Thimsey and Salome, b. 24 Nov 1779, bapt. 19 Nov 1780. Sponsors: Heinrich Mayer and wife Charlotta.
Joh. Wilhelm, of Wilhelm Moor and Susanna Maria, b. 11 Sep 1780, bapt. 12 Oct 1780. Sponsors: Joh. Benedict Schneider and wife Philippina Elisabeth.
Sahra, of Caspar Kribbel and Sahra, b. 1 Oct 1780, bapt. 8 Oct 1780. Sponsors: Johann Kribble and Catharina.
Catharina, of Joseph Siegfried and Elisabeth, b. 12 Oct 1780, bapt. 18 Oct 1780. Sponsors: Valentine Sorg and wife Anna Maria.
Catharina, of Christian Schaefer and Dorothea, b. 13 Oct 1780, bapt. 19 Oct 1780. Sponsors: the parents.
Catharina (twin), of Georg Seckel and Rebecca, b. 3 Oct 1780, bapt. 22 Oct 1780. Sponsors: the paretnts, and Catharina Seckel(in).
Isaac (twin), of Georg Seckel and Rebecca, b. 3 Oct 1780, bapt. 22 Oct 1780. Sponsors: same as above.
Sahra, of Jonathan Stanton and Jemina, b. 24 Oct 1780, bapt. 28 Oct 1780. Sponsors: Michael Ka[t]z and widow Steinert.
Jacob, of Jacob Filter [Fitler] and Margareta, b. 15 Oct 1780, bapt. 15 Oct 1780. Sponsors: the father, and the grandmother Mrs. Fitler.
Maria, of Philip Knecht and Maria, b. 9 Oct 1780, bapt. 3 Nov 1780. Sponsors: Jacob Vallentin and Rosina Rettinger(in).
Elisabeth, of Andreas Beck and wife Barbara, b. 24 Oct 1780, bapt. 9 Nov 1780. Sponsors: Georg Vogel and wife Elisab.
Grace, of Jacob Wegener and Grace, b. 2 Oct 1779, bapt. 5 Nov 1780, Sponsors: the parents.
Joh. Peter, of Mathias Goth and Fronica, b. 25 Oct 1780, Nov 5, 1780. Sponsors: Joh. Henrich Goth and wife Catharina Elisab.
Georg, of Leonhard Fischer and Susanna, b. 25 Oct 1780, bapt. 5 Nov 1780. Sponsors: Georg Fischer and Catharina Rigel(in).
Johann, of Georg Nonnemaker and Catharina, b. 24 Jul 1780, bapt. 5 Nov 1780. Sponsors: Johann Jacob and wife Anna Maria.
Margareta, of Jacob Reiser and Eva Christina, b. 31 Oct 1780, bapt. 12 Nov 1780. Sponsors: Martin Reiser and wife Catharina.
Joh. Thomas, of Johann Esch and Margareta, b. 20 Oct 1780, bapt. 12 Nov 1780. Sponsors: Thomas Fischer and wife Elisabeth.
Maria, of Jacob Beninghoff and Sibylla, b. 12 Oct 1780, bapt. 12 Nov 1780. Sponsors: Jacob Georg and wife (name not given).
Catharina Margar., of Johann Finck and Anna Maria, b. 25 Jul 1778, bapt. 14 Nov 1780. Sponsor: Cath. Margar. Kopp(in).
Joh. Wilhelm, of Johann Finck and Anna Maria, b. 8 Sep 1780, bapt. 14 Nov 1780. Sponsor: Anna Maria Trans__.

Elisabeth, of Christoph Bastian and Catharina, b. 15 Nov 1780, bapt. 19 Nov 1780. Sponsors: Johann Gredy and wife Elis.

Michael, of Michael Steinhauer and Barbara, b. 21 Oct 1780, bapt. 19 Nov 1780. Sponsors: the parents.

Catharina, of Johann Martin Foster and Catharina, b. 2 Oct 1780, bapt. 26 Nov 1780. Sponsors: Johann Hauck and wife Catharina.

Carl, of Carl Dight? and Christina, b. 2 Oct 1780, bapt. 27 Nov 1780. Sponsors: the parents.

Adam, of Adam Zantzinger and Susanna, b. 25 Oct 1780, bapt. 26 Nov 1780. Sponsors: Henrich Keppele, Sr., and Catharina Keppele.

Maria, of Abraham Bachmann and Philippina, b. 22 Nov 1780, bapt. 1 Dec 1780. Sponsors: Caspar Graff and dau. Maria.

Phil. Jacob, of Johann Jacob Finckel and Anna Maria, b. 25 Nov 1780, bapt. 2 Dec 1780. Sponsors: Philip Jacob Kuhnzmann and dau. Maria Salome.

Maria Elisab., of Johann Tarte and Catharina Elisab., b. 23 Aug 1780, bapt. 3 Dec 1780. Sponsors: Fridrich Kaltoven and wife Maria Elisab.

Johanna, of Johann Eberhard and Christina Cath., b. 9 Nov 1780, bapt. 5 Dec 1780, Sponsors: Georg Walcker and wife Anna Dorothea.

Catharina, of Philip Pfläger and Wilhelmina, b. 1 Nov 1780, bapt. 7 Dec 1780. Sponsors: Eberhard Geiss and wife Catharina.

Elisab. Wilhelmina, of John Wright and Catharina, b. 8 Feb 1779, bapt. in Dec 1780. Sponsors: Phil. Pfläger and wife Wilhelmina.

Jacob, of Jacob Schreiber and Anna Margar., b. 22 Nov 1780, bapt. 10 Dec 1780. Sponsors: Jacob Schmidt and wife Eva.

Catharina, of Friedrich Yesch and Catharina, b. 30 Oct 1780, bapt. 11 Dec 1780. Sponsors: John Lehr and wife Catharina.

Jacob, of Jacob Sahns (alias Sones) and Agnes, b. 9 Nov 1780, bapt. 10 Dec 1780. Sponsors: Phil. Heidelmann and wife Anna Margareta.

Anna Cath., of Andreas Beck and Eva Margar., b. 20 Oct 1780, bapt. 11 Dec 1780. Sponsors: the parents.

Daniel, of Philip Neuhauss and Juliana, b. 22 Nov 1780, bapt. 11 Dec 1780. Sponsors: the parents.

Margareta, of Isaac Kelly and Elisabeth, b. 5 Dec 1780, bapt. 15 Dec 1780. Sponsors: Jacob Schnell and wife Elisabeth.

Anna Maria, of Jacob Buss and Barbara, b. 8 Jun 1780, bapt. 22 Dec 1780. Sponsors: Peter Liech and wife Eva Maria.

Elisab., of Christian Spellenberg and Catharina, b. 11 Dec 1780, bapt. 24 Dec 1780. Sponsors: Johann Georg Kier and Elisabeth Haas(in.)

Maria, of Valentin Berk and Maria, b. 11 Sep 1780, bapt. 23 Dec 1780. Sponsors: Peter Fritsch and wife Sahra.

Johann Martin, of Valentin Riess and Susanna, b. 6 Dec 1780, bapt. 26 Dec 1780. Sponsors: Balthasar Emmerich and wife Catharina.

Jacob, of Friedrich Weng and Christina, b. 22 Dec 1780, bapt. 31 Dec 1780. Sponsors: Jacob Deis and Magdalena Weng(in).

Johann Friedrich, of Georg Klein and Elisabeth, b. 3 Dec 1780, bapt. 31 Dec 1780. Sponsors: Johann Friedr. Hainemann and wife Catharina.

Henrich, of David Flickwir and Sophia, b. 13 Nov 1780, bapt. 31 Dec 1780. Sponsors: Henr. Wankauf and wife Elisabeth.

Johannes, of Zacharias Loesch and Maria, b. 19 Nov 1780, bapt. 31 Dec 1780.
Sponsors: Johannes Kiemle and Margareta Kraft(in)..
Elisabeth, of Heinrich Apfel and Christina, b. 23 Oct 1780, bapt. 31 Dec 1780.
Sponsors: Wilh. Willer and wife Elisab.
Sahra, of Franz Loescher and Maria Barbara, b. 18 Nov 1780, bapt. 31 Dec
1780. Sponsors: Joh. Kunckel and wife Maria.

1781, First List
(baptisms by pastor Kunze, from Book III)

Jacob, of Johann Huber and Catharina, b. 30 Dec 1780, bapt. 4 Jan 1781.
Sponsors: the father, and Maria Paul(in).
Maria [twin], of Johannes Weber and Veronica, b. 30 Dec 1780, bapt. 7 Jan
1781. Sponsors: Bernhard Seip and wife Hanna.
Hanna [twin], of Johannes Weber and Veronica, b. 30 Dec 1780, bapt. 7 Jan
1781. Sponsors: same as above.
Magdalena, of Simon Barret and Margareta, b. 17 Dec 1780, bapt. 7 Jan 1781.
Sponsors: Franz Braenninger and Magd. Seiler(n).
Henrich, of Peter Lex and Elisabet, b. 30 Dec 1780, bapt. 7 Jan 1781. Sponsors:
Henrich Herbst and wife Elisabet.
Elisabet Margareta, of Johann Georg Braun and Anna Maria Elisabeth, b.
22 Nov 1770, bapt. 14 Jan 1781. Sponsors: Johan Nicolaus Kroll and wife
Elisab. Margareta.
Johannes, of Henrich Traveller and Margareta, b. 30 Dec 1780, bapt. 14 Jan
1781. Sponsors: Johannes Salomon and wife Christina Maria.
Johanna Maria, of Stephan Sulger and Johanna, b. 28 Dec 1780, bapt. 14 Jan
1781. Sponsors: Jacob Sulger and wife Margareta.
Johann Peter, of Jacob Omensetter and Elisabet, b. 5 Jul 1780, bapt. 14 Jan
1781. Sponsors: Johann Peter Beier and Johanna Beier(in).
Catharina, of Johann Wilhelm Stirnkorb and wife Sybilla, b. 22 Dec 1780, bapt.
16 Jan 1781. Sponsors: Jacob Kiemle and wife Cath.
Robert, of Wilhelm Burckhard and Sarah, b. 31 Dec 1780, bapt. 18 Jan 1781.
Sponsors: William Predin? and wife Maria Christina.
Johann Peter, of Jacob Eckfeld and Elisabet, b. 4 Jun 1780, bapt. 21 Jan 1781.
Sponsors: Georg Michael Gutmann and wife Margareta.
Bernhard, of Johannes Hinckel and Magdalena Maria, b. 19 Jan 1781, bapt.
28 Jan 1781. Sponsors: Bernhard Bruchhol[t]z and wife Catharina.
Anna Maria, of Johann Georg Schahl and Christina, b. 22 Jan 1781, bapt. 28 Jan
1781. Sponsors: Johannes Baetsch and wife Maria Cath.
Thomas, of Christian Kühn and Maria, b. 9 Jan 1781, bapt. 28 Jan 1781.
Sponsors: Michael Blanckst__ and wife Maria.
Michael, of Philipp Kaltwasser and Elisab., b. 14 Aug 1780, bapt. 29 Jan 1781.
Sponsor: Anna Maria Gasler(in).
Catharina, of Michael Trisler and Catharina, b. 20 Jan 1781, bapt. 4 Feb 1781.
Sponsors: Philipp Trisler and Catharina Redinger(in).
Elisabeth, of Henrich Herbst and Elisabeth, b. 31 Jan 1781, bapt. 4 Feb 1781.
Sponsors: Peter Lex and wife Elisab.
Johan Ludew., of Wilhelm Hay and Maria, b. 17 Dec 1780, bapt. 4 Feb 1781.
Sponsors: Ludewig Schaefer and Christina Wal[c]ker.

Catharina, of Georg Farly and Anna Maria, b. 10 Jan 1781, bapt. 4 Feb 1781. Sponsors: Jacob Walter and wife Cathar.

Maria Magdalena, of Johannes Freiburger and Susanna, b. 15 Jan 1781, bapt. 4 Feb 1781. Sponsors: Jacob Commer and wife Maria Magdalena.

Peter, of Henry Divarrost and Maria, b. 22 Jan 1781, bapt. 4 Feb 1781. Sponsors: Peter Ozeus and wife Magd.

Catharina, of Friedrich A. Mühlenberg and Catharina, b. 25 Jan 1781, bapt. 11 Feb 1781. Sponsors: David Schaefer and wife Maria.

Elisabeth Catharine, of Carl Hay and Sophia, b. 26 Jan 1781, bapt. 14 Feb 1781. Sponsors: Andreas Walker and Cathar. Spiegel(in).

Georg, of Georg Kehlhauer and Salome, b. 23 Jan 1781, bapt. 15 Feb 1781. Sponsors: Bartholmaeus Schae[t]zlein and wife Cath..

Johann Michael, of Michael Pfeiffer and Regina, b. 29 Jan 1781, bapt. 15 Feb 1781. Sponsors: the parents.

Rosina Margareta., of Jesaias Peters and Elisabeth, b. 30 Jan 1781, bapt. 16 Feb 1781. Sponsor: Rosina Margareta Geret(in).

Peter, of Adam Molitor (deceased) and Catharina, b. 30 Jan 1781, bapt. 16 Feb 1781. Sponsors: Adam Grof and wife Catharina.

Catharina, of Christoh Mohr and Catharina, b. 9 Jan 1781, bapt. 18 Feb 1781. Sponsors: Georg Schmidt and wife Eva.

Magdalena, of Carl Preis and Maria Magdalena, b. 17 Feb 1781, bapt. 17 Feb 1781. Sponsors: Nicolaus Bender and wife (name not gven).

Sibylla, of Johann Loschet and Catharina, b. 27 Jan 1781, bapt. 17 Feb 1781. Sponsors: the father, and the grandmother Sibylla Loschet.

Margareta, of Johann Emmirich and Maria, b. 6 Feb 1781, bapt. 25 Feb 1781. Sponsors: Johann Georg Sturmfels and wife Margareta.

Samuel, of Johann Koof and Elisabeth, b. 7 Feb 1781, bapt. 25 Feb 1781. Sponsors: Sebastian Wulle, and Matt. Armbrüster and wife Maria.

Johann Adam, of William Atkinson and Elisabet, b. 27 Feb 1781, bapt. 4 Mar 1781. Sponsors: Johann Adam Haendel and Elisab. Kaemmer(in).

Johann Friedrich, of Johann Meier and Elisabet, b. 3 Feb 1781, bapt. 4 Mar 1781. Sponsors: Friedrich Reinecke and Cathar. Murray.

Johann Georg, of Jacob Hirneisen and Anna Maria, b. 10 Feb 1781, bapt. 11 Mar 1781. Sponsors: Georg Shae[t]zlein and Margareta Hirneisen.

Georg, of Johann Graefenstein and Dorothea, b. 28 Feb 1781, bapt. 18 Mar 1781. Sponsors: Georg Happacher and wife Maria.

Christian, of Christian Reddig and Catharina, b. 25 Jan 1781, bapt. 22 Mar 1781. Sponsors: the parents.

Susanna Maria, of Johannes Hoetzel and Catharina, b. 6 Feb 1781, bapt. 25 Mar 1781. Sponsor: Balthasar Staus.

Elisabeth, of William Hock and Susanna, b. 12 Mar 1781, bapt. 25 Mar 1781. Sponsors: Andreas Knauer and Maria Elisab. Uhl(in).

Catharina, of Johannes Frickhoefer and Hedwig, b. 22 Mar 1781, bapt. 1 Apr 1781. Sponsors: the father, and Catharina Frickhoefer.

Carl, of Friedrich Callwi[t]z (*alias* Calway) and Salome, b. 20 Mar 1781, bapt. 8 Apr 1781. Sponsor: Carl Schildbach__ .

Margareta, of Friedrich Vogel and Catharina, b. 22 Mar 1781, bapt. 8 Apr 1781. Sponsors: Johannes Riemet? and wife Elis.

Samuel, of Johannes Lehmann and Louisa, b. 6 Nov 1758, bapt. 13 Apr 1781.
Sponsors: all the confirmands in 1781.
Catharina, of Johannes Lehmann and Louisa, b. in Sep 1763, bapt. 13 Apr 1781.
Sponsors: all the confirmands in 1781.
Johann Friedrich, of Johann Friedrich Vogel and Elisabeth, b. 27 Mar 1781,
bapt. 15 Apr 1781. Sponsors: Georg Oe__sterk and Eva Schneider(in).
Johann Caspar, of Jacob Steinmeier and Catharina, b. 26 Mar 1781, bapt. 15 Apr
1781. Sponsors: Caspar Wahl and wife Elisabet.
Henrich, of Henrich Sommer and Catharina, b. 25 Mar 1781, bapt. 15 Apr 1781.
Sponsors: Martin Sommer and wife Barb.
Judith, of Michael Wolf (from across the river) and Margareta, b. 30 Oct 1780,
bapt. 15 Apr 1781. Sponsors: David Uber and wife Anna.
Johann Adam, of Lorentz Schuster and Maria, b. 2 Jan 1781, bapt. 5 Apr 1781.
Sponsors: Joh. Adam Schuster and wife Doroth.
Andreas Christoph, of Johann Christoph Schnellhard, b. 5 Nov 1780, bapt.
16 Apr 1781. Sponsors: Andr. Christoph. Popa and Maria.
Maria Philippina, of Joseph Mansfield and Ann. Magdal., b. 25 Dec 1775, bapt.
16 Apr 1781. Sponsors: Peter Matt. Abel and wife Mar. Philippina.
Johannes, of Friedrich Mog and Maria, b. 3 Jan 1781, bapt. 22 Apr 1781.
Sponsors: Tobias Adam Koenig and wife Barb.
Margareth, of Johannes Straub and Margareta, b. 9 Apr 1781, bapt. 22 Apr
1781. Sponsors: the parents.
Elisabet, of Daniel Gilbert and Catharina, b. 29 Mar 1781, bapt. 29 Apr 1781.
Sponsors: Anton Birkenbeit and wife Barbara.
Johann Georg, of Jacob Schneider and Elisabet, b. 7 Apr 1781, bapt. 29 Apr
1781. Sponsors: Georg Schneider and wife Cathar.
Elisabet, of Adam Grob and Elisabeth, b. 27 Apr 1781, bapt. 6 May 1781.
Sponsors: Georg Banzer and wife Dorothea.
Hanna, of Leonard Kesler and Maria, b. 5 May 1781, bapt. 13 May 1781.
Sponsors: the parents.
Daniel, of Johannes Pilliar and Margareta, b. 4 Mar 1781, bapt. 14 May 1781.
Sponsors: the parents.
Anna Margar., of Nicolaus Paulus and Margareta, b. 7 May 1781, bapt. 10 May
1781. Sponsors: Christian Beringer and wife Margareta.
Catharina, of Henrich Fuhrer and Elisabeth, b. 17 Mar 1781, bapt. 20 May 1781.
Sponsors: Christoph Schmidt and wife Catharina.
Hanna, of Dobling (a negro of Mr. Fr. Wade) and Elisabeth (illegitimate), b.
13 May 1781, bapt. 20 May 1781. Sponsor: Sarah Wa___.
Peter, of Peter Wagner and Rosina, b. 1 May 1781, bapt. 20 May 1781.
Sponsors: the parents.
Susanna Barbara, of Adam Knoblauch and Susanna Barbara, b. 1 May 1781,
bapt. 27 May 1781. Sponsors: the parents.
Catharina, of Jacob Reis and Maria Magdalena, b. 6 May 1781, bapt. 27 May
1781. Sponsors: Johannes Fri[t]z and wife Catharina.
William, of Christian Ruch and Sahra, b. 18 Feb 1781, bapt. 3 Jun 1781.
Sponsors: William Pfau and wife Barbara.
Johann Phillip, of Gottlieb Mayer and Magdalena, b. 28 Apr 1781, bapt. 4 Jun
1781. Sponsors: Gottlieb Kolmann and Margareta Sehler(in).

Daniel, of Peter Arnold and Maria, b. in Apr 1781, bapt. 9 Jun 1781. Sponsors: John Daniel Sommer and Cath. Beckmann(in).

Maria, of Henrich Meier and Catharina, b. 28 May 1781, bapt. 17 Jun 1781. Sponsors: the father, and Maria Schweizer(in).

Georg, of Georg Stur[t]z and Sara, b. 16 Nov 1779, bapt. 17 Jun 1781. Sponsors: Wilhelm Stur[t]z and Margaretha Schindel(in).

Wilhelm, of Johann Jost Schweickard and Hanna, b. 17 Apr 1781, bapt. 21 Jun 1781. Sponsor: Hanna Eduards.

Henrich, of Johann Braun and Catharina, b. 4 Sep 1780, bapt. 24 Jun 1781. Sponsors: Henrich Herbst and wife Elisab.

Esther, of Peter Gress and Rosina, b. 6 Jun 1781, bapt. 24 Jun 1781. Sponsors: Jacob Teis and wife Dorothea.

Maria Sibylla, of Cathar. Dorothea Egar(sin) and unnamed father (illegitimate), b. 29 May 1781, bapt. 28 Jun 1781. Sponsor: Georg Oestertag?.

Carl Heinrich, of Johann Christoph Kunze (pastor here) and wife Henrietta Margareta, b. 24 Jun 1781, bapt. 26 Jun 1781. Sponsors: Heinr. Melch. Muhlenberg, Carl Kunze and wife Elisab.

Gottfried, of Gottfried Seider and Catharina, b. 6 Jun 1781, bapt. 1 Jul 1781. Sponsors: the parents.

Henrich, of Henrich Schmidt and Magdalena, b. 25 Jan 1781, bapt. 1 Jul 1781. Sponsors: Jacob Miller and wife Barbara.

Elisabet, of Wilhelm Faerley and Elisab., b. 1 Jul 1781, bapt. 2 Jul 1781. Sponsor: Jacobina Seyfert?.

Wilhelm, of Wilhelm Nushag and Catharina, b. 2 Jul 1781, bapt. 8 Jul 1781. Sponsors: the parents.

Catharina, of Philipp Reibold and Elisabeth, b. 24 Jun 1781, bapt. 8 Jul 1781. Sponsors: Jacob Grub and wife Cathar.

Catharina, of Thomas Fischer and Elisab., b. 5 Jun 1781, bapt. 8 Jul 1781. Sponsors: Michael Immel and wife Catharina

Johann Bernhard, of Johannes Riep and Susanna, b. 28 Jun 1781, bapt. 15 Jul 1781. Sponsors: Bernhard Lard and wife Catharina.

Wilhelm, of Johann Georg Weidemann and Maria Eva, b. 21 Jun 1781, bapt. 15 Jul 1781. Sponsors: the parents.

Elisabeth, of Peter Sohnleitner and Elisabeth, b. 15 Jul 1781, bapt. 20 Jul 1781. Sponsors: the parents.

Catharina, of Heinrich Schrupp and Eva, b. 10 Jul 1781, bapt. 22 Jul 1781. Sponsors: the father, and Barbara Seibert.

Wilhelm, of Georg Gebhard and Rosina, b. 16 Apr 1781, bapt. 30 Jul 1781. Sponsors: Elisabeth Holzkamp and the grandfather Gerh. Holzkamp.

Henrich, of Jacob Naegel and Margareta, b. 7 Nov 1779, bapt. 3 Jul 1781. Sponsors: the parents.

Catharina, of Johannes Heims and Elisabeth, b. 13 Jul 1781, bapt. 4 Aug 1781. Sponsors: Georg Holzkamp and wife Elisabeth.

Susanna Dorothea, of Peter Die[t]z and Maria, b. 17 Jul 1781, bapt. 5 Aug 1781. Sponsors: Johannes Graefenstein and wife Dorothea.

Johann Georg, of Philipp Gerber and Maria, b. 24 Jul 1781, bapt. 5 Aug 1781. Sponsors: Johann Georg Sturmfels and wife Margareta.

Salome, of Johannes Kuch and Barbara, b. 15 Jul 1781, bapt. 5 Aug 1781.
Sponsors: Nicolaus Ricket? and wife Salome.
Johannes, of Jacob Kaufman and Margareta, b. 2 Aug 1781, bapt. 19 Aug 1781.
Sponsors: Johannes Strupp and wife Margareta.
David, of David Nies and Clara Dorothea, b. 27 Jul 1781, bapt. 19 Aug 1781.
Sponsors: David Ott and wife Catharina.
Margareta Elisabeth, of Carl Wolpert and Catharina, b. 18 Aug 1781, bapt.
26 Aug 1781. Sponsors: Wilhelm Engelfried and wife [sic] Margar. Wolpert.
Maria Rebecca, of Conrad Baethis and Barbara, b. 21 Aug 1781, bapt. 10 Sep
1781. Sponsors: Heinrich Leuthauser and wife Maria.
Joh. Nicolaus, of Joh. Nicolaus Hirt and Maria, b. 12 Aug 1781, bapt. 13 Sep
1781. Sponsor: Maria Margareta Hirt(in).
Georg Leonard, of (first name not given) Harkus and Maria, b. 24 Jun 1781,
bapt. 6 Sep 1781. Sponsors: Georg Huber and wife Louisa.
Catharina, of Martin Peusch and Maria Magdalena, b. 28 Aug 1781, bapt.
16 Sep 1781. Sponsors: Georg Gro[t]z and wife Dorothea.
Johann Georg, of Henrich Schlesmann and Catharina, b. 1 Sep 1781, bapt.
16 Sep 1781. Sponsors: the parents.
Elisabeth, of Jacob Freiberger and Maria, b. 24 Aug 1781, bapt. 16 Sep 1781.
Sponsors: Mercur McCloud and wife Margareth.
Elisabeth, of Philipp Sommer and Sarah, b. 1 Sep 1781, bapt. 30 Sep 1781.
Sponsors: Jacob Bast and Elisab. Riebel(in).
Clementina Juliana, of David Ott (the schoolmaster here) and Catharina, b.
11 Sep 1781, bapt. 1 Oct 1781. Sponsor: Bast. Martin Sommer.
Georg Friedrich, of Heinrich Meier and Catharina, b. 26 Sep 1781, bapt. 4 Oct
1781. Sponsors: Johann Friedr. Gress and wife Sophia.
Carl Ulrich, of Jacob Ranninger and Magdalena, b. 29 Sep 1781, bapt. 6 Oct
1781. Sponsors: Carl Schmidt and Ulrich.
Christian, of Johannes Wessenberger and Barbara, b. 2 Aug 1781, bapt. 7 Oct
1781. Sponsors: Christian Derrick? and wife Anna Cath.
Anna Barbara, of David Schaefer and Elisabeth, b. 16 Sep 1781, bapt. 7 Oct
1781. (Sponsors not given.)
Henrich, of Jacob Strumbeck and Maria, b. 16 Sep 1781, bapt. 7 Oct 1781.
Sponsors: Johann Bra__ and Cathar. Stro___.
Georg, of Wilhelm Noll and Christina, b. 27 Sep 1781, bapt. 9 Oct 1781.
Sponsors: the parents.
Wilh. Dietrich, of Johann Nicolaus Kroll and Elisab. Margareta, b. 29 Sep 1781,
bapt. 14 Oct 1781. Sponsors: Johann Goetz? and wife An. Dor.
Elisabeth, of Carl Jung and Catharina, b. 5 Oct 1781, bapt. 14 Oct 1781.
Sponsors: Johann H___ and wife Elis.
Cath. Elisab., of Henrich Bot(h) and Catharina Elisab., b. 4 Oct 1781, bapt.
13 Oct 1781. Sponsors: the father and mother.
Anna Maria, of Thomas Wenzel and Christina, b. 1 Oct 1781, bapt. 14 Oct 1781.
Sponsors: John Adam Bausch and wife An.
Catharina, of Peter Grof and Catharina, b. 15 Sep 1781, bapt. 16 Oct 1781.
Sponsors: the father, and Cath. Kunz?.
Jeremias, of Johan Georg Kehl and Veronica, b. 16 Sep 1781, bapt. 1 Oct 1781.
Sponsor: Jus.? Otts.

Anna Elisabeth, of Johann Koch and Rosina Dorothea, b. 1 Oct 1781, bapt. 21 Oct 1781. Sponsors: Joh. Gottlieb Freiberger and Christina (illegible).

Leonhard, of Leonhard Kraemer and Maria, b. 24 Sep 1781, bapt. 21 Oct 1781. Sponsors: the parents.

Wilhelm, of Christian Fuchs and Dorothea, b. 25 Oct 1781, bapt. 31 Oct 1781. Sponsors: the parents.

Elisabeth, of Henrich Nagel and Barbara, b. 23 Oct 1781, bapt. 31 Oct 1781. Sponsors: Johann Nagel and wife Elisab.

Anna Elisabeth, of Johannes Wilhelm Schneider and Regina Catharina, b. 21 Oct 1781, bapt. 22 Oct 1781. Sponsors: Johannes Miller and wife Anna Elisab.

Philipp, of Johann Philip Heide and Magdalena, b. 24 Sep 1781, bapt. 4 Nov 1781. Sponsors: Philipp Heide and wife Agnes.

Georg, of Johann Preis and Mar. Catharina, b. 9 Oct 1781, bapt. 4 Nov 1781. Sponsors: Georg Kiefer and wife Eva Mar.

Johann Georg, of Martin Die[t]z and Sophia Margareta, b. 23 Oct 1781, bapt. 4 Nov 1781. Sponsors: Johann Georg Hartmann and wife Sabina Margar.

Margareta, of Jacob Pierce and Anna Magdalena, b. 4 Oct 1781, bapt. 4 Nov 1781. Sponsors: the father, and Anna Maria Magdalena. Pierce.

Hanna, of Friedrich Beck (deceased) and Catharina , b. 4 Oct 1781, bapt. 4 Nov 1781. Sponsors: Carl Schildbach and wife Hanna.

Margareta, of Jacob Specht and Margareta, b. 8 Feb 1781, bapt. 5 Nov 1781. Sponsors: the parents.

Anna Susanna, of Peter Kraft and Margareta, b. 29 Oct 1781, bapt. 10 Nov 1781. Sponsors: Jacob Kiemle and wife Cathar.

Johann Conrad, of Johannes Waester and Catharina, b. 28 Oct 1781, bapt. 11 Nov 1781. Sponsors: Johann Conrad Spangenberg and wife Anna Elisab.

Daniel, of Daniel Knodel and Anna Maria, b. 7 Oct 1781, bapt. 11 Nov 1781. Sponsors: Georg Sorg and wife Magdal.

Friederich, of Philipp Stock and Catharina, b. 7 Nov 1781, bapt. 13 Nov 1781. Sponsors: the parents.

Magdalena, of Johannes Rosk and Catharina, b. 13 Oct 1781, bapt. 14 Nov 1781. Sponsors: Jacob Holl and Ann. Mar. Streht(in).

Elisabeth, of Johannes Wucher and Elisabeth, b. 12 Oct 1781, bapt. 18 Nov 1781. Sponsors: the parents.

Georg, of Georg Baetsch and Catharina, b. 29 Oct 1781, bapt. 18 Nov 1781. Sponsors: Georg Stauss and wife Esther.

Johann David, of Georg Kur[t]z and Margareta, b. 14 Nov 1781, bapt. 19 Nov 1781. Sponsors: the parents.

Anna Maria, of Johannes Chargeau and Catharina, b. 17 Mar 1781, bapt. 20 Nov 1781. Sponsors: the mother, and Johann Michael Bas__.

Elisabeth, of Philipp May and Maria, b. 22 Nov 1781, bapt. 2 Dec 1781. Sponsors: Henrich Rathschlag and wife Elisabeth.

Joseph, of Johann Butler and Susanna, b. 18 Nov 1781, bapt. 2 Dec 1781. Sponsors: Johann Welsh and wife Susanna.

Carl, of Christlieb Baehrdling and Elisab., b. 31 Oct 1781, bapt. 2 Dec 1781. Sponsors: the parents.

Johann Peter, of Johann Friedr. Armbach and Maria, b. 4 Dec 1781, bapt. 5 Dec 1781. Sponsor: the mother.

Maria Elisab., of Michael Kraft and Johanna Maria, b. 4 Nov 1781, bapt. 9 Dec
1781. Sponsors: Peter Kraft and wife Margar.
Elisabeth, of Georg Garlinger and Maria Elisabeth, b. 7 Nov 1781, bapt. 9 Dec
1781. Sponsors: Henrich Moser and Dietrich? Diensmann.
Jacob, of Johann Georg Schmidt and Maria Eva, b. 23 Nov 1781, bapt. 9 Dec
1781. Sponsors: Jacob Schmidt and wife [sic] Elisab. Kaemmet?.
Johann Georg, of Georg Sigismund Geleta (at Mr. Fischer's place) and Naomi,
b. 19 Nov 1781, bapt. 16 Dec 1781. Sponsors: Johann Motschittler and
Christina Hempel__.
Elisabeth, of Johann Christian Gesner and Magdalena, b. 7 Nov 1781, bapt.
16 Dec 1781. Sponsors: Philipp Jung and wife Elisab.
Esther, of Johannes Hiep? and Catharina, b. 7 Dec 1781, bapt. 16 Dec 1781.
Sponsors: Henr. Moeller and wife Esther.
Christoph Friedrich., of Christoph Friedr. Wegmann and Margareta, b. 3 Dec
1781, bapt. 23 Dec 1781. Sponsors: Friedrich Augustus Muhlenberg and
wife Catharina.

1781, Second List
(baptisms by pastor Helmuth; from Book III)
Anna Maria, of Joh. Bach and Elisabeth, b. 24 Dec 1780, bapt. 17 Jan 1781.
Sponsors: Leonhard Craemer and wife Anna Maria.
Elisabeth, of Phil. Springer and Eva, b. 10 Jan 1780, bapt. 13 Jan 1781.
Sponsors: Simon Moll and wife Elisabeth.
Johann, of Samuel Yetter and Maria, b. 8 Oct 1780, bapt. 12 Jan 1781.
Sponsors: Joh. Mutschitler and wife Anna Margareta.
Christoph Fridr., of Christoph Fridrich Pantleon and Cathar., b. 13 Dec 1780,
bapt. 14 Jan 1781. Sponsors: Christoph Fridr. Fischbach and Hanna Vetter.
Christina Maria, of Adam Werner and Maria, b. 30 Nov 1780, bapt. 14 Jan
1781. Sponsors: Fridr. Hager? and wife Christina.
Johann, of Rudolph Nagel and Susanna, b. 10 Jan 1781, bapt. 21 Jan 1781.
Sponsors: Heinr. Shalbach and wife Catharina.
Wilhelm, of Wilhelm Hehn and Maria, b. 2 Dec 1780?, bapt. 22 Jan 1781.
Sponsors: the parents.
Johann Christian, of Georg Death and Maria, b. 23 Sep 1780, bapt. 31 Jan 1781.
Sponsor: Christina Fahn(sin).
Anna Maria, of Abraham Lang and Elisabeth, b. 29 Jan 1781, bapt. 2 Feb 1781.
Sponsors: Joh. Georg Escher and Anna Maria Wood.
Joh. Michael, of Bernh. Weber and Catharina, b. 20 Dec 1780, bapt. 6 Feb 1781.
Sponsors: the mother, and Joh. Michl. Seifferd.
Jacob, of Fridr. Kessler and Anna, b. 29 Jan 1781, bapt. 7 Feb 1781. Sponsors:
the father and his sister Elisab.
Phil. Heinrich, of Carl Miller and Anna Barb., b. 3 Feb 1781, bapt. 11 Feb 1781.
Sponsors: Phil. Heinr. Knapp and wife Eva Cath.
Joh. Joseph, of Carl Fridr. Hensel and Anna Margar., b. 16 Jan 1781, bapt.
11 Feb 1781. Sponsors: Joh. Joseph Kraft and Maria Dor.
Michael, of Caspar Kinsch and Margareta, b. 26 Jan 1781, bapt. 11 Feb 1781.
Sponsors: Michl. Blankhorn and wife Maria.

Margareta, of Joh. Friess and Anna, b. 7 Jan 1781, bapt. 12 Feb 1781. Sponsors: Thomas Mayer and wife Margar.

Wilhelm, of Adam Widderstein and Sophia, b. 29 Jan 1781, bapt. 18 Feb 1781. Sponsors: Wilhelm Behno and wife Anna Elisab.

Elisabeth (twin), of Joh. Simon and Anna Cath., b. 23 Jan 1781, bapt. 22 Feb 1781. Sponsors: Joh. Krauss and wife Catharina.

Barbara (twin), of Joh. Simon and Anna Cath., b. 23 Jan 1781, bapt. 22 Feb 1781. Sponsors: Michael Ye[t]z and wife Barbara.

Johann, of Gottfried Krumbach and Barbara, b. 9 Jan 1781, bapt. 24 Feb 1781. Sponsors: the parents.

Catharina, of Heinr. Stock and Susanna, b. 9 Sep 1780, bapt. 25 Feb 1781, Sponsor: widow Catharina Stock(in).

Catharina, of Joh. Starkey and Catharina, b. 29 Jan 1781, bapt. 3 Mar 1781. Sponsors: Christian Klockner and Cath. Leuthauser.

Joh. Georg, of Christoph Hefft and Anna Maria, b. 11 Feb 1781, bapt. 11 Mar 1781. Sponsors: Joh. Georg Kiehr and Anna Elisab Haass(in).

Johann, of Carl Enoch Schildbach and Hanna, b. 22 Feb 1781, bapt. 11 Mar 1781. Sponsors: the father, and Elisab. Clark.

Elisabeth, of Fridr. Schumann and Anna Maria, b. 3 Mar 1781, bapt. 11 Mar 1781. Sponsors: Joh. Georg Rummele and wife Elisab.

Elisabeth, of Johann Bender and Susanna, b. 17 Feb 1781, bapt. 11 Mar 1781. Sponsors: Peter Sonnleiter and wife Elisab.

Anna Maria, of Wilhelm Stur[t]z and Ursula, b. 16 Jan 1781, bapt. 11 Mar 1781. Sponsors: the parents.

Johann, of Joh. Asmus and Catharina, b. 2 Mar 1781, bapt. 11 Mar 1781. Sponsor: Cath. Stur[t]z(in).

Georg Fridr., of Valentin Gosner and Maria Agnesa, b. 14 Feb 1781, bapt. 17 Mar 1781. Sponsors: Joh. Fridr. Renn and wife Catharina.

Anna Maria, of Heinr. Reiss and Hanna, b. 5 Mar 1781, bapt. 17 Mar 1781. Sponsors: Nicol. Weber and wife Christina.

Johann, of Peter Armbrüster and Margareta, b. 13 Mar 1781, bapt. 24 Mar 1781. Sponsors: Joh. Pfau and wife Elisabeth.

Pet. Wilhelm, of Phil. Mittmann and Veronica, b. 19 Feb 1781, bapt. 24 Mar 1781. Sponsors: the parents.

Maria Margar., of Heinrich Wester and Rosina, b. 22 Mar 1781, bapt. 1 Apr 1781. Sponsor: Margareta Wester(in).

Carl Heinrich, of Heinr. Leonh. deArendt and Carolina Friderica, b. 12 Mar 1781, bapt. 3 Apr 1781. Sponsor: Phil. Bloomberg.

Andreas, of Joh. Lippie and Elisabeth, b. 6 Feb 1781, bapt. 8 Apr 1781. Sponsors: Andr. Weber and wife Eva.

Anna Maria, of Anthon Eberhard and Philippina, b. 21 Mar 1781, bapt. 8 Apr 1781. Sponsors: Heinr. Lenz and wife Anna Maria.

Sabina, of Heinr. Cress and Anna Maria, b. 28 Feb 1781, bapt. 7 Apr 1781. Sponsor: Sabina Grünewald(in).

Christina, of Gottfried Schüssler and Elisabeth, b. 15 Mar 1781, bapt. 16 Apr 1781. Sponsors: Wilh. Stein and wife Christina.

Jacob, of Michael Trappel and Elisabeth, b. 2 Feb 1780, bapt. 16 Apr 1781. Sponsors: the father, and Sa(h)ra Luticat.

Sahra, of Daniel Rusch and Susanna, b. 19 Jul 1780, bapt. 16 Apr 1781.
Sponsors: Peter Fridrich and wife Sarah.
Carl Franz, of Michael Kühner and Charlotte, b. 5 Apr 1781, bapt. 16 Apr 1781.
Sponsors: Cath. Truckenmüller and son Carl Franz.
Johann, of Daniel Huber and Maria, b. 30 Mar 1781, bapt. 18 Apr 1781.
Sponsors: Joh. Kappel and Catharina Sinck(in).
Salome, of Johann Kribble and Christina, b. 30 Mar 1781, bapt. 16 Apr 1781.
Sponsors: Christian Kempf and wife Maria.
Christoph, of Jacob Stauch and Rosina, b. 26 Mar 1781, bapt. 28 Apr 1781.
Sponsors: Phil. Jacob Pechthold and wife Anna Maria.
Anna, of Peter Kur[t]z and Sahra, b. 1 Apr 1781, bapt. 29 Apr 1781. Sponsors:
Wilhelm Hederich and wife Anna.
Margareta, of Jacob Asch and Rosina, b. 20 Mar 1781, bapt. 7 May 1781.
Sponsor: the mother.
Andreas, of Andreas Foster and Hanna, b. 15 Apr 1781, bapt. 9 May 1781.
Sponsors: Georg Schneider and wife Maria.
Georg, of Johann Miller and Maria, b. 18 Jan 1781, bapt. 9 May 1781.
Sponsors: Georg Wegerley and widow Maria Spengler.
Johann, of Elias Frey and Maria, b. 19 Apr 1781, bapt. 13 May 1781. Sponsors:
Michael Remm and wife Elisab.
Joh. Jacob, of Jacob Schaeffer and Maria, b. 2 Feb 1781, bapt. 13 May 1781.
Sponsors: Joh. Bender and wife Susanna.
Peter, of Jacob Schreck and Maria, b. 23 Mar 1781, bapt. 29 Apr 1781.
Sponsors: Peter Auner and wife Anna.
Dorothea, of Gabriel Steinbach and Anna Christina, b. 4 Jan 1781, bapt. 27 May
1781. Sponsors: Georg Hoff and wife Dorothea.
Barbara, of Jacob Becker and Margareta, b. 14 May 1781, bapt. 27 May 1781.
Sponsors: Martin Sonner and wife Barb.
Dorothea, of Joh. Weickert and Anna Maria, b. 14 Jan 1781, bapt. 27 May 1781.
Sponsor: Dorothea Beils.
Margareta, of Joh. Mich. Johbst and Margareta, b. 6 Feb 1781, bapt. 27 May
1781. Sponsors: Daniel Sorg and wife Margar.
Doroth. Barb., of Georg Detzel and Catharina, b. 1 Oct 1780, bapt. 27 May
1781. Sponsor: Dorothea Ferch(in).
Daniel, of Phil. Sorg and Margar. Susanna, b. 4 Apr 1781, bapt. 16 Apr 1781.
Sponsors: Daniel Sorg and wife Margar.
Susanna, of Adam Schaeffer and Dorothea, b. 14 Apr 1781, bapt. 28 May 1781.
Sponsors: Jacob Kroener and wife Susanna.
Joh. Georg, of Joh. Georg Hoff and Maria Margar., b. 24 Dec 1779, bapt. 4 Jun
1781. Sponsor: the mother.
Catharina, of Jacob Rohn and Elisabeth, b. 17 Apr 1781, bapt. 3 Jun 1781.
Sponsors: Jacob Schlemmer and Catharina Rohn.
Joseph, of Jacob Frey and Margareta, b. 13 May 1781, bapt. 4 Jun 1781.
Sponsors: the parents.
Georg, of Wilhelm Schmidt and Barbara, b. 9 May 1781, bapt. 4 Jun 1781.
Sponsors: the parents.
Joh. Phil., of Gottlieb Mayer and Magdalena, b. 28 Apr 1781, bapt. 4 Jun 1781.
Sponsors: Phil. Kohlmann and Magdalena Seiler(in).

Nancy Mary, of Peter Sauermann and Marchery [Marjory?], b. 18 Jun 1779, bapt. 7 Jun 1781. Sponsor: Anna Maria Sauermann.

Jesias Phil., of Peter Sauermann and Marchery, b. 1 Dec 1780, bapt. 7 Jun 1781. Sponsor: Phil. Jacob Sauermann.

Elisabeth, of Nicol. Panzer and Elisabeth, b. 5 Jun 1781, bapt. 10 Jun 1781. Sponsors: the parents.

Catharina, of Anthon Riel and Hanna, b. 6 Jan 1781, bapt. 10 Jun 1781. Sponsors: Joh. Georg Schü[t]z and wife Catharina.

Elisabeth, of Johann Stein and Anna Maria, b. 27 May 1781, bapt. 10 Jun 1781. Sponsors: Gottfried Schüssler and wife Elisabeth.

Leonhard, of Joh. Kinzel and Margareta, b. 14 May 1781, bapt. 10 Jun 1781. Sponsors: Leonhard Craemer and wife Maria.

Elisabeth, of Martin Reble and Clara, b. 12 May 1781, bapt. 10 Jun 1781. Sponsors: the parents.

Elisabeth, of Christian Huber and Margareta, b. 19 Jan 1781, bapt.11 Jul 1781. Sponsors: the father, and Doroth. Walcmer.

Johann, of Johann Sullivan wife Rebecca, b. 23 Apr 1781, bapt. 12 Jul 1781. Sponsors: the mother, and Adam Weber.

Rebecca, of Johann Jaeger and Maria, b. 11 Jul 1781, bapt. 15 Jul 1781. Sponsors: Valentin Unbehend and Rebecca Jaeger.

John, of John Brewill and Mary, b. 16 Jul 1781, bapt. 22 Jul 1781. Sponsor: the father.

Joh. Bened[ict], of Joh. Bened. Schneider and Phib. Elisab., b. 10 Jun 1781, bapt. 26 Jul 1781. Sponsors: the parents.

Sybilla (twin), of Ludwig Kehl and Elisabeth, b. 27 Jul 1781, bapt. the same day. Sponsors: Joseah Haselton and wife Sibylla.

Catharina (twin), of Ludwig Kehl and Elisabeth, b. 27 Jul 1781, bapt. the same day. Sponsors: same as above.

Michael, of Joh. Weydemeyer and Anna Maria, b. 22 Feb 1781, bapt. 30 Jul 1781. Sponsors: Michael Bettinger and wife Eva.

Margareta, of Jacob Schnell and Elisabeth, b. 12 Jul 1781, bapt. 30 Jul 1781. Sponsors: Christoph Beringer and wife Margareta.

Anna Barb., of Abraham Hambrecht and Eleonora, b. 4 Feb 1776, bapt. 1 Aug 1781. Sponsors: Michael Lauer and wife Anna Barbara.

Eleonora, of Abraham Hambrecht and Eleonora, b. 16 Apr 1780, bapt. 1 Aug 1781. Sponsors: Gottfried Kretschmer and wife Sophia.

Esther, of Abraham Hambrecht and Eleonora, b. 16 Jun 1772, bapt. 18 Jul 1781. Sponsor: Elisabeth Hambrecht. (I [the pastor] baptised this child at Lancaster but entered it here in this book with the rest of the children.)

Mich. Francys, of Sebast. Reddinger and Regina, b. 26 Jul 1781, bapt. 5 Aug 1781. Sponsor: the father.

Andreas, of Georg Schneider and Maria, b. 14 Jul 1781, bapt. 5 Aug 1781. Sponsors: Andreas Lex and wife Maria.

Johann, of Andreas Jung and Catharina, b. 25 Jul 1781, bapt. 5 Aug 1781. Sponsors: Johann Mayer and Margareta Jung(in).

Maria, of Joh. Mohr and Barbara, b. 1 Jul 1781, bapt. 5 Aug 1781. Sponsors: the parents.

Wilhelmina, of Christoph Gutte and Catharina, b. 14 Jul 1781, bapt. 5 Aug 1781. Sponsors: Georg Degenhard and Wilhelmina Obstrass.

Johann, of Carl Fridr. Knery and Margareta, b. 2 Aug 1781, bapt. 10 Aug 1781. Sponsors: Joh. Jacob Geiger and wife Catharina.

Joh. Georg, of Henrich Polenz and Elisabeth, b. 25 Jul 1781, bapt. 11 Aug 1781. Sponsors: Joh. Georg Schleicker and wife Elisabeth.

Anna Magdalena, of Jacob Süss and Elisabeth, b. 5 Aug 1781, bapt. 11 Aug 1781. Sponsor: Anna Magdalena Them(in).

Lorenz Heinr., of Heinrich Mayer and Catharina, b. 28 Jul 1781, bapt. 11 Aug 1781. Sponsors: Lorenz Lapp and wife Dorothea.

Elisabeth, of Michl. Bamberger and Elisabeth, b. 6 Apr 1781, bapt. 24 Aug 1781. Sponsor: Elisabeth Schweizer(in).

Catharina, of Michl. Bamberger and Elisabeth, b. 13 Aug 1781, bapt. 14 Aug 1781. Sponsor: Catharina Stümler(in).

Elisabeth, of Peter Mayer and Anna Maria, b. 9 Aug 1781, bapt. 26 Aug 1781. Sponsors: Peter Sonnleiter and wife Elisab.

Jacob, of Jacob Riel and Catharina, b. 30 Jul 1781, bapt. 26 Aug 1781. Sponsors: Johann Miller and wife Elisab.

Gustavus, of Nicol. Rehb and Christina, b. 21 Aug 1781, bapt. 26 Aug 1781. Sponsors: the parents.

Barbara, of Henr. Mich. Donner and Maria Justinia, b. 20 Aug 1781, bapt. 26 Aug 1781. Sponsors: Jonas? Heberstreit and wife Anna Barbara.

Catharina, of Wendel Becker and Anna Maria, b. 16 Oct 1781, bapt. 29 Aug 1781. Sponsors: Jacob Grub and wife Cathar.

Catharina, of Thomas Gerum and Elisabeth, b. 23 Aug 1781, bapt. 2 Sep 1781. Sponsors: the mother, and Johann Ohnangst.

Johan, of Georg Bachholtz and Veronica, b. 1 Aug 1781, bapt. 2 Sep 1781. Sponsor: the mother.

Peter, of Joh. Michl. Klug and Magdalena, b. 15 Aug 1781, bapt. 2 Sep 1781. Sponsors: Peter Mann and wife Anna.

Catharina, of James Carter and Barbara, b. 26 Aug 1781, bapt. 3 Sep 1781. Sponsor: Mary Francys.

Johann, of Joh. Schneider and Margareta, b. 15 Aug 1781, bapt. 9 Sep 1781. Sponsors: Johann Lehr and wife Cathar.

Jacob (twin), of Peter Treidle and Catharina, b. 24 Aug 1781, bapt. 12 Sep 1781. Sponsors: the father, and widow Catharina Lehr(in).

Catharina (twin), of Peter Treidle and Catharina, b. 24 Aug 1781, bapt. 12 Sep 1781. Sponsors: same as above,

Johann, of Georg Stephens and Margareta, b. 25 Aug 1781, bapt. 16 Sep 1781. Sponsors: Johann Benker and Elisab. Riven.

Johann Fridr., of Wilhelm Weissmann and Margareta, b. 28 Aug 1781, bapt. 17 Sep 1781. Sponsors: Fridr. Linck and wife Charlotte.

Joh. Joseph, of Joh. Joseph Graaff? and Maria Doroth., b. 8 Sep 1781, bapt. 23 Sep 1781. Sponsors: the parents.

Maria, of Jacob Walter and Helena, b. 9 Sep 1781, bapt. 23 Sep 1781. Sponsors: Andreas Beck (Berk) and wife Elisabeth.

Andreas, of Joh. Miller and Maria, b. 23 Sep 1781, bapt. 23 Sep 1781. Sponsors: Andreas Kressmann and Elisabeth.

Joh. David, of Michael Uber and Maria Magdal., b. 19 Sep 1781, bapt. 25 Sep 1781. Sponsors: Joh. David Uber and wife Anna.
Magdalena (twin), of Jacob Duffene and Anna Magdalena, b. 24 Sep 1781, bapt. 26 Sep 1781. Sponsors: Jacob Dürr and wife Magdalena,
Hanna (twin), of Jacob Duffene and Anna Magdalena, b. 24 Sep 1781, bapt. 26 Sep 1781. Sponsors: Heinr. Riess and wife Hanna.
Andreas, of Andreas Philler and Margareta, b. 16 Sep 1781, bapt. 29 Sep 1781. Sponsors: the parents.
Christoph, of Joh. Flory and Elisabeth, b. 14 Sep 1781, bapt. 30 Sep 1781. Sponsors: the father, and the grandmother Cath. Flory.
Christian, of Joh. Schaeffer and Sophia Maria, b. 10 Sep 1781, bapt. 30 Sep 1781. Sponsors: Christian Schaeffer and wife Dorothea.
Elisabeth, of Martin Kuhn and Catharina, b. 13 Aug 1781, bapt. 30 Sep 1781. Sponsors: the parents.
Peter, of Peter Auner and Margareta, b. 18 Sep 1781, bapt. 30 Sep 1781. Sponsors: the parents.
Hanna, of Martin Walter and Barbara, b. 14 Aug 1781, bapt. 2 Oct 1781. Sponsors: Jacob Reiber and wife Hanna.
Elisabeth Magd., of Joh. Appel and Margareta, b. 26 Aug 1781, bapt. 2 Oct 1781. Sponsor: Elisab. Magdalena Yehn__.
Hanna, of Joh. Didrich Bayerle and Sabina, b. 7 Jul 1781, bapt. 3 Oct 1781. Sponsors: Philip Burg and Maria Opp(in).
Jacob, of Nicolaus Doebler and Catharina, b. 27 Sep 1781, bapt. 7 Oct 1781. Sponsors: Jacob Sohns and wife Catharina.
Salome, of John Georg Waass and Elisabeth, b. 22 Sep 1781, bapt. 7 Oct 1781. Sponsors: the parents.
Jacob Frid., of Heinr. Denzel and Maria Doroth., b. 12 Aug 1781, bapt. 14 Oct 1781. Sponsors: Jacob Nagele and wife Margareta.
Samuel, of Martin Reiser and Catharina, b. 30 Sep 1781, bapt. 14 Oct 1781. Sponsors: Georg Schwar[t]z and wife Barbara.
Salome, of Valentin Sorg and Anna Maria, b. 16 Oct 1781, bapt. 20 Oct 1781. Sponsor: widow Anna Maria Gabeleck(in)?.
Maria Magd., of Leonhard Roht and Maria Magdalena, b. 10 Oct 1781, bapt. 21 Oct 1781. Sponsors: Andreas Lex and wife Maria Magdalena.
Anna Elisabeth, of Francys Liporte and Anna Elisabeth, b. 1 Oct 1781, bapt. 21 Oct 1781. Sponsors: Joh. Georg Kier and Anna Elisab. Haas(in).
Anna Maria, of Heinr. Herberger and Susanna, b. 12 Oct 1781, bapt. 21 Oct 1781. Sponsors: Michael Milleberger and Anna Maria Herberger(in).
Catharina, of Johann Spa[t]z and Elisabeth, b. 6 Oct 1781, bapt. 22 Oct 1781. Sponsors: Margareta Spa[t]z and her son Johann.
Anna Maria, of Conrad Hester and Eleonora Cath., b. 15 Oct 1781, bapt. 28 Oct 1781. Sponsors: Andreas Mattern and wife Anna Maria.
Philippina, of Heinr. Moses and Susana, b. 9 Oct 1781, bapt. 28 Oct 1781. Sponsors: Georg Blum and wife Philippina.
Margareta, of Jacob Ehwald and Jenny, b. 27 Oct 1781, bapt. 1 Nov 1781. Sponsors: the parents, and Henrich Stiller and wife Margareta.
Wilhelmina Julia, of Friedr. Schmidt and Sahra, b. 26 Oct 1781, bapt. 3 Nov 1781. Sponsors: the parents.

Joh. Jacob, of Jacob Kieffer and Catharina, b. 16 Oct 1781, bapt. 3 Nov 1781.
Sponsors: Balthasar Clymer and wife Catharina.

Jacob, of Andreas Bauer and Anna Barbara, b. 6 Nov 1781, bapt. 7 Nov 1781.
Sponsors: Jacob Mercker and wife Elisabeth.

Andreas, of Jacob Miller and Barbara, b. 25 Oct 1781, bapt. 3 Nov 1781.
Sponsors: Andreas Arbitsch and wife Eva.

Sabine, of Joseph (a negro) and Catharina, b. 14 Oct 1781, bapt. 3 Nov 1781.
Sponsor: Catharine Freund(in).

Johann, of Jacob Klauss and Margreta, b. 3 Mar 1781, bapt. 9 Nov 1781.
Sponsors: Wilhelm Fackendus and wife Dorothea.

Wilhelm, of Franz Wilhelm Helmannsberger and Maria Magdal., b. 26 Oct
1781, bapt. 11 Nov 1781. Sponsors: Philip Klein and wife Elisab.

Elisabeth, of Phil. Mayerley and Anna Esther, b. 7 Nov 1781, bapt. 15 Nov
1781. Sponsors: the parents.

Joh. Adam, of Johann Gebhard and Regina, b. 7 Nov 1781, bapt. 18 Nov 1781.
Sponsors: Joh. Adam Weber and Anna Cath. Die[t]z(in).

Margareta, of Jacob Seger and Barbara, b. 2 Nov 1781, bapt. 16 Nov 1781.
Sponsors: Michael Stricker and wife Margareta.

Georg Fridr., of Fridr. Dick and Elisabeth, b. 17 Oct 1781, bapt. 19 Nov 1781.
Sponsors: Fridr. Dick and Elisabeth Drason.

Maria, of Heinr. Emmert and Maria, b. 10 Nov 1781, bapt. 25 Nov 1781.
Sponsors: David Seyfferheld and Sarah Klein(in).

Dorothea, of Jacob Schroeder and Juliana, bapt. 24 Nov 1781. Sponsor:
Dorothea Leib.

Wilhelm, of Georg Breuning and Elisabeth, b. 28 Oct 1781, bapt. 25 Nov 1781.
Sponsors: Christian Wieg and wife Elisabeth.

Jacob, of Heinr. Miller and Maria, b. 5 Nov 1781, bapt. 28 Nov 1781. Sponsors:

Susanna, of John Yayser and Elisabeth, b. 8 Nov 1781, bapt. 28 Nov 1781.
Sponsors: Fridrich Yayser and wife Susanna.

Sophia, of Heinr. Depperwiehl and Margareta, b. 22 Oct 1781, bapt. 2 Dec
1781. Sponsors: the parents.

Margareta, of Christian Kempf and Maria, b. 20 Nov 1781, bapt. 2 Dec 1781.
Sponsors: Georg Schaeffer and wife Margareta.

Johann, of Georg Adam Becker and Anna Catharine, b. 7, Nov 781, bapt. 2 Dec
1781. Sponsors: Joh. Ludwig Kling and wife Anna.

Catharina, of Peter Lohra and Maria, b. 14 Nov 1781, bapt. 2 Dec 1781.
Sponsors: John Hauck and wife Cathar.

Catharina, of Joh. Engelh. Haussmann and Charity, b. 21 Sep 1781, bapt. 2 Dec
1781. Sponsors: Georg Jacob Haussmann and wife Maria Appelonia.

Elisabeth, of Phil. Schindler and Margareta, b. 23 Nov 1781, bapt. 3 Dec 1781.
Sponsors: the parents.

Elisabeth, of Georg Stur[t]z and Sahra, b. 23 Oct 1781, bapt. 3 Dec 1781.
Sponsors: the father, and Ursula Stur[t]z(in).

Joh. Daniel, of Adam Henkel and Hanna, b. 25 Nov 1781, bapt. 4 Dec 1781.
Sponsors: Joh. Daniel Appel and wife Elisabeth.

Elisabeth, of Joh. Peter Bauer and Barbara, b. 26 Nov 1781, bapt. 9 Dec 1781.
Sponsors: Wilhelm Ritter and wife Elisabeth.

Elisabeth, of Johann Pfeil and Philippina, b. 21 Nov 1781, bapt. 9 Dec 1781. Sponsors: the father, and Philippina Christler(in).

Anna Maria, of Friedr. Thui and Elisabeth, b. 17 Nov 1781, bapt. 9 Dec 1781. Sponsors: the parents.

Johann, of Johann Heiler and Susanna, b. 22 Nov 1781, bapt. 9 Dec 1781. Sponsors: Johann Schutt and wife Margareta.

Georg Friedr., of Georg Phil. Weissmann and Catharina, b. 24 Nov 1781, bapt. 16 Dec 1781. Sponsors: Nicolaus Krier and wife Sophia.

Georg, of Georg Michael Heil and Maria Cathar., b. 9 Nov 1781, bapt. 16 Dec 1781. Sponsors: the parents, and Elisab. Shann(in).

Anna Maria, of Georg Moser and Anna Dorothea, b. 30 Nov 1781, bapt. 16 Dec 1781. Sponsors: Georg Strieper and wife Anna Maria.

Anna Maria, of Christian Lu[t]z and Susanna, b. 22 Nov 1781, bapt. 23 Dec 1781. Sponsors: Phil. Pfannekuch and wife Anna Maria.

Wilhelm, of Joh. Jacob Unbehend and Maria, b. 19 Nov 1781, bapt. 23 Dec 1781. Sponsor: the father.

Elisabeth, of John Brooks and Catharina, b. 10 Nov 1781, bapt. 23 Dec 1781. Sponsors: the parents.

James McCotzen, of Johann Jeremias and Jeany, b. 11 Nov 1781, bapt. 23 Dec 1781. Sponsor: the father.

Joh. Georg, of Friedr. Sebast. Mercker and Elisab. Charlott., b. 13 Dec 1781, bapt. 26 Dec 1781. Sponsors: Joh. Balthas. Kinzler and wife Elisabeth.

Rahel, of Phil. Meger and Salome, b. 6 Dec 1781, bapt. 26 Dec 1781. Sponsors: Mathias Sommer and wife Rahel.

Salome, of Johann Michael Moh[t]z and Barbara, b. 7 Nov 1781, bapt. 26 Dec 1781. Sponsors: Phil. Meger and wife Salome.

Anna Maria, of Jacob Ritter and Dorothea, b. 23 Dec 1781, bapt. 28 Dec 1781. Sponsors: David Seifferheld and Anna Maria Klein(in).

Susanna Margareta, of Jacob Seyfried and Anna Salome, b. 30 Nov 1781, bapt. 29 Dec 1781. Sponsors: Andr. Dreher and wife Margareta.

Maria Elisabeth, of Johann Christoph Senderling and Maria, b. 27 May 1781, bapt. 31 Dec 1781. Sponsors: the parents.

1782, First List
(baptisms by pastor Kunze, from Book III

Johannes, of Johannes Lindenberg and Anna Margareta, b. 24 Oct 1781, bapt. 1 Jan 1782. Sponsors: the parents.

Sarah, of Peter Schneider and Elisabeth, b. 15 Nov 1781, bapt. 1 Jan 1782. Sponsors: Johann Graefenstein and wife Dorothea.

Anna Louisa, of Johannes Schreier and Catharina, b. 30 Dec 1781, bapt. 6 Jan 1782. Sponsors: Georg Hubert and wife Anna Louisa.

Johann Jacob, of Wilhelm Weber and Elisabeth, b. 21 Dec 1781, bapt. 6 Jan 1782. Sponsors: Johann Matthew Motschittler and Ann. Cath. Weber(in).

Johanna Elisab., of Jacob Ulrich Sutzel and Maria Barbara, b. 19 Dec 1781, bapt. 6 Jan 1782. Sponsors: Johann Georg Flescher? and wife Joh[anna] Elisab.

Samuel, of Johannes Stok and Elisabeth, b. 7 Dec 1781, bapt. 9 Jan 1782. Sponsors: Michael Preuss and wife Elisab.

Benjamin Peter, of Georg Jung and Maria, b. 1 Dec 1781, bapt. 1 Jan 1782.
Sponsors: Peter Jung and wife Magd.
Paulina Catharina, of Christoph Becker and Catharina, b. 26 Dec 1781, bapt.
15 Jan 1782. Sponsors: Paul Caspar Briton and wife Susanna.
Anna Christina, of Friedrich Woelper and Margareta, b. 25 Dec 1781, bapt.
15 Jan 1782. Sponsors: Hilarius Becker and wife Catharina, Christian
Alberger, and Anna Christina Moxfeld(in).
Georg Friedrich, of Jacob Alborn and Elisabeth, b. 30 Dec 1781, bapt. 15 Jan
1782. Sponsors: Georg Kiefer and wife Maria Eva.
Michael, of Michael Wartmann and Sarah, b. 21 Dec 1781, bapt. 15 Jan 1782.
Sponsors: Adam Seiberts and wife Sophia.
Anna Maria, of Michael Pipp and Catharina, b. 1 Jan 1782, bapt. 13 Jan 1782.
Sponsors: Martin Schweizer and wife Catharina.
Wilhelm, of Jacob Hackemuller and Maria, b. 19 Dec 1781, bapt. 20 Jan 1782.
Sponsors: Simon Moll and wife Elisabeth.
Maria, of Conrad Deviter and Catharina, b. 18 Dec 1781, bapt. 20 Jan 1782.
Sponsors: Jacob Bechtold and wife Maria.
Susanna, of Georg Friedr. Linck and Juliana Elisabeth, b. 2 Jan 1782, bapt.
20 Jan 1782. Sponsors: Nicolaus Walter and wife Anna Rosina.
Johann Henrich, of Martin Sommer and Margareta, b. 13 Jan 1782, bapt. 22 Jan
1782 Sponsors: Henrich Stern and wife Catharina.
Georg Gottfried, of Gottfried Schwing and Margareta, b. 14 Jan 1782, bapt.
24 Jan 1782. Sponsors: Georg Voelker and Barbara Kochendoerfer(in).
Maria Elisab., of Michael Preusch and Maria, b. 18 Jan 1782, bapt. 27 Jan 1782.
Sponsors: Caspar Wahl and wife Elisabeth.
Elisabeth, of John Scharf and Catharina, b. 1 Feb 1782, bapt. 5 Feb 1782.
Sponsors: Martin Noll and wife Elisab.
Georg, of Georg Schett and Susanna, b. 9 Apr 1781, bapt. 5 Feb 1782.
Sponsors: Geret Holzkamp and wife Elisab.
Ann, of Martin Noll and Elisabeth, b. 2 Jan 1782, bapt. 5 Feb 1782. Sponsor:
[Joh.?] Gertraud and wife Elisab.
Georg, of Johann Fromberger and Anna, b. 5 Jan 1782, bapt. 10 Feb 1782.
Sponsors: Nicolaus Weber and wife Christina.
Christoph, of Michael Bauer and Christina, b. 20 Jan 1782, bapt. 10 Feb 1782.
Sponsors: Christoph Becker and wife Catharina.
Elisabeth, of Michael Ki[t]z and Margareta, b. 5 Feb 1782, bapt. 13 Feb 1782.
Sponsors: Jacob Kopp and wife Elisabeth.
Balthasar, of Michael Kinzler and Elisabeth, b. 29 Jan 1782, bapt. 17 Feb 1782.
Sponsors: Balthasar Kinzler and wife Elisabeth.
Johann Jacob, of Georg Schneck and Elisabeth, b. 19 Jan 1782, bapt. 17 Feb
1782. Sponsors: the parents.
Elisabeth, of Philipp Buck and Elisabeth, b. 9 Feb 1782, bapt. 23 Feb 1782.
Sponsors: Jacob Hempelmann and wife Elisabeth.
Elisabeth, of Isaac Stahl and Elisabeth, b. 14 Feb 1782, bapt. 23 Feb 1782.
Sponsors: Balthas. Fleischer and wife Catharina.
Johan Remigius, of Johann Nagel and Elisabeth, b. 15 Feb 1782, bapt. 24 Feb
1782. Sponsors: Johann Remigius Spiegel and wife Mar. Elis.

Samuel, of Georg Heidel and Salome, b. 7 Feb 1782, bapt. 23 Feb 1782.
Sponsors: the parents.
Johann Adam, of Caspar Schneider and Elisabeth, b. 6 Feb 1782, bapt. 24 Feb
1782. Sponsors: the parents.
Wilhelm, of Georg Kinzinger and Catharina, b. 6 Feb 1782, bapt. 23 Feb 1782.
Sponsors: the parents.
Jacob, of Christian Wilke and Rosina, b. 23 Feb 1782, bapt. 23 Feb 1782.
Sponsors: the father, and Susanna Schumacher(in).
Susanna, of Wilhelm Lehmann and Elisabeth, b. 24 Feb 1782, bapt. 7 Mar 1782.
Sponsors: Christian Hahn and wife Hanna.
Anna Maria, of Martin Brenneisen and Elisabeth, b. 1 Mar 1782, bapt. 9 Mar
1782. Sponsors: Philipp Seidelmann and wife Anna Maria.
Margaret, of Carl Rosen and Elis., b. 21 Feb 1782, bapt. 10 Mar 1782.
Sponsors: the parents, and Samuel Cockey and Barbara Albert(in).
Eva Maria, of Georg Barding and Catharina, b. 27 Feb 1782, bapt. 10 Mar 1782.
Sponsors: Henrich Jash? and wife Eva Maria.
Elisabeth, of Anthony Kern and Catharina, b. 4 Feb 1782, bapt. 10 Mar 1782.
Sponsors: Wilhelm Lorenz and wife Elisabeth.
Joh. Philipp, of Johann Georg Sohnleiter and Catharina, b. 8 Mar 1782, bapt.
10 Mar 1782. Sponsors: Joh. Philipp Fischer and Ann. Mar. Unbehend.
Georg, of Georg Vogel and Elisabeth, b. 27 Feb 1782, bapt. 17 Mar 1782.
Sponsors: Jacob Kiemle and wife Cath.
Friedrich Gottlieb, of Friedrich Ranck and Catharina, b. 3 Mar 1782, bapt.
21 Mar 1782. Sponsors: the parents.
Wilhelm Ernst, of Johann Michael Wolf and Elisab., b. 19 Jan 1782, bapt.
24 Mar 1782. Sponsors: Wilhelm Ernst Feld___ and wife Elisab.
Peter, of Philipp Waeger and Hanna, b. 12 Mar 1782, bapt. 27 Mar 1782.
Sponsors: Christian Wir[t]z and wife Margareta.
Anna Maria, of Georg Linck and Elisab., b. 25 Sep 1781, bapt. 28 Dec 1781.
Sponsor: Joseph Stauch's wife (name not given).
Michael, of Michael Triesler and Catharina, b. 26 Mar 1782, bapt. 31 Mar 1782.
Sponsors: the parents.
Michael, of Andreas Tag and Christina, b. 10 Mar 1782, bapt. 1 Apr 1782.
Sponsors: Michael Schnoenneck and wife Catharina.
Anna, of Carl Hey and Sophia, b. 24 Mar 1782, bapt. 1 Apr 1782. Sponsors:
Friedr. Wilt and wife Anna.
Susanna, of Johannes Chresler and Catharina, b. 15 Jan 1782, bapt. 1 Apr 1782.
Sponsors: the parents.
Johann, of Johann Rugan and Elisabeth, b. 15 Mar 1782, bapt. 7 Apr 1782.
Sponsors: Johann Haensmann and wife Anna.
Heinrich, of Ludew. Scheibele and Sophia, b. 8, Mar 1782, bapt. 7 Apr 1782.
Sponsors: Henrich Emmers and wife Martha.
Georg, of Johan Jacob Durr and Maria Magd., b. 25 Mar 1782, bapt. 7 Apr
1782. Sponsors: Georg Vogel and wife Elisabeth.
Margareta, of Johannes Teubs and Margareta, b. 10 Mar 1782, bapt. 12 Apr
1782. Sponsors: Georg Weidemann and wife Cathar.
William, of Joseph Morgan and Sophia, b. 7 Apr 1782, bapt. 14 Apr 1782.
Sponsors: Christian Hobbart? and wife Margareta.

Georg Friedrich, of Georg Faenzel and Salome, b. 20 Nov 1779, bapt. 25 Apr 1782. Sponsors: Georg Friedr. Conrad Haas and wife (name not given).

Elisabeth, of Anthon Hecht and Sophia, b. 19 Apr 1782, bapt. 28 Apr 1782. Sponsors: the parents.

Margaret, of John Bingham and Nicola, b. 3, Apr 782, bapt. 29 Apr 1782. Sponsor: Dr. Mans[field?].

Philipp, of Georg Habacher and Maria, b. 16 Apr 1782, bapt. 3 May 1782. Sponsors: Philipp Weger and wife Hanna.

Johann Jacob, of Johannes Wolf and Anna Maria, b. 11 Apr 1782, bapt. 5 May 1782. Sponsors: Johann Jacob Jacobs and Ann. Mar. Eva ___ander.

Johann Georg, of Peter Gabel and Elisabeth, b. 28 Apr 1782, bapt. 5 May 1782. Sponsors: Conrad [Wa]gener and wife Cath.

Jacob, of Johannes Reimet and Elisabeth, b. 29 Apr 1782, bapt. 12 May 1782. Sponsors: Friedrich Vogel and wife Cathar.

Anna Margareta, of Johann Martin Haertel and Margareta, b. 10 May 1781, bapt. 20 May 1782. Sponsors: the parents.

Catharina, of Ludewig Garlinger and Maria Catharine, b. 9, Apr 782, bapt. 20 May 1782 Sponsors: Henrich Moser and Cath?. Rabansin [Robinson?].

Michael, of Michael Ka[t]z and Elisabeth, b. 15 May 1782, bapt. 20 May 1782. Sponsors: the father, and the grandmother Elisabet Schaub.

Elisabeth, of William Pool (deceased) and widow Anna, b. in 1780, bapt. 21 May 1782. Sponsors: Johannes Reimet and wife Elisabeth.

Anna Cathar., of Johann Braun and Anna Catharin, b. 8 May 1782, bapt. 26 May 1782. Sponsors: Henrich Lehr and Cath.? Elisabeth Jung(in).

Susanna, of Johannes Heil and Maria, b. 12 Nov 1781, bapt. 26 May 1782. Sponsors: Friedr. Schinckel and wife Susanna.

Mar. Cathar., of Johann Michael Bartholomae and Catharine, b. 10 May 1782, bapt. 26 May 1782. Sponsors: Johannes Breisch and wife Maria Catharine.

Georg, of David Dreschler and Elisab., b. 13 May 1782, bapt. 26 May 1782. Sponsors: Georg Bender and wife Anna.

Johann Christoph, of Andreas Heim and Sarah, b. 13 May 1782, bapt. 26 May 1782. Sponsors: Johann Henr. Both and wife Elisab.

Catharina Elisab., of Johann Thomson and Elisab., b. 10 Nov 1781, bapt. 28 May 1782. Sponsors: Dietrich Me[t]zner and wife Catharina.

Joseph, of Johannes Greiner and Margareta, b. 2 May 1782, bapt. 2 Jun 1782. Sponsors: the parents.

William, of Isaac McKee and Eva, b. 20 Nov 1782, bapt. 3 Jun 1782. Sponsors: Georg Heil__ and Elisabeth Schei___.

Johann Heinrich, of John Mohr and Barbara, b. 7 Jun 1782, bapt. 7 Jul 1782. Sponsors: Johann Schaefer and wife Maria.

Sara, of Michael Schubart and Elisabeth, b. 29 May 1782, bapt. 7 Jun 1782. Sponsors: Friedr. Heiler and wife Christina.

Georg Adam, of Johann Ludewig Kling and Anna, b. 16 May 1782, bapt. 27 Jun 1782. Sponsors: Georg Adam Becker and wife Anna Cath.

Johann Adam, of Andreas Mattern and Anna Maria, b. 25 May 1782, bapt. 9 Jun 1782. Sponsors: Johann Georg Sturmfels and wife Anna Margareta.

Maria, of Christian Hag and Anna, b. 24 May 1782, bapt. 6 Jun 1782. Sponsors: the father, and Maria Rebhun.

Johann Georg, of Heinrich Schreiber (deceased) and Margareta, b. 12 Jun 1782, bapt. 20 Jun 1782. Sponsors: the mother, and Henrich Strub.

Georg, of Christoph Schleig and Elisabeth (who died), b. 20 Jan 1782, bapt. 23 Jun 1782. Sponsors: Georg Schaer and wife Barbara.

Margareta, of Andreas Burghardt and Susanna, b. 23 Jun 1782, bapt. 23 Jun 1782. Sponsors: the father, and Margareta Kunze.

Franciscus, of Leonhard Jacobi and Margareta, b. 11 Jun 1782, bapt. 23 Jun 1782. Sponsors: the father, and widow Hasenclener?.

Barbara, of Johann Gebhard and Anna Maria, b. 22 Jun 1782, bapt. 24 Jun 1782. Sponsors: Johann Melchior Gebhard and wife [sic] Anna Maria Both(in).

Johann Jacob, of Jacob Geiger and Catharina, b. 7 Jun 1782, bapt. 24 Jun 1782. Sponsors: Andreas Burghard and Catharina Schepherd.

Anna Maria, of Heinrich Meier and Ursula, b. 4 Jun 1782, bapt. 26 Jun 1782. (Sponsors not given.)

Catharine, of Conrad Haas and Maria Magdalena, b. 12 Jun 1782, bapt. 30 Jun 1782. Sponsors: Johannes Schneider and Maria Eva.

Johannes, of Johann Ehrhard Eisenbrey and Catharina, b. 26 Jun 1782, bapt. 30 Jun 1782. Sponsors: Peter Lex and wife Elisabeth.

Elisabeth, of Joseph Kemmel and Elisabeth, b. 15 Jun 1782, bapt. 30 Jun 1782. Sponsors: the mother, and Jacob Schwab.

Anna, of Georg Merkel and Anna, b. 4 Jun 1782, bapt. 30 Jun 1782. Sponsors: the parents.

Wilhelm, of Wilhelm Bicking and Elisabeth, b. 1 June 1782, bapt. 3 June 1782. Sponsors: the parents.

Anna Maria, of Johann Shu[t]z and Maria, b. 17 Sep 1781, bapt. 3 June 1782. Sponsors: the parents.

Adam, of Christian Schu[t]z and Margareta, b. 5 Jul 1782, bapt. 7 Jul 1782. Sponsors: the parents.

Georg, of Emanuel Meizerzeim and Margareta, b. 15 Apr 1782, bapt. 7 Jul 1782. Sponsors: Georg Brunner and wife Catharina.

Georg Henrich, of Henrich Weinkauf and Elisabeth, b. 22 Jun 1782, bapt. 7 Jul 1782. Sponsors: the parents.

Robert, of James Caer and Catharina, b. 25 Jun 1782, bapt. 10 Jul 1782. Sponsor: Lorenz Schwab.

Johann Georg, of Caspar Christ and Catharina, b. 25 Jun 1782, bapt. 14 Jul 1782. Sponsors: Georg Lizinger and wife Elisabeth.

Peter, of Peter Preis and Catharina, b. 21 Jun 1782, bapt. 21 Jul 1782. Sponsors: Peter Schranck and wife Sophia.

Johann Martin, of Jacob Sulger and Margareta, b. 12 Jun 1782, bapt. 21 Jul 1782. Sponsors: Stephan Sulger and wife Johanna.

Margareta Barbara, of Friedrich Meier and Margareta, b. 6 Jul 1782, bapt. 21 Jul 1782. Sponsors: Christian Alberger and Margareta.

Balthasar, of Balthasar Emmerich and Maria, b. 12 Jul 1782, bapt. 19 Jul 1782. Sponsors: the parents.

Margareta, of Jacob Schwab and Margareta, b. 19 Jul 1782, bapt. 4 Aug 1782. Sponsors: Johannes Fein and wife Catharina.

Margareta, of Joseph Gress and Barbara, b. 15 Jul 1782, bapt. 11 Aug 1782. Sponsors: Georg Rehn and wife Eva.

Johann Jacob, of Adam Pausch and Anna Maria, b. 23 Jul 1782, bapt. 11 Aug 1782. Sponsors: Johann Jacob Demand and wife Elisabet.

Anna Catharine, of Michael Schinneck and Anna Catharine, b. 4, Jul 782, bapt. 11 Aug 1782. Sponsors: Adam Hold and wife Maria Christina.

Georg Friedrich, of Friedrich Gesch and Catharina, b. 10 Aug 1782, bapt. 18 Aug 1782. Sponsors: George Huber and wife Louisa.

Elisabeth, of Dietrich Montseis and Catharina, b. 1 Aug 1782, bapt. 18 Aug 1782. Sponsors: Johann Gottlieb (illegible) and Elisab. Greb(?).

Elisabeth, of Johannes Kappel and Catharina, b. 15 Jun 1782, bapt. 18 Aug 1782. Sponsors: Henrich Eble? and wife Elisabeth.

Wilhelm, of Conrad Baerthling and Maria, b. 8 Mar 1782, bapt. 18 Aug 1782. Sponsors: the father and mother.

Georg, of Christian Reddig and Catharina, b. 4 Aug 1782, bapt. 19 Aug 1782. Sponsors: the parents.

Michael, of Henrich Boecle and Elisabeth, b. 14 Aug 1782, bapt. 20 Aug 1782. Sponsors: Michael Horrich? and wife Barbara.

Susanna, of Johann Bender and Margareta, b. 14 Aug 1782, bapt. 23 Aug 1782. Sponsors: Wilhelm Will and wife Elisab.

A child (name not given), of Johannes Eisenbrey and Barbara, bapt. in Aug 1782 (no other information given).

Elisabeth, of Georg Zwick and Anna Dorothea, b. 6 Oct 1782, bapt. 8 Sep 1782. Sponsors: Johann Oeschsle and wife (name not given).

Maria, of Christian Unger and Maria, b. 21 Aug 1782, bapt. 8 Sep 1782. Sponsors: Michael Horry and wife Sibylla.

John, of Patrick Fox and Rebecca, b. 15 Apr 1782, bapt. 7 Sep 1782. Sponsor: J. C. Kunze. (The child was near death.)

Anna Barbara, of Adam Schuster and Christine Dorothea, b. 31 Aug 1782, bapt. 8 Sep 1782. Sponsors: Johann Dav. Uber and wife Anna Barbara.

Johann Carl, of Carl Miller and Magdalena, b. 23 Jul 1782, bapt. 9 Sep 1782. Sponsors: the parents.

Adam, of Adam Meier and Frederica, b. 8 Sep 1782, bapt. 16 Sep 1782. Sponsor: the father.

Jacob, of Christian Turk (at Ohrmann's place) and Maria Elisabeth Gruner, b. 16 Sep 1782, bapt. 19 Sep 1782. Sponsor: Maria Rosina Turk(in).

Sophia, of Carl Knery and Margareta, b. 13 Sep 1782, bapt. 2 Sep 1782. Sponsors: Johannes Fries and wife Sophia.

Johann Jacob, of Johannes Albert and Anna Maria, b. 28 Aug 1782, bapt. 29 Sep 1782. Sponsors: Christian Uhl and wife Christina.

Catharine, of John Godfrey and Margareta, b. 20 Aug 1782, bapt. 23 Sep 1782. Sponsors: Christoph Redding and wife Cathar.

Elisab., of Peter Sohnleitner and Elisabeth, b. 12 Sep 1782, bapt. 26 Sep 1782. Sponsors: the parents.

William, of John Hook and Margareta, b. 19 May 1780, bapt. 27 Sep 1782. Sponsors: Franz Wilhelm Helmansperger and wife Maria Magdalena.

Daniel, of John Hook and Margareta, b. 21 May 1782, bapt. 27 Sep 1782. Sponsors: same as above.

Jacob, of Leonhard Rau and Anna, b. 14 Sep 1782, bapt. 30 Sep 1782. Sponsors: Jacob Hoerner and wife Maria.

Anna Regina, of Jacob Anthony and Jacobaea, b. 13 Sep 1782, bapt. 6 Oct 1782.
Sponsors: the parents.

Elisabet, of Jacob Kiemle and Christina Catharina, b. 24 Sep 1782, bapt. 13 Oct
1782. Sponsors: Peter Kraft and wife Margareta.

Maria Elisabeth, of Peter Armbrüster and Margareta, b. 24 Sep 1782, bapt.
13 Oct 1782. Sponsors: Johannes Pfau and wife Maria Elisabeth.

Elisabeth, of Johann Nicolaus Wendeling and Catharina, b. 31 Jan 1782, bapt.
14 Oct 1782. Sponsors: Friedr. Brabant? and Mar. Wendel(in).

Philippina, of Johannes Frickhoefer and Esther, b. 15 Oct 1782, bapt. 20 Oct
1782. Sponsors: Philippina Krauch and Andr. Huber?.

Catharina, of Friedrich Weng and Christina, b. 29 Sep 1782, bapt. 20 Oct 1782.
Sponsors: Jacob Kiemle.

Catharina, of Valentin Unbehend and Sophia, b. 15 Oct 1782, bapt. 20 Oct 1782.
Sponsors: Johann Lorenz and wife Catharina.

Henrich, of Valentin Ries and Susanna, b. 1 Sep 1782, bapt. 20 Oct 1782.
Sponsor: Elisab. Hess(in)?.

Elisabet, of Georg Braeunig and Elisabet, b. 15 Oct 1782, bapt. 20 Oct 1782.
Sponsors: the parents.

Georg Michael, of Leonhard Fischer and Susanna, b. 15 Oct 1782, bapt. 20 Oct
1782. Sponsors: Georg Mich. Fischer and wife Elisab.

Andreas, of Christoph Baierle and Elisabeth, b. 5 Oct 1782, bapt. 20 Oct 1782.
Sponsors: Balthasar Gl___ and wife Elisab.

Johann Daniel, of Andreas Eisenhut and Maria, b. 6 Oct 1782, bapt. 27 Oct
1782. Sponsors: Daniel Grub and wife Elisab.

Michael, of Martin Killhauer and Salome, b. 4 Oct 1782, bapt. 3 Nov 1782.
Sponsors: Michael Miller and wife Barbara.

Christiana Margareta, of Andreas Rohr and Maria Christina, b. 20 Oct 1781,
bapt. 3 Nov 1782. Sponsors: the parents.

Anna Margareta, of Johann Georg Goettling and Anna, b. 18 Oct 1782, bapt.
3 Nov 1782. Sponsor: Georg Adam Albert and Anna Cath. Bischofberg(in).

Joh. Georg Adam, of Anthon Miller and Anna Maria, b. 9 May 1781, bapt.
7 Nov 1782. Sponsors: Johann Georg Bauer and wife Anna Marg.

Johannes, of Georg Bastian and Eva, b. 12 Oct 1782, bapt. 10 Nov 1782.
Sponsors: the parents.

Elisabeth, of Georg Senf and Charlotte, b. 25 Oct 1782, bapt. 10 Nov 1782.
Sponsors: Johann Stuckard and wife Elisab.

Reinhard, of Johannes Retue? and Maria Barbara, b. 13 Nov 1782, bapt. 17 Nov
1782. Sponsors: Philipp Jacob Kunzman and wife (name not given).

Maria, of Carl Schildbach and Hanna, b. 8 Nov 1782, bapt. 17 Nov 1782.
(Sponsors not given.)

Johann Georg, of Johann Jacob Kesler and Anna Catharina, b. 27 Oct 1782,
bapt. 17 Nov 1782. Sponsors: Johann Georg Ruel? and wife Elisabeth.

Johannes, of Johannes Kunckel and Maria, b. 3 Nov 1782, bapt. 17 Nov 1782.
Sponsors: Joh. Kunckel and wife Mar. Christina.

Joh. Christian, of Christoph Miller and Elisabet, b. 4 Nov 1782, bapt. 17 Nov
1782. Sponsors: Joh. Christian Kunckel and wife Cath. Elisab.

Catharina, of Johannes Me[t]z and Anna Barbara, b. 4 Nov 1782, bapt. 17 Nov
1782. Sponsors: Eberhard Langhof? and wife Catharina.

Elisabeth, of Zacharias Losch and Maria, b. 11 Nov 1782, bapt. 24 Nov 1782.
Sponsors: Johannes Rugan and wife Elisabeth.

Sibylla, of Jacob Biegler and Dorothea Catharina, b. 1 Nov 1782, Sponsors:
Nov 29, 1782. Sponsors: Johannes Kiemle and wife Sibylla.

Johannes, of Peter Lex and Elisabeth, b. 19 Nov 1782, bapt. 1 Dec 1782.
Sponsors: Johannes Eissenbrey and wife Catharina.

Anna Dorothea, of Johannes Biegler and Hanna, b. 29 Oct 1782, bapt. 1 Dec
1782. Sponsors: Georg Walker and wife Anna Dorothea.

Elisabeth, of Johannes Fugel and Margareta, b. 17 Oct 1782, bapt. 1 Dec 1782.
Sponsors: the parents.

Johann Adam, of David Ober and Hanna, b. 28 Nov 1782, bapt. 8 Dec 1782.
Sponsors: Adam Schuster and wife Anna Dorothea.

David, of Jacob Ki[t]z and Elisabeth, b. 22 Nov 1782, bapt. 7 Dec 1782.
Sponsors: Georg Ki[t]z and wife Apollonia.

Elisabet, of Gottfried Grimm and Rosina, b. 13 Nov 1782, bapt. 12 Dec 1782.
Sponsors: the parents.

Eva Catharina, of Georg Kanzer and Salome, b. 29 Nov 1782, bapt. 13 Dec
1782. Sponsors: the parents.

Magdalena, of Johannes Emmerich and Maria, b. 24 Nov 1782, bapt. 15 Dec
1782. Sponsors: the father, and Magdalena Steinme[t]z(in).

Catharina, of Martin Rebele and Clara, b. 21 Nov 1782, bapt. 15 Dec 1782.
Sponsors: Johann Gottlieb Me[t]zger and wife Catharina.

Elisabeth Catharina, of unknown parents (the father was a soldier in the
barracks), b. about 1778, bapt. 15 Dec 1782. Sponsors: Johann Gottlieb
Me[t]zger and wife Catharina.

Johann Georg, of Johannes Hinckel and Maria, b. 18 Dec 1782, bapt. 19 Dec
1782. Sponsors: Georg Meier and wife Salome.

Magdalena, of Daniel Gilbert and Catharina, b. 9 Nov 1782, bapt. 22 Dec 1782.
Sponsors: Georg Schier and his sister Magdalena Schier(in).

Maria Magdalena, of Johannes Dehm and Maria Magdalena Schmidt
(illegitimate), b. 15 Nov 1782, bapt. 21 Dec 1782. Sponsor: Maria
Magdalena Dehm(in).

Wilhelm, of Johann Nicolaus Wagner and Magdalena, b. 23 Nov 1782, bapt.
22 Dec 1782. Sponsors: Jacob Teis and wife Dorothea.

Henrich, of Adam Erben and Margareta, b. 28 Nov 1782, bapt. 22 Dec 1782.
Sponsors: Henrich Leuthauser and wife Maria Eva.

Johannes, of Jacob Daudermann and Barbara, b. 22 Oct 1782, bapt. 25 Dec
1782. Sponsors: Johannes Haas and wife Anna Elisab.

Margareta, of Jacob Becker and Margareta, b. 2 Dec 1782, bapt. 26 Dec 1782.
Sponsors: Casimir Dolbig and wife Margareta.

Susanna, of Johannes Freyburg and Susanna, b. 4 Dec 1782, bapt. 25 Dec 1782.
Sponsors: the parents.

Barbara, of Martin Sommer and Barbara, b. 29 Nov 1782, bapt. 29 Dec 1782.
Sponsors: Catharine Sommer and husband Henr. Sommer.

1782, Second List
(baptisms by pastor Helmuth, from Book III)

Catharina, of Joh. Christ. Rohn and Catharina, b. 6 Jan 1782, bapt. 1 Jan 1782. Sponsors: Jacob Jaenzer and Cath. Diel(in)?.

Jeany, of Joseph Kroks and Barbara, b. 17 Oct 1781, bapt. 2 Jan 1782. Sponsors: Joh. Heinr. Fuhr and wife Anna Elisab.

Billy, of Landiff Dracon (a negro) and Judith, b. 15 Aug 1781, bapt. 1 Jan 1782. Sponsors: Adam John and Christian Neger.

Catharina, of Nicolaus Senderling and Rosina, b. 17 Dec 1781, bapt. 6 Jan 1782. Sponsors: Friedr. Linck and wife Barbara.

Jacob, of Phil. Werner and Magdalena, b. 27 Mar 1781, bapt. 6 Jan 1782. Sponsors: John McNehr? and wife Elisab.

Joh. Wilhelm, of Jonathan Stanton and Jemina, b. 2 Jan 1782, bapt. 11 Jan 1782. Sponsors: John Bach and wife Elisab.

Johan (twin), of Christian Fleisch and Dorothea, b. 4 Jan 1782, bapt. 11 Jan 1782. Sponsor: the father.

Anna Maria (twin), of Christian Fleisch and Dorothea, b. 4 Jan 1782, bapt. 11 Jan 1782. Sponsor: the father.

Catharina, of Samuel Prinz and Anna, b. 27 Nov 1781, bapt. 13 Jan 1782. Sponsors: Joh. Peter Hartmann and wife Cath.

Maria Cath., of Fridr. Anthony and Susanna, b. 30 Dec 1781, bapt. 13 Jan 1782. Sponsors: Michael Anthony and wife Catharina.

Andreas (twin), of Bernhard Buck (mother's name not given), b. 5 Jan 1782, bapt. 19 Jan 1782. Sponsors: Andreas Bach__ and Margaret Katz(in).

Michael (twin), of Bernhard Buck (mother's name not given), b. 5 Jan 1782, bapt. 19 Jan 1782. Sponsors: Michael Katz and wife Elisab.

Joh. Jacob, of Georg Thürnis and Maria Cathar., b. 3 Jan 1782, bapt. 20 Jan 1782. Sponsors: Sarah Licht(in) and son Christian.

Magdalena, of Heinr. Hert and Barbara, b. 17 Nov 1782, bapt. 20 Jan 1782. Sponsors: Heinr. Schmidt and wife Magdalena.

Elisabeth, of Christian Spellenberg and Cathar., b. 21 Jan 1782, bapt. the same day. Sponsors: Joh. Georg Kier and Elisab. Haass(in).

Johanna Maria, of Wilhelm Mohr and Susanna Maria, b. 20 Jan 1782, bapt. 21 Jan 1782. Sponsors: the father, and Anna Maria Lochmann(in).

Elisabeth, of Joh. Shaetzlein and Barbara, b. 31 Dec 1781, bapt. 28 Jan 1782. Sponsors: Georg Schaetzlein and wife Veronica.

Wilhelm, of Johann Fuchs and Dorothea, b. 25 Oct 1781. Sponsors: the parents. (No baptism date given, and a line was drawn through this entry.)

Jacob, of Christoph Bastian and Catharina, b. 15 Jan 1782, bapt. 28 Jan 1782. Sponsor: Jacob Griesy.

Joh. Georg, of Michael Immel and Catharina, b. 18 Jan 1782, bapt. 31 Jan 1782. Sponsors: Thomas Fischer and wife Elisab.

Peter, of Georg Pop and Maria, b. 22 Jan 1782, bapt. 31 Jan 1782. Sponsors: the mother, and Peggy Schreiber.

Sarah, of Christian Schaeffer and Dorothea, b. 26 Dec 1781, bapt. 3 Feb 1782. Sponsors: the parents.

Elisabeth, of Johann Beck and Anna Maria, b. 17 Dec 1781, bapt. 3 Feb 1782. Sponsor: Catharina Lask(in).

Jacob, of David Kreider and Catharina, b. 4 Feb 1782, bapt. 10 Feb 1782.
Sponsors: Jacob Daudelmann and wife Barb.

Susan. Magdal., of Joh. Feltenberger and Elisab., b. 29 Jan 1782, bapt. 17 Feb
1782. Sponsors: Rudolph Nagel and wife Sus. Magdalena.

Simon, of Andreas Geger and Barbara, b. 25 Jan 1782, bapt. 17 Feb 1782.
Sponsors: Andreas Boshard and wife Cathar.

Catharina, of Daniel Enzle and Lucia, b. 13 Dec 1781, bapt. 17 Feb 1782.
Sponsor: the mother.

Sally, of Patrick Shaw and Maria, b. 22 Jan 1782, bapt. 19 Feb 1782. Sponsors:
the parents.

Elisab., of Joh. Weilman and Margareta, b. 7 Jan 1782, bapt. 21 Feb 1782.
Sponsors: the parents.

Dorothea, of Enoch Bayley and Dorothea, b. 22 Feb 1782, bapt. 23 Feb 1782.
Sponsor: Anna Barbara Wingartner(in).

Elisabeth, of Joh. Kinzler and Magdalena, b. 10 Feb 1782, bapt. 24 Feb 1782.
Sponsors: Balthaser Kinzler and wife Elisabeth.

Johann, of Joh. Krauss and Nancy, b. 20 Feb 1782, bapt. 24 Feb 1782.
Sponsors: the parents.

John Adam, of Phil. Werner and Anna Magdal., b. 5 Feb 1782, bapt. 24 Feb
1782. Sponsors: Joh. Adam Ohrlapp and wife (name not given).

William, of Jacob Jung and Sarah, b. 3 Jan 1782, bapt. 1 Mar 1782. Sponsors:
the parents.

Georg, of Fridr. Kerles and Elisabeth, b. 9 Dec 1781, bapt. 1 Mar 1782.
Sponsors: Georg Kerles and wife Eleonora.

Carl, of Michael Hag and Maria, b. 23 Feb 1782, bapt. 3 Mar 1782. Sponsors:
Carl Truckenmüller and wife Anna.

Catharina, of Michael Miller and Barbara, b. 12 Feb 1782, bapt. 3 Mar 1782.
Sponsors: the father, and Catharina Bottam.

Wilhelm, of Conrad Drumm and Susanna, b. 15 Feb 1782, bapt. 3 Mar 1782.
Sponsors: Andr. Riegler and wife Cath.

Georg, of Fridr. Paul and Elisab., b. 14 Feb 1782, bapt. 3 Mar 1782. Sponsors:
the parents.

Christina, of Georg Haffner and Magdalena, b. 3 Dec 1781, bapt. 3 Mar 1782.
Sponsors: Georg Lufft and Christina Beck(lin).

Johann, of Ruben Tappen and Elisabeth, b. 7 Dec 1781, bapt. 3 Mar 1782.
Sponsors: Fridr. Paul and wife Elisab.

Barbara, of Mathias Schü[t]z and Barbara, b. 22 Feb 1782, bapt. 3 Mar 1782.
Sponsor: the mother.

Michael, of Michael Schreyhoff and Anna Maria, b. 4 Jan 1782, bapt. 10 Mar
1782. Sponsors: Michael Kauffer and wife Barbara.

Susanna, of Wilhelm Jung and Elisabeth, b. 17 Feb 1782, bapt. 10 Mar 1782.
Sponsors: Rudolph Nagel and wife Susanna.

Joh. Wilh., of Caspar Seybert and Elisabet, b. 16 Feb 1782, bapt. 10 Mar 1782.
Sponsors: the parents.

Regina, of Andreas Wag and Regina, b. 27 Jan 1782, bapt. 10 Mar 1782.
Sponsors: the parents.

Susanna, of Wilhelm Kahst and Elisab., b. 9 Mar 1782, bapt. 13 Mar 1782.
Sponsors: the parents.

Georg, of Georg Millenberger and Catharina, b. 13 Feb 1782, bapt. 17 Mar 1782. Sponsors: the father, and Agatha Wolff(in).

Doroth. Magd., of Heinrich Habig and Anna Christina, b. 28 Jan 1782, bapt. 17 Mar 1782. Sponsors: Wilhelm Schmidt and wife Dorothea Margaretha.

Catharina, of Heinr. Kremle and Sophia, b. 15 Feb 1782. Sponsors: Thomas Kramle and wife Magdalena.

Elisab., of Joh. Weger and Sarah, b. 17 Mar 1782, bapt. 23 Mar 1782. Sponsor: Anna Marg. Frank__.

Sarah, of Jacob Reiser and Eva, b. 8 Mar 1782, bapt. 24 Mar 1782. Sponsors: Joh. Fritz and wife Cath.

Anna Maria, of Wilhelm Quire? and Jeany, b. 11 Jul 1760, bapt. and confirmed 24 Mar 1782.

Christoph, of Abrah. Hartranfft and Susanna, b. 5 Oct 1748, bapt. and confirmed 24 Mar 1782.

Barbara, of Abrah. Hartranfft and Susanna b. 20 Dec 1752, bapt. and confirmed 24 Mar 1782.

Anna Maria, of Abrah. Hartranfft and Susanna, b. 20 Dec 1762, bapt. and confirmed 24 Mar 1782.

Edward Georg, of Georg Foster and Maria, b. 10 Apr 1758, bapt. and confirmed 24 Mar 1782.

Jacob, of Carl Cist and Maria, b. 13 Mar 1782, bapt. 31 Mar 1782. Sponsors: the mother, and Rebecca Weiss(in).

Johann, of Johann Carl Hartman and Maria, b. 10 Mar 1782, bapt. 1 Apr 1782, Sponsors: the mother, and Joh. Mich. Bauer.

Anna Maria, of Johann Neu and Catharina, b. 28 Mar 1782, bapt. 1 Apr 1782. Sponsors: Anna Maria Kelmann(in) and Peter Neu.

Anna Maria, of James Humphreys and Maria, b. 28 Feb 1782, bapt. 1 Apr 1782. Sponsor: Anna Maria Hohl.

Elisabeth, of Andr. Barenstecher and Maria, b. 7 Mar 1782, bapt. 1 Apr 1782. Sponsors: John Krabbel and wife Elisab.

Philip, of Andreas King and Maria Elis., b. 23 Aug 1781, bapt. 2 Apr 1782. Sponsor: Elisab. Lahr(in).

Ann, of John Berrys and Sarah, b. 7 Dec 1781, bapt. 7 Apr 1782. Sponsors: Joseph Dorwill and Molly Schnyder.

Anna Cath., of Peter Bingemann and Anna Rosina, b. 18 Mar 1782, bapt. 7 Apr 1782. Sponsors: Peter Schwar[t]z and wife Anna Catharina.

Sarah, of Johann Edelmann and Sarah, b. 28 Jan 1782, bapt. 8 Apr 1782. Sponsors: Joh. Jacob Heine and wife Anna.

Sarah, of Peter Heimbach and Elisabeth, b. 24 Feb 1782, bapt. 14 Apr 1782. Sponsors: Adam Heimbach and wife Susanna.

Elisabeth, of Fridrich Bach and Margareta, b. 22 Mar 1782, bapt. 14 Apr 1782. Sponsors: Wilhelm Hantzel and Elis. Zimmermann(in).

Anna Christina, of Catharina Mohr(in) and Samuel Deal (illegitimate), b. 5 Apr 1782, bapt. 14 Apr 1782. Sponsor: Matthew Feyring and wife Christina.

Margareta, of Martin Boreff and Catharina, b. 5 Apr 1782, bapt. 14 Apr 1782. Sponsors: Valentin Riess and Marg. Zimmermann(in).

Heinrich, of Wilhelm Keppele and wife Susanna, b. 6 Mar 1782, bapt. 14 Apr 1782. Sponsor: the father.

Heinrich, of Leonhard Schmidt and Barbara, b. 1 Mar 1782, bapt. 15 Apr 1782.
Sponsors: Heinr. Schmidt and Magdalena.
Catharina, of Georg Seckel and Rebecca, b. 24 Jan 1782, bapt. 16 Apr 1782.
Sponsor: Maria Kunckel.
Joh. Georg, of Valentin Krieg and Maria, b. 16 Apr 1782, bapt. 20 Apr 1782.
Sponsors: the parents.
Margar., of Adam Munzer and Rosina, b. 28 Jan 1782, bapt. 20 Apr 1782.
Sponsors: Johann Fischer and wife Margareta.
Johann, of Hieronimus Werner and Christina, b. 1 Apr 1782, bapt. 21 Apr 1782.
Sponsors: John Lauden and wife Elisabeth.
Susanna, of Adam Cressmann and Elisabeth, b. 6 Mar 1782, bapt. 21 Apr 1782.
Sponsors: Valentin Riess and wife Susanna.
Joh. Michael, of Johann Kohff and Elisabeth, b. 21 Mar 1782, bapt. 23 Apr
1782. Sponsor: Margar. Wester.
Johanna, of Daniel Kappel and Catharina, b. 29 Aug 1782, bapt. 25 Apr 1782.
Sponsors: Joh. Latsch and wife Margareta.
Anna Cath., of Joh. Georg Süss and Anna Margar., b. 31 Mar 1782, bapt. 27 Apr
1782. Sponsors: Gottfried Schisler and wife Anna Elisabeth.
Dorothea, of Heinr. Homüller and Catharina, b. 30 Mar 1782, bapt. 27 Apr
1782. Sponsors: Michael Bauer and wife Dorothea.
Maria, of John Geyer and Christina, b. 7 Apr 1782, bapt. 27 Apr 1782.
Sponsors: Balthaser Clymer and wife Elisabeth.
Adam Reichhard, of Samuel Garder and Charlotta, b. 10 Sep 1782, bapt. 27 Sep
1782. Sponsors: Adam Custor and wife Anna Margareta.
Michael, of Adam Koch and Eva, b. 6 Apr 1782, bapt. 5 May 1782. Sponsors:
Michael Regenbogen and wife Catharina.
Anna, of Michael Schmidt and Maria, b. 29 Jan 1782, bapt. 5 May 1782.
Sponsors: Georg Loescher and Nancy Lehmann.
Elisab., of Fridr. Jeremias and Magdalena, b. 29 Mar 1782, bapt. 5 May 1782.
Sponsors: the parents.
Georg, of Georg Mallidore and Elisabeth, b. 12 Apr 1782, bapt. 9 May 1782.
Sponsors: the mother, and Georg Lufft.
Anna Maria, of Stephan Sulger and Johanna, b. 26 Apr 1782, bapt. 12 May
1782. Sponsors: Jacob Sulger and wife Anna Margareta.
Polly, of Fridr. Fischer and Nancy, b. 23 Apr 1782, bapt. 12 May 1782.
Sponsors: Johann Weiss and Polly Burckhard.
Maria Rosina (twin), of Conrad Wachler and Maria, b. 28 Mar 1782, bapt.
12 May 1782. Sponsors: Joh. Seyfferheld and wife Maria Rosina.
Anna Barbara (twin), of Conrad Wachler and Maria, b. 28 Mar 1782, bapt.
12 May 1782. Sponsors: Peter Staut and wife Barbara.
Anna, of Thomas Haal and Hanna, b. 6 Feb 1782, bapt. 16 May 1782. Sponsors:
William Krels and Elisab. Klein(in).
Maria Christina, of Daniel Braeutigam and Margareta, b. 1 May 1782, bapt.
20 May 1782. Sponsors: the father, and the widowed grandmother
Braeuligam(in).
Susanna, of Adam Zantzinger and Susanna, b. 21 Apr 1782, bapt. 23 May 1782.
Sponsors: Henrich Keppele, Sr., and Cath. Steinme[t]z.

Johann, of Phil. Pannekuchen and Maria, b. 8 May 1782, bapt. 26 May 1782. Sponsors: John Starky and wife Catharina.

Susanna Charlotte, of Carl Truckenmüller and Anna, b. 4 May 1782, bapt. 14 May 1782. Sponsors: Michael Koenner and wife Charlotte.

Han. Cath. Eleonora, of Benj. Armbrüster and Barbara, b. 7 May 1782, bapt. 28 May 1782. Sponsors: Conrad Schlemmer and wife Han. Cath. Eleonora.

Elisabeth, of Sebastian Heiler and Elisabeth, b. 18 May 1782, bapt. 7 Jun 1782. Sponsors: the father, and Margar. Gelzer(in).

Michael, of Lorenz Schwab a 1d Margareta, b. 20 May 1782, bapt. 9 Jun 1782. Sponsors: Jacob Fechthold and wife Maria.

Christina Salome, of James Burg and Elisabeth, b. 2, Nov 782, bapt. 9 Jun 1782. Sponsors: John Schlater and Salome Seybert(in)..

Joh. Peter, of Joh. Peter Lütsch and Eva Maria, b. 6 Jun 1782, bapt. 16 Jun 1782. Sponsors: Peter Rose and Elis. Preis.

Jacob, of Jacob Graff and Sophia, b. 2 Jun 1782, bapt. 16 Jun 1782. Sponsors: Jacob Ehringer and wife Esther?.

Wilhelm, of William Kahr and Sarah, b. 4 Oct 1781, bapt. 16 Jun 1782. Sponsors: Christian Sinck and wife Margareta.

Georg, of Martin Kinzel and Margareta, b. 25 May 1782, bapt. 16 Jun 1782. Sponsors: Michael Stricker and wife Margareta.

Johann, of Conrad Ort and Catharina, b. 1 Jun 1782, bapt. 16 Jun 1782. Sponsors: Jacob Kleiber and wife Catharina

Catharina, of Gottlieb Spannagel and Elisabeth, b. 15 Jun 1782, bapt. 20 Jun 1782. Sponsor: Anna Cathar. Weicht(in).

Johann, of Peter Klein and Maria, b. 8 Jun 1782, bapt. 20 Jun 1782. Sponsors: Thomas Haal and wife Hanna.

Maria, of John Sprocel and Elisabeth, b. 3 Jun 1782, bapt. 20 Jun 1782. Sponsors: Peter Klein and wife Maria.

Wilhelm, of Math. Berkheimer and Elisabeth, b. 29 May 1782, bapt. 23 Jun 1782. Sponsors: William Weber and wife Elisabeth.

Margareta, of Adam Reininger and Susanna, b. 22 May 1782, bapt. 23 Jun 1782. Sponsors: John Lenemann and wife Margareta.

Elisabeth, of Adam Schae[t]zlein and Hanna, b. 3 May 1782, bapt. 23 Jun 1782. Sponsors: Christian Pearsy and wife Elisabeth.

Susanna Cath., of Zacharias Endres and Maria, b. 8 Jun 1782, bapt. 23 Jun 1782. Sponsors: Joh. Nicol. Wagner and wife Anna Magdalena.

Sarah, of Heinr. Anderson and Susanna, b. 22 Aug 1781, bapt. 23 Jun 1782. Sponsors: Jacob Miller and wife Sarah.

Maria, of Heinr. Anderson and Susanna, b. 23 Jan 1779, bapt. 30 Jun 1782. Sponsors: Jacob Bast and Elis. Heil(in).

Mathias, of Gottfr. Heinrich and Elisabeth, b. 1 May 1782, bapt. 30 Jun 1782. Sponsors: Matthias Gilbert and wife Christina.

Maria, of Edward Rivels and Eva, b. 7 Dec 1781, bapt. 1 Jul 1782. Sponsor: the mother.

Anna Margar., of Nicol. Brumm and Anna Maria, b. 16 Oct 1781, bapt. 2 Jul 1782. Sponsors: the parents.

Joseph, of Fridr. Walter and Patty, b. 15 May 1782, bapt. 4 Jul 1782. Sponsors: the mother, and Johann Fischer.

Elisabeth, of Georg Dorn and Christina, b. 15 Jun 1782, bapt. 7 Jul 1782.
Sponsors: the parents.

Fridr. Jacob, of Georg Fleger and Maria Cath., b. 25 Jun 1782, bapt. 14 Jul
1782. Sponsors: Jacob Seger and wife Barbara

Margaretha, of Joh. Pet. Bihswanger and Eva, b. 26 Feb 1782, bapt. 14 Jul 1782.
Sponsors: the father, and Elis. Umbach.

Joh. Conrad, of Joh. Conr. Escher and wife Maria Felicitas, b. 19 Jun 1782, bapt.
16 Jul 1782. Sponsors: Jacob Seger and wife Barbara.

Fridrich, of Christ. Frid. Gobetbauer and Catharina, b. 15 Apr 1782, bapt. 16 Jul
1782. Sponsors: the parents.

Joh. Phil., of Phil. Krebs and Margareta, b. 3 Dec 1780, bapt. 19 Jul 1782.
Sponsor: the father.

Joh. Christian, of Phil. Krebs and Margareta, b. 7 Apr 1782, bapt. 19 Jul 1782.
Sponsors: Franz Loescher and wife Barbara.

Johann, of Johann Glaser and Christina, b. 23 Jun 1782, bapt. 21 Jul 1782.
Sponsors: Heinr. Debald and wife Margareta.

Elisabeth, of John Rindelmann and Catharina, b. 15 Mar 1782, bapt. 21 Jul
1782. Sponsors: Adam Spiegelmeyer and wife Catharina.

Johann, of Johann Engel and Maria, b. 19 Nov 1781, bapt. 21 Jul 1782.
Sponsors: Michael Pfeiffer and wife Regina.

Wilhelm, of Phil. Klein and Elisab., b. 6 Jul 1782, bapt. 21 Jul 1782. Sponsors:
the father, and widow Lehr(in).

Maria, of Jacob Kroener and Susanna, b. 30 Jun 1782, bapt. 21 Jul 1782.
Sponsors: Caspar Strubel and widow Libs.

Anna Margar., of Jacob Schreiber and Anna Margareta, b. 19 Jun 1782, bapt.
21 Jul 1782. Sponsors: the parents.

Johann, of Adam Jaeger and Veronica, b. 5 Jul 1782, bapt. 21 Jul 1782.
Sponsors: Johann Staat and widow Jaeger(in).

Heinr. Kepple, of Peter Kuhn and Elisabeth, b. 13 Jul 1782, bapt. 27 Jul 1782.
Sponsors: the parents.

Abraham, of Joh. Peter Meck and Sarah, b. 12 Apr 1782, bapt. 28 Jul 1782.
Sponsors: the parents.

Nathaniel Green, of Joh. Welsch and Susanna, b. 14 Jun 1782, bapt. 28 Jul 1782.
Sponsor: Judith Streckfus.

Georg, of Georg Welsch and Sarah, b. 15 Jul 1782, bapt. 28 Jul 1782. Sponsors:
Joh. Haenser and wife Agnesa.

Margareta, of Bernhard Simon and Margareta, b. 27 Jun 1782, bapt. 28 Jul 1782.
Sponsors: Fridr. Brenninger and Magdalena Seidel(in).

Georg, of Johann Kachler and Maria, b. 29 Jul 1782, bapt. 29 Jul 1782.
Sponsor: the father, and the midwife Wall(in).

Elisabeth, of Joh. Gertraut and Catharina, b. 12 Jul 1782, bapt. 31 Jul 1782.
Sponsors: Jacob Mayer and Elis. Koch(in).

Peter, of Matthias Armbrüster and Maria, b. 19 Jul 1782, bapt. 4 Aug 1782.
Sponsors: Peter Armbrüster and wife Margareta.

Joh. Georg, of Edw. Georg Foster and Susanna Barb., b. 22 Jul 1782, bapt.
4 Aug 1782. Sponsors: the parents.

Margareta, of Theophilus Cossart and Hanna, b. 1 Jul 1782, bapt. 4 Aug 1782.
Sponsors: Carl Knery and wife Margareta.

Jacob, of Joseph Beringer and Anna, b. 1 Oct 1780, bapt. 5 Aug 1782.
Sponsors: Gottfried Mayer and wife Margareta.

Georg Fridrick, of Joh. Jacob Riegelmeyer and Magdalena, b. 1 Aug 1782, bapt.
5 Aug 1782. Sponsors: Joh. Georg Riegelmeyer and wife Anna Margareta.

Joseph, of Joh. Nicolaus Die[t]z and Catharina, b. 4 Jul 1782, bapt. 7 Aug 1782.
Sponsors: Joseph Die[t]z and Maria Cath. Kelly.

Joh. Georg, of Georg Yessramm and Anna, b. 20 Jul 1782, bapt. 11 Aug 1782.
Sponsors: Simon Moll and wife Elisabeth.

Beniamin, of Beniamin Gassmann and Maria, b. 16 Jul 1782, bapt. 17 Aug 1782.
Sponsor: (first name not given) Thomson.

Catharina, of Jacob Kramlich and Christina, b. 31 Jul 1782, bapt. 17 Aug 1782.
Sponsors: Andreas Stahl and wife Christina.

Israel, of Israel Clark and Margareta Schmidt(in) (illegitimate), b. 30 May 1782,
bapt. 17 Aug 1782. Sponsor: Elisab. Cath. Wully.

Joh. Wilhelm, of Daniel Andreas and Anna Maria, b. 26 Jun 1782, bapt. 17 Aug
1782. Sponsors: Ehrhard Miller and wife Anna Barbara.

Johann, of Daniel Johns and Elisabeth, b. 1 Aug 1782, bapt. 23 Aug 1782.
Sponsors: Joh. Hehner and wife Anna Catharina.

Susanna, of Joh. David Seckel and Maria, b. 8 Aug 1782, bapt. 23 Aug 1782.
Sponsors: Georg David Seckel and dau Susanna.

Margareta, of Johann Herwey and Margareta, b. 3 Jun 1782, bapt. 24 Aug 1782.
Sponsors: the parents.

Georg, of Johann Yerger and Anna Maria, b. 3 Aug 1782, bapt. 25 Aug 1782.
Sponsors: Georg Mayer and his sister (name not given).

Salome, of Conrad Rohrmann and Elisabeth, b. 5 Aug 1782, bapt. 23 Aug 1782.
Sponsor: Elisabeth Fuchs(in).

Magdalene, of Andreas Abbisch and Eva, b. 17 Aug 1782, bapt. 25 Aug 1782.
Sponsors: Heinrich Schmidt and wife Maria.

Maria Magdal., of Adam Johann Johst Frikhefer and Anna Maria, b. 1 Aug
1782, bapt. 25 Aug 1782. Sponsors: Christian Frikhefer and Christina
Breimer(in).

Esther, of Joh. Fridr. Heine and Anna, b. 21 Aug 1782, bapt. 26 Aug 1782.
Sponsors: Johann Heine and wife Catharina.

Maria Elisab., of Jacob Merker and Elisab., b. 23 Aug 1782, bapt. 27 Aug 1782.
Sponsors: the parents.

Johann, of Christian Oberstech and Margareta, b. 26 Jul 1782, bapt. 1 Sep 1782.
Sponsors: Joh. Fischer and wife Magdalena.

Joh. Jacob, of Phil. Fleger and Wilhelmina, b. 26 Jul 1782, bapt. 4 Sep 1782.
Sponsors: Joh. Jacob Seger and wife Barbara.

Salome, of Johann Pfeiffer and Salome Oberdorffer(in) (illegitimate), b. 24 Jul
1782, bapt. 12 Sep 1782. Sponsor: Mr. Steiner and others in attendance.

Johann, of Fran[c]is Haffner and Susanna Wespe (illegitimate), b. 24 Aug 1782,
bapt. 12 Sep 1782. Sponsors: same as above.

Martin, of Michael Geilinger and Catharina, b. 28 Aug 1782, bapt. 15 Sep 1782.
Sponsor: Martin Gaul.

Elisab., of Fridr. Ulrich and Catharina, b. 1 Feb 1782, bapt. 22 Sep 1782.
Sponsor: Maria Eva Faenner(in).

Georg, of Georg Herley and Maria, b. 11 Sep 1782, bapt. 28 Sep 1782.
Sponsors: Georg Walter and wife Catharina.
Johann, of Joh. Guttmann and Elisabeth, b. 2 Mar 1782, bapt. 28 Sep 1782.
Sponsors: the parents.
Anna Marg., of Fridr. Lauterbrunn and Margareta, b. 20 Sep 1782, bapt. 28 Sep
1782. Sponsors: Anna Margar. Wenzel(in) and Johann Wenzel.
William, of Wilhelm Stewart and Juliana, b. 20 Sep 1782, bapt. 6 Oct 1782.
Sponsors: Johann Sonnleiter and wife Maria.
Margareta, of Joh. Georg Escher and Elisabeth, b. 30 Sep 1782, bapt. 6 Oct
1782. Sponsors: Georg Licht and wife Margar.
Henrich, of Fridr. Callway and Sarah, b. 25 Aug 1782, bapt. 6 Oct 1782.
Sponsors: Heinr. Blettermann and wife Elisabeth.
Magdalena, of Georg Book and Magdalena, b. 5 Oct 1782, bapt. 13 Oct 1782.
Sponsors: Ludwig Book and wife Juliana.
Andreas, of Jacob Crüger and Maria, b. 30 Sep 1782, bapt. 13 Oct 1782.
Sponsors: Andreas Philler and wife Margareta.
Joh. Georg, of Joh. Huber and Catharina, b. 13 Sep 1782, bapt. 14 Oct 1782.
Sponsors: the parents.
Phil. Nathaneal, of Phil. Burkhard and Jeany, b. 1 Mar 1780, bapt. 14 Oct 1782.
Sponsors: Johann Weber and wife Maria Magdalena.
Venable, of Phil. Burkhard and Jeany, b. 18 Sep 1782, bapt. 14 Oct 1782.
Sponsors: same as above.
Catharina, of Adam Hoffmann and Susanna, b. 9 Sep 1782, bapt. 20 Oct 1782.
Sponsors: Christian Lutz and wife Susanna.
Joh. Peter, of Carl Miller and Anna Barbara, b. 5 Oct 1782, bapt. 20 Oct 1782.
Sponsors: Joh. Peter Fri[t]z and wife (name not given).
Elisabeth, of Owen David and Margareta, b. 15 Sep 1782, bapt. 20 Oct 1782.
Sponsors: Johann Weissmann and wife Margareta.
Catharina, of Andreas Ohler and Regina Barbara, b. 8 Jul 1782, bapt. 20 Oct
1782. Sponsors: Johann Weissmann and wife Margareta.
Joseph, of Jacob Fitler and Margareta, b. 20 Sep 1782, bapt. 23 Oct 1782.
Sponsors: the parents.
Maria, of William Roberts and Catharina, b. 4 Oct 1782, bapt. 27 Oct 1782.
Sponsors: Georg Schneider and wife Margareta.
Margareta, of Johann Schumann and Elisabeth, b. 12 Oct 1782, bapt. 27 Oct
1782. Sponsors: Peter Benzel and wife Christina.
Anna Margar., of Joh. Kribble and Christina, b. 5 Oct 1782, bapt. 27 Oct 1782.
Sponsors: Christian Kempf and wife Maria.
Cathar., of Adam Heimbach and Hanna Magdalena, b. 17 Sep 1782, bapt.
27 Oct 1782. Sponsor: Catharina Heim(in).
Ernst Fridr., of Joh. Luger and wife Maria Magdal., b. 17 Sep 1782, bapt. 28 Oct
1782. Sponsors: the parents.
Joh. Eberhard, of Daniel Kayse and Regina, b. 14 Aug 1782, bapt. 3 Nov 1782.
Sponsors: Joh. Eberhard Miller and wife Barbara.
Elisab., of Johann Wright and Catharina, b. 25 Sep 1782, bapt. 9 Nov 1782.
Sponsor: the mother.
Elisabeth, of Jacob Süss and Elisabeth, b. 4 Nov 1782, bapt. 10 Nov 1782.
Sponsors: Jacob Christmann and wife Elisabeth.

William, of Georg Quinop and Christina, b. 3 Nov 1782, bapt. 10 Nov 1782. (Sponsors not given.)

Christina, of Johann Assmus and Catharina, b. 20 Oct 1782, bapt. 10 Nov 1782. Sponsors: Christian Hantzel and Elisabeth Kreab.

Elisabeth, of Peter Adam and Magdalena, b. 18 Oct 1782, bapt. 10 Nov 1782. Sponsors: Jacob Scheible and wife Elisab.

Carl, of Phil. Walter and Magdalena, b. 30 Jul 1777, bapt. 13 Nov 1782. Sponsors: the mothe,r and Margareta Brown.

Hanna, of Phil. Walter and Magdalena, b. 23 Mar 1779, bapt. 13 Nov 1782. Sponsors: same as above..

Philip, of Phil. Walter and Magdalena, b. 5 Jul 1782, bapt. 13 Nov 1782. Sponsors: same as above.

Phil., of Phil. Meyerley and Hanna Esther, b. 9 Nov 1782, bapt. 14 Nov 1782. Sponsors: the parents.

Anna Marg., of Joh. Esch and Anna Margar., b. 31 Oct 1782, bapt. 17 Nov 1782. Sponsors: the father, and Elisab. Fischer(in).

Maria Magd., of Phil. Schroeder and Maria Cath., b. 10 Nov 1782, bapt. 17 Nov 1782. Sponsor: Maria Magdalena Diestmann(in).

William, of Johann Bender and Susanna, b. 15 Nov 1782, bapt. 17 Nov 1782. Sponsors: Wilhelm Will and wife Elisabeth.

Carl, of Christoph Gutt and Christina, b. 10 Nov 1782, bapt. 24 Nov 1782. Sponsors: Carl Hantzel and Elis. Zimmermann.

Johann, of Adam Me[t]z and Barbara, b. 20 Oct 1782, bapt. 24 Nov 1782. Sponsors: the mother, and Joh. Me[t]z.

Wilhelm, of Bened[ict] Schneider and Philippina Elis., b. 14 Nov 1782, bapt. 25 Nov 1782. Sponsors: Wilhelm Mohr and wife Susanna Maria.

Johann, of Gottlieb Mayer and Magdalena, b. 28 Oct 1782, bapt. 28 Nov 1782. Sponsors: Johann Michael and wife Susanna Cathar.

Elisabeth, of Franz Ganss and Anna, b. 31 Sep 1780, bapt. 30 Nov 1782. Sponsors: Johann Fugel and wife Sarah.

Jacob, of Franz Ganss and Anna, b. 3 Oct 1782, bapt. 30 Nov 1782. Sponsors: same as above.

Johanna Elis., of Johann Christoph Heidel and Elisabeth, b. 12 Nov 1782, bapt. 31 Nov 1782. Sponsors: Joh. Georg Escher and wife Johanna Elisab.

Molly, of Wilhelm Wyart and Elisabeth, b. 20 Aug 1777, bapt. 7 Dec 1782, Sponsors: Franz Gaast and wife Anna.

William, of Wilhelm Wyart and Elisabeth, b. 26 Aug 1779, bapt. 7 Dec 1782. Sponsors: same as above.

Margareta, of Wilhelm Wyart and Elisabeth, b. 31 Mar 1782, bapt. 7 Dec 1782. Sponsors: Johann Fugel and wife Margareta

Johann, of Georg Dannecker and Margareta, b. 28 Jan 1775, bapt. 7 Dec 1782. Sponsors: Christian Dannecker and wife Juliana.

Magdalena, of Georg Dannecker and Margareta, b. 21 Feb 1782, bapt. 7 Dec 1782. Sponsors: Peter Ozeas and wife Magdalena..

Carl, of Heinrich Herbst and Elisabeth, b. 28 Nov 1782, bapt. 8 Dec 1782. Sponsors: Carl Jung and wife Catharina.

Maria Eva, of Jacob Beck and Elisabeth, b. 22 Jan 1782, bapt. 8 Dec 1782. Sponsors: Michael Regenbogen and wife Catharina.

Georg, of Jacob Miller and Sarah, b. 3 Dec 1782, bapt. 15 Dec 1782. Sponsors:
Georg Schumann and Elis. Renn(in).
Susanna, of William Scheaff and Barbara, b. 20 Nov 1782, bapt. 14 Dec 1782.
Sponsors: Georg David Seckel and dau. Susanna.
Elisabeth, of Samuel Gardner and Charlotta, b. 25 Nov 1782, bapt. 15 Dec 1782.
Sponsors: Joh. Adam Custer and wife Anna Margareta.
Joh. Nicol., of Joh. Krieger and Catharina, b. 1 Dec 1782, bapt. 15 Dec 1782.
Sponsors: Nicolaus Krieger and wife Sophia.
Thomas, of Ludwig Bender and Margareta, b. 11 May 1782, bapt. 15 Dec 1782.
Sponsors: Christian Schaeffer and wife Doroth.
Margaretha, of Daniel Butler and Martha, b. 23 Dec 1776, bapt. 18 Dec 1782.
Sponsor: Margaretha Fischer.
William, of Daniel Butler and Martha, b. 12 Mar 1779, bapt. 18 Dec 1782.
Sponsors: Johann Bender and wife Susanna.
Sarah, of Daniel Butler (a Quaker) and wife Martha, b. 21 Dec 1781, bapt.
18 Dec 1782. Sponsors: same as above.
Maria, of Jacob Jung and Margarethe, b. 27 Nov 1782, bapt. 18 Dec 1782.
Sponsors: (Sponsors not given.).
Salome, of Matthias Gilbert and Christina, b. 12 Dec 1782, bapt. 22 Dec 1782.
Sponsors: Michael Wardmann and wife Salome.
Wilh. Heinr., of Martin Christ and Elisabeth, b. 6 Dec 1782, bapt. 22 Dec 1782.
Sponsors: Wilhelm Heinrich Gr___ and Sarah Weber(in).
William, of Georg Facundus and Maria, b. 5 Dec 1782, bapt. 23 Dec 1782.
Sponsors: Adolph Dill and wife Catharina.
Elisabeth, of Gottfried Hamlet and Barbara, b. 25 Nov 1782, bapt. 29 Dec 1782.
Sponsors: Christoph Hartranfft and Elis. Reible.
Joh. Peter, of Heinr. Conrad and Maria, b. 10 Dec 1782, bapt. 29 Dec 1782.
Sponsors: Peter Kress and wife Maria Rosina.
Anna, of John Breise and Rahel, b. 10 Dec 1782, bapt. 29 Dec 1782. Sponsor:
Catharine Foster.
Joh. Georg, of Jacob Meger and Hanna, b. 12 Dec 1782, bapt. 29 Dec 1782.
Sponsors: Georg Moser and wife Hanna.
Joh. Phil., of Johann Bach and Elisabeth, b. 9 Dec 1782, bapt. 29 Dec 1782.
Sponsors: Phil. Haffner and wife Margar.
Maria Felicia, of Leonhard Scheld and Catharina, b. 20 Mar 1782, bapt. 29 Dec
1782. Sponsors: Joh. Conrad Aescher and wife Maria Felicitas.
Sarah, of Wilhelm Burghard and Sarah, b. 17 Dec 1782, bapt. 30 Dec 1782.
Sponsors: the father, and Maria Magdalena Weber(in).

1783, First List
(baptisms by pastor Kunze, from Book III)
Samuel, of Johannes Hetzel and Catharine, b. 29 Dec 1782, bapt. 1 Jan 1783.
Sponsors: the parents.
Samuel, of Melchior Weissinger and Maria, b. 17 Nov 1783, bapt. 1 Jan 1783.
Sponsors: the parents.
Johann, of Johann Well and Gertraud, b. 2 Dec 1782, bapt. 2 Jan 1783.
Sponsors: Margaret Bischof(in).

482   PHILADELPHIA GERMAN LUTHERAN CHURCH

Philipp, of Adam Dieter and Catharine, b. 16 Nov 1782, bapt. 3 Jan 1783.
Sponsors: Philipp Stock and wife Cath.
Carl, of Carl Jung and Catharina, b. 22 Dec 1782, bapt. 4 Jan 1783. Sponsors:
Carl Steinme[t]z and wife Marg.
Johann Christian, of Jacob Moo[t]z and Barbara, b. 29 Sep 1782, bapt. 16 Jan
1783. Sponsors: Christian Jung and wife Carol.
Anna Maria, of Paulus Scharaddin and Hanna, b. 7 Dec 1782, bapt. 15 Jan 1783.
Sponsors: the parents.
Maria, of Jacob Holt and Catharina, b. 13 Jan 1783, bapt. 16 Jan 1783.
Sponsors: Thomas Fischer and wife Elis.
Magdalena, of Heinrich Schmidt and Magdalena, b. 6 Jan 1783, bapt. 29 Jan
1783. Sponsors: Andr. Abitsch and wife Eva.
Susanna, of Georg Bickham and Christiana, b. 1 Jan 1783, bapt. 19 Jan 1783.
Sponsors: the parents.
Isaac (twin), of Georg Gasner and Christina, b. 21 Jan 1783, bapt. 24 Jan 1783.
Sponsors: the parents.
David (twin), of Georg Gasner and Christina, b. 21 Jan 1783, bapt. 24 Jan 1783.
Sponsors: the parents.
Anna Magdalena, of Fridrich Kesler and Anna Maria, b. 14 Dec 1782, bapt.
26 Jan 1783. Sponsors: the parents.
Maria Magdalena, of Leonhard Rosch and Maria Magdal., b. 26 Jan 1783, bapt.
26 Jan 1783. Sponsors: Andreas Lex and wife Mar. Magd.
Veronica, of Johann Friedr. Wegmann, b. 11 Jan 1783, bapt. 29 Jan 1783.
Sponsors: Richard Franck and Catharina Me[t]zger(in).
Sophia, of Conrad Seibert and Christina Maria, b. 17 Jan 1783, bapt. 27 Jan
1783. Sponsors: Adam Seibert and wife Sophia.
Catharina, of Humphrey McCumbre and Catharina, b. 2 Dec 1782, bapt. 2 Feb
1783. Sponsors: Peter Frei? and [wife] Catharina.
Johann Matthaeus, of Johann Matthaeus Tollmann and Catharina, b. 14 Jan
1783, bapt. 2 Feb 1783. Sponsors: Jacob? Gratter? and wife Cath.
Sarah, of Georg Schae[t]zlein and Veronica, b. 3 Jan 1783, bapt. 9 Feb 1783.
Sponsors: Bartholmes Shae[t]zlein and wife Cath.
Juliana, of Ludewig Book and Juliana, b. 18 Jan 1783, bapt. 9 Feb 1783.
Sponsors: Georg Bok and wife Magdalena.
Charlotte Philippina, of Georg Henrich Dehn and Maria Clara, b. 27 Feb 1783,
bapt. 23 Feb 1783. Sponsors: Georg Senf and wife Charlotta Phil[ippina].
Johannes Carl, of Georg Daum and Sarah, b. 4 Feb 1783, bapt. 25 Feb 1783.
Sponsors: Carl Billes and wife Clara.
Jacob, of Andreas Lobstein and Elisabeth, b. 23 Feb 1783, bapt. 28 Feb 1783.
Sponsors: Jacob Graf and Sophia Graf.
Elisabeth, of Christian Kuhn and Maria, b. 6 Feb 1783, bapt. 2 Mar 1783.
Sponsors: Wilhelm Weber and wife Elis.
Georg, of Henrich deForrest and Maria, b. 7 Feb 1783, bapt. 2 Mar 1783.
Sponsors: Peter Osias and wife Maria.
Johann, of Michael Huber and Maria, b. 16 Feb 1783, bapt. 2 Mar 1783.
Sponsors: Johann Hempel and Elisab. Grobb(in).
Johann Christian, of Christian Kinzle and Anna Margareta, b. 25 Feb 1783, bapt.
3 Mar 1783. Sponsors: Johann Reifschneider and wife (name not given).

Maria Margareta, of Heinrich Meier and Catharine, b. 21 Feb 1783, bapt. 4 Mar
1783. Sponsors: Thomas Meier and wife Anna Margareta.
Catharina, of Valentin Hofmann and Susanna, b. 25 Feb 1783, bapt. 6 Mar 1783.
Sponsors: Marcus Rot(h) and Cath. (surname obscured).
Jacob, of Heinrich Meier and Catharina, b. 7 Mar 1783, bapt. 14 May 1783.
Sponsors: Friedrich Gresler and wife Sophia.
Johann Conrad, of Philipp Tennis and Maria, b. 5 Jul 1782, bapt. 22 Mar 1783.
Sponsors: Johann Conrad Fergler? and Catharina Armbruster.
Elisabet, of Christoph Jelte and Anna Catharina, b. 23 Feb 1783, bapt. 23 Mar
1783. Sponsors: Johann Georg Degenhard and wife Wilhelmina.
Georg, of Georg Pauel and Anna Maria, b. 24 Mar 1783, bapt. 25 Mar 1783.
Sponsors: the mother, and old widow Thuringer(in).
Johann Georg, of Valentin Gesner and Maria, b. 6 Feb 1783, bapt. 30 Mar 1783.
Sponsors: Johann Georg Schaer and Elisab. Renn(in).
Johannes, of Joseph Mansfeld and Anna Magdalena, b. 5 Mar 1783, bapt. 6 Apr
1783. Sponsors: Johann Abel and Cath. Werner(in).
Christina, of Ehrhard Miller and Barbara, b. 1 Apr 1783, bapt. 7 Apr 1783.
Sponsors: Michael Preus and wife Maria.
Elisabeth, of Georg Aescherig and Elisabeth, b. 4 Apr 1783, bapt. 13 Apr 1783.
Sponsors: Georg Rummel and wife Elisabeth.
Catharina, of Heinrich Blaettermann and Elisabeth, b. 27 Mar 1783, bapt.
13 Apr 1783. Sponsors: Peter Weidner and wife Catharina.
David, of David Sutor (who died 20 years ago) and Margareta Catharina, b.
24 Sep 1752 at Germantown, bapt. 16 Apr 1783. Sponsors: all the
confirmands in the class of 1783.
Maria Elisab., of Georg Dannecker and Margareta, b. 27 Apr 1766, bapt. 16 Apr
1783. Sponsors: all the confirmands.
Anna Maria, of Joh. Jacob Pob and Elisabeth, b. in 1762 at Germantown, bapt.
16 Apr 1783. Sponsors: all the confirmands.
Elisabeth, of Joh. Jacob Pob and Elisabeth, born at Germantown (date not
given), bapt. 16 Apr 1783. Sponsors: all the confirmands.
Johannes, of Joh. Jacob Pob and Elisabeth, born at Germantown (date not
given), bapt. 16 Apr 1783. Sponsors: all the confirmands.
Georg, of Philipp Hirsch and Susanna, b. 11 Apr 1779, bapt. 14 Apr 1783.
Sponsors: Henr. Schrefler and wife Christina.
Anna, of Philipp Hirsch and Susanna, b. 20 Oct 1781, bapt. 14 Apr 1783.
Sponsors: same as above.
Michael, of Daniel Frischmuth and Barbara, b. 30 Mar 1783, bapt. 21 Apr 1783.
Sponsors: Henrich Schrefler, and Michael Sto[t]z and wife Cathar.
Maria Elisabeth, of Bernard Alberti and Catharina, b. 11 Mar 1783, bapt. 22 Apr
1783. Sponsors: Peter Kohl and Margaretha nee Kohl(in) in the place of
Thomas Fischer and [wife] Elisab..
Samuel, of Thomas Cook and Magdalena, b. 22 Feb 1783, bapt. 23 Apr 1783.
Sponsors: Jacob Schubart and wife Ursula.
Daniel, of Henrich Schrefler and Christina, b. 10 Feb 1783, bapt. 23 Apr 1783.
Sponsor: Philipp Hirsch.
Jacob, of Jacob Koeth? and Elisabeth, b. 19 Apr 1783, bapt. 4 May 1783.
Sponsors: Johannes Braun and wife Cath.

Rebecca, of Peter Gress and Rosina, b. 27 Apr 1783, bapt. 11 May 1783. Sponsors: Jacob Teis and wife Dorothea.

Johann Jacob, of Nicolaus Jacob and Anna Maria, b. 30 Apr 1783, bapt. 18 May 1783. Sponsors: Jacob Anthony and wife An. Cath.

Maria Barbara, of Daniel Benner and Catharina, b. 3 Apr 1783, bapt. 18 May 1783. Sponsors: Johann Gürge and wife Mar. Barb.

Johannes, of Christian Kaemph and Maria, b. 5 May 1783, bapt. 18 May 1783. Sponsors: Johann Krubel? and wife Christina.

Johann Philipp, of Johann Philipp Reibold and Elisab., b. 5 May 1783, bapt. 19 May 1783. Sponsors: the parents.

Juliana, of Heinrich Miller (preacher and rector [where?]) and Juliana, b. 13 May 1783, bapt. 20 May 1783. Sponsors: Jacob Mayer and wife Juliana.

Margareta, of Jacob Klein and Margareta, b. 12 Mar 1783, bapt. 25 May 1783. Sponsors: Johannes Fahn and wife Marg.

Johann Martin, of Friedrich Schik and Barbara, b. 16 May 1783, bapt. 25 May 1783. Sponsors: Johann Martin Schneider and wife Magdalena.

Johann, of Georg Feuchtenberger and Johanna Elisabeth, b. 22 May 1783, bapt. 2 Jun 1783. Sponsors: Johann Gottfried Bechtel? and Elisabet Kuhn(sin).

Georg, of (first name not given) Lehmann (deceased) and (mother's name and child's birthdate not given), bapt. 7 Jun 1783. Sponsors: all the "Baustanders" of 1783.

Peter, of Lorenz Schuster and Maria, b. 15 Jan 1783, bapt. 8 Jun 1783. Sponsors: Peter Schuster, and in his place Adam Schuster's wife Maria.

Johannes, of Friedrich Mog and Maria, b. 24 Mar 1783, bapt. 31 May 1783. Sponsors: Adam Koenig and wife Barb.

Johann, of Jacob Hoerner and Maria, b. 4 Jun 1783, bapt. 8 Jun 1783. Sponsors: the father, Leonard Rau, and Ann Rau(in).

Jacob, of Johannes Fulton and Philippina, b. 11 May 1783, bapt. 9 Jun 1783. Sponsors: Jacob Kochendoerfer and [his?] mother Barbara Kochendoerfer..

Elisabeth, of Conrad Denckfelder and Elisabeth, b. 9 Apr 1782, bapt. 23 Jun 1783. Sponsors: the parents.

Elisabeth, of (first name not given) Habbich and (mother's name not given), b. 24 Jun 1783, bapt. the same day. Sponsors: the father, and Elis. Cath. Walter?.

Elisabeth, of James Bourg and Elisab., b. 19 Apr 1783, bapt. 28 Jun 1783. Sponsors: Christian Vetter and wife [sic] Elis. Wisper(tin)?.

Wilhelm, of Friedrich Schuhmann and Anna Maria, b. 18 Jun 1783, bapt. 29 Jun 1783. Sponsors: William Henrich Ga___ and Regina Weber(in).

Elisabeth, of Wilhelm Weismann and Margareta, b. 14 Jun 1783, bapt. 29 Jun 1783. Sponsors: Andreas Uhler and wife Regina.

Johannes, of Johannes McCloud (deceased) and Maria, b. 17 Mar 1783, bapt. 30 Jun 1783. Sponsors: Adam Knoblauch and wife Barbara.

Susanna, of Friedrich Heine and Anna, b. 2 Jul 1783, bapt. the same day. (Sponsors not given.)

James, of [a daughter of] James Smith, the father is unknown, b. in 1782, bapt. 8 Jul 1783. Sponsors: Johann Jacob Durr and wife Maria.

Margareta Barbara, of Daniel Schrob and Catharina, b. 4 Jul 1783, bapt. 6 Jul 1783. Sponsors: Tobias Koenig and wife Barb.?.

Carl, of Johannes Cap and Maria, b. 9 Jun 1783, bapt. 6 Jul 1783. Sponsors: the parents.

Anna Catharina, of Johann Nicolaus Kroll and Elisab. Margareta, b. 22 Jun 1783, bapt. 6 Jul 1783. Sponsors: Jacob Keimle and wife Christina Cath.

Elisab., of Jacob Ries and Magdalena, b. 30 Jun 1783, bapt. 12 Jul 1783. Sponsors: Johann Fri[t]z and wife Cath.

Friedrich, of Friedrich Heinemann and Anna Catharine, b. 26 Jun 1783, bapt. 13 Jul 1783. Sponsors: Georg Huber and wife Ann. Louisa.

Johann Georg, of Peter Schreier and Barbara, b. 30 Jun 1783, bapt. 13 Jul 1783. Sponsors: Georg Krebs and wife Dorothea.

Philipp, of Johann Heinrich Wahl and Justina, b. 8 Jun 1783, bapt. 13 Jul 1783. Sponsors: Friedr. Vogel and wife Cathar.

Sophia, of Anthon Eberhard and Philippina, b. 30 Jun 1783, bapt. 13 Jul 1783. Sponsors: Jacob Grof and wife Sophia.

Johannes, of Johannes Hepp and Catharina, b. 26 Mar 1783, bapt. 13 Jul 1783. Sponsors: the parents, and Maria Frey(in).

Martha, of Johann Adams and Margareta, b. 6 Mar 1783, bapt. 13 Jul 1783. Sponsors: John Keimle and wife Margar. Reg[ina].

Henrich, of Henrich Treveller and Margareta, b. 2 Jul 1783, bapt. 20 Jul 1783. Sponsors: Johannes Solomo? and wife Christina.

Charlotte, of Rudolf Kinzle (deceased) and Anna Maria, b. 23 Jun 1783, bapt. 23 Jul 1783. Sponsors: the parents.

Jacob, of Johannes Faesemius and Catharina, b. 24 Jul 1783, bapt. 25 Jul 1783. Sponsors: Henrich Nagel and wife Cath. Ursula.

Friedrich [twin], of Georg Weckerle and Catharine, b. 24 Jul 1783, bapt. 26 Jul 1783. Sponsors: David Dietrich and wife Christina.

Elisabet, [twin], of Georg Weckerle and Catharine, b. 24 Jul 1783, bapt. 26 Jul 1783. Sponsors: same as above.

Johannes, of Johann Ehrhard Eisenbren and Catharina, b. 22 Jul 1783, bapt. 26 Jul 1783. Sponsors: Henrich Rathschlag and wife Maria.

Elisabeth, of Michael Endres and Margaret, b. 2 Jul 1783, bapt. 27 Jul 1783. Sponsor: Elisabeth Scheaffer(in).

Michael, of Michael Albrecht and Juliana, b. 20 Jul 1783, bapt. 27 Jul 1783. Sponsors: the parents.

A child (name not given), of Johann Georg Zeissinger and Anna Maria. (No other information given.)

Elisabeth, of Daniel Kirstner? and Barbara, b. 4 Feb 1782, bapt. 5 Aug 1783. Sponsors: the parents.

Jacob, of Jacob K___emeier and Maria, b. 25 Jul 1783, bapt. 9 Aug 1783. Sponsors: Jacob Kehl and wife Christina.

Joh. Martin, of Martin Die[t]z and Sabina Margareta, b. 31 Jul 1783, bapt. 9 Aug 1783. Sponsors: Joh. Conrad Seybert and wife Maria Christina.

Sarah, of Friedrich Vogel and Catharina, b. 3 Aug 1783, bapt. 10 Aug 1783. Sponsors: Johann Reimel and wife Elisab.

Christiana Cath., of Wilhelm Stockel and Susanna, b. 28 Jul 1783, bapt. 17 Aug 1783. Sponsors: Reinhard Valentin? and wife Anna Catharine.

Jacob, of Christoph Bechtel and Elisabeth, b. 13 Jul 1783, bapt. 20 Aug 1783. Sponsors: Jacob Seler and [wife] Margar.

Maria, of Wilhelm Kaempf and Sabina, b. 14 Aug 1783, bapt. 29 Aug 1783. Sponsors: Christian Kaempf and wife Maria.

Elisabet, of Friedrich Vogel and Elisabet, b. 17 Aug 1783, bapt. 24 Aug 1783. Sponsors: Johannes Schneider and wife Mar. Eva.

Wilhelm, of Jacob Strumbeck and Maria, b. 23 Jul 1783, bapt. 26 Aug 1783. Sponsors: the parents.

Gottfried, of Gottfried Schwing and Margareta, b. 16 Aug 1783, bapt. 27 Aug 1783. Sponsors: Christian Danecker and wife Juliana.

Anna Margareta, of Christian Elbel and Susanna, b. 15 Aug 1783, bapt. 31 Aug 1783. Sponsors: Henr. Nagel and wife Barbara.

Margareta, of Wilhelm Warner and Wilhelmina, b. 16 Aug 1783, bapt. 7 Sep 1783. Sponsors: Peter Litsch and wife Eva Maria.

Hanna Friederica, of Johann Boehler and Catharina, b. 28 Aug 1783, bapt. 7 Sep 1783. Sponsors: Friedrich Reinboot and wife Anna Barbara.

Jacob, of Georg Richter and Eva, b. 10 Aug 1783, bapt. 7 Sep 1783. Sponsors: Jacob Orn and Sus. Rens.

Johanna Beata, of Johann Christoph Kunze and Margareta, b. 11 Sep 1783, bapt. 13 Sep 1783. Sponsor: Gen. Johann Peter Jac. Muhlenberg, Joh[anna] Beata Kunz(in), and Maria Eppel(in).

Anna Margareta, of Johannes Wenzel and Christina, b. 30 Aug 1783, bapt. 14 Sep 1783. Sponsors: Christina Wenzel and her mother Anna Margareta.

Johann Georg, of Johannes Emmerich and Maria Cath., b. 9 Apr 1783, bapt. 14 Sep 1783. Sponsors: Johann Georg Seifferheld and wife Christina Elisab.

Henrich, of Jacob Appel and Anna Margareta, b. 3 Aug 1783, bapt. 14 Sep 1783. Sponsors: Henrich Shuller and Cath. Bod(in) [Both(in)].

Anna Catharina, of Johannes Rieb and Susanna, b. 3 Sep 1783, bapt. 21 Sep 1783. Sponsors: Michael Lennert and wife Anna Catharina.

Maria Margareta, of Johannes Wester and Catharine (who died), b. 25 Sep 1783, bapt. 26 Sep 1783. Sponsors: Daniel vanderSchleis and Maria Wester(in).

Magdalena, of Georg Schaerer and Elisabeth, b. 22 Sep 1783, bapt. 28 Sep 1783. Sponsors: Friedr. Renn and wife (name not given).

Johann Jacob, of Caspar Wittebach and Hanna, b. 12 Jun 1781 bapt. 30 Sep 1783. Sponsor: Catharina Vogel(in).

Anna Victoria, of Adolf Christian Wilhelm Hederich and Anna, b. 15 Sep 1783, bapt. 5 Oct 1783. Sponsors: the parents, and Capt. David Ziegler.

Joseph, of Daniel Jones and Elisab., b. 12 Sep 1783, bapt. 5 Oct 1783. Sponsors: the mother.

Anna, of Jacob Hackenmiller and Maria, b. 7 Sep 1783, bapt. 20 Oct 1783. Sponsors: the parents.

Maria Magdalena, of Andreas Boehmer and Margareta, b. 23 Sep 1783, bapt. 5 Oct 1783. Sponsors: Conrad Weber and wife (name not given).

Elisabet Catharina, of Henrich Bot(h) and Elisabeth, b. 18 Sep 1783, bapt. 10 Oct 1783. Sponsors: Peter Dick? and wife Elisab.

Wilhelm, of Peter Wagner and Rosina, b. 26 Sep 1783, bapt. 11 Oct 1783. Sponsors: the father, and Catharina Rudolph(in).

Henrich, of Jacob Duffiner and Anna Magdalena, b. 29 Sep 1783, bapt. 19 Oct 1783. Sponsors: Henr. Reiss and wife Hanna.

Johannes, of Philipp Jacob Burg and Elisabeth, b. 9 Oct 1783, bapt. 26 Oct 1783. Sponsors: Johannes Strup and wife Margareta.
Jacob, of Carl Wilhelm Nushag and Catharina, b. 4 Oct 1783, bapt. 26 Oct 1783. Sponsors: Jacob Keimle and wife Cathar. Christiana.
Michael, of Michael Zepf and Catharina, b. 12 Oct 1783, bapt. 26 Oct 1783. Sponsors: Michael Schweizer and wife Magdalena.
Johann Christian, of Johannes Frickhoefer and Hedwig, b. 14 Oct 1783, bapt. 26 Oct 1783. Sponsors: Johan Just Frickhoefer and wife Marg.
William, of Robert Frimouth and Elisab., b. 11 Sep 1783, bapt. 6 Oct 1783. Sponsors: Jacob Fimbel and wife Maria.
Anna Maria, of Philipp Schindler and Margareta, b. 7 Sep 1783, bapt. 6 Oct 1783. Sponsors: the parents.
Benjamin Erdman (twin), of John Freymuth and Elisabeth, b. 17 Nov 1783, bapt. 6 Dec 1783. (Sponsors not given.)
Dorothea, (twin), of John Freymuth and Elisabeth, b. 17 Nov 1783, bapt. 6 Dec 1783. (Sponsors not given.)
Johann David, of Jacob Wolf and Elisabet, b. 25 Jan 1783, bapt. 26 Oct 1783. Sponsors: Johann Friedr. Renn and wife Cathar.
Friedrich, of Johannes Schreier and Catharina, b. 31 Oct 1783, bapt. 9 Nov 1783. Sponsors: Friedr. Linck and wife Barbara.
Johann Georg, of Franz Wilhelm Hetmansperger and Maria, b. 22 Oct 1783, bapt. 9 Nov 1783. Sponsors: Georg Pest and wife Charlotta.
Johann Gottlieb, of Henrich Bohn and Elisabeth, b. 5 Oct 1783, bapt. 9 Nov 1783. Sponsors: Johann Litsch and wife Maria.
Georg, of John Justice and Catharina, b. 15 Oct 1783, bapt. 9 Nov 1783. Sponsors: Georg Sei[t]z and wife (name not given.).
Thomas, of Johannes Stock and Elisabet, b. 21 Sep 1783, bapt. 16 Nov 1783. Sponsors: Edward Miller and wife Barbara.
Georg, of Johann Friedrich Woelpert and Margareta, b. 3 Oct 1783, bapt. 16 Nov 1783. Sponsors: Georg Wilpert and wife Margar.
Elisabet, of Johann Georg Linck and Elisabet, b. 11 Sep 1783, bapt. 16 Nov 1783. Sponsors: the parents.
Johann Martin, of Johann Martin Haertle and Anna Margareta, b. 22 Oct 1783, bapt. 23 Nov 1783. Sponsor: John Jacob Scheppach and wife Maria Ursula.
Friedrich, of Friedrich Fischer and Anna Regina, b. 3 Oct 1783, bapt. 23 Nov 1783. Sponsors: Friedr. Zent and wife Barbara.
Margareta, of David Kries and Clara, b. 7 Nov 1783, bapt. 26 Nov 1783. Sponsors: Johann Seidel and Margar. Berrens.
Margareta, of Michael Preus and Maria, b. 8 Nov 1783, bapt. 30 Nov 1783. Sponsors: Michael Bartholomes and wife Cathar.
Johann Georg, of Johann Rugan and Elisabet, b. 30 Oct 1783, bapt. 30 Nov 1783. Sponsors: Johann Haensmann and wife Anna.
Margaret, of Joseph Morgan and Sophia, b. 16 Nov 1783, bapt. 7 Dec 1783. Sponsors: Christian Huber and wife Mar__.
Samuel, of Peter Gabel and Elisabet, b. 6 Dec 1783, bapt. 7 Dec 1783. Sponsors: the parents.
Georg, of Georg Grün and Catharina, b. 27 Nov 1783, bapt. 7 Dec 1783. Sponsors: the parents.

Margareta, of Daniel Boecle and Abigail, b. 19 Nov 1783, bapt. 4 Dec 1783. Sponsors: the father, and Margareta Boecle.

Elisabet, of David Ott and Catharina, b. 28 Nov 1783, bapt. 9 Dec 1783. Sponsors: Jacob Ki[t]z and wife Elisabet.

Anna Maria, of Johann Me[t]z and Barbara, b. 1 Nov 1783, bapt. 14 Dec 1783. Sponsors: Philipp Meger and wife Cathar. Salome.

Johann Georg, of Johan Fischer and Anna Maria, b. 5 Dec 1783, bapt. 21 Dec 1783. Sponsors: George Dehn and wife (name not given)..

Philipp, of Johan Heil and Maria, b. 5 Dec 1783, bapt. 2 Dec, 1783. Sponsors: Philipp Heil and wife? Philippina.

Barbara, of Jacob Seger and Barbara, b. 28 Nov 1783, bapt. 21 Dec 1783. Sponsors: Michael Stricker and wife Margareta.

Anna Maria, of Isaac Stahl and Elisabet, b. 8 Dec 1783, bapt. 21 Dec 1783. Sponsor: Balthasar Fleischer and wife Catharina.

Catharina, of Carl Hay and Sophia, b. 12 Dec 1783, bapt. 21 Dec 1783. Sponsors: Johann Loschet and wife Catharina.

Elisab. Catharina, of Johann Georg Shall and Maria Christina, b. 21 Dec 1783, bapt. 26 Dec 1783. Sponsors: Jacob Schmidt and wife (name not legible).

1783, Second List
(baptisms by pastor Helmuth, from Book III)

Johann, of Christian Huber and Margareta, b. 31 Oct 1782, bapt. 1 Jan 1783. Sponsors: the father, and Dorothea Walter.

Catharina, of Jacob Facundus and Juliana, b. 19 Dec 1782, bapt. 1 Jan 1783. Sponsors: Adolph Dill and wife Cathar.

Samuel Wilhelm, of Georg Phil. Weissmann and Catharina, b. 14 Dec 1782, bapt. 1 Jan 1783. Sponsors: Christoph Hansmann and wife (name not given).

Jacob, of David Breckley and Magdalena, b. 10 Dec 1782, bapt. 5 Jan 1783. Sponsors: Jacob Seger and wife Cathar.

Catharina, of Joh. Ludwig Reuschle and Margareta, b. 8 Dec 1782, bapt. 5 Jan 1783. Sponsors: Thomas Thürmer and wife Catharina.

Anna Barbara, of Joh. Hoffmann and Philippina, b. 3 Dec 1782, bapt. 5 Jan 1783. Sponsor: the mother.

Peter, of Ludwig Tiess and Catharina, b. 9 Dec 1782, bapt. 12 Jan 1783. Sponsors: John Peter Fri[t]z and wife Sahra.

Bernhard, of Leonhard Repscher and Barbara, b. 14 Dec 1783, bapt. 19 Jan 1783. Sponsors: Bernh. Schwenk and wife Rebecca.

Elisab., of Thomas Gerum and Elisabeth, b. 2 Jan 1783, bapt. 19 Jan 1783. Sponsors: the parents.

Elisabeth, of Joh. Fridr. Spatz and Elisabeth, b. 2 Jan 1783, bapt. 19 Jan 1783. Sponsors: Joh. Kappel and wife Cath.

Johann, of Jacob Sohns and Catharina, b. 4 Jan 1783, bapt. 26 Jan 1783. Sponsors: Nicol. Dobler and wife Catharina.

Hanna, of John Wilson and Catharina, b. 9 Dec 1782, bapt. 26 Jan 1783. Sponsors: Jonathan Stanton and wife Jemima.

Peter, of Balthasar Schenkel and Catharina, b. 6 Dec 1782, bapt. 2 Feb 1783. Sponsors: Peter Krafft and wife Margar.

Cathar., of Jacob Valentin and Rosina, b. 20 Jan 1783, bapt. 2 Feb 1783.
Sponsors: Phil. Knecht and wife Molly.
Christina, of Heinr. Reiss and Hanna, b. 12 Jan 1783, bapt. 2 Feb 1783.
Sponsors: Nicol. Weber and wife Christina.
William, of Thomas Ewinger and Sarah, b. 13 May 1782, bapt. 2 Feb 1783.
Sponsors: the parents, and Wilhelm Stein.
James, of John Porter and Catharina, b. 28 Dec 1783, bapt. 26 Jan 1783.
Sponsors: the father, and Doroth. Dixon.
Daniel, of Joh. Mich. Johbst and Margareta, b. 23 Jan 1783, bapt. 4 Feb 1783.
Sponsors: Daniel Sorg and wife Margar.
Anna Maria Salo[me], of Phil. Sorg and Susanna, b. 20 Jan 1783, bapt. 4 Feb
1783. Sponsors: Daniel Sorg and wife Margar.
Elisab., of Jacob Beydermann and Catharina, b. 21 Jan 1783, bapt. 4 Feb 1783.
Sponsor: widow Catharina Muht(in).
Peter, of Barbara Küntsch(in) and Peter Kühn (illegitimate), b. 29 Jan 1783,
bapt. 4 Feb 1783. Sponsors: Caspar Küntsch and wife Marg.
Maria, of Heinr. Depperwin and Margar., b. 25 Dec 1782, bapt. 9 Feb 1783.
Sponsors: Joh. Mann and Marg. Ren_.
Johann, of Christian Frieheffer and Maria, b. 30 Jan 1783, bapt. 9 Feb 1783.
Sponsors: John Friehefer and wife Esther.
Heinrich, of Jacob Schaeffer and Maria, b. 14 Feb 1783, bapt. 14 Feb 1783.
Sponsors: the parents.
Joh. Ludw. of Joh. Niemand and Polly, b. 5 Feb 1783, bapt. 16 Feb 1783.
Sponsors: Joh. Kunckler and Lud. Sch__.
David, of Michael Shumacher and Susanna, b. 20 Dec 1782, bapt. 16 Feb 1783.
Sponsors: Christian Wilkinson and wife Rosina
Margar., of Joh. Starke and Catharina Margar., b. 26 Dec 1782, bapt. 16 Feb
1783. Sponsors: Phil. Pannekuchen and wife Catharina
Joh. Georg, of Adam Widderstein and Sophia, b. 29 Jan 1783, bapt. 16 Feb
1783. Sponsors: the father, and Cath. Kribbel.
Carl, of Gottfried Seyder and Catharina, b. 5 Feb 1783, bapt. 16 Feb 1783.
Sponsors: Heinr. Lenz and wife Maria.
Johann, of Conrad Bernhard and Barbara, b. 20 Feb 1783, bapt. 20 Feb 1783.
Sponsor: Joh. Sonnleiter.
Jacob, of Heinr. Kress and Anna Maria, b. 23 Dec 1782, bapt. 23 Feb 1783.
Sponsors: the parents.
Anna Cath., of Nicol. Georg Book and Catharine, b. 15 Feb 1783, bapt. 2 Mar
1783. Sponsors: Gottfried Schling and wife Marg.
Sarah, of Edward Laske and Catharina, b. 5 Feb 1783, bapt. 2 Mar 1783.
Sponsors: Conrad Hoff and wife Sibylla.
Esther, of Georg Duncker and Eva Maria, b. 21 Dec, 1782, bapt. 2 Mar 1783.
Sponsors: Adam Knoblauch and wife Barbara..
Anna Marg., of David Jones and Elisabeth, b. 1 Dec 1782, bapt. 3 Mar 1783.
Sponsor: Margareat Burckhart(in).
Nancy [twin], of Richhard Schaffels and Rosina, b. 5 Mar 1783, bapt. 8 Mar
1783. (Sponsors not given.)
Elisabeth [twin], of Richhard Schaffels and Rosina, b. 5 Mar 1783, bapt. 8 Mar
1783. (Sponsors not given.)

Georg, of John Heartline and Gertraut, b. 4 Mar 1783, bapt. 9 Mar 1783.
Sponsors: Georg Rummel and wife Elisabeth.
Carl, of Georg Wood and Elisabeth, b. 29 Sep 1782, bapt. 9 Mar 1783.
Sponsors: Heinr. Kress and wife Anna Maria.
Rosina, of Joh. Straup and Margareta, b. 14 Mar 1783, bapt. 14 Mar 1783.
Sponsors: the parents.
Johann, of Georg Forbach and Margareta, b. 20 Feb 1783, bapt. 16 Mar 1783.
Sponsor: Christoph Mayer.
Magdalena, of Joh. Mich. Hans and Susanna, b. 20 Feb 1783, bapt. 21 Mar
1783. Sponsors: Gottl. Mayer and wife Magdal.
Hanna, of William Carter and Elisabeth, b. 2 Feb 1783, bapt. 21 Mar 1783.
Sponsors: the parents.
Henr. Wilhelm, of Christoph Moor and Catharina, b. 19 Feb 1783, bapt. 24 Mar
1783. Sponsors: Heinr. Wilh. Geiss and wife Mar.
Christina Elisab., of Joh. Mayer and Elisabeth, b. 10 Mar 1783, bapt. 24 Mar
1783. Sponsors: Georg Seyfferheld and wife Christ. Elis.
Georg, of Georg Krauskopp and Anna Maria, b. 8 Feb 1783, bapt. 25 Mar 1783.
Sponsors: Georg Krauskopp and wife Marg.
Julia Margar., of Gottfried Bender and Sarah, b. 7 Mar 1783, bapt. 26 Mar 1783.
Sponsors: Joh. Bender and wife Julianna Marg.
Phebe, of Isaac Kelly and Elisabeth, b. 23 Jul 1782, bapt. 29 Mar 1783.
Sponsor: Henry Allen.
Cath. Elis., of Heinr. Homüller and Catharina, b. 7 Mar 1783, bapt. 6 Apr 1783.
Sponsors: Michael Bauer and wife Christina Dorothea.
Elisabeth, of Jacob Messner and Elisabeth, b. 24 Feb 1783, bapt. 7 Apr 1783.
Sponsor: Elisabeth Bartsch.
Wilhelm [twin], of Fridr. Pontleon and Regina Cath., b. 30 Mar 1783, bapt.
7 Apr 1783. Sponsors: the parents.
Susanna [twin], of Fridr. Pontleon and Regina Cath.., b. 30 Mar 1783, bapt.
10 Apr 1783. Sponsors: the parents.
Nancy, of Wilhelm Ross and Anna, b. 4 Apr 1783, bapt. 13 Apr 1783.
Sponsors: Christoph Braun and wife Nancy.
Catharina, of Phil. Thomas and Salome, b. 16 Mar 1783, bapt. 15 Apr 1783.
Sponsors: Cath. Loescher(in).
Elisabeth, of Andr. Beck and Eva Marg., b. 25 Mar 1783, bapt. 16 Apr 1783.
Sponsors: Maria Grimm and Cath. Sei[t]z.
Joh. Thomas, of Leonh. Lutz and Magdal., b. 8 Apr 1783, bapt. 19 Apr 1783.
Sponsors: Nicol. Kaiser and wife Elisab.
Jacob, of Jacob Mayer and Margareta, b. 7 Jan 1783, bapt. 24 Apr 1783.
Sponsors: Jacob Weiser and wife Elisab.
Philippina, of John Finck and Anna Catharine, b. 10 Jan 1783, bapt. 24 Apr
1783. Sponsors: widow Cath. Kop(in).
Georg, of Joh. Weber and Fanny, b. 21 Mar 1783, bapt. 27 Apr 1783. Sponsors:
the parents.
Maria, of Joh. Heine and Catharina, b. 7 Apr 1783, bapt. 27 Apr 1783.
Sponsors: Carl Cuben and wife Maria.
Carl, of Rudolph Nagel and Susanna, b. 10 Apr 1783, bapt. 27 Apr 783.
Sponsors: Carl Sing and wife Margar.

Wilhelm, of Joh. Otto and Hanna, b. 21 Apr 1783, bapt. 4 May 1783. Sponsors: Wilhelm Hantzel and Marg. Carpenter.

Georg, of Mich. Miltenberger and Dorothea, b. 14 Apr 1783, bapt. 4 May 1783. Sponsors: Georg Miltenberger and wife Cathar.

Georg, of Friedrich Linck and Barbara, b. 29 Apr 1783, bapt. 5 May 1783. Sponsors: the parents.

Johanna, of Joh. Hartranfft and Catharina, b. 23 Mar 1783, bapt. 10 May 1783. Sponsors: Christoph Kucker and wife Doroth.

Catharina, of Georg Schneider and Margaretha, b. 30 Apr 1783, bapt. 11 May 1783. Sponsor: Cathar. Robisin.

Charlotte, of Georg Schutz and Catharina, b. 10 Apr 1775, bapt. 11 May 1783. Sponsors: Conrad Hester and wife Leona Cath.

Joh. Christoph., of Georg Sterr and Margaret, b. 16 Mar 1783, bapt. 11 May 1783. Sponsors: Christoph Rauch and wife Rosina.

Maria, of Thom. Chillingsworth and Rosina, b. 17 Jan 1783, bapt. 11 May 1783. Sponsors: Conrad Hester and wife Leona Cath.

Elisab., of Phil. Springer and Eva, b. 20 Apr 1783, bapt. 11 May 1783. Sponsors: Simon Mohl and wife Elisab.

Maria, of Francys Sweet and Maria, b. 24 Apr 1783, bapt. 11 May 1783. Sponsor: the mother.

Georg, of Heinr. Kur[t]z and Rosina, b. 14 Apr 1783, bapt. 11 May 1783. Sponsors: the parents.

Maria, of Georg Habacher and Maria, b. 29 Apr 1783, bapt. 15 May 1783. Sponsors: the parents, and Maria Dor. Dick(in).

Johann, of Fridr. Reible and wife Elisab., b. 24 Mar 1783, bapt. 25 May 1783. Sponsors: Joh. Sonnleiter and wife Maria.

Daniel, of Heinr. Mayer and Catharine, b. 22 May 1783, bapt. 25 May 1783. Sponsors: Daniel Bergmayer and wife Marg.

Joh. Georg, of Wilhelm Heins and Maria Cath., b. 29 Oct 1782, bapt. 25 May 1783. Sponsors: Joh. Georg Hoffmann and wife.

Elisab., of Andr. Rot(h) and Anna Maria, b. 25 Apr 1783, bapt. 25 May 1783. Sponsors: Christian Schaeffer and Elis. Rot(hin).

Anna Marg., of Jacob Swain and Anna Maria, b. 28 Feb 1783, bapt. 25 May 1783. Sponsor: An. Marg. Dingiss(in).

Joh. Phil., of Joh. Georg Hoff and Maria Marg., b. 7 Mar 1783, bapt. 26 May 1783. Sponsor: the mother.

Valentin, of Martin Will and Elisabeth, b. 14 May 1783, bapt. 27 May 1783. Sponsor: widow Eva Helder(in).

An. Elisab. [twin], of Fridr. Kaltoven and Maria Elis., b. 14 May 1783, bapt. 28 May 1783. Sponsors: the parents.

Georg Fridr. [twin], of Fridr. Kaltoven and Maria Elis., b. 14 May 1783, bapt. 28 May 1783. Sponsors: the parents

Elisabeth, of Joh. Mut(h) and Elisab., b. 28 Mar 1781, bapt. 28 May 1783. Sponsors: Jac. Beidermann and [wife] Elisab.

Catharina, of Joh. Mut(h) and Elisab., b. 30 Mar 1783, bapt. 28 May 1783. Sponsors: Brunne? and Catharina Reiss(in).

Fanny, of Georg Flowers and Elisab., b. 1 May 1783, bapt. 30 May 1783. Sponsors: the parents?.

Adam, of Jacob Fimpel and Maria, b. 7 May 1783, bapt. 2 Jun 1783. Sponsors: Adam Phister and Cath. Lochmann(in).

Cathar., of Jacob Buss and Barbara, b. 2 Jun 1782, bapt. 3 Jun 1783. Sponsors: Joh. Ellwood and Barb. Buss.

Elisab., of Joh. Kappel and Catharina, b. 10 May 1783, bapt. 8 Jun 1783. Sponsors: Joh. Spatz and wife Elisab.

Cathar., of Wilh. Kirls and Margar., b. 28 May 1783, bapt. 9 Jun 1783. Sponsors: Joh. Lorenz and wife Cathar.

Dorothea, of Leonh. Walter and Philippina, b. 19 May 1783, bapt. 9 Jun 1783. Sponsors: Jacob Baum and wife Doroth. Elisab.

Peter, of Daniel Ernst and Catharina, b. 20 Dec 1782, bapt. 9 Jun 1783. Sponsors: Peter Dill and wife Elisab.

Henrich, of Joh. Miller and Maria, b. 10 Mar 1783, bapt. 9 Jun 1783. Sponsors: Heinr. Huber and wife Maria.

Philip, of Adam Schaeffer and Dorothea, b. 28 May 1783, bapt. 9 Jun 1783. Sponsors: the parents.

Jacob, of Joh. Wagner and Elisabeth, b. 9 Sep 1782, bapt. 9 Jun 1783. Sponsors: the parents.

Philip, of Jacob Scherff (alias Sharp) and Elisabeth, b. 31 Mar 1782, bapt. 10 Jun 1783. Sponsors: Phil. Scherff and Eva Kidler.

Joh. Conrad, of Phil. Weitzel and Eva, b. 24 Jan 1783, bapt. 10 Jun 1783. Sponsors: Conr. Wagner and wife Catharina.

Andr., of Andrew Bauer and Anna Barbara, b. 6 Jun 1783, bapt. 13 Jun 1783. Sponsors: the parents.

Margareta, of Mich. Bamberger and Elisabeth, b. 20 May 1783, bapt. 14 Jun 1783. Sponsors: the father, and Margar. Goddard.

Joh. Christoph, of Joh. Nicol. Paulus and Margareta, b. 7 Jun 1783, bapt. 14 Jun 1783. Sponsors: Christ. Boehringer and wife Margareta.

Maria Margar., of Joh. Kressel and Catharina, b. 15 Jun 1782, bapt. 3 May 1783. Sponsors: Martin Rapp and wife Maria Margar.

Michael, of Jacob Schneider and Elisabeth, b. 20 May 1783, bapt. 23 Jun 1783. Sponsors: Michael Kitz and wife Margareta.

Johann, of Susanna Biel(in) and reportedly John Krob (illegitimate), b. 9 May 1783, bapt. 23 Jun 1783. Sponsors: Joh. Sailer and wife Catharina.

Elisabeth, of Wendel Wendling and Maria, b. 27 May 1783, bapt. 23 Jun 1783. Sponsors: Heinr. Reiss and wife Elisabeth.

Joh. Peter, of Joh. Pet. Walter and Antonetta, b. 8 Jun 1783, bapt. 23 Jun 1783. Sponsor: the father.

Maria, of Joh. Schütz and Maria, b. 27 May 1783, bapt. 28 Jun 1783. Sponsors: the parents.

Barbara, of Daniel Huber and Maria, b. 20 May 1783, bapt. 6 Jul 1783. Sponsors: Joh. Schae[t]zlein and wife Barbara.

Jacob, of Georg Mauti and Margareta, b. 25 Jun 1783, bapt. 6 Jul 1783. Sponsors: Jacob Hempelmann and wife Elisab.

Maria Cath., of Nicol. Panzer and Elisabeth, b. 5 Jul 1783, bapt. 13 Jul 1783. Sponsors: Maria Cath. Panzer(in).

Anna Maria, of Jacob Schreiner and Anna Margar., b. 2 July 1783, bapt. 1 July 1783. Sponsors: the parents.

Joh. Fridr., of Jacob Shcnell and Elisabeth, b. 3 Jul 1783, bapt. 13 Jul 1783.
Sponsors: Fridr. Weiss and wife Cathar.

Johann, of Wilh. Farley and Elisabeth, b. 9 Jul 1783, bapt. 14 Jul 1783.
Sponsors: the father, and Susanna Ehrenfeuchter?.

Jacob, of Magnus Neiss and Anna Spetz, b. 9 Jan 1783, bapt. 14 Jul 1783.
Sponsor: Anna Ottilia Conrad(in).

Margar., of David Griffin and Nancy, b. 10 Dec 1782, bapt. 16 Jul 1783.
Sponsors: Robert Collins and wife Elisab.

Joh. Peter, of Joh. Peter Bauer and Anna Barb., b. 11 Jul 1783, bapt. 17 Jul
1783. Sponsors: the father.

Michael, of Jacob Retzer and Susanna, b. 15 Apr 1783, bapt. 19 Jul 1783.
Sponsors: Joh. Ferg? and son Michael.

Mar. Magdal., of Elias Frey and Maria, b. 7 Jul 1783, bapt. 20 Jul 1783.
Sponsors: Mich. Riem and Maria Schmidt.

Margaret, of Georg Nonnemacher and Catharina, b. 28 May 1783, bapt. 20 Jul
1783. Sponsors: Leon. Rupert and Maria Leb(in).

Margar., of Jac. Wagner and Grace, b. 18 Jul 1783, bapt. 20 Jul 1783. Sponsors:
the parents.

Georg, of Joh. Eberhard and Christ. Cath., b. 15 Jul 1783, bapt. 20 Jul 1783.
Sponsors: George Walcker and wife Dorothea.

Wilhelm, of Wilhelm Stur[t]z and Ursula, b. 18 Jul 1783, bapt. 24 Jul 1783.
Sponsors: the parents.

Anna Maria, of Joh. Mart. Ludwig and Elisab., b. 12 Jan 1783, bapt. 26 Jul
1783. Sponsors: Anna Cath. Strupp(in).

Elisab., of Georg Gebhard and Rosina, b. 6 Jun 1783, bapt. 28 Jul 1783.
Sponsors: Gerhard Hol[t]zkamm and wife Elis.

Adam, of Nic. Wolff and Elisab., b. 22 Jun 1783, bapt. 28 Jul 1783. Sponsors:
the parents.

Johann, of Bernh. Weber and Cathar., b. 10 Jul 1783, bapt. 3 Aug 1783.
Sponsors: Joh. Lenz and Cath. Bahl.

Joh. Georg, of Joh. Bisans and Christina, b. 25 Jul 1783, bapt. 3 Aug 1783.
Sponsors: Georg Kur[t]z and wife Margaret.

Elisabeth, of Lucas Bittenhaus and Catharina, b. 5 Jun 1783, bapt. 5 Aug 783.
Sponsor: Anna Maria Kraft.

Martin, of Albertus Weber and Magdalena, b. 10 Jul 1783, bapt. 8 Aug 1783.
Sponsors: Heinr. Krimm and wife Magdal.

Georg Adam, of Georg Adam Becker and Anna Cath., b. 2 July 1783, bapt.
9 Aug 1783. Sponsors: the parents.

Margaret, of Andr. Jung and Catharina, b. 3 May 1783, bapt. 10 Aug 1783.
Sponsors: Richhard Jung and wife Margar.

Johann, of Jacob Luger and Elisabeth, b. 18 Sep 1783, bapt. 10 Aug 1783.
Sponsors: Joh. Georg Seifferheld and wife Christina Elisab.

Martin, of John Ehr[hard] Schnellhard and Christina, b. 29 Jul 1783, bapt. 1 Aug
1783. Sponsors: Martin Rapp and wife Maria Sabina.

Wilhelm, of Michael Katz and Elisab., b. 2 Aug 1783, bapt. 10 Aug 1783.
Sponsors: the father and Elis. Scheub(in).

Johann, of Nicol. Hirt and Maria, b. 17 Jul 1783, bapt. 10 Aug 1783. Sponsors:
John Hirt and Mar. Marg. Hirt(in).

494   PHILADELPHIA GERMAN LUTHERAN CHURCH

Adam, of Ludw. Preiss and Anna Maria, b. 19 Feb 1783, bapt. 12 Aug 1783.
Sponsors: the mother.
Joh. Peter, of Philipp Jung and Elisab., b. 30 Jul 1783, bapt. 30 Aug 1783.
Sponsors: Joh. Peter Jung and wife Mar. Magdal.
Nicol., of Gabr. Steinbock and Christina, b. 10 Jul 1783, bapt. 16 Aug 1783.
Sponsors: Nicol. Deahl and Polly Stock(in).
Mar. Ludw., of Joseph Kaiser and Anna, b. 20 Jul 1783, bapt. 17 Aug 1783.
Sponsors: Joh. Martin Rapp and wife Mar. Sabina.
Johann, of Joh. Jac. Heitz and Anna, b. 9 Aug 1783, bapt. 17 Aug 1783.
Sponsors: the father, and Cath. Hei[t]z(in).
Anna Cath., of Joh. Jacob Pobb? and Marg. Elisab., b. 14 Sep 1770, bapt.
17 Aug 1783. Sponsors: Gottfried Weiland and wife Cath., and Michael Kitz
and wife Anna Mar.
Joh. Wilh., of Joh. Jacob Pobb? and Marg. Elisab., b. 14 Nov 1774, bapt.
17 Aug 1783. Sponsors: same as above.
Hannetta, of Joh. Jacob Pobb? and Marg. Elisab., b. 20 Sep 1778, bapt. 17 Aug
1783. Sponsors: same as above.
Susanna, of Charles Dupoh and Johann[a], b. 25 Jul 1783, bapt. 21 Aug 1783.
Sponsor: Susanna Schumacher(in).
Christina, of Nicol. Rehb and Christina, b. 22 Aug 1783, bapt. the same day.
(Sponsors not given.)
Mar. Juliana, of Joh. Ring and Maria, b. 8 Aug 1783, bapt. 25 Aug 1783.
Sponsors: Conrad Ring and wife Mar. Juliana.
Ludw. Ernst, of Martin Baischt and Mar. Magdal., b. 4 Aug 1783, bapt. 24 Aug
1783. Sponsors: Georg Gro[t]z and wife Dorothea.
Elisab., of Heinr. Herberger and Susanna, b. 11 Aug 1783, bapt. 31 Aug 1783.
Sponsors: Georg Mildenberger and wife Cath.
Georg Washington, of Martin Parry and Maria, b. 15 Nov 1777, bapt. 2 Sep
1783. (Sponsors not given.)
James, of Martin Parry and Maria, b. 17 Oct 1782, bapt. 2 Sep 1783. (Sponsors
not given.)
Wilhelm, of Joh. Stein and Maria, b. 14 Aug 1783, bapt. 7 Sep 1783. Sponsors:
Wilh. Stein and wife Christina.
Elisabet, of Wilh. Jung and Elisab., b. 21 Aug 1783, bapt. 7 Sep 1783.
Sponsors: Rudolph Nagel and wife Susanna.
Carl Fridr., of Carl Fridr. Hensel and Anna Margareta, b. 15 Aug 1783, bapt.
7 Sep 1783. Sponsors: the parents.
Joh. Fridr., of Joh. Fridr. Lutz and Anna Catharine, b. 23 Aug 1783, bapt. 7 Sep
1783. Sponsors: Joh.Thom. Lu[t]z and wife Maria Barb.
Anna Barb., of Catharina Albach and reportedly Georg Alley, b. 3 Mar 1783,
bapt. 7 Sep 1783. Sponsors: Fridr. Lutz and [wife] Anna Barb.
Elisab., of Heinr. Moser and Christina, b. 28 Mar 1783, bapt. 8 Sep 1783.
Sponsors: Jacob Weisert and wife Elisab.
Hanna, of Joh. Georg Aescher and Elisab., b. 6 Sep 1783, bapt. 14 Sep 1783.
Sponsors: Heinr. Reiss and wife Hanna.
Wilhelm, of Gottf. Heinrich and Elisab., b. 17 Jul 1783, bapt. 8 Sep 1783.
Sponsor: Jacob Volckradt.

Magdalena, of Conrad Mul[l]er and Margar., b. 17 Sep 1782, bapt. 16 Sep 1783. Sponsors: Joh. Georg Krauskop and wife Maria.

Johann, of Joh. Dienstmann and Anna, b. 19 May 1783, bapt. 15 Sep 1783. Sponsor: Anna Marg. Miltenberger(in).

Mar. Magdal., of Joh. Joseph Graff and Mar. Dorothea, b. 6 Sep 1783, bapt. 21 Sep 1783. Sponsors: the parents.

Esther, of Joh. Breviehl and Maria, b. in 1783, bapt. 21 Sep 1783. Sponsors: the parents.

Anna Maria, of Joh. Wucherer and Elisab., b. 21 Aug 1783, bapt. 21 Sep 1783. Sponsors: the parents.

Jacob, of Gottfr. Krumbach and Barbara, b. 15 Aug 1783, bapt. 24 Sep 1783. Sponsors: the parents.

Joh. Peter, of Peter Klein and Maria, b. 17 Sep 1783, bapt. 25 Sep 1783. Sponsors: Joh. Peter Heinrich, Anna Maria Gebhard, and K__(illegible).

Cathar., of Phil. Ehwald and Hanna, b. 18 Sep 1783, bapt. 27 Sep 1783. Sponsor: Catharina Ehwald.

Wilhelm, of Abraham Sinck and Hanna, b. 12 Sep 1783, bapt. 28 Sep 1783. Sponsor: Regina Sinck(in).

Johann, of Georg Bauer and Margar., b. 29 Aug 1783, bapt. 28 Sep 1783. Sponsors: Joh. Haass and wife Elisab.

Elisab., of Benoni Baetz and Sophia, b. 12 Sep 1783, bapt. 28 Sep 1783. Sponsors: Joh. Kuehr? and Elis. Haasli.

Elisab., of Joh. Adam Wagner and Catharina, b. 7 Sep 1783, bapt. 28 Sep 1783. Sponsors: Christ. Vian? and wife Elisab.

Maria, of Valent. Breneisen and Elisabeth, b. 5 Sep 1783, bapt. 24 Sep 1783. Sponsors: Phil. Seidelmann and wife Maria.

Johann, of Michael Miller and Margareta, b. 29 Sep 1783, bapt. 30 Sep 1783. Sponsors: Jacob Hartmann and Polly Hirt?.

Eva Elisab., of Conrad Dewitter and Cath. Elis., b. 4 Sep 1783, bapt. 28 Sep 1783. Sponsors: Wilh. Geiss and wife Eva Elisab.

Anna, of Francy Loescher and Maria Barbara, b. 8 Mar 1783, bapt. 29 Sep 1783. Sponsors: the mother, and Christ. Krebs.

Catharina, of Mich. Lapp and Margareta, b. 24 Sep 1783, bapt. 5 Oct 1783. Sponsors: Cath. Schutz(in) and Peter Kochendoerffer.

Sarah, of Michael Frappel and Elisabeth, b. 3 Jul 1783, bapt. 5 Oct 1783. Sponsors: the father, and Sarah Lutket.

Georg, of Mich. Bayer and Elisab., b. 5 Oct 1783, bapt. 5 Oct 1783. Sponsors: the parents.

Jacob, of Peter Rotter and Prunelopy, b. 21 Aug 1783, bapt. 5 Oct 1783. Sponsor: Jacob Rotter.

Elisab., of Phil. Knecht and Maria, b. 15 Sep 1783, bapt. 5 Oct 1783. Sponsors: Georg Spiel and wife Elisab.

Georg, of Philipp Wager and Hanna, b. 20 Sep 1783, bapt. 8 Oct 1783. Sponsors: Georg Aebacher and wife Maria.

Margar., of Caspar Oberdorff and Margar., b. 16 Mar 1779, bapt. 17 Oct 1783. Sponsor: the mother.

Joh. Georg, of Joh. Heims and Deborah, b. 1 Sep 1783, bapt. 19 Oct 1783. Sponsors: Georg Holzkamm and wife Cath. Elisab.

Maria, of Andr. Haak and Philippina, b. 2 Oct 1783, bapt. 21 Oct 1783.
Sponsors: Fridr. Reinbold and wife Barbara.

Anna Eva, of Casp. Dunckelmayer and Anna Eva, b. 19 Sep 1783, bapt. 23 Oct
1783. Sponsor: the mother.

Maria Elisab., of Wilh. Weber and Elisab., b. 10 Oct 1783, bapt. 26 Oct 1783.
Sponsors: Mich. Goe[t]z and wife Maria.

Adam, of Joh. Dav. Seckel and Maria, b. 9 Oct 1783, bapt. 26 Oct 1783.
Sponsors: Adam Geyer and Maria Cath. Seckel.

Magdalena, of Georg Heitel and Salome, b. 16 Oct 1783, bapt. 2 Nov 1783.
Sponsors: the parents.

Anna Cath., of Mathias Joth? and Veronica, b. 13 Oct 1783, bapt. 27 Oct 1783.
Sponsor: Anna Cath. Schmidt(in).

Georg Phil., of Fridr. Gross and Esther, b. 21 Oct 1783, bapt. 27 Oct 1783.
Sponsors: Georg Fridr. H___ing and wife Ann. Ottilia.

Wilhelm, of Jacob Niglie and Susanna, b. 23 Nov 1774, bapt. 1 Nov 1783.
Sponsors: Gehrhard Holzkam and wife Cath. Elis.

Joh. [twin], of Adam Schwager and Maria Magdal., b. 21 Aug 1783, bapt. 2 Nov
1783. Sponsors: Joh. Hess and wife Elisabeth.

Georg Adam [twin], of Adam Schwager and Maria Magdal., b. 21 Aug 1783,
bapt. 2 Nov 1783. Sponsors: Georg Bauer and wife Margar.

Wilhelm, of Joh. Weiss and Elisab., b. 6 Oct 1783, bapt. 2 Nov 1783. Sponsors:
the parents.

Elisab., of Leonhard Eger and Charlotta, b. 8 Feb 1782, bapt. 3 Nov 1783.
Sponsor: Mathias Stohl.

Anna Elis., of Heinr. Lud. Loewe and Cathar., b. 3 Nov 1783, bapt. 6 Nov 1783.
Sponsors: Anna Kehr and Anthon Weiss.

Johann, of Joh. Friess and wife Anna, b. 30 Aug 1783, bapt. 7 Nov 1783.
Sponsors: Joh. Friess and wife (name not given).

Mar. Juliana, of Joh. Jacob Gauer and Elisab., b. 29 Oct 1783, bapt. 9 Nov 1783.
Sponsors: Jacob Jung and wife Maria Juliana.

Hanna, of Georg Seckel and Rebecca, b. 3 Oct 1783, bapt. 9 Nov 1783.
Sponsors: the parents.

Polly, of Peter Heston and Elisab., b. 17 Aug 1783, bapt. 11 Nov 1783.
Sponsors: the mother, and Susanna Jordan.

Polly, of Georg Adam Hellermann and Charlotta, b. 1 May 1783, bapt. 12 Nov
1783. Sponsor: the mother.

Joh. Mart., of Georg Schneider and Margareta, b. 9 Nov 1783, bapt. 13 Nov
1783. Sponsors: Martin Genzel and wife Margar.

Joh. Mich., of Mich. Immel and Catharina, b. 1 Nov 1783, bapt. 12 Nov 1783.
Sponsors: Joh. Thomas Fischer and wife Elisab.

Georg, of Joh. Schneider and Margaret, b. 20 Oct 1783, bapt. 16 Nov 1783.
Sponsors: Joh. Lehr and wife Catharina.

Maria, of Heinr. Brosius and Catharina, b. 26 Aug 1783, bapt. 15 Nov 1783.
Sponsor: the mother.

Elisab., of Peter Lohra and Maria, b. 19 Oct 1783, bapt. 16 Nov 1783.
Sponsors: Phil. Clamberg and dau. Elisab.

Catharina, of Michael Hains and Cath., b. 23 Oct 1783, bapt. 16 Nov 1783.
Sponsors: Valentin Klayus? and wife Mar. Margar.

Elisabeth, of Heinr. Spiel and Barbara, b. 14 Nov 1783, bapt. 22 Nov 1783.
Sponsors: Fridr. Froele and wife Catharina.

Georg Wilh., of Jacob Friderici and Anna, b. 3 Nov 1783, bapt. 22 Nov 1783.
Sponsors: Wilh. Hefft and wife Maria Cathar.

Jacob, of Jacob Steinmayer and Catharina, b. 11 Nov 1783, bapt. 23 Nov 1783.
Sponsors: Caspar Wahl and wife Elisab.

Samuel, of Joh. Georg Kieffer and Dorothea, b. 4 Nov 1783, bapt. 22 Nov 1783.
Sponsors: Georg Kieffer and wife Maria.

Jacob, of Heinrich Krammel and Sophia, b. 10 Oct 1783, bapt. 28 Nov 1783.
Sponsors: Jacob Sailer and wife Anna Maria.

Georg Fridr., of Carl Schmidt and Sophia, b. 11 Nov 1783, bapt. 30 Nov 1783.
Sponsors: Fridr. Schaumkessel and wife Elisab.

Elisab., of Georg Schneider and Maria, b. 12 Nov 1783, bapt. 30 Nov 1783.
Sponsors: Joh. Brown and wife Maria.

Peter, of Joh. Flory and Elisab., b. 20 Oct 1783, bapt. 2 Dec 1783. Sponsors: the
parents.

Margar., of James Densham and Sarah, b. 27 Oct 1783, bapt. 5 Dec 1783.
Sponsors: Christian Fleisch and Marg. Abel?.

Daniel, of Joh. Engelh. Haussmann and Charity, b. 29 Aug 1783, bapt. 7 Dec
1783. Sponsors: Fridr. Kochendoerffer and wife Rahel.

Joh. Mich., of Heinr. Allen and Eva, b. 6 Nov 1783, bapt. 7 Dec 1783.
Sponsors: Georg Jacob Haussmann and wife Mar. Apoll[onia].

Cathar., of Adam Handel and Hanna, b. 21 Nov 1783, bapt. 9 Dec 1783.
Sponsors: Heinr. Mayer and wife Catharina.

Simon, of Joh. Mart. Reinhard and Anna, b. 21 Aug 1783, bapt. 14 Dec 1783.
Sponsors: Simon Brunner and wife Anna Dorothea.

Anna, of Simon Brunner and Anna Dorothea, b. 22 Nov 1783, bapt. 14 Dec
1783. Sponsors: Joh. Mart. Reinhard and wife Anna.

Mathias, of Mathias Gilbert and Christina, b. 23 Nov 1783, bapt. 14 Dec 1783.
Sponsors: Mich. Hartmann and wife Sarah.

Margareta, of Jeremias Steelmann and Rosina, b. in Dec 1773, bapt. 14 Dec
1783. Sponsors: Nicol. Rehb and wife Christina.

Charlotta, of Jeremias Steelmann and Rosina, b. 5 Dec 1776, bapt. 14 Dec 1783.
Sponsors: Jacob Henrigel and wife Catharina.

Anna Elisab., of Heinr. Lüpke and Anna Maria, b. 1 Nov 1783, bapt. 15 Dec
1783. Sponsors: the parents.

Georg, of Jacob Ochs and Barbara, b. 25 Nov 1783, bapt. 17 Dec 1782.
Sponsors: Joh. Georg Schacka and Marg. Mer[t]z(in).

Lydia, of Jacob Rohn and Lydia, b. 29 Mar 1783, bapt. 18 Dec 1783. Sponsors:
the father, and Magdalena Rohn(in).

Thomas, of George Whig_ and Maria, b. 15 Dec 1783, bapt. 18 Dec 1783.
Sponsors: the mother, and Thomas Quail.

Polly, of Fridr. Anthony and Susanna, b. 5 Dec 1783, bapt. 21 Dec 1783.
Sponsors: the parents.

Catharina, of Georg Bressler and Catharina, b. 9 Nov 1783, bapt. 21 Dec 1783.
Sponsors: Georg Koch and wife Catharina.

Catharina, of Ludwig Wolff and Maria, b. 28 Nov 1783, bapt. 22 Dec 1783.
Sponsor: Christina Schlater.

Susan. Elis., of Joh. Georg Hess and Margareta, b. 7 Dec 1783, bapt. 25 Dec 1783. Sponsors: Susanna Elis. Euler(in).

Joh. Georg, of Joh. Simon and wife Anna Cath., b. 14 Nov 1783, bapt. 25 Dec 1783. Sponsors: Joh. Krause and wife Anna Cath.

Elisab., of Carl Truckenmüller and Anna, b. 15 Nov 1783, bapt. 25 Dec 1783. Sponsors: Joh. Hay and Elisab. Hay.

Martin, of Martin Boreff and Catharina, b. 19 Nov 1783, bapt. 28 Dec 1783. Sponsors: Valentin Riess and wife Susanna.

Anna Mar., of Georg Sonneleiter and Catharina, b. 2 Nov 1783, bapt. 30 Dec 1783. Sponsors: the father, and the grandmother (name not given).

Elisabeth, of Jacob Walter and Helena, b. 1 Nov 1783, bapt. 30 Dec 1783. Sponsors: the parents.

Elisabeth, of Benomy Bates and Sophia, b. 20 Nov 1783, bapt. 30 Dec 1783. Sponsors: Joh. Georg Käse and wife Elisabeth.

1784, First List
(baptisms by pastor Kunze, from Book III)

Sarah, of Johannes Fromberger and Anna, b. 4 Nov 1783, bapt. 4 Jan 1784. Sponsors: Nicol. Weber and wife An. Magd.

Dorothea, of Georg Krebs and Dorothea, b. 27 Dec 1783, bapt. 3 Jan 1784. Sponsors: Georg Gro[t]z and wife Marg. Dor.

Maria Christina, of Emannuel Jacob Alborn and Elisabet, b. 25 Sep 1783, bapt. 3 Jan 1784. Sponsors: the parents.

Johannes, of Johann Krause and Nancy, b. 28 Dec 1783, bapt. 9 Jan 1784. Sponsors: Johann Linnemann and wife (name not given).

Joh. Michael, of Peter Die[t]z and Anna Maria, b. 3 Jan 1784, bapt. 25 Jan 1784. Sponsors: Johann Michael Goe[t]z and wife Eva Barbara.

Maria, of Georg Dreier and Sara, b. 7 Jan 1784, bapt. 25 Jan 1784. Sponsors: Philipp Kraft and wife Mar.

Philipp, of Friedr. Jeremias and Magdalena, b. 17 Sep 1783, bapt. 25 Jan 1784. Sponsors: Phil. Rot(h) and wife Maria.

Georg, of Stephan Sulger and Hanna, b. 25 Jan 1784, bapt. 25 Jan 1784. Sponsors: Georg Mirkel and wife Magdal.

Anna Catharina, of Georg Stauss and Esther, b. 24 Jan 1784, bapt. 1 Feb 1784. Sponsors: Paul Cober and wife Barb.

Samuel, of Samuel Hempel and Catharina, b. 3 Jan 1784, bapt. 1 Feb 1784. Sponsors: the parents.

Georg, of Jacob Fiedler and Margareta, b. 17 Sep 1773, bapt. 4 Feb 1784. Sponsors: Georg Fiedler and wife Elisab.

Johannes, of Johann Georg Schmidt and Eva, b. 12 Jan 1784, bapt. 8 Feb 1784. Sponsors: Jacob Schmidt and wife Margareta.

Anna Margareta, of Carl Schmidt and Catharina, b. 28 Jan 1784, bapt. 13 Feb 1784. Sponsors: Johann Elliot and wife Anna Margareta.

Augusta Henrietta, of Ludewig Weiss and Christina Elisab., b. 22 Jan 1784, bapt. 15 Feb 1784. Sponsors: August Will and wife Nanette Elisab.

Catharina, of Henrich Nagel and Barbara, b. 5 Feb 1784, bapt. 15 Feb 1784. Sponsors: Johannes Nagel and wife Elisab.

Maria Elisabet, of Johannes Lengfelder and Catharina, b. 22 Dec 1783, bapt. 19 Feb 1784. Sponsors: Johann Lechend? and Elisab. Meier(in).

Anna, of Henrich Poecle and Elisabeth, b. 25 Jan 1784, bapt. 19 Feb 1784. Sponsors: the parents.

Maria, of Wilhelm Lehmann and Elisabet, b. 13 Feb 1784, bapt. 22 Feb 1784. Sponsors: Melchior Steiner and Mariana Steiner.

Catharina, of Johannes Emmerich and Maria, b. 23 Jan 1784, bapt. 22 Feb 1784. Sponsors: the father, and Magdal. Steinme[t]z(in).

Ge[org] Friedrich, of Georg Friedrich Linck and Jud. Elisabet, b. 27 Feb 1784, bapt. 24 Feb 1784. Sponsors: the parents.

Anna Maria, of Jacob Hirneissen and Anna Maria, b. 1 Mar 1784, bapt. 4 Mar 1784. Sponsors: Andreas Bertsch and wife Anna Maria.

Catharina, of Georg Vogel and Elisabeth, b. 18 Feb 1784, bapt. 7 Mar 1784. Sponsors: Jacob Keimle and wife Cath.

Johann Samuel, of Michael Gilbert and Anna, b. 13 Feb 1784, bapt. 7 Mar 1784. Sponsors: Johann Henr. Gilbert and wife Cathar.

Elisabet, of Balthasar Graf and Catharina, b. 2 Mar 1784, bapt. 14 Mar 1784. Sponsors: Georg Senf and wife Charlotte.

Eva Elisab., of Michael Bartholome and Maria Cathar., b. 22 Feb 1784, bapt. 21 Mar 1784. Sponsors: Johann Rugam and wife Elisab.

Josua, of Johannes Preuss and Maria Cath., b. 25 Feb 1784, bapt. 1 Mar 1784. Sponsors: Georg Kiefer and wife Eva Mar.

Juliana [twin], of Christian Statemar and Susanna, b. 13 Feb 1784, bapt. 21 Mar 1784. Sponsors: Conrad Hinkel and wife Barbara.

Barbara [twin], of Christian Statemar and Susanna, b. 13 Feb 1784, bapt. 21 Mar 1784. Sponsors: Lud. Schaefer and wife Juliana.

Maria Margareta, of Melchior Ki[t]z and Margareta, b. 4 Mar 1784, bapt. 21 Mar 1784. Sponsor: Apollonia Ki[t]z(in).

Margareta, of Peter Arnold and Maria, b. 11 Oct 1773, bapt. 24 Mar 1784. Sponsors: Ludwig Knauer and wife Margareta.

Henrich, of Henrich Moser and Susanna, b. 6 Mar 1784, bapt. 28 Mar 1784. Sponsors: Georg Blum and wife Philippina.

Anna Maria, of Andreas Eisenhut and Anna Maria, b. 30 Jan 1784, bapt. 28 Mar 1784. Sponsors: the parents.

Georg, of Carl Kugler and Catharina, b. 17 Dec 1783, bapt. 28 Mar 1784. Sponsors: Georg Bisbin and wife Elisab.

Peter, of Georg Kinzinger and Catharina, b. 9 Mar 1784, bapt. 4 Apr 1784. Sponsors: Magdalena Ulmann and David Schnek.

Elisabet, of Johann Jacob Durr and Elisabet, b. 31 Mar 1784, bapt. 9 Apr 1784. Sponsors: Georg Vogel and wife Elisab.

Andreas, of David Flickwier and Sophia, b. 8 Jan 1784, bapt. 11 Apr 1784. Sponsor: Andreas Meier.

Johannes, of Johann Straub and Margareta, b. 31 Mar 1784, bapt. 12 Apr 1784. Sponsors: the parents.

Anna Maria, of Thomas Gerum and Elisabet, b. 30 Mar 1784, bapt. 18 Apr 1784. Sponsors: Johann Rebschneider and wife Anna Maria.

Georg Ludwig, of Johannas Reisser and Magdalena, b. 8 Mar 1784, bapt. 18 Apr 1784. Sponsors: Johannes Kampfer and wife Elisabet.

Johann Georg, of Johann Hans and Eva Elisabet, b. 7 Apr 1784, bapt. 18 Apr
1784. Sponsor: Elisabet Hollweg(in).
Wilhelm, of Christian Fuchs and Dorothea, b. 12 Mar 1784, bapt. 29 Apr 1784.
Sponsors: the parents.
Johannes, of Marcus Ring and Elisabet, b. 15 Mar 1784, bapt. 2 May 1784.
Sponsors: Johann Heil and wife Maria.
Maria Elisabet, of Jacob Kemper and Catharina, b. 8 Feb 1784, bapt. 2 May
1784. Sponsors: Catharina Riddel(sin) and Mr. Joh. Ahardt?.
Maria Margareta, of Christian Miller and Maria Catharina, b. 13 Sep 1783, bapt.
9 May 1784. Sponsors: Johann Henrich Fischer and wife Margareta.
Maria Catharina, of Johannes Nagel and Magdalena Elisab., b. 10 May 1784,
bapt. 20 May 1784. Sponsors: Johannes Spiegel and wife Maria Catharina.
Anthony, of Johann Jacob Wisser and Susanna, b. 26 Feb 1784, bapt. 20 May
1784. Sponsors: Alexander Bärrey? and wife Jeanne.
Anna, of Conrad Harf and Anna, b. 29 Jan 1784, bapt. 20 May 1784. Sponsors:
the parents.
Christian, of Christian Kinzel and Margareta, b. 18 May 1784, bapt. 30 May
1784. Sponsors: the parents, and Catharina He___.
Adam, of Adam Erben and Margareta, b. 18 May 1784, bapt. 30 May 1784.
Sponsors: the parents.
Leonhard [twin], of Leonard Jacobi and Margareta, b. 10 May 1784, bapt.
30 May 1784. Sponsors: the parents
Johann Christoph [twin], of Leonard Jacobi and Margareta, b. 10 May 1784,
bapt. 30 May 1784. Sponsor: Georg Heppele.
Johannes Love, of unknown parents, b. in Feb 1784, bapt. 11 Jun 1784.
Sponsors: Johannes Elgart and wife Anna Marg.
Anna Catharine, of Philipp Werner and Anna Magdalena, b. 11 May 1784, bapt.
12 Jun 1784. Sponsors: Adam Lap and wife Anna Cath.
Elisabet, of Martin Will and Elisab., b. 3 Jun 1784, bapt. 12 Jun 1784.
Sponsors: Eva Held(in) and Valentin Boyer.
Georg, of Nicolaus Quast and Maria, b. 2 Jun 1784, bapt. 20 Jun 1784.
Sponsors: the parents.
Regina, of Jacob Kaufmann and Margareta, b. 2 Jun 1784, bapt. 20 Jun 1784.
Sponsors: the parents.
Heinrich, of Georg Schae[t]zlein and Veronica, b. 11 May 1784, bapt. 27 Jun
1784. Sponsors: the parents.
Elisabet, of Benjamin Smith and Mary, b. 14 Mar 1784, bapt. 27 Jun 1784.
Sponsors: Georg Smith and Elisabeth Schmidt(in).
Johann, of Conrad Ort and Catharina, b. in 1784, bapt. 27 Jun 1784. Sponsor:
Johann Silver.
Johannes, of Johann Thomas Fischer and Elisabet, b. 6 May 1784, bapt. 6 May
1784. Sponsors: Michael Immel and wife Catharina.
Regina, of Peter Kraft and Margareta, b. 20 Jun 1784, bapt. 1 Jul 1784.
Sponsors: Jacob Keimle and wife Anna?.
Charlotte Philippina, of Jacob Graff and Sophia, b. 18 Jun 1784, bapt. 4 Jul
1784. Sponsors: Georg Senf and wife Charlotte.
Margareta, of Christian Wilke and Rosina, b. 22 Jun 1784, bapt. 4 Jul 1784.
Sponsors: the parents.

Johanna Maria, of Michael Kraft and Johanna Maria, b.   June 1784, bapt. 8? Jul
    1784.   Sponsors: Georg Oesterle and Elisabet Kirst(in)?.
Johann Carl, of Friedrich Jacob Rap and Elisabeth, b. 27 Jan 1784, bapt. 10 Jul
    1784.   Sponsors: the parents, in place of Johannes Rap [who resides] at
    erlenheim in Alsace.
Carl, of Philipp Werner and Maria Magdalena, b. 3 Mar 1784, bapt. 10 Jul 1784.
    (Sponsors not given.)
Isaac, of Christian Rediger and Catharina, b. 19 Jun 1784, bapt. 8 Jul 1784.
    Sponsors: the parents.
Georg, of Henrich Knerr and Elisabet, b. 24 Jun 1784, bapt. 11 Jul 1784.
    Sponsors: the parents.
Maria Catharina, of Georg We[i]chert and Catharina, b. 26 Jun 1784, bapt.
    11 Jul 1784. Sponsors: Reinhardt Kammerer and wife Maria.
Johannes, of Johannes Heide and Martha, b. 26 Mar 1784, bapt. 18 Jul 1784.
    Sponsors: the parents.
Georg, of Michael Bauer and Christina, b. 6 Mar 1784, bapt. 18 Jul 1784.
    Sponsors: Georg Henr. Dehn and wife Mar. Marg.
Elisabet, of Joseph Jew and Maria, b. 1 Apr 1784, bapt. 19 Jul 1784. Sponsors:
    the grandmother Maria Barbara Weber(in).
Jonathan, of Jonathan Stanton and Gemi[m]a, b. 9 Mar 1784, bapt. 23 Jul? 1784.
    Sponsors: Georg Jessro and Elisabeth.
Michael, of Johann Andreas Weber and Phoebe, b. 15 Apr 1784, bapt. 18 Jul
    1784. Sponsors: the parents.
At this time pastor Kunze went to New York

1784, Second List
(baptisms by pastor Helmuth, from Book IV)
Samuel, of Peter Gabel and wife Elisabeth, b. 9 Dec 1783, bapt. 1 Jan 1784.
    Sponsors: the parents.
Catharina, of Elisabeth Schmidt and reportedly "W.", b. 13 Dec 1783, bapt.
    4 Jan 1784. Sponsors: Adam Mussky and wife Catharina.
Anna Barbara, of Michael Schenneck and wife Anna Catharina, b. 17 Dec 1783,
    bapt. 4 Jan 1784. Sponsors: Adam Hold and wife Maria Christina.
Catharina, of Andreas Peyer and wife Barbara, b. 14 Dec 1783, bapt. 4 Jan 1784.
    Sponsors: Andreas Bosshard and wife Christina Catharina.
Maria Margareta, of Peter Nicholson and wife Esther, b. 4 Jan 1784, bapt. 7 Jan
    1784. Sponsor: Maria Margareta Wester(in).
Magdalena, of Conrad Bernhard and wife Barbara, b. 8 Jan 1784, bapt. 18 Jan
    1784. Sponsors: Johannes Sonnleiter and wife Maria.
Christoph Eberhard, of Jacob Klohs and wife Anna Margareta, b.7 Nov 1783,
    bapt. 17 Jan 1784. Sponsors: Wilhelm Facundus and wife Dorothea.
Anna Maria, of Valentin Unbehend and wife Sophia, b. 12 Jan 1784, bapt.
    18 Jan 1784. Sponsors: Johann Lorenz and wife Catharina.
Elisabeth, of Andreas Walker and wife Maria, b. 31 Oct 1783, bapt. 18 Jan
    1784. Sponsors: the parents.
Johann Peter, of Peter Jung and wife Maria Magdalena, b. 30 Dec 1783, bapt.
    21 Jan 1784. Sponsors: Conrad Scheller and wife Elisabeth.

Friedrich, of Friedr. Fischer and wife Nancy, b. 17 Jan 1784, bapt.1 Jan 1784. Sponsors: Friedrich Zent and wife Barbara.

Andreas, of Georg Haffner and wife Magdalena, b. 27 Dec 1783, bapt. 22 Jan 1784. Sponsors: Georg Haffner and wife Christina.

Nicolaus, of Nicolaus Doebler and wife Catharina, b. 18 Jan 1784, bapt. 22 Jan 1784. Sponsors: the parents.

Enoch Frey, of Enoch Bagley and wife Dorothea, b. 4 Jan 1784, bapt. 24 Jan 1784. Sponsor: the mother.

Joseph, of Caspar Seybert and wife Elisabeth, b. 24 Dec 1783, bapt. 25 Jan 1784. Sponsors: the parents.

Anna Maria, of Jacob Ehwald and wife Jane, b. 12 Jan 1784, bapt. 25 Jan 1784. Sponsors: Adam Rex and Anna Maria Still(in).

Margareta Eva, of Johann Nick and wife Regina, b. 16 Dec 1783, bapt. 25 Jan 1784. Sponsors: Johann Besserer and wife Eva.

Maria Magdalena, of Georg Quinop and wife Christina, b. 14 Dec 1783, bapt. 25 Jan 1784. Sponsors: Jacob Rohn and his mother Magdalena.

Johann, of Friedrich Yesch and wife Catharina, b. 1 Jan 1784, bapt. 2 Feb 1784. Sponsors: Johann Lehr and wife Catharina.

Johann Conrad, of Conrad Hester and wife Eleonora Catharina, b. 13 Jan 1784, bapt. 2 Feb 1784. Sponsors: Johann Kunkel and wife Maria Christina.

Friedrich, of Nicolaus Senderling and wife Rosina, b. 21 Jan 1784, bapt. 1 Feb 1784. Sponsors: Gottfried Kühner and wife Elisabeth.

Catharina, of Anthon Kern and wife Catharina, b. 5 Jan 1784, bapt. 1 Feb 1784. Sponsors: the parents.

Caspar, of Adam Jaeger and wife Veronica, b. 2 Feb 1784, bapt. the same day. Sponsors: the parents.

Elisabeth, of Jacob Walther and wife Helena, b. 6 Dec 1783, bapt. 8 Feb 1784 Sponsors: Georg Hauser and wife Elisabeth.

Christian, of Christian Gasner and wife Magdalena, b. 24 Dec 1783, bapt. 15 Feb 1784. Sponsors: Phil. Jung and wife Elisabeth.

Dorothea (twin), of Johann Freymuth and wife Elisabeth, b. 8 Feb 1784, 15 Feb 1784. Sponsors: Johann Braun and wife Catharina.

Benjamin Erdmann (twin), of Johann Freymuth and wife Elisabeth, b. 8 Feb 1784, 15 Feb 1784. Sponsors: Jacob Meyer and wife Susanna.

Elisabeth, of Anna Catharina Schreiber and reportedly Daniel Woelker, b. 6 Feb 1784, bapt. 16 Feb 1784. Sponsor: Maria Catharina Fleider(in).

Philipp, of Christian Lutz and wife Susanna, b. 23 Jan 1784, bapt 18 Feb 1784. Sponsors: Philipp Pfannekuch and wife Catharina.

Maria, of Balthasar Emmerig and wife Anna Maria, b. 1 Feb 1784, bapt. 22 Feb 1784. Sponsors: the father, and Catharina Lasky.

Michael, of Michael Schmidt and wife Maria, b. 7 Feb 1784, bapt. 22 Feb 1784. Sponsors: the parents.

Barbara,of Adam Hoffmann and wife Susanna, b. 6 Feb 1784, bapt 22 Feb 1784. Sponsors: Daniel Barkhard and wife Catharina.

Sophia, of Leonhard Haah? and wife Catharina, b. 8 Jan 1784, bapt. 22 Feb 1784. Sponsors: the parents.

Thomas of Friedr. Heimberger and wife Maria, b. 5 Feb 1784, bapt. 22 Feb 1784. Sponsors: Thomas Heimberger and wife Margareta.

Elisabeth, of Georg Gatlinger and wife Maria Christina, b. 7 Jan 1784, bapt. 22 Feb 1784. Sponsors: Heinrich Moser and Margar. Elisabeth Christ.

Elisabeth, of Ludwig Parlinger and wife Maria Catharina, b. 23 Jan 1784, bapt. 22 Feb 1784. Sponsors: Heinrich Moser and wife Christina.

Heinrich of Catharina Rawahness (father's name not given), b. 26 Dec 1783, bapt. 22 Feb 1784. Sponsors: Margareta Elisabeth Christ and Heinrich Moser.

Margareta, of Christian Schoen and wife Margareta, b. 30 Jan 1783, bapt. 23 Feb 1784. Sponsor: Margareta Schoen.

Johann Peter, of Johann Kanty and wife Maria, b. 16 Sep 1783, bapt. 29 Feb 1784. Sponsors: Christoph Peter Bensel and wife Anna Christina.

Anna Catharina, of Carl Miller and wife Anna Barbara, b. 20 Feb 1784, bapt. 29 Feb 1784. Sponsors: Johann Commil? and wife Anna Catharina.

Anna Maria, of Carl Black and wife Nancy, b. 10 Jan 1784, bapt. 29 Feb 1784. Sponsors: Martin Barry and wife Sophia.

Johann, of Johann Pfeil and wife Philippina, b. 13 Feb 1784, bapt. 6 Mar 1784. Sponsors: Jacob Christler and Philippina Christler.

Elisabeth, of James Christie and wife Elisabeth, b. 27 Feb 1784, bapt. 6 Mar 1784. Sponsor: Elisabeth Later(in).

Mathias, of Johann Weickard and wife Anna Maria, b. 29 Feb 1784, bapt. 6 Mar 1784. Sponsors: Mathias Craemer and wife Susanna.

Catharina, of Philipp Schroeder and wife Catharina, b. 27 Jan 1784, bapt. 6 Mar 1784. Sponsor: Magdalena Rohn.

Johann, of Johann Neu and wife Elisabeth, b. 6 Mar 1784, bapt. 14 Mar 1784. Sponsors: Johann Leonhard and wife Catharina.

Friedrich, of Philipp Werner and wife Magdalena, b. 17 Feb 1784, bapt. 14 Mar 1784. Sponsors: Carl Johst and wife Christina.

Catharina, of Johann Hook and wife Elisabeth, b. 8 Feb 1784, bapt. 14 Mar 1784. Sponsors: Johann Linker and wife Catharina.

Maria, of Georg Stephans and wife Margareta, b. 24 Oct 1783, bapt. 17 Mar 1784. Sponsors: Georg Albert and wife Maria.

Adam of Georg Moser and wife Hanna, b. 14 Mar 1784, bapt. 17 Mar 1784. Sponsors: Adam Strieby and [wife] Anna Maria.

Johann Philipp, of Philipp Krebs and wife Anna Margareta, b. 25 Feb 1784, bapt. 27 Mar 1784. Sponsors: Johann Kunkel and wife Maria Clara.

Jane, of James Martin and wife Nancy, b. 1 Mar 1784, bapt. 22 Mar 1784. Sponsor: Elisabeth Catharina Wully.

Jonathan, of Jonathan Stanton and wife Mima, b. 10 Mar 1784, bapt 24 Mar 1784. Sponsors: Georg Jessro and wife Elisabeth.

Elisabeth, of Peter Neu and wife Maria, b. 17 Mar 1784, bapt. 27 Mar 1784. Sponsors: Johann Neu and wife Elisabeth.

Samuel, of Marin Roner and wife Sophia, b. 13 Mar 1784, bapt. 28 Mar 1784. Sponsors: Georg Haussman and Barbara Rohner.

Margareta, of Jeremias Wahrlich and wife Elisabeth, b. 11 Feb 1784, bapt. 30 Mar 1884. Sponsors: Georg Hess and wife Margareta.

Elisabeth, of Johann Starke and wife Catharina, b. 27 Mar 1784, bapt. 2 Apr 1784. Sponsors: Philipp Pfannekuch and wife Catharina.

Maria, of Johann Becker and wife Elisabeth Margareta, b. 29 Feb 1784, bapt
4 Apr 1784. Sponsors: James Becker and Maria Rohner.
*(Note: in the original, pastor Schmidt's list of 53 baptisms in 1785 is inserted
here; see 1785 Second List, below.) Pastor Helmuth's baptisms in 1784 then
continue, as follows:*
Maria Margareta, of Friedr. Sebastian. Mercker and wife Elis. Charlotta, b.
8 Feb 1784, bapt. 4 Apr 1784. Sponsors: Balthasar Künzler and wife Maria
Elisabeth.
Georg Leonhard, of Georg Dollmann and wife Polly, b. 3 Dec 1782, bapt. 4 Apr
1784. Sponsors: Georg Leonhard Huber and wife Anna Lowisa.
Joseph, of David Deiber and wife Hanna, b. 25 Mar 1767, bapt and confirmed
7 Apr 1784.
Hanna Hei[t]zin, of Abraham Carpenter and wife Sarah, b. 21 Apr 1757, bapt.
and confirmed 7 Apr 1784.
Johann Abraham, of Georg Weiss and wife Susanna, b. 4 Mar 1784, bapt. 9 Apr
1784. Sponsors: Abraham Rex and wife Nancy.
Joh. Heinrich, of Johann Christoph Rohn and wife Cathar., b. 9 Mar 1784, bapt.
11 Apr 1784. Sponsors: Johann Lauder and wife Catharina.
Margareta, of Bernhard Buck and wife Maria, b. 16 Mar 1784, bapt. 11 Apr
1784. Sponsors: Alexander Benson and wife Margareta.
Anna Maria, of Daniel Knodel and wife Anna Maria, b. 25 Feb 1784, bapt.
11 Apr 1784. Sponsors: Johann Schaeffer and wife Maria Sophia.
Margareta, of Daniel Braeudigam and wife Margareta, b. 18 Mar 1784, bapt.
12 Apr 1784. Sponsors: Andreas Pfiller and wife Margareta.
Samuel Andreas, of Peter Burckhard and wife Elisabeth, b. 23 Oct 1783, bapt.
12 Apr 1784. Sponsors: Andreas Beck and wife Barbara.
Barbara, of Georg Bauer and wife Catharina, b. 4 Mar 1784, bapt. 12 Apr 1784.
Sponsors: Joseph Herlemann and Sophia Küntseh(in).
Catharina, of Christian Beck and wife Elisabeth, b. 9 Mar 1784, bapt. 12 Apr
1784. Sponsors: Adolph Dill and wife Catharina.
Johann James, of Jacob Leimenzetter and wife Christina, b. 10 Jun 1783, bapt.
12 Apr 1784. Sponsors: James Wallace and wife Elisabeth.
Johann Wilhelm, of Philipp Meger and wife Maria Salome, b. 22 Mar 1784,
bapt. 12 Apr 1784. Sponsors: Johann Wilhelm Hef(f)t and wife Mar.
Catharina.
Anna Catharina, of Henrich Diel and wife Margareta, b. 5 Mar 1784, bapt.
12 Apr 1784. Sponsors: the parents.
Maria, of Martin Rebley and wife Clara, b. 3 Apr 1784, bapt. 12 Apr 1784.
Sponsors: the parents.
Johann, of John Rosck and wife Catharina,, b. 29 Feb 1784, bapt. 18 Apr 1784.
Sponsors:Thomas Fischer and wife Elisabeth.
Johann, of Georg Dorn and wife Christina, b. 10 Mar 1784, bapt. 18 Apr 1784.
Sponsors: the parents.
Elisabeth, of Heinrich Mayer and wife Maria, b. 24 Oct 1783, bapt. 19 Apr
1784. Sponsors: the parents.
Johann Martin, of Philipp Pfleger and wife Wilhelmina, b. 4 Apr 1784, bapt.
2 Apr 1784. Sponsors: Martin Weiland and wife (name not given).

Michael, of Christoph Hartranft and wife Elisabeth, b. 2 Mar 1784, bapt. 25 Apr 1784. Sponsors: Michael Rebly and wife Margareta.

Jacob, of Thomas Grün and wife Catharina, b. 21 Mar 1784, bapt. 25 Apr 1784. Sponsor: the mother.

Catharina (twin), of Ludwig Koehl and wife Elisabeth, b. 20 Apr 1784, bapt. 27 Apr 1784. Sponsors: Jacob Koehl and wife Christina.

Maria, (twin), of Ludwig Koehl and wife Elisabeth, b. 20 Apr 1784, bapt. 27 Apr 1784. Sponsors: Jeremia Koehl and Elisabeth Faehry.

Benjamin, of Jacob Seyfried and wife Salome, b. 16 Apr 1784, bapt. 27 Apr 1784. Sponsors: the parents.

Maria Elisabeth.of Martin Ritzenthaler and wife Dorothea, b. 26 Apr 1784, bapt. 30 Apr 1784. Sponsors: Joh. Jacob Blocher and wife Elisabeth.

Lydia, of Johann Kuchler and wife Maria, b. 20 Mar 1784, bapt. 2 May 1784. Sponsors: the parents.

Maria Elisabeth, of Fridr. Burckhard and wife Maria, b. 25 Apr 1784, bapt. 1 May 1784. Sponsors: Johann Kayser and wife Elisab.

Polly, of Jacob Frey and wife Margareta, b. 9 Dec 1783, bapt. 2 May 1784. Sponsors: the parents.

Johann Hartmann, of Johann Kreiner and wife Margareta, b. 26 Mar 1784, bapt. 2 May 1784. Sponsors: the parents.

Catharina, of Johann Kribbel and wife Christina, b. 7 Apr 1784, bapt. 2 May 1784. Sponsors: Christian Kempf and wife Maria.

(In a special baptism entered on the first page of Vol. 4): Carl Fridrich Wilhelm, son of the prince's lord high steward Wilhelm Carl vonZiegesar and wife Caroline Henriette Maria Sophia née Holzhausen, b. 1 May 1779, bapt. 2 May 1784. Sponsors present: the ruling prince his serene highness Durlaucht of Nassau-Usinger; lord tutor Oberhorstmeister of Hayn; and sovereign professor vonGünderade of Wiesbaden. Sponsors in absentia: the inheritor prince of Darmstadt-Durch....; Prince Georg of Darmstadt-D....; widowed countess Guntersblum of Leiningen; countess Harange Busch; etc.

Maria Sabina, of Peter Kuhn and wife Elisabeth, b. 5 Apr 1784, bapt. 4 May 1784. Sponsors: the parents.

Andreas, of John Heitel and wife Elisabeth, b. 26 Apr 1784, bapt. 8 May 1784. Sponsors: Andreas Kirchner and wife Anna Friderica

Elisabeth, of Johann Feldenberger and wife Magdalena, b. 24 Apr 1784, bapt. 9 May 1784. Sponsors: Rudolph Nagel and wife Susanna.

Johann, of Howard Night and wife Elisabeth, b. 21 Dec 1783, bapt. 13 May 1784. Sponsor: Elisabeth Mills.

Elisabeth, of Daniel Kappel and wife Catharina, b. 18 Apr 1784, bapt. 16 May 1784. Sponsors: Joh. Spols and wife Elisabeth.

Fridrich August, of Fridrich Bach and wife Margareta, b. 5 Oct 1783, bapt. 15 May 1784. Sponsors: Fridrich August Kaji.

Johann, of Georg Michael Heil and wife Maria Catharina, b. 10 May 1784, bapt. 15 May 1784. Sponsors: the parents.

Philipp, of Philipp Dressler and wife Maria, b. 2 May 1784, bapt. 15 May 1784. Sponsors: the father, and Elisabeth Rummel?.

Salome, of Dennys Delany and wife Barbara, b. 2 May 1784, bapt. 16 May 1784. Sponsor: Jacobina Grob(in).

Elisabeth, of Johann Weber and wife Maria, b. 2 May 1784, bapt. 16 May 1784. Sponsors: Georg Stoy? and wife Barbara.

Johann Adam, of Christoph Bastian and wife Cathar., b 6 May 1784, bapt. 23 May 1784. Sponsors: Joh. Adam Kerchner and Anna Eva Bastian.

Johann Georg, of Joh. Haertlein and wife Gertraut, b. 28 Apr 1784, bapt. 23 May 1784. Sponsors: Georg Rommel and wife Elisab.

Johann Carl, of Franz Martin and wife Elisabeth, b. 8 Jan 1784, bapt. 23 May 1784. Sponsor: Dorothea Bauer(in).

Anna Catharina, of Johann Kittler and wife Susanna, b. 15 May 1784, bapt. 24 May 1784. Sponsors: Carl Miller and wife Barbara.

Johann (twin), of Michael Rebly and wife Margar., b. 19 May 1784, bapt. 22 May 1784. Sponsors: the parents.

Elisabeth, (twin), of Michael Rebly and wife Margar., b. 19 May 1784, bapt. 22 May 1784. Sponsors: Christoph Hartranft and wife Elisabeth.

A child (name not given), of Lorenz Seckel and wife (name not given), birthdate not given, bapt. 23 May 1784. (Sponsors not given.)

Catharina, of Johann Schae[t]zlein and wife Barbara, b. 20 Apr 1784 bapt. 30 May 1784. Sponsors: Bartholomae Schae[t]zlein and wife Catharina.

Johann, of Nicol. Krieger and wife Sophia, b. 13 May 1784, bapt. 30 May 1784. Sponsors: John Krieger and wife Catharina.

Anna Barbara, of Joh. Jacob Karg and wife Ottilia, b. 26 Apr 1784, bapt. 30 May 1784. Sponsors: Anthon Frey and wife (name not given).

Georg Fridrich, of Georg Bock and wife Magdalena,b. 13 May 1784, bapt. 30 May 1784. Sponsors: Georg Schaumkessel and wife Elisabeth.

Johann Georg, of Christian Schreiber and wife Magdalena, b. 23 Apr 1784, bapt. 30 May 1784. Sponsors: Johann Georg Spiel and wife Elisabeth.

Elisabeth, of Johann Gottschall and wife Maria, b. 7 May 1784 bapt. 30 May 1784. Sponsors: Georg Schively and wife Elisabeth.

Wilhelm, of Hugh Hughs and wife Christina, b. 23 Jan 1783, bapt. 30 May 1784. Sponsors: Jacob Christmann and wife Elisabeth.

Eleonora, of Hugh Hughs and wife Christina, b. 15 Sep 1780, bapt. 30 May 1784. Sponsor: Maria Horre(in).

Barbara, of Jacob Specht and wife Margareta, b. 15 Feb 1784, bapt. 30 May 1784. Sponsors: Barbara Kochendoerffer(in) and son Fridrich.

Maria Catharina, of Fridrich Habecker and wife Christina, b. 8 Oct 1780, bapt. 31 May 1784. Sponsors: Johann Veits and wife Catharina.

Anna Maria, of Joh. Christian Uhl and wife Isabella, b. 24 May 1784, bapt. 6 Jun 1784. Sponsors: Christian Uhl and wife Christiana Cathar.

Jacob, of Jacob Beidermann and wife Catharina, b. 14 May 1784, bapt. 30 May 1784. Sponsors: Jacob Hill and wife Anna Maria.

Susanna, of Georg Miltenberger and wife Catharina, b. 24 Apr 1784, bapt. 4 Jun 1784. Sponsors: the father, and Agatha Wolf(in).

Johann Fridrich, of Anthony Hecht and wife Sophia, b. 30 May 1784, bapt. 6 Jun 1784. Sponsors: the parents.

Johann Thomas, of Thomas Jon's [Jones] and wife Anna Maria, b. 12 Apr 1784, bapt. 6 Jun 1784. Sponsors: Johann Freyburg and wife Susanna.

Jacob, of Georg Hutz and wife Sarah, b. 3 Jun 1784, bapt. 27 Jun 1784. Sponsors: the father, and Margareta Schindler.

Sarah, of Adam Zantzinger and wife Susanna, b. 14 May 1784, bapt. 10 Jun 1784. Sponsor: Henry Keppele.

Johann, of Andreas Cressmann and wife Elisab., b. 11 May 1784, bapt. 14 Jun 1784. Sponsors: Johann Graeff and wife Magdalena.

Johann, of Adam Reininger and wife Susanna, b. 30 Apr 1784, bapt. 20 Jun 1784. Sponsors: Johann Lenemann and wife Margareta.

Elisabeth, of Isaac McKee and wife Eva, b. 3 Aug [1783], bapt. 22 Jun 1784. Sponsors: Wilhelm Brooks and wife Elisabeth.

Magdalena, of Gottlieb Mayer and wife Magdalena, b. 12 Jun 1784, bapt. 23 Jun 1784. Sponsors: Jacob Becker and wife Magdalena.

Jacob, of Michael Kinzler and wife Elisab., b. 9 Jun 1784, bapt. 27 Jun 1784. Sponsors: Jacob Ahner and Margareta Kinzler.

Michael, of Heinrich Homüller and wife Cathar., b. 4 Jun 1784, bapt. 27 Jun 1784. Sponsors: the parents.

Johann, of Alexander Benson and wife Margar., b. 13 Jun 1784, bapt. 27 Jun 1784. Sponsors: Bernhard Bock and wife Molly.

Anna Margareta, of Georg Herrmann and wife Elisabeth, b. 30 May 1784, bapt. 30 Jun 1784. Sponsors: the father, and Margareta Herrman.

John, of Robert Colliard and wife Elisabeth, b. 3 May 1784, bapt. 27 Jun 1784. Sponsor: the father.

Anna Maria (the names of the parents are not known; Gottfried Heinrich and wife Elisabeth are the child's foster parents), b. 17 Jan 1784, bapt. 29 Jun 1784. Sponsors: Gottfried Heinrich and wife Elisabeth.

Georg, of Georg Habacher and wife Maria, b. 4 Jun 1784, bapt. 9 Jun 1784. Sponsors: the parents.

Phillis, of Georg Loyd and wife Sylvia, b. 30 Jan 1784, bapt. 29 Jun 1784. Sponsor: Maria Dick.

Johann, of Georg Faster and wife Susanna Barb., b. 3 May 1784, bapt. 4 Jul 1784. Sponsors: the parents.

Anna Catharina, of Georg Fridr. Schaumkessel and wife Elisab., b. 17 Jun 1784, bapt. 4 Jul 1784. Sponsors: Fridr. Heinemann and wife Anna Catharina.

Elisabeth, of Jacob Jung and wife Elisabeth, b. 28 May 1784, bapt. 4 Jul 1784. Sponsors: Joh. Gawers and wife Elisab.

Maria Catharina, of Philipp Clamphord and wife Maria Catharina, b. 12 Jun 1784, bapt. 4 Jul 1784. Sponsors: Heinrich Schwalber and wife Maria Catharina.

Martin, of Fridr. Schick and wife Barbara, b. 27 Jun 1784, bapt. 11 Jul 1784. Sponsors: the parents.

Rebecca, of John Kramp and wife Dorothea, b. 1 Oct 1783, bapt. 11 Jun 1784. Sponsors: Valentin Beck and Maria Beck.

Maria, of William Rot(h) and wife Christina, b. 25 Jun 1784, bapt. 13 Jul 1784. Sponsors: Christoph Bochringer and wife Margareta.

Jacobus, of Fridrich Toblebauer and wife Catharina, b. 14 Apr 1784, bapt. 14 Jul 1784. Sponsors: the parents.

Sarah, of Peter Mayers and wife Maria, b. 13 Jul 1784, bapt. 15 Jul 1784. Sponsors: the parents.

Ludwig, of Carl Cist and wife Maria, b. in Jul 1784, bapt. 18 Jul 1784. Sponsors: Ludwig Weiss and wife (her name not given).

Sophia Elisabeth, of Joh. Nicol. Die[t]z and wife Cathar., b. 24 Jun 1784, bapt. 15 Jul 1784. Sponsors: David Flickweher and wife Anna Sophia.

Mathias, of Gerry Haal and wife Elisabeth, b. 7 May 1784, bapt. 16 Jul 1784. Sponsor: the mother.

Johann, of Michael Klein and wife Margar., b. 13 Jun 1784, bapt. 17 Jul 1784. Sponsor: Lydia Schweiger.

Catharina, of Jacob Schmidt and wife Polly, b. 11 Jul 1784, bapt. 18 Jul 1784. Sponsors: Christian Weils and wife Catharina.

Margareta, of Johann Whitemann and wife Margareta, b. 8 Mar 1784, bapt. 20 Jul 1784. Sponsors: the parents.

Johann, of Johann Geyer and wife Christian, b. 14 Jul 1784, bapt. 25 Jul 1784. Sponsors: Balthasar Cleisner and wife Elisabeth.

Elisabeth, of Johann Wagner and wife Margareta, b. 22 Jul 1784, bapt. 27 Jul 1784. Sponsors: the father, and Elisabeth Hoffmann(in).

Georg Jacob, of Jacob Barkhard and wife Catharina, b. 24 Jul 1784, bapt. 27 Jul 1784. Sponsors: the parents.

Johann Michael, of Michael Krauss and wife Dorothea, b. 6 Jul 1784, bapt. 27 Jul 1784. Sponsors: Heinrich Hopmüller and wife Catharina.

Sally, of Gottlieb Leinhoff and wife Anna Margareta, b. 2 Jul 1784, bapt. 30 Jul 1784. Sponsors: the parents.

Catharina, of Jacob Miller and wife Margareta, b. 16 Jun 1784, bapt. 1 Aug 1784. Sponsors: Peter Miller and wife Catharina.

Elisabeth, of Martin Kielhauer and wife Sarah, b. 28 Jun 1784, bapt. 1 Aug 1784. Sponsors: Johann Krauss and wife Catharina.

Jacob, of Christian Haag and wife Anna, b. 17 Jul 1784, bapt. 1 Aug 1784. Sponsors: Jacob Ulrich Sulzel and wife Anna Barbara.

Anthony, of James Finley and wife Mary, b. 25 Apr 1784, bapt. 1 Aug 1784. Sponsor: the mother.

Johann, of Wilhelm Kürzel and wife Charlotte, b. 23 Jun 1784, bapt. 1 Aug 1784. Sponsors: Balthasar Kürzler and wife Elisab.

Wilhelm, of Michael Goener and wife Sarah, b. 10 Jul 1784, bapt. 1 Aug 1784. Sponsors: Balthasar Cleimer and wife Elisabeth.

Margareta Barbara, of Owen Donnel and wife Margareta, b. 17 Jul 1784, bapt. 1 Aug 1784. Sponsors: Johann Weissmann and wife Margareta Barbara.

Sarah, of Heinrich Eppger and wife Maria, b. 4 Jan 1780, bapt. 4 Aug 1784. Sponsor: the father.

Elisabeth, of Heinrich Eppger and wife Maria, b. 19 Mar 1782, bapt. 4 Aug 1784. Sponsor: the father.

William, of Heinrich Eppger and wife Maria, b. 22 May 1784, bapt. 4 Aug 1784. Sponsor: the father.

Sarah, of James Humphrys and wife Maria, b. 13 Jul 1784, bapt. 5 Aug 1784. Sponsors: Elisabeth Loveberry.

Johann, of Wilhelm Wunderlich and wife Elisabeth, b. 19 Jul 1784, bapt. 18 Aug 1784. Sponsors: Nicol. Andrea and wife (her name not given).

Sarah, of Andreas Heim and wife Sophia, b. 18 Jul 1784, bapt. 8 Aug 1784. Sponsors: Peter Diel and wife Catharina.

Philipp, of Joh. Fachsmeyer and wife Catharina, b. 4 Aug 1784, bapt. 8 Aug 1784. Sponsors: Philipp Haal and wife Catharina.

Georg, of Georg Facundus and wife Maria, b. 22 Jul 1784, bapt. 8 Aug 1784.
Sponsors: the parents.

Anna Maria, of Johann Peck and wife Anna Maria, b. 26 Jun 1784, bapt. 8 Aug 1784. Sponsors: Jacob Mayer and wife Elisabeth.

Johann, of Johann Georg Ki[t]z and wife Maria, b. 12 Jul 1784, bapt. 8 Aug 1784. Sponsors: Johann Graeffenstein and wife Dorothea.

Anna Margareta, of Jacob Süss and wife Elisabeth, b. 8 Aug 1784, bapt. 12 Aug 1784. Sponsors: William Kerls and wife Margareta.

Anna Elisabeth, of Johann Koch and wife Rosina Doroth., b. 24 Jul 1784, bapt. 14 Aug 1784. Sponsors: the parents.

Elisabeth, of Fridrich Kerls and wife Elisabeth, b. 11 Jul 1784, bapt. 14 Aug 1784. Sponsors: William Kerls and wife Margareta.

Johann, of Johann Mayer and wife Maria, b. 18 Jul 1784, bapt. 14 Aug 1784. Sponsors: the father, and Elisabeth Strupp(in).

Elisabeth, of Daniel Rosch and wife Susanna, b. 7 Apr 1782, bapt. 20 Aug 1784. Sponsors: Heinrich Ernst and Elis. Rosch.

Catharina, of Daniel Rosch and wife Susanna, b. 11 Feb 1784, bapt. 20 Aug 1784. Sponsors: same as above.

Georg, of Christian Ungar and wife Maria, b. 8 Aug 1784, bapt. 22 Aug 1784. Sponsors: Georg Schmidt and Elisabeth Schmidt(in).

Catharina, of Carl Fuhg and wife Catharina, b. 18 Aug 1784, bapt. 22 Aug 1784. Sponsors: Heinrich Herbst and wife Elisabeth.

Georg, of Johann Braun and wife Catharina, b. 6 Aug 1784, bapt. 22 Aug 1784. Sponsors: Georg Voelcker and wife Anna.

Juliana, of David Suter and wife Martha, b. 21 Jul 1784, bapt. 22 Aug 1784. Sponsors: Michael Albrecht and wife Juliana.

Susanna, of Adam Bausch and wife Anna Maria, b. 1 Aug 1784, bapt. 22 Aug 1784. Sponsors: Johann Wenzel and Elisab. Demend.

Catharina, of Johann Kern and wife Elisabeth, b. 4 Jul 1784, bapt. 22 Aug 1784. Sponsors: Daniel Kayser and wife Rahel.

Esther, of Fridr. Heine? and wife Anna, b. 20 Jan 1784, bapt. 20 Aug 1784. Sponsor: the father.

Maria Juliana, of John Ring and wife Maria, b. 4 Aug 1784, bapt. 23 Aug 1784. Sponsors: Conrad Ring and wife Juliana.

Johann Theobald, of Johann Gerhard Stiegeler and wife Elisab. Cathar., b. 10 Aug 1784, bapt. 25 Aug 1784. Sponsors: Johann Ernst Fuchs, Joh. Caffel?, Theobald Emmerich, Elisab. Petri(n), and Elisabeth Margar. Held(in).

Christina Margareta (twin), of Fridrich Paul and wife Elisabeth, b. 26 Aug 1784, bapt. the same day. Sponsors: the father, and Christina Margareta Seybert(in).

Catharina, (twin), of Fridrich Paul and wife Elisabeth, b. 26 Aug 1784, bapt. the same day. Sponsors: same as above.

Jacob, of Isaac Koch and wife Eva, b. 6 Aug 1784, bapt. 29 Aug 1784. Sponsors: Balthasar Reim and wife Eva.

Dorothea Magdalena, of Heinrich Habig and wife Anna Catharina, b. 15 Aug 1784, bapt. 29 Aug 1784. Sponsors: Wilhelm Schmidt and wife Doroth. Magdalena.

Christoph, of Christoph Gut and wife Christina, b. 12 Aug 1784, bapt. 29 Aug 1784. Sponsors: Christoph Assmus and wife Catharina.

Hetty, of Georg Mallidore and wife Elisabeth, b. 6 Jan 1784, bapt. 29 Aug 1784. Sponsors: Johann Benner and wife Hanna.

Maria, of Phil. Hagener and wife Catharina, b. 1 Aug 1784, bapt. 19 Aug 1784. Sponsors: Fridr. Hagener and Maria Magdal. Schaeffer.

Christina, of Fridr. Gericke and wife Angelica, b. 23 Aug 1784, bapt. 29 Aug 1784. Sponsors: Hieronimus Warder and wife Christina.

Georg, of Heinr. Spangler and wife Maria, b. 26 Jul 1784, bapt. 29 Aug 1784. Sponsors: Georg Gasner and Barbara Krook.

Augustus, of Ludwig Peter and wife Elisabeth, b. 22 Aug 1784, bapt. 29 Aug 1784. Sponsor: Wilhelm Lackmann.

Fridrich David, of Joh. Georg Paetsch and wife Catharina, b. 4 Jul 1784, bapt. 30 Aug 1784. Sponsors: Joh. Georg Schacky and [his?] mother Elisabeth.

Johann, of Michael Katz and wife Elisabeth, b. 29 Aug 1784, bapt. 31 Aug 1784. Sponsors: widow Elisabeth Schaub(in).

Anna Margareta, of Wilhelm Stotz? and wife Ursula, b. 24 Aug 1784, bapt. 1 Sep 1784. Sponsors: the father, and Anna Margareta Schinker(in).

Maria, of Fridrich Mitchel and wife Christine, b. 22 Aug 1784, bapt. 5 Sep 1784. Sponsors: Martin Heinrich and wife Maria.

Elisabeth, of Jacob Luger and wife Elisabeth, b. 15 Aug 1784, bapt. 5 Sep 1784. Sponsors: Heinrich Grigemeyer and wife Elisabeth.

Elisabeth, of Fridrich Künzel and wife Anna, b. 30 Aug 1782, bapt. 6 Sep 1784. Sponsors: Jacob Alborn and wife Elisabeth.

Jacob Benjamin, of Jacob Alborn and wife Anna, b. 7 Aug 1784, bapt. 6 Sep 1784. Sponsors: same as above.

Jacob, of Johann Cleimer and wife Margareta, b. 22 Dec 1783, bapt. 7 Sep 1784. Sponsors: Jacob Ritter and wife Dorothea.

Elisabeth, of Johann Cleimer and wife Margareta, b. 22 Dec 1780, bapt. 7 Sep 1784. Sponsors: Maria Elisabeth Schauk(in).

Johann Jacob, of Thomas Cook and wife Maria, b. 15 Aug 1784, bapt. 10 Sep 1784. Sponsors: Johann Jacob Prinz and wife Barbara.

Johann, of Conrad Drumm and wife Susanna, b. 22 Aug 1784, bapt. 12 Sep 1784. Sponsors: Johann Krier and wife Catharina.

Elisabeth, of Johann Georg Gottfree and wife Maria, b. 30 Aug 1784, bapt. 12 Sep 1784. Sponsors: Adam Seybert and Elisab. Cammerer.

Sara Margareta, of Andreas Barenstecher and wife Maria, b. 24 Aug 1784, bapt. 12 Sep 1784. Sponsors: Adam Fanck and Anna Margar. Kres(in).

Catharina, of Carl Rose and wife Ally, b. 8 Aug 1784, bapt. 12 Sep 1784. Sponsors: Jacob Blocher and Margar. Engel(in).

Margareta, of Leonhard Hoch and wife Margareta, b. 18 Aug 1784, bapt. 19 Sep 1784. Sponsors: Georg Hoch and wife Dorothea.

Heinr. Wilhelm, of Christian Schoen and wife Margareta, b. 3 Sep 1784, bapt. 19 Sep 1784. Sponsors: Heinrich Wilhelm Geise and wife Eva.

Elisabeth, of Heinrich Lehr and wife Elisabeth, b. 6 Sep 1784, bapt. 19 Sep 1784. Sponsors: Jacob Kehl and wife Elisabeth.

Georg, of Johann Spatz and wife Elisabeth, b. 23 Aug 1784, bapt. 19 Sep 1784. Sponsors: Johann Kappel and wife Catharina.

Eva Maria, of Michael Hay and wife Maria, b. 1 Sep 1784, bapt. 19 Sep 1784.
Sponsors: the parents.
Carl, of Johann Berris and wife Sarah, b. 15 Sep 1784, bapt. 19 Sep 1784.
Sponsors: Johann Weber and wife Maria.
Catharina, of Jacob Viehl and wife Christina, b. 16 Aug 1784, bapt. 22 Sep
1784. Sponsors: Catharina Schumann(in) and Johann Wester.
Maria Margareta, of John Hazelton and wife Rahel, b. 11 Sep 1784, bapt. 22 Sep
1784. Sponsor: Maria Margareta Underweg(in).
Sarah, of Richard Shovins and wife Rosina, b. 15 Sep 1784, bapt. 23 Sep 1784.
Sponsor: Margareta Künzle.
Johann Fridrich, of Thomas Kahn and wife Catharina, b. 20 Nov 1782, bapt.
22 Sep 1784. Sponsors: Fridr. Vogel and wife Catharina.
Erdmann, of Erdmann French and wife Sabina Margar., b. 16 Nov 1782, bapt.
22 Sep 1784. Sponsor: the grandmother (name not given).
Adam, of Heinrich Benner and wife Catharin, b. 11 Sep 1784, bapt. 22 Sep
1784. Sponsors: Adam Handel and wife Hanna.
Peter, of Wilhelm Burckhard and wife Sarah, b. 16 Aug 1784, bapt. 23 Sep
1784. Sponsors: the father, and Barbara Dominic.
Johann Zacharias, of Samuel Lehmann and wife Elisabeth, b. 12 Sep 1784, bapt.
23 Sep 1784. Sponsors: Zacharias Endress and wife Maria.
Margareta, of Wilhelm Gibson and wife Eleonora (at the request of her parents it
is recorded here that this child has a cut in her left ear), b. 13 Mar 1784, bapt.
24 Sep 1784. Sponsors: Caspar Strubel and wife Catharina.
Johann Michael, of Jacob Gross and wife Anna Dorothea, b. 15 Sep 1784,bapt.
26 Sep 1784. Sponsor: Elisabeth Schaeffer(in).
Elisabeth, of Samuel Wanright and wife Catharina, b. 16 Sep 1784, bapt 25 Sep
1784. Sponsor: Dorothea Lag(in).
Catharina, of Johann Kappel and wife Catharina, b. 28 Aug 1784, bapt. 26 Sep
1784. Sponsors: Johann Spats and wife Elisabeth.
Susanna, of Christian Krug and wife Sarah, b. 24 Aug 1784, bapt. 26 Sep 1784.
Sponsors: Johann Painter and wife Susanna.
Jacob, of Jacob Becker and wife Margareta, b. 22 Sep 1784, bapt. 26 Sep 1784.
Sponsors: Jacob Henriegel and wife Catharina.
Catharina Barbara, of Jacob Ritter and wife Dorothea, b. 27 Aug 1784, bapt.
26 Sep 1784. Sponsor: Catharina Barbara Schmidt(in).
Anna Maria, of Heinrich Klemmer and wife Magdalena, b. 17 Sep 1784, bapt.
26 Sep 1784. Sponsors: Jacob Ritter and wife Dorothea.
Sarah, of Daniel Miller and wife Margareta, b. 24 Oct 1783, bapt. 27 Sep 1784.
Sponsors: the parents.
Johann Georg, of Richard Patterson and wife Barbara, b. 19 Sep 1784, bapt.
27 Sep 1784. Sponsors: Nicol. Heart and wife Anna Magdalena.
Polly, of Georg Lehmann and wife Catharina, b. 1 Sep 1784, bapt. 30 Sep 1784.
Sponsors: Wilhelm Eckard and wife Maria.
Christina, of Peter Heimbach and wife Elisabeth, b. 6 Sep 1784, bapt. 30 Sep
1784. Sponsors: Johann Birckenbeiler and wife Christina.
Anna Rosina, of Michael Ehrhard and wife Anna Cath., b. 16 Sep 1784, bapt.
3 Oct 1784. Sponsors: Andreas Winemor and wife Anna Rosina.

Johann, of Elias Fischer and wife Barbara, b. 5 Sep 1784, bapt. 3 Oct 1784. Sponsors: Johann Heinrich Fischer and wife Margareta.

Maria, of Mathias Schütz and wife Barbara, b. 3 Sep 1784, bapt. 3 Oct 1784. Sponsors: Johann Pfau and wife Maria.

Maria Magdalena, of Leonhard Emmerig and wife Maria Catharina, b. 14 Sep 1784, bapt. 2 Oct 1784. Sponsors: Mathias Kucker and wife Maria Magdalena.

Johann, of Johann Bender and wife Margareta, b. 4 Sep 1784, bapt. 3 Oct 1784. Sponsors: the parents.

Fridrich, of Andreas Abitsch and wife Eva, b. 19 Sep 1784, bapt. 3 Oct 1784. Sponsors: Fridrich Kielhefer and wife Margareta.

Johann Christian, of Daniel Andreas and wife Maria, b. 17 Aug 1784, bapt. 3 Oct 1784. Sponsors: Christian Seybert and wife Christina.

Heinrich, of Heinrich Daser and wife Margareta, b. 25 Jul 1782, bapt. 3 Oct 1784. Sponsors: the parents.

Maria, of Heinrich Daser and wife Margareta, b.25 Feb 1779, bapt. 3 Oct 1784. Sponsors: the parents.

Adam (twin), of Conrad Schelter and wife Maria Elisab. (birth date not given), bapt. 4 Oct 1784. Sponsors: Peter Jung and wife Magdalena.

Anna (twin), of Conrad Schelter and wife Maria Elisab. (birth date not given), bapt. 4 Oct 1784. Sponsors: same as above.

Michael, of Martin Kuhn and wife Catharina, b. 28 Sep 1784, bapt. 6 Oct 1784. Sponsors: the parents.

Maria, of Johann Pott and wife Elisabeth, b. 28 Sep 1784, bapt. 6 Oct 1784. Sponsors: the parents.

Jacob, of Jacob Schroeder and wife Juliana, b. 28 Aug 1784, bapt. 9 Oct 1784. Sponsors: Johan? Jacobs and wife (name not given).

Peter, of Johann Rotter and wife Maria, b. 30 Sep 1784, bapt. 9 Oct 1784. Sponsors: Mathias Rose and wife Susanna.

Johann David, of Adam Schüster and wife Christina Doroth., b. 18 Sep 1784, bapt. 9 Oct 1784. Sponsors: Johann David Uber and wife Anna.

Margareta, of Lorenz Schwaab and wife Margareta, b. 20 Sep 1784, bapt. 9 Oct 1784. Sponsors: Phil. Jacob Pechthold and wife Maria.

Sebastian, of Sebastian Heiler and wife Elisabeth, b. 28 Sep 1784, bapt. 9 Oct 1784. Sponsors: the parents.

Johann Heinrich, of Johann Andreas Schaeffer and wife Catharina, b. 27 Aug 1784, bapt. 9 Oct 1784. Sponsors: Joh. Heinr. Schach and wife Maria.

Margareta, of Georg Hazelton and wife Dorothea, b. 8 Sep 1784, bapt. 11 Oct 1784. Sponsors: Wilhelm Stans and wife Margareta,

David, of Martin Sommer and wife Margareta, b. 8 Oct 1784, bapt. 12 Oct 1784. Sponsors: Heinrich Krimm and wife Catharina.

Wilhelm, of Heinrich Apfel and wife Christina, b. 27 Apr 1784, bapt. 13 Oct 1784. Sponsors: Wilhelm Weile and wife Elisabeth.

Elisabeth, of Fridr. Weng and wife Christina, b. 26 Sep 1784, bapt. 17 Oct 1784. Sponsors: Georg Vogel and wife Elisabeth.

Johann, of Joh. Georg Krausskop and wife Anna Maria, b. 30 Sep 1784, bapt. 17 Oct 1784. Sponsors: Johann Krausskopp and Dorothea Dannecker(in).

Elisabeth, of Marcus Roh and wife Catharina, b. 10 Sep 1784, bapt. 17 Oct 1784. Sponsors: Michael Sinzer and wife Margareta.

Heinrich, of Heinr. Michael Demmer and wife Maria Jacobina, b. 2 Oct 1784, bapt. 17 Oct 1784. Sponsors: Christian Welthe and wife Rosina.

Johann, of Joh. Martin Künzel and wife Anna Margar., b. 5 Oct 1784, bapt. 17 Oct 1784. Sponsors: Johann Kaiser and wife Elisabeth.

Salome, of Joh. Mich. Fuchs and wife Salome, b. 19 Sep 1784, bapt. 17 Oct 1784. Sponsors: the mother, and Christian Leibbrand.

Johann Fridrich, of Fridr. Reinbot(h) and wife Barbara, b. 22 Sep 1784, bapt. 17 Oct 1784. Sponsors: Jacob Mayer and wife Juliana.

Georg, of Valentin Riess and wife Susanna, b. 16 Sep 1784, bapt. 17 Oct 1784. Sponsors: Georg Oesterle and wife Charlotte.

Joh. Georg, of Johann Cress and wife Elisabeth, b. 17 Sep 1784, bapt. 21 Oct 1784. Sponsor: Anna Maria Cress(in).

Maria Elisabeth, of Jacob Daudermann and wife Barbara, b. 15 Oct 1784, bapt. 22 Oct 1784. Sponsor: Maria Elisabeth Werner.

Nancy, of Simon Bounot and wife Margareta, b. 25 Sep 1784, bapt. 24 Oct 1784. Sponsors: Johann Seidel and Nancy Fleming.

Carl, of Heinrich Mayer and wife Maria, b. 7 Oct 1784, bapt. 24 Oct 1784. Sponsor: Maria Schweizer(in).

Elisabeth, of Joh. Heinr. Commendore and wife Christian, b. 3 Oct 1784, bapt. 24 Oct 1784. Sponsors: the father, and Gertraut Elisabeth Walter(in).

Louis, of Louis Bisayade_ and wife Margareta, b. 15 Oct 1784, bapt. 24 Oct 1784. Sponsors: Michael Miller and wife Rosina.

Catharina, of Georg Albert and wife Maria, b. 24 Oct 1784, bapt. 28 Oct 1784. Sponsors: Christoph Adam and Catharina Gassner(in).

Elisabeth, of Johann Breckle and wife Polly, b. 6 Oct 1784, bapt. 31 Oct 1784. Sponsors: Philipp Klein and wife Elisabeth.

Emanuel Wilhelm Conrad, of Johann Conrad Metsch and wife Jenny, b. 6 Oct 1784, bapt. 1 Nov 1784. Sponsors: the parents.

Elisabeth, of Caspar Schneider and wife Elisabeth, b. 12 Oct 1784, bapt. 30 Oct 1784. Sponsors: the parents.

Heinrich, of Johann Linck and wife Maria, b. 15 Oct 1784, bapt. 31 Oct 1784. Sponsors: Heinrich Kiess and wife (name not given).

Johann Andreas, of Thomas Lorenz Schreiber and wife Anna Maria, b. 28 Oct 1784, bapt. 31 Oct 1784. Sponsors: Johann Andreas Rohr and wife Maria Christina.

Johann Andreas, of Johann Schumann and wife Elisabeth, b. 25 Sep 1784, bapt. 31 Oct 1784. Sponsors: Michael Haehns and wife Susanna.

Leonhard, of Leonhard Repscher and wife Barbara, b. 1 Oct 1784, bapt. 31 Oct 1784. Sponsors: Berhard Wenz and wife Rebecca Margareta.

Georg, of Carl Achilles and wife Elisabeth, b. 9 Oct 1784, bapt. 31 Oct 1784. Sponsors: Georg Daum and wife (name not given).

Elisabeth, of Matheaus Armbrüster and wife Maria, b. 3 Oct 1784, bapt. 31 Oct 1784. Sponsors: John Schweizer and Elisab. Buck.

Margareta, of Conrad Wachter and wife Maria, b. 21 Jun 1784, bapt. 1 Nov 1784. Sponsor: Margareta Deiss.

William, of William Ward and wife Elisabeth, b. 15 Mar 1775, bapt. 2 Nov 1784. Sponsors: Michael Reble and wife Margareta, and Humphry Donnehew.

Johann, of William Ward and wife Elisabeth, b. 10 Apr 1779, bapt. 2 Nov 1784. Sponsors: same as above.

Abraham, of William Ward and wife Elisabeth, b. 2 Jan 1782, bapt. 2 Nov 1784. Sponsors: same as above.

Isaac, of William Ward and wife Elisabeth, b. 2 Sep 1784, bapt. 2 Nov 1784. Sponsors: same as above.

Maria, of Nicol. Panzer and wife Elisabeth, b. 28 Oct 1784, bapt. 7 Nov 1784. Sponsor: Maria Leech.

Margareta, of Adam Heimbach and wife Anna Magadalena, b. 23 Oct 1784, bapt. 7 Nov 1784. Sponsor: widow Catharina Heimann.

Johann, of Albrecht Weber and wife Magdalena, b. 1 Sep 1784, bapt. 7 Nov 1784. Sponsors: Heinr. Krimm and wife Appellonia.

Johann, of David Dreihsler and wife Elisabeth, b. 27 Sep 1784, bapt. 7 Nov 1784. Sponsors: Johann Valentin Edling and wife Maria Barbara.

Andreas, of Johann Krieger and wife Catharina, b. 16 Oct 1784, bapt. 7 Nov 1784. Sponsors: Andreas Riegler and wife Catharina.

Johan Albrecht, of Georg Fischer and wife (name not given), b. 1 Jun 1779, bapt. 7 Nov 1784. Sponsors: Albrecht Weber and Magdalena Weber(in).

Catharina Elisabeth. of Georg Fischer and wife (name not given), b. 9 Mar 1784, bapt. 7 Nov 1784. Sponsors: Albrecht Weber and [wife] Catharina Elisabeth.

Heinrich, of Didrich Monsch? and wife Catharina, b. 4 Oct 1784, bapt. 14 Nov 1784. Sponsors: Heinrich Mayer and wife Catharina.

Maria, of Georg Michael Vockinson and wife Maria, b. 31 Oct 1784, bapt. 14 Nov 1784. Sponsors: Johann Daum and wife Maria.

Maria, of Heinrich Herbst and wife Elisabeth, b. 10 Nov 1784, bapt. 14 Nov 1784. Sponsors: Joahnn Braun and wife Maria.

Anna Maria, of Heinr. Pot(h) and wife Elisabeth, b. 4 Nov 1784, bapt. 14 Nov 1784. Sponsors: Peter Diel and wife Elisabeth.

Elisabeth, of Georg Metzinger and wife Maria, b. 19 Sep 1784, bapt. 14 Nov 1784. Sponsors: Elisabeth Metzinger and Adam Metzinger.

Nancy, of Gottlieb Kohp and wife Maria, b. 28 Oct 1784, bapt. 14 Nov 1784. Sponsors: Jacob Franz and wife Nancy.

Susanna, of Johann Wolf and wife Maria, b. 6 Nov 1784, bapt. 15 Nov 1784. Sponsors: Valentin Hofmann and wife Susanna.

Georg, of Georg Meaty and wife Margareta, b. 3 Nov 1784, bapt. 21 Nov 1784. Sponsors: the parents.

Andreas, of William Cunningham and wife Juliana, b. in Sep 1779, bapt. 21 Nov 1784. Sponsors: Georg Meaty and wife Margareta.

Johann Georg, of Johann Schmidt and wife Anna Maria, b. 7 Nov 1783, bapt. 1 Nov 1784. Sponsor: Johann Georg Diel.

Isaac, of Balthasar Heim and wife Eva, b. 27 Oct 1784, bapt. 21 Nov 1784. Sponsors: Isaac Koch and wife Eva.

Veronica, of Fridr. Brown and wife Elisabeth, b. 5 Nov 1784, bapt. 21 Nov 1784. Sponsors: Gottfried Münnich and wife Veronica.

Catharina, of Martin List and wife Maria Elisab., b. 21 Sep 1784, bapt. 21 Nov 1784. Sponsors: the parents.

Elisabeth, of Jacob Klein and wife Margareta, b. 8 Oct 1784, bapt. 21 Nov 1784. Sponsors: Fridr. Schumann and wife Anna Maria.

Heinrich, of Adolph Riel and wife Hanna, b. 5 Aug 1784, bapt. 28 Nov 1784. Sponsors: Johann Heinr. Riel and wife Maria.

Georg, of Georg Sterr and wife Margareta, b. 11 Nov 1784, bapt. 28 Nov 1784. Sponsors: Christoph Rau and wife Rosina.

Maria Catharina, of David Schaeffer, Jr., and wife Elisabeth, b.27 Nov 1784, bapt. the same day. Sponsors: David Schaeffer and wife Maria Catharina

Molly, of David vonZobern and wife Hanna, (birth date not given), bapt. 28 Nov 1784. Sponsors: Heinrich Schul[t]z and wife Molly.

Henrica, of David vonZobern and wife Hanna, b. 24 Oct 1784, bapt. 28 Nov 1784. Sponsors: same as above.

John, of William Weiler and wife Maria, b. 23 Sep 1784, bapt. 30 Nov 1784. Sponsor: the mother.

Carolina Barbara, of Carl Benjamin Thannphels? and wife Barbara, b. 28 Nov 1784, bapt. 3 Dec 1784. Sponsors: Joh. David Haussmann and Anna Barbara Bastian(in).

Magdalena,of Heinrich Miller and wife Anna Elisab., b. 11 Nov 1784, bapt. 5 Dec 1784. Sponsors: Johann Trangenstein (or Frangenstein)and wife Magdalena.

Maria, of Peter Armbrüster and wife Margareta, b. 20 Nov 1784, bapt. 5 Dec 1784. Sponsors: Georg Gilbert and Maria Gilbert.

Catharina, of Johann Rickard and wife Catharina Elisab., b. 4 Dec 1784, bapt. 5 Dec 1784. Sponsors: Jacob Koehler and wife Catharina.

Johann Michael, of Carl Conrad and wife Regina, b. 21 Nov 1784, bapt. 5 Dec 1784. Sponsors: Carl Vie[t]z and Biddy Welsch.

Johann Peter, of Heinrich Blettermann and wife Elisabeth, b. 11 Nov 1784, bapt. 5 Dec 1784. Sponsors: Johann Peter Witner and wife Cath. Elisabeth.

Christina, of Johann Gechter and wife Dorothea, b. 13 Nov 1784, bapt. 5 Dec 1784. Sponsors: Christina Stadelma(e)nn(in).

Christina Catharina, of Zacharias Lesch and wife Maria Barbara, b. 26 Nov 1784, bapt. 5 Dec 1784. Sponsors: Jacob Keimle and wife Christina Catharina.

Carl, of Georg Merkley and wife Anna ,b. 4 Nov 1784, bapt. 5 Dec 1784. Sponsors: the parents.

Georg, of Jacob Happel and wife Margareta, b. 7 Nov 1784, bapt. 5 Dec 1784. Sponsors: Georg Schneider and wife Maria.

Barbara, of Johann Haalmann and wife Maria, b. 28 Nov 1784, bapt. 5 Dec 1784. Sponsors: Heinr. Schneider and wife Barbara.

Peter, of Jacob Whitemann and wife Elisabeth, b. 9 Mar 1784, bapt. 5 Dec 1784. Sponsors: Peter White and wife Susanna.

Jacob, of Leonhard Schmidt and wife Barbara, b. 6 Oct 1784, bapt. 12 Dec 1784. Sponsors: Jacob Hirneisen and wife Maria.

Johann Jacob, of Johann Gauer and wife Elisabeth, b. 17 Nov 1784, bapt. 12 Dec 1784. Sponsors: Jacob Young and wife Elisabeth.

Joseph, of Andreas Mayer and wife Maria, b. 29 Nov 1784, bapt. 11 Dec 1784. Sponsors: Joseph Leacock and Margareta Hinch.

Catharina, of Christian Fleisch and wife Dorothea, b. 10 Nov 1784, bapt. 12 Dec 1784. Sponsors: Catharina Roh and Heinrich Benner.

Christian, of Johann Wittig and wife Elisabeth, b. 13 oct 1784, bapt. 12 Dec 1784. Sponsors: the parents.

Johann Fridrich, of Heinrich Schreffler and wife Christina, b. 16 Oct 1784, bapt. 12 Dec 1784. Sponsors: Fridr. Feltebaum and Anna Maria Richard.

Johann, of Adam Schae[t]zlein and wife Hanna, b. 30 Nov 1784, bapt. 16 Dec 1784. Sponsors: Christian Pearsey and wife Elisabeth.

Peter, of Andreas Tag and wife Christina, b. 3 Dec 1784, bapt. 19 Dec 1784. Sponsors: Peter Schneider and wife Elisab.

Barbara, of Jacob Schmidt and wife Margareta, b. 5 Dec 1784, bapt. 19 Dec 1784. Sponsors: Johann Westenberger and wife Barbara.

Simon, of Johann Henkel and wife Maria Magdalena, b. 4 Dec 1784, bapt. 19 Dec 1784. Sponsors: Simon Schockard? and wife Barbara.

Michael, of Caspar Christ and wife Catharina, b. 30 Nov 1784, bapt. 19 Dec 1784. Sponsors: Michael Krauss and wife Dorothea.

Johann Jacob, of Philipp Mayerley and wife Anna Esther, b. 6 Nov 1784, bapt. 20 Dec 1784. Sponsors: Jacob Schiebley and wife Elisabeth.

Catharina, of Gottfried Cyder and wife Catharina, b. 22 Aug 1784, bapt. 21 Dec 1784. Sponsors: the parents.

Franzis, of Georg Herrley and wife Maria, b. 16 Nov 1784, bapt. 25 Dec 1784. Sponsors: Francys Cooper and wife Maria.

Johann, of Christian Kunkel and wife Catharina, b. 11 Dec 1784, bapt. 26 Dec 1784. Sponsors: Johann Kunkel and wife Eleonora.

Johann Michael, of Johann Hempel and wife Elisabeth, b. 9 Dec 1784, bapt. 26 Dec 1784. Sponsors: Johann Michael Haber? and wife Maria.

Rebecca, of Christian Friehefer and wife Maria, b. 1 Dec 1784, bapt. 26 Dec 1784. Sponsor: Anthon? Mut(h).

Sarah Elisabeth, of Johann Freyburg and wife Susanna, b. 12 Dec 1784, bapt. 26 Dec 1784. Sponsors: the parents.

Jacob, of Hieronimus Wagner and wife Christina, b. 6 Dec 1784, bapt. 26 Dec 1784. Sponsors: Johann Hack and wife Elisabeth.

Rebecca, of Philipp Burkhard and wife Jean, b. 16 Oct 1784, bapt. 26 Dec 1784. Sponsors: Christina Scheibli(n).

Joh. Georg. of Conrad Denckfelder and wife Elisabeth, b. 1 Sep 1784, bapt. 27 Dec 1784. Sponsors: Joh. Georg Escherig and wife Elisabeth.

Johann Conrad, of Joh. Georg Escherig and wife Elisabeth, b . 2 Oct 1784, bapt. 27 Dec 1784. Sponsors: Joh. Conrad Denckfelder and wife Elisabeth.

Maria Catharina, of Heinrich Schmidt and wife Catharina, b. 18 Dec 1784, bapt. 28 Dec 1784. Sponsors: the father, and Maria Cath. Bedichmann(in)?.

Elisabeth, of Johann Wagner and wife Salome, b. 29 Apr 1784, bapt. 31 Dec 1784. Sponsor: widow Elisabeth Working.

Esther, of Georg Yessero and wife Elisabeth, b. 23 Nov 1784, bapt. 31 Dec 1784. Sponsors: Michael Stricker and wife Maria Margareta.

1785, First List
(baptisms by pastor Helmuth, from Book IV)

Johann, of Johann Niemand and wife Maria, b. 23 Dec 1784, bapt. 2 Jan 1785. Sponsors: the parents.

Johann, of Jacob Scharff and wife Elisabeth, b. 6 Oct 1784,bapt. 2 Jan 1785. Sponsors: Joh. Kittler and wife Susanna.

Joh. Peter, of Peter Schreyer and wife Barbara, b. 19 Dec 1784, bapt. 2 Jan 1785. Sponsors: Georg Krebs and wife Dorothea.

Georg, of Fridrich Walter and wife Martha, b. 17 Sep 1784, bapt. 1 Jan 1785. Sponsor: Michael Diedrich.

Elisabeth, of Johann Weilmayer and wife (name not given), b. 5 Dec 1784, bapt. 2 Jan 1785. Sponsors: the parents.

Appellonia, of Jacob Schreiber and wife Anna Margar., b. 30 Dec 1784, bapt. 7 Jan 1785. Sponsors: Michael Schweyer and Appellonia Götz(in).

Margareta, of Phil. Pfannekuchen and wife Catharina, b. 26 Dec 1784, bapt. 9 Jan 1785. Sponsors: Joh. Schütz and wife Margareta.

Fridrich, of Michael Schwei[t]zer and wife Elisabeth, b. 23 Dec 1784, bapt. 9 Jan 1785. Sponsors: Fridrich Schumann and wife Maria.

Thomas, of Joseph Wolbert and wife Catharina, b. 26 Dec 1784, bapt. 9 Jan 1785. Sponsors: Thomas Hanneberger and Maria Barbara Michel?.

Catharina Elisab., of Heinrich Wester and wife Ruth, b. 1 Aug 1784, bapt. 8 Jan 1785. Sponsor: Catharina Wester.

Catharina, of Johann Sagler and wife Margareta, b. 27 Oct 1784, bapt. 8 Jan 1785. Sponsor: Catharina Wester.

Peter, of Caspar Wittebach and wife Anna Gertraut, b . 4 Dec 1784, bapt. 8 Jan 1785. Sponsors: the parents.

Anna Maria, of Philip Sorg and wife Susanna Magdalena, b. 1 Jan 1785, bapt. 11 Jan 1785. Sponsors: Johann Krausskopp and Anna Maria Sorg(in).

Johann, of Johann Assmus and wife Catharina, b. 26 Dec 1784, bapt. 9 Jan 1785. Sponsors: Johann Gut and wife Catharina.

Elisabeth, of Georg Breuning and wife Elisabeth, b. 27 Dec 1784, bapt. 11 Jan 1785. Sponsors: the parents.

Rebecca or Margaret (to be called Becky [or Peggy]), of Christian Oberstech and wife Margar., b. 3 Jan 1785, bapt. 14 Jan 1785. Sponsors: Phil. Scharf(f) and Margar. Tempel.

Thomas, of Jacob Kramlich and wife Christina, b. 1 Jan 1785, bapt. 16 Jan 1785. Sponsors: Thomas Kramlich and wife Magdalena.

Fridrich, of Georg Christoph Reinhold and wife Maria, b. 8 Jun 17<u>82</u>, bapt. 17 Jan 1785. Sponsor: Georg Alberti.

Anna Maria (twin), of Johann Jerger and wife Anna Maria, b. 24 Dec 1784, bapt. 19 Jan 1785. Sponsors: the parents.

Catharina (twin), of Johann Jerger and wife Anna Maria, b. 24 Dec 1784, bapt. 19 Jan 1785. Sponsors: Peter Walter and Charlotte Weid___.

Maria Margareta, of David Niess and wife Clara, b. 19 Dec 1784, bapt. 19 Jan 1785. Sponsor: Maria Margareta Bernhardt(in).

Anna Charlotta, of Johann Eberhard and wife Christiana Cathar., b. 4 Jan 1785, bapt. 20 Jan 1785. Sponsors: Georg Oesterley and wife Anna Charlotta.

Conrad, of Michael Bamberger and wife Magdalena, b. 25 Dec 1784, bapt. 20 Jan 1785. Sponsors: the father, and Margareta Schwei[t]zer(in).

Elisabeth, of Georg Forbach and wife Margareta, b. 22 Dec 1784, b at. 21 Jan 1785. Sponsors: Christoph Mayer and Eva Forbach.

Maria Magdalena, of Louis Barsel and wife Maria Elisab., b. 16 Dec 1784, bapt. 23 Jan 1785. Sponsors: Martin Henterich and wife Anna Maria.

Johann Michael, of Jacob Bast and wife Elisabeth, b. 29 Dec 1784, bapt. 23 Jan 1785. Sponsors: Joh. Michael Bast and Ros. Len[t]z.

Eleonora, of Carl Knery and wife Margareta, b. 13 Jan 1785, bapt. 23 Jan 1785. Sponsors: Johann Friess and wife Sophia Eleonora.

William, of Christian Kühn and wife Maria, b. 5 Jan 1785, bapt. 23 Jan 1785. Sponsors: Wilhelm Weber and wife Elisab.

Catharina, of Jacob Holl and wife Catharina, b. 8 Jan 1785, bapt. 23 Jan 1785. Sponsors: Thomas Fischer and wife Elisab.

Maria, of Thomas Bignell and wife Maria, b. 7 Jan 1785, bapt. 23 Jan 1785. Sponsors: Georg Savel and wife Maria.

Maria Salome, of Johann Ridge and wife Maria Barbara, b. 29 Sep 1783, bapt. 24 Jan 1785. Sponsors: Joh. Heinr. Homberger and Maria Salome Kunzmann.

William, of Charles Alexander and wife Elisabeth, b. 15 Jan 1785, bapt. 24 Jan 1785. Sponsor: Wilhelm Sparrehack.

Fridrich, of Fridr. Winckler and wife Cath. Magdal., b. 6 Jan 1785, bapt. 30 Jan 1785. Sponsors: the parents.

Caspar, of Caspar Schoen and wife Debora, b. 16 Jan 1785, bapt. 31 Jan 1785. Sponsors: the parents.

Georg, of Georg Wood and wife Elisab., b. 27 Dec 1784, bapt. 4 Feb 1785. Sponsor: Dorothea Walcker(in).

Catharina, of Heinr. Linck and wife Magdalena, b. 22 Jan 1784, bapt. 6 Feb 1785. Sponsors: Fridr. Linck and wife Cath. Barbara.

Georg, of Christoph Mohr and wife Catharina, b. 23 Jan 1785, bapt. 6 Feb 1785. Sponsors: Georg Mohr and Margar. Weisert.

Catharina, of Georg Senft and wife Charlotta, b. 18 Jan 1785, bapt. 6 Feb 1785. Sponsors: Joh. Stackert? and wife Elisabeth.

Maria Magdalena, of Joh. Schaeffer and wife Sophia Maria, b. 4 Jan 1785, bapt. 7 Feb 1785. Sponsors: the parents.

Veronica [twin], of Arthur French and wife Sabine Cathar., b. 3 Feb 1785, bapt. 6 Feb 1785. Sponsor: Veronica Pariss.

Sarah [twin], of Arthur French and wife Sabine Cathar., b. 3 Feb 1785, bapt. 6 Feb 1785. Sponsor: Sarah Fahns.

Jacob, of Eberhard Miller and wife Barbara, b. 30 Dec 1784, bapt. 6 Feb 1785. Sponsors: Jacob Mercker and wife Elisabeth.

Maria, of Christoph Wilpert and wife Margaret, b. 7 Nov 1784, bapt. 6 Feb 1785. Sponsors: Wilhelm Stein and wife Maria.

Joh. Adam, of Jonas Klaser (or Kleser) and wife Anna Elisab., b. 21 Nov 1784, bapt. 10 Feb 1785. Sponsors: Adam Oppermann and wife Maria, and Joh. Buk___ and wife Elisab.

Christian, of Melchior Kempf and wife Maria, b. 4 Jan 1785, bapt. 12 Feb 1785. Sponsors: Christian Kempf and wife Maria.

Sarah, of Conrad Gebhard and wife Maria, b. 10 Feb 1785, bapt. 13 Feb 1785.
Sponsors: Heinrich Pot(h) and wife Cath. Elisab.

Georg, of Adam Metz and wife Barbara, b. 4 Jan 1785, bapt. 13 Feb 1785.
Sponsors: Johann Lennemann and wife Margar.

Samuel, of Mathaeus Fuss and wife Hanna, b. 17 Jan 1785, bapt. 13 Feb 1785.
Sponsors: Samuel Moller and wife (name not given).

Johann Caspar, of Caspar Graeff and wife Rebecca, b. 24 Jan 1785, bapt. 16 Feb
1785. Sponsor: Caspar Graeff, Sr.

Sarah, of Thomas Weiss and wife Rachel, b. 26 Jan 1785, bapt. 16 Feb 1785.
Sponsors: Christoph Behringer and wife Margareta.

Johann, of Johann Mut(h) and wife Elisabeth, b. 14 Feb 1785, bapr. 17 Feb
1785. Sponsors: Caspar Schüster and wife Regina.

Susanna, of Jacob Jucher? and wife Maria Magdalena, b. 7 Jan 1785, bapt.
17 Feb 1785. Sponsor: Susanna Kramp(in).

Heinrich, of Georg Scheible and wife Elisabeth, b. 17 Oct 1784, bapt. 17 Feb
1785. Sponsors: the mother, and Heinrich Scheible.

Catharina, of Balthasar Schoener and wife Cathar., b. 5 Jan 1785, bapt. 20 Feb
1785. Sponsors: Peter Kraft and dau. Catharina.

Dorothea, of Peter Lex and wife Elisabeth, b. 16 Feb 1785, bapt. 20 Feb 1785.
Sponsors: Georg Krips and wife Dorothea.

Anna Catharina, of Fridrich Rohrer and wife Margareta, b. 4.Feb 1785, bapt.
20 Feb 1785. Sponsors: Joh. Wolfgang Gemeinbauer and wife Anna
Catharina.

Joh. Gerhard, of Johann Scharp and wife Catharina, b. 26 Dec 1784, bapt.
19 Feb 1785. Sponsors: Gerhard Hol[t]zkamm and wife Elisabeth.

Henry, of Henry deForrest and wife Mary, b. 7 Jan 1785, bapt. 20 Feb 1785.
Sponsors: Peter Ozeas and wife Mary.

Daniel, of Fridrich Mayer and wife Margareta, b. 27 Jan 1785, bapt. 20 Feb
1785. Sponsors: Daniel Schaub and wife Catharina.

Andreas, of Andreas Bosshart and wife Christina, b. 4 eb 1785, bapt. 20 Feb
1785. Sponsors: Andreas Bosshart and wife Christina [the parents?].

Anna, o f Georg Bantleon and wife Regina, b. 3 Oct 1784, bapt. 21 Feb 1785.
Sponsors: the parents.

Barbara, of Fridr. Kochendoerf(f)er and wife Regina, b. 14 Feb 1785, bapt.
23 Feb 1785. Sponsors: Barbara Kochendoerf(f)er.

Mathias, of Jacob Masoner and wife Elisabeth, b. 30 Jan 1785, bapt. 24 Feb
1785. Sponsors: Mathias Landeberger and wife Maria.

Catharina, of William Reyley and wife Elisabeth, b. 27 Sep 1784, bapt. 27 Feb
1785. Sponsors: Philipp Ohler and wife Catharina.

Georg Ludwig, of Georg Ludw. Cistler and wife Anna Margar., b.18 Feb 1785,
bapt. 1 Mar 1785. Sponsors: the parents.

Elisabeth, of Jacob Trumbeck and wife Maria, b. 27 Dec 1784, bapt. 6 Mar
1785. Sponsors: the parents.

Maria, of Johan Kunckel and wife Maria Clara, b. 5 Feb 1785, bapt. 6 Mar 1785.
Sponsors: Andreas Mattern and wife Maria.

Elisabeth, of Johann Jaeger and wife Catharina, b. 21 Feb 1785, bapt. 6 Mar
1785. Sponsors: the father, and Elisab. Frideric.

Apellonia, of William Douglas and wife Elisabeth, b. 18 Nov 1784, bapt. 7 Mar 1785. Sponsors: Georg Haussmann and wife Apellonia.

Maria, of bs and wife Dorothea, b. 6 Mar 1785, bapt. 13 Mar 1785. Sponsors: Georg Grotz and wife Margar Dorothea.

Barbara, of Magnus Neiss and wife Anna, b. 18 Jan 1785, bapt. 13 Mar 1785. Sponsors: Isaak King and wife Barbara.

Elisabeth, of Wilhelm Bicking and wife Elisabeth, b. 20 Feb 1785, bapt. 16 Mar 1785. Sponsors: the parents.

Carl Ludwig, of Heinrich Daser and wife Margareta, b. 28 Feb 1785, bapt. 16 Mar 1785. Sponsors: Christoph Behringer and wife Margar.

Wilhelm, of Johann Hartranft and wife Catharina, b. 30 Jan 1785, bapt. 20 Mar 1785. Sponsors: Jacob Kucker and wife Maria.

Hanna, of Jacob Kehl and wife Anna Maria Elisab., b. 20 Feb 1785, bapt. 20 Mar 1785. Sponsors: Heinr. Lehr and wife Elisabeth.

Wilhelmina Elisabeth, of Wilhelm Hederich and wife Anna, b. 25 Feb 1785, bapt. 20 Mar 1785. Sponsors: Wilhelm Will and wife Anna.

Elisabeth, of Jacob Facundus and wife Juliana, b. 6 Mar 1785, bapt. 21 Mar 1785. Sponsors: Adolph Dill and Elisab. Ritter(in)?.

Joseph, of Adam Wedderstein and wife Sophia, 17 Mar 1785, bapt. 26 Mar 1785. Sponsors: the parents.

Catharina, of Adam Bohl and wife Catharina, b. 15 Dec 1766, bapt. 23 Mar 1785. Sponsors: Christian Lenz and wife (name not given), Johann Bohl and wife (name not given), and the other children.

Adam, of Adam Bohl and wife Catharina, b. in Oct 1769, bapt. 23 Mar 1785. Sponsors: same as above.

Susanna, of Adam Bohl and wife Catharina, b. 10 Nov 1774, bapt. 23 Mar 1785. Sponsors: same as above.

Margareta, of Adam Bohl and wife Catharina, b. 6 Jul 1777, bapt. 23 Mar 1785. Sponsors: same as above.

Georg, [adult son] of Jacob Steinmetz and wife Catharina, b. 15 Jul 1765, bapt. 23 Mar 1785.

Maria Miller, [adult dau.] of Thomas Birch and wife Sarah, b. 11 Nov 1755, bapt. 23 Mar 1785.

Johann, of Jacob Mayer and wife Anna Maria, b. 7 Mar 1785, bapt. 28 Mar 1785. Sponsors: Johann Kaiser and wife Elisabeth.

Anna Sarah, of Johann Heinrich Die[t]z and wife Hanna, b. 11 Feb 1785, bapt. 25 Mar 1785. Sponsors: Joh.Peter Die[t]z and wife Anna Maria.

Elisabeth, of John Justus and wife Catharina, b. 8 Mar 1785, bapt. 27 Mar 1785. Sponsors: Georg Seitz and wife Elisabeth.

Sarah, of Johann Schwar[t]z and wife Susanna, b. 7 Mar 1785, bapt 28 Mar 1785. Sponsors: James Stover and wife Sarah.

Charlotte (twin), of Carl Truckenmuller and wife Anna, b. 26 Feb 1785, bapt. 28 Mar 1785. Sponsors: Peter Hay and wife (name not given).

Henrietta, (twin), of Carl Truckenmuller and wife Anna, b. 26 Feb 1785, bapt. 28 Mar 1785. Sponsors: same as above.

Susanna [adult dau.] of Jacob Colleday and wife Veronica (wife of Joh. Schwar[t]z), b. 3 Mar 1762, bapt. 28 Mar 1785.

Sarah, of Regina Betzler and allegedly John Borris, b. 29 May 1784, bapt. 2 Apr
1785. Sponsor: Sarah Betzler
Christina Dorothea, of Johann Nicol. Groll and wife Elisabeth, b. 1 Apr 1785,
bapt. 3 Apr 1785. Sponsors: Jacob Keimle and wife Christina Catharina.
Anna Margareta, of Jacob Riess and wife Maria Magdalena, b. 21 Mar
1785,bapt. 3 Apr 1785. Sponsors: Phil. Zeller and wife Anna Margareta.
Catharina, of Michael Miltenberger and wife Dorothea, b. 3 Mar 1785, bapt.
3 Apr 1785. Sponsor: Catharina Miltenberger.
Anna Elisabeth, of Carl Miller and wife Magdalena, b. 5 Mar 1785, bapt. 3 Apr
1785. Sponsors: Johann Miller and wife Anna Elisab.
Heinrich, of Daniel Boeckle and wife Elisabeth, b. 4 Feb 1785, bapt 3 Apr 1785.
Sponsors: Heinrich Boeckle and wife Elisab.
Anna, of Conrad Bertling and wife Maria, b . 12 Oct 1784, bapt. 3 Apr 1785.
Sponsors: Jacob Kitz and wife Elisabeth.
Mathias, of Fridrich Heimberger and wife Maria, b. 12 Mar 1785, bapt. 3 Apr
1785. Sponsors: Fridrich Heimberger and Christina Stemble.
Lucretia, of Albert Hencke and wife Christina, b. 5 Apr 1785, bapt. 6 Apr 1785.
Sponsor: Patrick Green.
Sarah, of Albert Hencke and wife Christina, b. 4 Sep 1783, bapt. 6 Apr 1785.
Sponsors: same as above.
Rahel, of William Fitzgerald and wife Eleonora, b. 7 Mar 1779, bapt. 6 Apr
1785. Sponsors: Jacob Henrigel and wife Eleonora.
Elisabeth, of William Fitzgerald and wife Eleonora, b. 1 Nov 1780, bapt. 6 Apr
1785. Sponsors: same as above.
William, of William Fitzgerald and wife Eleonora, b. 23 Nov 1784, bapt. 6 Apr
1784. Sponsors: same as above.
Hanna, of Jacob Beck and wife Elisabeth, b. 22 Mar 1785, bapt. 10 Apr 1785.
Sponsors: Adam Handel and wife Hanna.
Johann David Wilhelm, of Wilhelm Clemens and wife Maria Magdalena, b.
14 Jan 1785, bapt. 10 Apr 1785. Sponsors: David Schaeffer and wife Maria
Catharina.
Joseph,of Georg Fuchs and wife Sarah, b. 21 Feb 1785, bapt. 10 Apr 1785.
Sponsors: Fridr. Forbach and Maria Fuchs.
Joseph, of Fridr. Fischer and wife Anna, b. 22 Mar 1785, bapt. 17 Apr 1785.
Sponsors: Joseph Graff and wife (name not given).
Johann, of Wilhelm Weissmann and wife Rebecca, b. 15 Oct 1784, bapt. 17 Apr
1785. Sponsors: Joh. Weissmann and wife Barbara.
Georg, of Fridrich Schütz and wife Barbara, b. 27 Jan 1785, bapt. 17 Apr 1785.
Sponsors: Conrad Paethys and wife Barbara.
Sarah, of Nicol. Quast and wife Maria, b. 9 Dec 1784, bapt. 19 Apr 1785.
Sponsors: the parents.
A child (name not given), of Joh. Fridrich Krebs and wife Anna Maria, b. 20 Apr
1785, bapt. 21 Apr 1785. Sponsors: the parents.
Johann David, of David Uber and wife Anna, b. 1 Apr 1785, bapt. 15 Apr 1785.
Sponsors: the parents.
Hanna, of Wilhelm Wer[t]z and wife Margareta (who died), b. 1 Apr 1785, bapt.
22 Apr 1785. Sponsors: Phil. Weger and wife Hanna.

Margareta, of Heinrich Lübecke and wife Anna Maria, b. 7 Apr 1785, bapt.
24 Apr 1785. Sponsors: Johann Wester and Margar. Schumacher(in).
Elisabeth, of Enoch Bayley and wife Dorothea, b. 23 Apr 1785, bapt. the same
day. Sponsor: Barbara Weingaertner(in).
Catharina, of Philipp Kohlmann and wife Anna Margareta, b. 18 Mar 1785, bapt.
24 Apr 1785. Sponsors: Catharina Kohlmann and Heinr. Heil.
David, of Johann Weber and wife Veronica, b. 1 Apr 1785, bapt. 24 Apr 1785.
Sponsors: the parents.
Johann Fridrich, of Christoph Hef(f)t and wife Maria, b. 8 Dec 1784, bapt.
24 Apr 1785. Sponsor: widow Elisabeth Mayers.
Philipp, of Georg Snake and wife Elisabeth, b. 2 Apr 1785, bapt. 24 Apr 1785.
Sponsors: Philipp Losch and wife Maria.
Michael, of Michael Wolf and wife Elisabeth, b. 1 Mar 1785, bapt. 28 Apr 1785.
Sponsors: the parents.
John, of James Cooper and wife Catharina, b. 28 Feb 1785, bapt. 26 Apr 1785.
Sponsors: the parents.
Esther, of Johann Jeremias and wife Jean, b. 11 Nov 1783, bapt. 28 Apr 1785.
Sponsor: the mother.
Anna Eva, of Caspar Dunckelmeyer and wife Anna Eva, b. 20 Mar 1785,bapt.
28 Apr 1785. Sponsor: the mother.
Maria, of Johann Seidelmann and wife Catharina, b. 13 Apr 1785, bapt. 1 Mar
1785. Sponsors: Phil. Seidelmann and wife Maria.
Maria Louisa, of Christoph Becker and wife Catharina, b. 17 Apr 1785, bapt.
1 May 1785. Sponsors: Elisabeth Kreuter(in), and Paul Caspar Briton and
wife Susanna Louisa.
Heinrich, of Heinrich Depperwin and wife Margareta, b. 28 Feb 1785, bapt.
1 May 1785. Sponsors: the parents.
Elisabeth, of Johann Edelmann and wife Sarah, b. 26 Jan 1785, bapt. 1 May
1785. Sponsors: Georg Kress and wife Elisabeth.
Leonhard, of Fridrich Kessler and wife Anna, b. 21 Feb 1785, bapt. 1 May 1785.
Sponsors: the father, and Elisab. Baff(in)?.
Johann, of Leonhard Eger and wife Charlotta, b. 4 Apr 1785, bapt. 1 May 1785.
Sponsors: Christoph Miller and Marg. Bender.
William, of John Silber and wife Christina, b. 27 Apr 1785, bapt. 8 May 1785.
Sponsors: John Annear? and wife Elisabeth.
Jacob, of Jacob Hermann and wife Maria Barbara, b. 20 Aug 1784, bapt. 9 May
1785. Sponsors: Jacob Raesler and wife (name not given).
Anna Dorothea, of Martin Reinhard and wife Anna, b. 21 Feb 1785, bapt.
15 May 1785. Sponsors: Georg Simon Brunner and wife Anna Dorothea.
Maria, of Georg Schneider and wife Margareta, b. 1 May 1785, bapt. 15 May
1785. Sponsors: Andreas Walcker and wife Maria.
Philippina, of Fridrich Kehlhefer and wife Margareta, b. 2 May 1785, bapt.
15 May 1785. Sponsors: Georg Blim and wife Philippina.
Sally, of Peter Burckhard and wife Elisabeth, b. 3 Jan 1785, bapt. 15 May 1785.
Sponsors: Margareta Ganzen and Jacob Sauber.
Jacob, of Georg Happel and wife Christina, b. 26 Nov 1784, bapt. 15 May 1785.
Sponsors: Johann Gutermann and Catharina Happel.

Georg David, of David Johns and wife Elisabeth, b. 22 Jan 1785, bapt. 16 May 1785. Sponsor: Margareta Burckhard(in).
Sally, of Heinrich Reiss and wife Hanna, b. 4 May 1785, bapt. 16 May 1785. Sponsors: Nicolaus Weber and wife Christina.
Elisabeth, of Johann Wagner and wife Elisabeth, b. 1 Dec 1784, bapt. 16 May 1785. Sponsors: the parents.
Maria Susanna, of Georg Stephans and wife Margareta, b. 28 Apr 1785, bapt. 16 May 1785. Sponsors: Jacob Schaeffer and wife Maria Elisabeth.
Maria, of Michael Billmeyer and wife Maria, b. 24 Dec 1784, bapt. 16 May 1785. Sponsor: Dorothea Krebs.
Conrad, of Georg Hembold and wife Elisabeth, b. 29 Sep 1784, bapt. 19 May 1785. Sponsors: Conrad Schütz and Anna Maria Stel___.
Jacob, of Fridr. Ulrich and wife Catharina, b. 11 Dec 1784, bapt. 21 May 1785. Sponsor: the mother.
Samuel, of Henry Stock and wife Susanna, b. 22 May 1784, bapt. 22 May 1785. Sponsors: William Clarck and wife Breilla.
Johann Georg, of Georg Bardeck and wife Catharina, b. 20 Sep 1784, bapt. 2 May 1785. Sponsors: Johann Wilkens and wife (name not given).
Margareta, of Edward Laske and wife Catharina, b. 24 Apr 1785, bapt. 24 May 1785. Sponsors: Jacob Mayer and wife Elisabeth.
Heinrich, of Adam Rex and wife Anna Maria, b. 18 May 1785, bapt. 26 May 1785. Sponsors: Heinrich Steller and wife Anna Margar.
A child of (first name not given Stinchmann, bapt. 27 May 1785. (No other information given.)
Maria, of Rudolph Nagel and wife Susanna, b. 12 May 1785, bapt. 29 May 1785. Sponsors: Lorenz Herbert and wife Margareta.
Christian, of Georg Dürr and wife Catharina, b. 8 Apr 1785, bapt. 29 May 1785. Sponsors: the parents.
A child (name not given) of Wilhelm Scheaff, Sr., bapt. 29 May 1785. (No other information given.)
Juliana, of Heinrich Mayer and wife Maria, b. 4 Apr 1785, bapt. 30 May 1785. Sponsors: the parents.
Georg, of Johann Meidinger and wife Elisabeth, b. 29 Apr 1785, bapt. 30 May 1785. Sponsors: the parents.
Jacob, of Leonhard Lutz and wife Magdalena, b. 12 Dec 1784, bapt. 31 May 1785. Sponsors: Jacob Sailer and wife Maria.
Georg Michael, of Heinrich Haffner and wife Anna Maria, b. 15 May 1785, bapt. 31 May 1785. Sponsors: Georg Krebs and wife Dorothea.
Maria, of Johann Weitmann and wife Margareta, b. 11 May 1785, bapt. 2 Jun 1785. Sponsors: the parents.
Johann Georg, of Martin Stepp and wife Catharina, b. 28 Apr 1785, bapt. 5 Jun 1785. Sponsors: Joh. Georg Seyfferheld and wife Christina Elisabeth.
Georg Christian, of Philipp Kalckbrenner and wife Maria, b. 18 May 1785, bapt. 5 Jun 1785. Sponsors: Georg Butz and wife Margareta.
Johann, of Martin Rebeley and wife Clara, b. 5 Apr 1785, bapt. 5 Jun 1785. Sponsors: the parents.
Elisabeth, of Adam Rebley and wife Maria, b. in 1776, bapt. 5 Jun 1785. Sponsors: Martin Rebley and wife Clara.

Christiana Catharina, of Joh. Albert and wife Anna Maria, b. 17 May 1785, bapt. 5 Jun 1785. Sponsors: Reinhard Uhl and wife Christina Catharina.

Sarah, of Leonhard Rost and wife Maria Christina, b. 28 May 1785, bapt. 5 Jun 1785. Sponsors: Andreas Lex and wife Maria Magdalena.

Johann Andreas, of Johann Andreas Rohr and wife Maria Christina, b. 27 May 1785, bapt. 11 Jun 1785. Sponsors: the parents.

Johann Caspar, of Johann Caspar Falck and wife Helena, b. 7 Jun 1785, bapt. 12 Jun 1785. Sponsor: (first name not given) Wully.

Elisabeth, of Thomas Chillingsworth and wife Rosina, b. 29 Jan 1785, bapt. 10 Jun 1785. Sponsors: Ludwig Gallinger and wife Maria Catharina.

Catharina Elisabeth, of Andreas Lapp and wife Anna Dorothea, b. 5 Jun 1785, bapt. 11 Jun 1785.

Elisabeth, of Philipp Stout and wife Margareta, b. 23 May 1785, bapt. 12 Jun 1785. Sponsors: Andreas Beck and wife Barbara.

Johann Heinrich, of Johann Georg Hess and wife Anna Margar., b. 3 Jun 1785, bapt. 12 Jun 1785. Sponsors: Johann Dudel and wife Susanna.

Johann Jacob, of Isaak Stoh and wife Anna Regina, b. 26 Apr 1785, bapt. 12 Jun 1785. Sponsors: Johann Zacharias Schneider and wife Anna Eva.

Samuel, of Samuel Gardner and wife Charlotta, b. 11 Mar 1785, bapt. 12 Jun 1785. Sponsors: Adam Koshert and wife Margareta.

Georg, of Georg Janus and wife Margareta, b. 18 May 1785, bapt. 14 Jun 1785. Sponsors; the parents.

Georg, of Gottfried Bender and wife Sarah, birthdate not given, bapt. 14 Jun 1785. Sponsors: Georg Reboldt and Margareta Reboldt(in).

Maria, of Johann Haens and wife Elisabeth, b. in Apr 1780, bapt. 14 Jun 1785. Sponsor: Susanna Rosch(in).

Johann, of Johann Haens and wife Elisabeth, b. 27 Sep 1781, bapt. 14 Jun 1785. Sponsor: the father.

Albert, of Johann Haens and wife Elisabeth, b. 27 Apr 1785, bapt. 14 Jun 1785. Sponsor: Catharina Lutz.

Johann, of Fridrich Linck and wife Barbara, b. 1 Jun 1785, bapt. 19 Jun 1785. Sponsors: Johann Schreyer and wife Catharina.

Johann, of Johann Schreyer and wife Catharina, b. 24 May 1785, bapt. 19 Jun 1785. Sponsors: Fridrich Linck and wife Barbara.

Jacob, of Fridrich Mayer and wife Catharina, b. 18 May 1785, bapt. 19 Jun 1785. Sponsors: Bartholomae Schaetzlein and wife Anna.

Johann, of Philipp Klein and wife Elisabeth, b. 2 Jun 1785, bapt. 19 Jun 1785. Sponsors: Johann Hoefflein and wife Catharina.

Maria, of Fridrich Reibley and wife Elisabeth, (birth date not given), bapt. 19 Jun 1785. Sponsors: Johann Sonnleiter and wife Maria.

Clara, of Fridrich Breuninger and wife Christina, b. 7 Jun 1785, bapt. 19 Jun 1785. Sponsors: David Niess and wife Clara.

Anna Maria, of Johann Hef(f)t and wife Catharina, b. 29 Feb 1785, bapt. 19 Jun 1785. Sponsor: Anna Maria Frey(in).

Rebecca, of Mansfield Banton and wife Elisabeth, b. 30 May 1785, bapt. 19 Jun 1785. Sponsors: Charles Hake and Liddy Hirst.

Michael, of Michael Schubert and wife Elisabeth, b. 4 Jun 1785, bapt, 22 Jun 1785. Sponsors: Fridrich Heiler and wife Christina.

Elisabeth, of Johann Peter Oster and wife Elisab. Cathar., b. 18 Jun 1785, bapt.
24 Jun 1785. Sponsors: Johann Schlaechter and wife Elisabeth.
Johann, of Joh. Michael Hans (deceased) and wife Susanna, b. 4 Jun 1785, bapt.
26 Jun 1785. Sponsors: Johann Heiler and wife Susanna.
Catharina, of Martin Die[t]z and wife Sabina Margar., b. 25 Apr 1785, bapt.
26 Jun 1785. Sponsors: Georg Hartmann and wife Catharina.
Elisabeth, of Caspar Seybert and wife Elisabeth, b. 2 Jun 1785, bapt. 26 Jun
1785. Sponsors: the parents.
Jeany, of Jeremias Kehl and wife Elisabeth, b. 11 Apr 1785, bapt. 26 Jun 1785.
Sponsors: the parents.
Hanna, of Wilhelm Kerls and wife Margareta (who died), b. 14 Jun 1785, bapt.
26 Jun 1785. Sponsors: Thomas Haal and wife Hanna.
Johann Peter, of Jeremias Thiel (deceased) and wife Maria Rosina, b. 11 Jun
1785, bapt. 26 Jun 1785. Sponsors: Peter Staut and wife Anna Barbara.
Thomas, of Samuel Napp and wife Rebecca, b. 15 May 1785, bapt. 26 Jun
1785. Sponsor: Elisabeth Trautmann.
Eve Margareta, of Abraham Walters and wife Maria, b. 18 Jun 1785, bapt.
28 Jun 1785. Sponsors: Andreas Beck and wife Eva Margareta.
Sarah, of Thomas Themblin and wife Rebecca, b. 26 Oct 1784, bapt. 28 Jun
1785. Sponsors: Michael Wartmann and wife Sarah.
James, of Valentin Wenholz and wife Anna, b. 9 Apr 1782, bapt. 28 Jun 1785.
Sponsors: Heinrich Dason and wife Margareta.
Elisabeth, of Valentin Wenholz and wife Anna, b. 17 Jun 1785, bapt. 28 Jun
1785. Sponsors: same as above.
Christina Elisabeth, of Heinrich Mayer and wife Catharina, b. 18 Jun 1785, bapt.
28 Jun 1785. Sponsors: the parents.
Georg, of Jacob Geiger and wife Catharina, b. 14 Jun 1785, bapt. 1 Jul 1785.
Sponsors: Georg Weiss and wife Susanna.
Johann, of Melchior Lehrer and wife Maria, b. 3 Feb 1785, bapt. 3 Jul 1785.
Sponsors: the parents.
Maria, of Jacob Krieger and wife Maria Eva, b. 17 Jun 1785, bapt. 3 Jul 1785.
Sponsors: the parents.
Susanna, of Fridrich Anthony and wife Susanna, b. 11 Jun 1785, bapt. 3 Jul
1785. Sponsors: Jacob Anthony and Susanna Laud (or Land).
Maria, of Johann Stock and wife Elisabeth, b. 29 May 1785, bapt. 3 Jul 1785.
Sponsors: Johann Hinckel and wife Christina.
Georg, of Nicolaus Brum and wife Anna Maria, b. 19 Mar 1785, bapt. 6 Jul
1785. Sponsors: the parents.
Maria, of Johann Stock and wife Maria Elisabeth, b. 29 May 1785, bapt. 7 Jul
1785. Sponsors: Johann Hinckel and wife Christina.
Jacob, of Jacob Mercker and wife Elisabeth, b. 30 Jun 1785, bapt. 7 Jul 1785.
Sponsors: Ehrhard Miller and wife Barbara.
Catharina, of Thomas Lehmann and wife Catharina, b. 18 Aug 1777, bapt. 9 Jul
1785. Sponsors: Caspar Strubel and wife Catharina.
Elisabeth, of Thomas Lehmann and wife Catharina, b. 18 Sep 1779, bapt. 9 Jul
1785. Sponsors: same as above.
Caspar, of Thomas Lehmann and wife Catharina, b. 8 Jun 1780, bapt. 9 Jul
1785. Sponsors: same as above.

Nancy, of Thomas Lehmann and wife Catharina, b. 20 Nov 17_82_, bapt. 9 Jul 1785. Sponsors: same as above.

Thomas, of Thomas Lehmann and wife Catharina, b. in Mar 1784, bapt. 9 Jul 1785. Sponsors: same as above.

Catharina, of John Adams and wife Margareta, b. 14 Jun 1785, bapt. 10 Jul 1785. Sponsors: Peter Kraf(f)t and dau. Catharina.

Johann Philipp, of Jacob Hammerbach and wife Maria Susanna, b. 3 Jul 1785, bapt. 17 Jul 1785. Sponsors: Philipp Volckroth and wife Barbara.

Margareta, of Christian Bock and wife Maria, b. 11 Jun 1785, bapt. 17 Jul 1785. Sponsors: Bernhard Bock and wife Maria.

Polly, of Philipp Neuhauss and wife Juliana, b. 30 Jun 1785, bapt. 17 Jul 1785. Sponsors: Jacob Walter and wife Maria.

Heinrich, of Johann Kohp and wife Maria, b. 16 Jun 1785, bapt. 17 Jul 1785. Sponsors: the parents.

Sarah,of Mathias Brooks and wife Rose Hanna [Rosanna], b. in Oct 17_79_, bapt. 17 Jul 1785. Sponsors: Fridrich Reinbot(h) and Christina Louisa Kres__.

Barbara, of Christian Miller and wife Maria Catharina, b. 11 Jul 1785, bapt. 17 Jul 1785. Sponsors: Elias Fischer and wife Elisabeth.

Georg, of Andreas Bauer and wife Barbara, b. 9 Jul 1785, bapt. 19 Jul 1785. Sponsors: Georg Fischer and wife Elisabeth.

Sarah Elisabeth, of Johann Hoel[t]zel and wife Catharina, b. 25 Jun 1785, bapt. 24 Jul 1785. Sponsors: the parents.

Abraham, of Paul Scherratin [Sheridan?] and wife Hanna, b. 25 Jun 1785, bapt. 24 Jul 1785. Sponsors: Abraham Scherratin and wife (name not given).

Jacob, of Jacob Likenham and wife Catharina, b. 19 Mar 1785, bapt. 24 Jul 1785. Sponsor: Maria Neu.

Gottfried, of Gottlieb Lehnof and wife Anna Margar., b. 23 Jul 1785, bapt. 24 Jul 1785. Sponsors: the parents.

Georg, of Georg Vogel and wife Dorothea, b. 23 Dec 1784, bapt. 26 Jul 1785. Sponsors: August Kaget and wife Maria.

Elisabeth, of Abel Abraham Morris and wife Catharina, b. 17 Aug 1784, bapt. 28 Jul 1785. Sponsor: Elisabeth (surname not given).

Maria, of Johann Stohe and wife Barbara, b. 10 Jul 1785, bapt. 28 Jul 1785. Sponsors: Joh. Georg Stohe and wife Barbara.

Henrietta, of Johann Lenckfelder and wife Anna Cath., b. 22 May 1785, bapt. 29 Jul 1785. Sponsor: Henrietta Hammond.

Elisabeth, of Heinrich Hof(f)mann and wife Margareta, b. 5 Jul 1785, bapt. 30 Jul 1785. Sponsors: Johann Schü[t]z and wife Margareta.

Christina Charlotta, of Christoph Fridr. Tieffenbach and wife Anna Maria, b. 16 Jul 1785, bapt. 31 Jul 1785. Sponsors: Christian Braun and [wife] Charlotta

Rebecca, of Jacob Kitz and wife Elisabeth, b. 27 Jul 1785, bapt. 31 Jul 1785. Sponsors: Georg Kitz, Sr., and wife Apellonia.

Maria, of Johann Georg Kitz and wife Maria, b. 8 Jul 1785, bapt. 31 Jul 1785. Sponsors: Georg Kitz, Sr., and wife Apellonia.

Georg Caspar, of Ludwig Schauf(f)ly and wife Susanna, b. 13 Jul 1785,bapt. 31 Jul 1785. Sponsors: Caspar Seyf(f)erheld and wife Elisabeth.

Caspar, of Jacob Kroener and wife Susann, b. 27 Jul 1785, bapt. 1 Aug 1785.
Sponsors: Caspar Steubel and wife Catharina.

Catharina, (twin), of Jacob Sohns and wife Catharina, b. 27 Jul 1785, bapt.
2 Aug 1785. Sponsors: Philipp Seidelmann and wife Anna Maria.

Anna Maria, (twin), of Jacob Sohns and wife Catharina, b. 27 Jul 1785, bapt.
2 Aug 1785. Sponsors: same as above.

Johann, of Jacob Wolf(f) and wife Elisabeth, b. 15 Jan 1785, bapt. 4 Aug 1785.
Sponsor: the mother.

Peter, of Johann Kuhn and wife Elisabeth, b. 23 Jun 1785, bapt. 7 Aug 1785.
Sponsors: the father, and Elisabeth Kammer.

Johann, of Johann Haertlein and wife Gertraut, b. 20 Jul 1785, bapt. 7 Aug 1785.
Sponsors: the parents.

Fridrich, of Heinrich Wahl and wife Justina, b. 18 Jul 1785, bapt. 7 Aug 1785.
Sponsors: Fridrich Vogel and wife Catharina.

Johanna (twin), of William Wire and wife Elisabeth, b. 4 Dec 1784, bapt.
11 Aug 1785. Sponsor: Elisabeth Atkinson.

Elisabeth, (twin), of William Wire and wife Elisabeth, b. 4 Dec 1784, bapt.
11 Aug 1785. Sponsor: same as above.

Elisabeth, of Valentin Krieg and wife Maria Eva, b. 30 Jul 1785, bapt. 18 Aug
1785. Sponsors: Fridrich Die[t]z and wife Christina.

Salome, of Salomon Die[t]z and wife Barbara, b. 30 Jul 1785, bapt. 13 Aug
1785. Sponsors: Valentin Krieg and wife Maria Eva.

Abigail, of Johann Stein and wife Margareta, 23 Jul 1785, bapt. 14 Aug 1785.
Sponsors: Fridrich Schwar[t]z and wife Abigail.

Georg Adam, of Thomas Dixon and wife Catharina, b. 21 Jun 1785, bapt.
13 Aug 1785. Sponsors: Michael Scharf(f) and wife Susanna.

Christina, of Carl Dupont and wife Johanna, b. 24 Jul 1785, bapt. 14 Aug 1785.
Sponsors: Johann Stadelmann and wife Christina.

Rebecca, of Christian Schaeffer and wife Dorothea, b. 13 Jun 1785, bapt.
14 Aug 1785. Sponsors: the parents.

Wilhelm, of Peter Mayers and wife Maria, b. 3 Aug 1785, bapt. 14 Aug 1785.
Sponsors: Christian Schaeffer and wife Dorothea.

Catharina Elisab., of Georg Keidel and wife Elisabeth, b. 22 Jul 1785, bapt.
14 Aug 1785. Sponsors: Heinrich Pot(h) and wife Catharina.

Charlotta, of Adam Funck and wife Margareta, b. 31 Jul 1785, bapt. 14 Aug
1785. Sponsor: Charlotta Gress(in).

Georg Jacob, of Conrad Seybert and wife Christina, b. 1 Aug 1785, bapt. 14 Aug
1785. Sponsors: Jacob Frey and wife Maria Veronica.

Jacob, of Elisas Joy and wife Barbara, b. 2 Oct 1782, bapt. 15 Aug 1785.
Sponsors: James Joy and wife Eleonora.

James (twin), of Elias Joy and wife Barbara, b. 13 Nov 1784, bapt. 15 Aug 1785.
Sponsors: Daniel Pohlmann and wife Sophia Catharina.

Eleonora (twin), of Elias Joy and wife Barbara, b. 13 Nov 1784, bapt. 15 Aug
1785. Sponsors: same as above.

Elijah, of James Joy and wife Eleonora, b. 25 Nov 1774, bapt. 15 Aug 1785.
(Sponsors not given.)

Peter, of James Joy and wife Eleonora, b. 28 Mar 1771, bapt. 15 Aug 1785.
(Sponsors not given.)

Maria Magdalena, of Johann Künzler and wife Magdalena, b. 14 Nov 1784, bapt. 15 Aug 1785. Sponsors: Balthasar Künzler and wife Maria Elisab.

Johann, of Johann Baum and wife Nancy, b. 29 Jul 1785, bapt. 20 Aug 1785. Sponsors: Johann Wilhelm Schüb and Maria Bender.

Susanna, of Johann Martin Haertle and wife Margareta, b. 13 Jul 1785, bapt. 28 Aug 1785. Sponsors: the parents.

Maria, of Jacob Hei[t]z and wife Anna, b. 14 Aug 1785, bapt. 28 Aug 1785. Sponsors: Maria Camp and Wilhelm Gauss (or Hauss).

Conrad, of Georg Escher and wife Elisab. Hanna, b. 16 Aug 1785, bapt. 28 Aug 1785. Sponsors: Conrad Reiss and wife Hanna.

Maria, of Jacob Trion and wife Elisabeth, b. 14 Aug 1785, bapt 28 Aug 1785. Sponsors: Ludwig Rosch and Maria Teichel.

Veronica, of Peter Klein and wife Maria, b. 18 Aug 1785, bapt. 28 Aug 1785. Sponsors: Mathias Poth and wife Veronica.

Maria, of James Moddick and wife Elisabeth, b. 17 Aug 1785, bapt. 28 Aug 1785. Sponsor: the mother.

Elisabeth, of Johann Weber and wife Anna Eva, b. 25 Sep 1784, bapt. 29 Aug 1785. Sponsors: Thomas Griffith and wife Elisab.

A child of Adam Zantzinger, bapt. 29 Aug 1785 (no other information given).

Hanna, of Georg Habacher and wife Maria, b. 12 Aug 1785, bapt. 31 Aug 1785. Sponsors: Philipp Wager and wife Hanna.

Jacob, of Jacob Christler and wife Maria, b. 4 Aug 1785, bapt. 26 Aug 1785. Sponsors: the father, and (her first name not given) Weber(in).

Elisabeth, of Martin Bohreff and wife Catharina, b. 19 Aug 1785, bapt. 2 Sep 1785. Sponsor: Elisabeth Carpenter.

Sarah, of Adam Rebley and wife Maria, b. 28 Jan 1785, bapt. 3 Sep 1785. Sponsors: Christoph Hartranft and wife Elisabeth.

Elisabeth, of Henrich Spiel and wife Barbara, b. 28 Aug 1785, bapt. 4 Sep 1785. Sponsors: Georg Spiel and wife Elisabeth.

Johann Wilhelm, of Elias Frey and wife Maria, b. 10 Aug 1785, bapt. 4 Sep 1785. Sponsors: Michael Rehn and Maria Schmidt(in).

Sarah, of Adam Keller and wife Maria, b. 5 Aug 1785, bapt. 6 Sep 1785. Sponsors: Jacob Schubert and Sarah (last name crossed out).

Anna Maria, of Johann Walter and wife Margareta, b. 18 Aug 1785, bapt. 8 Sep 1785. Sponsors: the mother, and Barbara Kochendoerfer.

Anna Maria, of Conrad Ott and wife Magdalena, b. 1 Jul 1785, bapt. 9 Sep 1785. Sponsors: Georg Ott and Anna Maria Lohra.

Christian, of Johann Bender and wife Susanna, b. 27 Aug 1785, bapt. 11 Sep 1785. Sponsors: Johann Christian Jung and wife Carolina.

Johann, of Wolf(f)gang Hof(f)mann and wife Maria Philippina, b. 28 Aug 1785, bapt. 11 Sep 1785. Sponsors: Gottfried Weiland and wife Catharina.

Margareta, of Phil. Reibold and wife Elisabeth, b. 18 Aug 1785, bapt. 11 Sep 1785. Sponsors: Peter Treitz and wife Margareta.

Johann, of Neal Martin and wife Maria, b. 4 Feb 1785, bapt. 11 Sep 1785. Sponsors: Thomas Sterges? and Caty Ely.

Margareta, of Johann Radler and wife Margarta, b. 4? Aug 1785, bapt. 11 Sep 1785. Sponsors: Michael Ehrhard and wife Margareta.

Isaack, of Ludwig Bender and wife Margareta, b. 1 Dec 1784, bapt. 11 Sep 1785. Sponsors: Wilhelm Will and wife Elisab.

Johann, of Johann Landle and wife Maria, b. 1 Aug 1785, bapt. 11 Sep 1785. Sponsors: the parents.

Johann, of Georg Prinz and wife Magdalena, b. 13 Apr 1785, bapt. 4 Sep 1785. Sponsors: Jacob Prinz and wife Barbara.

Johann, of Johann Specht and wife Catharina, b. 7 Sep 1785, bapt. 14 Sep 1785. Sponsors: the parents.

Elisabeth, of Fridrich Yesch and wife Catharina, b. 8 Sep 1785, bapt. 16 Sep 1785. Sponsors: Johann Lehr and wife Catharina.

Johann Carl, of Carl Miller and wife Anna Barbara, b. 9 Sep 1785, bapt. 18 Sep 1785. Sponsors: Johann Kittler and wife Susanna.

Johann, of Lucas Bettenhaus and wife Catharina, b. 12 Sep 1785, bapt. 18 Sep 1785. Sponsors: Johann Dihm and wife Maria.

Georg, of Georg Treuer and wife Salome, b. 27 Aug 1785, bapt. 18 Sep 1785. Sponsors: Nicolaus Rehb and wife Christina Regina.

Magdalena, of Nicolaus Klein and wife Margareta, b. 7 Sep 1785, bapt.. 18 Sep 1785. Sponsor: Magdalena Duffie.

Catharina, of Georg Krieg and wife Catharina, b. 28 Aug 1785, bapt. 18 Sep 1785. Sponsors: the parents.

Johann Heinrich, of Johann Nuske and wife Maria Elisab., b. in Sep 1785, bapt. 21 Sep 1785. Sponsors: Heinrich Herrmann and wife Maria.

Heinrich, of Joh. Schneider and wife Margareta, b. 14 Sep 1785, bapt. 22 Sep 1785. Sponsors: the parents.

Elisabeth Regina, of Georg Bastian and wife Maria Eva, b. 8 Sep 1785, bapt. 24 Sep 1785. Sponsors: Georg Vogel and wife Elisabeth.

Susanna, of Christian Lutz and wife Susanna, b. 10 Aug 1785, bapt. 29 Sep 1785. Sponsors: Phil. Pfannekuch and wife Cathar.

Johann Gottfried Philip, of Johann Graeb and wife Maria Philippina, b. 12 Sep 1785, bapt. 30 Sep 1785. Sponsor: the mother.

Georg, of Wilhelm Weber and wife Elisabeth, b. 18 Sep 1785, bapt. 2 Oct 1785. Sponsors: Georg Reinhard and wife Magdalena.

Maria, of Heinrich Benner and wife Catharina, b. 20 Sep 1785, bapt. 2 Oct 1785. Sponsors: Fridrich Feltebaum and wife Maria.

Anna Catharina, of Georg Adam Becker and wife Anna Catharina, b. 13 Sep 1785, bapt. 2 Oct 1785. Sponsors: Christoph Becker and wife Anna Catharina.

Maria, of Andreas Hay and wife Rahel, b. 9 Jul 1785, bapt. 2 Oct 1785. Sponsors: the parents.

Georg, of Georg Schoen and wife Maria, b. 2 Sep 1785, bapt. 1 Oct 1785. Sponsor: Caspar Schoen.

Hanna, of Georg Piessman and wife Catharina, b. 17 Sep 1785, bapt. 2 Oct 1785. Sponsors: (first name not given) Mayer and wife Hanna.

Andreas, of Andreas Rot(h) and wife Anna Maria, b. 14 Aug 1785, bapt. 2 Oct 1785. Sponsors: Johann Fachs and wife Margareta.

Johann, of Christoph Baierle and wife Elisabeth, b. 13 Sep 1785, bapt. 2 Oct 1785. Sponsors: the parents.

Peter, of Peter Adam and wife Magdalena, b. 5 Sep 1785, bapt. 2 Oct 1785.
Sponsors: the parents.
Catharina, of Johann Esch and wife Margareta, b. 25 Jan 1785, bapt. 2 Oct 1785.
Sponsors: the parents.
David, of David Suter and wife Martha, b. 3 Oct 1785, bapt. the same day.
Sponsors: the father, and Juliana Albrecht(in).
Johann, of Jacob Kraf(f)t and wife Elisabeth, b. 14 Sep 1785, bapt. 9 Oct 1785.
Sponsors: Johann Schaeffer and Susanna Miller.
Barbara, of Adam Schiefferer and wife Dorothea Barbara, b. 27 Sep 1785, bapt.
9 Oct 1785. Sponsors: the father, and Barbara Strauss.
Susanna Maria, of Heinrich Herberger and wife Susanna, b. 11 Sep 1785, bapt.
9 Oct 1785. Sponsors: Georg Miltenberger and wife Catharina.
Anna Maria, of Peter Weit and wife Susanna, b. 5 Sep 1785, bapt. 9 Oct 1785.
Sponsors: Andreas Bertsch and wife Anna Maria.
Johann, of Johann Miller and wife Maria, b. 25 Sep 1785, bapt. 14 Oct 1785.
Sponsors: the parents.
Anna Maria, of Georg Fridr. Vogel and wife Catharina, b. 4 Oct 1785, bapt.
16 Oct 1785. Sponsors: Johann Reimel and wife Elisabeth.
Catharina, of William Burckit and wife Maria, b. 1 Dec 1785, bapt. 16 Oct 1785.
Sponsors: William Henderson and wife Catharina.
Jacob, of Jaocb Leap and wife Anna, b. 18 Sep 1785, bapt. 16 Oct 1785.
Sponsors: Jacob Prinz and wife Barbara.
Maria, of John Reyley and wife Salome, b. 20 Sep 1785, bapt. 18 Oct 1785.
Sponsors: Georg Leib and wife Dorothea.
Peter, of Abraham Grandson and wife Agness, b. 4 Nov 1781, bapt. 16 Oct
1785. Sponsors: Jacob Schroeder and wife Juliana.
Georg, of Abraham Grandson and wife Agness, b. 16 Jul 1785, bapt. 16 Oct
1785. Sponsors: same as above.
Christian, of Phil. Ehwald and wife Hanna, b. 14 Oct 1785, bapt. 19 Oct 1785.
Sponsors: Christian Fleischer and wife Dorothea.
Molly, of Peter Saarmann and wife Margaret, b. 1 Dec 1784, bapt. 20 Oct 1785.
Sponsors: Anna Maria Saarmann and son Martin.
Catharina, of Michael Immel and wife Catharina, b. 6 Oct 1785, bapt. 20 Oct
1785. Sponsors: Thomas Fischer and wife Elisabeth.
John Samuel, of Philipp Jung and wife Elisabeth, b. 24 Sep 1785, bapt. 23 Oct
1785. Sponsors: Peter Jung and wife Magdalena.
Georg, of Peter Kress and wife Rosina, b. 3 Oct 1785, bapt. 23 Oct 1785.
Sponsors: Jacob Deiss and wife Dorothea.
Elisabeth, of Francis Lescher and wife (name not given), b. 13 Sep 1785, bapt.
23 Oct 1785. Sponsors: the parents.
Jacob, of Daniel Johns and wife Elisabeth, b. 25 Jul 1785, bapt. 23 Oct 1785.
Sponsors: Jacob Nonnecker and wife Catharina.
Elisabeth, of Carl Geissler and wife Catharina, b. 27 Jul 1785, bapt. 23 Oct
1785. Sponsors: Gottfried Kinder and wife Elisabeth.
William, of John Flowers and wife Elisabeth, b . 25 Oct 1785, bapt. the same
day. Sponsor: Barbara Stein.
Johann, of Jacob Blocher and wife Elisabeth, b. 23 Oct 1785, bapt. 26 Oct 1785.
Sponsors: Jacob Blocher and wife Elisabeth [the parents?].

Elisabeth Friderica, of Christian Hummel and wife Phebe, b. 1 Sep 1785, bapt. 28 Oct 1785. Sponsors: Jacob Alborn and wife Elisab., and Georg Weiss and wife Susanna.

Maria, Magdalena, of Heinrich Krammle and wife Sophia, b. 17 Sep 1785, bapt. 29 Oct 1785. Sponsors: Thomas Krammle and wife Magdalena.

Wilhelm, of Johann Pfeil and wife Philippina, b. 7 Oct 1785, bapt. 30 Oct 1785. Sponsors: the father, and widow Philippina Christler.

Jacob, of Jacob Kessler and wife Catharina, b. 30 Sep 1785, bapt. 30 Oct 1785. Sponsors: Jacob Weisert and wife Elisabeth.

Elisabeth, of Franz Wilhelm Hetmansberger and wife Maria Magdalena, b. 6 Oct 1785, bapt. 30 Oct 1785. Sponsors: Philipp Klein and wife Elisabeth.

Johann, of Jacob Schnell and wife Elisabeth,, b. 16 Jul 1785, bapt. 1 Nov 1785. Sponsors: the parents.

Anna Barbara, of Adam Mayer and wife Hanna, b. 24 Oct 1785, bapt. 3 Nov 1785. Sponsor: Barbara Burckhard.

Anna Catharina, of Andreas Jung and wife Catharina, b. 25 Oct 1785, bapt. 3 Nov 1785. Sponsor: widow Margareta Jung(in).

Hanna, of Heinrich Knerr and wife Elisabeth, b. 25 Oct 1785, bapt 6 Nov 1785. Sponsors: the parents.

Anna, of Jacob Reiser and wife Eva Christina, b. 12 Oct 1785, bapt. 6 Nov 1785. Sponsors: Jacob Riess and wife Maria.

Elisabeth, of Peter Bingemann and wife Maria Rosina, b. 14 Aug 1785, bapt. 6 Nov 1785. Sponsors: Christian Schwar[t]z and Cath. Reiser(in).

Anna Catharina, of Anton Eberhard and wife Philippina, b. 22 Oct 1785, bapt. 6 Nov 1785. Sponsors: Philipp Heinrich Diel and Elis. München.

Johann, of Michael Huber and wife Maria, b. 16 Oct 1785, bapt. 6 Nov 1785. Sponsors: Johann Hempel and wife Elisabeth.

Catharina Lovisa, of Hilarius Becker and wife Maria, b. 7 Oct 1785, bapt. 6 Nov 1785. Sponsors: widow Catharina Becker(in) and the grandparents Paul Caspar Breton and wife Susanna Louisa.

A child (name not given), of (first name not given) Fromberger and wife Anna, b. 2 Sep 1785, bapt. 6 Nov 1785. Sponsors: (first name not given) Christler and wife Maria.

Johann Georg, of Johann Mathaeus Tollmann and wife Anna Maria, b. 30 Sep 1785, bapt. 6 Nov 1785. Sponsor: Rosina Koch(in).

Jacob, of Jacob Fimpel and wife Maria, b. 23 Sep 1785, bapt. 6 Nov 1785. Sponsors: the parents.

Johann, of Alexander Braunin and wife Maria, b. 3 Feb 1785, bapt. 6 Nov 1785. Sponsors: Margareta Kibler and Regina Merk(in).

Abraham, of Christian Reddig and wife Catharina, b. 13 Oct 1785, bapt. 13 Nov 1785. Sponsors: Abraham Bollebach and wife Catharina.

Anna Barbara, of Johann Weber and wife Maria, b. 25 Oct 1785,bapt. 13 Nov 1785. Sponsors: Johann Hoh and wife Anna Barbara.

Catharina, of Michael Goering and wife Margareta, b. 15 Oct 1785, bapt. 15 Nov 1785. Sponsor: Maria Dorothea Peil(sin).

Elisabeth, of Michael Kur[t]z and wife Elisabeth, b. 31 Oct 1785, bapt. 20 Nov 1785. Sponsors: Joh, Ulrich Schaub and wife Elisab.

Georg Gottfried, of Jacob Fridrich and wife Anna, b. 11 Nov 1785, bapt. 20 Nov 1785. Sponsors: Gottfried Mayer and wife Anna Margar.

Jacob, of Jacob Weiss and wife Christina, b. 9 Nov 1785, bapt. 20 Nov 1785. Sponsors: Jacob Fridrich and wife Eva.

Elisabeth, of Georg Richter and wife Eva, b. 15 Oct 1785, bapt. 20 Nov 1785. Sponsors: (first name not given) Schaumkessel and wife Elisabeth.

Abraham, of John Line and wife Maria, b. 22 Jun 1785, bapt. 20 Nov 1785. Sponsors: Abraham Pater and wife Maria.

Wilhelm, of Jacob Schmidt and wife Maria, b. 8 Nov 1785, bapt. 20 Nov 1785. Sponsors: Wilhelm Rudolph and wife Magdalena.

Maria, of John Copper and wife Catharina, b. 19 Sep 1785, bapt. 20 Nov 1785. Sponsors: Fridrich Schumann and wife Anna Maria.

Georg, of Georg Bickham and wife Christiana, b. 2 Nov 1785, bapt. 20 Nov 1785. Sponsors: the parents.

Anna Margareta, of Philipp Wager and wife Hanna, b. 26 Oct 1785, bapt. 24 Nov 1785. Sponsors: Christian Wir[t]z and wife Margareta.

Georg, of Johann Eysenbrey and wife Catharina, b. 18 Nov 1785, bapt. 26 Nov 1785. Sponsors: Heinrich Rathschlag and wife Maria.

Johann, of Beng_y Bates and wife Sophia, b. 10 Nov 1785, bapt. 26 Nov 1785. Sponsors: Johann Hanss and wife Elisabeth.

Hanna, of Johann Waeger and wife Sarah, b. 3 Sep 1785, bapt. 24 Nov 1785. Sponsors: Philipp Waeger and wife Hanna.

Johann, of Adam Jaeger and wife Fanny, b. 19 Oct 1785, bapt. 4 Dec 1785. Sponsors: Johann La_sht and Rebecca Jung.

Christian, of Conrad Winter and wife Maria, b. 19 Nov 1785, bapt. 4 Dec 1785. Sponsor: Christian Jauch.

Anna Maria, of Ludwig Wolf and wife Maria, .b 12 Nov 1785, bapt. 4 Dec 1785. Sponsors: the parents.

Margareta, of Christoph Herley and wife Catharina, b. 23 Oct 1785, bapt. 7 Dec 1785. Sponsor: Margareta Maxeimer.

Maria Elisabeth, of Christian Schneider and wife Maria Elisab., b. 30 Nov 1785, bapt. 10 Dec 1785. Sponsors: Georg Heinr. Spiel and wife Barbara.

Eva Barbara, of Georg Brunner and wife Catharina, b. 5 Nov 1785, bapt. 8 Dec 1785. Sponsors: Joh. Michael Goe[t]z and wife Eva Barbara.

Johann David, of William Farley and wife Elisabeth, b. 7 Dec 1785, bapt. 10 Dec 1785. Sponsors: Johann Ehrenfechter and wife Maria.

Margareta, of Christoph Peters and wife Elisabeth, b. 11 Nov 1785, bapt 10 Dec 1785. Sponsor: Margareta Crehk.

Jacob, of Christian Kempf and wife Maria, b. 25 Nov 1785, bapt. 10 Dec 1785. Sponsors: the parents.

Elisabeth Magdalena, of Joh. Stephan Schirm and wife Margareta, b. 9 Nov 1785, bapt. 10 Dec 1785. Sponsors: Jacob Behring and wife Elisab. Magdalena.

Maria, of Johann Heinr. Biehler and wife Catharina, b. 10 Nov 1785, bapt. 10 Dec 1785. Sponsors: the parents.

Georg, of Johann Steinmetz and wife Catharina, b. 7 Dec , bapt. 14 Dec 1785. Sponsors: Heinrich Helmuth and wife Barbara.

Anna Margareta, of Johann Fridr. Woelper and wife Margareta, b. 30 Nov 1785, bapt. 18 Dec 1785. Sponsors: David Huber and wife Anna.

Johann Wilhelm, of Jacob Schaeffer and wife Maria, b. 16 Nov 1785, bapt. 18 Dec 1785. Sponsors: Georg Krauskopp and wife Maria.

Johann Heinrich, of Joh. Christian Gessner and wife Magdalena, b. 5 Dec 1785, bapt. 20 Dec 1785. Sponsors: Johann Heinrich Gessner and wife Margareta.

John, of Samuel Carpenter and wife Catharina, b. 5 Nov 1785, bapt. 25 Dec 1785. Sponsors: Charl. Linnenschied and wife Margareta.

Johann Adam, of Adam Handel and wife Hanna, b. 12 Dec 1785, bapt. 26 Dec 1785. Sponsors: the parents.

Anna Maria, of Jacob Stein and wife Anna Maria, b. 25 Dec 1785, bapt. the same day. Sponsors: the parents.

Esther, of Samuel Clemens and wife Martha, b. 13 Sep 1778, bapt. 26 Dec 1785. Sponsors: Carl Linnenschied and wife Margareta.

1785, Second List
(baptisms by pastor Schmidt, from Book IV)
In the original, this list is found as a group inserted within pastor Helmuth's
1784 list of baptisms, in Book IV)

Christian, of Philip Leisten and wife Louisa, b. 19 Jun, bapt. 10 Jul 1785. Sponsors: Christian Schneider and wife A. Gottliebin.

Maria Barbara, of Johann Georg Engert and wife Maria Magdalena, b. 27 Jun 1785, bapt. 10 Jul 1785. Sponsors: Maria Barbara Schütz(in) and son Joh. Schütz.

Johanna Catharina, of Joseph Klatterbuch and wife Sophia, b. 21 Oct 1785, bapt. 16 Jul 1785. Sponsor: Johanna Christina Lapp(in).

Adam, of Adam Seibert and wife Sabina, b. 6 Jul 1785, bapt. 17 Jul 1785. Sponsors: the parents.

Agnes, of Elias Reiker and wife Sara, b. 14 Aug 1785, bapt. 20 Jul 1785. Sponsors: Henrich Riebert and wife Agnes.

Sara, of Andreas Lehr and wife Elisabeth, b. 9 Jul 1785, bapt. 27 Jul 1785. Sponsor: the mother.

Susanna, of Peter Korch and wife Elisabeth, b. 7 Apr 1785, bapt. 31 Jul 1785. Sponsors: the parents.

Margareta, of Jacob Meyer and wife Elisabeth, b. 6 Jul 1785, bapt. 31 Jul 1785. Sponsors: the father, and Margaret Backerig?

Wilhelm, of Johannes Flegel? and wife Margarete, b. 7 Jul 1785, bapt. 19 Aug 1785. Sponsors: the parents.

Catharina, of Heinrich Haalman and wife Catharina, b. 14 Jun 185, bapt. 19 Aug 1785. Sponsors: the parents.

Elisabeth, of Johann Heims and wife Ilebora, b. 22 Jul 1785, bapt. 20 Aug 1785. Sponsors: Adam Lutz and dau. Elisabeth.

Abraham, of Michael Wortman and wife Sara, b. 29 Jul 1785, bapt. 21 Aug 1785. Sponsors: Abraham Rex and wife Anna.

Maria Magdalena, of Michael Seps and wife Catharina, b. 13 Aug 1785, bapt. 28 Aug 1785. Sponsors: Martin Schweitzer and wife Mar. Magdalena.

Anna Maria, of Valentin Hofman and wife Susanna, b. 12 Jul 1785, bapt. 28 Aug 1785. Sponsors: Joh. Henzelman and wife A. Maria.

534   PHILADELPHIA GERMAN LUTHERAN CHURCH

Jacob, of Johannes Gahn and wife Margareta, b. 4 Jun 1785, bapt. 10 Sep 1785.
Sponsor: Jacob Baum.
Elisabeth, of Johannes Gahn and wife Margareta, b. 17 Sep 1782, bapt. 10 Sep
1785. Sponsor: Emanuel (surname not given).
Georg, of Johannes Gahn and wife Margareta, b. 4 Nov 1783, bapt. 10 Sep
1785. Sponsors: Wilhem Heims and wife Catharina.
Elisabeth, of Jacob Henrich and wife Agnes, b. 22 Jul 1785, bapt. 28 Aug 1785.
Sponsors: the mother, and Elisabeth Gräfly.
Philip, of Philip Jost? and wife Maria, b. 27 Aug 1785, bapt. 28 Aug 1785.
Sponsors: Jacob Kraft and Margarite Weit(h).
Catharina, of Andreas Waa[l]ker and wife Maria, b. 5 Aug 1785, bapt. 10 Sep
1785. Sponsors: Catharina Wagener(in).
Louisa, of Salomon Stenger and wife Quina, b. 17 Aug 1785, bapt. 11 Sep 1785.
Sponsors; Christian Seifert and wife Christina Margarete.
Maria, of Peter Preiss and wife Catharina, b. 13 Aug 1785, 11 Sep 1785.
Sponsor: Peter Litsch.
Catharina, of Jacob Becker and wife Barbara, b. 7 Sep 1785, bapt. 16 Sep 1785.
Sponsors: Jacob Henriegel and wife Catharina.
Eva Catahrina, of Elias Horst and wife Catharina, b. 28 Aug 1785, bapt. 1 Oct
1785. Sponsors: Peter Uxorer and wife Barbara.
Valentin, of Friedrich Gross and wife Ester, b. 3 Sep 1785, bapt. 2 Oct 1785.
Sponsors: the father, and Catharina Gross(in).
Maria, of Johann Lambart and wife Sara, b. 20 Sep 1785, bapt. 3 Oct 1785.
Sponsors: the parents.
Johannes, of Johann Schofferich and wife Anna Maria, b. 11 Mar 1783, bapt.
7 Oct 1785. Sponsors: Conrad Steund and wife Catharina.
Philip Jacob, of Jacob Omensetter and wife Elisabeth, b. 17 Nov 1784, bapt.
10 Oct 1785. Sponsors: the parents.
Michael, of Johannes Meyer and wife A. Maria, b. 5 Sep 1785, bapt. 16 Oct
1785. Sponsors: Michael Polmer and wife Catharina.
Margrete, of Jacob Miller and wife Cathar. Dorothea, b. 25 Aug 1785, bapt.
23 Oct 1785. Sponsors: Johann Friedrich Wilpert and wife Margrete.
Joseph Isaac, of Johann Conrad Schrel and wife Margrete, b. 9 Oct 178, bapt.
23 Oct 1785. Sponsors: the parents.
Johann Jacob, of Georg Sahl and wife (name not given), b. 23 Oct 1785, bapt.
25 Oct 1785. Sponsors: Jacob Schuler and wife (name not given).
Dorothea, of Christian Huber and wife Margrete, b. 17 Sep 1784, bapt. 24 Oct
1785. Sponsors: the father, and Dorothea Wa[l]ker(in).
Georg, of Georg Scherer and wife Elisabeth, b. 22 Oct 1785, bapt. 30 Oct 1785.
Sponsors: the father, and Magdalena Braun(in).
Jacob, of Jac. Seger (deceased) and wife Barbara, b. 6 Oct 1785, bapt. 31 Oct
1785. Sponsors: Jacob Keimly and wife Catharina.
Anna Maria, of Henrich Hersel and wife Barbara, b. 4 Oct 1785, bapt. 6 Nov
1785. Sponsor: Anna Maria Hermann(in).
Maria Christina, of Johann Pitt? and wife Elisabeth, b. 20 Nov 1784, bapt.
11 Nov 1785. Sponsor: Maria Christina Beckman(in)?.
Sibille, of Conrad Neischwenner and wife Sibille, b. 9 Oct 1785, bapt. 20 Nov
1785. Sponsors: Jacob Kuder? and Barbara Miller.

Susanna, of Henrich Bohn and wife Elisabeth, b. 9 Oct 1785, bapt. 18 Nov 1785.
Sponsors: the mother, and Joh. Gottlieb Bohn.
Maria Catharina, of Johannes Rugan and wife Elisabeth, b.16 Oct 1785, bapt.
19 Nov 1785. Sponsors: Michael Bartholome and wife Maria Catharina,
Maria, of Christian Schneider and wife Catharina, b. 30 Sep 1785, bapt. 20 Nov
1785. Sponsors: Jacob Schneider and wife A. Maria.
Antonius, of Gottfried Velte and wife Elisabeth, b. 1 Nov 1785, bapt. 20 Nov
1785. Sponsors: Anton Kern and wife Catharina.
Georg, of Jacob Fischer and wife Jeanne, b. 12 May 1785, bapt. 20 Nov 1785.
Sponsors: Friedrich Heiler and Catharina Metzger(in).
Elisabeth, of Wilhelm Batt(h)o and wife Elisabeth, b. 12 Nov 1785, bapt.
27 Nov 1785. Sponsors: the parents.
Michael, of Leonhard Rau and wife Anna, b. 14 Nov 1785, bapt. 4 Dec 1785.
Sponsors: Michael Oberdorf and wife Catharina.
Maria, of Bernhard Will and wife Maria, b. 17 Nov 1785, bapt. 4 Dec 1785.
Sponsors: Christian Huber and wife Margrete.
Nancy, of James Halloday and wife Margaret, b. 15 Jun 1780, bapt. 6 Nov 1785.
Sponsors: Christian Huber and wife Margrete.
Anna, of Albert Joh. Buchtman and wife Margrete, b. 27 Oct 1785, bapt. 4 Dec
1785. Sponsor: Dorothea Bernhard.
Johann, of Johann Michael Breisch and wife Maria, b. 3 Dec 1785, bapt. 12 Dec
1785. Sponsors: Casper Waal and wife Elisabeth.
Philip Jacob, of Johannes Reib and wife Susanna, b. 18 Nov 1785, bapt. 18 Dec
1785. Sponsors: Philip Jacob Lescher and wife Anna Maria
Margrete, of Henrich Meyer and wife Margrete, b. 12 Oct 1785, bapt. 25 Dec
1785. Sponsors: the father, and Catharina Kitman.
Henrich, of Georg Rhen and wife Catharina, b. 19 Dec 1785, bapt. 25 Dec 1785.
Sponsors: Henrich Meyer and Margrete Kitman.
*In the list of baptisms in 1785 at Philadelphia are found here also "a few which
belong to the congregation at Germantown," as follows:*
Elsbeth, of Johann Gordan and wife Maria, b. 18 Mar 1784, bapt. in Jul 1785.
Sponsor: Elisabeth Keil.
Jacob, of Henrich Meyer and wife Anna, b. 10 Aug 1785, bapt. 16 Oct 1785.
Sponsors: the parents.
Maria, of Johann Krieger and wife Maria, b. 2 Sep 1785, bapt. 7 Nov 1785.
Sponsors: Jacob Krieger and wife Maria.

1786, First List
(baptisms by pastor Helmuth, from Book IV)
Elisabeth, of Georg Schmidt and wife Maria Eva., b. 13 Dec 1785, bapt. 1 Jan
1786. Sponsors: Elisabeth Schmidt and Fridr. Schmidt.
Ra[c]hel, of Martin Kochersberger and wife Rosina, b. 13 Aug 1785, bapt. 1 Jan
1786. Sponsors: Georg Bastian and wife Eva.
Georg, of Andreas Geyer and wife Barbara, b. 7 Dec 1785, bapt. 1 Jan 1786.
Sponsors: Andreas Bosshard and wife Christina.
Georg Peter, of Adam Fister and wife Catharina, b. 17 Dec 1785, bapt. 1 Jan
1786. Sponsors: Georg Lochman and [his?] mother Anna Maria.

Susanna, of Philipp Klebe and wife Maria, b. 18 Dec 1785, bapt. 1 Jan 1786. Sponsors: Rudolph Nagel and wife Susanna.

Georg, of Jeremias Wahrlich and wife Elisabeth, b. 14 Nov 1785, bapt. 1 Jan 1786. Sponsors: Georg Zei[t]z and Elisabeth Witz(in).

Georg, of Andreas Epple and wife Maria, b. 20 Dec 1785, bapt. 1 Jan 1786. Sponsors: Georg Epple and wife Juliann.

Jacob, of Heinrich Moser and wife Christina, b. 5 Aug 1785, bapt. 6 Jan 1786. Sponsors: Jacob Weisert and wife Elisabeth.

Wilhelm, of Samuel Winright and wife Catharina, b. 9 Oct 1785, bapt. 12 Jan 1786. Sponsors: the mother, and Dorothea Logan.

William, of Jacob Fidler and wife Margareta, b. 18 Sep 1785, bapt. 13 Jan 1786. Sponsors: the father, and Elisabeth Fidler.

Hanna, of Heinrich Jaeger and wife Anna Barbara, b. 1 Jan 1786, bapt. 13 Jan 1786. Sponsors: Heinrich Die[t]z and Hanna Jaeger(in).

Jacob, of Jonas Cleser and wife Anna Elisabeth, b. 8 Jan 1786, bapt. 13 Jan 1786. Sponsors: Heinrich Sell and Maria Weiss.

Heinrich Christian, of Johann Wogus and wife Rebecca, b. 12 Dec 1785, bapt. 13 Jan 1786. Sponsors: Christian Oberstech and wife Anna Margareta.

Margareta, of Joseph Behringer and wife Sarah, b. 18 Nov 1785, bapt. 15 Jan 1786. Sponsors: Valentin Hagener and wife Margareta.

Johann Zacharias, of Christoph Crass and wife Maria Barbara, b. 10 Jan 1786, bapt. 15 Jan 1786. Sponsors: the parents.

Elisabeth, of Heinrich Linck and wife Magdalena, b. 31 Dec 1785, bapt. 15 Jan 1786. Sponsors: Henry Knery and wife Elisabeth.

Thomas, of John Berris and wife Sarah, b. 1 Aug 1785, bapt. 15 Jan 1786. Sponsors: Jacob Colladay and wife Sarah.

Susanna Regina, of Joh. Peter Die[t]z and wife Anna Maria, b. 14 Dec 1785, bapt. 22 Jan 1786. Sponsors: the parents.

Maria, of Johann Kalckbrenner and wife Elisabeth, b. 8 Jul 1785, bapt. 22 Jan 1785. Sponsors: the father, and Maria Pepper.

Anna Maria, of Adam Hauber and wife Hanna, b. 22 Jan 1786, bapt. 23 Jan 1786. Sponsor: widow Krebs-lampt?.

Catharina, of Johann Moser and wife Catharina, b. 13 Jan 1786, bapt. 24 Jan 1786. Sponsors: Johann Haack and wife Catharina.

Joseph, of Georg Schneider and wife Maria, b. 7 Jan 1786, bapt. 25 Jan 1786. Sponsors: Johann Braun and wife Maria.

Elisabeth, of Georg Lehmann and wife Catharina, b. 1 Jan 1786, bapt. 29 Jan 1786. Sponsors: the father, and Elisab. Lehmann.

Johann Georg, of Georg Fridrich Linck and wife Juliana Elisab., b. 22 Jan 1786, bapt. 29 Jan 1786. Sponsors: Joh. Georg Mayer and wife Susanna.

Georg, of Johann Cooper and wife Dorothea (who died), b. 15 Jan 1786, bapt. 29 Jan 1786. Sponsors: Johann Rupp and wife Dorothea.

Jacob, of Johann Reide and wife Margareta, b. 17 Jan 1786, bapt. the same day. Sponsors: the father, and Doroth. Deiss.

Michael, of John Little and wife Catharina, birthdate not given, bapt. 25 Jan 1786. Sponsors: Tobias Koenig and wife Anna Barbara.

Anna, of John Little and wife Catharina, b. 8 Aug 1785, bapt. 25 Jan 1786. Sponsors: same as above.

Johann, of John Breviehl and wife Anna Maria, b. 18 Jan 1786, bapt. 29 Jan 1786. Sponsors: John Richards and Cath. Kohlmann.

Johann, of Jacob Schubert and wife Sarah, b. 27 Dec 1785, bapt. 29 Jan 1786. Sponsors: Johann Adam Keller and wife Maria.

Johann, of Martin Ronner and wife Sophia, b. 18 Jan 1786, bapt. 5 Feb 1786. Sponsors: Johann Ronner and Maria Haussmann.

Carl, of Heinrich Lehr and wife Elisabeth, b. 21 Jan 1786, bapt. 5 Feb 1786. Sponsors: Carl Jung and wife Catharina.

Elisabeth, of Peter Burcky and wife Elisab., b. 6 Dec 1785, bapt. 5 Feb 1786. Sponsors: Georg Liess and wife Catharina.

Theobald, of Jacob Daudermann and wife Barbara, b. 20 Jan 1786, bapt. 3 Feb 1786. Sponsors: Theobald Storch and wife Regina.

Samuel, of Johann Keimle and wife Sybilla, b. 23 Nov 1785, bapt. 8 Feb 1786. Sponsors: Zacharias Lesch and wife Maria Barbara.

Joh. Mathias, of Joh. Mathias Pote and wife Veronica, b. 29 Jan 1786, bapt. 10 Feb 1786. Sponsors: the father, and Anna Maria Pot(in).

Maria, of Carl Schmidt and wife Cath. Elisab., b. 9 Dec 1785, bapt. 10 Feb 1786. Sponsors: Johann Keyler and Maria Erben.

Wilhelm, of Joh. Freymuth and wife Elisab., b. 22 Jan 1786, bapt. 1 Feb 1786. Sponsors: the parents.

Anna, of Thomas Cook and wife Maria, b. 18 Jan 1786, bapt. 12 Feb 1786. Sponsors: Johann Wildfang, Anna Thomson, and Maria Long.

Johann, of Joseph Siegfried and wife Elisab. (who died), b. 22 Jan 1786, bapt. 12 Feb 1786. Sponsors: Martin Cramp and Anna Maria Becker(in).

Georg, of Joseph Kayser and wife Maria, b. 18 Jan 1786, bapt. 12 Feb 1786. Sponsors: Georg Turner and wife Maria Susanna.

Susanna, of Georg Johy and wife Sarah, b. 18 Dec 1785, bapt. 12 Feb 1786. Sponsors: Michael Acker and wife Elisabeth.

Jacob, of Jacob Walter and wife Helena (who died?), b. 6 Jan 1786, bapt. 12 Feb 1786. Sponsors: the parents.

Nicolaus, of Jacob Noel and wife Margareta, b. 6 Feb 1786, bapt. 12 Feb 1786. Sponsors: Nicolaus Klein and wife Margareta.

Jacob, of Johann Seyfried and wife Christina, b. 9 Feb 1786, bapt. 12 Feb 1786. Sponsors: Jacob Buck and Maria Taylor.

Anna Maria, of Martin Weiss and wife Agatha, b. 15 Jan 1786, bapt. 12 Feb 1786. Sponsors: Andreas Hay and wife Anna Maria.

Johann Georg, of Carl Hay and wife Sophia, b. 30 Jan 1786, bapt. 19 Feb 1786. Sponsors: the father, and Maria Braun.

Jacob, of Jacob Frey and wife Maria, b. 29 Jan 1786, bapt. 19 Feb 1786. Sponsors: the parents.

Elisabeth, of Joh. Andreas Phil. Ludwig and wife Anna, b. 18 Feb 1786, bapt. 21 Feb 1786. Sponsors: Jacob Mercker and wife Elisabeth.

Johann David, of David Seckel and wife Maria, b. 5 Feb 1786, bapt. 26 Feb 1786. Sponsors: Georg David Seckel and wife Maria.

Elisabeth, of Jacob Kehl and wife Christina, b. 19 Feb 1786, bapt. 26 Feb 1786. Sponsors: Christoph Miller and wife Elisabeth.

Anna, of Georg Herrmann and wife Elisabeth, b. 30 Jan 1786, bapt. 26 Feb 1786. Sponsors: the father, and Anna Braun.

Jeany, of Johann Graeff and wife Maria, b. 20 Feb 1786, bapt. 27 Feb 1786. Sponsors: the father, and Jean Hall.
Charlotta, of Friedrich Vogel and wife Elisabeth, b. 3 Feb 1786, bapt. 5 Mar 1786. Sponsors: the parents.
Sarah, of Fridrich Fahltebaum and wife Maria, b. 17 Feb 1786, bapt. 5 Mar 1786. Sponsors: Martin Die[t]z and wife Sabina.
Johann, of Christoph Sanderling and wife Maria, b. 10 Feb 1786, bapt. 5 Mar 1786. Sponsor: John Grace.
Catharina, of August Kay and wife Dorothea, b. 15 Feb 1786, bapt. 5 Mar 1786. Sponsors: Fridrich Linck and wife Barbara.
Maria, of Daniel Braeutigam and wife Margar., b. 26 Jan 1786, bapt. 5 Mar 1786. Sponsors: the parents.
Ludwig, of Georg Schneider and wife Margareta, b. 19 Feb 1786, bapt. 5 Mar 1786. Sponsors: Ludwig Winckler and Catharina Schneider(in).
Johanna Rosina, of Joh. Peter Roeder and wife Friderica Dorothea, b. 24 Jan 1786, bapt. 6 Mar 1786. Sponsor: the mother.
Johann Georg, of Johann Weiss and wife Elisabeth, b. 6 Feb 1786, bapt. 6 Mar 1786. Sponsors: the parents.
Daniel, of Heinrich Dickhaut and wife Catharina, b. 30 Dec 1785, bapt. 11 Mar 1786. Sponsors: the father, and Helena Teichert.
Christiana, of Johann Phister and wife Maria Sophia (birthday not given), bapt. 11 Mar 1786. Sponsors: (first name not given) Deal and Christiana Gussmann.
Jacob, of Johann Clemmer and wife Margareta, b. 1 Feb 1786, bapt. 12 Mar 1786. Sponsors: Peter Schack and wife Catharina.
Maria, of Albert Warneck and wife Maria, b. 13 Feb 1786, bapt. 13 Mar 1786. Sponsors: Heinrich Miller and wife Maria.
Carl, of Johann Ko_e and wife Rosina Elisab., b. 6 Mar 1786, bapt 17 Mar 1786. Sponsors: Christoph Carl Behringer and wife Margareta.
Jacob, of Fridrich Heimmann and wife Catharina, b. 26 Feb 1786, bapt. 19 Mar 1786. Sponsors: Fridrich Schaumkessel and wife Elisabeth.
Adam, of Carl Dedecke and wife Maria, b. 23 Feb 1786, bapt. 19 Mar 1786. Sponsors: Adam Meyer and wife Hanna.
Johann, of Georg Gottfried and wife Elisabeth, b. 27 Feb 1786, bapt. 26 Mar 1786. Sponsor: Elisabeth Kuhn.
Wilhelm, of Adam Wagner and wife Catharina, b. 19 Feb 1786, bapt. 26 Mar 1786. Sponsors: the parents.
Wilhelm, of William Burckhard and wife Sarah, b. 26 Feb 1786, bapt. 18 Mar 1786. Sponsors: the parents.
Susanna, of Francys Cooper and wife Elisabeth, b. 1 Mar 1786, bapt. 26 Mar 1786. Sponsors: the parents.
Johann, of Andreas Fritsch and wife Maria, b. 12 Oct 1782, bapt. 26 Mar 1786. Sponsors: Phil. Kunzmann and wife Catharina.
Maria Salome, of Andreas Fritsch and wife Maria, b. 24 Feb 1786, bapt. 26 Mar 1786. Sponsors: Abraham Eichle and wife Maria.
Hanna, of Joh. Westenberger and wife Salome, b. 26 Feb 1786, bapt. 2 Apr 1786. Sponsors: Joh. Westenberger and wife Barbara.

Maria, of Carl Feicht and wife Elisabeth, b. 15 Jul 1782, bapt. 30 Mar 1786.
Sponsors: the parents.
Elisabeth, of Carl Feicht and wife Elisabeth, b. 1 Apr 1785, bapt. 30 Mar 1786.
Sponsors: the parents.
Wilhelm (twin), of Fridrich Kaltoven and wife Elisabeth, b. 23 Mar 1786, bapt.
2 Apr 1786. Sponsors: the parents.
Heinrich (twin), of Fridrich Kaltoven and wife Elisabeth, b. 23 Mar 1786, bapt.
2 Apr 1786. Sponsors: the parents.
Maria Barbara, of Johann Georg Buttler and wife Christina, b. 5 Mar 1786, bapt.
3 Apr 1786. Sponsors: Martin Sigismund Ziepold and wife Maria Barbara.
David, of David Kreider and wife Catharina, b. 27 Mar 1786, bapt. 2 Apr 1786.
Sponsors: the parents.
Maria Magdalena, of Johann Yechter and wife Dorothea, b. 21 Mar 1786, bapt.
2 Apr 1786. Sponsor: Maria Magdal. Schumacher(in), single.
Heinrich, of Johann Sharp and wife Catharina, b. 5 Feb 1786, bapt. 5 Apr 1786.
Sponsor: Heinrich Bedken.
Wilhelm, of Wilhelm Kohp and wife Maria, b. 29 Jan 1786, bapt. 9 Apr 1786.
Sponsors: Mathias Ross and Catharina Kohp.
James, of James Burck and wife Elisabeth, b. 11 Nov 1785, bapt. 9 Apr 1786.
Sponsors: Christian Vetter and Elisab. Wester(lin).
Hanna Preiss, of Georg Fridrich Alberti and wife Hanna, b. 31 Dec 1785, bapt.
9 Apr 1786. Sponsors: the parents.
Anna Maria, of Johann Creiner and wife Margareta, b. 6 Mar 1786, bapt. 9 Apr
1786. Sponsors: the father, and Barbara Fritz.
Rebecca, of Carl List and wife Maria, b. 19 Mar 1786, bapt. 9 Apr 1786.
Sponsors: Maria Weiss.
Maria, of Johann Weilemeyer and wife Barbara, b. 18 Mar 1786, bapt. 9 Apr
1786. Sponsors: the parents.
Esther, of Johann Wucherer and wife Elisabeth, b. 22 Mar 1786, bapt. 10 Apr
1786. Sponsors: the parents.
Johann Georg, of Joh. Georg Rummel and wife Maria, b. 13 Mar 1786, bapt.
11 Apr 1786. Sponsors: Johann Leckrum and wife Catharina.
Peter, of Philipp Walter and wife Catharina, b. 25 Mar 1786, bapt. 16 Apr 1786.
Sponsors: the parents.
Philipp, of Daniel Dick and wife Catharina, b. 2 Apr 1786, bapt. 16 Apr 1786.
Sponsors: Philipp Dick and wife Catharina.
Johann Michael, of Johann Metts and wife Anna Barbara, b. 16 Mar 1786, bapt.
17 Apr 1786. Sponsors: the parents.
Jacob, of Bathasar Graff and wife Catharina, b. 1 Apr 1786, bapt. 17 Apr 1786.
Sponsors: Jacob Graff and wife Sophia.
Anna Maria, of Robert Freinold (now deceased) and wife Elisabeth, b. 5 Mar
1786, bapt. 18 Apr 1786. Sponsor: the mother.
A child (name not given), of Margareta (surname not given) and Georg Ried
(illegitimate), b. 13 Apr 1786, bapt. 18 Apr 1786. (Sponsors not given.)
Anna Margareta, of Jacob Ochs and wife Barbara, b. 14 Feb 1786, bapt. 20 Apr
1786. Sponsors: the parents.
Peter, of Michael Hay and wife Maria, b. 4 Apr 1786, bapt. 23 Apr 1786.
Sponsors: Peter Mühlenberg and wife Anna.

Elisabeth, of Andreas Heid and wife Maria, b. 7 Apr 1786, bapt. 12 Apr 1786. Sponsors: Reinhard Cammer and wife Maria.

Johann, of Georg Bauer and wife Catharina, b. 7 Apr 1786, bapt. 23 Apr 1786. Sponsors: Barbara French and Johann Wagner.

Heinrich, of Ludwig Garlinger and wife Maria Cath., b. 16 Nov 1785, bapt. 30 Apr 1786. Sponsors: Michael Garlinger and wife Maria.

Susanna, of Philipp Clumberg, Jr., and wife Catharina, birthdate not given, bapt. 30 Apr 1786. Sponsors: Johann Painter and wife Susanna.

Conrad Wilhelm, of Conrad Dewitter and wife Catharina Elisabeth, b. 1 Apr 1786, bapt. 30 Apr 1786. Sponsors: Wilhelm Geiss and wife Eva.

Joseph, of Wilhelm Hockel and wife Maria Susanna, b. 23 Mar 1786, bapt. 7 May 1786. Sponsors: Joseph Faster and wife Anna Maria.

Elisabeth, of Valentin Brenneisen and wife Elisabeth, b. 23 Apr 1786, bapt. 14 May 1786. Sponsors: Peter Kraft and wife (name not given).

Nancy, of Wilhelm Trautwein, Jr., and wife Maria, b. 20 Apr 1786, bapt. 14 May 1786. Sponsor: Nancy Trautwein.

Maria Elisabeth, of Andreas Eisenhuth and wife Maria, b. 12 Mar 1786, bapt. 14 May 1786. Sponsors: Daniel Grub and dau. Maria Elisabeth.

Margareta, of Martin Perry and wife Maria, b. 17 Nov 1785, bapt. 3 May 1786. Sponsors: the parents.

Sarah, of Johann Fettenberger and wife Susanna, b. 4 May 1786, bapt. 14 May 1786. Sponsors: the father, and Sarah Lutket.

Michael, of Carl Wilhelm Nushag and wife Maria Catharina, b. 4 May 1786, bapt. 21 May 1786. Sponsors: the parents.

Catharina, of Enoch Bayley and wife Dorothea, b. 19 May 1786, bapt. 24 May 1786. Sponsors: Charles Caldwel and wife Catharina.

Charles, of Charles Robison and wife (name not given), b. 18 Feb 1786, bapt. 25 May 1786. Sponsors: Mathaeus Hohl and wife Maria Magdal.

Johann Ernst, of Heinrich Voelcker and wife Hanna, b. 29 Jan 1786, bapt. 25 May 1786. Sponsors: Johann Sophia [sic] Elsrüche.

Johann Georg, of Heinrich Klein and wife Elisabeth, b. 25 Apr 1786, bapt. 28 May 1786. Sponsors: Christoph Bayer and wife Apellonia.

Johann, of Gabriel Steinbach and wife Christina, b. 12 Feb 1786, bapt. 30 May 1786. Sponsors: Adolph Dill and wife Catharina.

Elisabeth, of Johann Sauter and wife Margareta, b. 13 Feb 1786, bapt. 4 Jun 1786. Sponsors: Georg Sterr? and [wife?] Elisabeth.

Johann, of Georg Gerlinger and wife Maria Christina, b. 28 Mar 1786, bapt. 4 Jun 1786. Sponsors: Johann Christ and Anna Diess.

Michael, of Jaocb Hoff and wife Elisabeth, b. 3 Jun 1786, bapt. the same day. Sponsors: Michael Diderich and wife Magdalena.

Georg David, of Heinrich Seckel and wife Sophia, b. 27 Apr 1786, bapt. 4 Jun 1786. Sponsors: Georg David Seckel and wife Maria Cathar.

Margareta, of Johann Spatz and wife Elisabeth, b. 7 May 1786, bapt. 4 Jun 1786. Sponsors: the father, and Margareta Spatz.

Adam, of Johann Adam Bausch and wife Anna Maria, b. 8 May 1786, bapt. 6 Jun 1786. Sponsors: the parents.

Elisabeth, of Heinrich Herbst and wife Elisabeth, b. 1 Jun 1786, bapt. 11 Jun 1786. Sponsors: Peter Lex and wife Elisabeth.

Sarah, of Johann Kressel (deceased) and wife Catharina, b. 25 Feb 1786, bapt. 11 Jun 1786. Sponsors: David Drechsler and wife Elisabeth.

Margareta, of Philipp Schroeder and wife Catharina, b. 3 May 1786, bapt. 11 Jun 1786. Sponsors: Johann Miller and wife Margareta.

Johann Georg, of Balthasar Emmerich and wife Maria, b. 24 May 1786, bapt. 11 Jun 1786. Sponsors: Johann Emmerigh and Cath. Ries(in).

A child (name not given), of Georg Vogel, bapt. 19 Jun 1786. (No other information given.)

Catharina, of Daniel Kappel and wife Catharina, b. 25 May 1786, bapt. 25 Jun 1786. Sponsors: Caspar Schneider and wife Elisabeth.

Maria Magdalena, of Georg Bock and wife Catharina, b. in Feb 1786, bapt. 25 Jun 1786. Sponsors: the mother, and Maria Magd. Schli__.

Wilhelm, of Wilhelm Schneider and wife Maria, b. 27 Mar 1786, bapt. 25 Jun 1786. Sponsors: the parents.

Daniel, of Johann Kern and wife Elisabeth, b. 13 Apr 1786, bapt. 26 Jun 1786. Sponsors: the parents.

Johann, of Georg Miltenberger and wife Catharina, b. 7 Jun 1786, bapt. 28 Jun 1786. Sponsors: the parents.

Johann Fridrich, of Andreas Lobstein and wife Elisabeth, b. 18 Jan 1786, bapt. 2 Jul 1786. Sponsors: Johann Leibinger and wife Catharina.

Joh. Jacob, of Leonhard Lutz and wife Catharina, b. 23 Apr 1786, bapt. 2 Jul 1786. Sponsors: Jacob Sayler and wife Maria.

Ammy, of Jeremias Hornkocher and wife Elisabeth, b. 13 Jun 1786, bapt. 2 Jul 1786. Sponsor: widow Ammy Mann.

Ruth, of Johann Ferdinand Rohn and wife Liddy, b. 1 Apr 1786, bapt. 2 Jul 1786. Sponsors: Johann Christoph Rohn and wife Catharina.

Jeremias, of Johann Schmidt and wife Magdalena, b. 15 Apr 1786, bapt. 2 Jul 1786. Sponsor: Jeremias Hornkocher.

Elisabeth, of Christian Schütz and wife Magdalena, b. 26 Nov 1784, bapt. 3 Jul 1786. Sponsors: the parents.

Catharina, of Michael Craemer and wife Maria, b. 17 Feb 1786, bapt. 9 Jul 1786. Sponsors: Joh. Gottlieb Me[t]zger and wife Catharina.

Maria, of Johann Jacob Dürr and wife Maria, b. 25 Jun 1786, bapt. 9 Jul 1786. Sponsors: Johann Preiss and wife Catharina.

Elisabeth, of Johann Eberhard and wife Dorothea, b. 23 Jun 1786, bapt. 10 Jul 1786. Sponsors: the parents.

Anna Maria, of Christoph Bechtel and wife Elisabeth, b. 2 Jul 1786, bapt. 16 Jul 1786. Sponsors: Jacob Bechtel and wife Anna Maria.

Catharina, of Johann Geyer and wife Christina, b. 2 Jul 1786, bapt. 16 Jul 1786. Sponsors: Balthasar Cleimer and wife Elisab.

Maria, of Adam Weber and wife Anna, b. 19 Jul 1784, bapt. 15 Jul 1786. Sponsors: the parents.

Johann, of Adam Weber and wife Anna, b. 21 Sep 1785, bapt 15 Jul 1786. Sponsors: the parents.

Catharina, of John Sullivan and wife Margareta, b. 25 Nov 1782, bapt. 15 Jul 1786, Sponsor: the mother.

Elisabeth, of Johann Dürr and wife Susanna, b. 15 Jun 1786, bapt. 15 Jul 1786. Sponsors: Nicolaus Dürr and Christina Eckli(n).

Johann, of Heinrich Depperwihn and wife Margareta, b. 7 Jul 1786, bapt. 17 Jul 1786 (the child soon died). Sponsors: the parents.

Sarah, of Heinrich Kur[t]z and wife Rosina, b. 12 May 1786, bapt. 17 Jul 1786. Sponsors: the parents.

Sarah, of James Manfield and wife Elisabeth, b. 18 Mar 1786, bapt. 2 Aug 1786. Sponsor: the mother.

Michael, of Andreas Oberdorf(f) and wife Elisabeth, b. 19 Jun 1786, bapt. 6 Aug 1786. Sponsors: Michael Oberdorf(f) and wife Catharina.

Michael, of Michael Kitz and wife Margareta, b. 15 Jul 1786, bapt. 6 Aug 1786. Sponsors: Georg Kitz, Jr., and wife Maria.

Johann, of Caspar Graeff and wife Rebecca, b. 21 Jul 1786, bapt. 8 Aug 1786. Sponsors: the father, and Elisabeth Link.

Jacob, of Phil. Kohlmann and wife Maria Margareta, b. 19 Jul 1786, bapt. 12 Aug 1786. Sponsors: Jacob Kohlmann and wife Maria Margareta.

Johann, of Joh. Joseph Bernard and wife Gertraut, b. 17 Jul 1786, bapt 13 Aug 1786. Sponsors: Johann Reinhard and wife Anna Barbara.

Johann, of Michael Stauch and wife Rosina, b. 12 Nov 1785, bapt. 15 Aug 1786. Sponsors: Joseph Stauch and wife Euphrosina.

Joh. Heinrich, of Fridr. Sebastia Mercker and wife Elis. Charlotte, b. 9 Aug 1786, bapt. 19 Aug 1786. Sponsors: Balthasar Kinzler and wife Elisabeth.

Johann, of Christoph Meyer and wife Maria, b. 10 Apr 1786, bapt. 19 Aug 1786. Sponsors: the parents.

A child of Johann Graeff, Jr., bapt. in Aug 1786. (No other information given.)

Eva Margareta, of Andreas Beck and wife Eva Margareta, b. 25 Dec 1785, bapt. 20 Aug 1786. Sponsors: Johann Kitz, Cath. Heimann, and John Laitz? and wife (name not given).

David, of Johann Lauch and wife Hanna, b. 17 Nov 1785, bapt. 22 Aug 1786. Sponsor: Barbara Bauer (in).

Barbara, of Georg Boehm and wife Maria, b. 7 Mar 1785, 26 Aug 1786. Sponsors: Anna Maria Gabriel.

Johann, of Fridrich Mayer and wife Maria, b. 5 Aug 1786, bapt. 27 Aug 1786. Sponsors: the parents.

Wilhelm, of Jacob Wunderlich and wife Sophia, b. 14 Aug 1786, bapt. 27 Aug 1786. Sponsors: Anthon Hecht and wife Sophia.

Anna Eva, of Heinrich Wahl and wife Justina, b. 16 Aug 1786, bapt. 27 Aug 1786. Sponsors: Georg Fridr. Vogel and wife Catharina.

Wilhelm, of Philip Werner and wife Magdalena, b. 16 Aug 1786, bapt. 27 Aug 1786. Sponsors: Johann McNear and wife Elisabeth.

Elisabeth, of Jacob Schreiber and wife Anna Margareta, b. 12 Aug 1786, bapt. 27 Aug 1786. Sponsors: Johann Georg Bock and wife Elisabeth.

Maria Sophia, of Michael Garlinger and wife Maria, b. 8 Aug 1786, bapt. 20 Aug 1786. Sponsors: the parents.

Eva Catharina, of Balthasar Stein and wife Eva, b. 11 Aug 1786, bapt. 27 Aug 1786. Sponsors: Isaac Koch and wife Eva.

Jacob, of Jacob Happel and wife Margareta, b. 22 Jul 1786, bapt. 27 Aug 1786. Sponsors: the parents.

Elisabeth, of Fridrich Burckhard and wife Maria, b. 10 Jul 1786, bapt. 23 Jul 1786. Sponsors: Martin Heinrich and wife Maria.

Adam, of Michael Steinhauer and wife Barbara, b. 4 Jul, bapt. 23 Jul 1786.
Sponsor: Adam Logan.

Elisabeth, of Georg Weckerley and wife Catharina, b. 10 Jul 1786, 23 Jul 1786.
Sponsors: Emanuel Fridr. Weckerley and wife Maria Elisabeth.

Johann Nicolaus, of Jacob Anthony and wife Jacobina, b. 18 Aug 1786, 3 Sep
1786. Sponsors: Nicolaus Walter and wife Rosina.

James, of James Cooper and wife Catharina, b. 26 Jul 1786, bapt. 3 Sep 1786.
Sponsor: Catharina Cooper.

Anna Margareta, of Peter May and wife Catharina b. 21 Aug 1786, bapt. 3 Sep
1786. Sponsor: Anna Margareta Bauer(in).

Wilhelm, of Andreas Kirch and Maria Elisabeth, b. 14 Aug 1786, bapt. 4 Sep
1786. Sponsors: Wilhelm Kerl and wife Margareta.

Heinrich, of Johann Kunckel and wife Maria Clara, b. 26 Aug 1786, bapt. 6 Sep
1786. Sponsors: Joh. Kunckel and wife Maria Christina.

Polly, of James Christe and wife Elisabeth, b. 15 Aug 1786, bapt. 7 Sep 1786.
Sponsors: Michael Schweyer and wife Hanna.

Anna Elisabeth, of Peter Ostermann and wife Elisabeth Cathar., b. 29 Aug 1786,
bapt. 10 Sep 1786. Sponsors: Joh. Holdaufderheyde and wife Anna
Elisabeth.

Susanna, of Balthasar Wolf(f) and wife Magdalena, b. 8 Jun 1786, bap. 10 Sep
1786. Sponsors: the parents.

Johann, of Christian Fischer and wife Anna Catharina, b. 24 Oct 1785, bapt.
10 Sep 1786. Sponsors: the parents.

Leonhard, of Leonhard Jacobi and wife Margareta, b. 14 Aug 1786, bapt. 10 Sep
1786. Sponsors: the parents.

Benjamin, of Gottfried Cyder and wife Catharina, b. 7 Sep 1786, bapt. 13 Sep
1786. Sponsor: the mother.

Jacob, of Bernhard Weber and wife Catharina, b. 23 Aug 1786, bapt. 17 Sep
1786. Sponsors: Jacob Schmidt and wife Margareta.

Eva Elisabeth, of Isaac Hoch and wife Eva, b. 5 Sep 1786, bapt. 17 Sep 1786.
Sponsors: Balthasar Stein and wife Eva.

Georg, of Georg Bantleon and wife Regina, b. 10 Aug 1786, bapt. 24 Sep 1786.
Sponsors: the parents.

Fridrich, of Bernhard Schranck and wife Philippina, b. 19 Sep 1786, bapt.
14 Sep 1786. Sponsors: Fridrich Briney and wife Christina, and Philipp
Weng and wife Catharina.

Catharina, of Martin Sackman and wife Maria Elisabeth, b. 13 Sep 1786, bapt.
24 Sep 1786. Sponsors: Peter Bahr and wife Margareta.

Margareta, of Jacob Schoch and wife Margareta, b. 4 Sep 1786, bapt. 24 Sep
1786. Sponsors: Michael Schoch and wife Margareta.

Christina, of Lorenz Schwab and wife Margareta, b.8 Sep 1786, bapt. 24 Sep
1786. Sponsors: the father, and Christina Brentli(n).

Catharina, of Jonathan Stanton and wife Jemima, b. 16 Aug 1786, bapt. 24 Sep
1786. Sponsors: Wilhelm Roberts and wife Catharina.

Margareta, of Jacob Schock and wife Margareta, b. 4 Sep 1786, bapt. 24 Sep
1786. Sponsors: Michael Schock and wife Margareta.

Wilhelm, of Owen Dan[n]y Daniel and wife Margareta, b. 14 Aug 1786, bapt. 24
Sep 1786. Sponsors: Wilhelm Weissmann and wife Margareta.

Joseph, of Johann Georg Eschrig and wife Elisabeth, b. 4 Jul 1786, bapt. 24 Sep 1786. Sponsors: the parents.

Catharina Sarah, of Wilh. Lehmann and wife Elisabeth, b. 28 Aug 1786, bapt. 7 Sep 1786. Sponsors: Georg Daum and wife Catharina.

Johann Georg, of Fridrich Mayer and wife Catharina, b. 9 Sep 1786, bapt. 1 Oct 1786. Sponsors: the parents.

Josua, of Gottfried Lehnhof(f) and wife Margareta, b. 19 Sep 1786, bapt. 1 Oct 1786. Sponsors: the parents.

Justina Maria, of Gottlieb Meinecke and wife Anna, b. 27 Sep 1786, bapt. 1 Oct 1786. Sponsors: Justus Albring and wife Maria.

Catharina, of Jacob Kroener and wife Susanna, b. 27 Sep 1786, bapt. 7 Oct 1786. Sponsors: Caspar Strubble and wife Catharina.

Daniel, of Peter Kuhn and wife Elisabeth, birthdate not given, bapt. 6 Oct 1786. Sponsors: the parents.

Anna Catharina, of Christian Dannecker and wife Catharina, b. 25 Sep 1786, bapt. 7 Oct 1786. Sponsors: the father, and the grandmother (name not given).

A child (name not given), of David Ott and wife (name not given), birthdate not given, bapt. 8 Oct 1786. Sponsors: the parents.

Johann Martin, of Joh. Fridrich Schick and wife Eva Barbara, b. 1 Oct 1786, bapt. 8 Oct 1786. Sponsors: the parents.

Ludwig, of Michael Wolf(f) and wife Elisabeth, b. 12 Sep 1786, bapt. 9 Oct 1786. Sponsors: the parents.

Georg, of Gottlieb Mayer and wife Magdalena, b. 29 Sep 1786, bapt. 13 Oct 1786. Sponsors: the parents.

Heinrich, of Johann Mayer and wife Maria, b. 26 Aug 1786, bapt. 15 Oct 1786. Sponsors: the father, and grandmother Catharina Heinrich.

Margareta, of Georg Steer and wife Margareta, b. 25 Sep 1786, bapt. 15 Oct 1786. Sponsors: Johann Sauder and wife Margareta.

Aleck?, of Neal Martin and wife Mary, b. 2 Oct 1786, bapt. 15 Oct 1786. Sponsors: John McCallister and Peggy Schinck.

Maria, of Elias? Pissied (*alias* Besayade) and wife Margareta, b. 8 Oct 1786, bapt. 19 Oct 1786. Sponsors: the mother, and Jacob Rust.

August Heinrich, of Heinrich Blettermann and wife Elisabeth, b. 23 Sep 1786, bapt. 22 Oct 1786. Sponsors: the parents.

Johann, of Jacob Messner and wife Elisabeth, b. 4 Oct 1786, bapt. 22 Oct 1786. Sponsors: Johann Weitmann and wife Catharina.

Elisabeth, of Anton Kern and wife Catharina, b. 15 Oct 1786, bapt. 21 Oct 1786. Sponsor: Elisabeth Wagener.

Joh. Georg of Georg Michael Vockinson and wife Maria, b. 4 Oct 1786, bapt. 22 Oct 1786. Sponsors: Joh. Christian Steinhauer and Maria Elisab. Weincot(in).

Elisabeth, of Martin Ludwig and wife Elisabeth, b. 12 Dec 1785, bapt. 18 Oct 1786. Sponsors: the mother, and Johann Mayer.

Andreas, of Johann Facundus and wife Maria, b. 10 May 1786, bapt. 16 Oct 1786. Sponsors: the parents.

Johann Ludwig, of Heinrich Hornberger and wife Magdalena, b. 26 Apr 1786, bapt. 20 Oct 1786. Sponsors: Johann Ludw. Reuschle and wife Margareta.

Anna Margareta, of Joh. Neu and wife Elisab., b. 24 Sep 1786, bapt. 22 Oct 1786. Sponsor: Anna Margareta Misterzen(in).

Aaron?, of Wilhelm Rockhill and wife Anna, b. 10 Jul 1786, bapt. 22 Oct 1786. Sponsors: Jacob Fridrich and wife Anna.

Catharina, of Peter Sonnleiter and wife Elisabeth, b. 19 Oct 1786, bapt. 24 Oct 1786. Sponsors: the parents.

Anna Elisabeth, of Georg Molledore and wife Anna Elisabeth, b. 3 Jan 1786, bapt 26 Oct 1786. Sponsor: the mother.

Jacob, of Jacob Schneider and wife Elisabeth, b. 6 Oct 1786, bapt. 29 Oct 1786. Sponsors: the father, and Sarah Reinhard.

Catharina Margareta, of Heinrich Hof(f)mann and wife Margareta, b. 4 Oct 1786, bapt. 29 Oct 1786. Sponsors: Phil. Pfankuche and wife Catharina.

Johann Michael, of Johann Justus and wife Catharina, b. 9 Oct 1786, bapt. 29 Oct 1786. Sponsors: Michael Miller and wife Christina.

Anna Maria, of Peter Neu and wife Margareta, b. 22 Oct 1786, bapt. 19 Nov 1786. Sponsors: Joh. Becker and wife Maria.

Elisabeth, of Adam Wagner and wife Elisabeth, b. 6 Nov 1786, bapt. 27 Nov 1786. Sponsors: Fridrich Diess and Elisab. Rosch.

Georg, of Lorenz Seckel and wife Maria, birthdate not given, bapt. 27 Nov 1786. Sponsor: Georg David Seckel.

Maria, of Joh. Craemer and wife Catharina, b. 12 Nov 1786, bapt. 17 Dec 1786. Sponsors: Andreas Lex and wife Maria.

Sarah, of Joh. Haalmann and wife Maria, b. 26 Nov 1786, bapt. 17 Dec 1786. Sponsors: the parents.

Josua, of Heinrich Scheible and wife Nancy, b. 9 Nov 1786, bapt. 17 Dec 1786. Sponsors: the parents.

Sarah, of Daniel Huber and wife Anna Maria, b. 2 Dec 1786, bapt. 24 Dec 1786. Sponsors: Martin Kielhauer and wife Sarah.

Wilhelm, of Wilhelm Wunderlich and wife Elisab., b. 1 Dec 1786, bapt. 24 Dec 1786. Sponsors: the parents.

Maria, of Heinrich Miller and wife Maria, b. 24 Nov 1786, bapt. 24 Dec 1786. Sponsors: the parents.

Catharina, of Carl Achilles and wife Elisabeth, b. 7 Dec 1786, bapt. 24 Dec 1786. Sponsor: Catharina Johst.

Johann Christian, of Michael Blümke and wife Johanna Esther, b. 19 Dec 1786, bapt. 24 Dec 1786. Sponsors: Johann Schreyer and wife Catharina, and Johanna Margar. Bollen.

Catharina, of Fridrich Paul and wife Elisabeth, b. 16 Dec 1786, bapt. 25 Dec 1786. Sponsors: Heinrich Grots? and wife Catharina.

Margareta, of Georg Britt and Wife Maria, b. 20 Jan 1785, bapt. 25 Dec 1786. Sponsors: John Ruling and wife Elisabeth.

Margareta, of Johann Heinr. Kressel and wife Agnesa, b. 17 Oct 1785, bapt. 26 Dec 1786. Sponsors: Johann Schneider and wife Margareta.

1786, Second List
(baptisms by pastor Schmidt, from Book IV)

Elisabeth, of Anton Stock and wife Maria, b. 5 Aug 1785, bapt. 1 Jan 1786. Sponsors: Samuel Stock and wife Elisabeth.

Johann Philipp, of Henrich Hohmüller and wife Catharina, b. 16 Dec 1785, bapt. 3 Jan 1786. Sponsors: the parents.

Catharina, of Philip Burk and wife Elisabeth, b. 21 Dec 1785, bapt. 8 Jan 1786. Sponsors: Friedrich Link and wife Cath. Barbara.

Johannes, of Margretha Milseld(in)? and allegedly (first name not given) Bensel, b. 1 Jan 1786, bapt. 8 Jan 1786. Sponsors: Ludwig Winkler and wife Margretha.

Elisabeth of Georg Volkrot(h) and wife Barbara, b. 31 Oct 1785, bapt. 8 Jan 1786. Sponsors: Jacob Esler and wife Susanna.

Jacobi, of Jacob Toffein and wife A. Magdalena, b. 8 Dec 1785, bapt. 8 Jan 1786. Sponsors: the parents.

Margrethe, of Martin Will and wife Elisabeth, b. 17 Dec 1785, bapt. 8 Jan 1786. Sponsors: Valentin Boyer and Margreth Carpenter.

Maria, of Johannes Tarrear? and wife Margrethe, b. 16 Dec 1785, bapt. 9 Jan 1786. Sponsors: Philip Rot(h) and wife Maria.

Georg, of Georg Son[n]leiter and wife Catharina, b. 15 Dec 1785, bapt. 10 Jan 1786. Sponsors: the parents.

Elisabeth, of Isaac Stahl and wife Elisabeth, b. 1 Jan 1786, bapt. 21 Jan 1786. Sponsors: Baltes Fleischer and wife Catharina.

Susanna Magdalena, of Georg Casper Seiferheld and wife Elisabeth, b. 25 Dec 1785, bapt. 29 Jan 1786. Sponsors: Ludwig Scheibly and [wife] Susanna Magdalena.

Christian, of Christman Baum and wife Elisabeth, b. 14 Dec 1785, bapt. 29 Jan 1786. Sponsors: Georg Led___, and Henrich Scheffler and wife Christina.

Elisabeth, of Henrich Velte and wife Regina, b. 25 Sep 1785, bapt. 29 Jan 1786. Sponsors: Henrich Velte and wife Eva.

A child (name not given), of Elias Fischer and wife Barbara, b. 7 Jun 1785, bapt. 29 Jan 1786. (Sponsors names not given.)

Anna Maria, of Georg Schahl and wife Maria, b. 26 Jan 1786, bapt. 5 Feb 1786. Sponsors: Jacob Seiner? and Elisabeth Pop(in).

Georg, of Georg Volkrot(h) and wife Elisabeth, b. 7 Nov 1785,bapt. 10 Feb 1786. Sponsors: Georg Volkrot(h) and wife Catharina.

Elisabeth, of Lorentz Ramin? and wife Elisabeth, b. 15 Feb 1786, bapt. 21 Feb 1786. Sponsors: the parents.

Andreas, of Adam Riess and wife Elisabeth, b. 22 Jan 1786, bapt. 26 Feb 1786. Sponsors: Christoph Stutzbach and Maria Wulmann.

Carl, of Johann Fabricus and wife Christina, b. 25 Jan 1786, bapt. 26 Feb 1786. Sponsors: the parents.

Johann Georg, of Georg Straus and wife Regina, b. 17 Dec 1785, bapt. 26 Feb 1786. Sponsors: Georg Meyer and Anna Maria Fischer.

Johann Adam, of Adam Krop? and wife Elisabeth, b. 26 Feb 1786, bapt. the same day. Sponsors: the parents.

Philip, of Eve Kochersburg(in) and reportedly Philip Velte, b. 21 Jan 1786, bapt. 28 Feb 1786. Sponsor: the mother.

Anna, of Johannes Kiffler and wife Susanna, b. 25 Feb 1786, bapt. 6 Mar 1786. Sponsors: Carl Miller and wife Barbara.

Anna, of Benjamin Baily and wife Maria, b. 3 Mar 1786, bapt. 7 Mar 1786. Sponsor: Hanna Rink__.

Christiana, of Michael Bartholome and wife Christine Eva Maria Catharine, b. 23 Feb 1786, bapt. 19 Mar 1786. Sponsors: Joh. Rugen and wife Eva Elisabeth.

Catharine, of Georg Rehbold and wife Elisabeth, b. 22 Jan 1786, bapt. 19 Mar 1786. Sponsors: Henrich Sommer and wife Catharine.

Johann Michael, of Georg Müller and wife Margrethe, b. 13 Feb 1786, bapt. 19 Mar 1786. Sponsors: the parents.

Anna Elisabeth, of Jacob Krügmeyer and wife Magdalena, b. 9 Mar 1786, bapt. 21 Mar 1786. Sponsors: Anton Ludwig Muff and Elisabeth Ferry(n).

Catharine, of Christ. Henrich Habich and wife Anna Christina, b. 4 Mar 1786, bapt. 23 Mar 1786. Sponsors: the father, and Dorothea Magdalene Schmidt(in).

Sophia Friderica, of Jacob Alborn and wife Elisabeth, b. 26 Feb 1786, bapt. 23 Mar 1786. Sponsors: Mr.? Secker and wife (name not given).

Sara, of Michael Bohler? and wife Anna, b. 1 Mar 1786, bapt. 24 Mar 1786. Sponsors: Georg Denzel and wife Sara.

Philip, of Gottfried Grumbach and wife Barbara, b. 2 Mar 1786, bapt. 29 Mar 1786. Sponsors: the parents.

Susanna, of Georg Dorn and wife Christine, b. 14 Jan 1786, bapt. 5 Apr 1786. Sponsors: the parents.

Peter, of Jacob Solender and wife Wilhelmine, b. 15 Mar 1786, bapt. 6 Apr 1786. Sponsors: Peter Grim and wife Elisabeth.

Alexander, of Georg Cress and wife Elisabeth. b. 6 Jan 1786, bapt. 6 Apr 1786. Sponsors: Alexander Grimm? and wife Sara.

Benjamin, of Peter Klein and wife Margrethe, b. 16 Feb 1786, bapt. 6 Apr 1786. Sponsors: Benjamin Kei__s and wife Maria.

Georg, of Wilhelm Will and wife Elisabeth, b. 20 Feb 1786, bapt. 12 Apr 1786. Sponsors: Joh. Georg Steiby and wife Anna Maria.

Sara, of Sara Weber(in) and Andreas Baum, b. 8 Apr 1786, bapt. 13 Apr 1786. Sponsors: Elisabeth Rap and Susanna Schmidt.

Joh. Georg, of Friedrich Schuman and wife Maria, b. 22 Mar 1786, bapt. 16 Apr 1786. Sponsors: Georg Knerl? and wife A. Maria.

Margrethe, of Johannes Fink and wife Regina, b. 10 Mar 1786, bapt. 16 Apr 1786. Sponsors: Friedrich Schmidt and Margreth Weber(in).

Jacob, of Johann Nicolaus Wagner and wife Anna Magdalene, b. 2 Apr 1786, bapt. 17 Apr 1786. Sponsors: Jacob Weiss? and wife Dorothea.

Johann Catharine, of Conrad Faster and wife Catharine, b. 1 Sep 1785, bapt. 20 Apr 1786. Sponsors: Philip Faster and Catharine Faster(in).

Thomas, of Henrich Cress and wife A. Maria, b. 7 Mar 1786, bapt. 30 Apr 1786. Sponsors: the parents.

Johannes, of Johannes Herby and wife Margrethe, b. 17 Jan 1786, bapt. 30 Apr 1786. Sponsors: the parents.

Anna, of Georg Schüssler and wife Veronica, b. 27 Nov 1785, bapt. 14 May 1786. Sponsor: Catharine Schüssler(in).

Johannes, of Martin Kilhauer and wife Salome, b. 9 Apr 1786, bapt. 14 May 1786. Sponsors: Johannes Schatzlein and wife Barbara.

Philip Conrad, of Conrad Hester and wife Eleonore Catharine, b. 26 Apr 1786, bapt 14 May 1786. Sponsors: Johannes Kunkel and wife Mar. Christine.

548   PHILADELPHIA GERMAN LUTHERAN CHURCH

Fridrich, of Wilhelm Egers and wife Margrethe, b. 6 Mar 1786, bapt 14 May 1786. Sponsors: Fridrich Eschel and Elisabeth Gilbert.
Catharine, of Henrich Krugemeyer and wife Elisabeth, b. 23 Apr 1786, bapt. 14 May 1786. Sponsors: Bernhard Bruchhol[t]z and wife A. Catharine.
Maria Magdalene, of Andreas Cressman and wife Elisabeth, b. 22 Mar 1786, bapt. 20 May 1786. Sponsors: Joh. Gräf and wife Mar. Magdalene.
Friederich, of Wilhelm Higgins and wife Margrethe, b. 6 Mar 1786, bapt. 14 May 1786, Sponsors: Friederich Gänser and Elisabeth Gilbert.
Sara Elisabeth, of Joh. Georg Kur[t]z and wife Margrethe, b. 7 Mar 1786, bapt. 20 May 1786. Sponsors: the father, and Sara Elisabeth Müntzer(in).
Rahel, of Johannes Holden and wife Agnes, b. 10 Feb 1786, bapt. 24 May 1786. Sponsors: Jacob Kenze_er and Barbara Strauss(in).
Johann Henrich, of Johannes Nagel and wife Elisabeth, b. 14 May 1786, bapt. 28 May 1786. Sponsors: Henrich Nagel and wife (name_not given).
Sara, of John Hughs and wife Elisabeth, b. 28 Apr 1786, bapt. 28 May 1786. Sponsors: Daniel Bender and Christine McClur.
Anna Catharine, of Valentin Unbehend and wife Sophia, b. 16 May 1786, bapt. 28 May 1786. Sponsors: Johannes Lorenz and wife Catharine.
Johannes, of Albert Weber and wife Magdalene, b. 16 Apr 1786, bapt. 28 May 1786. Sponsors: Joh. Philip and Margreth Volmer(in).
Elisabeth, of Georg Kiesinger and wife Catharine, b. 2 Apr 1786, bapt. 1 Jun 1786. Sponsors: David Schäfer and wife Elisabeth.
Johann Jacob, of Henrich Klammer and wife Magdalene, b. 22 Jan 1786, bapt. 8 Jun 1786. Sponsors: Jacob Solender and wife Catharine.
Georg, of Georg Tunker and wife Maria, b. 7 Jun 1785, bapt. 3 Jun 1786. Sponsors: Adam Knoblauch and wife Barbara.
Elisabeth, of Johann Woltensdorf and Barbara Miller(in), b. 4 Mar 1786, bapt. 4 Jun 1786. Sponsors: Conrad Neischwenner and wife Sibilla.
Jacob, of Michael Rebele and wife Margrethe, b. 24 Jan 1786, bapt. 7 Jun 1786. Sponsors: the father, and Susanna Herberger.
Johannes, of Jacob Scheran? and wife A. Maria, b. 14 Feb 1786, bapt. 8 Jun 1786. Sponsors: the mother, and Andreas Baum and wife Barbara.
Anna Barbara, of Michael Hans and wife Catharine, b. 24 May 1786, bapt. 9 Jun 1786. Sponsors: the parents.
Elisabeth, of Johannes Baum and wife Magdalene, b. 11 May 1786, bapt. 17 Jun 1786. Sponsors: Georg Scherer and wife Elisabeth.
Maria Magdalene, of Brighty Way Hips, and wife Mar. Clara, b. 11 Apr 1784, bapt. 18 Jun 1786. Sponsors: Baltzer Geyer and wife Mar. Magdalene.
Elisabeth, of unnamed parents, b. 11 May 1786, bapt. 18 Jun 1786. Sponsor: Elisabeth Geyer.
Anna, of Jacob Seyfried and wife Salome, b. 26 May 1786, bapt. 18 Jun 1786. Sponsors: the parents.
William Benjamin, of Benjamin Harris and wife Margrethe, b. 25 May 1786, bapt. 25 Jun 1786. Sponsors: the parents.
Christian, of Ludwig Buck and wife Juliane, b. 1 Jun 1786, bapt. 25 Jun 1786. Sponsors: Henrich Book and wife Elisabeth.
Anna Maria, of Valentin Flegler and wife Eva, b. 24 Jun 1786, bapt. 28 Jun 1786. Sponsor: Anna Maria Endres.

Eva, of Andreas Abeth and wife Eva, b. 31 May 1786, bapt. 2 Jul 1786.
Sponsors: the parents.

Sara, of Philip Springer and wife Eva, b. 16 May 1786, bapt. 2 Jul 1786.
Sponsor: the mother.

Johannes, of Peter Neischwenner and wife Eva, b. 26 May 1786, bapt. 3 Jul
1786. Sponsors: Johannes Böhn and wife Magdalene.

Isaac, of Casper Volmer and wife Maria, b. 5 Jun 1786, bapt. 9 Jul 1786.
Sponsors: the father, and (illegible).

Johannes, of Johannes Gahn and wife Margrethe, b. 11 Jun 1786, bapt. 12 Jun
1786. Sponsors: Johannes Baum and wife Anne.

Johannes, of Christoph Bastian and wife Sophia Cathar., b. 12 May 1786, bapt.
13 Jul 1786. Sponsors: Jacob Kreiter? and wife Elisabeth.

Maria, of Jacob Kaufman and wife Margrethe, b. 3 Jul 1786, bapt. 18 Jul 1786.
Sponsors: Henrich Cress and wife Maria.

Jeremias, of Georg Kaiser and wife Elisabeth, b. 23 Jul 1786, bapt. the same
day. Sponsors: the parents.

Anna Maria, of Michael Kraft and wife Maria, b. 18 Jun 1786, bapt. 24 Jul 1786.
Sponsors: Peter Kraft and wife Margrethe.

Johannes, of Jacob Beideman and wife Elisabeth, b. 2 Jul 1786, bapt. 18 Jul
1786. Sponsors: Johannes Mut(h) and wife Elisabeth.

Johannes, of Georg Kier (alias Kühr) and wife Elisabeth, b. 16 Jul 1786, bapt.
29 Jul 1786. Sponsors: Johannes Haas and wife Elisabeth.

Friedrich, of Andreas Dering and wife Maria, b. 3 Jul 1786, bapt. 29 Jul 1786.
Sponsors: Friedrich Schuman and wife Magdalene.

Ester, of Georg Fischer and wife Elisabeth, b. 14 Jul 1786, bapt 30 Jul 1786.
Sponsors: Joh. Philip Fischer and wife A. Maria.

Johannes, of Johannes Seidelman and wife Catherine, b. 19 Jul 1786, bapt.
30 Jul 1786. Sponsors: Philip Seidelman and wife Maria.

Catharine, of John Mengs and wife Maria. b. 6 Aug 1786, bapt. 18 Aug 1786.
Sponsors: Justus Bloch and Cathar. Bauer(in)?.

Joh. Henrich, of Henrich Schmidt and wife Magdalene, b. 27 Jul 1786, bapt.
13 Aug 1786. Sponsors: the parents.

Catharine, of Thomas Gerum (alias Kohrum) and wife Elisabeth, b. 12 Jun 1786,
bapt. 26 Jul 1786. Sponsors: the parents.

Maria Catharine, of Philip Meyer and wife Mar. Salome, b. 27 Jul 1786, bapt.
20 Aug 1786. Sponsors: Georg Maunty and Cathar. Maunty(n).

Catharine, of Wilhelm P__ty and wife Anne, b. 9 Apr 1786, bapt. 24 Aug 1786.
Sponsor: the mother.

Joh. Philip, of Johannes Buck and wife Maria, b. 15 Aug 1786, bapt. 26 Aug
1786. Sponsors: Philip Lescher and wife Maria.

Elisabeth, of Georg Burkenbein and wife Elisabeth, birthdate not given, bapt.
3 Sep 1786. Sponsors: Jacob Omensetter and wife Elisabeth.

Georg, of Johannes Krauskopf and wife Margrethe, b. 1 Sep 1786, bapt. 7 Sep
1786. Sponsors: the father, and the grandmother Margr. Krauskopf(in).

Peter, of David Jenkins and wife Elisabeth, b. 29 Aug 1786, bapt. 8 Sep 1786.
Sponsors: Peter Lietsch and wife Eva Maria.

Georg, of Johannes Nieman? and wife Maria, b. 30 Aug 1786, bapt. 8 Sep 1786.
Sponsors: Georg Prinz and Catharine Prinz.

Catharine, of Henrich Nagel and wife Barbara, b. 30 Aug 1786, bapt. 10 Sep 1786. Sponsors: Catharina Fischer(in) and Jacob Fischer.

Philip, of Philip Hirsch and wife Susanna, 2 years old, bapt. 10 Sep 1786. Sponsors: Samuel Carpenter and wife Catharine.

Maria, of Johannes Haas and wife Elisabeth, b. 1 Sep 1786, bapt. 10 Sep 1786. Sponsors: the parents.

Anna Catharine, of Johannes Schäfer and wife Margrethe, b. 28 Jun 1786, bapt. 11 Sep 1786. Sponsors: Johannes Böhm and wife Barbara.

Elisabeth, of Jacob Schwab and wife Margrethe, b. 23 Aug 1786, bapt. 11 Sep 1786. Sponsors: Johannes Feyen and wife Catharine.

Jacob, of Johann? Kaprel? and wife Catharine, b. 11 Aug 1786, bapt. 12 Sep 1786. Sponsors: Jacob Sink and wife Catharine.

Johann Henrich, of Ernst Taubert and wife Elisabeth, b. 8 Jul 1784, bapt. 13 Sep 1786. Sponsors: the parents and Magdalena Taubert..

Maria, of Ernst Taubert and wife Elisabeth, b. 2 Jul 1786, bapt. 13 Sep 1786. Sponsors: same as above.

Anna, of Johannes Müller and wife Catharine, b. 7 Sep 1786, bapt. 15 Sep 1786. Sponsor: Anna Beyer(in).

Jacob, of Ludwig Preiss and wife Maria, b. 7 Mar 1785, bapt. 16 Sep 1786. Sponsor: the mother.

Christian, of Christian Müller and wife Maria, b. 14 Aug 1786, bapt. 16 Sep 1786. Sponsors: the parents.

Elisabeth, of Jacob Dresler and wife Regina, b. 24 Aug 1786, bapt. 21 Sep 1786. Sponsors: Jacob Kitz and wife Elisabeth.

Jacob, of Daniel Jung and wife Eva, b. 16 Sep 1786, bapt. 21 Sep 1786. Sponsors: the parents.

Magdalene Elisabeth, of Michael Spiegel and wife Elisabeth, b. 9 Sep 1786, bapt. 24 Sep 1786. Sponsors: the parents.

Maria, of Henrich Apfel and wife Christina, b. 12 Jan 1786, bapt. 24 Sep 1786. Sponsors: the parents.

Wilhelm, of Johannes Reit? and wife Catharine, b. 16 Sep 1785, bapt. 24 Sep 1786. Sponsors: the parents.

Johannes, of Johannes Volmer and wife Maria, b. 3 Sep 1786, bapt. 24 Sep 1786. Sponsors: the father, and Margr. Krauskopf.

Margrethe, of Henrich Bäckly and wife Elisabeth, b. 12 Jan 1786, bapt. 24 Sep 1786. Sponsors: Adam Erwin and wife Margrethe.

Catharine Sara, of Jacob Eckfeld and wife Cathar. Sara, b. 12 Sep 1786, bapt. 26 Sep 1786. Sponsors: Georg Daum and wife Cathar. Sara.

Joseph, of Bernhard Kaufman and wife A. Margr., b. 30 Aug 1786, bapt. 28 Sep 1786. Sponsors: Joseph Volkrot(h) and Hätty Neff.

Jacob, of Daniel Müller and wife Margrethe, b. 9 Oct [1785], bapt. 28 Sep 1786. Sponsors: Johannes Adolph and Caspar Müller.

Johannes, of Peter Sost and wife Maria, 5 weeks old, bapt. 24 Sep 1786. Sponsors: the parents.

Johannes, of Johannes Fässmeyer and wife Catharine, b. 23 Sep 1786, bapt. 30 Sep 1786. Sponsors: Joh. Sauter and wife Margrethe.

Susanne Louise, of Nicolaus Wagener and wife Sara, b. 9 Sep 1786, bapt. 5 Oct 1786. Sponsors: Paul Casper Britton and wife Sus. Louise.

Johannes, of Bernhard Beck and wife Maria, b. 18 Sep 1786, bapt. 7 Oct 1786. Sponsors: Alexander Pensen and wife Margreth.

Wilhelm, of Joh. Christoph Gut and wife Christina, b. 26 Sep 1786, bapt. 8 Oct 1786. Sponsors: Wilhelm Lohn and wife Veronica.

Johannes, of Mark Rot(h)s and wife Catharine, b. 17 Sep 1786, bapt. 8 Oct 1786. Sponsors: Joh. Rugen and wife Elisabeth.

Susanna, of Peter Kraft and wife Margreth, b. 27 Sep 1786, bapt. 8 Oct 1786. Sponsors: the parents and the grandmother Keimli(n).

Johannes, of Casper Wirschon and wife A. Maria, b. 5 Oct 1786, bapt. 15 Oct 1786. Sponsors: Joh .Jacob and wife Maria.

Rebecca, of Andreas Böhmer and wife Margrethe, b. 25 Sep 1786, bapt. 15 Oct 1786. Sponsors: Conrad Weber and wife Maria.

Ludwig, of Johannes Freiburg and wife Susanna, b. 1 Oct 1786, bapt. 15 Oct 1786. Sponsors: Ludwig Roner and wife Maria.

Anna Maria, of Thomas Fischer and wife Elisabeth, birthdate not given, bapt. 15 Oct 1786. Sponsors: Michael J__mel and wife Catharine.

Johann Simon, of Jacob Hademüller and wife Marie, b. 14 Oct 1786, bapt. 17 Oct 1786. Sponsors: Simon Moll and wife Elisabeth.

Elisabeth, of Johannes Hecker and wife Catharine, b. 19 Oct 1784, bapt. 18 Oct 1786. Sponsor: Magdalene Rohn(in).

Johann, of Philip Jung and wife Elisabeth, birthdate not given, bapt. in Oct 1786. (Sponsors not given.)

Joseph, of Johannes Ebel and wife Catharine, b. 13 Sep 1786, bapt. 22 Oct 1786. Sponsors: Joseph Mansfeld and wife Maria.

Margrethe, of Jacob Hall and wife Catharine, b. 17 Sep 1786, bapt. 22 Oct 1786. Sponsors: Thomas Fischer and wife Elisabeth.

Friederich, of Fried. Jacob Rapp and wife Elisabeth, b. 14 Oct 1786, bapt. 22 Oct 1786. Sponsors: the parents.

Wilhelm, of Wilhelm Wheler and wife Maria, b. 16 Oct 1786, bapt. 26 Oct 1786. Sponsors: Jacob Seger and wife Barbara.

Michael, of Michael Lapp and wife Margrethe, b.10 Oct 1786, bapt. 29 Oct 1786. Sponsors: the parents.

Elisabeth, of Christian Unger and wife Maria, b. 25 Sep 1786, bapt. 29 Oct 1786. Sponsors: Christoph Sonderlin and wife Maria.

Friedrich, of Johannes Wimly and wife Maria Magdalene, b. 6 Sep 1786, bapt. 29 Oct 1786. Sponsors: Fridrich Feltebaum and wife Maria.

Maria Dorothea, of Joh. Nick and wife Regine, b. 1 Oct 1786, bapt. 29 Oct 1786. Sponsors: Joh. Georg Streiby and wife Mar. Dorothea.

Johannes, of Joh. Betsch and wife Cath. Margrethe, b. 29 Sep 1786, bapt. 29 Oct 1786. Sponsors: Christian Velte and wife Maria.

Maria Dorothea, of Philip Horree? and wife Mar. Elisabeth, b. 13 Sep 1786, bapt. 3 Nov 1786. Sponsors: A. Dorothea Flicker(in), single.

Johannes, of Jacob Christler and wife Maria, b. 15 Oct 1786, bapt. 5 Nov 1786. Sponsors: Nicolaus Weber and Maria Philippina Christler(in).

Wilhelm, of Gottfr. Ernst Schmidt and wife Margrethe, b. 2 Oct 1786, bapt. 8 Nov 1786. Sponsors: Wilhelm Weber and wife Margrethe,

Carl, of Carl Wishach and wife Johanette, b. 6 Nov 1786, bapt. 9 Nov 1786. Sponsors: the parents.

David, of Johannes Krieger and wife Catharine, b. 28 Oct 1786, bapt. 12 Nov 1786. Sponsors: David Eberhard and wife Elisabeth.

Isaac Werner, of Peter Bauschon and wife Margreth. Magd., b. 24 Oct 1786, bapt. 13 Nov 1786. Sponsors: Isaac Werner and wife Cath. Maria.

Benjamin, of Hieronimus Werner and wife Christine, b. 7 Oct 1786, bapt. 12 Nov 1786. Sponsors: Johannes Huck and wife Elisabeth.

Joh. Georg, of Samuel Henzel and wife Catharine, b. 20 Oct 1786, bapt. 12 Nov 1786. Sponsors: Georg Tossky and wife Christine.

Johann, of Isaac Pallen? and wife Anna, b. 22 Apr 1786, bapt. 13 Nov 1786. Sponsor: Maria Dorothea Meister(in).

Philip Christian, of Nicolaus Ferdinand Wesphal and wife Sara, b. 4 Jul 1786, bapt. 14 Nov 1786. Sponsor: Philip Christian Möller.

Jacob, of Andreas Bossert and wife Christine, b. 3 Nov 1786, bapt. 14 Nov 1786. Sponsors: Jacob Dietrich and Christine Cath. Bossert(in).

Margrethe, of Jacob Riess and wife Magdalene, b. 8 Nov 1786, bapt. the same day. Sponsors: the parents.

Elisabeth, of Michael Kreppel and wife Elisabeth, 1 Mar 1786, bapt. 11 Nov 1786. Sponsors: Joh. Ludwig and wife Magdalene.

Johann David, of Wilhelm Clemens and wife Maria, b. 14 Sep 1786, bapt. 13 Nov 1786. Sponsors: Joh. David Schäfer and wife Mar. Cathar.

Maria Elisabeth, of Jacob Trion and wife Elisabeth, b. 3 Nov 1786, bapt. 17 Nov 1786. Sponsors: Gabriel Kern and wife Maria.

Jacob, of Martin Sommer and wife Barbara, b. 17 Oct 1786, bapt. 19 Nov 1786. Sponsors: Jacob Becker and wife Maria.

Barbara, of Johannes Meyer and wife Elisabeth, b. 1 Nov 1786, bapt. 19 Nov 1786. Sponsors: Tobias König and wife Barbara.

Margrethe, of Philip Werner and wife Magdal., b. 8 Sep 1786, bapt. 19 Nov 1786. Sponsors: Michael Rebele and wife Margrethe.

Anton, of Anton Balleck and wife Maria, b. 13 Nov 1786, bapt. 19 Nov 1786. Sponsor: Johannes Fontaneau.

Philip Henrich, of Joh. David Neess and wife Clara, b. 7 Oct 1786, bapt. 19 Nov 1786. Sponsor: Philip Henrich Diehl.

Richard, of Friedrich Heimberger and wife Maria, b. 27 Oct 1786, bapt. 21 Nov 1786. Sponsors: the parents.

Elisabeth, of Valentin Heger and wife Sara, 3 years old, bapt. 23 Nov 1786. Sponsors: Dewald Storch and wife Rosina.

Joh. Georg, of Abraham Bachman and wife Philippina, b. 22 Nov 1786, bapt. the same day. Sponsors: the parents.

Henrich, of Georg Christhilf and wife Sabina, b. 20 Nov 1786, bapt. 23 Nov 1786. Sponsors: the parents.

Georg, of Nicolaus Quast and wife Maria, b. 5 Nov 1786, bapt. 26 Nov 1786. Sponsors: the parents.

Elisabeth, of Johannes Klein and wife Hanna, b. 18 Nov 1786, bapt. 29 Nov 1786. Sponsors: Joh. Miller and Elisabeth Klein

Margrethe, of Wilhelm Reily and wife Elisabeth, b. 20 Nov 1786, bapt. 3 Dec 1786. Sponsors: Philip Alberger and wife Margrethe.

Johannes, of Christian Graf and wife Eva, b. 26 Nov 1786, bapt. 3 Dec 1786. Sponsors: the parents.

Jacob, of Johannes Straus and wife Margr., b. 29 Nov 1786, bapt. 9 Dec 1786. Sponsors: Jacob Kaufman and wife Margrethe.
Henrich, of Johannes Rotter and wife Maria, b. 17 Oct 1786, bapt. 16 Dec 1786. Sponsors: the mother, and Mattheas Rooss.
Margrethe, of Christoph Mohr and wife Catharine, b. 12 Nov 1786, bapt. 17 Dec 1786. Sponsors: Georg Mohr and wife Margrethe.
Elisabeth, of Johannes Ungar and wife Susanna. 6 weeks old, bapt. 17 Dec 1786. Sponsors: Joh. Wack and wife Elisabeth.
Georg, of Georg Flouers and wife Elisabeth, b. 17 Nov 1786, bapt. 17 Dec 1786. Sponsors: Joh. Linneman and wife Margrethe.
Maria Magdalene, of Adam Seibert and wife Sabina, b. 2 Dec 1786, bapt. 17 Dec 1786. Sponsors: Georg Gottfr[ied] and wife Maria Magdalene.
Hanna, of Mark Jung and wife Rebecca, b. 3 Dec 1786, bapt. 17 Dec 1786. Sponsors: the father, and Hanna Jäger.
Johan Georg, of Jacob Stein and wife Maria, b. 18 Dec 1786, bapt. 19 Dec 1786. Sponsors: Johannes Rup and wife Dorothea.
Andreas, of Adam Ratts and wife Rosina, b. 17 Dec 1786, bapt. 24 Dec 1786. Sponsors: Andreas Treyer and wife Margrethe.
Joh. Wolfgang, of Friedrich Rohr and wife Margrethe, b. 1 Dec 1786, bapt. 24 Dec 1786. Sponsors: Joh. Wolfg. Gemeindbauer and wife Catharine.
Maria Magdalene, of Johannes Hempel and wife Elisabeth, b. 19 Nov 1786, bapt. 24 Dec 1786. Sponsors: the parents.
Sara, of Christian Elwel and wife Susanna, b. 31 Mar 1786, bapt. 24 Dec 1786. Sponsors: the parents.
Eva Maria, of Johannes Breisch and wife Maria Catharine, b. 6 Dec 1786, bapt. 26 Dec 1786. Sponsors: Georg Kiefer (alias Cooper) and wife Eva Maria.
Anna Barbara, of Christoph Wilpert and wife Margrethe, b. 2 Sep 1786, bapt. 26 Dec 1786. Sponsors: Barbara Burkhart(in).
Nicolaus, of Nicolaus Friedrich and wife Elisabeth, b.24 Dec 1786, bapt 26 Dec 1786. Sponsors: Peter Friedrich and Elisab. Friedrich.
Joseph, of Jacob Moh[t]z and wife Barbara, b. 2 Nov 1786, bapt. 28 Dec 1786. Sponsors: the parents.
Johann Carl, of Carl Schmidt and wife Sophia, b. 28 Oct 1786, bapt. 31 Dec 1786. Sponsors: Johann Krebs and wife Barbara.
Adam, of Christian Beck and wife Elisabeth, b. 20 Oct 1786, bapt. 31 Dec 1786. Sponsors: Adam Beck and wife Susanna.
Maria, of Henrich Schröpler and wife Christine, b.1 Oct 1786, bapt. 31 Dec 1786. Sponsors: (first name not given) Schuler and wife (name not given).
Anna Maria, of Zacharias Töpf and wife Mar. Barbara, b. 4 Dec 1786, bapt. 31 Dec 1786. Sponsors: Johann Hänsman and wife Anna Maria.

INDEX

ABB, Anna Maria, 366, Michael, 366
ABBISCH, Andreas, 478; Eva, 478;
  Magdalene, 478
ABEL, Conrad, 277, 293, 316; Elis., 414;
  Isaac, 331; Joh., 317, 414, 483; Joh.
  Georg, 277; Mar. Philippina, 453;
  Marg., 277, 316, 331, 497; Maria,
  316; Maria Magd., 390; Maria
  Philippina, 317; Peter Mat., 317, 453;
  Salomon, 331
ABETH, Andreas, 549; Eva, 549
ABITSCH, Andr., 482; Andreas, 512;
  Eva, 482, 512; Frdr., 512; Maria
  Rosina Cath., 348; Martin, 348
ABRAHAM, Jonas, 399; Rachel, 399;
  Sarah, 399
ACHILLES, Carl, 513, 545; Cath., 545;
  Elis., 513, 545; Georg, 513
ACKER, Elis., 537; Michael, 537
ADAM, Barbara, 287; Bartholomaeus,
  331; Cath., 281, 287, 331, 363;
  Christoph, 327, 338, 363, 513;
  Daniel, 327; Elis., 480; Ernst
  Christoph, 281; Joh., 287, 331;
  Magdalena, 480, 530; Marg., 327;
  Peter, 480, 530; Susannah, 281;
  Wilhelm, 363
ADAMS, Anna Barbara, 367; Cath., 370,
  526; Esther, 370; Joh., 370, 485;
  John, 526; Marg., 485, 526; Martha,
  485; Salome, 349
ADAMSON, Alex. Henry, 374; Alexan.,
  374; Maria, 374
AEBACHER, Georg, 495; Maria, 495
AERTIUS, Anna, 349
AESCH, Barbara, 360; Jac., 392; Jacob,
  360; Joh., 392; Lovina, 392; Marg.,
  392; Maria, 392; Rosina, 360
AESCHER, Elis., 494; Hanna, 494; Jacob
  Ulrich, 401; Joh. Conrad, 481; Joh.
  Georg, 401, 494; Maria Felicitas, 481;
  Maria Regina, 401
AESCHERIG, Elis., 483; Georg, 483
AESTEN, Maria, 336; Maria Cath., 336;
  William, 336
AGRICOLA, Ludewig, 326
AHARDT, Joh., 500
AHL, Elis., 373; Frdr., 373; Mat., 373
AHNER, Jacob, 507
AHRN, Cath., 443; Rudolf, 443
ALBACH, Anna Barb., 494; Cath., 494
ALBERGER, Adam, 352; Christian, 465,
  468; Marg., 468, 552; Maria Elis.,
  352; Phil., 435; Philip, 552
ALBERLY, Barbara, 331; Philip, 331
ALBERT, Anna Maria, 469, 524;
  Barbara, 466; Cath., 513; Christian,

429; Christiana Cath., 524; Georg, 503,
  513; Georg Adam, 470; Hanna Maria,
  429; Joh., 469, 524; Joh. Jacob, 469;
  John, 429; Maria, 503, 513
ALBERTI, Anna Barbara, 314, 323;
  Barbara, 324; Bernard, 483; Cath., 483;
  Georg, 517; Georg Frdr., 539; Hanna,
  539; Hanna Preiss, 539; Joh. Phil., 314;
  Joh. Philipp, 324; Maria Elis., 483;
  Philipp, 323
ALBERTY, Philip, 351
ALBORN, Elis., 440, 465, 498, 510, 531,
  547; Eman. Jacob, 440; Emmanuel
  Jacob, 498; Georg Frdr., 465; Jacob,
  465, 510, 531, 547; Jacob Benjamin,
  510; Maria Christina, 498; Sophia
  Frdr., 547
ALBRECHT, Anna Magdalena, 424;
  Cath., 304; Christina, 298; Elias, 304,
  353; Elis., 384, 391; Georg Philip, 353;
  Jacob, 424; Joh., 424; Joh. Frdr., 367;
  Joh. Philipp, 304; Juliana, 384, 391,
  424, 485, 509, 530; Leonard, 298;
  Maria Cath., 353; Michael, 384, 391,
  424, 485, 509
ALBRING, Justus, 544; Maria, 544
ALEXANDER, Charles, 518; Elis., 518;
  Maria, 418; Rebecca, 418; William,
  418, 518
ALLEN, Ambros, 411; Eleonor, 411; Eva,
  497; Henry, 490; Hnr., 497; Joh. Mich.,
  497; Marg., 411
ALLERT, Anna, 306; Joseph, 306; Ruben,
  306; Thomas, 306
ALLEY, Georg, 494
ALSTER, Anna Maria, 397; Conrad, 397
ALTBERGER, Cath., 391
AMMON, Cath., 322; Jacob, 322
AMOUR, Adam, 278; John, 278; Mary,
  278
ANDERSON, Andreas, 440; Elis., 418,
  440; Hnr., 476; Isaac, 418, 440; Joh.
  Jacob, 418; Maria, 476; Sarah, 476;
  Susanna, 476
ANDREA, Nicol., 508
ANDREAS, Anna Maria, 478; Daniel,
  478, 512; Joh. Christian, 512; Joh.
  Wilhelm, 478; Maria, 512
ANDRES, Maria, 296; Philip Jacob, 296;
  Zacharias, 296
ANGEL, Anna Maria, 439; Joh., 439;
  Michael, 439
ANNEAR, Elis., 522; John, 522
ANNICK, Anna Barbara, 430; Hanna, 430;
  Joh. Andr., 430
ANTHONY, An. Cath., 484; Anna Maria,
  280; Anna Regina, 470; Cath., 280,

472; Elis., 430; Frdr., 472, 497, 525; Jacob, 428, 430, 470, 484, 525, 543; Jacobaea, 430, 470; Jacobina, 543; Joh. Nicolaus, 543; Maria Cath., 472; Michael, 280, 472; Polly, 497; Susanna, 472, 497, 525
ANTONI, Cath. Elis., 357; Christina, 303; Jacob, 303, 357; Jacobea, 357; Johanna Jacobina, 303
ANTONY, Jacob, 336, 396; Jacobea, 336; Jacobine, 396; Joh. Hnr., 396; Salome, 336
APFEL, Cath., 310, 388; Christian, 310; Christina, 422, 451, 512, 550; Christine, 388; Elis., 451; Hnr., 388, 422, 451, 512, 550; Joh. Frdr., 422; Marg., 310; Maria, 550; Wilhelm, 512
APIELMAN, Philip, 338
APP, Anna Maria, 436; Michael, 436
APPEL, Anna Magd., 357; Anna Marg., 486; Christian, 278, 282; Elis., 463; Elis. Magd., 462; Georg, 357; Hnr., 486; Jacob, 486; Joh., 462; Joh. Daniel, 463; Joh. Hnr., 357; Marg., 278, 282, 462
ARBITSCH, Andreas, 463; Eva, 463
ARCHUR, Joshua, 397
AREN, Maria Philippine, 369; Peter Mat., 369
ARMBACH, Joh. Frdr., 456; Joh. Peter, 456; Maria, 456
ARMBRUSTER, Anna Cath., 447; Anthon, 312, 348; Anthony, 380; Anton, 430; Barbara, 430, 447, 476; Benj., 476; Benjamin, 430, 447; Cath. Regina, 380; Catharina, 483; Christina Maria, 348; Eleonora, 368; Elis., 513; Han. Cath. Eleonora, 476; Joh., 458; Joh. Cath. Eleonora, 430; Mar. Christina, 380; Marg., 424, 458, 470, 477, 515; Maria, 452, 477, 513, 515; Maria Cath., 312; Maria Elis., 424, 470; Maria Magdalena, 368; Maria Rosina Cath., 348; Mat., 452, 477, 513; Peter, 312, 339, 368, 424, 458, 470, 477, 515
ARMITAGE, Susan, 406
ARN, Cath., 427; Elis., 427; Frdr., 427
ARNOLD, Daniel, 454; Joh. Georg, 350; Joh. Hnr., 316; Marg., 499; Maria, 316, 350, 384, 454, 499; Peter, 316, 350, 384, 454, 499; Wilhelm, 384
ARON, Elis., 410; Frdr., 410; Magdalena, 410
ARPENGAST, Maria Elis., 295; Maria Magdalena, 295
ASCH, Jacob, 301, 459; Marg., 459; Rosina, 301, 459

ASCHTON, Bernhard, 355; Cath., 386; Joh. Jacob, 386; Will., 386; William, 355
ASHTON, Cath., 322; Georg, 322; William, 322
ASMUS, Cath., 425, 458; Joh., 425, 458; Valentin, 425
ASSMUS, Cath., 480, 510, 517; Christina, 480; Christoph, 510; Joh., 480, 517
ATKINSON, Cath., 431; Elis., 431, 452, 527; Joh. Adam, 452; William, 431, 452
AUNER, Anna, 459; Cath., 447; Marg., 447, 462; Peter, 447, 459, 462
BABCOCK, Gideon, 351; Marg., 351
BACH, Andreas, 472; Anna, 323; Anna Elis., 299; Anna Maria, 457; Cath., 309, 314, 323; Elis., 343, 348, 390, 419, 457, 472, 474, 481; Frdr., 474, 505; Frdr. August, 505; Hnr., 323; Joh., 343, 348, 390, 419, 457, 481; Joh. Phil., 481; Joh. Thomas, 309, 314; John, 472; Marg., 348, 424, 505; Maria Regina, 419; Susanna Marg., 348
BACHHOLTZ, Georg, 394, 420, 461; Joh., 461; Maria, 420; Veronica, 394, 461
BACHMAN, Abraham, 337, 420, 552; Andreas, 347; Anna Marg., 347; Cath., 347; Joh., 364, 420; Joh. Caspar, 337; Joh. Georg, 552; Maria Philippina, 337; Philippina, 552; Philippine, 420
BACHMANN, Abr., 388; Abraham, 363, 450; Cath., 363; Jacob, 388; Maria, 450; Philippina, 363, 388, 450
BACHOLTZ, Elis., 373; Georg, 373; Veronica, 373
BACKERIG, Marg., 533
BACKLY, Elis., 550; Hnr., 550; Marg., 550
BACKOS, Joh. Georg, 347; Salome, 347
BACKWIK, Joh. Georg, 330; John, 330; Marg., 330
BADEMAN, Jac., 378; Susanna, 378
BAEHRDLING, Carl, 456; Christlieb, 361, 427, 456; Elis., 361, 427, 456; Sophia, 427
BAERDLING, Christlieb, 388; Cornelia, 388; Elis., 388
BAERENS, Daniel, 339; Jacob, 339; Maria, 339
BAERENSTECHER, Andr., 435
BAERTHLING, Conrad, 469; Maria, 469; Wilhelm, 469
BAETHIS, Barbara, 369, 374, 415, 422, 455; Cath., 422; Conrad, 369, 374, 415, 422, 455; Maria Rebecca, 455; Wilhelm, 369
BAETIS, Barbara, 440; Conrad, 440

BAS, Joh. Michael, 456
BASLEY, Cath., 317; Jacob, 317; Magdalena, 317
BAST, Elis., 296, 389, 518; Jac., 379; Jacob, 455, 476, 518; Joh., 296, 389; Joh. David, 389; Joh. Frdr., 296, 351; Joh. Georg, 351; Joh. Michael, 518; Lorentz, 296, 326
BASTIAN, Anna Barbara, 515; Anna Magdel., 357; Cath., 379, 443, 450, 472, 506; Cath. Salome, 364; Christoph, 450, 472, 506, 549; Daniel, 379; Elis., 450; Elis. Regina, 529; Eva, 443, 470, 535; Georg, 364, 366, 386, 415, 421, 443, 470, 529, 535; Hnr., 443; Jacob, 472; Joh., 470, 549; Joh. Adam, 506; Johanna, 379; M. Magdalena, 361; Magd., 421; Maria Eva, 364, 366, 386, 415, 529; Michael, 359, 361; Sophia Cath., 549
BATES, Beng., 532; Benomy, 498; Elis., 498; Joh., 532; Sophia, 498, 532
BATH, Mr., 315
BATHO, Elis., 340, 434; Wilh., 434; Wilhelm, 340
BATHOS, Elis., 373; Peter, 373; Wilh., 373
BATTEAN, Elis., 422; Wilh., 422
BATTEAU, Elis., 438; Wilhelm, 438
BATTHO, Elis., 535; Wilhelm, 535
BAUER, Adam, 394; Andr., 377, 384, 492; Andreas, 280, 297, 332, 359, 435, 463, 526; Andrew, 492; Anna, 399; Anna Barb., 493; Anna Barbara, 297, 332, 463, 492; Anna Marg., 292, 343, 438, 448, 470, 543; Anna Maria, 377, 394; Barbara, 280, 309, 311, 332, 359, 384, 389, 435, 463, 504, 526, 542; Cath., 318, 325, 351, 359, 371, 405, 504, 540, 549; Chloe, 338; Christina, 465, 501; Christina Dorothea, 490; Christoph, 465; Dorothea, 298, 358, 365, 475, 506; Elis., 332, 463; Georg, 292, 320, 328, 343, 351, 365, 389, 401, 438, 448, 495, 496, 501, 504, 526, 540; Hanna, 308, 358; J., 389; Jacob, 320, 337, 338, 345, 383, 405, 463; Joh., 292, 318, 332, 371, 495, 540; Joh. Georg, 470; Joh. Hnr., 309, 394; Joh. Jac., 377; Joh. Mich., 474; Joh. Palatin, 308; Joh. Peter, 463, 493; John, 311; Marg., 320, 365, 401, 435, 495, 496; Maria, 345, 439; Maria Cath., 308; Maria Clara, 337, 377, 383; Mat., 308; Michael, 298, 332, 351, 358, 371, 405, 465, 475, 490, 501; Regina, 318; Sophia Elis., 448; Valentin, 358, 399; Wilhelm, 399; Wolf, 325

BAUM, Andreas, 547, 548; Anne, 549; Barbara, 548; Christian, 546; Christman, 546; Doroth. Elis., 492; Elis., 353, 546, 548; Jacob, 353, 492, 534; Joh., 528, 548, 549; Magdalene, 548; Nancy, 528
BAUMAN, An. Eva, 392; Carl, 288, 336, 390; Elis., 338, 346, 392; Jacob, 294; Joh., 336, 346, 392; Joh. Georg, 338; Maria, 288, 336, 390
BAUMANN, Carl, 391; Elis., 372; Joh., 341, 372; Maria, 391; Mary Marg., 294
BAUSCH, Adam, 286, 364, 509, 540; An., 455; Anna Maria, 286, 311, 364, 509, 540; Joh., 311, 540; Joh. Adam, 311; Joh. Georg, 364; John Adam, 455; Susanna, 509
BAUSCHON, Isaac Werner, 552; Marg., 552; Peter, 552
BAUSH, Martin, 428
BAYER, Ann, 433; Apellonia, 540; Barbara, 303; Blasius, 299; Christoph, 540; Elis., 420, 495; Elis. Marg., 353; Georg, 495; Georg Frdr., 353; John, 433; Mich., 495; Michael, 420; Sara, 433; Sarah, 420; Wm., 296
BAYERLE, Dietrich, 366; Hanna, 462; Joh. Didrich, 462; Joh. Jac., 368; Michael, 366; Sabina, 366, 462
BAYLEY, Cath., 540; Dorothea, 473, 522, 540; Elis., 522; Enoch, 473, 522, 540
BDYBAKER, Abraham, 312
BEATHO, Elis., 395; Wilh., 395
BECHMAN, Andreas, 300; Cath., 300; Elis., 300
BECHTEL, Anna Maria, 541; Christoph, 485, 541; Daniel, 317; Elis., 290, 292, 317, 369, 384, 485, 541; Georg, 292, 361, 369, 384; Jacob, 485, 541; Joh. Georg, 290, 361; Joh. Gottfried, 484; Matthaeus, 300; Susanna, 361; William, 317
BECHTHOLD, Anna Maria, 293, 341, 415; Jacob, 415; Joh. Conrad, 293; Philip Jacob, 341; Philipp Jacob, 293; Philippina, 415
BECHTOLD, Anna Cath., 338; Anna Maria, 314, 316, 338, 382; Elis., 423; Georg, 314, 423; Georg Adam, 382; Jacob, 444, 465; Maria, 433, 444, 465; Phil. Jac., 382, 433; Phil. Jacob, 338; Philip, 314; Philip Jacob, 316
BECK, Adam, 553; Andr., 375, 490; Andreas, 281, 354, 371, 386, 404, 427, 429, 449, 450, 461, 504, 524, 525, 542; Anna Cath., 430, 450; Anna Maria, 343, 472; Barbara, 354, 371, 404, 427, 429, 449, 504, 524; Bernhard, 338, 551; Carl, 437; Cath., 437, 456, 504; Christian, 504, 553; Christina, 473;

Christina Dorothea, 281; Conrad, 321; Elis., 285, 329, 375, 383, 426, 449, 461, 472, 480, 490, 504, 521, 553; Eva Marg., 375, 450, 490, 525, 542; Frdr., 437, 456; Hanna, 456, 521; Hnr., 427; Jacob, 298, 342, 345, 383, 426, 430, 480, 521; Jacob Frdr., 404; Joh., 343, 354, 472, 551; Joh. Adam, 352; Joh. Christian, 285; Joh. Jacob, 383; Joh. Peter, 329; Joh. Wilhelm, 354; Marg., 281, 426, 427; Margretha, 354; Maria, 338, 507, 551; Maria Barbara, 386; Maria Elis., 298, 342, 345, 430; Maria Eva, 480; Maria Magdalena, 317; Michael, 345; Paulus Michael, 317; Peter, 285; Susanna, 553; Valentin, 426, 507
BECKELY, Elis., 413; Hnr., 413; Marg., 413
BECKER, Adam, 300, 307; Ann Cath., 467; Anna Cath., 336, 463, 493, 529; Anna Maria, 293, 301, 336, 356, 461, 537; Arnold, 300, 307, 346, 389; Barbara, 459, 534; Cath., 358, 373, 396, 402, 435, 437, 461, 465, 522, 531, 534; Cath. Elis., 340; Cath. Lovisa, 531; Christina, 330, 335; Christina Barbara, 316; Christoph, 373, 437, 465, 522, 529; Conrad, 349; Elis., 285, 300, 307, 324, 327, 340, 346, 366, 389; Elis. Marg., 504; Frdr., 335; Georg Adam, 435, 463, 467, 493, 529; Hilarius, 435, 465, 531; Jacob, 293, 316, 330, 335, 336, 389, 434, 459, 471, 507, 511, 534, 552; James, 504; Joh., 306, 324, 356, 358, 396, 434, 463, 504, 545; Joh. Christoph, 402; Joh. Hilarius, 373, 402; Joh. Jacob, 346; Joh. Stuckert, 340; Magdalena, 507; Marg., 331, 346, 434, 459, 471, 511; Maria, 324, 331, 504, 531, 545, 552; Maria Cath., 349; Maria Louisa, 437, 522; Maria Magdalena, 331, 367; Mich., 301; Paulina Cath., 465; Peter, 331, 367; Regina, 316, 346; Susanna Cath., 373; Wendel, 331, 461; Wenzel, 356
BECKMAN, Maria Christina, 534
BECKMANN, Cath., 350, 454; Joh. Andreas, 350
BECKMEIER, Cath. Marg., 429; Hnr., 429
BEDICHMANN, Maria Cath., 516
BEDINGER, Eva, 314; Michael, 314
BEDKEN, Hnr., 539
BEHLER, Anna Maria, 362; David, 362, 379; Joh., 379; Joh. David, 362; Maria, 379
BEHNER, Anna Marg. Magdalena, 289; Jacob, 289; Marg., 289

BEHNO, Anna Elis., 458; Wilhelm, 458
BEHRENS, Agnes Henrica, 277; Daniel, 277; Maria, 277
BEHRES, Christoph, 279; Dorothea, 279
BEHRING, Elis. Magdalena, 532; Jacob, 532
BEHRINGER, Christoph, 519, 520; Christoph Carl, 538; Joseph, 536; Marg., 519, 520, 536, 538; Sarah, 536
BEHRNS, Mrs., 281
BEIDEMAN, Elis., 549; Jacob, 549; Joh., 549
BEIDER, Joh. Georg, 300
BEIDERMANN, Cath., 506; Elis., 491; Jac., 491; Jacob, 506
BEIER, Joh. Peter, 451; Johanna, 451
BEIL, Anna Barb., 391; Will., 391
BEILS, Dorothea, 459
BEISCH, Andreas, 286; Cath., 286; Jacob, 286
BEK, John Peter, 338; Marg., 338
BEKELY, Hnr., 304; Marg., 304; Maria Barbara, 304
BELIER, An. Marg., 344; Cath. Elis., 344; John Pater, 344
BELL, Anna Marg., 381; Joh. Jacob, 381; Peter, 381
BEN, Wm., 413
BENDER, Anna, 467; Barb., 368; Barbara, 301; Cath., 415, 417; Christian, 528; Daniel, 280, 338, 548; Dorothea, 333, 388, 415, 441; Dorothea Regina, 416; Elis., 287, 333, 388, 415, 458; Georg, 292, 333, 425, 467, 524; Gottfried, 490, 524; Isaack, 529; Jacob, 279, 310, 333, 368, 388, 415; Joh., 307, 386, 387, 417, 430, 431, 441, 458, 459, 469, 480, 481, 490, 512, 528; Joh. Frdr., 287, 333; Joh. Georg, 368, 431; Julia Marg., 490; Julianna, 279; Julianna Marg., 490; Ludw., 388; Ludwig, 416, 481, 529; Marg., 388, 416, 430, 441, 469, 481, 512, 522, 529; Maria, 279, 301, 310, 333, 528; Maria Ann, 394; Maria Marg., 441; Nicolaus, 452; Philip, 301; Rosina Marg., 425; Sarah, 490, 524; Sophia Susanna, 280, 338; Susanna, 386, 458, 459, 469, 480, 481, 528; Susanne, 431; Thomas, 481; William, 480
BENDERI, Georg, 361
BENDLER, Barbara, 287; Esther, 287; Jacob, 287
BENEDICT, Joh., 290
BENINGHOFF, Jacob, 449; Maria, 449; Sibylla, 449
BENK, Cath., 392; Joseph, 392; Mary Elis., 392
BENKER, Joh., 461
BENN, Philip, 396; Rosine, 396

BENNER, Adam, 511; Cath., 353, 423, 484, 511, 529; Cath. Elis., 330; Daniel, 484; Georg, 353; Hanna, 510; Hnr., 330, 511, 516, 529; Joh., 353, 510; John, 423; Maria, 529; Maria Barbara, 484
BENNIFORD, Joh., 310; Joh. Hnr., 310; Susanna, 310
BENNO, Joh., 442; Maria Elis., 423, 428, 442; Wilh., 428; Wilhelm, 423
BENSEL, Anna Christina, 503; Christoph Peter, 503; Mr., 546
BENSON, Alexander, 504, 507; Jacob, 322; Joh., 507; Marg., 504, 507
BENZEL, Christina, 444, 479; Joh. Peter, 444; Peter, 444, 479
BEREIFF, Cath., 446; Valentin, 446
BEREND, Barbara, 354, 395; Joh., 395
BERERUNG, Joh., 381; Joh. Conrad, 381; Marg., 381
BERG, Hanna, 371; Hnr., 371; Polly, 371
BERGMAYER, Daniel, 491; Marg., 491
BERGS, Joh., 440; Salome, 440
BERINGER, Anna, 478; Christian, 453; Christoph, 460; Christoph Carl, 429; Jacob, 478; Joseph, 478; Marg., 429, 453, 460
BERK, Andreas, 461; Elis., 461; Maria, 450; Valentin, 450
BERKHARDT, Andreas, 416; Joseph Reed, 416; Susanna, 416
BERKHEIMER, Elis., 476; Mat., 476; Wilhelm, 476
BERNARD, Gertraut, 542; Joh., 542; Joh. Joseph, 542
BERNDT, Joh., 304
BERNHARD, Barbara, 489, 501; Conrad, 489, 501; Dorothea, 535; Joh., 489; Magdalena, 501
BERNHARDT, Cath., 404; Conrad, 404; Gottlieb, 404; Maria Marg., 517
BERNHOLD, Cath., 391; Dorothea, 420; Joh., 391, 420; Joh. Frdr., 287, 420; Maria, 287, 391
BERON, Rosina, 341
BERRENS, Marg., 487
BERRICK, Hnr., 333; Joh., 333
BERRIS, Carl, 511; Joh., 511; John, 536; Sarah, 511, 536; Thomas, 536
BERRYS, Ann, 474; John, 474; Sarah, 474
BERTHHOLD, Cath., 415
BERTLING, Anna, 521; Conrad, 521; Maria, 521
BERTSCH (PERTSCH), Andreas, 499, 530; Anna Maria, 499, 530; Maria, 357; Wilh., 364
BESAYADE, Elias, 544
BESCH, Cath., 428; Georg, 428; Maria Elis., 428

BESSERER, Eva, 502; Joh., 502
BETS, Barbara, 358; Eva Maria, 358; Jacob, 358
BETSCH, Cath., 353; Cath. Marg., 551; Georg, 353; Joh., 551; Marg., 353
BETTENHAUS, Cath., 529; Joh., 529; Lucas, 529
BETTINGEN, Eva, 297; Michael, 297; Michael Joh., 297
BETTINGER, An. Barb., 321; Andreas, 395; Anna Maria, 321; Cath., 395; Eva, 460; Jacob, 321; Michael, 460
BETTON, Anna Elis., 354; Thomas, 354
BETZELER, Caspar, 442; Joh., 442
BETZLER, Regina, 521; Sarah, 521
BEUERLE, Christop, 302; Elis., 302; Wilhelm, 302
BEUSCH, Andreas, 410; Cath., 410; Georg, 410; Joseph, 410; Thomas, 410
BEVERING, John, 345; Sara, 345; Sarah, 345
BEYDEMANN, Jacob, 285
BEYDERMANN, Cath., 489; Elis., 489; Jacob, 489
BEYER, Anna, 550; Barbara, 277; Elis., 309; Marg., 309; Michael, 309
BEYERLE, Frdr., 383
BICHLER, Cath., 532; Joh., 532; Maria, 532
BICK, Christian, 333; Christina, 333
BICKENBEILER, Anna Maria, 372; Joh., 372
BICKHAM, Ann, 442; Christiana, 482; 532; Christina, 442; Georg, 442, 482, 532; Susanna, 482
BICKING, Dieter, 395; Dietr. Wilh., 375, 405; Elis., 375, 395, 405, 468, 520; Sus. Cath., 395; Wilhelm, 468, 520
BIEGLER, Anna, 321, 338, 346, 405, 424; Anna Cath., 361, 365, 389, 419, 431; Anna Dorothea, 471; Cath., 298, 385; Dorothea Cath., 338, 471; Hanna, 471; Hanna Rosina, 338; Jacob, 298, 338, 385, 471; Joh., 321, 338, 346, 361, 365, 389, 405, 419, 424, 431, 471; Maria, 298; Philip, 338; Sibylla, 471
BIEL, Joh., 492; Susanna, 492
BIGLER, Anna, 278, 294; Anna Cath., 284, 406; Anna Soph., 406; Christopher, 406; David, 294; Joh., 278, 284, 294
BIGNELL, Maria, 518; Thomas, 518
BIHSWANGER, Eva, 477; Joh. Pet., 477; Marg., 477
BILER, Barbara, 352
BILGER, Anna Cath., 406; Anna Soph., 406; Cath., 306; Christopher, 406; Daniel, 306; Marg., 306
BILL, Anna Marg., 313; Joh. Peter, 313; Joh. Philip, 313

BOETTINGER, Andreas, 360; Anna Maria, 360; Cath., 360; Jacob, 360; Joh. Georg, 360; Wilhelm, 360
BOHL, Adam, 520; Cath., 520; Elis., 330; Joh., 520; Marg., 520; Susanna, 520
BOHLER, Anna, 547; Michael, 547; Sara, 547
BOHM, Barbara, 550; Joh., 550
BOHMER, Andreas, 551; Marg., 551; Rebecca, 551
BOHN, Elis., 487, 535; Hnr., 487, 535; Joh., 549; Joh. Gottlieb, 487, 535; Magdalene, 549; Susanna, 535
BOHNE, Elis., 367
BOHR, Thomas, 308
BOHREFF, Cath., 528; Elis., 528; Martin, 528
BOHT, Cath. Elis., 326; Joh. Hnr., 326
BOIER, Elis. Marg., 388; Georg Frdr., 388
BOK, Anna, 403; Georg, 482; Magdalena, 482
BOLD, Elis., 318
BOLLEBACH, Abraham, 531; Cath., 531
BOLLEN, Johanna Marg., 545
BOLT, Hnr., 427; Mat., 427; Veronica, 427
BOND, Joh., 394; Thorn, 394
BONDY, Ann, 429; William, 429
BOOK, Anna Cath., 489; Cath., 489; Elis., 548; Georg, 479; Hnr., 548; Juliana, 479, 482; Ludewig, 482; Ludwig, 479; Magdalena, 479; Nicol. Georg, 489
BOOT (see also POT(H), BOT(H), Anna Cath., 402; Hnr., 402; Mat., 402
BORDER, Cath., 414
BOREF, Cath., 415; Joseph Martin, 415; Martin, 415
BOREFF, Cath., 474, 498; Marg., 474; Martin, 474, 498
BORRIS, John, 521
BORSTEIN, Eva, 308; Eva Cath., 308; Georg, 308
BORSTEL, Cath., 382; Frdr., 382
BOSARD, Andr., 387; Cath., 387
BOSHARD, Andreas, 446, 473; Barbara, 446; Cath., 473
BOSSARD, Andreas, 359
BOSSERT, Andreas, 552; Christine, 552; Christine Cath., 552; Jacob, 552
BOSSHARD, Andreas, 501, 535; Christina, 535; Christina Cath., 501
BOSSHART, And., 321; Andreas, 519; Christina, 519; Mar. Barbara, 321
BOT(H) (see also BOTT, POOT(H), POT(H), POTT), Anna Maria, 360, 468; Cath., 486; Cath. Elis., 297, 437, 455379; Elis., 425, 467, 486; Elis.

Cath. 486; Hnr., 425, 455, 486; Joh., 379; Joh. Hnr., 379, 437, 467; Maria Anna, 304; Mat., 417; Peter, 304, 360, 411; Susanna, 411
BOTT, Elis., 430; Joh. Hnr., 430
BOTTAM, Cath., 473
BOTTINGER, Andrew, 282; Balthas., 282; Cath., 282; Michael, 281, 309; Ottilia, 281
BOUCHER, Ann, 444
BOULE, Christina, 429; Michael, 429; Paul Caspar, 429
BOUNOT, Marg., 513; Nancy, 513; Simon, 513
BOURG, Elis., 484; James, 484
BOURGAL, Elis., 379; Jean, 379; Marg., 379
BOWIZER, Francis, 393; James, 393; Rosanna, 393
BOWMANN, Anna, 445; Elis., 445; Joh., 445
BOYD, Joh., 371
BOYER, Valentin, 500, 546
BRABANT, Frdr., 470
BRACKING, Elis., 430; Georg Ludewig, 430; Hanna Cath., 430
BRADLER, Jacob, 300; Sarah Cath., 300
BRAENNINGER, Franz, 451
BRAEUDIGAM, Daniel, 504; Marg., 504
BRAEULIGAM, Widow, 475
BRAEUNIG, Elis., 470; Georg, 470
BRAEUTIGAM, Daniel, 436, 475, 538; Marg., 538; Margareta, 475; Maria, 538; Maria Christina, 475
BRAND, Christina Cath., 299, 402; Elis., 407; Jacob, 407
BRANDT, Elis., 351; Jacob, 351
BRANNON, Ann, 417; Christoph, 417
BRANT, Elis., 361, 418; Eve, 431; Isaac, 418; Jacob, 361
BRATLER, Cath., 412
BRAUN, Andreas, 435; Anna, 537; Anna Cath., 358, 413, 467; Anna Maria, 302, 316, 354, 359, 412; Anna Maria Elis., 451; Cath., 387, 405, 435, 454, 483, 502, 509; Charlotta, 526; Christian, 526; Christoph, 490; Cornelius, 316; Dorothea, 443; Elis., 443; Elis. Marg., 451; Georg, 509; Hnr., 454; Jacob, 283, 358, 435; Joahnn, 514; Joh., 378, 387, 394, 405, 413, 436, 454, 467, 483, 502, 509, 536; Joh. Carl, 412; Joh. Conrad, 378; Joh. Georg, 451; Joseph, 302; Lud., 359; Ludwig, 315; Magdalena, 534; Maria, 378, 436, 514, 536, 537; Maria Elis., 387; Maria Magdalena, 316, 354; Maria Sarah, 359; Martin, 378, 412; Michael, 413; Nancy, 490; Nicolaus, 354; Sarah, 315; Wilhelm, 443

BRAUNHOLTZ, Anna Barbara, 287,
310; Barbara, 362; Frantz, 287, 310;
Franz, 362; Joh. Fransciscus, 310;
Maria Barbara, 287; Susanna, 362
BRAUNIN, Alexander, 531; Joh., 531;
Maria, 531
BREAKFIELD, Anna Maria, 394; Cath.,
394; Joh., 394; John, 420; Mary, 420;
Philip William, 420
BRECHEL, Barbara, 327; Cath., 311
BRECHLE, Anna, 423; Joh., 423; Maria
Barbara, 423
BRECHT, Anna Maria, 390; Joh. Georg,
286
BRECHTL, Marg. Barb., 436
BRECKLE, Anna, 397; Elis., 513; Joh.,
397, 513; Polly, 513
BRECKLEY, David, 488; Jacob, 488;
Magdalena, 488
BREIMER, Christina, 478
BREISCH, Eva Maria, 553; Joh., 467,
535, 553; Joh. Michael, 284, 535;
Maria, 535; Maria Cath., 467, 553
BREISE, Anna, 481; John, 481; Rahel,
481
BREMMER, George, 278
BRENDLE, Christina, 278; Philip, 278
BRENEISEN, Elis., 495; Maria, 495;
Valent., 495
BRENNEISEN, Anna Maria, 466; Elis.,
466, 540; Martin, 466; Valentin, 540
BRENNINGER, Frdr., 477
BRENTLER, Christina Cath., 366
BRENTLI, Christina, 543
BRESSLER, Cath., 497; Georg, 497
BRETON, Paul Caspar, 386, 531; Paul
Casper, 437; Susanna, 386, 437;
Susanna Louisa, 531
BREUNING, Elis., 463, 517; Georg, 463,
517; Wilhelm, 463
BREUNINGER, Christina, 524; Clara,
524; Frdr., 524
BREVIEHL, Anna Maria, 537; Esther,
495; Joh., 495, 537; John, 537; Maria,
495
BREVILL, Joh., 441; Mary, 441
BREWILL, John, 460; Mary, 460
BRICKS, Agnes Maria, 374; Anna
Magd., 374; Frdr., 374
BRINEY, Christina, 543; Frdr., 543
BRIT, Robert, 362; Sara, 362
BRITON, Paul, 410; Paul Caspar, 429,
465, 522; Susanna, 410, 429, 465;
Susanna Louisa, 522
BRITT, Georg, 545; Marg., 545; Maria,
545
BRITTON, Paul Casper, 550; Sus.
Louise, 550
BROBANST, Mrs., 432
BRODBECK, Frdr., 422; Marg., 422

BROENNING, Elis., 428; Georg, 428
BROM, Anna Maria, 324; Nicolaus, 324
BROOKS, Benjamin, 445; Cath., 439, 464;
Elis., 464, 507; Georg, 439; John, 439,
464; Marg. Cath., 445; Mat., 526;
Rosanna, 526; Rose Hanna, 526; Sarah,
526; Wilhelm, 507
BROSIUS, Cath., 364, 405, 445, 496;
Daniel, 364; Hnr., 364, 405, 445, 496;
Joseph, 405; Maria, 496; Sarah, 445
BROTHENECK, Charles, 338
BROWN, Elis., 514; Frdr., 514; Joh., 497;
Marg., 480; Maria, 497; Veronica, 514;
Will., 420
BRUCHHOLTZ, A. Cath., 548; Bernhard,
451, 548; Cath., 451
BRUDERSON, Joh., 431
BRUGER, Anna Marg., 360
BRUGGES, Cath., 416; Joh., 416; Samuel,
416
BRUM, Anna Maria, 295, 525; Georg,
525; Nicolaus, 295, 305, 525; Philip,
295
BRUMM, Anna Marg., 476; Anna Maria,
447, 476; Georg, 447; Joh., 447; Marg.,
447; Nicol., 476; Nicolaus, 447
BRUN, Christian Georg, 389; Elis., 389;
Geo. Simon, 288; Georg Simon, 389;
George, 280; Jacob, 288; Ludewig,
280; Maria Elis., 288; Nicolaus, 305;
Sarah, 280
BRUNNER, Anna, 497; Anna Dorothea,
497, 522; Anna Maria, 404; Cath., 468,
532; Eva Barbara, 532; Georg, 404,
468, 532; Georg Simon, 522; Simon,
497
BRYAN, Barbara, 393; Cath., 436;
Cath.Dorothea, 286; Elis., 299; Joh.,
436; Joh. Georg, 286; John, 286; Marg.
Barbara, 436; Maria, 393; Matthew,
299; Samuel, 393
BRYER, Apollonia, 350; Christoph, 350;
Hnr., 350
BUB, Anna, 348; Cath., 280, 344; Georg,
415; Georg Adam, 280; Joh., 348;
John, 348; Marg., 415; Maria, 415
BUCHTMAN, Albert Joh., 535; Anna,
535; Marg., 535
BUCK, Andreas, 283, 472; Anna Cath.,
283; Anna Marg., 283; Berhard, 504;
Bernhard, 343, 357, 414, 415, 472;
Bernhardt, 307, 400; Caspar, 283;
Cath., 304, 348, 377, 409, 437;
Christian, 548; Elis., 357, 377, 465,
513; Jacob, 304, 348, 377, 409, 437,
537; Joh., 549; Joh. Bernhard, 443;
Joh. Jacob, 283, 409; Joh. Philip, 549;
Juliane, 548; Leonhard, 413; Ludwig,
548; Marg., 504; Maria, 343, 357, 400,

413, 415, 443, 504, 549; Michael, 472; Philipp, 437, 465; Wilhelm, 304
BUCKELI, Joh. Adam, 288; Johannetta, 288
BUCKHOLTZ, Georg, 437; Veronica, 437
BUCKINHAM, John, 313
BUCKLEY, Cath., 408; Tenes, 408; Thomas, 408
BUDINGER, Anna Maria, 322; Jac., 322
BUDO, Elis., 351; Georg, 351
BUETKIS, Anna Barbara, 348; Conrad, 348; Joh., 348
BUG, Bernhard, 302
BUGHARDT, Andreas, 371; Elis., 371; Susanna, 371
BUHLER, Dorothea Cath., 429; Jacob, 429; Joh. Jacob, 429
BUK, Elis., 518; Joh., 518
BULGEAN, William, 322
BULLER, Cath., 384
BULLMANN, Joh., 339; Mar. Eleon, 339
BUMM, Elis., 323; Joh. Jacob, 323
BUNTER, Andreas, 285; Anna Maria, 285; Georg, 285
BURCK, Elis., 539; James, 539
BURCKARD, Andreas, 440; Susanna, 440
BURCKERD, Mary, 423
BURCKHARD, Barbara, 531; Elis., 504, 522, 542; Frdr., 505, 542; Marg., 523; Maria, 505, 542; Maria Elis., 505; Peter, 504, 511, 522; Polly, 475; Robert, 451; Sally, 522; Samuel Andreas, 504; Sarah, 451, 511, 538; Wilhelm, 451, 511, 538; William, 538
BURCKHARDT, Andras, 293; Andreas, 340; Andreas Samuel, 340; Barbara, 286; Jacob, 286; Susanna, 293; Susanna Elis., 293
BURCKHART, Marg., 489
BURCKIT, Cath., 530; Maria, 530; William, 530
BURCKY, Elis., 537; Peter, 537
BURDENHEIM, Anna Maria, 383; Georg, 383
BURES, Joh., 404; Sarah, 404; Wilhelm, 404
BURG, Anna, 417; Christina Salome, 476; Elis., 411, 417, 476, 487; James, 476; Joh., 487; Philip, 462; Philip Jacob, 417; Philipp, 411; Philipp Jacob, 487
BURGDORF, Joh. Fridrich, 286
BURGELT, Daniel, 409; James, 409; Marg., 409
BURGER, Michael, 279
BURGHARD, Andreas, 284, 468; Andreaus, 441; Anna Barbara, 359; Cath., 333, 367; Daniel, 333, 367;

Jacob, 359; Joh., 367; Joh. Wilh., 424; Joh. William, 424; Magdalena, 444; Sara, 410; Sarah, 481; Wilhelm, 410, 481
BURGHARDT, Andreas, 442, 468; Barbara, 313; Cath., 310, 332, 347; Daniel, 332, 347; Jacob, 313; Joh. Daniel, 347; Marg., 286, 293, 328, 468; Maria, 442; Susanna, 442, 468
BURGHART, Marg., 417
BURIAL, Daniel, 428; George, 428; Marg., 428
BURK, Anna Maria, 439; Bernard, 336; Cath., 546; Elis., 439; Ellis., 546; Maria, 336; Philip, 546; Philip Jacob, 439
BURKENBEIN, Elis., 549; Georg, 549
BURKERT, Abigail, 431; Jean, 431; John, 377; Philip, 431; Sara, 377; William, 377
BURKHARD, Casp. Daniel, 386; Cath., 386; Daniel, 279; Elis., 279; Jean, 516; Jeany, 479; Peggy, 446; Phil., 479; Phil. Nathaneal, 479; Philipp, 516; Rebecca, 516; Sophia, 279; Venable, 479
BURKHARDT, Andr., 350; Susanna, 350
BURKHART, Barbara, 553; Cath., 384; Joh., 435; Wilh., 384
BURSTEL, Joh. Frdr., 366
BUSCH, Christian, 300; Elis., 300; Sara, 300; Susanna Maria, 447
BUSKIRK, Cath., 336
BUSS, Anna, 348; Anna Maria, 450; Barbara, 416, 450, 492; Cath., 492; Elis., 416; Jacob, 416, 450, 492; Joh., 348; John, 348
BUTLER, Daniel, 481; Frdr., 427; Georg, 357; James, 423; Joh., 427, 456; Joseph, 456; Marg., 481; Martha, 481; Mary, 423; Richard, 406; Sarah, 481; Susanna, 427, 456; William, 409, 481
BUTTLER, Christina, 539; Joh. Georg, 539; Maria Barbara, 539
BUTZ, Christina, 427; Georg, 523; Marg., 523
CAEMMER, Cath., 305; Frantz Hnr., 305; Marg., 305
CAEMMERER, Cath., 339; Hnr., 339
CAER, Cath., 468; James, 468; Robert, 468
CAFFEL, Joh., 509
CALDWEL, Cath., 540; Charles, 540
CALLINS, Rebecca, 308
CALLWAY, Frdr., 479; Hnr., 479; Sarah, 479
CALLWITZ, Carl, 452; Frdr., 452; Salome, 452
CALWAY, Frdr., 452
CAMMER, Maria, 540; Reinhard, 540

CLEIMER, Balthasar, 508, 541; Elis.,
    508, 510, 541; Jacob, 510; Joh., 510;
    Marg., 510
CLEISNER, Balthasar, 508; Elis., 508
CLEMENS, Esther, 533; Joh. David, 552;
    Joh. David Wilhelm, 521; Joh. Peter,
    301; Maria, 315, 552; Maria
    Magdalena, 301, 521; Martha, 533;
    Peter, 301, 315; Samuel, 533;
    Wilhelm, 521, 552
CLEMMER, Jacob, 538; Joh., 538;
    Marg., 538
CLESER, Anna Elis., 536; Jacob, 536;
    Jonas, 536
CLIFFORD, Anna, 310; Jane, 310;
    William, 310
CLODING, Abr., 378; Abraham, 356;
    Cath., 356; Juliana, 356, 378; Marg.,
    378
CLOSS (see KLOSS), Susanna, 322;
    Theobald, 322
CLUMBERG, Cath., 540; Christine, 358;
    Philipp, 358, 540; Susanna, 540
CLUNIE, James, 313; Mary, 313; Robert,
    313
CLYMER, Balthasar, 426, 448, 463;
    Balthaser, 475; Cath., 463; Elis., 426,
    448, 475
COBER, Barb., 498; Paul, 376, 498
COCKEY, Samuel, 466
COCKS, Cath., 299
COHLMAN, Mary, 420; Philip Wilh.,
    420
COLLADAY, Jacob, 536; Sarah, 536
COLLEDAY, Jacob, 520; Susanna, 520;
    Veronica, 520
COLLER, Cath. Marg., 391; Daniel, 391;
    Marg., 391
COLLIARD, Elis., 507; John, 507;
    Robert, 507
COLLIN, Georg, 432; Susanne, 432;
    William, 432
COLLINS, Ann, 277; Elis., 493; Jeremia,
    277; Joseph, 292; Rebecca, 292;
    Robert, 493; Sara, 277
COLLY, John, 318; Maria, 318
COMAL, Benjamin, 284; Charlotte
    Sophia, 284; Joh. Georg, 284
COMINS, Judith, 289; Tobias, 289
COMMAT, Benj., 379; Benjamin, 356;
    Charlotte, 356, 379; John, 379;
    Sophia, 356
COMMENDORE, Christian, 513; Elis.,
    513; Joh. Hnr., 513
COMMENS, Abraham, 289; Judy, 289,
    290; Ledischie, 289; Lidia, 289;
    Tobias, 289, 290
COMMER, Jacob, 452; Maria
    Magdalena, 452
COMMIL, Anna Cath., 503; Joh., 503

CONNALY, Barbara, 404; John, 404;
    Simeon, 404
CONNER, Carl Joseph, 410; John, 410;
    Rachel, 410
CONNING, Christine, 414; Joh., 414;
    Marg., 414
CONNOR, Cath., 426
CONRAD, Anna Maria, 345, 408; Anna
    Ottilia, 493; Carl, 515; Conrad, 408;
    Hnr., 396, 422, 481; Joh. Hnr., 345;
    Joh. Jacob, 345; Joh. Michael, 515;
    Joh. Peter, 481; Johann, 408; Mar.
    Rosina, 396; Maria, 396, 422, 481;
    Regina, 515; Susanna, 422
COOK, Anna, 339, 537; Elis., 414;
    George, 288, 318; Hannah, 288; Joh.
    Jacob, 510; Magdalena, 483; Maria,
    510, 537; Robert, 288; Samuel, 483;
    Thomas, 483, 510, 537
COOP, Carl Philip, 355; Cath., 355; Joh.,
    355; Joh. Wilhelm, 355; Marg., 355
COOPER, Cath., 522, 543; Dorothea, 536;
    Elis., 538; Eva Maria, 553; Francys,
    516, 538; Georg, 536, 553; James, 522,
    543; Joh., 536; John, 522; Maria, 516;
    Susanna, 538
COPIA (see also KOPIA), Conrad, 300;
    Elis., 413; Jemima, 300; Magdalena
    Sophia, 324; Maria, 300; Peter, 345;
    Siegesmund, 324; Sigemund, 361;
    Sigmund, 338, 345, 413; Sophia, 338;
    Sophia Magd., 361; Sophia Magdalena,
    345, 413
COPPER, Cath., 532; John, 532; Maria,
    532
CORB, Cath., 310
CORDES, Cord, 362; Joh. Gottfried, 362;
    Marg., 362
CORTE, Hnr., 314; Marg., 314
COSSART, Hanna, 477; Marg., 477;
    Theophilus, 477
COTBUS, Edward, 318; Mr., 318
COTIG, Barbara, 290; Joh., 290
COTUS, Cath., 309; Hnr., 309
COURT, Hnr., 331; Joh., 331; Maria, 331;
    Regina, 331
COVER, Paul, 319
COX, Caspar, 383, 419; Cath., 358; Elis.,
    358, 383; George, 419; Martha, 419;
    Martin, 358; Thomas, 383; Wilhelm,
    358
CRAEMER (see also GRAEMER,
    KRAEMER), Albert, 435; Anna Maria,
    425, 457; Cath., 541, 545; Cath. Elis.,
    425; Christina, 435; Joh., 545;
    Leonhard, 425, 448, 457, 460; Maria,
    460, 541, 545; Mat., 503; Michael,
    541; Peter, 355; Susanna, 355, 503
CRAMER, Balthas, 302; Elis., 302
CRAMP, Martin, 537

Joh. Georg, 399; Marg., 335; Maria, 457; Maria Elis., 375; Mary, 375, 399
DEBALD, Hnr., 477; Marg., 477
DEBRUIN, Henr., 404; Joh. Peter, 404; Marg., 404
DECHERT, Gertrude, 313; Maria Elis., 313; Peter, 313
DEDECKE, Adam, 538; Carl, 538; Maria, 538
DEFORREST, Georg, 482; Hnr., 423, 482, 519; Magdalena, 423; Maria, 423, 482; Mary, 519
DEGEN, Eva, 335, 385; Joh., 335; Ludwig, 335, 385
DEGENHARD, Georg, 461; Joh. Georg, 483; Wilhelmina, 483
DEHM, Joh., 471; Maria Magdalena, 471
DEHN, Caspar, 351; Charlotte Philippina, 482; Eleonor, 441; Georg, 441, 488; Georg Hnr., 482, 501; Mar. Marg., 501; Marg., 351; Maria Clara, 482; Susanna, 441
DEHNER, Anna Marg., 308; Jacob, 308; Marg., 308; Maria Elis., 308
DEIBELIN, Joh., 333; Patrick, 333
DEIBER, David, 504; Hanna, 504; Joseph, 504
DEIS, Doroth., 405; Dorothea, 405; Jacob, 405, 450; Joh. Jac., 405
DEISS, Doroth., 536; Dorothea, 530; Jacob, 530; Marg., 513
DEITZ, Hnr., 407; Joh., 407; Maria Barb., 407
DELANY, Barbara, 505; Dennys, 505; Salome, 505
DELAPP, Anna Maria, 292; Barbara, 292; Nathaniel, 292
DEMAND, Elis., 435, 469; Jacob, 435; Joh. Jacob, 469
DEMANT, Elis., 442; Jacob, 442
DEMEND, Elis., 509
DEMER, Flora Rosina, 395; Hnr. Michael, 395; Maria Jacobina, 395
DEMMER, Hnr., 513; Hnr. Mich., 445; Hnr. Michael, 513; Joh. Jonas, 445; Maria Jacobina, 445, 513
DENCKFELDER, Conrad, 484, 516; Elis., 484, 516; Joh. Conrad, 516; Joh. Georg, 516
DENKFELDER, Elis., 431; Joh. Conr., 431; Joh. Georg, 431
DENNEST, Christian, 448; Maria, 448; Phil., 448
DENNINGER, Clara, 379; Magdalena, 315
DENNISON, James, 308; James Conrad, 308; Mary, 308
DENROS, Joseph, 346; Marg., 346
DENSHAM, James, 497; Marg., 497; Sarah, 497

DENZEL, Dorothea Elis., 389; Georg, 547; Hnr., 389, 445, 462; Jacob Frdr., 462; Joh. Georg, 400; Maria, 389; Maria Doroth., 462; Maria Dorothea, 445; Regina Dorothea, 445; Sara, 547; Sarah, 400
DEORINGER, Maria, 339
DEPPENWEIN, Elis. Julia, 339; Hnr., 339
DEPPERWIEHL, Hnr., 463; Marg., 463; Sophia, 463
DEPPERWIHN, Hnr., 542; Joh., 542; Marg., 542
DEPPERWILL, Hnr., 448; Marg., 448
DEPPERWIN, Cath., 371; Hnr., 371, 489, 522; Marg., 371, 489, 522; Maria, 489
DEPRUIN, Anna Marg., 364; Cath., 364; Hnr., 364
DERICK, Cath., 366; Christian, 383; Gottfried, 366; Marg. Cath., 366; Maria Ros., 383; Maria Rosina, 383
DERING, Andreas, 549; Anna Barbara, 404; Frdr., 549; Joh. Georg, 404; Maria, 549
DERINGER, Christina, 300; Maria, 300, 339, 383; Peter Paul, 383
DERK, Jacob, 366; Joh., 366
DERN, Christine, 337; Joh., 337; Joh. Georg, 337; Marg., 337
DERR, Adam, 323; Cath., 323
DERRICK, Anna Cath., 455; Christian, 455
DERRY, Charles, 377; Elis., 318, 343; Joh. Caspar, 318; Maria, 377; Martin, 377; Peter, 318, 343; Susanna, 362; William, 343
DESOHNER, Cath., 300; Georg, 300; Salome, 300
DETER, Joh., 348
DETZEL, Cath., 459; Doroth. Barb., 459; Georg, 459
DEVITER, Cath., 465; Conrad, 465; Maria, 465
DEWALD, Benjamin Jacob, 352; Elis., 352; Hanna, 320; Isaac, 320; Joh. Andreas, 320; Marg. Elis., 320; Michael, 352; Sara, 320
DEWEESE, Hanna, 297; Joshua, 297; William, 297
DEWESE, Eleonor, 353; Hanna, 353; William, 353
DEWETER, Cath., 377; Conrad, 377; Joh., 377
DEWHERST, Elizabeth, 316; Isaac, 316
DEWITER, Cath., 406; Conr., 406; Joh., 406
DEWITTER, Cath. Elis., 495, 540; Conrad, 495, 540; Conrad Wilhelm, 540; Eva Elis., 495
DEY, Jacob, 325
DEZEDWITZ, Juliana, 444

DICHANG, Anna Marg., 295; Frdr., 295
DICK, Anna Maria, 283, 352; Cath., 310,
  372, 397, 422, 539; Christian, 347;
  Christiana, 347; Daniel, 539; Elis.,
  463, 486; Frdr., 463; Georg Frdr.,
  463; Henrietta Cath., 338; Henriette,
  407; Juliana, 385; Maria, 312, 345,
  507; Maria Dor., 491; Melchior, 407;
  Peter, 283, 312, 345, 352, 385, 486;
  Phil., 397; Philip, 310; Philipp, 372,
  422, 539; Sophia, 347
DICKFELDER, Adam, 443; Conrad
  Adam, 443; Elis., 443
DICKHAUT, Cath., 538; Daniel, 538;
  Hnr., 538
DICKINSON, Marg., 369; Thomas, 369
DICKLAUCH, Elis., 385
DIDERICH, Charlotta, 447; Christina,
  447; Christoph, 447; Elis., 447, 448;
  Jacob, 447, 448; Joh. Phil., 447;
  Magdalena, 540; Marg., 448;
  Michael, 540; Rosina, 447
DIEBOLD, Carl, 443; Eva, 443; Joh.
  Georg, 443; Joh. Philipp, 443
DIEDEL, Barbara, 277
DIEDERICH, Barbara, 295; Magdalena,
  295; Michael, 295
DIEDERLE, Cath., 309; Joh. Adam, 309;
  Maria Elis., 316; Michael, 316
DIEDRICH, Michael, 517
DIEGEL, Hanna, 309; Jacob, 309
DIEHL, Philip Hnr., 552
DIEL (see also TIEL), Anna Cath., 504;
  Anna Maria, 352; Anna Sophia, 367;
  Cath., 294, 333, 389, 415, 472, 508;
  Eberhard, 294, 333, 389, 415; Elis.,
  514; Elizabeth, 352; Hnr., 428, 504;
  Jacob, 294; Joh., 333; Joh. Christoph,
  294; Joh. Georg, 389, 514; Joh. Hnr.,
  367; Joh. Jacob, 415; Marg., 443,
  504; Maria, 315, 384; Niclaus, 315;
  Nicol., 384; Nicolaus, 352; Peter,
  508, 514; Philipp Hnr., 531; Thomas,
  384; Wilhelm, 443
DIEM, Christian, 427; Magdalena, 427
DIEMANT, Anna Elis., 443; Elis., 443;
  Hnr., 443; Wilhelm, 443
DIENSMANN, Dietrich, 457
DIENSTMANN, Anna, 495; Anna Maria,
  447; Joh., 447, 495; Susanna Maria,
  447
DIERK, Christian, 283; Maria Rosina,
  283
DIERY, Georg, 326; Maria, 326
DIESS, Anna, 540; Dorothea, 365; Frdr.,
  545; Jacob, 365
DIESTMANN, Anna Maria, 324; Elis.,
  324; Jacob, 324; Joh., 324; Maria
  Magdalena, 480
DIET, Anna Cath., 284

DIETER, Adam, 370, 440, 482; Cath.,
  370, 440, 482; Dorothea, 354; Eva
  Christina, 441; Jacob, 354; Joh. Adam,
  440; Maria Elis., 314; Melchior, 370;
  Michael, 314; Philipp, 482
DIETERICH, Christina, 413, 439; David,
  413, 439; Frdr., 439; Georg, 442;
  Jacob, 413; Joh., 442
DIETHRICH, Anna Rosina, 350; Jacob,
  350
DIETRICH, Augustina, 315, 375; Cath.,
  287; Christina, 485; Christoph, 287,
  350; David, 485; Dorothea, 327; Elis.,
  287, 315, 350; Georg, 375; Georg
  Christoph, 287; Jac., 375; Jacob, 287,
  315, 327, 413, 552; Joh. Jacob, 287;
  Marg., 413; Peter, 350; Rosina, 287
DIETZ, Adam, 305; Anna Barbara, 314,
  334, 444; Anna Cath., 463; Anna
  Marg., 444; Anna Maria, 301, 305,
  326, 498, 520, 536; Anna Sarah, 520;
  Barbara, 372, 527; Carl, 376; Cath.,
  320, 321, 360, 478, 508, 525; Cath.
  Elis., 334; Christina, 282, 310, 341,
  371, 527; Elis., 368; Frde., 282; Frdr.,
  310, 321, 341, 527; Georg Nicholaus,
  403; Hanna, 520; Hnr., 279, 334, 372,
  418, 444, 536; Jacob, 310; Joh., 314;
  348; Joh. Daniel, 371; Joh. Frdr., 371;
  Joh. Georg, 282, 456; Joh. Hnr., 314,
  520; Joh. Martin, 485; Joh. Michael,
  498; Joh. Nicholaus, 438; Joh. Nicol.,
  508; Joh. Nicolaus, 478; Joh. Peter,
  301, 326, 520, 536; Joseph, 478;
  Magdalena, 438; Marg., 348, 368;
  Maria, 316, 372, 454; Maria Barbara,
  279, 418; Maria Cath., 317; Maria
  Elis., 317; Maria Eva, 320; Maria
  Marg., 403; Martin, 348, 376, 403,
  456, 485, 525, 538; Peter, 326, 368,
  454, 498; Philip, 320, 360; Sabina,
  538; Sabina Marg., 376, 485, 525;
  Salome, 527; Salomon, 527; Samuel,
  341; Sophia Elis., 508; Sophia Marg.,
  456; Susanna Dorothea, 454; Susanna
  Regina, 536; Wilhelm, 279, 317, 360
DIGHT, Carl, 450; Christina, 450
DIHM, Joh., 529; Maria, 529
DILL, Adam, 385; Adolf, 350; Adolph,
  288, 340, 346, 352, 370, 385, 388, 481,
  488, 504, 520, 540; Cath., 288, 340,
  346, 350, 352, 370, 385, 388, 435, 481,
  488, 504, 540; Elis., 340, 492; Joh.,
  288; Joh. Adam, 435; Joh. Jacob, 435;
  Juliana, 418; Julianna, 384; Peter, 492;
  Sabina Marg., 370
DILLER, Barbara, 278; Hannah, 278;
  Jacob, 278
DILLMANN, Cath., 291; Frdr., 291;
  Georg, 291

DUNCKELMEYER, Anna Eva, 522;
Caspar, 522
DUNLAP, Elis., 385; Mary, 385;
Neamian, 385
DUNN, Mary, 294; Patrick, 294
DUPOH, Charles, 494; Johanna, 494;
Susanna, 494
DUPONT, Carl, 527; Christina, 527; Joh.,
527
DURCK, Christian, 281; Maria, 281
DURR, Cath., 523; Christian, 523;
Christine, 357; Dorothea, 357; Elis.,
499, 541; Georg, 280, 396, 466, 523;
Jacob, 462; Joh., 541; Joh. Georg,
357; Joh. Jacob, 280, 466, 484, 499,
541; Joh. Maria, 396; Magdalena,
462; Marg., 431; Maria, 484, 541;
Maria Christina, 280; Maria Christine,
396; Maria Magd., 466; Nicolaus,
541; Susanna, 541
DUSCHANT, Frdr., 376
EASTIE, John, 372; Sarah, 372; Thomas,
372
EATS, Barbara, 284; Joh., 284; Thomas,
284
EBEL, Cath., 551; Joh., 551; Joseph, 551
EBERHARD, Anna Cath., 531; Anna
Charlotta, 517; Anna Dor., 374; Anna
Maria, 458; Anthon, 458, 485; Anton,
400, 531; Barbara, 354; Cath., 338,
418; Christ. Cath., 493; Christiana
Cath., 517; Christina Cath., 450;
David, 320, 354, 388, 419, 552;
Dorothea, 541; Elis., 320, 388, 419,
541, 552; Georg, 354, 493; Joh., 338,
374, 418, 450, 493, 517, 541; Johanna
Elis., 400; Maria Elis., 418;
Philippina, 400, 458, 485, 531;
Sophia, 485
EBERHARDT, Barbara, 292; Catah.,
336; Georg, 292; Joh., 313, 336;
Salome, 292
EBERHART, David, 369; Elis., 369
EBERLE, Adam, 335; Christina, 335;
Israel, 335; Joh. Gottlieb, 355; Joh.
Hnr., 355; Louisa, 355; Marg., 433;
Maria Cath., 433; Maria Sophia, 356;
Michael, 433; Simon, 356
EBERT, Carl Philip, 379
EBLE, Elis., 469; Hnr., 469
ECKARD, Anna Marg., 279; Cath., 430;
Elis., 392; Joh., 304; Maria, 304, 334,
392, 511; Wilhelm, 304, 334, 392,
511; Wm., 279
ECKARDT, Maria, 320; Wilhelm, 320
ECKERT, Anna Maria, 405; Wilhelm,
405
ECKFELD, Anna Elis., 422; Cath. Sara,
550; Elis., 366, 370, 394, 451; Georg
Michael, 422; Jacob, 366, 394, 422,

451, 550; Joh. Jacob, 394; Joh. Peter,
451; Joh. Philip, 366; John, 370
ECKLI, Christina, 541
EDELMANN, Elis., 522; Isaac, 448; Joh.,
414, 448, 474, 522; Regina, 414;
Sahra, 448; Sarah, 414, 474, 522
EDERS, Barbara, 342; Christina, 342;
Joh., 342
EDLING, Joh. Valentin, 514; Maria
Barbara, 514
EDUARDS, Hanna, 454
EDWARDS, Cath., 322
EGAR, Cath. Dorothea, 454; Maria
Sibylla, 454
EGER, Cath., 298; Charlotta, 496, 522;
Charlotte, 316; Elis., 322, 496; Joh.,
522; Leonard, 316; Leonhard, 496,
522; Philip Jacob, 298; Philipp, 322
EGERS, Frdr., 548; Marg., 548; Wilhelm,
548
EGY, Charlotta, 294; Charlotte, 400;
Jacob, 373; Joh., 359; Joh. Georg, 294,
373; Leon., 400; Leonhard, 294; Marg.,
373; Mat., 400; Sarah, 400
EHR, Elis., 361
EHRENFECHTER, Joh., 532; Maria, 532
EHRENFEUCHT, Elis., 363
EHRENFEUCHTER, An. Maria, 375;
Anna Maria, 280; Jac., 375, 379; Jacob,
302, 338; Joh. Jacob, 280, 302; Mat.,
338; Susanna, 280, 338, 379, 493;
Susanna Marg., 280, 302, 375
EHRHARD, Anna Cath., 511; Anna
Rosina, 511; Eleonora, 336; Jac., 336;
Marg., 528; Michael, 511, 528
EHRHARDT, Christina Marg., 345; Jacob,
345; Johanetta, 345; Johanna Eleonora,
285
EHRINGER, Esther, 476; Jacob, 476
EHWALD, Anna Maria, 330, 502; Cath.,
495; Christian, 530; Christina, 291;
Hanna, 495, 530; Jacob, 448, 462, 502;
Jane, 502; Jeany, 448; Jenny, 462;
Justina Elis., 324; Marg., 462; Maria,
342; Phil., 495, 530
EICHLE, Abraham, 538; Maria, 538
EICHLER, Elis., 406; Marg., 406; Peter,
406
EIHENPRAEGER, John, 328
EISENBREN, Cath., 485; Joh., 485; Joh.
Ehrhard, 485
EISENBREY, Barb., 469; Cath., 468;
Dorothea, 350, 357; Joh., 468, 469;
Joh. Dorothea, 402; Joh. Ehrhard, 468;
Peter, 350, 357, 402
EISENBRY, Cath., 356; Joh. Ehrhardt,
356
EISENHUT, Andreas, 470, 499; Anna
Maria, 499; Joh. Daniel, 470; Maria,
470

ERDMANLEINER, Andr., 390; Elis., 390; Rosina, 390
ERLINGER, Christina, 428; Georg, 428; Maria Magdalena, 428
ERMANTRAUD, Cath., 424; Frdr., 424; Joh. Frdr., 424
ERMENTRAUD, Cath., 342; Frdr., 342; Maria Charlotte, 342
ERNST, Anna Cath., 297; Cath., 329, 393, 432, 492; Cath. Elis., 297; Daniel, 297, 393, 432, 492; Elis., 351, 393; Frdr., 314, 334, 349, 351; Hnr., 349, 509; Joh. Dan., 329; Joh. Georg, 432; John Philipp, 314; Maria Cath., 329; Maria Clara, 314, 349, 351; Peter, 492
ERWIN, Adam, 550; Marg., 550
ESCH, Anna Marg., 480; Cath., 530; Joh., 449, 480, 530; Joh. Thomas, 449; Marg., 449, 530
ESCHART, John Conrad, 315; Maria, 315
ESCHEL, Frdr., 548
ESCHER, Anna, 366; Anna Cath., 399; Conrad, 285, 337, 528; Elis., 479; Elis. Hanna, 528; Ester, 292; Eva, 435; Georg, 435, 528; Jacob Frdr., 292; Joh., 366; Joh. Conrad, 477; Joh. Georg, 399, 457, 479, 480; Johanna Elis., 480; Marg., 479; Maria Barb., 435; Maria Barbara, 337; Maria Felice, 337; Maria Felicitas, 285, 477; Maria Magdalena, 366; Theodorus Wilhelm, 285
ESCHERIG, Elis., 516; Joh. Conrad, 516; Joh. Georg, 516
ESCHMANN, Christina, 286; Georg, 286
ESCHRIG, Elis., 544; Joh. Georg, 544; Joseph, 544
ESHER, Maria Barbara, 337
ESLER, Jacob, 424, 546; Susanna, 546
ESSER, Joh. Conr., 367; Joh. Maria, 367; Maria, 367
ESSIG, Barbara, 302; Christiana, 290, 302; Christina, 291, 319; Joh., 302, 323; Maria Barbara, 323
ESSLING, Anna Cath., 380; Nicolaus, 380; Philipp, 380
ESTERLE, Georg, 310; Maria, 310
ESTERLY, Joh. Georg, 386; Maria Sybille, 386
ETTER, Cath., 288, 348; Maria Marg., 348; Philip, 288, 348
EULER, Susanna Elis., 498
EVAN, Polly, 434
EVANS, Anthony, 413; Benjamin, 334; Cath., 303, 334, 413; Ephraim, 303, 413; Ephrem, 334; Eva, 313; John, 413; Joseph, 413; Ludwig, 369;

Rebecca, 406; Samuel, 313; Thomas, 303; William Carl, 313
EVINGER, Anna Elis., 402; Anna Marg., 402; Marg. Cath., 402
EWALD, Elis., 407; Jacob, 407; Jane, 407
EWERT, Marg., 348; Wilhelm, 348
EWINGER, Sarah, 489; Thomas, 489; William, 489
EYSENBREY, Cath., 532; Georg, 532; Joh., 532
FABER, Adam, 408; Cath., 408
FABRICUS, Carl, 546; Christina, 546; Joh., 546
FACHS, Joh., 529; Marg., 529
FACHSMEYER, Cath., 508; Joh., 508; Philipp, 508
FACKENDUS, Dorothea, 463; Wilhelm, 463
FACUNDUS, Andreas, 544; Anna Marg., 365; Cath., 488; Cath. Doroth., 445; Dorothea, 365, 417, 445, 501; Dorothy, 303; Elis., 520; Georg, 481, 509; Jacob, 488, 520; Jacob Ferdinand, 417; Jacob Wilhelm, 417; Joh., 544; Juliana, 488, 520; Lorreth, 373; Maria, 481, 509, 544; Maria Marg., 303; Wilh., 365; Wilhelm, 373, 445, 501; William, 303, 481
FACUS, Ann, 379
FACY, Christina, 309; Salome, 309
FAEHRY, Elis., 505
FAENNER, Maria Eva, 478
FAENZEL, Georg, 467; Georg Frdr., 467; Salome, 467
FAERLEY, Elis., 454; Wilhelm, 454
FAESEMIUS, Cath., 485; Jacob, 485; Joh., 485
FAESLER, Anna Barbara, 304; Georg, 304
FAGAN, Elis., 420
FAGNER, Mrs., 309
FAHL, Cath., 404; Joh., 404; Susanne, 404
FAHLTEBAUM, Frdr., 538; Maria, 538; Sarah, 538
FAHN, Christina, 457; Joh., 484; Marg., 484
FAHNS, Hnr., 346, 430; Joh., 296; Marg., 296; Sarah, 518; Veronica, 430
FAIRLE, Elis., 317; Susanna Elis., 317; William, 317
FAIRLEY, Cath., 367; Elis., 379; Jacob, 379; Regina, 367; Simon, 367; Will., 379
FAIRLY, Elis., 363; Maria, 363; William, 363
FAIRY, Eve Elizabeth, 288; James, 288
FALCK, Helena, 524; Joh. Caspar, 524
FALKENSTEIN, Ludewig, 325; Maria, 325
FALKNER, Marg., 387

FALLER, Andreas, 436; Elis., 436; Marg., 436
FALLKLE, Christina, 322; Hnr., 322; Maria, 322
FALMANN, Debora, 370; Georg, 370; Maria, 370
FAN, John, 370
FANCK, Adam, 510
FARBY, Elis., 345; William, 345
FARLAENDER, Elis., 399
FARLEY, Elis., 338, 493, 532; Joh., 493; Joh. David, 532; Joh. Mathias, 338; Wilh., 493; William, 338, 532
FARLY, Anna Maria, 452; Cath., 452; Georg, 339, 452; Marg., 339
FARMER, Anna, 326; Anna Maria, 295, 326, 415; Ludewig, 295, 326; Ludwig, 326, 368, 415; Maria, 368; Sara, 300; Septima, 312; William, 300
FARRA, Doroth., 433
FARY, Elis., 417
FASELER, Georg, 279
FASSMEYER, Cath., 550; Joh., 550
FASTEN, Cath., 403
FASTER (see also FORSTER), Anna Maria, 426, 540; Cath., 547; Conrad, 547; Georg, 507; Joh., 507; Johann Cath., 547; Joseph, 540; Philip, 547; Susanna Barb., 507
FASY, Christina, 340; John, 340, 380
FAUIET, Waker Dason, 412
FAUNS, Hnr., 388; Veronica, 388
FEAL, Cath., 432; Hanna, 432; Thomas, 432
FECHTHOLD, Jacob, 476; Maria, 476
FEDERER, Casp., 372; Cath., 372
FEHM, Barb., 386
FEICHT, Carl, 539; Elis., 539; Maria, 539
FEIL (see also PIEL, PFEIL), Cath., 428; Frdr., 399; Joh., 414, 428; Maria, 399, 414; Philippina, 414
FEIN, Cath., 468; Joh., 468
FEISE, Edward, 448; Elis., 448; Jeany, 448
FEISSINGER, Anna Maria Marg., 438; Joh. Georg, 438; Maria Salome, 438
FEITENBERGER, Elis., 385; Georg, 385; Maria, 385
FELD, Elis., 466; Wilhelm Ernst, 466
FELDENBERGER, Elis., 505; Joh., 315, 505; Magdalena, 505; Susanna, 315
FELDS, Maria Eva, 288
FELIX, Catharina, 368; Elis., 368; Joh., 368; Maria, 391
FELLON, James, 311
FELTEBAUM, Frdr., 516, 529; Maria, 529
FELTEBERGER, Joh., 394; Magdalena, 394

FELTEN, Hnr., 363; Joh. Ludwig, 363; Maria Dorothea, 363
FELTENBERGER, Elis., 473; Joh., 355, 473; Peter, 355; Susan. Magdal., 473; Susanna, 355
FENSTERMACHER, Frdr. Abraham, 294
FENZEL, Hnr., 367; Joh. Adam, 367; Joh. Georg, 426; Maria Dorothea, 367, 426; Salome, 426
FERCH, Dorothea, 459
FERG, Joh., 493; Michael, 493
FERGLER, Joh. Conrad, 483
FERRY, Elis., 547
FETTENBERGER, Joh., 540; Sarah, 540; Susanna, 540
FETTER, George, 313; Maria, 313
FETZER, Joh. Jacob, 368; Magdalena, 368; Maria Elis., 368
FEUCHTENBERG, Elis., 404; Georg, 404
FEUCHTENBERGER, Elis., 443, 444; Georg, 443, 444, 484; Joh., 484; Joh. Michael, 443; Johanna Elis., 484
FEYEN, Cath., 550; Joh., 550
FEYRING, Christina, 474; Mat., 474
FICHLIN, Elis., 341; Leonhard, 341; Maria Magdalena, 341
FIDER, Adam, 409; Cath., 409; Elis., 409
FIDLER, Christian, 285; Elis., 310, 326, 330, 341, 371, 536; Georg, 326, 330, 341, 371, 432; George, 310; Jacob, 310, 536; Marg., 536; Susan., 394; Susanne, 432; William, 536
FIEDLER, Christian, 378; Elis., 351, 498; Georg, 498; Jacob, 498; Marg., 498
FIES, Cath., 374; Dorothea, 374, 406; Jacob, 374; Martin, 374, 406; Peter, 406
FIESS, Adam, 336; Anna Maria, 330; Dorothea, 336; Dorothy, 308; Emanuel, 330; Martin, 308, 336; Peter, 330; William, 308
FIESTENTHAL, Joh., 357; Marg., 357; Peter, 357
FIFE, Edward, 406; Jane, 355; Jean, 406
FIGEL, Ann Marg., 333; Joh., 333
FILLER (see also PFILLER, PHILLER), Andrew, 362; Christoph, 440; Marg., 362; Maria Christina, 440; Sophia, 440; William, 362
FILTER, Jacob, 449; Marg., 449
FIMBEL, Jacob, 487; Maria, 487
FIMPEL, Adam, 492; Jacob, 492, 531; Maria, 492, 531
FINCK, Anna Cath., 490; Anna Maria, 449; Cath. Marg., 449; Joh., 449; Joh. Wilhelm, 449; John, 490; Philippina, 490
FINCKEL, Anna Maria, 450; Joh. Jacob, 450; Phil. Jacob, 450

FINK, Christoph, 388; Dorothea, 388; Joh., 388, 547; Marg., 547; Regina, 547

FINLEY, Anthony, 508; James, 508; Mary, 319, 508; Susanna, 319; William, 319

FIRELOCK, John, 385

FISCHBACH, Christoph Frdr., 457

FISCHER, A. Maria, 549; An. Maria, 385; Anna, 521; Anna Cath., 543; Anna Maria, 287, 312, 321, 332, 368, 380, 405, 408, 418, 437, 488, 546, 551; Anna Regina, 487; Barbara, 512, 546; Cath., 350, 392, 415, 417, 454, 550; Cath. Elis., 514; Christian, 543; David, 417; Elias, 512, 526, 546; Elis., 407, 425, 427, 437, 448, 449, 454, 470, 472, 480, 482, 483, 496, 500, 504, 518, 526, 530, 549, 551; Ester, 549; Eva Cath., 321; Frdr., 437, 475, 487, 502, 521; Georg, 392, 413, 449, 514, 526, 535, 549; Georg Adam, 304; Georg Michael, 470; Hnr., 350; Jacob, 535, 550; Jeanne, 535; Joh., 304, 321, 332, 350, 385, 390, 392, 417, 437, 475, 476, 478, 488, 500, 512, 543; Joh. Albrecht, 514; Joh. Burghard, 415; Joh. Dietr., 356; Joh. Frdr., 408; Joh. Georg, 488; Joh. Hnr., 500, 512; Joh. Jacob, 408; Joh. Michael, 390; Joh. Philip, 287, 312, 549; Joh. Philipp, 466; Joh. Thomas, 496, 500; John, 332; Joseph, 521; Leonhard, 415, 449, 470; Magdalena, 478; Marg., 475, 481, 500, 512; Maria, 356, 419; Maria Elis., 356; Maria Hermann, 425; Maria Marg., 304; Maria Regina, 322; Mariana, 290; Martin, 290; Mich., 384; Michael, 425; Nancy, 475, 502; Phil., 380, 393; Philip, 405, 418, 419; Philipp, 368; Polly, 475; Rahel, 329; Regina, 390; Rony, 380; Roxy, 380; Rudolf, 415; Samuel, 405; Susanna, 415, 449, 470; Thom., 380; Thomas, 423, 427, 437, 448, 449, 454, 472, 482, 483, 504, 518, 530, 551

FISHER, Cath., 349; Hanna, 322; Joh., 349; Joh. Georg, 349; John, 409

FISS, Doroth., 447; Elis., 373

FISTER (see also PFISTER, PISTER), Adam, 535; Cath., 535; Georg Peter, 535

FITLER, Jacob, 449, 479; Joseph, 479; Marg., 449, 479; Mrs., 449

FITTLER, Elis., 282; Georg, 282

FITZGERALD (see also Vitzgerald), Eleonora, 521; Elis., 521; Rahel, 521; William, 521

FITZGERLAND, Patrick, 367; Thomas, 367

FLAUER, Elis., 423; Joh., 423

FLEEMAN, Elis., 324; Joh., 324; Joh. Philipp, 324

FLEGEL, Joh., 533; Marg., 533; Wilhelm, 533

FLEGER, Frdr. Jacob, 477; Georg, 477; Joh. Jacob, 478; Maria Cath., 477; Phil., 478; Wilhelmina, 478

FLEGLER, Anna Maria, 548; Eva, 548; Valentin, 548

FLEIDER, Maria Cath., 502

FLEISCH, Anna Maria, 472; Cath., 516; Christian, 369, 472, 497, 516; Dorothea, 472, 516; Elis., 388; Joh., 472; Joh. Christian, 345; Joh. Georg, 345; Maria Marg., 369; Rosina Dorothea, 345, 369

FLEISCHER, Anna Cath., 444; Baltes, 546; Balth., 417; Balthas., 465; Balthasar, 287, 444, 488; Balthsar, 337; Cath., 287, 337, 417, 465, 488, 546; Christian, 530; Dorothea, 530

FLEMING, Elizabeth, 302; Joh., 302; Marg., 302; Nancy, 513

FLESCHER, Conrad, 410; Jacob, 410; Joh. Elis., 464; Joh. Georg, 464; Maria, 410

FLICK, Hnr., 431; Maria Cath., 431

FLICKER, A. Dorothea, 551

FLICKINGER, Cath., 293

FLICKWEHER, Anna Sophia, 508; David, 508

FLICKWIER, Andreas, 499; Anna Sophia, 429; David, 429, 499; Sophia, 499

FLICKWIR, Anna Sophia, 353; Cath. Maria, 353; David, 450; Elis., 398; Gotthard David, 353; Gotthelf David, 398; Hnr., 450; Sophia, 398, 450

FLOR, Anna Marg., 308; Joh. Philipp, 308; Maria, 308

FLORI, Bernhard, 404; Cath., 404; James, 404

FLORY, Cath., 462; Christoph, 395, 462; Elis., 395, 462, 497; Joh., 395, 462, 497; Peter, 497

FLOUERS, Elis., 553; Georg, 553

FLOWERS, Elis., 491, 530; Fanny, 491; Georg, 491; John, 530; William, 530

FOCHEROD, Maria Barbara, 323; Philip, 323

FOERRICH, Dorothea, 396; Joh., 396

FOERSTER, Andreas, 347, 401; Christian, 401; Hanna, 347, 401; Hnr., 347

FOGGEROD, Christina, 310; Joh., 310

FOHR, Joh., 360; Maria Cath., 360

FOLIKER, Christina Barbara, 316

FOLK, Adam, 304, 382, 425; Anna Cath., 304; Cath., 304, 382, 425; Dorothea

Susanna, 382; Georg, 382; Maria, 304; Sarah, 425
FOLKROT, Cath., 546; Elis., 546
FOLLING, Marg., 399
FOLN, Joh. Frdr., 338; Marg., 338
FONTANEAU, Joh., 552
FORBACH, Anna Marg., 313; Elis., 518; Eva, 345, 518; Eva Cath., 313; Frdr., 521; Georg, 313, 446, 490, 518; Joh., 490; Joh. Georg, 294; Marg., 294, 446, 490, 518; Maria, 446; Wilhelm, 446
FOREPAUGH, Anna Marg., 348; Georg, 348
FORER, Cath., 325; Cath. Dorothea, 325; John Georg, 325
FORNY, Cath., 333
FORRES, Elis., 430; Ludewig, 430
FORRESTER, Anna Cath., 428; Marg., 428; Rudolf, 428
FORST, Hanna, 436
FORSTER, An. Sybilla, 378; Andr., 378; Andreas, 284, 341, 361, 436; Anna, 436; Anna Sybila, 361; Anna Sybilla, 284; Cath., 409; Dorothea Maria, 284; Ernst, 340; Georg, 378; Mary, 340; Sophia Dorothea, 341
FORT, Barbara, 342; Cath., 382; Christoph, 382
FORTUN, Elis., 416
FORTZ, Carl, 284; Cath., 284
FOSTER, Andreas, 459; Cath., 450, 481; Edw. Georg, 477; Edward Georg, 474; Georg, 474; Hanna, 459; Joh. Georg, 477; Joh. Martin, 450; Maria, 474; Susanna Barb., 477
FOULCK, Adam, 329; Catharina, 329; Elis., 329
FOX, Jergan Michael, 307; John, 469; Joseph, 307; Patrick, 469; Phil., 435; Rebecca, 469; Salome, 307
FRANCK, Anna Marg., 446; Anna Maria, 324; Barbara, 324; Elis., 415; Jacob, 324, 362; Richard, 482
FRANCYS, Mary, 461
FRANGENSTEIN, Joh., 515; Magdalena, 515
FRANK, Anna Marg., 474; Elis., 301; Joh., 322; Marg., 322, 448
FRANKENBERGER, Joseph, 347; Maria, 347; Mary, 347
FRANKS, Elis., 357
FRANZ, Jacob, 514; Nancy, 514
FRAPPEL, Elis., 495; Michael, 495; Sarah, 495
FRAZER, Archibald, 419; James, 370, 419; Juliana, 370, 419; Mat., 370
FREEBORN, Anna Maria, 367; Dorothea, 367; Jacob, 367
FREEMAN, Elis., 438; Joh., 438

FREI, Cath., 482; Elias, 358; Joh., 358; Maria, 358; Peter, 482
FREIBERG, Anna Elis., 374; Joh., 374, 422; Joh. Jacob, 422; Susanna, 374, 422
FREIBERGER, Elis., 455; Jacob, 455; Joh. Gottlieb, 456; Maria, 455
FREIBURG, Elis., 327; Joh., 327, 551; Ludwig, 551; Susanna, 327, 551
FREIBURGER, Cath., 351; Joh., 351, 452; Maria Magdalena, 452; Susanna, 351, 452
FREICHEL, Elias Ludwig, 292; Maria Elis., 292
FREIDEL, Elias Ludwig, 283
FREIHEFER, Anna Maria, 435; Christina, 435; Joh., 435
FREIMUTH, Elis., 439; Jacob, 439; Joh., 439
FREINOLD, Anna Maria, 539; Elis., 539; Robert, 539
FRENCH, Arthur, 518; Barbara, 540; Erdmann, 511; Sabina Marg., 511; Sabine Cath., 518; Sarah, 518; Veronica, 518
FREUHEIM, Elis., 363
FREUND, Cath., 463; Christian, 299; Elis., 299; Jesse, 299
FREY, Anna Maria, 524; Anthon, 506; Elias, 320, 431, 459, 528; Elias Frey, 493; Elis., 431; Georg, 429; Jacob, 459, 505, 527, 537; Joh., 459; Joh. Wilhelm, 528; Joseph, 459; Mar. Magdal., 493; Marg., 459, 505; Maria, 320, 391, 431, 459, 485, 493, 528, 537; Maria Veronica, 527; Mich., 391; Michael, 320, 391; Polly, 505
FREYBURG, Joh., 397, 471, 506, 516; Sarah Elis., 516; Susann, 397; Susanna, 471, 506, 516
FREYMUTH, Benjamin Erdman, 487; Benjamin Erdmann, 502; Dorothea, 487, 502; Elis., 487, 502, 537; Joh., 502, 537; John, 487; Wilhelm, 537
FREYTAG, Hnr., 399
FRIBELI, Barbara, 355; Urban, 355
FRICK, Marg., 366; Michael, 366
FRICKHOEFER, Cath., 452; Esther, 470; Hedwig, 452, 487; Joh., 452, 470, 487; Joh. Christian, 487; Joh. Just, 487; Marg., 487; Philippina, 470
FRICKHOFER, Joh., 378; Marg. Stucker, 378
FRIDERIC, Elis., 519
FRIDERICI, Anna, 497; Georg Wilh., 497; Jacob, 497
FRIDRICH, Anna, 532, 545; Eva, 532; Georg Gottfried, 532; Jacob, 532, 545; Peter, 459; Sarah, 459

GEIS, Cath., 429; Joh. Eberhard, 429
GEISE, Eva, 510; Hnr. Wilhelm, 510
GEISER, Anna Maria, 353; Elis., 312;
  Jacob, 367; Joh., 312, 346, 367;
  Joseph, 353; Maria, 353; Maria Elis.,
  346
GEISS, Cath., 450; Eberhard, 450; Eva,
  540; Eva Elis., 495; Hnr. Wilh., 490;
  Mar., 490; Wilh., 495; Wilhelm, 540
GEISSER, Elis., 401; Joh., 401; Wilhelm,
  401
GEISSLER, Carl, 530; Cath., 530; Elis.,
  530
GELETA, Georg Sigismund, 457; Joh.
  Georg, 457; Naomi, 457
GELZER, Marg., 476
GEMEINBAUER, Anna Cath., 359, 405,
  439, 519; Anna Maria, 359; Cath.,
  284, 299, 319, 383; Joh., 405; Joh.
  Georg, 439; Joh. Michael, 319; Joh.
  Peter, 284; Joh. Wolf, 319; Joh.
  Wolf., 359; Joh. Wolfg., 299, 405;
  Joh. Wolfgang, 284, 519; Maria Elis.,
  376; Wolfg., 383; Wolfgang, 439
GEMEINDBAUER, Cath., 553; Joh.
  Wolfg., 553
GENSEMER, Maria Cath., 281
GENSER, Cath., 411; Georg, 411; Joh.
  Jacob, 411
GENZEL, Cath., 375; Christian, 375;
  Marg., 496; Martin, 496
GEORG, Carl, 365; Charles, 297;
  Euphemia Sus., 365; Jacob, 449;
  Prince, 505; Rosina Christiana, 297;
  Veronica, 297; Wilhelm, 365
GEORGE, Agnes, 340; Joseph, 340;
  Rosa, 340; William, 340
GERARD, Anton, 379
GERBER, Eva Maria, 411; Joh. Georg,
  454; Joh. Phil., 411; Maria, 418, 454;
  Maria Elis., 418; Philip, 418; Philipp,
  454
GERET, Christina, 400; Rosina Marg.,
  346, 413, 452; Sophia Marg., 309
GERHARD, Anna Marg., 429; Anna
  Maria, 378; Daniel, 429; Elis., 429;
  Joh. Jac. Ehrhard, 378; Johanetta
  Eleonor, 378
GERICH, Adam, 302, 333, 356; Susanna,
  302, 333
GERICKE, Angelica, 510; Christina, 510;
  Frdr., 510
GERIER, Maria, 315
GERIH, Adam, 289; Susanna, 289
GERLACH, An. Maria, 373; Anna Maria,
  317, 400; Elis., 392; Joh., 317, 373
GERLING, Anna Marg. Magdalena, 289;
  Christina, 368; Elis., 335; Georg, 335,
  368; Joh., 289; Ludwig, 368; Maria
  Cath., 368; Maria Christina, 335

GERLINGER, Christ., 406; Georg, 296,
  406, 540; Joh., 540; Ludwig, 387, 406;
  Magdalena, 296; Maria Christina, 296,
  540
GERRET, Anna Maria, 378; Elis., 411;
  Joh. Jac. Ehrhard, 378; Johanetta
  Eleonor, 378; Robert, 411; Sophia,
  411; William, 289
GERRICK, Ros. Marg., 391
GERTLING, Georg, 387
GERTRAUD, Elis., 465; Joh., 465
GERTRAUT, Cath., 477; Elis., 477; Joh.,
  477
GERUM, Anna Maria, 499; Cath., 461,
  549; Elis., 461, 488, 499, 549; Thomas,
  461, 488, 499, 549
GESCH, Cath., 421, 469; Frdr., 421, 469;
  Georg, 421; Georg Frdr., 469
GESNER, Christian, 446; Daniel, 327;
  Elis., 327, 457; Hnr., 298, 330; Joh.
  Christian, 457; Joh. Georg, 483; Joh.
  Hnr., 330; Magdalena, 446, 457;
  Marg., 298, 330; Maria, 298, 446, 483;
  Maria Agnes, 330; Maria Marg., 298;
  Valentin, 298, 330, 483
GESSNER, Joh. Christian, 533; Joh. Hnr.,
  533; Magdalena, 533; Marg., 533
GETBHARDT, Cath., 306; Conrad, 306
GETTER, Anna Marg., 305; Anna Maria,
  434; Christoph, 305; Elis., 305; Hnr.,
  305; Joh., 434; Maria Magdalena, 305;
  Samuel, 434
GETTLING, Joh. Georg, 315; Joh. Martin,
  315; Maria Christina, 315
GETTMAN, Anna Marg., 364; Joh. Leon.,
  364; Joh. Nicolaus, 364
GEYER, Adam, 370, 496; Andreas, 446,
  535; Baltzer, 548; Barbara, 446, 535;
  Caspar, 280; Cath., 541; Christian,
  508; Christina, 448, 475, 541; Elis.,
  280, 448, 548; Georg, 535; Joh., 448,
  508, 541; John, 475; Mar. Magdalene,
  548; Maria, 370, 475; Wilhelm, 446
GIBBINS, William, 330
GIBBONS, Georg, 412; Jeane, 412;
  Theresia, 412
GIBSON, Eleonora, 511; Marg., 511; Mr.,
  327; Wilhelm, 511
GIE, Christophel, 407; Elis., 407
GIEBEL, Hanna, 368
GIEBELHAUS, Christian Carl, 394;
  Ehrhard, 363, 394; Ehrhardt, 314;
  Georg Adam, 314; Maria Barbara, 314,
  363, 394; Maria Martha, 363
GIESS, Caspar, 277; Christina, 277;
  Christina Marg., 277; Marg., 277;
  Michael, 277
GIHL, Christoph, 350; Elis., 350; Joh.
  Peter, 350

GILBERT, Andreas, 341; Anna, 417, 499; Anthon, 340; Anthony, 391; Anton, 324, 357; Antoni, 307; Barbara, 420; Cath., 316, 407, 420, 453, 471, 499; Christina, 415, 476, 481, 497; Christoph, 341; Daniel, 420, 453, 471; Elis., 300, 317, 332, 391, 453, 548; Georg, 415, 515; Hanna, 440; Hnr., 357, 440; Jacob, 407; Joh., 332; Joh. Hnr., 316, 499; Joh. Michael, 417; Joh. Samuel, 499; Magdalena, 324, 471; Magdalene, 357; Marg., 347; Maria, 515; Mat., 332, 415, 476, 481, 497; Matthaeus, 300; Michael, 417, 440, 499; Salome, 481; Samuel, 407; Sophia, 324, 341, 357
GILLMAN, Adolph, 336; Cath., 336
GILLMANN, Susanna Louwisa, 296
GILMAN, Joh. Adolph, 337
GIMELL, George, 295
GINNENS, David, 306; Marg., 306; Peter, 306
GINSLER, Balthas, 278; Maria Elis., 278; Michael, 278
GISSON, Mary, 319
GLASER, Christina, 477; Joh., 477
GLASGOW, Cath., 377; Edward, 377
GLASSER, Cath., 428; Christina, 428; Joh., 428
GLAUBFLUGER, Joh. Christian, 376
GLOCKNER, Magdalena, 307
GLODIN, Abraham, 302, 317; Juliana, 302, 317
GLYN, Bartholom, 418; Elis., 418; Mary, 418
GOBETBAUER, Cath., 477; Christ. Frdr., 477; Frdr., 477
GODDARD, Marg., 492
GODFREW, Charles, 439; John, 439; Marg., 439
GODFREY, Cath., 469; John, 469; Marg., 469
GOEBLER, Joh., 400; Joh. Adam, 400; Susanna, 400
GOENER, Michael, 508; Sarah, 508; Wilhelm, 508
GOENNER, Charlotte, 340; Christina Elis., 290; Marg. Cath., 290; Michael, 290, 340
GOENTNER, Cath., 437; Jacob, 437
GOERING, Cath., 531; Marg., 531; Michael, 531
GOETHLING, Eva Maria, 286; Salome, 286; Wilhelm, 286
GOETLING, Christina Elis., 423; Eva Maria, 325; Georg David, 325; Henriette, 423; Joh. Georg, 423; Wilh., 325
GOETTLE, Anna, 348; Georg, 418; Hanna, 418; Joh. Georg, 348

GOETTLING, Anna, 470; Anna Marg., 470; Joh. Georg, 470
GOETZ, An. Dor., 455; Anna Dorothea, 285; Anna Elis., 395; Dorothea, 381, 423; Eva Barbara, 345, 498, 532; Joh., 285, 381, 423, 455; Joh. Michael, 345, 498, 532; Maria, 303, 395, 496; Mich., 496; Michael, 303, 395
GOHT, Christian, 306; Christina, 306; Joh., 306
GON, Cath. Elis., 325; Joh., 325; Joh. Thomas, 325
GONNER, Charlotta, 319, 329; Charlotta Elis., 311; Marg. Charlotta, 329; Michael, 311, 319, 329
GONTER, Cath., 354; Jacob, 354
GONTNER, Carl, 376; Cath., 376; Jacob, 376
GORDAN, Elsbeth, 535; Joh., 535; Maria, 535
GORDON, John, 430; Mary, 430; Stephan, 430
GORGER, An. Maria, 405; Joh., 405
GOSNER, Georg Frdr., 458; Joh. Joseph, 414; Maria Agnes, 414; Maria Agnesa, 458; Valentin, 414, 458
GOT, Anna Maria, 446
GOTH, Cath. Elis., 449; Fronica, 449; Joh. Hnr., 449; Joh. Peter, 449; Mat., 449
GOTTFREE, Elis., 510; Joh. Georg, 510; Maria, 510
GOTTFRIED, Elis., 538; Georg, 538, 553; Joh., 538; Maria Magdalene, 553
GOTTINGER, Anna Marg., 277; Francis, 277; Jacob, 277
GOTTLE, Georg, 375; Hanna, 375
GOTTLIEBIN, A., 533
GOTTSCHALL, Elis., 506; Joh., 506; Maria, 506
GOTTSCHULD, Rosina, 338
GOTZ, Anna, 365; Appellonia, 517; Barbara, 281; Dor., 386; Dorothea, 358; Eva Barbara, 379; Maria, 390; Mich., 390; Michael, 281, 365
GOUCHER, Ann, 380; Hanna, 380; Hannah, 327; Thomas, 327, 380; William, 327
GRAAF, Elis., 354; Samuel, 291
GRAAFF, Joh. Joseph, 461; Maria Doroth., 461
GRABEL, Adam, 399; Christine, 389; Elis., 389, 392, 399; Joh., 355, 389; Regina Dorothea, 355
GRABER, Anna Maria, 301; Georg, 301
GRACE, Jacob, 371; John, 538; Marg., 371
GRAEB, Joh., 529; Joh. Gottfried Philip, 529; Maria Philippina, 529
GRAEBER, Anna Maria, 294; Elis., 339; Frdr., 294; Joh., 294, 339

GRAEF, Adam, 363; Anna Maria, 403; Anna Maria Rosina, 351; Carl, 428; Casp., 391, 403; Caspar, 323, 337, 343, 363; Cath., 317, 323, 337, 343, 351, 356, 363; Elis., 343, 351, 372, 397; Frdr., 372; Hesther, 403; Hnr., 403; Jac., 356; Jacob, 317, 343, 372, 397, 400, 428; Joh., 307, 323, 338, 391, 403; Joh. Jacob, 343; Joh. Philipp, 372; Magdalena, 338, 356; Mar. Elis., 391; Maria, 372, 400, 428; Maria Magd., 307; Maria Magdalena, 323; Mat., 351; Mr., 352; Osborne, 403; Samuel, 403; Sara, 323; Susanne, 391; Wilhelm, 397
GRAEFEL, Christoph, 304; Eva, 304; Joh. Philipp, 304
GRAEFENSTEIN, Dorothea, 454, 464; Joh., 454, 464
GRAEFF, Caspar, 519, 542; Cath. Marg., 295; Elis., 327; Jacob, 295, 327; Jeany, 538; Joh., 507, 538, 542; Joh. Caspar, 519; Magdalena, 507; Marg., 295; Maria, 538; Maria Cath., 327; Rebecca, 519, 542
GRAEFFENSTEIN, Dorothea, 509; Joh., 509
GRAEFLY, Christoph, 318; Eva, 318; Joh. Georg, 318; Philipp, 318
GRAEKER, Adam, 415; Jacob, 415; Susanna, 415
GRAEMER (see also KRAEMER), Cath., 402; Mat., 403
GRAES, Anna, 415; Susanna, 415
GRAESEL, Elis., 348; Joh., 348; Magdalene, 348
GRAESS, Caspar, 314; Cath., 281, 314; Hnr., 281; Jacob, 281
GRAETER, Ambros, 375; Andreas, 375; Ann, 375
GRAF, Balthasar, 499; Caspar, 388, 420; Cath., 422, 499; Charl., 378; Christian, 552; Daniel, 342; Dorothea, 397; Elis., 366, 407, 499; Eva, 552; Frdr., 366; Jacob, 420, 482; Joh., 548, 552; Joh. Joseph, 397; Mar. Elis., 397; Mar. Magdalene, 548; Marg., 342; Maria, 407, 420; Michael, 342; Peter, 366, 407, 422; Sophia, 482; Wilhelm, 422
GRAFENSTEIN, Dorothea, 452; Georg, 452; Joh., 452
GRAFF, Balthasar, 539; Caspar, 425, 450; Cath., 539; Charlotte Philippina, 500; Elis., 425; Jacob, 425, 476, 500, 539; Joh. Joseph, 495; John, 435; Joseph, 521; Magdalena, 344; Mar. Dorothea, 495; Mar. Magdal., 495; Marg., 435; Maria, 450; Sophia, 476, 500; Susanna, 435

GRAFLY, Christoph, 365; Elis., 534; Eva, 365; Marg., 365
GRANDSON, Abraham, 530; Agness, 530; Georg, 530; Peter, 530
GRANT, Daniel, 409; Robert Francys, 446
GRASS, Christine, 354; Widow, 354
GRATTER, Cath., 482; Jacob, 482
GRATZ, Joh. Joseph, 422; Maria Dorothea, 422; Maria Marg., 422
GRAUAN, Anna Albertine, 392; Joh. Jac., 392
GRAUER, Ludewig, 347
GREB, Anna Magdalena, 424; Christina Marg., 424; Elis., 424, 469; Peter, 424
GREDY, Elis., 450; Joh., 450
GREEN, George, 363; John, 398; Maria, 398; Patrick, 521
GREENAWAY, Anna, 363; Benjamin, 363; Valentinus, 363
GREENWOOD, Alexander, 320, 356; Salome, 356
GREIFENSTEIN, Dorothea, 362, 393; Joh., 362, 393; Simon, 393
GREIFFENSTEIN, Christian, 327; Dorothea, 281, 282, 312, 327, 350; Joh., 277, 281, 282, 312, 327, 350, 426; Joh. Michael, 277; Mar. Dorothea, 426; Maria Dorothea, 277
GREINER, Cath., 323; Daniel, 323; Elis., 364, 395; Frdr., 364, 395; Joh., 467; Joseph, 467; Marg., 467; Sophia, 364
GRENADIER, Abraham, 354
GREON, Elis., 357
GRESEL, Cath., 384; Joh., 384; Maria Doroth., 384
GRESLER, Frdr., 483; Sophia, 483
GRESS (see also CRESS, CHRESS, KRESS), Anna Christina, 287; Anna Maria, 325, 423; Anna Rosina, 287; Barbara, 468; Charlotta, 527; Doroth., 375; Elis., 408; Esther, 454; Hnr., 308, 325, 423; Jacob, 288, 396, 408, 422; Joh., 349; Joh. Frdr., 455; Joh. Jacob, 308, 349; Joh. Ludwig, 287; Joh. Peter, 287; Joseph, 468; Mar. Rosina, 396; Marg., 396, 468; Maria, 325; Peter, 317, 375, 396, 422, 454, 484; Rebecca, 484; Rosina, 317, 375, 422, 454, 484; Sophia, 455; Susanna, 288, 308, 349
GRESSEL, Andreas, 314; Anna, 429; Barbara, 323; Cath., 314, 323, 429; Dorothea Sophia, 314; Joh., 314, 323, 429
GRESSL, Barbara, 323
GREUS, Anna Elis., 306; Anna Maria], 306; Barbara, 427; Georg, 427; Joh., 306, 427
GRIECH, Valentin, 316
GRIEFFENSTEIN, Dorothea, 416; Joh., 416

GRIEFFICH, Georg, 308; Grieffich, 308; Sarah, 308
GRIER, Charles, 394; Georg, 387; Joseph, 387; Maria, 387
GRIES, Barbara, 309; Joh., 309
GRIESS, Barbara, 314, 356, 394; Elis., 356; Joh., 314, 356, 394; Philipp, 394
GRIESY, Jacob, 472
GRIFFENSTEIN, Joh., 399; Maria Dorothea, 399
GRIFFIN, David, 493; Marg., 493; Nancy, 493
GRIFFITH, Elis., 528; Thomas, 528
GRIGEMEYER (see also KRIEGEMEYER, KRUGEMEIER), Elis., 510; Hnr., 510
GRIM, Dorothea Sophia, 288; Elis., 547; Peter, 288, 547; Susanna Cath., 288
GRIMM, Alexander, 547; Anna Barbara, 398; Cath., 383; Deder, 324; Doroth. Soph, 361; Dorothea, 398, 413; Elis., 471; Georg David, 437; Gottfried, 383, 407, 437, 471; Joh. Jacob, 407; Joh. Nic., 397; Joh. Sophia, 324; Mar. Magdal., 397; Maria, 490; Peter, 361, 398, 413; Rosina, 383, 437, 471; Rosina Magdalena, 407; Sara, 547; Sophia Dorothea, 324; Sophia Magd., 361
GRIND, Joh., 315
GRIST, Elis., 375
GROB (see also KROB), Adam, 279, 365, 443, 453; Anna Maria, 293; Cath., 421; Christoph, 279; Elis., 279, 313, 365, 443, 453; Jacobina, 505; Joh. Adam, 313; Sebastian, 313
GROBB, Elis., 482
GRODIAN, Catharina, 289; Hnr., 289
GROF, Adam, 350, 452; Balthasar, 429; Cath., 328, 350, 354, 381, 429, 452, 455; Elis., 381, 391; Georg, 328, 429; Jacob, 485; Marg., 391; Maria, 354; Michael, 391; Peter, 328, 354, 381, 455; Sophia, 485
GROFF, Barb., 431; Christina Friderica, 344; Samuel, 344
GROH, Cath., 368; Elis., 368; Hnr., 368
GROLL, Christina Dorothea, 521; Elis., 521; Joh. Nicol., 521
GROLY, Anna Maria, 431; Wilhelm, 431
GROMMEL, Maria Marg., 414
GROS, Cath., 328; Georg, 328; Maria, 397; Peter, 328
GROSS, Anna Dorothea, 511; Anna Elis., 367; Anna Maria, 301; Cath., 335, 429, 534; Christian Bastian, 399; Dorothea, 292; Elis., 425; Ester, 534; Esther, 496; Frdr., 410, 496, 534; Georg Hnr., 301; Georg Phil., 496; Jacob, 335, 429, 511; Joh. Michael,

511; Marg., 399; Maria Marg., 425; Michael, 302; Philipp, 399; Valentin, 534
GROTHAUSS, Cath. Sibella, 303; Jacob, 303
GROTIUS, Amalia, 308; Georg, 308; Marg., 308
GROTLER, Cath., 339; Hnr., 339
GROTS, Cath., 545; Hnr., 545
GROTZ, Dorothea, 283, 331, 343, 372, 401, 455, 494; Dorothia, 428; Georg, 331, 343, 344, 372, 401, 412, 416, 428, 455, 494, 498, 520; Joh. Georg, 283; Marg., 344; Marg. Dor., 498; Marg. Doroth., 412; Marg. Dorothea, 416, 520; Maria Magdalena, 416
GROVES, Dorothea, 350; John, 350; William, 350
GROWL, Laetitia, 408
GRUB, Cath., 454, 461; Daniel, 342, 470, 540; Elis., 470; Jacob, 454, 461; Maria Elis., 540; Mrs., 342
GRUBBEL, Joh., 303
GRUBEL (see also KRUBEL), Andr., 420; Andreas, 278, 304; Casp., 390; Christina, 302, 337, 373, 411; Joh., 302, 337, 373, 411; Joh. Georg, 302; Joh. Wilhelm, 411; John, 279; Maria, 279; Maria Dorothea, 337; Maria Elis., 304; Regina, 278, 390, 420; Sara, 390; Wilhelm, 278
GRUMBACH, Barbara, 348, 416, 547; Georg Michael, 348; Gottfried, 348, 416, 547; Joh. Gottfried, 416; Philip, 547
GRUN, Cath., 487, 505; Georg, 487; Jacob, 505; Thomas, 505
GRUNER, Christian, 282; Elis., 282; Maria Elis., 469
GRUNEWALD, Sabina, 458
GRUT, Cath., 432; Joh. Jacob, 432
GUMMI, An. Cath., 397; Cath., 374, 427; Joh., 374, 397, 427
GUMMY, Cath., 351; Joh., 327, 351
GUNSEL, Joh., 431; Leonard, 431; Marg., 431
GUNTERSBLUM, Countess, 505
GUNTNER, Cath., 341; Jacob, 341; Maria, 341
GURGE, Joh., 484; Mar. Barb., 484
GUSE, Cath., 392; John, 392
GUSSMANN, Christiana, 538; Deal, 538
GUT, Cath., 338, 517; Christina, 510, 551; Christoph, 510; Jacob, 432; Joh., 517; Joh. Christoph, 551; Joh. Michael Jacob, 432; Marg., 432; Maria Susanne, 432; Wilhelm, 551
GUTEL, Georg, 389; Mar. Sabina, 389
GUTERMAN, Agnes, 323; Georg, 323; Michael, 323

GUTERMANN, Joh., 522; Michael, 365;
  Susanna, 365
GUTHEIM, Cath., 338
GUTMAN, Michael, 328, 369; Regina
  Marg., 328, 369
GUTMANN, Georg Michael, 434, 451;
  Marg., 422, 451; Maria, 299; Michael,
  401, 422; Regina Marg., 401, 434
GUTT, Carl, 480; Christina, 480;
  Christoph, 480
GUTTE, Cath., 461; Christoph, 461;
  Wilhelmina, 461
GUTTMANN, Elis., 479; Joh., 479
GUTTON, Maria, 441
HAACK, Cath., 536; Joh., 536
HAAF, Joh., 387
HAAG, Anna, 334, 361, 392, 403, 440,
  508; Anna Barbara, 440; Christian,
  334, 361, 392, 403, 440, 508; Jacob,
  361, 508; Joh. Hnr., 334; Peter, 403;
  Philip, 392
HAAH, Cath., 502; Leonhard, 502;
  Sophia, 502
HAAKS, Cath., 402; Hnr., 402; Jacob,
  402
HAAL, Anna, 475; Cath., 508; Elis., 445,
  508; Gerry, 508; Hanna, 445, 475,
  476, 525; Mat., 508; Philipp, 508;
  Thomas, 445, 475, 476, 525
HAALMAN, Cath., 533; Hnr., 533
HAALMANN, Barbara, 515; Joh., 515,
  545; Maria, 515, 545; Sarah, 545
HAAS, Anna Cath., 359; Anna Elis., 462,
  471; Caspar, 284, 288, 313, 398;
  Casper, 359; Cath., 284, 288, 313,
  359, 398, 468; Christoph Frdr., 288;
  Conrad, 400, 425, 468; Elis., 384,
  391, 417, 450, 549, 550; Eva, 425;
  Frdr., 398; Georg Conrad, 371; Georg
  Frdr., 371; Georg Frdr. Conrad, 467;
  Joh., 346, 384, 391, 400, 417, 471,
  549, 550; Magdalena, 400;
  Magdalene, 425; Maria, 313, 550;
  Maria Elis., 346; Maria Magdalena,
  371, 468; Salome, 346
HAASER, Joh. Georg, 392; Sophia, 392
HAASLI, Elis., 495
HAASS, Anna Elis., 458; Elis., 472, 495;
  Joh., 495
HABACHER, Beorg, 528; Georg, 467,
  491, 507; Hanna, 528; Maria, 467,
  491, 507, 528; Philipp, 467
HABBICH, Elis., 484
HABECHER, Georg, 448; Marg., 448;
  Maria, 448
HABECKER, Christina, 506; Frdr., 506;
  Maria Cath., 506
HABER, Gerog, 424; Joh. Michael, 516;
  Maria, 516; Maria Marg., 424;
  Salome, 424

HABICH, Anna Christina, 547; Cath., 547;
  Christ. Hnr., 547; Christina, 293;
  Henrich, 293
HABIG, Anna Cath., 509; Anna Christina,
  350, 474; Christian Hnr., 350; Doroth.
  Magd., 474; Dorothea Magdalena, 509;
  Hnr., 474, 509; Joh. Hnr., 350
HABKISON, Maria, 354; Peter, 354;
  Rebecca, 354
HABMERICH, Maria Elis., 288
HACK, Elis., 516; Joh., 516
HACKENMILLER, Anna, 486; Jacob,
  486; Maria, 486
HACKENMULLER, Elis., 445; Jacob,
  445, 465; Maria, 465; Polly, 445;
  Wilhelm, 465
HACKINBACH, Elis., 325; Georg, 325
HACKINLOCH, Anna Maria, 305; Joh.
  Georg, 305; Juliana Elis., 305
HADEMULLER, Jacob, 551; Joh. Simon,
  551; Marie, 551
HAEFLER, Jacob, 306
HAEHN, Anton, 412; Cath., 412; Jacob,
  412
HAEHNLEY, Cath., 403; Georg, 403
HAEHNS, Anna Cath., 435; Anna Marg.,
  435; Cath., 293, 306, 359; Hnr., 293;
  Jacob, 306; John Mich., 435; Maria
  Marg., 293; Michael, 306, 359, 513;
  Susanna, 513
HAELSCH, Cath., 354; Joh., 354; Maria
  Cath., 354
HAENDEL, Joh. Adam, 452
HAENS, Albert, 524; Elis., 443, 524; Joh.,
  443, 524; Maria, 524
HAENSER, Agness, 477; Joh., 477
HAENSMANN, Anna, 466, 487; Barbara,
  331, 388; Cath., 314; Christoph, 314,
  331, 346, 388, 407; Hanna Marg., 346;
  Joh., 466, 487; Mar. Barb., 407
HAERDT, Cath., 287; Henry, 287; Marg.,
  287
HAERLE, Georg, 442
HAERLING, Anna Maria, 341; Joh.
  Georg, 341; Marg., 341
HAERLY, Barbara, 399; Georg, 399
HAERTEL, Anna Marg., 467; Hnr., 344;
  Joh. Martin, 402, 467; Marg., 344, 467;
  Maria, 402; Maria Ursula, 402
HAERTLE, Anna Marg., 487; Joh. Martin,
  487, 528; Marg., 413, 528; Martin,
  413; Susanna, 528
HAERTLEIN, Gertraut, 506, 527; Joh.,
  506, 527; Joh. Georg, 506
HAFFNER, Andreas, 502; Anna Maria,
  523; Christina, 473, 502; Francis, 478;
  Georg, 473, 502; Georg Michael, 523;
  Hnr., 523; Joh., 478; Magdalena, 473,
  502; Marg., 481; Phil., 481

HAFNER, Anna Elis., 344; Barbara, 386; Cath., 303, 365; Christin Elis., 277; Christina, 322; Daniel, 277; Elis., 365; Frdr. Wilhelm, 365; Georg, 307, 361, 386, 397, 410, 430, 445; Hnr., 344; Hnr. Wilh., 365; Jacob, 445; Joh. Georg, 322, 342, 386, 410; Joh. Hnr., 344; Joh. Jacob, 386; Magdalena, 342, 361, 410, 445; Maria, 344; Maria Magdal., 361; Maria Magdalena, 386; Maria Marg., 342; Mrs., 314; Susanna, 386
HAG, Anna, 467; Carl, 473; Christian, 467; Maria, 467, 473; Michael, 473
HAGELGANS, Joh. Carl, 319; Marg., 319, 329; Siegmund, 319, 329
HAGELGANSS, Marg. Cath., 290; Sigmund, 290
HAGENER, Cath., 510; Frdr., 510; Marg., 536; Maria, 510; Phil., 510; Valentin, 536
HAGENLOCH, Elis., 363; Georg, 363; Hnr., 363
HAGENLOCHER, Anna Cath., 308; Joh. Georg, 308
HAGER, Anna Cath., 317; Cath., 352; Christina, 457; Frdr., 457; Gottfried, 352, 391; Joh., 317; Peter, 352
HAGINLOCH, Elis., 406; Georg, 406
HAGNER, Ann Marg., 390; Anna, 362; Christina, 301; Frdr., 301; Joh., 301; Joh. Peter, 321; M. Barbara, 362; Marg., 280, 321, 351, 401; Maria Elis., 280; Valentin, 280, 321, 351, 362, 390; Valentine, 401
HAHL, Cath., 290, 294; Joh. Gottfried, 290; Maria Cath., 290, 293; Philip, 290, 294; Philipp, 293, 327; Sarah, 290; Susanna, 327
HAHN, Anna Magdalena, 384; Cath., 393, 403; Christian, 466; Hanna, 466; Joh., 384; Magdal., 384; Peter, 393, 403; Rachel, 316
HAHNS, Anna Cath., 328; Joh. Georg, 328; Joh. Michael, 328
HAILER, Christina, 397; Frdr., 397
HAINE, Anna, 377; Anna Christina, 377; Esther, 414; Jacob, 377, 414, 439; Joh. Frdr., 439; Marg., 439; Salome, 439
HAINEMANN, Cath., 410, 450; Elis., 410; Frdr., 410; Joh. Frdr., 450
HAINS, Andreas, 326; Cath., 326, 357, 363, 496; Elis., 326, 357; Frdr., 357; Hnr., 326, 363; Joh., 363; Michael, 496; Wilhelm, 357
HAINY, Anna Marg., 434; Jacob, 434; Joh., 434; Sara, 434
HAKE, Charles, 524
HALBERGER, Joh. Adam, 353

HALES, Phil., 377
HALL, Cath., 318, 551; Elis., 394; Hanna, 394; Henry, 318; Jacob, 551; Jean, 538; Joh. Gottfr., 318; John, 326; Marg., 551; Maria, 419; Maria Cath. Susanna, 323; Mary, 326; Philip, 318, 323, 360, 388, 395; Sarah, 318, 375; Sus. Cath., 395; Susanna, 360; Susanna Cath., 388; Thomas, 394
HALLODAY, James, 535; Marg., 535; Nancy, 535
HAM, Maria, 381
HAMBER, Maria Eva, 348
HAMBRECHT, Abraham, 460; Anna Barb., 460; Eleonora, 460; Elis., 460; Esther, 460
HAMILTON, Rosina, 316; William, 316
HAMLET, Barbara, 420, 481; Elis., 481; Godfrey, 420; Gottfried, 481; Mary, 420
HAMM, Maria, 403
HAMMER, Christina, 309; Joh., 309; Moses, 309
HAMMERBACH, Jacob, 526; Joh. Philipp, 526; Maria Susanna, 526
HAMMOND, Henrietta, 526
HAMPTON, Agnes, 404; Ann, 431; Isabel, 431; Thomas, 404, 431; William, 404
HANDEL, Adam, 497, 511, 521, 533; Cath., 497; Hanna, 497, 511, 521, 533; Joh. Adam, 533
HANDERING, John, 362
HANNEBERGER, Thomas, 517
HANS, Anna Barbara, 548; Anna Mar., 377; Cath., 377, 548; Eva Elis., 500; Joh., 500, 525; Joh. Georg, 500; Joh. Mich., 377, 490; Joh. Michael, 525; Magdalena, 490; Michael, 548; Susanna, 490, 525
HANSEL, Christoph, 328; Elis., 328; Susanna, 328
HANSMAN, Anna Maria, 553; Barbara, 301; Christoph, 301; Joh., 553; Joh. Christoph, 294; Maria Barbara, 294
HANSMANN, Christoph, 488
HANSS, Elis., 532; Joh., 532
HANTZEL, Carl, 480; Christian, 480; Wilhelm, 474, 491
HANTZELMAN, Anna, 283; Anna Barbara, 283; Joh., 283
HANTZMAN, Andreas, 280; Cath., 280; Joh. Michael, 280
HAPPACHER, Georg, 452; Maria, 452
HAPPASHER, Magdalena, 436
HAPPEL, Ann Marg., 373; Cath., 522; Christina, 522; Georg, 515, 522; Georg Caspar, 373; Jacob, 515, 522, 542; Joh. Joseph, 373; Marg., 515, 542
HARANGE BUSCH, Countess, 505

HARF, Anna, 293, 351, 414, 443, 500;
Anna Maria, 351; Conrad, 293, 351,
414, 443, 500; Elis., 414; Jacob, 293;
Joh. Georg, 443
HARGUS, Abraham, 408; Maria, 408;
Martin, 408
HARGYS, Abraham, 445; Cath., 445;
Marg., 445
HARKUS, Georg Leonard, 455; Maria,
455
HARLEY, George, 300; Jacob, 300;
Marg., 300
HAROLD, Hans Georg, 292; Regina,
292; Sybilla, 292
HARPER, Thomas, 405
HARRER, Anna Maria, 303; Daniel, 436;
Joh., 303, 436; Lydia, 436; Marianna,
436
HARRIS, Adam, 282; Anna Maria, 282;
Benjamin, 548; Christina, 282; Marg.,
548; William Benjamin, 548
HARRISON, Benja., 365; Cath., 317,
391; Conrad, 365; Georg, 317; Joh.,
391; John, 428; Marg., 365, 391;
Mary, 428; William, 428
HART, Elis., 422
HARTER, Dorothea, 312; Mat., 312
HARTERICH (see also HEIDRICH),
Andreas, 287; Elis., 287
HARTMAN, An. Barbara, 391; Cath.,
284; Dorothea, 367; Joh., 391, 474;
Joh. Carl, 474; Joh. Peter, 284; Maria,
391, 474; Peter, 367; Phil., 366
HARTMANN, Cath., 429, 472, 525;
Fronica, 345; Georg, 525; Jacob, 495;
Joh., 408; Joh. Georg, 456; Joh. Peter,
472; Mich., 497; Peter, 429; Sabina
Marg., 456; Sarah, 497
HARTON, Charles, 327
HARTRANFFT, Anna Maria, 474;
Barbara, 474; Cath., 491; Christoph,
474, 481; Joh., 491; Johanna, 491;
Susanna, 474
HARTRANFT, Cath., 520; Christoph,
505, 506, 528; Elis., 505, 506, 528;
Joh., 520; Michael, 505; Wilhelm,
520
HARVAY, Anna Marg., 385; Jacob, 385;
Joh., 385
HAS, Cath, 375
HASE, Anna Maria, 299; William, 299
HASELTON, Joseah, 460; Sibylla, 460
HASK, Andr., 496; Maria, 496;
Philippina, 496
HASO, Maria, 416
HASSENCLENER, Widow, 468
HATERMANN, Susanna Marg., 305;
William, 305

HAUBER, Adam, 536; Anna Maria, 536;
Georg, 284, 320; Hanna, 536; Jacob,
320; Salome, 284, 320
HAUBINSAC, Barb., 384; Joh., 384
HAUCK, Anna Cath., 340; Cath., 298,
359, 447, 450, 463; Joh., 298, 340,
359, 447, 450; John, 463
HAUK, Cath., 381, 383; Joh., 381, 383;
Maria, 432
HAULER, Anna Maria, 416; Cath.
Barbara, 416; Nicolaus, 416
HAUPT, Cath., 290
HAUS, Barb., 369; Marg., 330
HAUSEL, Anna Elis., 351; Cath., 351;
Georg, 351
HAUSER, Cath., 283, 363; Elis., 363, 394,
502; Georg, 294, 502; Jacob, 363, 398;
Joh., 398; Joh. Georg, 283, 364; Joh.
Jac., 394; John Jacob, 283; Magdalena,
398; Maria, 363; Maria Anna, 394;
Sophia, 283, 294, 364
HAUSMANN, Elis., 318; Georg Jacob,
311, 362; Mar. Apollonia, 362; Maria,
311; Maria Magdal., 311
HAUSS, Georg, 330; Peter, 284, 317;
Wilhelm, 528
HAUSSER, Elis., 333; Joh. Georg, 439;
John Jacob, 333; Maria Magdalena,
333
HAUSSMAN, Georg, 503
HAUSSMANN, Apellonia, 520; Cath.,
463; Charity, 463, 497; Daniel, 497;
Georg, 520; Georg Jacob, 463, 497;
Joh. David, 515; Joh. Engelh., 463,
497; Mar. Appoll., 497; Maria, 537;
Maria Appelonia, 463
HAWKIN, Susanna, 368; Theophilus, 368
HAWKINS, Cath., 314; Joh., 314; Philipp,
314
HAWRICH, Christina, 385; Elis., 385;
Hnr., 385
HAY, Adam, 421; Andreas, 529, 537;
Anna Maria, 537; Carl, 452, 488, 537;
Cath., 488; Elis., 403, 498; Elis. Cath.,
452; Eva Maria, 511; Joh., 446, 498;
Joh. Georg, 537; Joh. Ludew., 451;
Maria, 421, 446, 451, 511, 529, 539;
Michael, 421, 446, 511, 539; Peter,
399, 446, 520, 539; Philip, 342; Rahel,
529; Sophia, 452, 488, 537; Wilhelm,
451
HAYER, Andreas, 280; Maria Clara, 280;
Mat., 280
HAYS, Christine, 420; Maria, 420;
Wilhelm, 420
HAZELTON, Dorothea, 512; Georg, 512;
John, 511; Marg., 512; Maria Marg.,
511; Rahel, 511

HEART, Anna Magdalena, 511; Barbara, 442; Cath., 442; Georg, 442; Nicol., 511
HEARTLINE, Georg, 490; Gertraut, 490; John, 490
HEBERLE, Anna, 278; Simon, 278
HEBERSTREIT, Anna Barbara, 461; Barbara, 445; Jonas, 445, 461
HECHT, Anna Marg., 294, 309; Anthon, 294, 342, 467, 542; Anthony, 309, 506; Anton, 361, 392, 412, 442; Elis., 467; Frdr., 342, 442; Joh. Frdr., 506; Marg., 361; Maria Magdalene, 412; Michael, 392; Sophia, 294, 309, 342, 361, 392, 412, 442, 467, 506, 542
HECK, Anna Cath., 434; Georg Michael, 434
HECKER, Cath., 551; Elis., 551; Joh., 551
HECKERT, Anna Cath., 335; Anna Maria, 313; Joh., 313, 335
HEDERIC, James, 295; Rebecca, 295; William, 295
HEDERICH, Adolf Christian, 416; Adolf Christian, Wilhelm, 486; Anna, 459, 486, 520; Anna Victoria, 486; Maria Aletta, 416; Nancy, 416; Wilhelm, 459, 520; Wilhelmina Elis., 520
HEDERICK, Adolf, 441; Anna, 441
HEFER, Andreas, 281; Eva Elis., 281
HEFFT, Anna Maria, 458, 524; Cath., 524; Christoph, 458, 522; Joh., 524; Joh. Frdr., 522; Joh. Georg, 458; Joh. Wilhelm, 504; Mar. Cath., 504; Maria, 522; Maria Cath., 497; Wilh., 497
HEFTRIG, Elis., 379
HEG, Anrdr., 431; Hnr., 431; Maria, 431
HEGE, Cath., 403
HEGER, An. Cath., 391; Anna Cath., 414; Cath., 362, 423, 441; Elis., 552; Georg Jacob, 414; Joh., 403, 414; Joh. Christian, 362; Phil., 441; Philip, 362; Philipp, 391, 414, 423; Sara, 552; Valentin, 552
HEHN, Maria, 457; Wilhelm, 457
HEHNER, Anna Cath., 478; Joh., 478
HEHR, Bastian, 358
HEIBEL, Anna Maria, 353; Joh. Christoph, 353
HEID, Andreas, 540; Anna, 317; Barbara, 366; Elis., 540; Joh. Georg, 366; Maria, 540; Mary, 317; Thomas, 317; Valentin, 366
HEIDE, Agnes, 456; Joh., 501; Joh. Philip, 456; Magdalena, 456; Martha, 501; Philipp, 456
HEIDEL, Elis., 480; Georg, 441, 466; George, 290, 312; Joh., 441; Joh. Christoph, 480; Joh. Hnr., 299;

Johanna Elis., 480; Maria Marg., 312; Maria Salome, 290, 312; Salome, 441, 466; Samuel, 466; Simon, 307
HEIDELMANN, Anna Marg., 450; Phil., 450
HEIDENICK, Andreus Nicolaus, 305; Elis. Marg., 305
HEIDERICH, Andreas, 367, 440, 447; Elis., 367, 440, 447; Joh. Peter, 367
HEIDRICH, Andreas, 435; Elis., 435
HEIDTEL, Anna Maria, 337; Christoph, 337
HEIL, Adam, 320; Ann Cath., 380; Anna Maria, 380, 381, 418; Cath., 336, 339; Dorothea, 307, 353, 390; Elis., 339, 423, 425, 476; Frdr., 418; Georg, 307, 336, 353, 373, 390, 464, 467; Georg Mich., 373; Georg Michael, 306, 336, 401, 423, 464, 505; Hnr., 522; Jacob, 400; Jacobina, 285, 306, 321, 364, 425; Joh., 306, 320, 347, 364, 371, 390, 400, 467, 488, 500, 505; Joh. Leon., 380, 381; John, 371; Leonard, 418; Mar. Cath., 401; Maria, 320, 347, 364, 371, 390, 400, 415, 467, 488, 500; Maria Cath., 306, 336, 373, 423, 464, 505; Michael, 336; Philip, 285; Philipp, 306, 321, 364, 425, 488; Philippina, 488; Sebastian, 339; Susanna, 306, 381, 467; Thomas, 321, 347; Wilhelm Georg, 353
HEILEMAN, Eva, 433; Martin, 433
HEILEMANN, Eva Christina, 386; Maria, 386; Martin, 386
HEILER, Ann, 318; Cath., 368; Christina, 291, 308, 340, 365, 467, 524; Daniel, 431; Elis., 316, 365, 387, 431, 476, 512; Frdr., 291, 308, 312, 340, 365, 430, 467, 524, 535; Georg, 316, 318; Joh., 358, 387, 464, 525; Joh. Jacob, 365; Marg., 318; Sebastian, 316, 365, 368, 387, 431, 476, 512; Susanna, 464, 525
HEILINS, Elis., 303
HEILMAN, Christian, 386
HEILMANN, Adam, 355; Ann. Mar., 423; Elis., 355; Eva, 306; Hnr., 355; Martin, 306; Michael, 306, 355; Susanna, 355
HEILY, Caspar, 327; Elis., 327
HEIM, Andreas, 437, 467, 508; Balthasar, 514; Cath., 379, 479; Cath. Elis., 437; Eva, 514; Isaac, 514; Joh. Christoph, 467; Sabina, 437; Sarah, 467, 508; Sophia, 508
HEIMANN, Cath., 514, 542
HEIMAR, Cath., 335; Frdr., 335; Jacob, 335, 417; Martha, 335; Mercy, 417
HEIMBACH, Adam, 360, 474, 479, 514; Anna Magadalena, 514; Anna Maria, 372; Cath., 403, 479; Christina, 511;

HENDEL, Adam, 380
HENDERSON, Cath., 530; William, 530
HENERTON, Daniel, 388; Hanna, 388;
John, 388
HENG, Andreas, 414; Anna Maria, 414
HENKE, Henrich, 279; Maria Elis., 279
HENKEL, Adam, 463; Christoph, 361;
Eva, 361; Hanna, 463; Joh., 516; Joh.
Daniel, 463; Maria Magdalena, 516;
Simon, 516
HENRICH, Agnes, 534; Anna, 400; Anna
Maria, 330, 344, 360; Cath., 350, 360,
385; Christoph, 344, 360; Elis., 534;
Georg, 385, 400; Gottfried, 350, 385;
Jacob, 360, 534; Joh., 306, 344, 350;
Maria, 306; Maria Magd., 306; Maria
Marg., 360; Sophia, 400
HENRICHEL, Baltus, 332; Cath., 332,
334; Jacob, 332, 334; Wilhelmine,
332
HENRIEGEL, Cath., 381, 409, 511, 534;
Jacob, 381, 409, 511, 534
HENRIGEL, Cath., 497; Eleonora, 521;
Jacob, 497, 521
HENRY, Georg, 340; Hanna, 340; Joh.,
340
HENSCHEL, Anna Doroth., 395; Carl
Frdr., 395; Dorothea Elis., 395
HENSEL, Anna Marg., 457, 494; Carl,
307; Carl Frdr., 457, 494; Dorothea,
307; Joh. Joseph, 457; Peter David,
307
HENSLER, Conrad, 331, 428; Eleonora
Cath., 428; Maria Marg., 428
HENSLY, William, 362
HENTERICH, Anna Maria, 518; Martin,
518
HENTZMAN, Joh. Jacob, 280
HENZEL, Anna Dorothea, 280; Anna
Marg., 371; Cath., 552; Christian
Frdr., 371; Christina, 371; Elis., 280;
Frdr., 371; Joh. Georg, 552; Maria
Dorothea, 371; Peter David, 280;
Samuel, 552
HENZELMAN, A. Maria, 533; Anna
Mar., 444; Joh., 444, 533
HENZLER, Christina Cath., 367; Conrad,
367; Eleonora, 367
HENZMANN, Christoph, 435; Maria
Barbara, 435
HEPP, Cath., 407, 429, 485; Elis., 407;
Joh., 407, 429, 485; Susanna, 429
HEPPELE, Georg, 428, 500; Juliana, 428
HERA, Charlotte Louise, 304; Christian,
304; Elis., 398; Sophia, 304; Thomas,
304
HERBERGER, Anna Cath., 430; Anna
Maria, 462; Elis., 494; Hnr., 430, 462,
494, 530; Susanna, 430, 462, 494,
530, 548; Susanna Maria, 530

HERBERT, Lorenz, 523; Marg., 523
HERBST, Carl, 480; Elis., 403, 421, 451,
454, 480, 509, 514, 540; Georg Hnr.,
421; Hnr., 398, 421, 451, 454, 480,
509, 514, 540; Joh. Hnr., 403; Maria,
514; Susanna, 398
HERBY, Joh., 547; Marg., 547
HERGESHEIM, Rosina, 377
HERGESHEIMER, Barbara, 322; Georg,
322; Rosina, 322
HERLEMANN, Joeph, 504
HERLEY, Cath., 532; Christoph, 532;
Georg, 479; Marg., 532; Maria, 479
HERMAN, Anna Marg., 279, 295, 325;
Anna Maria, 279, 295, 323, 328, 361;
Anna Regina, 328; Cath., 325, 334,
354, 369, 404, 433; Jacob, 295, 334,
369, 404, 433; Joh., 334, 354; Joh.
Georg, 328; Joh. Jacob, 405; Leonhard,
323; Marg., 414; Maria, 405; Mich.,
405; Michael, 295, 323, 361, 404;
Philip, 433; Sarah, 369; Wilhelm, 279,
325; Wm., 414
HERMANN, Anna Marg., 507; Anna
Maria, 311, 534; Christian, 334;
Christina, 398; Christina Marg., 345;
Christine, 405; Elis., 507; Georg, 507;
Jacob, 522; Marg., 386, 448; Maria
Barbara, 522; Maria Elis., 376;
Michael, 311, 345, 386; Susanna
Marg., 376; Wilhelm, 376, 448
HERMSTAD, Cath., 376; Nicol., 376
HERMSTADT, Maria, 390; Maria Barb.,
390; Martin, 390; Nancy, 390
HERMSTADTER, Anna, 331; Lorenz,
331; Martin, 331
HERN, Elisabet, 303
HERO, Charlotte Louise, 395; Christian,
395
HEROLD, Joh. Georg, 400; Regina, 400
HERRLEY, Franzis, 516; Georg, 516;
Maria, 516
HERRMAN, Anna Maria, 358; Marg.,
507; Michael, 358
HERRMANN, Anna, 537; Anna Regina,
292; Elis., 292, 537; Georg, 537; Hnr.,
529; Joh. Georg, 292; Marg., 284;
Maria, 529; Wilhelm, 284
HERSEL, Anna Maria, 534; Barbara, 534;
Hnr., 534
HERT, Barbara, 472; Georg, 358, 472;
Joh., 427; Magdalena, 472; Marg., 427
HERTEL, Joh. Jacob, 384; Marg., 384;
Martin, 384
HERTLE, Anna Marg., 377; Joh. Martin,
377
HERTZBACH, Cath., 316; Regina, 337
HERTZOG, Andreas, 286; Eva, 298;
Maria Dorothea, 298; Wilhelm, 298

HERVEY, Elis., 407; Joh., 407; Marg., 407
HERVY, Joh. Hnr., 320; Maria Marg., 320; Thomas, 320
HERWEY, Joh., 478; Marg., 478
HERZBACH, Eva Maria, 368, 430; Joh. Nicol., 368; Nicol., 430; Regina, 368, 430
HERZEBACH, Joh. Jacob, 312; Nicolaus, 306, 312; Regina, 306, 312
HERZENBERGER, Carl, 376
HESCH, Elis., 423; Jacob, 411; Joh., 423; Marg., 423; Rosina, 411
HESLER, Hanna, 389; Jacob, 389; Joh. Georg, 389
HESS, Adam, 435; Anna Cath., 280; Anna Gertraut, 417; Anna Marg., 524; Anna Maria, 379; Cath., 285, 334; Charlotta, 291, 446; Charlotte, 336, 379, 415; Charlotte Christina, 421; Charlotte Susanna, 415; Conrad, 291, 379, 415, 421, 446; Daniel, 285, 333, 417; Elis., 368, 419, 435, 470, 496; Georg, 503; Gertraudt, 333; Joanna Charlotta, 446; Joh., 336, 496; Joh. Conrad, 336; Joh. Georg, 498, 524; Joh. Hnr., 524; Ludewig, 334; Ludwig, 280; Marg., 498, 503; Nicolaus, 440; Samuel, 291; Susan Elis., 498; Wilhelmina, 440
HESSE, Hnr., 319; Joh., 319; Sarah, 319
HESTER, Anna Maria, 462; Conrad, 462, 491, 502, 547; Eleonora Cath., 462, 502; Eleonore Cath., 547; Joh. Conrad, 502; Leona Cath., 491; Philip Conrad, 547
HESTON, Elis., 496; Peter, 496; Polly, 496
HETMANSBERGER, Elis., 531; Franz Wilhelm, 531; Maria Magdalena, 531
HETMANSPERGER, Andreas Philipp, 403; Francisc. Wilh., 368; Franz Wilh., 349; Franz Wilhelm, 403, 487; Joh. Georg, 487; Mar. Magdalena, 368; Maria, 487; Maria Magdalena, 403
HETMONSBERGER, Franz Wil., 435; Joh., 435; Maria Magdalena, 435
HETZEL, Cath., 481; Joh., 481; Samuel, 481
HEUMAN, Cath., 335; Dan., 335
HEUMANN, Cath., 357; Daniel, 357; Joh. Adam, 357
HEUSEL, Christina, 290; Joh. Georg, 290
HEUSER, Ernst, 340; Magdalena, 340
HEVERT, Joh., 285
HEY, Anna, 466; Carl, 466; Mar., 436; Peter, 436; Sophia, 466
HEYDEL, Georg, 349; Salome, 349

HICKCOX, Martha, 409; Mary, 409; William, 409
HICKS, Cath., 403; Joh., 403
HIEP, Cath., 457; Esther, 457; Joh., 457
HIGGINS, Frdr., 548; Marg., 548; Wilhelm, 548
HILARIUS, Joh., 402
HILARY, Abigail, 408
HILL, Anna, 318; Anna Maria, 506; Hnr., 340; Jacob, 506; John, 318, 400; Joseph, 340; Laetitia Mary, 408; Sara, 340; Sarah, 408; William, 400, 408
HILLER, Cath., 322; Elis., 322; Joseph, 322
HINCH, Marg., 516
HINCKEL, Anna Marg., 363; Anna Susanna, 363; Bernhard, 451; Christina, 339, 441, 525; Jacob, 322; Joh., 339, 441, 451, 471, 525; Joh. Georg, 471; Joh. Nicol., 363; Joh. Nicolaus, 322; Magdalena Maria, 451; Maria, 471; Susanna, 322
HINCKLE, Christina, 357; Hannah, 357; Joh., 357
HINKEL, Anna, 417; Barbara, 499; Christine, 389; Christoph, 349; Conrad, 499; Joh., 389, 417; Maria Eva, 349; Nicolaus, 388, 417; Sara Elis., 389; Susan., 388
HINKELMAN, Christina, 301; Joh., 301
HIPS, Brighty Way, 548; Mar. Clara, 548; Maria Magdalene, 548
HIRKISHEIMER, Elis., 359; Georg, 359; Rosina, 359
HIRNEISEN, Anna Maria, 452; Jacob, 452, 515; Joh. Georg, 452; Marg., 452; Maria, 515; Michael, 301, 312; Rosina, 301, 312; Sophia, 389
HIRNEISSEN, Anna Maria, 499; Jacob, 499
HIRSCH, Anna, 483; Barbara, 282; Georg, 483; Joh. Samuel, 282; John, 370; Michael, 282; Philip, 370, 550; Philipp, 483; Susanna, 483, 550
HIRSCHHORN, Ruth, 435
HIRSCHLER, Joh. Michael, 297
HIRST, Liddy, 524
HIRT, Anna Magdalena, 449; Christoph, 350, 383; Georg, 310, 374; Hnr., 436; Joh., 493; Joh. Hnr., 436; Joh. Nicolaus, 455; John, 493; Magdalena, 436; Mar. Marg., 493; Marg., 310; Maria, 455, 493; Maria Marg., 436, 455; Nicol., 436, 493; Peter, 350, 383; Polly, 495; Susanna, 350, 383
HOBBART, Christian, 466; Marg., 466
HOCH, Barbara, 317, 362; Dorothea, 510; Eva, 543; Eva Elis., 543; Georg, 510; Isaac, 543; Joh., 317, 362; Joh. Adam,

362; Leonard, 317; Leonhard, 510; Marg., 317, 362, 510
HOCHER, Joh. Michael, 391
HOCK, Cath., 328; Dorothea, 313; ELis., 452; Georg, 313; Georg Michael, 328; Regina Marg., 328; Susanna, 452; William, 452
HOCKEL, Joh. Wilhelm, 423; Joh. William, 423; Joseph, 540; Maria Susanna, 540; Susanna, 423; Wilhelm, 540
HOEFFLEIN, Cath., 524; Joh., 524
HOEK, Cath., 345; Wilhelm, 345
HOELSIKAMB, Cath. Elis., 303; Gerett, 303; Maria, 303
HOELTZEL, Cath., 526; Joh., 526; Sarah Elis., 526
HOERNER, Anna, 288; Elis., 288; Jacob, 469, 484; Joh., 484; Maria, 469, 484
HOETZEL, Cath., 416, 452; Joh., 416; Joh. Philipp, 416; Susanna Maria, 452
HOF, An. Marg., 382; Cath., 382; Conrad, 280, 299, 300, 352, 440; Dorothea, 429; Georg, 311, 382; Joh., 311; Joh. Conrad, 300; Joh. Georg, 429; Maria Elis., 280; Maria Marg., 311; Sibilla, 300, 352; Sibylla, 440; Sybilla, 280
HOFACKER, Hnr., 283; Marg., 283
HOFECKER, Cath., 341; Hnr., 341; Marg., 341
HOFF, Conrad, 366, 489; Dorothea, 459; Elis., 540; Georg, 459; Jacob, 540; Joh. Georg, 459, 491; Joh. Phil., 491; Maria Marg., 459, 491; Maria Sybila, 366; Michael, 540; Sibylla, 489
HOFFMAN, Adam, 354; Barbara, 354; Maria, 354
HOFFMANN, Adam, 479, 502; Anna Barbara, 488; Barbara, 502; Cath., 479, 483; Cath. Marg., 545; Daniel, 435; Elis., 508, 526; Hnr., 526, 545; Joh., 488, 528; Joh. Georg, 491; Marg., 435, 526, 545; Maria Philippina, 528; Philippina, 488; Susanna, 479, 483, 502; Valentin, 483; Wolffgang, 528
HOFLEIN, Anna Cath., 281, 316; Anna Elis., 316; Cath., 281, 364, 397; Joh., 316, 364, 397; Maria, 364; Philip, 397
HOFLINGER, Andreas, 277; Joh. Jacob, 277; Marg., 277; Susanna Marg., 277
HOFMAN, Adam, 304; Anna Marg., 317; Anna Maria, 284, 533; Barbara, 304; Carl Bernhard, 360; Christina Barbara, 284; Daniel, 284, 298, 317, 396; Georg, 374; Jacob, 298; Jeremias, 284; Magd., 374; Magdalene, 420; Mar. Marg., 390;

Marg., 284, 298, 396; Philip, 284, 374; Rosina, 304; Samuel, 396; Sus. Regina, 360; Susan., 390; Susanna, 533; Susanne, 420; Valent., 390; Valentin, 336, 420, 533
HOFMANN, Albertina Philippa, 388; Anna Marg., 291; Barbara, 345; Carl, 415; Charles, 315; Daniel, 291, 320, 350; Elis., 366; Georg, 401; Georg Jacob, 320; Joh., 339, 345; Magdalena, 401; Marg., 286, 320, 350; Maria, 371, 379; Paul, 286, 339, 388; Regina, 286, 339, 388; Susanna, 350, 365, 371, 425, 442, 444, 514; Susanna Regina, 315, 415; Valentin, 345, 365, 371, 425, 442, 444, 514; Wm., 349
HOFSAS, Georg, 328
HOGAL, Marg. Barbara, 299; Nicolaus, 299; Sara, 299
HOGEL, Nicolaus, 299; Sarah, 299; Ursula, 299
HOH, Adam, 438; Anna Barbara, 531; Joh., 531; Leonhard, 323; Mar. Christina, 438
HOHL, Anna Maria, 474; Joh., 298; Maria, 298; Maria Magdal., 540; Maria Magdalena, 326; Mat., 326, 540
HOHLWAGER, Anna Elis., 386
HOHMULLER, Cath., 546; Cath. Elis., 299; Christopher, 299; Hnr., 546; Joh. Philipp, 546
HOLD, Adam, 277, 342, 469, 501; Anna Maria, 301; Elis., 400; Jacob, 400; Joh., 385; Joh. Adam, 301; Mar., 385; Maria Cath., 277; Maria Christina, 342, 469, 501
HOLDAUFDERHEYDE, Anna Elis., 543; Joh., 543
HOLDEN, Agnes, 548; Joh., 548; Rahel, 548
HOLDER, Elis., 342; Martin, 342; Widow, 407
HOLL, Cath., 518; Elis., 424; Jacob, 424, 456, 518; Joh., 286; Maria, 286
HOLLER, Anna Philippina, 277; Cath., 277; Mathias, 277
HOLLOWEL, Mary, 328
HOLLWEG, Elis., 500
HOLT, Adam, 368, 394; Cath., 482; Jacob, 482; Mar. Christina, 368, 394; Maria, 482
HOLTZ, Joh. Hnr., 406; Susanne, 406
HOLTZCAMP, Cath. Elis., 354; Elis., 397; Gerard, 354; Gerhard, 397; Joh., 397; Marg., 397; Salome, 354
HOLTZEL, Anna Susanna, 298; Cath., 298; Joh., 298
HOLTZKAMM, Elis., 493, 519; Gerhard, 493, 519
HOLTZKAMP, Elis., 295; Gerhard, 295

HOLZCOMB, Elis., 361; Garett, 361
HOLZHAUSEN, Caroline,
Henr.Mar.Sophia, 505
HOLZKAM, Cath. Elis., 496; Gehrhard,
496
HOLZKAMM, Cath Elis., 495; Georg,
495
HOLZKAMP, Cath., 402; Elis., 454, 465;
Georg, 454; Geret, 465; Gerh., 454
HOMBERGER, Joh. Hnr., 518
HOMULLER, An. Maria, 383; Cath.,
475, 490, 507; Cath. Elis., 490;
Christoph, 383; Dorothea, 475; Hnr.,
475, 490, 507; Joh. Jacob, 345;
Magdal., 383; Michael, 507
HONCK, Anna, 328
HONIG, Barbara, 347, 382; Georg, 347,
382
HONOLD, Andreas, 322; Joh., 322; Joh.
Georg, 361; Regina, 322, 361
HOOD, Barbara, 375
HOOK, Anna, 426; Cath., 503; Daniel,
469; Elis., 278, 503; Esther, 387, 425;
Joh., 425, 426, 503; John, 278, 387,
469; Marg., 278, 387, 425, 426, 469;
Mary, 387; William, 469
HOPKINS, Mary, 391; Peter, 391; Peter
Ervin, 391
HOPMULLER, Cath., 508; Hnr., 508
HORF, Anna, 387; Cath., 387; Conr., 387
HORING, Frederica Sophia, 356
HORNBERGER, Christina Regina, 325;
Hnr., 325, 544; Joh. Ludwig, 544;
Magdalena, 325, 544
HORNE, Joh. Georg, 318; Louis, 446
HORNER, Elis., 313, 352; Jacob, 352;
Marg., 313; Melchior, 313, 352
HORNKOCHER, Ammy, 541; Elis., 541;
Jeremias, 541
HORR, Jacob, 331; Maria Magdalena,
331; Rosina Barbara, 331
HORRE, Maria, 506
HORREE, Mar. Elis., 551; Maria
Dorothea, 551; Philip, 551
HORRICH, Barbara, 469; Michael, 469
HORRY, Michael, 469; Sibylla, 469
HORST, Cath., 534; Elias, 534; Eva
Cath., 534; Joh. Nicolaus Weber, 302;
Maria, 302
HOSS, Joh. Georg, 350; Joh. Joseph, 350;
Marg., 350
HOTT, Elis., 423
HOTZ, Cath., 277, 281, 312, 352, 385,
415; Elis., 362; Joh., 281; Joh. Peter,
312; Michael, 277, 281, 312, 352,
385, 415
HOUCK, Cath., 329; Joh., 329
HOVOCKS, Christina, 385; Elis., 385;
Hnr., 385

HOW, Eva Barbara, 356; John, 356;
Salome, 356
HOWARD, Elis., 325; John, 325; Marg.,
325
HOWEL, Gen., 421
HOWWER, Elis., 325; John, 325; Marg.,
325
HOY, Amalia, 383; Peter, 383
HUBER, Agnes, 422; Andr., 470; Ann.
Louisa, 485; Anna, 381, 383, 385, 533;
Anna Cath., 295; Anna Lowisa, 504;
Anna Maria, 545; Barbara, 373, 492;
Cath., 335, 383, 410, 451, 479;
Christian, 460, 487, 488, 534, 535;
Christina Marg., 424; Daniel, 406, 459,
492, 545; David, 351, 381, 533;
Dorothea, 534; Elis., 460; Eva, 406;
Georg, 358, 406, 455, 469, 485; Georg
Leonard, 431; Georg Leonhard, 504;
Hanna, 351; Hnr., 412, 422, 492;
Jacob, 335, 451; Joh., 295, 302, 335,
383, 410, 433, 451, 459, 479, 482, 488,
531; Joh. David, 385; Joh. Georg, 479;
Joh. Ludwig, 385; Louisa, 431, 455,
469; Mar., 487; Marg., 277, 385, 422,
460, 488, 534, 535; Maria, 459, 482,
492, 531; Maria Salome, 358; Michael,
482, 531; Peter, 302; Sarah, 545;
Sophia, 358; Wilhelm, 410
HUBERT, Anna Louisa, 464; Georg, 464
HUCK, Elis., 552; Joh., 552
HUGHS, Christina, 506; Eleonora, 506;
Elis., 548; Hugh, 506; John, 548; Sara,
548; Wilhelm, 506
HULER, Barbara, 441; Joseph, 441; Maria
Barbara, 441
HULMUTH, Pastor, 535
HUMMEL, Anna Barbara, 406; Elis., 319,
357, 406; Georg, 319, 357, 406; Jacob,
357
HUMMELL, Christian, 531; Elis.
Friderica, 531; Phebe, 531
HUMPHREYS, Ann, 393; Anna Maria,
474; James, 474; John, 408, 419; Jost,
419; Marg., 419; Maria, 394, 474;
Mary, 393; Nancy, 394; Robert, 393;
Samuel, 394
HUMPHRYS, James, 508; Maria, 508;
Sarah, 508
HUNT, Elis., 361
HUNTER, Anna Maria, 423; Joh., 423;
Joh. Georg, 423
HURLEY, Ann, 402; Cath., 402; John, 402
HUSER, Anna Cath., 304; Cuniganda,
304; John Jacob, 304
HUSHER, Eva Elis., 386; Joh. David, 386;
William Thomas, 386
HUTHMAN, Anna Cath., 297; Christian
Frdr., 297

KAMPF, Anna Sabina, 344; Jacob, 344; Wilhelm, 344
KAMPFER, Elis., 499; Joh., 499; Mich., 378; Susanna, 378
KAN, Elis. Cath., 353; Jacob, 353; Thomas, 353
KANDLER, Barbara, 283; Bernd, 283; Elis., 283
KANTY, Joh., 503; Joh. Peter, 503; Maria, 503
KANZER, Elis., 399; Eva Cath., 471; Georg, 399, 471; Salome, 471; Sarah, 399
KAPP, Elis., 431
KAPPEL, Cath., 469, 475, 488, 492, 505, 510, 511, 541; Daniel, 475, 505, 541; Elis., 469, 492, 505; Joh., 459, 469, 475, 488, 492, 510, 511
KAPREL, Cath., 550; Jacob, 550; Joh., 550
KARCH, Barbara, 350; Elis., 302, 350; Jacob, 350; Maria Marg., 302; Peter, 302, 350
KARE, Hnr., 289; Jane, 289; William, 289
KARFT, Elis., 360; Mary, 360; William, 360
KARG, Anna Barbara, 506; Joh. Jacob, 506; Ottilia, 506
KARLING, Jacob, 322; Joh. Hnr., 322; Marg. Magdalena, 322
KARST, Philippine, 282
KASE, Elis., 498; Joh. Georg, 498
KASLER, Josua, 302; Magdalena, 302; Susanna Elis., 302
KASSEN, Eleonore, 353; Joh., 353; Samuel, 353
KATH, Georg, 357; Jacob, 357; Maria, 357
KATZ, Agnes Henrica, 277; Anna Maria, 307; Elis., 443, 467, 472, 493, 510; Joh., 510; Joh. Jacob, 443; John Hnr., 307; Marg., 472; Michael, 357, 360, 432, 443, 449, 467, 472, 493, 510; Rosina, 307; Wilhelm, 493
KAUFFER, Barbara, 473; Michael, 473
KAUFMAN, A. Marg., 550; An. Marg., 345; An. Maria, 415; Anna Marg., 384; Bernard, 372; Bernh., 345; Bernhard, 384, 550; Jacob, 376, 415, 455, 549, 553; Joh., 345, 384, 396, 455; Joseph, 550; Marg., 372, 455, 549, 553; Maria, 396, 549; Maria Barb., 376; Regina, 345; Veronica, 376
KAUFMANN, Anna Marg., 289; Bernhard, 301, 364; Bernhardt, 289; Cath., 301; Jacob, 289, 399, 427, 500; Joh., 350; Marg., 301, 427, 500; Maria Barbara, 399; Regina, 399, 500

KAY, August, 538; Cath., 538; Dorothea, 538
KAYSE, Daniel, 479; Joh. Eberhard, 479; Regina, 479
KAYSER, Anna Maria, 367; Daniel, 509; Elis., 505; Georg, 537; Hnr., 418; Joh., 505; Joh. Hnr., 367; Joseph, 537; Maria, 537; Rahel, 509
KEATES, Elis., 382
KEHL, Anna, 403; Anna Cath., 420; Anna Marg., 359, 376; Anna Maria, 398; Anna Maria Elis., 520; Barbara, 391; Cath., 460; Cath. Magd., 354; Christina, 485, 537; Elis., 376, 417, 460, 525, 537; Elis. Marg., 417; Frdr., 371; Georg, 398, 403, 420; Hanna, 520; Jacob, 485, 520, 537; Jeany, 525; Jeremia, 417; Jeremias, 455, 525; Joh., 340, 359, 391; Joh. Georg, 455; Ludwig, 376, 417, 460; Marg., 340, 391; Maria, 340; Maria Magdalena, 371; Sybilla, 460; Veronica, 398, 403, 420, 455
KEHLER, Frdr., 371
KEHLHAUER, Georg, 452; Salome, 452
KEHLHEFER, Frdr., 522; Marg., 522; Philippina, 522
KEHN, Cath., 361; Eva, 372; Georg, 372; Joh. Frdr., 361; Maria Eva, 361; Wilhelm, 372
KEHR, Anna, 496; Elis., 510; Hnr., 510; Jacob, 510; Joh., 277; Pamelia, 277; Sophia, 277
KEHRLMANN, Elis., 413; Georg, 413; Joh. Michael, 413
KEIDEL, Cath. Elis., 527; Elis., 527; Georg, 527
KEIL, Elis., 535
KEILER, Barbara, 413; Georg, 413
KEIMEL, Elis., 432; Jacob, 432
KEIMLE (see also KIEMLE), Anna, 500; Barbara, 370; Cath., 316, 383, 499; Cath. Christiana, 487; Christina Cath., 286, 373, 395, 485, 515, 521; Georg, 404; Jacob, 286, 347, 373, 383, 395, 485, 487, 499, 500, 515, 521; Joh., 537; Joh. Frdr., 395; Joh. Georg, 347; Joh. Jacob, 286; John, 485; Marg., 347; Marg. Reg., 485; Maria Dorothea, 373; Samuel, 537; Susanne Marg., 404; Sybilla, 537; Ursula, 404; Ursula Barbara, 395
KEIMLI, Mrs., 551
KEIMLY, Cath., 534; Jacob, 534
KEIMSLI, Maria Barbara, 321
KEINLE, Cath. Dorothea, 378; Jacob, 378
KEIS, Benjamin, 547; Maria, 547
KEITEBACH, Sabina, 385
KEITHE, Caspar, 357; Charlotte, 357

KELLER, Adam, 528; Cath., 306;
Christian, 318; Christoph, 321; Elis.,
306; Elis. Barbara, 284, 324; Georg,
284, 306; Joh. Adam, 537; Maria,
321, 528, 537; Maria Marg., 318;
Maria Susanna, 318; Sarah, 528
KELLOR, Elis., 414; Joh. Jacob, 414
KELLY, Cath., 422; Elis., 363, 405, 432,
450, 490; Georg, 422; Isaac, 363, 405,
432, 450, 490; John, 363; Marg., 450;
Maria Cath., 478; Phebe, 490;
William, 432
KELMANN, Anna Maria, 474
KEMEIER, Jacob, 485; Maria, 485
KEMMEL, Elis., 426, 468; Joseph, 426,
468
KEMMINGER, Adam, 396, 404, 417;
Susanne, 404, 417
KEMP, Anna Sabina, 307; Joh. Nicolaus,
307; William, 307
KEMPER, Cath., 500; Jacob, 500; Maria
Elis., 500
KEMPF, Anna Sabina, 434; Christian,
459, 463, 479, 505, 518, 532; Jacob,
532; Marg., 463; Maria, 459, 463,
479, 505, 518, 532; Maria Elis., 434;
Melchior, 518; Sabina, 380; Wilh.,
380; Wilhelm, 434
KENDEL, An. Maria, 404
KENNEDY, Andr., 384; Joh., 419; Sus.
Christine, 419; Susanna, 419
KENNER, Charlotte, 387; Mich., 387
KENSEL, Christian, 424; Joh., 388;
Marg., 388, 424; Michael, 388
KENZER, Jacob, 548
KEPPEL, Christina, 411; Elis., 349
KEPPELE, Andreas, 389, 429, 444; Anna
Cath., 351; Anna Maria, 369; Anna
Maria Cath., 367; Cath., 325, 343,
344, 350, 365, 367, 381, 418, 450;
Elis., 299, 331; Esther, 389; Georg
Hnr., 343; Henr., 381; Henrietta, 418;
Henry, 365; Hnr., 325, 343, 350, 351,
354, 367, 376, 381, 418, 425, 427,
442, 450, 474, 475, 507; Joh., 282,
299, 331, 349; Joh. Hnr., 344; Maria,
389, 429, 444; Peter, 444; Susanna,
282, 474; Valentin, 369; Wilhelm,
474
KEPPLER, Michael, 359
KERCH, Susanna, 435
KERCHNER, Anna Eva Bastian, 506;
Joh. Adam, 506
KERL, Elis., 405; Joh., 408; Marg., 543;
Maria Elis., 408; Robert, 405; Wilh.,
405; Wilhelm, 543
KERLES, Eleonora, 473; Elis., 473;
Frdr., 473; Georg, 473
KERLS, Anna Cath., 373; Charlotta, 409;
Elis., 509; Frdr., 509; Hanna, 525;

Joh., 373; Joh. Michael, 409; Marg.,
509, 525; Wilh., 373; Wilhelm, 525;
William, 509
KERMAN, Elis., 315; Georg, 315; Jacob,
315
KERN, Anthon, 502; Anthony, 466;
Anton, 425, 535, 544; Cath., 285, 425,
466, 502, 509, 535, 544; Daniel, 541;
Elis., 466, 509, 541, 544; Gabriel, 384,
415, 421, 552; Joh., 425, 509, 541;
Magdalena, 415; Magdalene, 421;
Maria, 552
KERREL, Elis., 360; Joseph, 360;
Wilhelm, 360
KESLER, Anna Cath., 368, 412, 470;
Anna Maria, 322; Apollonia, 399;
Cath., 403; Hanna, 453; Jacob, 368,
403; Joh., 470; Joh. Georg, 470; Joh.
Jacob, 322, 412; Leonard, 399, 453;
Leonhard, 322, 359, 398; Maria, 399,
453; Maria Susanna, 359; Susanna, 359
KESSLER, Anna, 457, 522; Anna Cath.,
413; Anna Magdalena, 482; Anna
Marg., 377; Anna Maria, 291, 482;
Cath., 347, 377, 531; Cath. Elis., 347;
Elis., 457; Frdr., 457, 482, 522; Jacob,
347, 377, 457, 531; Joh., 413; Joh.
Jacob, 413; Leonhard, 522; Leonhardt,
291; Maria Magdalena, 413; Martin,
413; Samuel, 413
KESTLER, Anna Cath., 302; Balthasar,
302; Jacob, 302
KETTMANN, An. Maria, 399; Anna
Marg., 399; Leonard, 399
KEULER, Barbara, 280; Christina, 280;
Joh. Georg, 280
KEYLER, Joh., 537
KIBLER, Marg., 531
KIDD, Georg, 342; Marg., 342
KIDLER, Adam, 435; Elis., 435; Eva, 492;
Sahra Susanna, 435
KIEBLER, Cath., 320; Jacob, 320; Joh.,
320
KIEFER, Elis., 366; Eva Mar., 456, 499;
Eva Marg., 368; Eva Maria, 286, 329,
352, 377; Georg, 280, 286, 329, 352,
456, 465, 499, 553; Jacob, 293, 313,
358, 366; Joh. Georg, 368, 377; Joh.
Jacob, 293; Joh. Michael, 366; Maria
Eva, 465; Torothea, 293
KIEFFER, Cath., 463; Dorothea, 497;
Elis., 350; Eva, 324; Georg, 446;
Jacob, 350, 463; Joh. Georg, 497; Joh.
Jacob, 463; John Georg, 324; Maria,
497; Samuel, 497
KIEGLER, Elis., 283; Stephan, 283
KIEHR, Joh. Georg, 458
KIEL, Anna Marg., 411; Christoph, 411;
Elis., 411

KIELHAUER, Elis., 508; Martin, 508,
545; Sarah, 508, 545
KIELHEFER, Frdr., 512; Marg., 512
KIEMLE (see also KEIMLE), Barbara,
401; Cath., 422, 451, 456, 466; Cath.
Christina, 415; Christina, 444;
Christina Cath., 407, 416, 437, 470;
Conrad, 310; Elis., 470; Jacob, 346,
407, 415, 416, 422, 437, 444, 451,
456, 466, 470; Joh., 451, 471; Joh.
Peter, 444; Leonh., 427; Marg., 346;
Marg. Barbara, 416; Maria Sophia,
310; Mrs., 428; Sibylla, 471; Ursula,
386; Ursula Barbara, 427
KIEMLI, Ursula Barbara, 416
KIEN, Georg Hnr., 374; Joh. Georg, 374;
Maria Marg., 374
KIENSCH, Caspar, 307; Marg., 307
KIENSLE, Elis., 387; Joh. Balt., 387;
Maria, 385; Martin, 385
KIENSLI, Anna Marg., 327; Christian,
327
KIENTZEL, Anna Marg., 312; Christian,
312; Joh., 312
KIER, Elis., 549; Georg, 549; Joh., 549;
Joh. Georg, 450, 462, 472
KIERMANN, Daniel, 374; Elis., 374;
Sophia, 374
KIESER, Eva Maria, 315; Joh. Georg,
315
KIESINGER, Cath., 548; Elis., 548;
Georg, 548
KIESLER, Charlotta, 434; Elis., 359;
Michael, 359; Wilhelm, 434
KIESS, Hnr., 513
KIET, Joh. Wilhelm, 355; Maria Marg.,
355
KIFFERT, Elis., 375; Joh., 375; Maria,
400; Mat., 400
KIFFLER, Anna, 546; Joh., 546;
Susanna, 546
KIFSORT, Anna Eva, 316
KIHL, Anna Marg., 363; Barbara, 363;
Joh., 363
KILE, Samuel, 355
KILHAUER, Joh., 547; Martin, 547;
Salome, 547
KILLHAUER, Martin, 470; Michael,
470; Salome, 470
KILLMANN, Daniel, 323
KIMMERLE, Joh., 326; Marg., 326;
Maria, 326
KIMMERLI, Joh., 307; Marg., 307
KINDER, Elis., 530; Gottfried, 530
KINDISCH, Anna Marg., 371; Anna
Maria, 417; Caspar, 371, 417; Marg.,
417; Susanna, 371
KING, Andreas, 474; Anna, 296, 336;
Barbara, 520; Conr., 387; Conrad,
430; Debora, 296; Elis., 412; Elis.

Charlotta, 387; Hanna, 430; Issak, 520;
James, 412; Joh., 430; Joh. Michael,
296; John, 336, 363; Juliana, 387;
Magdalene, 363; Maria, 412; Maria
Elis., 474; Philip, 474; Samuel, 427;
Sarah, 427; William, 427
KINGSTON, Mary, 405; Paul, 405
KINSCH, Caspar, 457; Marg., 457;
Michael, 457
KINSEY, Ann, 409
KINSINGER, Anna Maria, 290; Joh.
Balthasar, 290; Michael, 290
KINSLE, Joh., 350; Joh. Wilhelm, 350;
Marg., 350
KINSLER, Baltasar, 407; Elis., 407; Joh.
Balthasar, 434; Maria, 359; Maria Elis.,
434; Michael, 407
KINST, Peter, 422
KINTZLER, Elis., 308; Martin, 308;
Michael, 308
KINZEL, Anna Maria, 443; Cath., 347;
Christian, 347, 443, 500; Georg, 476;
Jh., 460; Leonhard, 460; Marg., 347,
443, 460, 476, 500; Martin, 476
KINZINGER, Cath., 304, 384, 416, 466,
499; Georg, 304, 384, 416, 466, 499;
Joh. Christoph, 304; Peter, 499; Philipp
jacob, 416; Wilhelm, 466
KINZLE, Anna Marg., 482; Anna Maria,
485; Charlotte, 485; Christian, 482;
Joh. Christian, 482; Rudolf, 485
KINZLER, Anna Marg., 380; Balthasar,
288, 353, 446, 465, 542; Balthaser,
473; Christian, 380; Christoph Carl,
429; Elis., 288, 379, 464, 465, 473,
507, 542; Elis. Charlotte, 379; Jacob,
507; Joh., 473; Joh. Balthas., 464;
Magdalena, 473; Marg., 353, 507;
Maria Elis., 429, 446; Michael, 379,
429, 465, 507
KINZLI, Christian, 308; Joh., 308; Marg.,
308
KIRCH, Andreas, 543; Maria Elis., 543;
Wilhelm, 543
KIRCHEN, Marg., 316; Maria, 316; Owen,
316
KIRCHNER, Andreas, 296, 505; Anna
Elis., 287; Anna Friderica, 505;
Susanna, 296
KIRCK, Andreas, 356, 398; Maria, 356;
Maria Elis., 356, 398
KIRLS, Cath., 492; Elis., 383, 429; Frdr.,
383, 429; Marg., 492; Maria Elis., 383;
Wilh., 492
KIRN, Cath., 427; Maria, 427; Wilhelm,
427
KIRSCHNER, Anna Magdalena, 302;
Cath., 302; Daniel, 316; Joh., 302;
Maria, 316; Philippina, 316
KIRST, Elis., 501

KIRSTNER, Barbara, 485; Daniel, 485; Elis., 485
KITMAN, Cath., 535; Marg., 535
KITTLER, Anna Cath., 506; Joh., 506, 517, 529; Susanna, 506, 517, 529
KITZ, Anna Mar., 494; Apellonia, 526; Apoll., 394; Apollonia, 359, 361, 399, 416, 441, 471, 499; Appol., 372; Appollonia, 433; Appolonia, 421; David, 471; Elis., 372, 394, 416, 422, 441, 465, 471, 488, 521, 526, 550; Esther, 441; Georg, 359, 372, 399, 416, 421, 433, 441, 471, 526, 542; Jacob, 372, 394, 416, 422, 441, 471, 488, 521, 526, 550; Joh., 509, 526, 542; Joh. Georg, 361, 509; Joh. Jacob, 394; Marg., 416, 421, 422, 465, 492, 499, 542; Maria, 417, 445, 509, 526, 542; Maria Marg., 499; Melchior, 422, 499; Michael, 445, 465, 492, 494, 542; Rebecca, 526
KLAG, David, 409; Maria Magdalena, 409
KLAGER, Elis., 332; Valentin, 332
KLAMMER, Hnr., 548; Joh. Jacob, 548; Magdalene, 548
KLAMPER, Anna Christina, 280; Joh. Philip, 280
KLAMPFORT, Adam, 336
KLASER, Anna Elis., 518; Joh. Adam, 518; Jonas, 518
KLATTERBUCH, Joh. Cath., 533; Joseph, 533; Sophia, 533
KLAUER, Marg., 297, 311; Wilhelm, 297, 311
KLAUS, Jacob, 413; Marg., 413; Samuel, 413
KLAUSS, Jacob, 338, 368, 392, 463; Joh., 392, 463; Joh. Wilhelm, 338; Marg., 338, 368, 392, 463
KLAYUS, Mar. Marg., 496; Valentin, 496
KLEBE, Maria, 536; Philipp, 536; Susanna, 536
KLEES, Joh., 356; Joh. Cath., 356
KLEIBER, Cath., 476; Jacob, 476
KLEIM, Elis., 531; Philipp, 531
KLEIN, Adam, 314; Andr., 390; Andreas, 445; Anna, 313; Anna Cath., 295, 324, 348, 364; Anna Marg., 348, 376, 406; Anna Maria, 301, 464; Barb., 359; Barbara, 319, 323; Benjamin, 547; Cath., 301, 314, 344, 353, 376, 406; Cath. Elis., 298; Elis., 297, 319, 329, 334, 348, 353, 359, 362, 383, 390, 393, 400, 403, 410, 432, 441, 443, 445, 450, 463, 475, 477, 513, 515, 524, 540, 552; Elis. Cath., 344; Eva Mar., 403; Eva Maria, 277, 291, 297, 298, 313, 339, 343, 346, 358,

376, 393, 416; Frdr., 295, 432; Georg, 319, 342, 348, 362, 393, 410, 432, 450; Hanna, 376, 552; Hnr., 301, 540; Jacob, 301, 484, 515; Joh., 295, 314, 324, 341, 348, 364, 376, 476, 508, 524, 552; Joh. Balthas., 400; Joh. Balthasar, 348; Joh. Frdr., 376, 450; Joh. Georg, 329, 342, 540; Joh. Mat., 383; Joh. Matthaeus, 297; Joh. Peter, 495; Louisa, 342; Magdalena, 529; Marg., 376, 387, 447, 484, 508, 515, 529, 537, 547; Maria, 345, 377, 381, 382, 405, 443, 476, 495, 528; Maria Cath., 387; Michael, 297, 383, 508; Nicol., 376, 406; Nicolaus, 301, 344, 529, 537; Peter, 277, 291, 297, 298, 313, 324, 332, 339, 343, 345, 346, 358, 376, 377, 382, 443, 476, 495, 528, 547; Phil., 345, 359, 477; Philip, 319, 353, 373, 463; Philipp, 333, 334, 403, 441, 513, 524; Rehanna, 324; Ruldop, 319; Sarah, 463; Sophia, 301; Susan Marg., 345; Susanna Elis., 333; Theobald, 387, 447; Veronica, 528; Wilhelm, 477; Wilhelmine, 332
KLEINSY, Elis., 314; James, 314; Jonas, 314; Rachel, 314
KLEM, Anna, 317
KLEMMER, Anna, 373; Anna Maria, 511; Cath., 286; Hnr., 511; Joh. Wilhelm, 287; Magdalena, 511
KLEPPER, Carl, 324; Christina, 324; Elis., 412; Hnr., 324
KLESER, Anna Elis., 518; Joh. Adam, 518; Jonas, 518
KLESS, Jacob, 310; Sabina, 310
KLETT, Hnr., 353; Marg., 353; Wilhelm, 353
KLETTNER, Joh. Georg, 410; Sara, 410
KLING, Anna, 309, 463, 467; Anna Cath., 326; Anna Marg., 360, 393; Anna Maria, 309, 326; Anna Susanna, 393; Elis., 442; Georg Adam, 467; Jacob Ernst, 411; Joh., 309, 326, 360, 393, 436, 442; Joh. Ludewig, 467; Joh. Ludwig, 463; Maria Christina, 411; Philip, 360
KLINGESCHMIDT, Dorothea, 300
KLINGMANN, Anna Elis., 323, 324, 350, 381; Barbara, 283, 323; Cath., 324; Elis., 323, 368, 381; Georg Philip, 324; Hanna, 324; Jacob, 324; Joh., 350, 368; Michael, 323, 324, 350, 381; Regina, 323
KLOCKNER, Christian, 458
KLOHR, Anna Cath., 362; Joh. Christian, 362
KLOHS, Anna Marg., 501; Christoph Eberhard, 501; Jacob, 501
KLOOS, Jacob, 300; Sabina, 300

KLOSS (see also GAHN), Jacob, 289;
   Sabyna, 289
KLUG, Anna, 340; Joh. Michael, 340;
   Joh. Michl., 461; Magdalena, 461;
   Peter, 461; Wilhelm, 340
KNAPP, Cath., 406, 423; Eva Cath., 457;
   Joh. Georg, 406; Phil. Hnr., 457;
   Philip, 406; Philipp, 423
KNAUER, Andreas, 452; Ludwig, 499;
   Marg., 499
KNECHT, An. Cath., 369; Anna Maria,
   317, 369; Elis., 495; Maria, 449, 495;
   Molly, 489; Phil., 489, 495; Phil.
   Georg, 369; Philip, 449; Philipp
   Georg, 317; Rosina, 317
KNEIS, Christian, 288; Christina, 288
KNERL, A. Maria, 547; Georg, 547
KNERR, Barb., 390; Cath., 285, 332,
   347, 355, 375, 418; Elis., 501, 531;
   Georg, 285, 332, 347, 355, 375, 390,
   418, 501; Hanna, 531; Hnr., 501, 531;
   Joh. Simon, 418; Marg., 332
KNERY, Carl, 469, 477, 518; Carl Frdr.,
   461; Eleonora, 518; Elis., 536; Hnr.,
   536; Joh., 461; Marg., 461, 469, 477,
   518; Sophia, 469
KNIES, Anna Clara Doroth., 359;
   Christoph, 378; Clara, 393; David,
   393; Joh., 359; Joh. David, 359;
   Maria, 393
KNOBLAUCH, Adam, 312, 348, 383,
   388, 412, 453, 484, 489, 548; Anna
   Barbara, 312; Anna Maria, 312;
   Barbara, 348, 383, 484, 489, 548;
   Cath., 388; Elis. Barbara, 412; Elis.
   Marg., 383; Hnr., 348; Maria Agnes,
   355; Martin, 355; Susanna Barbara,
   453
KNODEL, Anna Maria, 313, 316, 327,
   349, 378, 403, 427, 456, 504;
   Christian, 427; Daniel, 313, 316, 327,
   349, 378, 403, 427, 456, 504; Elis.,
   340; Georg, 340, 403; Jacob, 313;
   Joh., 378; Magdalene, 349; Wilhelm,
   340
KNOP, Christina, 289
KNORR, Cath., 305, 332; Georg, 332;
   Joh. Georgt, 305
KOBER, Anna Barbara, 343; Barbara,
   412, 442; Paul, 343, 412, 442
KOBLER, Barbara, 435; Isaac, 435
KOBUT, John, 339
KOCH, Adam, 420, 475; Anna, 420;
   Anna Cath., 352; Anna Elis., 456,
   509; Anna Maria, 365, 429; Balthasar,
   438; Barbara, 322, 331, 374; Cath.,
   397, 497; Dorothea, 374; Elis., 365,
   477; Eva, 438, 475, 509, 514, 542;
   Georg, 397, 497; Hnr., 365, 421;
   Isaac, 402, 438, 509, 514, 542; Jacob,

322, 509; Joh., 331, 374, 420, 429,
   456, 509; John, 322; Joshua Archir,
   397; Martin, 421; Michael, 475;
   Rosina, 531; Rosina Doroth., 509;
   Rosina Dorothea, 429, 456
KOCHEN, Albertina Philippina, 388
KOCHENDOERFER, Anna, 322; Barbara,
   344, 465, 484, 528; Jacob, 484; Joh.
   Jac., 322; Philippina, 362
KOCHENDOERFFER, Barbara, 506, 519;
   Frdr., 497, 506, 519; Peter, 495; Rahel,
   497; Regina, 519
KOCHENDORFER, Widow, 370
KOCHER, Christoph, 279; Joh. Georg,
   279; Juliana, 279
KOCHERSBERGER, Martin, 535; Rachel,
   535; Rosina, 535
KOCHERSBURG, Eve, 546; Philip, 546
KOCHLER, Cath., 315; Jacob, 315; Joh.
   Frdr., 422, 440; John Georg, 422;
   Joseph, 440; Maria, 422, 440; Maria
   Elis., 422
KOE, Carl, 538; Joh., 538; Rosina Elis.,
   538
KOEHL, Cath., 505; Christina, 505; Elis.,
   505; Jacob, 505; Jeremia, 505; Ludwig,
   505; Maria, 505
KOEHLER, Cath., 515; Hnr., 334; Jacob,
   515; Maria, 334; Nicol., 334
KOENIG, Adam, 329, 352, 484; Anna
   Barbar, 329; Anna Barbara, 352, 435,
   536; Anna Maria, 306; Barb., 453, 484;
   Barbara, 388, 401, 406, 443; Maria
   Barb., 432; Tobias, 388, 401, 406, 443,
   484, 536; Tobias Adam, 435, 453
KOENNER, Charlotte, 476; Michael, 476
KOETH, Elis., 483; Jacob, 483
KOHFF, Elis., 475; Joh., 475; Joh.
   Michael, 475
KOHL, Elis., 342; Esther, 361, 433; Jacob,
   433; Joh., 342, 354, 361, 433;
   Magdalena, 372; Marg., 483; Maria,
   342; Maria Esther, 354; Peter, 483;
   Sophia, 372
KOHLMANN, Anna Marg., 522; Cath.,
   522, 537; Jacob, 542; Maria Marg.,
   542; Phil., 459, 542; Philipp, 522
KOHM, Joh., 418; Mar. Cath., 418
KOHP (see also GAAB), Cath., 539;
   Gottlieb, 514; Hnr., 526; Joh., 526;
   Maria, 514, 526; Nancy, 514
KOHR, Anna Maria, 365
KOHRMAN, Anna, 418; Conrad, 418;
   Elis., 418
KOHRT, Cath., 418; Georg, 418; William,
   418
KOHRUM, Thomas, 549
KOLB, Anna Maria, 397; Cath., 397;
   Philip, 397

KOLE, Euphronica, 335; Georg, 335; Joh.
   Georg, 335; Thomas, 335
KOLLER, Elis., 287; Georg, 287
KOLMAN, Andreas, 409; Martin, 409;
   Mary, 409
KOLMANN, Gottlieb, 453
KOLN, Euphronica, 335; Georg, 335;
   Joh. Georg, 335; Thomas, 335
KOLP, Maria, 539; Wilhelm, 539
KONIG, Anna Barbara, 283, 290, 297;
   Barbara, 334, 353, 552; Tobias, 283,
   334, 353, 552; Tobias Adam, 290,
   297
KOOF, Elis., 452; Joh., 452; Samuel, 452
KOP, Cath., 490
KOPIA (see also COPIA), Joh., 446
KOPP, Cath. Marg., 449; Elis., 465;
   Jacob, 465; Joh., 446; Maria, 446
KOPPENHAVER, Rosina Barbara, 355
KORBMANN, Susanna Elis., 294
KORCH, Elis., 533; Peter, 533; Susanna,
   533
KORN, Anna Maria, 286; Caspar, 286;
   Maria Marg., 369
KOSCH, Christian, 373; Daniel, 406;
   Laban, 373; Sarah, 373
KOSHERT, Adam, 524; Marg., 524
KOSTING, Joh. Frdr., 344
KOT, Cath., 357; Joh. Jacob, 357; Marg.
   Magdalena, 357
KOTSCH, Elis., 434; Wilhelm, 434
KOTTER, Anna, 418
KRABBEL, Elis., 445, 474; John, 474;
   Mat., 445
KRAEMER (see also CRAEMER,
   GRAEMER), Adam, 381; An. Maria,
   381; Anna Maria, 334, 344; Cath.,
   408; Jacob, 398, 449; Joh. Georg,
   352, 408; Joh. Jacob, 352; Joh. Peter,
   398; Leon., 381; Leonard, 344, 431;
   Leonhard, 334, 456; Maria, 431, 449,
   456; Mat., 394; Otillia, 352; Ottilia,
   398; Philipp, 334; Susanna, 449
KRAENDER, Maria, 437
KRAFFT, Cath., 526; Elis., 530; Jacob,
   530; Joh., 530; Johanna Maria, 446;
   Marg., 488; Michael, 446; Peter, 488,
   526
KRAFT, Anna Maria, 379, 493, 549;
   Anna Susanna, 456; Cath., 289, 519;
   Dorothea, 366; Georg Michael, 319,
   364; George Michael, 280; Jacob,
   422, 534; Joh. Georg, 366, 386; Joh.
   Joseph, 457; Joh. Maria, 367, 386,
   457; Joh. Michael, 366; Joh. Peter,
   340, 444; Johanna Maria, 280, 319,
   421, 501; John Jacob, 319; Mar., 498;
   Marg., 279, 289, 321, 340, 358, 386,
   399, 422, 444, 451, 456, 457, 470,
   500, 549, 551; Maria, 364, 365, 549;

Maria Barbara, 321; Maria Charlotte,
   421; Maria Dor., 457; Maria Elis., 457;
   Michael, 364, 367, 379, 386, 396, 421,
   457, 501, 549; Peter, 279, 289, 321,
   358, 365, 386, 399, 404, 422, 456, 457,
   470, 500, 519, 540, 549, 551; Philipp,
   498; Regina, 500; Sara, 358; Susanna,
   551
KRAMER, Ann. Marg., 408; Arnold, 331;
   Cath., 331; Joh. Hnr., 299; Joh. Jacob,
   299; Leonard, 408; Leonhard, 299;
   Magdalena, 408; Ottilia, 299
KRAMLE, Hnr., 445; Magdalena, 474;
   Thomas, 474
KRAMLICH, Cath., 478; Christina, 478,
   517; Jacob, 478, 517; Magdalena, 517;
   Thomas, 517
KRAMMEL, Hnr., 497; Jacob, 497;
   Sophia, 497
KRAMMLE, Hnr., 531; Magdalena, 531;
   Maria Magdalena, 531; Sophia, 531;
   Thomas, 531
KRAMP, Dorothea, 330, 420, 507; Joh.,
   420; Joh. Georg, 330; John, 507;
   Rebecca, 507; Susanna, 519
KRAUCH, Joh. Georg, 432; Philippina,
   470
KRAUS, Ann, 430; Cath., 418; Elis., 336,
   383; Jacob, 336; Joh., 418, 430;
   Magdalena, 336; Marg., 353; Stephan,
   353; Susanne, 430
KRAUSE, Anna, 365; Anna Cath., 365,
   498; Georg, 365; Joh., 498; Nancy, 498
KRAUSKOP, Joh. Georg, 495; Maria, 495
KRAUSKOPF, Georg, 316, 549; Joh., 549;
   Marg., 316, 549, 550
KRAUSKOPP, Anna Maria, 490; Georg,
   490, 533; Marg., 490; Maria, 533
KRAUSNER, Anna, 440; Joh., 440
KRAUSS, Anna, 442; Anna Cath., 287;
   Cath., 305, 341, 396, 411, 424, 458,
   508; Dorothea, 508, 516; Elis., 306,
   442; Jacob, 306; Joh., 341, 411, 424,
   442, 458, 473, 508; Joh. Georg, 287,
   305, 396; Joh. Jurg, 287; Joh. Michael,
   287, 508; Michael, 508, 516; Nancy,
   473; Rosina, 411
KRAUSSKOP, Anna Maria, 512; Joh.,
   512; Joh. Georg, 512
KRAUSSKOPF, Christina, 322; Georg,
   322; Jacob, 322; Marg., 322
KRAUSSKOPP, Joh., 517
KRAUTER, Joh., 417; Marg., 417
KREAB, Elis., 480
KREB, Christina Barbara, 339; David,
   339; Georg, 281
KREBS, Adam, 284, 285, 320, 358, 359,
   420, 424; Anna Barbara, 297; Anna
   Marg., 503; Anna Maria, 323, 358,
   359, 420, 521; Barbara, 349, 553;

Cath., 279; Christ., 495; Christian, 297, 307; Dorothea, 485, 498, 517, 523; Elis., 307; Georg, 485, 498, 517, 523; Joh., 422, 553; Joh. Christian, 307, 477; Joh. Frdr., 521; Joh. Michael, 279; Joh. Phil., 477; Joh. Philip, 323, 349; Joh. Philipp, 503; Magdalena, 307; Marg., 422, 477; Maria, 306, 320, 424; Maria Marg., 284; Michael, 279; Phil., 477; Philipp, 422, 503
KREBS-LAMPT, Widow, 536
KREIDER, Cath., 473, 539; David, 473, 539; Jacob, 473
KREINER, Joh., 505; Joh. Hartmann, 505; Marg., 505
KREINMEIER, Anne Maria, 398; Jacob, 398
KREIS (see also CREIS), Anna Marg., 284; Georg, 284; John Jacob, 345; Susanna Cath., 345
KREISEL, Cath., 355; Joh., 355
KREISMEIER, Anne Maria, 398; Jacob, 398
KREISS, Anna Marg., 332; Cath., 332; Georg, 332; Joh. Georg, 332
KREITER, Elis., 549; Jacob, 549
KRELS, William, 475
KREMLE, Cath., 474; Hnr., 474; Sophia, 474
KREPER, Anna Maria, 329; Georg, 329; Joh., 329
KREPPEL, Elis., 552; Michael, 552
KRES, Anna Marg., 510; Christina Louisa, 526
KRESS (see also CRESS, CHRESS, GRESS), Anna Maria, 280, 295, 343, 489, 490; Anne Elis., 355; Elis., 280, 342, 522; Georg, 522, 530; Henrich, 280; Hnr., 295, 343, 348, 489, 490; Jacob, 405, 489; Joh., 355; Maria, 348; Maria Magdal., 314; Maria Rosina, 481; Peter, 342, 405, 481, 530; Philip, 355; Rosina, 342, 405, 530; Salome, 342; William, 295
KRESSEL, Cath., 492, 541; Joh., 492, 541; Joh. Hnr., 545; Marg., 545; Maria Marg., 492; Sarah, 541
KRESSMANN, Andreas, 461; Elis., 461
KRETSCHMER, Gottfried, 460; Sophia, 460
KREUDER, Maria, 402
KREUTER, Cath., 336; Elis., 522; Martin, 296, 336; Susanna Louisa, 296
KREUTZ, Elis., 312; Samuel, 312; Sarah, 312
KRIBBEL, Andr., 445; Anna Regina, 445; Caspar, 449; Cath., 449, 489,

505; Christina, 434, 505; Elis., 434; Joh., 434, 449, 505; Sahra, 449
KRIBBLE, Anna Marg., 479; Christina, 459, 479; Joh., 459, 479; Salome, 459
KRIECHENMEIER, Anna Marg., 411; Georg, 411
KRIEG, Cath., 372, 529; Elis., 527; Georg, 529; Joh. Daniel, 412; Joh. Georg, 475; Maria, 475; Maria Eva, 412, 527; Martin, 412; Philip, 372; Valentin, 372, 475, 527
KRIEGEMEIER, Jacob, 354
KRIEGER, Andreas, 514; Cath., 481, 506, 514, 552; David, 552; Jacob, 525, 535; Joh., 481, 506, 514, 535, 552; Joh. Nicol., 481; John, 506; Maria, 525, 535; Maria Eva, 525; Nicol., 506; Nicolaus, 481; Sophia, 481, 506
KRIER, Cath., 510; Joh., 510; Nicolaus, 464; Sophia, 464
KRIES, Clara, 487; David, 487; Marg., 487
KRIESMEIER, Anna Marg., 384; Georg, 384; Jacob, 384; Joh. Georg, 384; Magdalena, 384
KRIGER, Cath., 442; Joh., 442; Maria Magdalena, 442
KRIMM, Appellonia, 514; Cath., 512; Hnr., 493, 512, 514; Magdal., 493
KRIPS, Dorothea, 519; Georg, 519
KROB (see also GROB), John, 492
KROENER, Caspar, 527; Cath., 544; Jacob, 459, 477, 527, 544; Maria, 477; Susann, 527; Susanna, 459, 477, 544
KROKS, Barbara, 472; Jeany, 472; Joseph, 472
KROLL, Anna Cath., 485; Elis. Marg., 451, 455, 485; Joh. Nicolaus, 451, 455, 485; Wilh. Dietrich, 455
KROOK, Barbara, 510
KROP, Adam, 546; Elis., 546; Joh. Adam, 546
KRUBEL (see also GRUBEL), Christina, 484; Joh., 484
KRUG, Christian, 511; Georg, 411; Maria Eva, 336; Peter, 295; Sarah, 511; Susanna, 511; Valentin, 336
KRUGEMEIER, Anna Marg., 376; Georg, 376
KRUGEMEYER (see also GRIGEMEIER), Cath., 548; Elis., 548; Hnr., 548
KRUGER, Anna Cath., 287, 321; Cath., 408; Cath. Barbara, 325; Eleonore, 325; Francis, 325; Joh., 321, 408; John Christian, 287
KRUGMEYER, Anna Elis., 547; Jacob, 547; Magdalena, 547

KRUMBACH, Barbara, 382, 458, 495;
Gottfr., 495; Gottfried, 382, 458;
Jacob, 495; Joh., 458; Michael, 382
KRUMMEL, Elis., 448; Hnr., 448;
Sophia, 448
KUBEL, Marg., 387
KUBLER, Cath., 326; David, 385; Jacob,
326; Marg., 385; Regina, 385
KUCH, Anna Barbara, 286; Barbara, 455;
Jacob, 286; Joh., 286, 455; Salome,
455
KUCHER, An. Mar., 382; Anna Elis.,
278; Anna Maria, 355; Christian, 278;
Christoph, 355, 382; Maria Cath.,
355; Wilhelm, 382
KUCHERER, Esther Elis., 397; Joh.
Frdr., 397
KUCHLER, Joh., 505; Lydia, 505; Maria,
505
KUCKER, Christoph, 491; Doroth., 491;
Jacob, 520; Maria, 520; Maria
Magdalena, 512; Mat., 512
KUDER, Jacob, 534
KUEHR, Joh., 495
KUFER, Elis., 355
KUG, Cath., 409; Georg, 409; William,
409
KUGLER, Carl, 499; Cath., 499; Georg,
499
KUHL, Cath., 381; Frdr., 285, 320, 371;
Hnr. Frdr., 320; Joh. Hnr., 305;
Marcus, 285; Sophia, 305; Susanna,
285, 320
KUHLE, Cath., 392; Marg., 392; Sigm.,
392
KUHLI, Elis., 315; Susanna, 315;
William, 315
KUHN, Adam Simon, 416; Anna Maria,
292, 353, 389, 431; Cath., 462, 512;
Christian, 395, 421, 451, 482, 518;
Daniel, 544; Elis., 327, 376, 416, 447,
462, 477, 482, 484, 505, 527, 538,
544; Hnr. Kepple, 477; Jac., 376;
Jacob, 390; Joh., 395, 527; Joh.
Georg, 431; Joh. Jacob, 292; Joh.
Wilhelm, 353; John Ludwig, 319;
Mar., 395; Mar. Sabina, 376; Maria,
319, 366, 407, 421, 451, 482, 518;
Maria Sabina, 505; Martin, 462, 512;
MIchael, 284; Michael, 292, 319,
353, 389, 512; Peter, 376, 416, 447,
477, 489, 505, 527, 544; Samuel, 389;
Sara Doroth., 331; Thomas, 451;
Vincents, 327; William, 518
KUHNER, Carl Franz, 459; Charlotte,
459; Elis., 502; Gottfried, 502;
Michael, 459
KUHNHAUER, Cath., 418; ELis., 418;
Martin, 418
KUHNS, Gertraut, 347; Michael, 347

KUHNZMANN, Maria Salome, 450;
Philip Jacob, 450
KUHR, Georg, 549
KUNCKEL, Anna Maria, 429; Cath., 331,
363, 429; Cath. Elis., 470; Christian,
331, 363, 429; Christina, 363;
Christina Cath., 363; Eleanora, 441;
Eleonor, 331; Eleonora Cath., 331;
Hnr., 543; Joh., 363, 400, 422, 439,
441, 451, 470, 519, 543; Joh. Christian,
470; Mar. Christina, 470; Maria, 451,
470, 475, 519; Maria Christina, 400,
439, 543; Maria Cla., 422; Maria Clara,
441, 519, 543; Philipp Conrad, 441
KUNCKLER, Joh., 489
KUNKEL, Anna Marg., 375; Cath., 516;
Christian, 516; Christina, 367;
Eleonora, 516; Joh., 367, 502, 503,
516, 547; Mar. Christine, 547; Maria
Christina, 502; Maria Clara, 503
KUNS, Cath., 376; Christian, 394; Hnr.,
345; Maria Juliana, 345; Michael, 376
KUNSMAN, Maria Cath., 300; Philip, 300
KUNTSCH, Barbara, 489; Caspar, 489;
Marg., 489; Peter, 489
KUNTSEH, Sophia, 504
KUNTZ, Anna, 349; Cath. Elis., 389; Joh.
Christoph, 389; Marg. Henrietta, 389
KUNTZE, Rev., 313
KUNTZLER, Balthasar, 302; Elis., 302
KUNZ, Cath., 434, 455; Georg, 377; Joh.,
434; Joh. Beata, 486; Joh. Christoph,
362; Marg., 336, 354, 428; Marg.
Henrietta, 362; Maria Cath., 362
KUNZE, Anna Maria Cath., 417; Carl,
454; Carl Hnr., 454; Christoph, 309,
330; Elis., 454; Henr. Marg., 395, 440;
Henrietta Marg., 339, 454; Joh. Chr.,
395; Joh. Christ., 344; Joh. Christoph,
304, 339, 417, 440, 454, 486; Johanna
Beata, 486; John, 379; Marg., 330,
468, 486; Marg. Henrietta, 344, 417;
Maria, 339; Pastor, 277, 288, 293, 303,
309, 327, 346, 362, 376, 393, 394, 404,
407, 421, 426, 428, 434, 436, 437, 439,
451, 464, 481, 498, 501
KUNZEL, Anna, 510; Anna Marg., 513;
Elis., 510; Frdr., 510; Joh., 513; Joh.
Martin, 513
KUNZLE, Marg., 511
KUNZLER, Balthasar, 504, 528; Joh., 528;
Magdalena, 528; Maria Elis., 504, 528;
Maria Magdalena, 528
KUNZMAN, Philipp Jacob, 470
KUNZMANN, Cath., 538; Maria Cath.,
422; Maria Salome, 518; Phil., 538;
Philip, 394; Philipp, 422
KUPPER, Eva Maria, 286; Georg, 286
KURTZ, Anna, 459; Anna Cath., 361;
Anna Maria, 344; Christopher, 341;

Dorothea, 344; Elis., 343, 400, 434, 531; Eva Barbara, 296, 324; Georg, 328, 344, 361, 397, 412, 425, 456, 491, 493; Georg Jacob, 412; Hnr., 324, 343, 354, 363, 373, 406, 414, 442, 491, 542; Hnr. Peter, 324; Jacob, 360; Jacob Ulrich, 425; Joh. Bernhardt, 373; Joh. David, 456; Joh. Georg, 415, 548; Juliana Henrietta, 366; Marg., 341, 361, 412, 425, 456, 493, 548; Maria, 441; Michael, 531; Peter, 296, 324, 360, 400, 421, 459; Regina, 442; Ros., 406; Rosina, 343, 354, 363, 373, 414, 491, 542; Sahra, 459; Sara, 296, 324, 360; Sara Barbara, 296; Sara Elis., 397, 548; Sarah, 400, 421, 542
KURZEL, Charlotte, 508; Joh., 508; Wilhelm, 508
KURZLER, Balthasar, 508; Elis., 508
LACHTLEBEN, Cath., 448; Christian, 448; Christina, 448
LACKMANN, Wilhelm, 510
LAD, Anna Barb., 408
LADER, Elis., 279, 289, 309, 337; Philip, 279, 289, 337; Philipp, 309
LADERS, Philip, 432
LAEMLE, Eva, 385
LAEMMEL, Joh., 337; Sarah, 337
LAG, Dorothea, 511
LAGER, Joh., 445; Marg., 445
LAHR, Elis., 474
LAIB, Dorothea, 278, 302, 337, 369; Georg, 278, 283, 302, 312, 337, 369; George Ludewig, 283; Marg. Dorothea, 283, 312; Maria Elis., 312
LAIKY, Cath., 414; Edward, 414; Elis., 414
LAININGER, Maria Elis., 294
LAITZ, John, 542
LAMBADER, Maria Cath., 361
LAMBART, Joh., 534; Maria, 534; Sara, 534
LAMBARTER, Joh., 331, 433; Joh. Adam, 331; Marcus, 433; Salome, 433; Sarah, 331
LAMLE, John, 385; Jonathan, 385; Sarah, 385
LAMLIN, James, 285; Joh., 285; Sarah, 285
LAMPADER, Anna Marg., 332
LAMPARDER, Cath., 425; Joh., 355, 409; Joh. Thomas, 355; Josua, 286; Sarah, 355, 409
LAMPARTER, George, 352; Joh., 297, 346; Josua, 288, 352; Marg., 297; Maria Cath., 288; Salome, 297; Sarah, 346; Sophia, 352
LAMPATER, Cath., 310; Josua, 310; Marg., 328; Salome, 310

LAMPATHER, Joh., 293; Salome, 293
LAMPE, Joh., 393
LAMPERTER, Joh., 377; Joh. Georg, 377; Sara, 377
LAND, Susanna, 525
LANDEBERGER, Anna Maria, 279; Joh., 335; Magdalena, 335; Maria, 406, 519; Maria Magdalena, 279; Mat., 406, 519; Matthias, 279; Susanne, 406
LANDENBERGER, Maria, 354, 440; Mat., 315, 354, 440; Regina, 315; Sarah, 354
LANDGRAF, Georg, 284, 316; Magdalena, 284, 316; Marg. Anna, 316
LANDLE, Joh., 529; Maria, 529
LANDVESS, Cath., 346; Elias, 346; Joh. Georg, 346
LANG, Abraham, 457; Anna Maria, 457; Cath., 386; Charles, 317; Chrisina, 413; Christian, 413; Christopher, 317; Elis., 457; Marg., 317
LANGBECHT, Cath., 411; Christian, 411; Elis., 411
LANGE, Georg, 281, 306, 339, 349, 384; Maria, 306; Maria Susanna, 349; Susanna, 281, 306, 349, 384; Wilhelm, 384
LANGHOF, Cath., 470; Eberhard, 470
LANIARD, Anna, 327; Mr., 327
LANKEP, Cath., 348; Eberhard, 348; Joh. Samuel, 348
LANTZ, Jacob, 281; Juliana, 281; Martin, 281
LAP(P) (see also LAUB), Adam, 500; Andr., 445; Andreas, 304, 311, 362, 445, 524; Anna Cath., 500; Anna Dorothea, 524; Cath., 495; Cath. Elis., 524; Christina, 311, 445; Christina Cath., 304; Dorothea, 331, 461; Joh., 423; Joh. Martin, 311; Johanna Christina, 533; Lorenz, 331, 461; Marg., 423, 495, 551; Mich., 495; Michael, 362, 423, 551
LARD, Bernhard, 454; Cath., 454
LASHT, Joh., 532
LASK, Cath., 472
LASKE, Cath., 489, 523; Edward, 489, 523; Marg., 523; Sarah, 489
LASKY, Alexander, 299; Anna Maria, 343; Cath., 299, 343, 440, 502; Edward, 299, 343, 440
LASS, Dorothea, 398; Lorenz, 398; Regina Cath., 398
LATER, Elis., 296, 503; Philip, 296
LATSCH, Joh., 475; Marg., 475
LAUB, Andreas, 284; Anna Cath., 284; Christina, 284; Christine, 366; Marg., 350; Peter, 350
LAUCH, David, 542; Hanna, 542; Joh., 542

LINNENBERG, Anna Marg., 377; Joh., 377; Joh. Georg, 377
LINNENSCHIED, Carl, 533; Charl., 533; Marg., 533
LINTSCH, Alexander, 418; Ros. Magd., 418; Rosina Magdalene, 418
LINTZ, Anna Maria, 280; Georg Adam, 280; Jacob, 280
LIPORTE, Anna Elis., 462; Francys, 462
LIPPENCOT, Abel, 390; Cath., 390; Samuel, 390
LIPPIE, Andreas, 458; Elis., 458; Joh., 458
LIPPINCOT, Abel, 316; Cath., 316
LIPPY, Elis., 298; Joh., 298; Rachel, 298
LIPS, Ann. Mar., 380
LIST, Carl, 539; Cath., 515; Maria, 539; Maria Elis., 515; Martin, 515; Rebecca, 539
LITSCH, Eva Maria, 441, 486; Joh., 487; Joh. Peter, 441; Maria, 487; Peter, 486, 534
LITTLE, Anna, 536; Cath., 432, 536; Joh., 432, 536; John, 536; Maria Barbara, 432; Michael, 536
LIVINGSTON, Ann, 444; Daniel, 354; Elis., 444; Ellis, 419; Eva, 326, 354; John, 419; Mary, 326, 419; Samuel, 326, 354; William, 444
LIZINGER, Elis., 468; Georg, 468
LOB, Eva, 421
LOBSTEIN, Andr., 420; Andreas, 444, 482, 541; Cath., 420; Elis., 420, 444, 482, 541; Jacob, 482; Joh. Frdr., 541
LOCHMAN, Anna Maria, 317, 375, 535; Georg, 535; Johanna Maria, 317; Nicol., 375; Nicolaus, 317
LOCHMANN, Anna Mar., 424; Anna Maria, 298, 472; Cath., 492; Joh. Maria, 370; Nicolaus, 298
LOCK, Andreas, 374; Cath., 374; Emos, 374
LOECHER, Maria Magdalena, 307
LOESCH, Elis., 427; Joh., 451; Maria, 401, 427, 451; Maria Barbara, 370; Zachar., 370; Zacharias, 401, 427, 451
LOESCHER, Anna, 495; Barbara, 477; Cath., 403, 490; Catharina, 375; Eva, 375; Francy, 495; Franz, 451, 477; Georg, 475; Jacob, 398; Joh. Georg, 403; Maria, 398; Maria Barbara, 451, 495; Mr., 375; Sahra, 451; Wilhelm, 403
LOESHER, Anna Maria, 291; Jacob, 291; Maria, 291; Maria Magd., 376
LOEWE, Anna Elis., 496; Cath., 496; Hnr. Lud., 496
LOGAN, Adam, 543; Dorothea, 536
LOHN, Veronica, 551; Wilhelm, 551

LOHR, Anna Maria, 333; Elis., 325; Frdr., 282; Joh., 325; Rosina, 282; Rudolph, 333
LOHRA, Anna Maria, 528; Caspar, 298; Cath., 463; Elis., 358, 496; Maria, 463, 496; Peter, 463, 496; Sophia, 298
LOHRMANN, Anna Justina, 277, 318; Anna Justinia, 360; Anna Maria, 277; Joh. Andreas, 360; Joh. Georg, 277, 318, 360; Martha Rebecca, 318
LONG, Maria, 537
LORCHE, Carl, 411; Joh. Georg, 411; Johanna, 411
LORENTZ, Anna Cath., 294; Cath., 294; Joh., 294, 374; Sophia, 374
LORENZ, Cath., 333, 347, 424, 470, 492, 501, 548; Elis., 333, 366, 466; Joh., 347, 424, 470, 492, 501, 548; Joh. Lorenz, 333; Wilhelm, 466
LOSCH, Daniel, 295; Dorothea Elis., 295; Elis., 295, 471; Joh. Peter, 340; Magdalena, 349; Maria, 340, 471, 522; Philipp, 522; Zacharias, 340, 471
LOSCHE, Maria Cath., 364; Will., 364
LOSCHER, Anna, 379; Anna Maria, 336; Barba., 432; Barbara, 338, 379; Chloe, 338; Francis, 338, 379, 432; Frantz, 297; Georg, 308, 333, 376; Jacob, 300, 336, 432, 433; Leonard, 306; Mar. Cath., 333; Maria, 300, 306, 308, 333; Maria Barbara, 297; Maria Cath., 308, 376; Maria Elis., 333; Maria Magd., 376; Michael, 336; Susanna, 386; Wilhelm, 333, 376; William, 308
LOSCHET, Anna Cath., 290, 322; Anna Sybilla, 290; Cath., 406, 452, 488; Joh., 290, 322, 406, 452, 488; Maria Regina, 322; Sibylla, 452
LOSER, Joh., 319
LOSHER, Anna Maria, 352; Jacob, 352; Rahel, 352
LOTS, Cath., 306; Michael, 306
LOTZ, Anna Maria, 295
LOVE, Elis., 357; Joh., 357, 500; William, 317, 357
LOVEBERRY, Elis., 508
LOW, Eva, 379; Georg, 410; Joh., 379; Maria, 410; Maria Hanna, 379; Nancy, 410
LOYD, Georg, 507; Phillis, 507; Sylvia, 507
LUBECKE, Anna Maria, 522; Hnr., 522; Marg., 522
LUBEN, Anna, 309, 314; Hannah, 309, 314; Melchior, 309, 314
LUDCAPE, Richard, 301; Salome, 301
LUDEWIG, Elis., 330; Joh. Wilhelm, 330; John, 330
LUDWIG, Anna, 537; Anna Maria, 493; Elis., 438, 493, 537, 544; Joh., 438,

552; Joh. Andreas Phil., 537; Joh. Mart., 493; Magdalene, 552; Martin, 438, 544
LUFFT, Georg, 473, 475
LUGER, Elis., 493, 510; Ernst Frdr., 479; Jacob, 493, 510; Joh., 479, 493; Maria Magdal., 479
LUPKE, Anna Elis., 497; Anna Maria, 497; Hnr., 497
LUTENBERGER, Anna Doroth. Elis., 410; Eberhard, 410; Joh., 410
LUTHERLOW, Col., 416
LUTICAT, Sahra, 458
LUTKET, Sarah, 495, 540
LUTSCH, Eva Maria, 476; Joh. Peter, 476
LUTZ, Adam, 533; Anna Barb., 494; Anna Barbara, 443; Anna Cath., 494; Anna Maria, 319, 464; Cath., 323, 359, 374, 376, 412, 443, 524, 541; Christian, 287, 301, 323, 359, 365, 396, 411, 445, 464, 479, 502, 529; Elis., 533; Elis. Cath., 376; Frdr., 376, 412, 443, 494; Georg, 400; Hnr., 412; Jacob, 411, 523; Joh., 343; Joh. Frdr., 494; Joh. Jacob, 541; Joh. Phil., 319; Joh. Thom., 494; Joh. Thomas, 490; Leonh., 490; Leonhard, 523, 541; Magdal., 490; Magdalena, 343, 523; Maria Barb., 494; Martin, 287, 359, 374; Michael, 301, 343, 374, 400; Philipp, 502; Susanna, 287, 301, 323, 359, 365, 374, 400, 411, 445, 464, 479, 502, 529; Susanne, 396
LYON, Dorothea, 326, 327; James, 326, 327
MCBARRIEL, William, 410
MACCAITAU, Cath., 308; Elis. Cath., 308; John, 308
MCCALLISTER, John, 544
MCCANNY, Mary, 362
MACCARNIE, James, 335
MCCLAIN, Alex., 336; Anna Maria, 336; Marg., 336
MACCLAINE, James, 355
MACCLAINE, John, 331
MACCLAINE, John, 355
MACCLAINE, Mary, 331
MCCLEAN, Elis., 419; Joh. Hnr., 419; Thomas, 419
MCCLOUD, Joh., 484; Marg., 455; Maria, 484; Mercur, 455
MCCLOY, Cath., 406; Susanne, 406
MCCLUR, Christine, 548
MCCONDRE, Hugh, 431
MCCONNET, Canoth, 377; Susanna, 377
MCCORD, John, 447
MCCORMICK, Christiana, 420
MCCUMBRE, Cath., 482; Humphrey, 482

MCDOWEL, Hugh, 419
MCGINNY, James, 420; Mary, 420
MCGOMERY, Mary, 300
MCKEE, Elis., 507; Eva, 467, 507; Isaac, 467, 507; William, 467
MACKENIGHT, John, 438; Marg., 438; William, 438
MCKINDLEY, Charles, 438; Eva, 438; Thomas, 438
MCKINLEY, Martha, 285; Sarah, 285
MCLAWSEN, Cath., 343; John, 343; Mary, 343
MCMULLIN, William, 291
MCNEAR, Elis., 542; Joh., 542
MCNEHR, Elis., 472; John, 472
MCQUINY, James, 278
MADER, Elis., 317; Joh., 317; Ludewig, 317
MAEINER, Hnr. Adam, 402; Maria, 402
MAENGEN, Cath., 381; Ernst, 291, 381; Joh., 381; Mar. Magdalena, 381; Maria, 291
MAERKER, Cath. Elis., 402; Charlotte Elis., 402; Frdr., 402
MAHN, An. Mar., 438; Anna Marg., 346; Anna Maria, 361, 415; Jacob, 285; Laurence, 310; Lorentz, 285, 346; Marg., 285, 310; Maria, 393; Peter, 361, 393, 409, 415, 438; Sara, 317, 346; Sara Elis., 284, 348, 369; Sarah, 339, 398, 408
MAHRLIN, Joh. Peter, 310; Maria Dorothea, 310
MAHRLING, Maria Dorothea, 360; Peter, 360
MALLER, Joh. Wilhelm, 380
MALLERY, Hanna, 278; James, 278
MALLIDORE, Elis., 475, 510; Georg, 475, 510; Hetty, 510
MALLO, Elis., 392; Georg, 392; Marg., 392
MALMITON, ELis., 399; Ferdinand, 399
MALTER, Elis. Charlotta, 446; Frdr Sebast., 446; Maria Elis., 446
MANCH, Marg., 332
MANCHEN, Cath., 336, 397, 407; Ernst, 294, 336, 357, 407; Joh., 336, 397, 407; Joh. Georg, 294; Joh. Hnr., 418; Marg. Magd., 357; Maria, 336; Maria Magdalena, 294; Sara, 407
MANFIELD, Elis., 542; James, 542; Sarah, 542
MANGEN, Cath., 278; Ernst, 278; Joh., 278; Joh. Ernst, 278
MANKESON, Appolonia, 335; Cath., 335; Cath. Maria, 335; Joh., 335; Mich., 335
MANMEIER, Maria Cath., 397
MANN, Ammy, 541; Anna, 461; Anna Maria, 382; Joh., 325, 489; Maria, 325;

Maria Barbara, 294; Peter, 325, 382, 461; Sarah Elis., 382
MANS, Cath., 283; Dr., 467
MANSCHER, Cath., 413; Joh., 413
MANSFELD, Anna Magdalena, 483; Joh., 483; Joseph, 483, 551; Maria, 551
MANSFIELD, Ann. Magdal., 453; Joseph, 453; Maria Philippina, 453
MANSFILD, Anna Elis., 414; Anna Magdalena, 414; Joseph, 414
MANTELIUS, Carl, 414; Christine, 414; Marcus, 414
MARDER, Frdr., 379; Mar. Elis., 379
MARET, Barbara, 371; Joh., 371
MARKER, Elis., 368, 387; Elis. Cath., 387; Elis. Charlotte, 387; Frdr. Sebast., 330; Jacob, 368, 387; Joh. Baltz., 387; Sebast. Franz, 387
MARKS, Anna Marg., 438; Elis., 438; Robert, 438
MARLING, Maria Cath., 326; Maria Dorothea, 326; Peter, 326
MARMUTON, Ferdinand, 354; Ludwig, 354; Maria Cath., 354
MARSHAL, Mary, 343
MARSTELLER, Jacob, 392
MARTIN, Aleck, 544; Cath. Barbara, 326; Elis., 326, 506; Franz, 506; Georg, 326, 360; James, 503; Jane, 503; Joh., 528; Joh. Carl, 506; John, 287; Maria, 326, 360, 528; Mary, 544; Michael, 360; Nancy, 503; Neal, 528, 544
MASHOLDER, Anna Marg., 349; Jacob, 277, 349, 370; Marg., 277, 370
MASON, Henry, 425; Mary, 425; William, 425
MASONER, Elis., 519; Jacob, 519; Mat., 519
MASS, Joh., 318
MASSHOLDER, Joh. Jacob, 304; Maria Magdalena, 304
MAST, Anna Eva, 359; Joh., 359
MASTER, Joh., 292
MATMAKEL, Elis., 363; Martha, 363
MATTER, Andreas, 337; Anna Maria, 337; Joh. Georg, 337
MATTERN, Andreas, 369, 400, 429, 439, 462, 467, 519; Anna Maria, 369, 400, 429, 439, 462, 467; Joh., 400; Joh. Adam, 467; Joh. Georg, 369; Maria, 519; Maria Christina, 439
MATZ, Anna Barbara, 439; Elis., 439; Joh., 439; Joh. Frdr., 439
MATZINGER, Job. Michael, 352; Joh. Melchior, 352
MATZMAN, Marg., 315
MAUER, Anna, 394

MAUK, Elis. Cath., 290; Joh. David, 290; Rosina, 290
MAUNTY, Cath., 549; Georg, 549
MAUR, Anna, 358; Maria, 433
MAURER, Adam, 278; Jacob, 330; John Jacob, 342; Ludwig, 278; Maria, 278, 330
MAUS, Elis., 291
MAUSS, Anna, 281; Cath., 313; Joh., 281; Joh. Christian, 281; Maria Elis., 391
MAUTI, Georg, 492; Jacob, 492; Marg., 492
MAUTS, Dorothea, 302; Georg, 302
MAUTTY, David, 299; Elis. Cath., 299; Rosina, 299
MAXEIMER, Marg., 532
MAY, Adam, 335; Anna, 335, 359; Anna Marg., 543; Anna Maria, 317, 359, 406; Cath., 543; Elis., 333, 456; Hnr., 317, 333; Maria, 456; Peter, 543; Philip, 317, 359, 406; Philipp, 456
MAYENMODER, Cath., 317; Ferdinand, 317
MAYER, Adam, 531; Andreas, 516; Anna Barbara, 531; Anna Marg., 532; Anna Maria, 461, 520; Carl, 513; Cath., 311, 461, 491, 497, 514, 524, 525, 544; Charlotta, 449; Christina Elis., 490, 525; Christoph, 490, 518; Daniel, 491, 519; Elis., 461, 490, 504, 509, 523; Frdr., 519, 524, 542, 544; Georg, 478, 544; Gottfried, 478, 532; Gottl., 490; Gottlieb, 453, 459, 480, 507, 544; Hanna, 529, 531; Henr., 497; Hnr., 311, 449, 461, 491, 504, 513, 514, 523, 525, 544; Hnr. Alexander, 311; Jacob, 477, 484, 490, 509, 513, 520, 523, 524; Joh., 460, 480, 490, 509, 520, 542, 544; Joh. Georg, 536, 544; Joh. Phil., 459; Joh. Philib, 453; Joseph, 516; Juliana, 484, 513, 523; Lorenz Hnr., 461; Magdal., 490; Magdalena, 453, 459, 480, 507, 544; Marg., 293, 458, 478, 519; Margareta, 490; Maria, 504, 509, 513, 516, 523, 542, 544; Mr., 529; Nicolaus, 424; Peter, 461; Philipp, 424; Salome, 424; Susanna, 536; Thomas, 293, 458
MAYERLE, Cath., 445; Conrad, 445; Esther, 445; Georg Conrad, 445; Phil., 445
MAYERLEY, Anna Esther, 463, 516; Elis., 463; Joh. Jacob, 516; Phil., 463; Philipp, 516
MAYERS, Elis., 522; Maria, 507, 527; Peter, 507, 527; Sarah, 507; Wilhelm, 527
MAYS, Abby, 417; Jacob, 417; Michael, 417
MEATY, Georg, 514; Marg., 514

MECK, Abraham, 477; Joh. Peter, 477;
Sarah, 477
MECKES, Polly, 403
MEDSCHILLER, Anna Marg., 434; Joh.,
434
MEELS, Anna Maria, 409; Elis., 409;
John, 409
MEGER, Cath. Salome, 488; Hanna, 481;
Jacob, 481; Joh. Georg, 481; Joh.
Wilhelm, 504; Maria Salome, 504;
Phil., 464; Philip, 386, 428; Philipp,
488, 504; Rahel, 464; Salome, 386,
464
MEHL, Cath., 380; Elis., 351; Elis. Cath.,
293; Frdr., 343, 351; Joh. Frdr., 293,
380; Magdalena, 343
MEHLS, Elis. Cath., 308; Joh. Frdr., 308
MEHR, Ester, 358
MEHRELIN, Jacob, 421; Maria, 421;
Peter, 421
MEHRLING, Mar. Barb., 390; Mar.
Dorothea, 390; Peter, 390
MEIDINGER, Elis., 523; Georg, 523;
Joh., 523
MEIER, Adam, 469; Andreas, 291, 499;
Anna Eva, 392; Anna Marg., 483;
Anna Maria, 289, 315, 378, 381, 437,
468; Anna Ursula, 402, 439; Barbara,
402; Benjamin, 326; Cath., 318, 347,
382, 406, 408, 410, 423, 425, 429,
439, 454, 455, 483; Charlotta
Eleonora, 381; Christina, 292, 328;
Christoph, 313, 392; Dorothea, 328;
Elis., 422, 423, 452, 499; Esther, 389;
Eva Cath., 313; Eva Christ., 390;
Frdr., 398, 468; Frederica, 469;
Georg, 471; Georg Frdr., 455; Georg
Hnr., 390; Hnr., 315, 347, 382, 402,
408, 423, 439, 454, 455, 468, 483;
Hnr. Andr., 406; Jacob, 286, 289,
315, 326, 381, 390, 422, 437, 439,
483; Joh., 359, 410, 429, 452; Joh.
Adam, 408; Joh. Christian, 378; Joh.
Frdr., 397, 398, 425, 452; Joh. Hnr.,
437; Joh. Michael, 410; Joh. Peter,
378; John Jacob, 323; John Martin,
328; Juliana, 439; Marg., 315, 354,
364, 382, 388, 406, 422, 425, 426,
468; Marg. Barbara, 468; Marg.
Cath., 425; Maria, 390, 397, 454;
Maria Cath., 359, 397; Maria
Christina, 359; Maria Clara, 291;
Maria Juliana, 323; Maria Marg., 483;
Matthew, 292; Regina, 326, 330;
Salome, 471; Sarah Elis., 398;
Susanna, 291; Susanne, 406; Thomas,
315, 354, 388, 406, 426, 483; Ursula,
468; William, 364
MEIERLE, Anna Esther, 408;
Christopher, 408; Philipp, 408

MEIERS, Anna Maria, 433; Cath., 426;
Hnr., 426; Maria Marg., 433; Peter,
433; Thomas, 426
MEIN, Cath., 437; John Hnr., 437
MEINECKE, Anna, 544; Gottlieb, 544;
Justina Maria, 544
MEISINGER, Hnr., 310; Joh., 310;
Juliana, 310
MEISTER, Cath. Elis., 376; Dorothea,
297, 302, 341, 376; Joh., 297, 302,
334, 341, 376; Joh. Nicolaus, 341;
Juliana, 302; Maria Dorothea, 334, 552
MEISTERZEIM, Emanuel, 422; Marg.,
422; Salome, 422
MEISTERZIM, Ann Marg., 393; Emanuel,
393; Marg., 393
MEIZERZEIM, Emanuel, 468; Georg,
468; Marg., 468
MELCHEN, Conrad, 301; Wilhelmina,
301
MELLS, Elis., 438; Joh., 438; Peter, 438
MEMMINGER, Georg, 289; Joh., 360;
Ludwig, 311; Maria, 289, 311, 360;
Theodorus, 289, 311, 360
MENAT, Gottfried, 356
MENGS, Cath., 549; John, 549; Maria,
549
MENOLD, Joh. Frdr., 392; Martin, 392,
411; Rosina, 392, 411
MENSER, Adam, 395; Maria Barbara,
395; Rosine, 395
MENTZER, Adam, 395; Maria Barbara,
395; Rosine, 395
MENZ, Elis., 414; Franc., 414
MENZER, Barb., 355; Marc., 433;
Salome, 433
MERANT, John Sanders, 301; Martha,
301; Philip, 301
MERCKEL, Anna, 441; Elis., 381; Georg,
353, 441; Jacob, 381; Marg., 401;
Nancy, 401
MERCKEN, Cath., 286; Peter, 286
MERCKER, Cath., 447; Elis., 463, 518,
525, 537; Elis. Charlott., 464; Elis.
Charlotta, 504; Elis. Charlotte, 542;
Frdr. Sebast., 464; Frdr. Sebastia, 542;
Frdr. Sebastian, 504; Jacob, 463, 518,
525, 537; Joh. Georg, 464; Joh. Hnr.,
542; Maria Marg., 504; Peter, 447;
Rebecca Doroth., 447
MERCY, Anna, 408; Elis., 408; John, 408
MERG, Barbara, 336
MERK, Ann, 431; Joh. Peter, 431; Regina,
531; Sarah, 431
MERKEL, Anna, 468; Anne, 372; Georg,
372, 468; Peter, 372
MERKER, Elis., 392, 478; Jacob, 392,
478; Maria Elis., 478
MERKLEY, Anna, 515; Carl, 515; Georg,
515

MERNER, Anna Maria, 309; Ludew.,
309
MERTZ, Andreas, 283; Joh., 405; Marg.,
497
MESS, Elis. Cath., 308; Joh. Frdr., 308
MESSERSCHMIDT, Andreas, 291; Anna
Barbara, 378; Barbara, 314, 423;
Cath., 291; Joh., 314, 378, 423; Joh.
Conrad, 291
MESSINGER, Maria, 413
MESSNER, Elis., 490, 544; Jacob, 490,
544; Joh., 544
METABERGER, Anna, 427
METER, Georg, 387
METSCH, Emanuel Wilhelm, Conrad,
513; Jenny, 513; Joh. Conrad, 513
METTS, Anna Barbara, 539; Joh., 539;
Joh. Michael, 539
METZ, Adam, 342, 371, 407, 445, 480,
519; Amelia, 399; Andreas, 334;
Anna Barbara, 294, 329, 364, 407,
470; Anna Marg., 334; Anna Maria,
488; Barbara, 342, 347, 371, 407,
445, 480, 488, 519; Cath., 470;
Daniel, 334; Elis., 342; Georg, 519;
Hnr., 399; Joh., 294, 329, 347, 364,
407, 470, 480, 488; Joh. Georg, 364;
Maria Marg., 329, 407; Michael, 399;
Nancy, 445; Susanna, 334
METZGER, Anna Barbara, 352; Cath.,
292, 471, 482, 535, 541; Elis., 352;
Elis. Dorothea, 317; Georg, 352;
Jacob, 292; Joh., 285; Joh. Gottlieb,
471, 541; Josua, 285, 317; Sophia,
285, 317
METZINGER, Adam, 514; Christina,
410; Elis., 514; Francisca, 410;
Georg, 514; Joh. Georg, 410; Joh.
Melchior, 410; Maria, 514; Maria
Christina, 410
METZNER, Cath., 467; Cath. Elis., 293,
364; Dietrich, 293, 467; Elis., 293;
Joh. Dietrich, 293; Mr., 364
MEYER, A. Maria, 534; Adam, 381, 538;
Andreas, 308, 342, 446; Anna, 535;
Anna Marg., 279; Anna Maria, 341;
Anna Ursula, 361, 381; Barbara, 552;
Cath., 326, 344, 383; Cath. Elis., 341;
Christina Elis., 326; Christoph, 299,
419, 542; Dorothea, 303; Elis., 283,
533, 552; Georg, 546; Hanna, 538;
Hnr., 344, 361, 381, 383, 535; Hrn.,
535; Jacob, 301, 341, 502, 533, 535;
Joh., 308, 383, 534, 542, 552; Joh.
Frdr., 344; Joh. Gottfried, 326; Joh.
Jacob, 342; Mar. Salome, 549; Marg.,
533, 552; Maria, 542; Maria Cath.,
549; Maria Clara, 308, 342; Maria
Rosina, 354; Mat., 351; Mich., 284;
Michael, 534; Philip, 549; Reg., 345;

Sara, 419; Sebastian, 283; Susanna,
502; Thomas, 279
MEYERLE, Anna Esther, 347, 376;
Gertraut, 347; Maria Magd., 376; Phil.,
376; Philip, 347
MEYERLEY, Hanna Esther, 480; Phil.,
480
MEZGER, Apollonia Cath., 344; Gottlieb,
425; Jacob, 344; Josua, 360; Maria
Magdalena, 344; Sophia, 360; Sophia
Dorothea, 360
MICHAEL, Joh., 312, 480; Susanna Cath.,
480
MICHEL, Maria Barbara, 517
MIERKEN, Anna Elis., 350; Cath., 281,
350, 405, 406; Peter, 281, 350, 405,
406; Sara, 405
MIERKLE, Cath., 307; Peter, 307
MIET, Elis., 311; Hnr., 305, 311
MIETH, Eva Elis., 291; Hnr., 291; Joh.
Peter, 291
MIETMAN, Barbara, 382; Euphronica,
382; Phil., 376; Philip, 382; Veronica,
376
MIETMANN, Cath., 310; Euphronia, 310;
Philip, 310; Philipp, 422; Veronica,
422
MILAN, Elis., 409; Jemina, 409; Joseph,
409
MILDEBERG, Cath., 339; Georg, 339
MILDEBERGER, Ann. Marg., 380; Anna
Cath., 312; Anna Marg., 288, 299, 323,
357, 410; Cath., 312, 344; Christina,
312; Elis., 344; Georg, 312, 344;
Marg., 288; Michael, 312, 344
MILDENBERGER, Cath., 494; Georg,
494
MILEHAM, Jane, 302; Joseph, 302;
Marg., 302
MILES, Elis., 361; John, 361; Peter, 361
MILLEBERGER, Michael, 462
MILLENBERGER, Cath., 474; Georg,
474; Susanna, 446
MILLER, Andreas, 461, 463; Anna Barb.,
457; Anna Barbara, 402, 478, 479, 503,
529; Anna Cath., 503; Anna Elis., 456,
515, 521; Anna Marg., 396; Anna
Maria, 412, 470; Anthon, 470; Barbara,
426, 439, 454, 463, 470, 473, 479, 483,
487, 506, 518, 525, 526, 534, 546, 548;
Carl, 402, 437, 457, 469, 479, 503,
506, 521, 529, 546; Cath., 319, 391,
445, 448, 473, 508; Cath. Dorothea,
534; Charlotta Eleonora, 381;
Charlotte, 408; Christian, 500, 526;
Christina, 319, 351, 437, 448, 483,
545; Christoph, 437, 470, 522, 537;
Conrad, 391; Daniel, 511; Eberhard,
518; Edward, 487; Ehrhard, 478, 483,
525; Elis., 408, 437, 438, 461, 470,

537; Georg, 351, 408, 459, 481;
Hannah, 307; Hantis, 286; Hnr., 426,
463, 484, 492, 515, 538, 545; Hnr.
Adam, 402; Jacob, 396, 409, 426,
438, 454, 463, 476, 481, 508, 518,
534; Joh., 381, 434, 438, 445, 456,
459, 461, 492, 495, 521, 530, 541,
552; Joh. Carl, 469, 529; Joh.
Christian, 470; Joh. Eberhard, 479;
Joh. Georg, 437; Joh. Georg Adam,
470; Joh. Nicol., 412; Joh. Peter, 479;
Juliana, 484; Magdalena, 437, 469,
515, 521; Mar., 403; Marg., 409, 437,
438, 495, 508, 511, 534, 541; Maria,
412, 424, 428, 459, 461, 463, 492,
530, 538, 545; Maria Cath., 500, 526;
Maria Marg., 500; Mat., 359;
Michael, 351, 437, 439, 448, 470,
473, 495, 513, 545; Nicol., 414;
Nicolaus, 307, 403, 424; Peter, 409,
508; Phil. Hnr., 457; Rosina, 513;
Salome, 439; Sarah, 476, 481, 511;
Susanna, 530; Wilh., 319
MILLS, Elis., 284, 369, 393, 505; Joh.,
323, 369, 393; Joh. Peter, 369; John,
284; Maria, 323; Maria Barbara, 323;
Maria Magdalena, 284
MILSELD, Joh., 546; Marg., 546
MILTEBERGER, Anna Cath., 385; Anna
Marg., 385, 399; Cath., 434; Georg,
385, 434; John Michael, 387; Marg.,
307; Regina, 434
MILTENBERGER, Anna Marg., 495;
Cath., 421, 491, 506, 521, 530, 541;
Dorothea, 491, 521; Georg, 421, 491,
506, 530, 541; Joh., 541; Marg., 285;
Mich., 491; Michael, 521; Rachel,
421; Susanna, 506
MINCER, Adam, 321; Cath., 321;
Rosina, 321
MINCK, Anna Cath., 278; Christian, 278;
Johannes, 278; Maria Sabina, 369
MINK, Cath., 369; Christian, 369
MIRKEL, Georg, 498; Magdal., 498
MISER, Elis., 381; Philipp, 381
MISTERZEN, Anna Marg., 545
MITCHEL, Christine, 510; Frdr., 510;
Maria, 510
MITCHELL, Joh., 300; Marg., 300
MITHARDT, Cath., 287; Hnr., 287;
Marg., 287
MITMAN, Euphronica, 349; Joh., 349;
Joh. Philip, 349
MITSCHEL, Mary, 292
MITTMANN, Pet. Wilhelm, 458; Phil.,
458; Veronica, 458
MOCH, Anna Maria, 290, 329; Frdr.,
290, 329; Joh. Frdr., 329

MOCK, An. Maria, 406; Anna Cath., 406;
Frdr., 388, 406; Hnr., 391; Joh. Adam,
388; Maria, 388; Sara, 391
MODDICK, Elis., 528; James, 528; Maria,
528
MOELLER, Anna Maria, 399; Esther, 399,
457; Hnr., 399, 457
MOELS, Cath. Elis., 317; Jacob, 317; Joh.
Frdr., 317
MOG, Anna, 281; Frdr., 352, 453, 484;
Hnr., 333; Joh., 453, 484; Maria, 333,
352, 453, 484; Maria Barbara, 352
MOGEL, Valentin, 321
MOHL, Elis., 491; Simon, 491
MOHN, Sara, 412
MOHR, An. Maria, 375, 391; Anna
Christina, 474; Barbara, 460, 467;
Benedict, 350; Cath., 415, 426, 452,
474, 518, 553; Christine, 391;
Christoh, 452; Christoph, 415, 426,
518, 553; Conrad, 424; Elis., 426;
Georg, 518, 553; Georg Wilhelm, 325;
Joh., 460; Joh. Hnr., 467; Johanna
Maria, 472; John, 467; Lorenz, 391;
Marg., 553; Maria, 460; Maria Elis.,
298; Philippina Elis., 325; Susanna,
350, 403, 424; Susanna Elis., 325;
Susanna Maria, 298, 375, 472, 480;
Wilh., 375; Wilhelm, 298, 350, 403,
424, 472, 480
MOHTZ, Barbara, 464, 553; Jacob, 553;
Joh. Michael, 464; Joseph, 553;
Salome, 464
MOLIDOR, Adam, 325, 364; Anna Marg.,
364; Joh., 341; Joh. Adam, 341; Marg.,
341
MOLITOR, Adam, 385, 452; Anna Marg.,
385; Cath., 452; Elis., 400; Georg, 385,
400; Peter, 452; Sarah, 385, 400
MOLL, Elis., 457, 465, 478, 551; Simon,
457, 465, 478, 551
MOLLEDORE, Anna Elis., 545; Georg,
545
MOLLER, P. Mat., 356; Philip Christian,
552; Samuel, 519
MOLLIN, Cath., 303; John, 303; Robert,
303
MOMBAUER, Magdalena, 385; Nicol.,
385
MONCH, Marg., 325
MONCHE, Henrich, 295; Marg., 295
MONSCH, Cath., 514; Didrich, 514; Hnr.,
514
MONTELIUS, Christina, 434; Elis., 434;
Marcus, 434
MONTH, Helena, 290; Lonnen, 290
MONTSEIS, Cath., 469; Dietrich, 469;
Elis., 469
MONTSU, Cath., 437; Dietrich, 437

MOOR, Anna Dorothea, 405; Cath., 490;
Christoph, 490; Elis., 363; Hnr.
Wilhelm, 490; Joh. Wilhelm, 449;
John, 405; Mary, 294; Samuel, 294,
363; Sarah, 405; Susanna Maria, 449;
Wilhelm, 449
MOORE, Cath., 312; Elis., 328, 330;
Hnr., 312; James, 330; John, 328,
412, 424; Joseph, 424; Maria, 312;
Mary, 330; Sara, 328; Sarah, 412, 424
MOOS, Anna Cath., 410; Cath., 372, 409,
448; Christopher, 372; Joh., 372, 409,
410, 448
MOOTZ, Barbara, 482; Jacob, 339, 482;
Joh. Christian, 482; Maria Barbara,
339
MORE, Esy, 342
MORGAN, Benjamin, 335; David, 375;
Hesther, 335; Joh., 335; Joseph, 466,
487; Marg., 487; Sophia, 466, 487;
Thomas, 371; William, 466
MORRIS, Abel Abraham, 526; Cath.,
526; Elis., 526
MORST, Anna Eva, 423; Jacob, 423;
Joh., 423
MOS, Cath., 338; Joh., 338, 380; Joh.
Peter, 338; Susanna, 380
MOSER, Adam, 503; Ann Doroth., 383;
Anna Cath., 409; Anna Dorothea,
316, 409, 464; Anna Maria, 464;
Cath., 373, 536; Christina, 494, 503,
536; Elis., 494; Georg, 383, 409, 464,
481, 503; Hanna, 481, 503; Hnr., 373,
457, 467, 494, 499, 503, 536; Jacob,
383, 536; Joh., 536; Joh. Christian,
316; Joh. Georg, 316; Susanna, 373,
499
MOSES, Anna Marg., 334; Cath., 334;
Hnr., 311, 334, 419, 462; Joh. Georg,
311; Philippina, 462; Susana, 462;
Susanna, 311; Susanne, 419
MOTSCHITLER, Anna Marg., 439; Joh.,
439
MOTSCHITTLER, Joh., 457; Joh. Mat.,
464
MOTSCHUTTER, Joh., 378
MOTSCHUTTING, Joh., 408
MOTZ, Anna Maria, 428; Barbara, 383,
428; Jacob, 360, 383, 387; Joh., 386;
Joh. Michael, 428; Maria Barbara,
360; Sara, 383; Sus. Barb., 387
MOXFELD, Anna Christina, 465
MUDSCHIDLER, Joh., 438
MUFF, Anna Elis., 285; Anton Ludwig,
547; Elis., 285, 326, 375; Georg, 285,
375; Jac. Martin, 375; Joh. Georg,
326
MUHLBRE, Anna Maria, 301
MUHLENBERG, Anna, 427, 444, 539;
Anna Maria, 301, 324, 356; Carl

Frdr., 429; Cath., 366, 375, 376, 382,
388, 425, 452, 457; Elis., 382; Frdr.,
382, 425; Frdr. A., 452; Frdr. August
Conrad, 429; Frdr. Augustus, 457;
G.H.E., 362, 376, 404, 407, 417, 430;
H., 414; H.M., 277, 293, 303; Hanna,
356, 429; Hnr., 313, 324, 356, 362,
366, 375, 388, 389; Hnr. Melch., 454;
Joh. Peter Jac., 486; Mar., 371; Mar.
Cath., 389; Maria, 336, 339, 388;
Maria Cath., 339, 362, 388; Maria
Esther, 356; Mary, 319; Melchior, 339;
Pastor, 309, 327, 346, 393, 394, 404,
434; Peter, 427, 429, 444, 539; Petrus,
356; Polly, 347; Rev., 336, 344, 414
MUHLLER, Eleonora, 331
MUHT, Cath., 489
MULLER, Abraham, 291; Adam, 304,
411; An. Marg., 377; Ann, 383; Anna,
550; Anna Magdalena, 310; Anna
Maria, 284, 302, 337, 342, 351, 375,
377; Anna Rosina, 304; Anna Ursula,
321; Barb., 418; Barbara, 404; Carl,
310, 341, 351, 354, 395; Caspar, 550;
Cath., 280, 282, 291, 305, 309, 310,
325, 340, 342, 358, 365, 550; Cath.
Dorothea, 367; Cath. Elis., 344; Cath.
Magd., 395; Charlotta, 278; Christian,
375, 550; Christina, 304, 309, 336;
Christina Elis., 291; Christine, 396;
Christoph, 322, 358, 396; Conrad, 280,
282, 325, 365, 495; Daniel, 550; Elis.,
284, 302, 322, 323, 330, 350, 358, 372,
387, 396; Esther, 433; Frdr., 309;
Georg, 547; Georg Hnr., 433; Hanna,
367; Henry, 383; Hnr., 430, 433;
Jacob, 335, 352, 354, 367, 550; Joh.,
278, 315, 330, 384, 387, 396, 550; Joh.
Adolph, 550; Joh. Christ., 344; Joh.
Frdr., 367; Joh. Georg, 336, 337; Joh.
Hnr., 344; Joh. Jacob, 350; Joh.
Michael, 547; Joh. Nicolaus, 337; Joh.
Phil., 372; Joh. Wilhelm, 291;
Magdalena, 495; Marg., 335, 354, 367,
495, 547, 550; Marg. Elis., 396; Maria,
315, 335, 341, 384, 418, 430, 550;
Maria Louisa, 306; Maria Magdalene,
395; Mat., 394, 419; Michael, 309,
336, 370, 396, 404, 418; Nicol., 375;
Nicolaus, 284, 302, 342, 351, 377;
Philipp, 309, 322; Salome, 309;
Samuel, 404; Sara, 315; Sophia
Dorothea, 367; William, 291
MULLY, Christina, 311; Elis. Cath., 311;
Sebastian, 311
MUMBAUER, Magdalena, 353; Nicolaus,
353
MUNCH, Philippina, 312
MUNCHEN, Elis., 531
MUNNICH, Gottfried, 514; Veronica, 514

MUNSEAS, Cath., 367; Frdr., 367; Peter, 367
MUNSTER, Adam, 359; Alexander, 289; Philip Jacob, 289; Rosina, 359
MUNTZER, Sara Elis., 548
MUNZER, Adam, 427, 475; Barbara, 359; David, 321; Georg, 427; Jemima, 321; Lovina, 427; Marc., 377; Marg., 475; Richard, 321; Rosina, 475; Sara, 377
MURKEN, Jacob, 332
MURRAY, Cath., 452
MUSSKY, Adam, 501; Cath., 501
MUT, Anthon, 516; Cath., 491; Elis., 491, 519, 549; Joh., 491, 519, 549
MUTSCHIDLER, Joh., 310; Marg., 310
MUTSCHITLER, Anna Marg., 457; Joh., 457
MUTSCHITTLER, Joh., 312
MUTZFELD, Joh. Gerhard, 277; Joh. Jacob, 277; Maria Barbara, 277
MUTZHELD, Anna Marg., 349; Barbara, 349; Joh. Gerhard, 349
NAAS, Anne Elis., 355; Philip, 355
NAEF, Magd., 386; Marg., 394; Melchior, 386, 394
NAEGEL, Anna, 441; Hnr., 454; Jacob, 454; Marg., 454
NAEGELE, Mich., 378; Sophia, 378
NAEVE, Marg., 285
NAEVI, Cath., 314; Elis., 314; Joh., 314
NAGEL, Anna, 284, 317; Anna Elis., 416; Barbara, 424, 456, 486, 498, 550; Carl, 490; Cath., 498, 550; Cath. Ursula, 485; Christian, 295, 297, 349, 388; Christina, 418; Elis., 295, 297, 349, 388, 441, 456, 465, 498, 548; Georg, 295, 297; Hnr., 277, 374, 397, 424, 456, 485, 486, 498, 548, 550; Jacob, 397; Joh., 388, 441, 456, 457, 465, 498, 500, 548; Joh. Hnr., 348, 548; Joh. Remigius, 465; Joseph, 317; Magdalena, 441; Magdalena Elis., 500; Maria, 523; Maria Cath., 369, 500; Peter, 284; Rudolp, 348; Rudolph, 302, 315, 369, 397, 416, 422, 457, 473, 490, 494, 505, 523, 536; Sus. Magdalena, 473; Susanna, 348, 369, 397, 416, 422, 457, 473, 490, 494, 505, 523, 536
NAGELE, Cath., 323; Jacob, 323, 462; Marg., 462; Susanna, 323
NAGELI, Marg., 306; Thomas, 306
NAPP, Rebecca, 525; Samuel, 525; Thomas, 525
NASSAU-USINGER, Durlaucht, 505
NAUMANN, Daniel, 294, 390; Joh., 390; Maria, 390
NEBEL, Frdr., 309, 314; Joh. Hnr., 309, 314; Marg., 309, 314

NEES, Anna Clara Doroth., 359; Joh., 359; Joh. David, 359
NEESS, Clara, 552; Joh. David, 552; Philip Hnr., 552
NEFF, Hatty, 550
NEGELE, Anna, 371; Anna Maria, 359; Jacob, 371; Johna Wilh., 359; Sophia, 359; Wilhelm, 371
NEGER, Christian, 472
NEGRO, Cath., 463; David, 352; Devonshire, 352; Dobling, 453; Elis., 453; Euphronia, 414; Hanna, 453; Jacob, 414; Joseph, 463; Rosina, 352; Sabine, 463; Susanna, 352; Thomas, 352
NEIDLINGER, Maria Elis., 413; Samuel, 413
NEISCHWANGER, Anna, 320
NEISCHWENNER, Conrad, 534, 548; Eva, 549; Joh., 549; Peter, 549; Sibilla, 548; Sibille, 534
NEISS, Anna, 520; Barbara, 520; Jacob, 493; Magnus, 493, 520
NEISWANDER, Christine, 357
NELSON, James, 311; Marg., 311
NENNI, Anna Cath., 447; Jacob, 447
NESCH, Esther, 277; Maria Dorothea, 277
NESLE, Cath., 431; Jacob, 431; Marg., 431
NESSELSTRAW, Anna Maria, 413; Joh. Andreas, 413
NESSLER, Anna Marg., 366; Elis., 366; Jacob, 366
NEU, Anna Marg., 545; Anna Maria, 414, 474, 545; Cath., 474; Elis., 414, 435, 503, 545; Joh., 474, 503, 545; John, 435; Lud., 435; Mar. El. An., 435; Marg., 545; Maria, 503, 526; Maria Elis., 435; Peter, 474, 503, 545; Wilhelm Joh., 414
NEUHAUSS, Daniel, 450; Juliana, 450, 526; Philip, 450; Philipp, 526; Polly, 526
NEUHEUER, Jacob, 426; Juliana, 426; Philipp, 426
NEUMAN, Daniel, 381; Marg., 381
NEUMANN, Cath., 371; Daniel Peter, 371; Hnr., 371
NICHOLSON, Esther, 501; Maria Marg., 501; Peter, 501
NICHS, Cath., 434; David, 434; Dorothea, 434
NICK, Joh., 502, 551; Marg. Eva, 502; Maria Dorothea, 551; Maria Eva, 336; Regina, 502; Regine, 551; Wilhelm, 336
NICOLSIN, Hanna, 412; Wilh., 412
NIEMAN, Georg, 549; Joh., 549; Maria, 549

NIEMAND, Joh., 489, 517; Joh. Ludw., 489; Maria, 517; Polly, 489
NIES, Clara Dorothea, 455; David, 455; Dorothea, 412; Joh. David, 412
NIESS, Clara, 517, 524; David, 517, 524; Maria Marg., 517
NIGHT, Elis., 318, 505; Howard, 505; Joh., 505; John, 318; William, 318
NIGLIE, Jacob, 496; Susanna, 496; Wilhelm, 496
NITZEL, Anna Elis., 336; Pancratius, 322, 336
NOEL, Jacob, 537; Marg., 537; Nicolaus, 537
NOLE, Elis., 362; Martin, 362
NOLL, Ann, 465; Anton, 389; Barbara, 448; Christina, 455; Elis., 343, 465; Elis. Barbara, 389; Georg, 455; Martin, 343, 389, 448, 465; Martin Frdr., 343; Wilhelm, 455
NOLT, Christine, 372; Maria, 372; Wilhelm, 372
NONNECKER, Cath., 530; Jacob, 530
NONNEMACHER, Cath., 493; Georg, 493; Marg., 493
NONNEMAKER, Cath., 449; Georg, 449; Joh., 449
NORRIS, John, 300; Maria, 300
NORTH, Joh. Jacob, 311; William, 311
NOTZ, Christoph, 414; Marg., 323
NUNNEMACHER, Mich., 300; Salome, 300
NUSHAG, Carl, 413; Carl Wilhelm, 413, 487, 540; Cath., 413, 454, 487; Jacob, 487; Maria Cath., 540; Michael, 540; Wilhelm, 454
NUSHANG, Anna Cath., 365; Carl, 365
NUSKE, Joh., 529; Joh. Hnr., 529; Maria Elis., 529
NUSSACK, Anna Barbara, 305; Carl Wilhelm, 305; Maria Cath., 305
NUTTER, Anna Maria, 321; Henry, 321
OAR, Elis., 355; John, 355; Sarah, 355
OBER (see also UBER), David, 471; Hanna, 471; Joh. Adam, 471
OBERDOFT, Anna Maria, 413; Caspar, 413; Marg., 413
OBERDORF, Andreas, 285; Anna Cath., 365; Casp., 365; Caspar, 322; Casper, 291; Cath., 535; Elis., 322; Esther, 285; Jacob, 291; Joh. Andreas, 285; Marg., 291, 322; Michael, 535
OBERDORFF, Andreas, 542; Caspar, 495; Cath., 542; Elis., 542; Marg., 495; Michael, 542
OBERDORFFER, Salome, 478
OBERHORSTMEISTER, Lord Tutor, 505
OBERSLEY, Joh. Jacob, 408

OBERSTECH, Anna Marg., 536; Christian, 435, 478, 536; Jacob, 435; Joh., 478; Marg., 435, 478, 517; Rebecca, 517
OBERSTEG, Christian, 360, 387, 427; Elis., 387; Jacob, 427; Joh. Gerhard, 360; Marg., 360, 387, 427
OBSTRASS, Wilhelmina, 461
OCHS, Anna Marg., 539; Barbara, 497, 539; Georg, 497; Jacob, 497, 539
ODENHEIMER, Anna Cath., 351; Joh., 325, 351; Keppele, 325; Maria, 325, 351
ODENWALTER, Nicolaus, 285
ODMERALTER, Nicolaus, 285
OERINGER, Hanna, 328; Jacob, 328
OESCHSLE, Joh., 469
OESTERK, Georg, 453
OESTERLE, Charlotte, 513; Georg, 322, 374, 501, 513; Georg Jacob, 320; Maria, 320, 322, 374
OESTERLEY, Anna Charlotta, 517; Georg, 517
OESTERLI, Georg, 316; Maria, 316
OESTERLING, Georg, 336; Maria, 336
OESTERTAG, Georg, 454
OHL, Adam, 278, 300, 340; Anna Marg., 300; Cath. Elis., 340; Joh. Georg, 340; Maria Christina, 278, 300, 340
OHLER, Andreas, 479; Cath., 351, 479, 519; Philipp, 351, 519; Regina Barbara, 479
OHNANGST (see also UNANGST), Joh., 461
OHRLAPP, Joh. Adam, 473
OLDFIELD, Ann, 328; Cath., 328; William, 328
OLIVER, John, 404; Maria, 404; William, 404
OMENSETTER, Anna Sophia, 372; Cath., 318, 385, 421; Elis., 333, 386, 410, 451, 534, 549; Jac., 386; Jacob, 333, 410, 451, 534, 549; Joh., 369; Joh. Frdr., 385; Joh. Georg, 369; Joh. Peter, 451; Mich., 385, 421; Michael, 318; Paul Caspar, 410; Philip Jacob, 534; Salome, 333
OPERER, Barbara, 398; Peter, 398
OPMAN, Elis., 347; Lorentz, 347; Lorenz, 332; Marg., 332
OPMANN, Anna Maria, 311; Lorentz, 311; Maria Marg., 311
OPP, Maria, 462
OPPERMANN, Adam, 518; Maria, 518
OPPMAN, Lorenz, 295
OPPMANN, Anna Marg., 341; Lorenz, 326, 341; Marg., 326; Mat., 341
ORANGE, Hanna, 328; Jacob, 328
ORMAN, Albertina, 282; Andreas, 282; Charlotta, 282

ORN, Dorothea, 347; Elis., 347; Frdr.,
347; Jacob, 486
ORNER, Anna Maria, 292, 308; Michael,
292, 308
ORT, Cath., 476, 500; Conrad, 476, 500;
Joh., 476, 500
OSIAS, Maria, 482; Peter, 482
OSIOUS, Maria, 423; Peter, 423
OSTER, Elis., 525; Elis. Cath., 525; Joh.
Peter, 525
OSTERLIN, Georg, 323; Maria, 323
OSTERMANN, Anna Elis., 543; Elis.
Cath., 543; Peter, 543
OSTERTAG, Eva Cath., 363, 407; Joh.,
345, 363, 407; Joh. Adam, 363; Joh.
David, 407; Regina Cath., 345
OTMAN, Anton, 394
OTT, Anna Maria, 399, 528; Cath., 282,
427, 455, 488; Clementina Juliana,
455; Conrad, 528; Dav., 393; David,
393, 427, 455, 488, 544; Elis., 488;
Esther, 314; Georg, 528; Jacob, 282;
Joh., 427; Joh. Phil. David, 407;
Magdalena, 528; Regina, 411
OTTO, Anna Maria, 402; Hanna, 491;
Hnr., 353, 402; Joh., 491; Marg., 313;
Podo, 313; Wilhelm, 491
OTTS, Jus., 455
OXLE, Johannes, 285; Maria, 285
OXLEIN, Joh., 334; Joh. Casper, 334;
Magdalena, 334
OXSFEL, Hnr., 348
OZEAS, Magdalena, 480; Mary, 519;
Peter, 480, 519
OZEUS, Magd., 452; Peter, 452
PACHTEL, Elis., 448; Georg, 448
PAESCH, Anna Barb., 405
PAETHIS, Barbara, 320, 406; Conrad,
320, 406; Elis., 320; Wilhelm, 406
PAETHYS, Barbara, 521; Conrad, 521
PAETSCH, Anna Maria, 300, 337; Cath.,
403, 510; David, 300, 337; Frdr.
David, 510; Georg, 403; Joh. Georg,
510; Joh. Michael, 300; Regina Cath.,
300
PAFHAUSSER, Jacob, 346; Susanna,
346
PAIL, Cath., 303; Mary, 303; Nathaniel,
303
PAIN, Mary, 300
PAINTER (see also BENTER, PENTER),
Christina, 300; Elis., 300; Joh., 300,
511, 540; John, 300; Philip Wilhelm,
300; Susanna, 511, 540
PAIS, Anna Maria, 306
PAISCH (see also BAISCH), Dorothea
Magdalena, 317; Joh. Frdr., 279; Joh.
Martin, 317; Magdalena, 308, 317;
Maria Eva, 279; Martin, 308, 317

PALLEN, Anna, 552; Isaac, 552; Joh., 552
PANKUCH, Cath., 347; Maria, 347;
Philip, 347
PANKUCHEN, Ludw., 433; Magdalena,
433; Maria, 407; Philip, 407
PANNAKUCHE, John Ludwig, 319
PANNEKUCH, Anna Cath., 365; Maria,
413; Philip, 413
PANNEKUCHE, Cath., 398; Joh. Georg,
377; Maria, 377; Phil., 377, 398
PANNEKUCHEN, Cath., 489; Elis., 433;
Joh., 476; Maria, 433, 476; Phil., 433,
476, 489
PANNER, Anna Cath., 299; Joh., 299
PANNKUCHEN, Ludwig, 373; Maria,
373, 376; Maria Magd., 373; Phil., 376
PANTLEON (see also BANTHLEON,
PONTLEON), Cath., 457; Christoph
Frdr., 457
PANZER (see also BANZER, SPENCER),
Elis., 338, 367, 396, 400, 414, 436,
460, 492, 514; Joh. Adam, 338; Joh.
Gottlieb, 367; Maria, 514; Maria Cath.,
492; Nicol., 460, 492, 514; Nicolaus,
338, 400, 414, 436
PARISS, Veronica, 518
PARLINGER, Elis., 503; Ludwig, 503;
Maria Cath., 503
PARMER, Rachel, 277
PARROT, John, 333
PARRY, Alexander, 442; Georg
Washington, 494; Hnr., 442; James,
494; Jeaney, 442; Maria, 494; Martin,
494
PARTSCH, Andreas, 279
PASCHETOW, Christian, 380; Christine,
380
PASHETY, Christian, 412; Christina, 412;
Elis., 412
PATER, Abraham, 532; Georg, 381;
Marg., 381; Maria, 381, 532
PATSCHE (see also BETSCH), Joh., 337;
Michael, 337; Regina Marg., 337
PATT, Philippine Elis., 290
PATTERSON, Barbara, 511; Joh. Georg,
511; Richard, 511
PATTO, Elis., 401; Marg., 401; Wilhelm,
401
PATZ, Rosina, 328; Thomas, 328
PAUEL, Anna Maria, 483; Georg, 483
PAUER, An. Marg., 405; Anna Maria,
375; Joh. Georg, 405; Peter, 375
PAUL, Andreas, 426; Anna Barbara, 297;
Anna Maria, 295, 302, 346, 415;
Caspar, 441; Cath., 371, 509, 545;
Christina Marg., 509; Dor. Susanna,
441; Elis., 309, 329, 371, 426, 473,
509, 545; Frdr., 309, 329, 371, 426,
473, 509, 545; Georg, 473; Hnr., 309;
Joh., 295, 329, 424; Joh. Hnr., 297;

Joh. Wilhelm, 415; Joseph, 346; Mar.
Elis., 424; Maria, 410, 451; Mary,
335; Peter, 295, 302, 335, 346, 410,
415
PAULI, Anna Marg., 298, 303; Carl
Philip, 298; Christian, 298, 303
PAULSON, Marg., 363
PAULUS, Anna Marg., 453; Jacob, 294;
Joh. Christoph, 492; Joh. Nicol., 492;
Marg., 453, 492; Nicolaus, 453
PAUSCH, Adam, 343, 413, 442, 469;
Anna Marg., 343; Anna Maria, 343,
413, 442, 469; Elis., 442; Joh. Jacob,
469
PAYSCH, Joh. Martin, 344; Magdalena,
344; Marg., 344
PEARS, Elis., 448; Joh., 448; Maria, 448
PEARSEY, Christian, 516; Elis., 516
PEARSY, Christian, 448, 476; Elis., 447,
476; Hnr., 448; Jacob, 447; Maria,
447, 448
PEARY, Elis., 407; George, 407
PECHTEL (see also BECHTEL), Cath.,
287; Joh., 392; Joh. Georg, 287;
Susanna, 287, 392
PECHTHOLD, Anna Maria, 459; Maria,
512; Phil. Jacob, 459, 512
PECHTOLD, Elis., 353
PECK, Anna Maria, 509; Joh., 414, 509
PEGNAM, Barbara, 384; James, 384;
Maria, 384
PEIL (see also PFEIL, FEIL), Maria
Dorothea, 531
PEISCH, Dorothea, 401; Maria Magd.,
401; Martin, 401
PELLFORD, Elis. Marg., 421; Major,
421
PENDER, Daniel, 314; Esther, 314;
Sophia Susanna, 314
PENNIGHOF, Jacob, 360, 387; Sara,
360; Sibylla, 387; Susanna Barbara,
387
PENNIGHOFF, Jacob, 419; Maria, 419;
Sybilla, 419
PENNIHOF, Jacob, 383; Sara, 383
PENNIKOF, Jacob, 298, 302; Joh., 302;
Mrs., 350; Sibilla, 298; Sybilla, 302
PENNIKOP, Jacob, 353; Maria, 353;
Sybilla, 353
PENNROSE, Abigail Whyle David, 398;
Abraham, 398; Joseph, 398
PENNY, John Michael, 311; Michael,
311; Rosina, 311
PENROSE, Joseph, 369
PENSEN, Alexander, 551; Marg., 551
PENTER (see also BENTER, PAINTER),
Christopher, 279; Dorothea, 279, 353;
Elis., 354; Jacob, 279, 353, 354; Joh.,
353, 419; John, 340; Ludwig, 316;

Mary, 354; Susanna, 340, 353;
Susanne, 419
PENTOR, George, 328; Joh., 328;
Susanna, 328
PENZ, Franciscus Wulf, 304; Georg, 304;
Hanna, 304
PEPPER, Maria, 536
PERRY, Marg., 540; Maria, 342, 540;
Martin, 284, 342, 540; Mary, 284;
Robert, 284; William, 342
PERSIE, Anna Marg., 291; Anna Maria,
291; Christian, 279, 327, 346, 368;
Elis., 346; Georg, 327; Jacob, 291; Joh.
Jacob, 279; Maria, 327, 346, 368;
Maria Magdal., 279; Wilhelm, 368
PERSSEL, Christina, 314; Elis., 314
PERSY, Henrietta, 374; James, 374
PERTSCH (see also BERTSCH),
Christine, 309; Elis., 309
PESCHEL, Jacob, 326; Joh. Georg, 326;
Susanna, 326
PEST, Charlotta, 487; Georg, 487
PETER, Augustus, 510; Caspar, 286;
Daniel, 295; Elis., 510; Ludwig, 510;
Magdalena Maria, 286; Sophia
Susanna, 295
PETERS, Christoph, 532; Elis., 452, 532;
Jesaias, 452; Marg., 532; Rosina Marg.,
452
PETERSON, Anna Barbara, 295; Elis.,
382
PETRI, Elis., 509
PETRIE, Anna, 388; Jacob, 388; Rosina,
388
PEUSCH, Cath., 455; Joh. Georg, 428;
Maria Magdal., 428; Maria Magdalena,
455; Martin, 428, 455
PEW, Anna Cath., 429; Barbara, 412, 429;
William, 412, 429
PEYER, Andreas, 501; Barbara, 501;
Cath., 501
PFANKUCHE, Cath., 545; Phil., 545
PFANKUCHEN, Anna Marg., 309; Anna
Maria, 309; Maria, 437; Peter, 309;
Philipp, 309, 437
PFANNEKUCH, Anna Marg., 290; Anna
Maria, 290, 464; Cath., 502, 503, 529;
Peter, 290; Phil., 464, 529; Philip, 290;
Philipp, 502, 503
PFANNEKUCHEN, Cath., 517; Marg.,
517; Phil., 517
PFAU, Barbara, 453; Elis., 458; Joh., 458,
470, 512; Maria, 512; Maria Elis., 470;
William, 453
PFEIFER, Michael, 411; Regina, 411;
Susanna, 411; Susanna Cath., 411
PFEIFFER, Adam, 334; Barbara, 292, 334;
Hanna, 367; Hnr., 408; Jacob, 292,
334; Joh., 478; Joh. Michael, 452; Mar.
Elis., 367; Michael, 367, 452, 477;

POLMER, Cath., 534; Michael, 534
PONTEY, Anna, 384; Elis., 384; Will., 384
PONTIUS, An. Elis., 405; Anna Barb., 405; Elis., 370; Joh., 370; Joh. Adam, 370; Joh. David, 405
PONTLEON (see also PANTLEON), Frdr., 490; Regina Cath., 490; Susanna, 490; Wilhelm, 490
POOL, Anna, 467; Elis., 467; William, 467
POOLE, Anna, 282; Barbara, 282; Samuel, 282; William, 282
POP (see also BOP, BOB), Barbara, 380; Elis., 354, 546; Georg, 380, 472; Joh. Jacob, 354; Joh. Philip, 354; Maria, 380, 472; Peter, 472
POPA, Andr. Christoph, 453; Maria, 453
PORTER, Cath., 489; James, 489; John, 489
POSARD, Andreas, 412
POT, Anna Maria, 514, 537; Cath., 301, 527; Cath. Elis., 341, 347, 519; Elis., 514; Hnr., 514, 519, 527; Joh. Hnr., 301, 341, 347; Joh. Peter, 347
POTE, Joh. Mathias, 537; Veronica, 537
POT(H) (see also BOT(H), BOOT(H), POOT), Mathias, 528; Veronica, 528
POTT, Elis., 512; Joh., 512; Maria, 512
POTT(S), Elis., 335, 512; Joh., 512; John, 335; Maria, 512; Mary, 335
POWEL, Barbara, 432; Wilh., 373; William, 432
PREDIN, Maria Christina, 451; William, 451
PREFFONTAIN, Leah, 445; Peter, 445
PREIS, Anna, 414; Anna Maria, 419; Carl, 419, 420, 428, 443, 452; Cath., 468; Elis., 476; Georg, 456; Jacob, 414; Joh., 358, 456; Joh. Carl, 395; John, 414; Magdalena, 452; Magdalene, 395; Mar. Cath., 456; Marg. Dorothea, 395; Maria, 443; Maria Magd., 358, 420; Maria Magdalena, 428, 443, 452; Mr., 298; Peter, 468; Regina Barbara, 420
PREISS, Adam, 494; Anna Maria, 367, 494; Cath., 534, 541; Elis., 343; Jacob, 550; Joh., 344, 541; Ludw., 494; Ludwig, 550; Maria, 534, 550; Mat., 343; Michael, 367; Peter, 343, 534
PRENZ, Anna, 389; Jacob, 389; Samuel, 389
PREUS, Marg., 487; Maria, 483, 487; Michael, 483, 487
PREUSCH, Anna Maria, 334; Joh., 361, 412; Joh. Frdr., 334; Joh. Mat., 334; Joh. Michael, 334, 361, 412; Marg., 439; Maria, 361, 439, 465; Maria

Cath., 412; Maria Elis., 465; Michael, 439, 465
PREUSS, Carl, 344; Elis., 464; Joh., 499; Josua, 499; Maria Cath., 499; Maria Magdalena, 344; Michael, 464
PRICE, Elis., 376; Marg., 418; Mat., 376
PRINTZ, Anna, 277; Samuel, 277
PRINZ, Anna, 312, 349, 472; Anna Susanne, 432; Barbara, 510, 529, 530; Cath., 472, 549; Georg, 529, 549; Jacob, 529, 530; Joh., 349, 529; Joh. Jacob, 510; Magdalena, 529; Rosina, 312; Samuel, 312; Samuel, 349, 432, 472; Susanne, 432
QUADT, Benjamin, 420; Charlotte, 420; Joh. Benjamin, 420
QUAIL, Thomas, 497
QUAST, Georg, 500, 552; Maria, 500, 521, 552; Nicol., 521; Nicolaus, 500, 552; Sarah, 521
QUENDEL, Joh. Daniel, 412
QUIN, Anna Barbara, 359; Anna Cath., 359; Patrick, 359
QUINOP, Christina, 480, 502; Georg, 480, 502; Maria Magdalena, 502; William, 480
QUIRE, Anna Maria, 474; Jeany, 474; Wilhelm, 474
RAB, Joseph, 339; Maria, 339; Martin, 389; Sabina, 389
RABASIN, Cath., 467
RABATEAU, Cornelius, 301; Jacob, 301; Maria, 301
RADLERE, Joh., 528; Marg., 528
RAEDINGER, Wilhelm, 427
RAESLER, Jacob, 522
RAHN, Hnr., 336; Magdalena, 336
RAM, Joseph, 339; Maria, 339
RAMBO, Gabriel, 299; Theodor William, 299
RAMBOW, Cath., 341; Gabriel, 341; Mary, 341
RAMIN, Elis., 546; Lorentz, 546
RAMMINGER, Barb., 359; Barbara, 412
RANCK, Cath., 466; Frdr., 466; Frdr. Gottlieb, 466
RANNINGER, Carl Ulrich, 455; Jacob, 455; Magdalena, 455
RAP, Elis., 394, 501, 547; Frdr. Jacob, 501; Gottfried, 394; Joh., 501; Joh. Carl, 501; Mar. Salome, 412; Martin, 412; Regina, 394
RAPP, Elis., 443, 551; Frdr., 551; Frdr. Jacob, 551; Gottfried, 443; Joh. Martin, 315, 494; Mar. Sabina, 494; Maria Marg., 492; Maria Sabina, 493; Martin, 492, 493; Rosina Amelia, 443
RASS, Cath., 375
RATH, An. Maria, 392; Andr., 392; Conrad, 392

REIMEL, Cath., 441; Elis., 441, 485,
530; Joh., 441, 485, 530
REIMET, Elis., 467; Jacob, 467; Joh.,
467
REIN, Adam, 434; Anna Maria, 434;
Barb., 395; Cath., 332; Christina
Susanna, 434; Felix, 332; Joseph,
332; Maria, 390
REINBOLD, Barbara, 496; Frdr., 496
REINBOOT, Anna Barbara, 486; Frdr.,
486
REINBOT, Barbara, 513; Frdr., 513, 526;
Joh. Frdr., 513
REINECKE, Frdr., 452
REINHARD, Anna, 497, 522; Anna
Barbara, 297, 341, 542; Anna
Dorothea, 522; Elis., 440; Georg, 329,
369, 440, 529; Georg Valentin, 341;
Joh., 297, 341, 542; Joh. Hnr., 297;
Joh. Mart., 497; Joh. Michael, 329;
Johanna Elis., 446; Lorenz, 446;
Magdalena, 440, 529; Maria Magd.,
369; Maria Magdalena, 329; Martin,
522; Regina Marg., 369; Sarah, 545;
Simon, 497
REINHARDT, Anna, 291; Elis., 292;
Georg, 401; Joh., 291; Mar. Magdal.,
401
REINHOLD, Anna Cath., 332; Christoph,
335; Daniel, 441; Frdr., 332, 517;
Georg Christoph, 298, 366, 388, 441,
517; George, 298; Hnr., 388; Joh.
Lorenz, 332; Marg. Elis., 335; Maria,
298, 335, 366, 388, 441, 517; Maria
Elis., 335
REININGER, Adam, 476, 507; Cath.,
392; Jacob, 392; Joh., 507; Joh.
Georg, 392; Marg., 476; Susanna,
476, 507
REINTALER, Anna Maria, 329;
Christoph, 378; Elis., 378; Jacob, 329;
Wilh., 378
REINTHAL, Elis., 308; Jacob, 308; Joh.
Christoph, 308
REINTHALER, Christoph, 341, 446;
Elis., 341, 446; Jacob, 278, 292, 341;
Joh., 446; Maria, 278, 341
REIS, Andr., 382; Anna, 417; Cath., 453;
Elis., 411; Georg, 326; Hanna, 411,
430; Hnr., 411, 417, 430; Jacob, 453;
Joh., 382; Maria, 326; Maria
Magdalena, 453; Sus., 382; Valentin,
380; Zacharias, 326
REISE, Eva, 411; Jacob, 411
REISER, Anna, 531; Anna Maria, 292,
308; Cath., 292, 435, 449, 462, 531;
Christina, 292; Eva, 435, 474; Eva
Christina, 449, 531; Jacob, 292, 435,
449, 474, 531; Joh. Joseph, 435;

Marg., 449; Maria, 531; Martin, 292,
435, 449, 462; Samuel, 462; Sarah, 474
REISS, Anna Maria, 458; Brunne, 491;
Cath., 491; Christina, 489; Conrad,
528; Elis., 492; Hanna, 438, 458, 486,
489, 494, 523, 528; Hnr., 438, 458,
486, 489, 492, 494, 523; Nicolaus,
438; Sally, 523; Susan, 345; Susanna,
381
REISSER, Cath., 395, 398, 433; Elis., 398,
433; Eva, 398; Eva Christine, 433; Eva
Maria, 430; Georg Ludwig, 499; Jacob,
398, 430, 433; Joh., 499; Joh. Georg,
395; Magdalena, 499; Maria, 398;
Martin, 395, 398
REIT, Cath., 550; Joh., 550; Wilhelm, 550
REITE, Joh., 443
REITEBACH, Sab. Marg., 370
REITER, Philip, 433
REITZ, Anna Maria, 286
REMM, Elis., 459; Michael, 459
REN, Marg., 489
RENDSHEIMER, Christina, 410; Maria,
410
RENK, Joh., 325; Magdalena, 325;
Susanna, 325
RENN, Cath., 300, 458, 487; Elis., 481,
483; Frdr., 486; Joh. Frdr., 300, 458,
487
RENS, Sus., 486
REP, Christina, 409; Joh. Nicolaus, 409;
Nicolaus, 409
REPSCHER, Barbara, 488, 513; Bernhard,
488; Leonhard, 488, 513
RETTEN, Cath., 431; Christian, 431; Hnr.,
431
RETTINGER, Jacob Vallentin, 449;
Rosina, 449
RETUE, Joh., 470; Maria Barbara, 470;
Reinhard, 470
RETZ, Anna Marg., 303; Anna Maria, 303;
Joh. Georg, 303
RETZEL, Susanna, 315
RETZER, Georg, 366; Jacob, 303, 325,
396, 493; Joh., 303, 396; Joh. Hnr.,
325; Marg., 366; Michael, 493;
Rebecca, 366; Sophia, 366; Susanna,
303, 325, 396, 493
REUSCH, Jacobina, 313
REUSCHLE, Cath., 488; Joh. Ludw., 544;
Joh. Ludwig, 488; Marg., 488, 544
REUSS, Barbara, 357; Marg. Elis., 357;
Simon, 357
REUSSER, Anna Cath., 307, 360; Anna
Maria, 360; Cath., 349; Christina, 360;
Eva, 349; Jacob, 349, 360; Joh. Jacob,
307; Joh. Michael, 349; Martin, 307,
349, 360
REUT, Cath., 443; Michael, 443
REUTH, Rachel, 288

REX, Abraham, 504, 533; Adam, 373, 502, 523; Anna, 533; Anna Maria, 523; Hnr., 523; Maria Eva, 281; Nancy, 504
REYFELDSCHER, Wilhelm Reinhardt, 411
REYLEY, Cath., 519; Elis., 519; John, 530; Maria, 530; Salome, 530; William, 519
REZER, Georg, 366; Jacob, 366; Sophia, 366; Susanna, 366
RHEIN, Eva, 292; Georg, 292; Joh. Georg, 292
RHEINTALER, Anna Maria, 328; Jacob, 328
RHEINTHALER, Joh. Jacob, 308
RHEISLING, Jacob, 334; Maria Catharina, 334
RHEN, Cath., 535; Georg, 535; Hnr., 535
RIBBEL, Nicolaus, 328; Susanna, 328
RIBEL, Nicolaus, 340; Sara, 340
RICAS, Cath., 283; Martin, 283
RICE, Elizabeth, 285; John, 285, 302, 413; Susanna, 285, 302, 371
RICHARD, Anna Maria, 516; Cath., 332; Elis., 332; Hannah, 415; John, 332; Nathaniel, 415; William, 415
RICHARDS, John, 537
RICHARDSON, Ann, 279, 333; David, 279, 333; Rebecca, 333
RICHMOND, Cath., 419; Hnr., 419; Thomas, 419
RICHTER, Elis., 532; Eva, 486, 532; Georg, 486, 532; Jacob, 486
RICKARD, Cath., 515; Cath. Elis., 515; Joh., 515
RICKER, Joh. Martin, 385; Maria, 305
RICKET, Nicolaus, 455; Salome, 455
RIDDEL, Cath., 500
RIDEL, Cath., 286; Joh., 286; Joh. Gottfried, 286
RIDGE, Joh., 518; Maria Barbara, 518; Maria Salome, 518
RIEB, Anna Cath., 486; Anna Susanna, 344; Cath., 313; Elis., 416, 431; Joh., 332, 344, 416, 431, 486; Joh. Michael, 344; Joh. Philipp, 332; Leonard, 416, 431; Martha, 344; Peter, 313; Susanna, 332, 416, 486
RIEBEL, Elis., 455; Susanna, 307
RIEBERT, Agnes, 533; Hnr., 533
RIEBLE, Elis., 481
RIED, Georg, 539; Joh., 382; Joh. Hnr., 382; Mrs., 426; Susanna, 382
RIEDEL, Elis., 370; Joh. Gottfried, 370; Joh. Gottfriedt, 311; Magdalena, 370; Magdalena Cath., 311; Maria, 311
RIEGEL, Cath., 364; Jacob, 364; Joh. Georg, 364

RIEGELMEYER, Anna Marg., 478; Georg Frdr., 478; Joh. Georg, 478; Joh. Jacob, 478; Magdalena, 478
RIEGLER, Andr., 473; Andreas, 430, 442, 514; Cath., 430, 442, 473, 514
RIEHM, Maria Elis., 446; Michael, 446
RIEL, Adolph, 302, 428, 515; Anthon, 460; Cath., 408, 460, 461; Elis., 302; Hanna, 302, 460, 515; Hannah, 428; Hnr., 515; Jacob, 328, 408, 461; Joh., 328; Joh. Hnr., 515; Maria, 515; Rachel, 328; Thomas, 428
RIEM, Elis., 320; Mich., 493; Michael, 320
RIEMER, Elis., 428; Mat., 428; Salome, 428
RIEMET, Elis., 452; Joh., 452
RIEN, Barbara, 299
RIEP, Joh., 454; Joh. Bernard, 454; Susanna, 454
RIES, Anna Maria, 330; Cath., 330, 341, 397, 541; Christiana, 328; Christina, 329; Dieterich, 328, 329; Elis., 485; Hnr., 470; Jacob, 351, 421, 485; Joh., 385; Magdalena, 351, 485; Magdalene, 385; Mar. Magdalena, 421; Maria Magdalena, 351; Maria Marg., 421; Mart., 330; Martin, 330, 341, 373, 397; Susanna, 441, 470; Valentin, 470; Valentine, 441; Wilhelm, 328
RIESS, Adam, 546; Agnes, 312; Andreas, 546; Anna Marg., 521; Anna Maria, 280; Cath., 343; Elis., 546; Georg, 513; Hanna, 462; Hnr., 462; Jac., 315; Jacob, 293, 521, 552; Joh. Adam, 312; Joh. Diethrich, 280; Joh. Martin, 450; Magdalena, 315; Magdalene, 552; Marg., 552; Maria Magdalena, 521; Martin, 343; Michael, 315; Philip, 312; Rosina Christiana, 280; Susanna, 446, 450, 475, 498, 513; Valentin, 446, 450, 474, 475, 498, 513
RIGEL, Cath., 449
RIGER, Jacob, 371; Susanna, 371
RIHM, Elis., 326; Joh. Michael, 326
RIM, Cath., 331; Jacob, 331
RINDELMANN, Cath., 477; Elis., 477; John, 477
RING, Conrad, 302, 305, 308, 334, 373, 388, 432, 494, 509; Elis., 500; Joh., 494, 500; Joh. Wilhelm, 305; John, 509; Juliana, 302, 305, 308, 334, 373, 388, 432, 509; Mar. Juliana, 494; Marcus, 409, 500; Maria, 494, 509; Maria Dorothea, 334; Maria Juliana, 509; Regina Elis., 373
RINGSBACH, Elis., 316
RINK, Conrad, 280; Hanna, 546; Joh., 280; Magdalena, 280
RISCH, Elis., 391

RISCHONG, David, 448
RISH, Cath., 356
RISSART, Anna Eva, 294
RITTER, Anna Maria, 464; Brunella,
420; Cath., 279, 318, 319, 389, 420;
Cath. Barbara, 511; Christine, 389;
Dorothea, 464, 510, 511; Elis., 463,
520; Georg, 285, 318; Hnr., 279, 318;
Jacob, 285, 464, 510, 511; John, 319;
Marg., 279, 318, 389; Penelope, 318;
Peter, 318, 319, 420; Philippine, 420;
Prunella, 420; Susanna, 279; Wilh.,
389; Wilhelm, 463
RITZ, Georg, 415; Maria Elis., 415
RITZENTHALER, Dorothea, 505; Maria
Elis., 505; Martin, 505
RITZER, Jacob, 417; Susanne, 417
RIVELS, Edward, 476; Eva, 476; Maria,
476
RIVEN, Elis., 461
RIVERS, Cath., 313, 335; Cath. Elis.,
354; Cath. Eliza, 288; Cath.
Magdalena, 313; James, 288; Joseph,
288, 313, 335, 354
RIVERT, Edward, 437; Eva, 437; Joseph,
437
ROBAUST, Cath., 279, 367; Christoph,
279
ROBERTS, Anna, 349; Cath., 443, 479,
543; Francis, 349; Maria, 479;
Wilhelm, 543; William, 443, 479
ROBERTSON, Joh., 361; Marg., 408
ROBINSON, Cath., 467; Charles, 540;
Maria, 291; William, 291
ROBISIN, Cath., 491
ROCKENBERGER, Adam, 395
ROCKER, Cath., 298; Elis., 298; Jacob,
298
ROCKHILL, Aaron, 545; Anna, 545;
Wilhelm, 545
ROEDER, Friderica Dorothea, 538; Joh.
Peter, 538; Johanna Rosina, 538
ROEHM, Elis., 326; Michael, 326
ROEHN, Elis., 300; Michael, 300
ROEM, Elis., 358, 359; Joh. Michael,
359; Michael, 358
ROEMER, Michael, 360
ROGERS, Hanna, 298; Joseph, 298;
Rebecca, 298; Salome, 298
ROH, Barbara, 409; Cath., 513, 516;
Daniel, 361; Elis., 513; Hnr., 409;
Marcus, 513; Martin, 361, 408, 409
ROHL, Gottlieb, 396
ROHN, Cath., 459, 472, 504, 541;
Christine, 417; Elis., 417, 459; Hnr.,
346; Jacob, 417, 459, 497, 502; Jeane,
403; Joh. Christ., 472; Joh. Christoph,
504, 541; Joh. Ferdinand, 541; Joh.
Henr., 504; Liddy, 541; Lydia, 417,
497; Magdalena, 346, 497, 502, 503;

Magdalene, 551; Maria Elis., 397;
Maria Euphronica, 346; Peter, 403;
Ruth, 541; Susanna, 403
ROHNER, Barbara, 416, 503; Georg, 425;
Joh., 416; Ludwig, 425; Maria, 425,
504; Samuel, 416
ROHR, Andreas, 470; Christiana Marg.,
470; Frdr., 280, 553; Joh., 384, 444;
Joh. Andr., 296, 328, 377, 445; Joh.
Andreas, 285, 393, 440, 513, 524; Joh.
Hnr., 285; Joh. Wolfgang, 553; John,
317; Mar. Christina, 377, 384; Marg.,
553; Maria, 296, 317; Maria Christina,
285, 328, 393, 440, 444, 445, 470, 513,
524; Maria Elis., 328
ROHRER, Anna Cath., 519; Frdr., 519;
Marg., 519
ROHRMANN, Conrad, 448, 478; Elis.,
448, 478; Leonhard, 448; Salome, 478
ROHT, Charlotta, 344; Elis., 385; Jacob,
327; Joh. Leonhard, 344; Leonard, 432;
Leonhard, 344, 462; Maria Magd., 462;
Susanna, 327
ROL, Christine, 407
ROLL, Anna Cath., 376; Cath., 297, 335;
Gottlieb, 335, 376, 396; Jac. Gottlieb,
297; Joh. Jacob, 297, 335
ROMMEL, Elis., 506; Georg, 506
RONDECKER, Dorothea, 278; Joh.
Samuel, 278; Samuel, 278
RONDELS, Barbara, 308; David, 308;
Mary, 308; Michael, 308
RONDIGER, Dorothea, 361; Joh.
Christoph, 361; Samuel, 361
RONER, Anna Maria, 283; Barbara, 283,
393, 394; Joh., 283; Ludwig, 551;
Maria, 394, 551; Marin, 503; Samuel,
503; Sophia, 503
RONN, Barbara, 362; Joh., 362; John, 362
RONNER, Joh., 537; Martin, 537; Sophia,
537
RONSER, Barbara, 341; Joh., 341
ROOSS, Mat., 553
ROPER, Anna, 413; Richard, 413
ROS, Elis., 328; Mat., 394; Peter, 394;
Susanne, 394
ROSCH, Cath., 509; Christian, 331, 373;
Christine, 361; Conrad, 392, 425, 427;
Daniel, 425, 509; Elis., 509, 545;
Georg, 286; Joh., 331; Laban, 373;
Leonhard, 482; Ludwig, 528; Marg.,
286; Maria Magdalena, 482; Sarah,
331, 373; Susanna, 392, 425, 427, 509,
524
ROSCK, Cath., 504; Joh., 504; John, 504
ROSE, Ally, 510; Carl, 510; Cath., 510;
Elis., 277; Joseph, 277; Maria Marg.,
314; Mat., 313, 512; Peter, 277, 313,
476; Sarah Elis., 313; Sus., 370;
Susanna, 512

SAILER, Aemelia, 399; Anna Maria, 497;
   Cath., 492; Jacob, 399, 497, 523;
   Joh., 492; Maria, 523
ST. GOWAN, Cath., 409
SALOMON, Cath. Salome, 294;
   Christina Maria, 451; Elis., 294; Joh.,
   290, 301, 451; Mr., 417; Mrs., 417
SALSER, Anna Barb., 400; Jacob, 400
SAMUEL, Deborah, 361; Elis., 361;
   Georg, 361; Robert, 361
SANDER, Joh., 364
SANDERLING, Christoph, 538; Joh.,
   538; Maria, 538
SANDMANN, Georg, 347; Lorentz, 347;
   Maria Magdel., 347
SANER, Cath., 420
SANTOR, Mar. Magdalena, 422
SARNINGHAUSEN, Elis., 424; Georg
   Christoph, 424; Wilhelm, 424
SARTORIUS, Christina, 348
SASLIAN, Daniel, 332; Joh. Georg, 332;
   Maria Eva, 332
SATLER, Maria, 300; Philip, 300
SAUBER, Jacob, 522
SAUDER, Joh., 363, 544; Marg., 544;
   Maria Magdal., 363
SAUER, Anna Barbara, 320; Apollonia,
   313; Francis, 313; Georg, 399; Joh.
   Adam, 312; Joh. Hnr., 320; Joh.
   Leonhard, 313; Mar. Magdalena, 399
SAUERMANN, Anna Maria, 460; Jesias
   Phil., 460; Majory, 460; Marchery,
   460; Nancy Mary, 460; Peter, 460;
   Phil. Jacob, 460
SAUTER, Carl, 294; Elis., 540; Joh., 540,
   550; Marg., 447, 540, 550
SAVEL, Georg, 518; Maria, 518
SAVOIR, Elis., 307; John, 307; Peter,
   307
SAWTON, Cath., 448; Edward, 448;
   Maria Susanna, 448
SAYLER, Jacob, 541; Maria, 541
SCHAAB, Cath., 350; Daniel, 350
SCHAAL, John Georg, 366
SCHAB, Cath., 369; Daniel, 369
SCHABER, Anna, 392, 403
SCHACH, Joh. Hnr., 512; Maria, 512
SCHACK, Cath., 538; Peter, 538
SCHACKA, Joh. George, 497
SCHACKAR, Mat., 375
SCHACKSON, Math., 338
SCHACKY, Elis., 510; Joh. Georg, 510
SCHAD, Elis., 430; Georg, 430; Gertraut,
   351; Susanne, 430
SCHADE, Joh., 299
SCHAEF, Barbara, 355; Cath., 392;
   Maria, 355; Wilhelm, 355
SCHAEFER, Adam, 415, 418, 433, 446;
   Agatha, 393; Agnes, 353; Andreas,
   304; Anna, 359; Anna Barbara, 455;

Anna Marg., 359; Anna Maria, 393;
   Barbara, 304; Carl, 353; Cath., 284,
   307, 425, 434; Christ., 378; Christian,
   284, 356, 388, 416, 419; Christoph,
   359; Conrad, 393; Dav., 382; David,
   307, 355, 375, 419; DAvid, 425;
   David, 452, 455; Doroth., 419, 433;
   Dorothea, 284, 356, 378, 388, 416,
   418; Elis., 336, 373, 375, 376, 388,
   403, 425, 455; Franz, 336, 373; Georg,
   330; Jacob, 324, 330, 419, 425, 431;
   Jacobina, 425; Joh., 319, 376, 382,
   393, 398, 403, 418, 419, 422, 429, 467;
   Joh. Frdr., 319, 425; Joh. Michael, 382;
   Johan, 398; John, 361; Juliana, 499;
   Lud., 499; Ludewig, 451; Magdal.,
   431; Marg., 319; Marg. Dorothea, 446;
   Maria, 324, 330, 353, 356, 382, 419,
   452, 467; Maria Cath., 355; Maria
   Elis., 304, 375; Nicolaus, 431; Soph.
   Maria, 398; Susanna, 376, 398, 403,
   429; Susanna Dorothea, 422
SCHAEFF, Anna Cath., 387; Barbara, 387;
   Cath., 387; Wilhelm, 387
SCHAEFFER, Adam, 459, 492; Agata,
   435; Anna Barbara, 295; Anna Maria,
   435; Carl, 435; Cath., 512; Christian,
   462, 472, 481, 491, 527; David, 515,
   521; Doroth., 481; Dorothea, 459, 462,
   472, 492, 527; Elis., 295, 382, 511,
   515; Franz, 295; Georg, 463; Hnr.,
   489; Jacob, 297, 459, 489, 523, 533;
   Joh., 462, 504, 518, 530; Joh. Andreas,
   512; Joh. David, 346; Joh. Hnr., 512;
   Joh. jacob, 459; Joh. Wilhelm, 533;
   Juliana, 297; Marg., 463; Maria, 459,
   489, 533; Maria Cath., 297, 346, 515,
   521; Maria Elis., 523; Maria Magdal.,
   510; Maria Magdalena, 518; Maria
   Sophia, 504; Philip, 492; Rebecca,
   527; Sarah, 472; Sophia Maria, 462,
   518; Susanna, 459
SCHAER, Barbara, 468; Georg, 468; Joh.
   Georg, 483
SCHAERER, Elis., 486; Georg, 486;
   Magdalena, 486
SCHAETZL, Barbara, 295
SCHAETZLEIN, Adam, 303, 307, 319,
   403, 430, 476, 516; Anna, 524;
   Barbara, 424, 492, 506; Barth., 404;
   Barthol, 430; Barthol., 418;
   Bartholmaeus, 452; Bartholomae, 506,
   524; Bartholomaes, 319;
   Bartholomaius, 439; Cath., 319, 404,
   418, 430, 439, 452, 506; David, 403;
   Elis., 476; Georg, 482, 500; Hanna,
   303, 307, 319, 403, 430, 476, 516;
   Hnr., 500; Joh., 424, 492, 506, 516;
   Maria, 303; Sara, 482; Veronica, 482,
   500

SCHAFER, Anna Cath., 550; Cath., 449; Cath. Barbara, 294; Cath. Elis., 347; Christian, 320, 449; David, 301, 548; Dorothea, 320, 449; Elis., 320, 548; Jacob, 298, 301; Joh., 301, 349, 550; Joh. David, 552; Joh. Jacob, 294; Mar. Cath., 552; Marg., 550; Maria, 301; Maria Cath., 301; Maria Magdalena, 298; Michael, 294, 347; Sophia Maria, 349

SCHAFFELS, Elis., 489; Nancy, 489; Richhard, 489; Rosina, 489

SCHAFFER, Cath., 304; David, 304, 346; Elis., 346; Joh. David, 346

SCHAGAR, Mat., 338

SCHAHL, Anna Maria, 451, 546; Christina, 451; Georg, 546; Joh. Georg, 451; Joh. Martin, 285; Maria, 546

SCHAICH, Anna Magdalen, 280; Jacob, 280; Joh. Georg, 280

SCHAIKA, Barbara, 292; Carl, 292

SCHALL, Georg, 432; Maria Christine, 432; Maria Elis., 344

SCHAMMEL, Elis., 354; James, 354

SCHARADDIN, Anna Maria, 482; Hanna, 482; Paulus, 482

SCHARF, Cath., 465; Elis., 465; John, 465; Michael, 527; Phil., 517; Susanna, 527

SCHARFF, Elis., 517; Jacob, 517; Joh., 517

SCHARP, Cath., 519; Joh., 519; Joh. Gerhard, 519; Maria Susanna, 448

SCHATZLEIN, Adam, 300, 363; Barbara, 287, 547; Bartholomaeus, 331; Cath., 331; Georg, 422; Hanna, 300, 338, 363; Joh., 547; Joh. Adam, 338; Salome, 422; Sara, 363; Sarah, 363

SCHATZLER, Barbara, 396; Joh., 373, 396; Joh. Georg, 396

SCHAUB, Cath., 300, 519; Daniel, 300, 519; Dorothea, 300; Elis., 467, 510, 531; Joh. Ulrich, 531

SCHAUFFLY, Georg Caspar, 526; Ludwig, 526; Susanna, 526

SCHAUK, Maria Elis., 510

SCHAUMKESSEL, Anna Cath., 507; Elis., 497, 506, 507, 532, 538; Frdr., 497, 538; Georg, 506; Georg Frdr., 507; Mr., 532

SCHAUT, Cath., 401; Daniel, 401

SCHEAFF, Barbara, 481; Susanna, 481; Wilhelm, 523; William, 481

SCHEAFFER, Elis., 485

SCHEBACH, Carl Enoch, 434; Elis., 434; Hanna, 434

SCHED, Christine, 376; Hnr., 376

SCHEE, Barbara, 333; Georg, 333

SCHEELES, Georg Thomas, 343; John, 343

SCHEFFER, Ad., 391; Doroth., 391; Marg., 391

SCHEFFLER, Christina, 546; Hnr., 546

SCHEIB, Anna Elis., 354; Joh. Bernhard, 344; Johannes, 354

SCHEIBEL, Agnes, 330; Hanna Maria, 330; Theobald, 330

SCHEIBELE, Agnes, 370; Georg, 370; Hnr., 466; Ludew., 466; Sophia, 466; Theobald, 370

SCHEIBLE, Cath., 435; Elis., 480, 519; Geo., 435; Georg, 519; Hnr., 519, 545; Jacob, 480; Josua, 545; Nancy, 545

SCHEIBLI, Christina, 516

SCHEIBLY, Ludwig, 546; Susanna Magdalena, 546

SCHEID, Elis., 305

SCHEIG, Anna Magdal., 363; Anna Magdalena, 327; Jacob, 363; John Jacob, 327; Philipp, 327

SCHEKHORN, Cath., 368; Mat., 368

SCHELD, Cath., 481; Leonhard, 481; Maria Felicia, 481

SCHELDIAN, Joh., 366

SCHELHORN, Cath., 407; Elis., 407; Mat., 407

SCHELIER, Conrad, 309; Maria Elis., 309

SCHELL, Jacob, 306; Joh., 428; Marg., 428, 444; Peter, 428, 444

SCHELLEBERGER, Cath., 339; Dorothea, 339; Peter, 339

SCHELLER, Conr., 392; Conrad, 298, 362, 501; Elis., 362, 392, 501

SCHELLES, Conrad, 322; Maria Elis., 322

SCHELT, Christina, 303; Hnr., 303

SCHELTER, Adam, 512; Anna, 512; Conrad, 512; Maria Elis., 512

SCHENCK, Balthasar, 444; Barbara, 390; Elis., 380; Georg, 380, 390, 401; Jacob, 390; Joh., 444; Maria Cath., 444; Sophia, 401

SCHENECK, Anna Cath., 336; Cath., 389; Mich., 389; Michael, 336

SCHENERER, Cath., 407; Mich., 407

SCHENK, Cath., 431; Joh., 431

SCHENKEL, Balthasar, 488; Cath., 488; Frdr., 372; Peter, 488; Susanna, 372

SCHENNECK, Anna Barbara, 501; Anna Cath., 501; Michael, 501

SCHEP, Anna Maria, 279, 321; Elis., 321; Maria, 279; Philip, 321

SCHEPHERD, Cath., 468

SCHEPPACH, Jacob, 334, 384, 402; Joh., 340; Joh. Jacob, 311, 487; Mar. Ursula, 402; Maria, 340; Maria Ursula, 311, 334, 487; Ursula, 384

SCHEPPERD, Joseph, 446; Maria, 446; Maria Anna, 446

SCHER, Anna Barbara, 333; Hans Gurg, 333
SCHERAN, A. Maria, 548; Jacob, 548; Joh., 548
SCHERER, Elis., 534, 548; Georg, 383, 534, 548; Rosina, 409
SCHERFF, Elis., 492; Jacob, 492; Phil., 492; Philip, 492
SCHERRATIN, Abraham, 526; Hanna, 526; Paul, 526
SCHESING, Joh. Gottfried, 362
SCHETT, Georg, 465; Susanna, 465
SCHEUB, Elis., 493
SCHEUER, Barbara, 416; Mat., 416
SCHEULEMANN, Joh. Mat., 334
SCHICK, Barbara, 347, 507; Eva Barb., 392; Eva Barbara, 442, 544; Frdr., 280, 392, 442, 507; Joh. Frdr., 347, 544; Joh. Hnr., 347; Joh. Martin, 544; Martin, 507
SCHICKELE, Cath. Marg., 296; Mstr., 296
SCHIEBER, Jacob, 445; Magdalena, 445
SCHIEBLEY, Elis., 516; Jacob, 516
SCHIEFFERER, Adam, 530; Barbara, 530; Dorothea Barbara, 530
SCHIER, Georg, 471; Magdalena, 471
SCHIESSER, Dorothea, 317; Joh. Adam, 317
SCHIESSLER, Caspar, 334; Regina, 334
SCHIFFER, Adam, 357; Anna Maria, 357, 359; Dorothea, 357
SCHIFFERER, Dorothea, 292, 349; Jacob, 349; Joh., 292, 349; Joh. Adam, 292, 349; Maria Juliana, 349
SCHIK, Barbara, 484; Frdr., 484; Joh. Martin, 484
SCHILBACH, Carl, 437; Hanna, 437
SCHILDBACH, Carl, 452, 456, 470; Carl Enoch, 458; Hanna, 456, 458, 470; Joh., 458; Maria, 470
SCHINCK, Elis. Sophia, 381; Joh. Georg, 381; Joh. Hnr., 381; Peggy, 544
SCHINCKEL, Frdr., 306, 467; Susanna, 306, 467
SCHINDEL, Marg., 454
SCHINDLER, Anna, 293; Anna Maria, 487; Conrad, 293; Elis., 463; Joh. Wilhelm, 362; Marg., 362, 463, 487, 506; Phil., 463; Philip, 362; Philipp, 487
SCHINKEL, Frdr., 356; Susanna, 356
SCHINKER, Anna Marg., 510
SCHINKLER, Philipp, 327
SCHINNECK, Anna Cath., 469; Michael, 469
SCHIRM, Elis. Magdalena, 532; Joh. Stephan, 532; Marg., 532
SCHISLER, Anna Elis., 475; Gottfried, 475

SCHISTERER, Adam, 324; Dorothea, 324; Jacob, 324
SCHITTEL, Daniel, 406; Elis., 406; Rebecca, 406
SCHIVELY, Elis., 506; Georg, 506
SCHLAECHTER, Elis., 525; Joh., 525
SCHLATER, Christina, 303, 497; Conrad, 303; John, 476
SCHLATTER, An. Marg., 378; Ann Cath., 385; Anna Maria, 441; Christina, 310, 338, 393; Christine, 378; Conr., 393; Elis., 409; Eva, 433; Eva Christine, 441; Hanna, 310; Hnr., 441; Joh. Conrad, 310, 338, 378; Maria, 409; Maria Elis., 409; Mat., 409; Rosina, 338
SCHLECHTER, Elis., 440; Joh., 440
SCHLEICH, Anna Barbara, 333; Christoph, 327, 333, 383; Elis., 327, 333, 383
SCHLEICKER, Elis., 461; Georg, 461
SCHLEIG, Christoph, 468; Elis., 468; Georg, 468
SCHLEIGMANN, Maria, 341; Maria Magdalena, 341; Mat., 341
SCHLEIHOF, Anna Barbara, 312; Gottfried, 312; Jacob, 429; Maria, 429; Michael, 312, 429
SCHLEIHOFF, Anna Maria, 358; Barbara, 358; Hnr., 358; Michael, 358
SCHLEMER, Joh. Cath. Eleonora, 430
SCHLEMMER, Conrad, 476; Han. Cath. Eleonora, 476; Jacob, 459
SCHLESMANN, Cath., 305, 391, 455; Hnr., 391, 455; Joh., 305, 391; Joh. Georg, 455; Joh. Hnr., 305
SCHLESSMAN, Andreas, 356; Cath., 356; Hnr., 356
SCHLEUTER, Elis., 430; Georg, 430
SCHLI, Maria Magd., 541
SCHLIEPS, Maria, 449
SCHLING, Gottfried, 489; Marg., 489
SCHLUG, Christoph, 414; Elis., 414
SCHLUSTER, Eva, 312
SCHMALTZ, Marg., 353
SCHMID, Anna Maria, 284, 347; Cath., 304, 442; Conrad, 284; Jacob, 347; Joh. Daniel, 310; Joh. Georg, 337, 347; Martin, 442; Mat., 304; Mr., 302
SCHMIDT, Abrahan, 289; Adam, 281, 283, 315, 334, 365, 384, 439; Agnes Cath., 311, 383; An. Elis., 387; Andreas, 402; Anna, 295, 326, 351, 368, 475; Anna Barb., 432; Anna Barbara, 332; Anna Cath., 341, 427, 496; Anna Christina, 310, 341, 381; Anna Juliana, 314; Anna Marg., 350, 498; Anna Maria, 283, 514; Apollonia, 319; Barbara, 289, 344, 384, 438, 459, 475, 515, 516; Carl, 455, 497, 498,

537, 553; Cath., 281, 283, 284, 286, 293, 315, 323, 332, 334, 365, 384, 386, 399, 411, 438, 439, 441, 453, 498, 501, 508, 516; Cath. Barb., 511; Cath. Elis., 537; Christian, 283; Christine, 432; Christoph, 333, 453; Conrad, 351; Daniel Frdr., 344; Doroth., 364; Doroth. Magdalena, 509; Dorothea, 386; Dorothea Magdalene, 547; Dorothea Marg., 474; Elis., 358, 395, 500, 501, 509, 535; Eva, 429, 450, 452, 498; Frdr., 323, 326, 332, 386, 462, 535; Georg, 289, 301, 350, 368, 452, 459, 509, 535; Georg Adam, 310, 314, 341, 381, 432; Georg Frdr., 497; Gottfr. Ernst, 551; Hnr., 426, 427, 454, 472, 475, 478, 482, 516, 549; Jacob, 286, 293, 318, 391, 439, 450, 457, 488, 498, 508, 515, 516, 532, 543; Jeremias, 541; Joh., 446, 498, 514, 541; Joh. Adam, 315; Joh. Andreas, 332; Joh. Carl, 553; Joh. Frdr., 289, 332; Joh. Georg, 429, 457, 498, 514; Joh. Hnr., 319, 549; Joh. Jacob, 293; Joh. Martin, 311; Joh. Mat., 332; Joh. Michael, 318; Joh. Peter, 310; Joh. Sebastian, 281; Leonard, 438; Leonhard, 475, 515; Ludewig, 295; Magdalena, 344, 426, 454, 472, 475, 482, 541; Magdalene, 549; Marg., 446, 478, 498, 516, 543, 551; Maria, 391, 475, 478, 493, 502, 528, 532, 537; Maria Cath., 293, 323, 516; Maria Dorothea, 277; Maria Eva, 457, 535; Maria Magdalena, 293, 301, 318, 351, 471; Martin, 341, 399, 438; Mat., 358, 383, 411, 441; Matthias, 284; Michael, 475, 502; Pastor, 504, 533, 545; Philip, 395; Philip Jacob, 351; Philipp, 402; Polly, 508; Sahra, 462; Sara, 386; Sarah, 383; Sophia, 497, 553; Susanna, 402, 441, 547; Thomas, 386; Ulrich, 455; Wilh., 326, 431; Wilhelm, 295, 351, 368, 411, 459, 474, 509, 532, 551; Wilhelmina, 301; Wilhelmina Julia, 462
SCHMONKER, Cath., 386; Dietrich, 386; Susanna, 386
SCHNECK, Barbara, 332; Elis., 412, 429, 465; Georg, 332, 412, 429, 465; Georg Frdr., 429; Joh. Georg, 345; Joh. Jacob, 465; Marg. Dorothea, 412; Sara, 332
SCHNEEBERG, Magdalena, 333
SCHNEIDER, A. Maria, 535; Andreas, 460; Anna, 337; Anna Barbara, 332; Anna Elis., 337, 456; Anna Eva, 524; Anna Eva Elis., 288; Anna Marg., 414; Anna Maria, 308, 318, 337, 377,

423; Baltus, 361; Barbara, 515; Bened., 480; Benedict, 325, 345, 350, 370, 397, 427; Carl, 308, 378, 423; Carl Joseph, 382; Carl Preuss, 344; Caspar, 307, 329, 363, 388, 428, 444, 466, 513, 541; Cath., 346, 388, 406, 435, 453, 491, 535, 538; Cath. Barbara, 373; Cath. Elis., 299; Christian, 532, 533, 535; Christina Cath., 307; Christoph, 414; Conrad, 424; David, 352; Elis., 307, 329, 353, 363, 388, 391, 399, 428, 443, 444, 446, 453, 464, 466, 492, 497, 513, 516, 541, 545; Eva, 332, 374, 400, 425, 453; Felix, 285, 386; Georg, 321, 337, 357, 382, 407, 453, 459, 460, 479, 491, 496, 497, 515, 522, 536, 538; Georg Frdr., 337; Georg Jacob, 423; Hanna, 321; Hnr., 309, 318, 363, 428, 515, 529; Jacob, 337, 453, 492, 535, 545; Joh., 288, 307, 308, 332, 337, 346, 363, 374, 400, 404, 425, 431, 433, 435, 446, 461, 468, 486, 496, 529, 545; Joh. Adam, 466; Joh. Bened., 441, 460; Joh. Benedict, 299, 449; Joh. Carl, 307, 378; Joh. Conrad, 337; Joh. David, 406; Joh. Georg, 294, 337, 377, 414, 453; Joh. Hnr., 295, 337; Joh. Jacob, 345; Joh. Mart., 496; Joh. Martin, 484; Joh. Wilhelm, 456; Joh. Zacharias, 288, 344, 524; John Jacob, 322; Joseph, 536; Ludwig, 406, 538; Magdalena, 421, 484; Mar. Eva, 404, 486; Marg., 309, 361, 421, 431, 435, 461, 479, 491, 496, 522, 529, 538, 545; Maria, 307, 321, 357, 378, 407, 459, 460, 497, 515, 522, 535, 536, 541; Maria Barbara, 285; Maria Cath., 303; Maria Christina, 321; Maria Dorothea, 399; Maria Elis., 353, 532; Maria Eva, 468; Martin, 421; Mary Eliane, 295; Michael, 332, 492; Nancy, 352; Peter, 337, 353, 399, 464, 516; Phib. Elis., 460; Philip, 407; Philipine Elis., 397; Philippina, 427; Philippina Elis., 299, 325, 345, 350, 370, 441, 449, 480; Regina Cath., 456; Rosina, 373; Rosina Magdalena, 322; Sara, 464; Sibylla Cath., 288; Sophia Susanna, 295; Sybilla Rosina, 369; Valentin, 322, 373; Wilh. Frdr., 370; Wilhelm, 480, 541
SCHNEK, David, 499
SCHNELL, Elis., 426, 450, 460, 493, 531; Jacob, 426, 450, 460, 493, 531; Joh. Frdr., 493; Joh., 531; Marg., 460; Maria Magdal., 426
SCHNELLHARD, Andreas Christoph, 453; Christina, 493; Joh. Christoph, 453; John Ehr., 493; Martin, 493

SCHNEP, Anna Maria, 326; Martin, 326; Mat., 326
SCHNEPF, Joh. Martin, 277; Magdalena, 277
SCHNONECK, Anna Cath., 342; Elis., 342; Michael, 342
SCHNYDER, Molly, 474
SCHOBER, Elis., 333; Georg, 333; Samuel, 333
SCHOBERT, Elis., 282; Samuel, 282
SCHOCH, Andreas, 372; Bernard, 372; Cath., 372; Hans Georg, 383; Jacob, 388, 543; Joh. Michael, 303; Magd., 383; Marg., 303, 432, 543; Mich., 383; Michael, 303, 432, 543; Nicolaus, 432
SCHOCHT, Elis., 288; Maria Marg., 288; Martin, 288
SCHOCK, Jacob, 543; Marg., 543; Michael, 543
SCHOCKARD, Barbara, 516; Simon, 516
SCHOEICH, An. Cath., 368; Michael, 368
SCHOEMACHER, Christoph, 337; Michael, 337; Susanna Maria, 337
SCHOEN, Caspar, 518, 529; Christian, 503, 510; Debora, 518; Georg, 529; Hnr. Wilhelm, 510; Marg., 503, 510; Maria, 529
SCHOENECK, Anna Cath., 301, 394; Joh. Adam, 301; Joh. Jacob, 394; Michael, 394
SCHOENEKER, Cath., 425; Joh., 425
SCHOENER, Balthasar, 519; Cath., 519
SCHOENNECK, Cath., 438, 466; Michael, 466; Sophia, 438; Wilhelm, 438
SCHOENNEL, Balthas., 422
SCHOFFERICH, Anna Maria, 534; Joh., 534
SCHOG, Joh. Mat., 359; Marg., 359; Michael, 359
SCHOLBER, Elis., 297; Joh. Michael, 297; Samuel, 297
SCHONAU, Lorenz, 332; Marg., 332
SCHONECK, Cath., 277; Maria Christina, 277; Michael, 277
SCHOP, Elis., 432
SCHRACK, Elis., 345; Jacob, 345; John, 345; Mary, 345; Simon John, 345
SCHRAM, Anna Elis., 336; Anna Maria, 335; Cath., 336; Nicolaus, 335; Theobald, 336
SCHRANCK, Bernhard, 543; Cath., 400; Frdr., 543; Georg, 400; Joh. Georg, 400; Peter, 400, 468; Philippina, 543; Sophia, 400, 468
SCHRANK, Cath., 406; Joh. Georg, 406

SCHRECK, Jacob, 344. 383, 459; Joh. Georg, 310; John Bernhard, 344; Marg., 310, 383; Maria, 344, 383, 459; Peter, 459
SCHREFFLER, Christina, 516; Hnr., 516; Joh. Frdr., 516
SCHREFLER, Christina, 483; Daniel, 483; Hnr., 483
SCHREIBER, Anna Cath., 291, 502; Anna Marg., 450, 477, 517, 542; Anna Maria, 370, 513; Appellonia, 517; Cath., 370; Christian, 506; Daniel Woelker, 502; Elis., 280, 281, 369, 502, 542; Hanna, 319; Hnr., 288, 329, 369, 380, 428, 468; Jacob, 370, 450, 477, 517, 542; Joh., 280, 281, 291, 300; Joh. Andreas, 513; Joh. Georg, 468, 506; Magdalena, 506; Marg., 288, 329, 369, 380, 428, 468; Maria, 366; Maria Elis., 300; Michael, 318; Peggy, 472; Peter, 366; Thomas Lorenz, 513
SCHREIDER, Georg, 424; Joh. Nicolaus, 424; Maria, 424
SCHREIER, Anna Louisa, 464; Anna Rosina, 382; Barbara, 485; Cath., 464, 487; Frdr., 487; Joh., 464, 487; Joh. Georg, 328, 485; Joh. Hnr., 382; Martin, 382; Peter, 485
SCHREIHOF, Anna Maria, 413; Joh., 413; Michael, 413
SCHREIK, Elis., 281
SCHREINER, Anna Marg., 492; Anna Maria, 492; Anna Rosina, 346; Eva Maria, 346; Jacob, 492
SCHREL, Joh. Conrad, 534; Joseph Isaac, 534; Marg., 534
SCHRENCK, Georg, 448; Soph. Elis., 448
SCHREYER, Barbara, 517; Cath., 524, 545; Joh., 524, 545; Joh. Peter, 517; Peter, 517
SCHROB, Cath., 484; Daniel, 484; Marg. Barbara, 484
SCHRODER, Frdr., 369; Jacob, 365
SCHROEDER, Cath., 503, 541; Christina, 413; Christina Juliana, 413; Dorothea, 463; Elis., 448; Jacob, 379, 413, 448, 463, 512, 530; Juliana, 379, 448, 463, 512, 530; Marg., 379, 541; Maria Cath., 480; Maria Magd., 480; Phil., 480; Philipp, 503, 541
SCHROETER, Daniel, 408
SCHROPLER, Christine, 553; Hnr., 553; Maria, 553
SCHRUB, Eva, 440; Hnr., 440
SCHRUBB, Elis., 439; Eva, 439; Hnr., 439
SCHRUBER, Hnr., 415; Marg., 415
SCHRUPP, Cath., 454; Eva, 454; Hnr., 454
SCHUB, Joh. Wilhelm, 528

SCHUBART, Christina, 291; Elis., 291, 365, 467; Jacob, 483; Joh. Frdr., 365; Mich., 441; Michael, 291, 365, 467; Sara, 467; Ursula, 483
SCHUBARTH, Elis., 340; Michael, 340
SCHUBBART, Elis., 332; Michael, 312
SCHUBBERT, Anna Marg., 303; Joh. Jacob, 303; Ursula, 303
SCHUBERT, Elis., 285, 397, 430, 524; Esther, 397; Jacob, 528, 537; Joh., 537; Joh. Georg, 430; Michael, 285, 397, 430, 524; Sarah, 528, 537
SCHUCH, Cath. Marg., 447; Marg., 329, 447; Mat., 329; Michael, 329, 447
SCHUHMANN, Anna Maria, 484; Frdr., 484; Wilhelm, 484
SCHUL, Juliana, 318
SCHULER, Jacob, 534; Mr., 553
SCHULL, Elis., 391; Elis. Marg., 391; Joh. Peter, 391
SCHULM, Joh., 385; Joh. Fugel., 385; Marg., 385
SCHULTZ, Anna Maria, 280; Cath., 280; Charlotte, 344; Christian, 344; Elis., 382; Eva Elis., 389; Hnr., 515; Joh. Philip, 280; Maria, 344; Molly, 515; Pastor, 288, 303
SCHUMACHER, Abraham, 302; Adam, 426; Agnes, 328, 367; Barbara, 283; Benjamin, 395; Cath., 328; Christina, 426; Elis., 302; Joh., 302, 313, 328, 367; Joh. Hnr., 367; Magdalena, 358; Marg., 424, 522; Maria Magdal., 539; Michael, 283, 313, 358, 395; Rosina, 395; Susanna, 283, 313, 358, 395, 411, 466, 494
SCHUMAN, Frdr., 547, 549; Joh. Georg, 547; Magdalene, 549; Maria, 547
SCHUMANN, Anna, 286; Anna Maria, 458, 515, 532; Elis., 441, 458, 479, 513; Frdr., 458, 515, 517, 532; Georg, 481; Joh., 441, 479, 513; Joh. Andreas, 513; Marg., 479; Maria, 441, 517
SCHUMMANN, Cath., 511
SCHUSLER, Anna Elis., 296; Cath., 296; Gottfried, 296
SCHUSSLER, Anna, 547; Cath., 547; Christina, 458; Elis., 458, 460; Georg, 547; Gottfried, 458, 460; Veronica, 547
SCHUSTER, Adam, 420, 421, 422, 442, 469, 471, 484, 512; Anna, 310; Anna Barbara, 469; Anna Dorothea, 471; Caspar, 366, 398, 420, 519; Christina Doroth., 512; Christina Dorothea, 421, 422; Christine Dorothea, 420, 469; David, 421; Doroth., 453; Dorothea, 422, 442; Joh., 359; Joh. Adam, 453; Joh. David, 512; Joh.

Martin, 361; Jonathan, 422; Lorentz, 453; Lorenz, 422, 484; Maria, 422, 453, 484; Maria Elis., 361; Maria Magdalena, 305, 442; Mercy, 422; Peter, 484; Regina, 366, 398, 420, 519
SCHUT, Joh., 376; Marg., 376
SCHUTE, Joh., 397; Marg., 397
SCHUTT, Joh., 464; Marg., 464
SCHUTTEHELM, Elis., 312; Peter, 312
SCHUTZ, Anna, 325; Barbara, 317, 364, 421, 436, 473, 512, 521; Cath., 339, 358, 360, 364, 409, 460, 491, 495; Charlotte, 491; Christian, 406, 541; Conrad, 523; Daniel, 406; Dorothea, 409; Elis., 358, 360, 541; Frdr., 421, 521; Georg, 358, 360, 491, 521; Joh., 278, 341, 397, 429, 492, 517, 526, 533; Joh. Georg, 460; Magdalena, 541; Marg., 397, 406, 429, 517, 526; Maria, 492, 512; Maria Barbara, 533; Maria Magd., 436; Maria Marg., 278, 341; Mat., 364, 409, 436, 512; Mathias, 473; Rosina, 335
SCHUTZE, Joh., 298; Marg., 298
SCHUTZMAN, Barb., 387
SCHWAAB, Dorothea Maria, 298; Joh., 348; Joh. Adam, 348; Joh. Jacob, 348; Lorenz, 512; Marg., 348, 512; Walther, 298
SCHWAB, Adam Walter, 317; Anna Marg., 317, 366; Anna Maria, 325, 341; Anna Martha, 397, 426; Cath., 428; Christina, 543; Christina Barbara, 426; Elis., 550; Jacob, 325, 341, 366, 388, 426, 428, 468, 550; Joh. Adam, 366, 397, 426; Joh. Walter, 317; Lorenz, 374, 390, 433, 444, 468, 476, 543; Marg., 374, 390, 428, 433, 444, 468, 476, 543, 550; Maria, 388, 390, 433; Michael, 476; Peter, 284; Philipp Jacob, 444
SCHWABACH, Cath., 416; Hnr., 416
SCHWABEL, Anna Marg., 352; Jacob, 342, 352; Maria Marg., 342
SCHWAGER, Adam, 496; Georg Adam, 496; Joh., 496; Maria Magdal., 496
SCHWALBACH, Cath., 348, 369, 397; Hnr., 348, 369, 397; Susanna Elis., 302
SCHWALBER, Hnr., 507; Maria Cath., 507
SCHWANFELDER, Daniel, 368
SCHWANSELER, Marg., 389
SCHWARTZ, Abigail, 527; Anna Cath., 283, 336, 474; Barbara, 462; Cath., 438; Christian, 531; Christina, 289; Frdr., 527; Georg, 462; Joh., 520; Joh. Georg, 289; Joh. Peter, 283; Marg., 336; Maria Elis., 283; Peter, 336, 438, 474; Philip, 289; Sarah, 520; Susanna, 520

SHIPPY, Ann, 294; Benjamina, 294;
Christina Maria, 400; Maria, 371;
William, 294, 400
SHLEIGMAN, Mary, 383; Mat., 383
SHMILY, Joh. Wilhelm, 287; Magdalena,
287
SHOVINS, Richard, 511; Rosina, 511;
Sarah, 511
SHRACK, John, 345; John Charles, 345;
Marg., 345
SHULLER, Hnr., 486
SHULTZ, An. Maria, 374; Hnr. Conrad,
374
SHULZE, Elis., 289; Emannuel, 289
SHUMACHER, David, 489; Michael,
489; Susanna, 489
SHUTZ, Adam, 468; Anna Maria, 468;
Christian, 468; Joh., 349, 423, 468;
Marg., 349, 423, 468; Maria, 468
SIEGFRIED, Cath., 449; Elis., 449, 537;
Joh., 537; Joseph, 449, 537
SILBER, Christina, 522; John, 522;
William, 522
SILVER, Joh., 500
SIMION, Anna Cath., 360; Cath., 360;
Joh., 360
SIMON, Anna Cath., 458, 498; Anna
Marg., 282, 314; Anna Rosina, 282;
Anna Sophia, 314; Barbara, 458;
Bernhard, 477; Christoph, 282, 314;
Elis., 458; Joh., 458, 498; Joh. Georg,
498; Marg., 477; Maria Elis., 289;
Patrick, 408; Widow, 419
SIMPSON, John, 423
SIMSON, John, 431
SINCK (see also ZINCK), Abraham, 495;
Cath., 459; Christian, 476; Hanna,
495; Marg., 476; Regina, 495;
Wilhelm, 495
SING, Carl, 428, 490; Elis., 281; George,
281; Marg., 428, 490; Maria, 281
SINK, Cath., 550; Jacob, 550
SINZEL, Jacob Ulrich, 337
SINZER, Marg., 513; Michael, 513
SITTEN, Isaia, 409
SKIMPF, Joh., 319
SLESSEL, Cath., 296; Joh., 296; Maria
Cath., 296
SLEW, Elis., 281; Georg, 281; Regina,
281; Richard, 281
SMEILY, Jacob, 343; Maria, 343;
William, 343
SMICK, Peter, 344
SMITH, Abigail, 299; Anna, 293;
Benjamin, 500; Elis., 500; Georg,
500; James, 484; Joseph, 299; Mary,
500; William, 293
SNAKE, Elis., 522; Georg, 522; Philipp,
522

SOEFERENTZ, Anna Cath., 280; Cath.,
280; Georg, 280
SOEFFERENS, Anna Cath., 334; Cath.,
334; Georg, 334; Mr., 320; Sarah Elis.,
320
SOHN, Jacob, 359
SOHNLEITER, Cath., 466; Joh. Georg,
466; Joh. Philipp, 466
SOHNLEITNER, Cath., 442; Elis., 454,
469; Georg, 442; Peter, 454, 469
SOHNLEUTNER, Cath., 405, 418; Elis.,
419; Georg, 405, 418, 419; Joh. Georg,
418; Maria, 405; Peter, 419
SOHNS, Cath., 462, 488, 527; Jacob, 462,
488, 527; Joh., 488
SOLENDER, Cath., 548; Jacob, 547, 548;
Peter, 547; Wilhelmine, 547
SOLLIGER, Anna Marg., 351; Jacob, 351
SOLOMO, Christina, 485; Joh., 485
SOMMER, Andr., 393, 433; Andreas, 303,
310, 328, 366; Anna, 303, 328, 366,
393, 433; Anna Barbara, 320, 342, 358,
396; Anna Cath., 368; Anna Marg.,
332; Anna Maria, 328; Barb., 453;
Barbara, 440, 471, 552; Bast. Martin,
455; Cath., 289, 291, 332, 340, 358,
364, 366, 368, 378, 396, 404, 412, 453,
471, 547; Daniel, 357; David, 512;
Elis., 315, 455; Ernst, 291; Eva, 284;
Eva Cath., 396; Georg, 320; Hanna,
310; Hnr., 289, 319, 332, 340, 358,
368, 378, 412, 453, 471, 547; Jacob,
552; Joh., 284, 307, 357; Joh. Georg,
294, 397; Joh. Hnr., 340, 412, 465;
Joh. Jacob, 425; Joh. Martin, 279, 283,
320, 323, 342, 396; Joh. Peter, 415;
John Daniel, 454; Marg., 283, 320,
324, 357, 397, 425, 465, 512;
Margreth, 294; Maria, 279, 289, 323,
357; Maria Cath., 319, 332; Maria
Elis., 357; Maria Eva, 279, 396; Maria
Marg., 332; Maria Reg., 419; Martin,
283, 357, 358, 396, 397, 425, 440, 453,
465, 471, 512, 552; Mat., 315, 332,
360, 381, 419, 440, 464; Peter, 291,
332, 364, 368, 378, 396, 404; Philip,
290, 340; Philipp, 307, 415, 455;
Rahel, 381, 440, 464; Regina, 360;
Salome, 290, 307, 340, 415; Sara, 393;
Sarah, 455
SOMMERS, Anna Barbara, 290; Martin,
290; Philip, 290
SONDERLIN, Christoph, 551; Maria, 551
SONES, Jacob, 450
SONLEITNER, Marg., 315, 391; Maria
Marg., 335; Sebast., 335; Sebastian,
315
SONLEUTNER, Elis., 376; Joh. Peter,
376; Peter, 376, 379

STANTON, Cath., 543; Elis., 432;
  Gemima, 501; Jemima, 432, 488, 543;
  Jemina, 449, 472; Joh., 472; Joh.
  Wilhelm, 472; Jonathan, 432, 449,
  488, 501, 503, 543; Mima, 503;
  Sahra, 449
STARCK, Joh., 347; Joh. Ludewig, 341;
  Ludew., 332; Ludewig, 320; Maria
  Marg., 341
STARK, Cath., 398; Joh., 398; Joh.
  Ludwig, 354; Maria Marg., 354;
  Philip, 398
STARKE, Anna Cath., 376; Cath., 433,
  503; Cath. Marg., 489; Elis., 503;
  Joh., 365, 433, 489, 503; John, 376;
  Marg., 489; Maria, 376
STARKEY, Cath., 458; Joh., 458
STARKY, Cath., 476; John, 476
STARTER, Dorothea, 312; Mat., 312
STARTZ, Dorothea, 373
STAT, Nicol., 364
STATEMAR, Barbara, 499; Christian,
  499; Juliana, 499; Susanna, 499
STATS, Dorothea, 347, 410; Mat., 347
STAUCH, Anna Marg., 280, 381;
  Christina, 339; Christoph, 459; Elis.,
  400; Euphrosina, 542; Eva Rosina,
  381; Georg, 446; Jacob, 374, 400,
  446, 459; Joh., 542; Johanna, 437;
  Joseph, 381, 412, 466, 542; Marg.,
  322, 339, 342, 361, 378, 381, 437;
  Michael, 280, 339, 342, 361, 374,
  378, 381, 437, 542; Peter, 280;
  Rosina, 400, 412, 446, 459, 542; Sara,
  374
STAUS, Anna Maria, 343; Balt., 380,
  405; Balth., 418; Balthas., 440;
  Balthasar, 374, 416, 452; Esther, 343,
  376, 412; Esther Dorothea, 412;
  Georg, 343, 412; Joh. Georg, 376;
  Maria, 374, 380, 405, 416, 418
STAUSS, Anna Cath., 498; Balthasar,
  311, 346; Ester, 319; Esther, 442,
  456, 498; Georg, 319, 442, 456, 498;
  Joh. Daniel, 442; Joseph, 319; Maria,
  346
STAUT, Anna Barbara, 278, 325, 525;
  Barbara, 475; Christina, 278; Joh.
  Peter, 278, 325; Marg., 292, 319;
  Peter, 475, 525; Wilhelm, 319
STEBBER, Anna Marg., 326; Hnr., 326
STECHER, Joh. Conrad, 355; Maria
  Felicia, 355
STEELMANN, Charlotta, 497; Jeremias,
  497; Marg., 497; Rosina, 497
STEER, Georg, 544; Marg., 544
STEEVER, Anna Marg., 364; Georg, 364
STEGNER, Elis., 377
STEHLER, Christina, 372; Georg, 372
STEHN, William, 296

STEIBY, Anna Maria, 547; Joh. Georg,
  547
STEIERWALD, Anna Doroth., 369
STEIGEL, Cath., 320; Joh., 320
STEIGER, Christina, 328; Conrad, 328
STEIMETZ, Magdal., 499
STEIN, Abigail, 527; Anna Maria, 460,
  533; Balthasar, 542, 543; Barbara, 530;
  Christina, 458, 494; Elis., 460; Eva,
  542, 543; Eva Cath., 542; Jacob, 533,
  553; Joh., 460, 494, 527; Joh. Georg,
  553; Marg., 322, 527; Maria, 494, 518,
  553; Philip, 322; Wilh., 458; Wilhelm,
  489, 494, 518
STEINBACH, Anna Christina, 352, 459;
  Barbara, 352; Cath., 352; Christina,
  384, 540; Dorothea, 459; Gabriel, 352,
  384, 459, 540; Joh., 540; Joh. Adam,
  352; Juliana, 384
STEINBACHER, Elis., 390; Joh. Gott.,
  390; Maria Cath., 390
STEINBECHER, Christina, 368; Joh.
  Gottlieb, 368
STEINBECK, Anna Marg., 325; Joh.
  Gotlieb, 325; Maria Cath., 325
STEINBOCK, Christina, 494; Gabr., 494;
  Nicol., 494
STEINER, Marg., 353; Mariana, 499;
  Melchior, 499; Mr., 478; Philip, 353
STEINERT, Anna Maria, 290; Elis., 290;
  Joh. Georg, 290; Widow, 449
STEINFALS, Anna Marg., 337; Joh.
  Georg, 337
STEINFORTH, Balthasar, 438; Elis., 438
STEINFURTH, Balthasar, 303; Cath., 303;
  Elis., 303
STEINHAUER, Adam, 543; Barbara, 340,
  356, 380, 420, 450, 543; Cath., 340;
  Elis., 356; Joh. Christian, 544; Joh.
  Wilhelm, 420; Mich., 380; Michael,
  340, 356, 420, 450, 543; Sara, 380
STEINMANN, Anna Marg., 439; Joh.
  Georg, 439
STEINMAYER, Cath., 497; Jacob, 497
STEINMEIER, Anna Barbara, 286; Anna
  Cath., 315; Cath., 343, 386, 432, 453;
  David, 343; Dorothea, 386; Elis., 315;
  Georg, 343; Jac., 432; Jacob, 315, 386,
  453; Joh. Caspar, 453; Sebastian, 286
STEINMETZ, Andreas, 279; Anna Maria,
  285; Barbara, 279, 342, 396, 428; Carl,
  482; Cath., 334, 354, 393, 434, 442,
  475, 520, 532; Daniel, 434; Dorothea,
  357; Elis., 354, 410; Georg, 520, 532;
  Hnr., 279, 342, 396; Jacob, 357, 520;
  Joh., 393, 431, 532; Joh. Conrad, 306;
  Joh. Peter, 334, 431; John, 354, 434;
  Magdalena, 356, 471; Marg., 307, 482;
  Maria, 334, 393, 431; Maria Elis., 354;
  Peter, 307

STRAUS, Balthasar, 354; Georg, 546; Jacob, 553; Joh., 553; Joh. Georg, 546; Marg., 553; Maria, 354; Regina, 546
STRAUSS, Balthasar, 298; Barbara, 530, 548; Maria, 298
STRECHLEGER, Gottfried, 400; Joh. Jacob, 400; Nancy, 400
STRECHT, Ann. Mar., 456
STRECKER, Anna Marg., 310; Georg, 310; Georg Caspar, 373; Joh. Michael, 359; Maria Marg., 359; Michael, 310
STRECKFUS, Judith, 477
STREHL, Maria, 389
STREIBY, Joh. Georg, 551; Mar. Dorothea, 551
STREICH, Elisabeth, 292
STREIN, Elis.Henrica, 284; Esther, 379, 408; Georg, 408; George, 379; Jacob, 379; Joh. Georg, 284; Joh. Jacob, 408; Peter, 379
STREK, Cath., 408
STRENGE, Cath. Elis., 294; Johannes, 294; John, 294
STREPER, An. Maria, 398; Anna Marg., 286; Dorothea, 395, 398; Georg, 286, 381, 395, 398
STRETCH, Mr., 349
STRETH, Isaac, 336
STRIBY, Dorothea, 404, 443; Georg, 404, 443
STRICKER, Ad., 381; Adam, 320; An. Marg., 377; Joh., 286; Marg., 286, 388, 401, 415, 463, 476, 488; Maria Marg., 446, 516; Michael, 286, 377, 388, 401, 415, 446, 463, 476, 488, 516; Rebecca Elis., 320
STRICKLER, Jacob, 301
STRIEBY, Adam, 503; Anna Maria, 503
STRIEPER, Anna Maria, 464; Georg, 464
STRIY, Georg, 308; Maria, 308
STROBELE, Caspar, 351; Cath., 351
STROEBEL, Caspar, 331; Cath., 331
STROHBANCK, Eleanor, 366
STROHBANK, Joh., 396; Maria, 396; Maria Magdalena, 396
STROHM, Eva, 306; Joh., 306
STRUB, Anna Maria, 402; Hnr., 437, 468; Joh., 298, 402; Rachel, 298; Regina, 402; Susanna, 437
STRUBBLE, Caspar, 544; Cath., 544
STRUBEL, Caspar, 449, 477, 511, 525; Cath., 391, 511, 525
STRUMBECK, Hnr., 428, 455; Jacob, 428, 455, 486; Maria, 428, 455, 486; Wilhelm, 486
STRUP, Joh., 336, 390, 406, 487; John, 288; Marg., 487; Rachel, 336; Rahel, 390; Regina, 406

STRUPEL, Caspar, 391
STRUPP, Anna Cath., 493; Elis., 342, 509; Joh., 455; Marg., 455
STUART, Elis., 448; Juliana, 448; Wilhelm, 448
STUBER, Anna, 440; Christian Frdr., 311; Elis., 311, 378, 440; Eva, 435; Frdr., 378, 440; Joh. Daniel, 435; Maria, 311
STUCKARD, Elis., 470; Joh., 470
STUCKHARDT, Elis., 342; Joh., 342
STUMLER, Cath., 461
STUMP, Georg, 350; Jacob, 350; Maria, 350
STUPP, Joh., 438
STURG, Dorothea, 303; Joh., 303
STURMFELS, Anna Marg., 289, 302, 467; Georg, 302, 428; Joh. Georg, 289, 452, 454, 467; Mar. Marg., 428; Marg., 452, 454
STURNSFELS, Anna Marg., 433; Georg, 433
STURTZ, Anna Maria, 458; Cath., 458; Elis., 463; Eva Cath., 318; Georg, 415, 454, 463; Hannah, 415; Ludwig, 318; Regina, 415; Sahra, 463; Sara, 454; Ursula, 458, 463, 493; Wilhelm, 415, 454, 458, 493
STUTZ, Cath., 387; Frdr., 387; Joh. Wilh., 362; Marg., 327; Ursula, 362
STUTZBACH, Christoph, 546
STUTZER, Carl Bernhard, 360; Christian, 315, 360; Christina, 315; Christine, 360; Susanna Regina, 315
STUTZMAN, Barbara, 368; Cath., 284; Christian, 284; Eva Elis., 284
STUZ, Cath., 327; Philip, 327
STUZEL, Cath., 402; Georg Jacob, 402
STUZER, Carolina Susanna, 415; Christian, 415; Christina, 415
SULGER, An. Marg., 380; Anna Marg., 475; Anna Maria, 475; Dorothea, 334, 364; Georg, 498; Gottfried, 390; Hanna, 498; Jacob, 334, 364, 380, 394, 451, 468; Joh. Martin, 468; Johanna, 390, 451, 468, 475; Johanna Maria, 451; Marg., 364, 394, 451, 468; Maria, 334; Steph., 390; Stephan, 451, 468, 475, 498
SULLIGER, An. Marg., 421; Anna Eleonora, 402; Jacob, 402, 437; Joh. Jacob, 421; Joh. Marg., 402; Joh. Stephan, 421, 437; Johanna, 421, 437; Marg., 402, 437; Stephan, 402, 437
SULLIVAN, Cath., 541; Joh., 434, 460; John, 541; Magdalena, 434; Marg., 541; Rebecca, 434, 460; Thomas, 420
SULTZEL, Barbara, 425; Jacob, 423; Jacob Ulrich, 425; Maria Barb., 423

THIEL (see also DIEL, DEAL), Jeremias, 525; Joh. Peter, 525; Maria Rosina, 525
THIELMAN, Cath., 321; Frdr., 321; Salomon, 321
THIMSEY, Dennys, 449; Rahel, 449; Salome, 449
THOMAS, Anna Elis., 343; Barbara, 329; Cath., 490; Elis., 317, 404; Jacob, 371; John, 329, 371; Mary, 371; Phil., 490; Philipp, 404; Rachel, 375; Richard, 375, 417; Salome, 490; Sara, 417; Sarah, 375; William Godfrey, 417
THOMSDUN, Magdalena, 413
THOMSON, Alexander, 306; Anna, 537; Cath. Elis., 467; Elis., 364, 467; Joh., 432, 467; John, 364; John Leithaus, 364; Marg., 432; Maria, 306; Mark, 383; Martha, 419; Mary, 296; Sarah, 383; William, 296
THORN, Cath., 426, 447; Christina, 447; Georg, 447; Louis, 426; William, 426
THUI, Anna Maria, 464; Elis., 448, 464; Frdr., 448, 464; Joh., 448
THURINGER, Widow, 483
THURMER, Cath., 488; Thomas, 488
THURNIS, Georg, 472; Joh. Jacob, 472; Maria Cath., 472
TIEFFENBACH, Anna Maria, 526; Christina Charlotta, 526; Christoph, 526
TIERK, Elis., 343; Joh., 343; Wendel, 343
TIERKOP, Anna Maria, 413; Joh. Andreas, 413; Joh. Hnr., 413
TIES, Elis., 342; Frdr., 298, 342; George, 298; Maria, 298, 342
TIESS, Cath., 488; Ludwig, 488; Peter, 488
TILE, Adam, 310; Cath., 310
TIMBROOK, Marg., 344; Peter, 344
TIRELOCK, John, 385
TIRNIS, Elis., 432; Georg, 432; Maria Cath., 432
TOBELBAUER, Cath., 444; Frdr., 444; Louis, 444
TOBLEBAUER, Cath., 507; Frdr., 507; Jacobus, 507
TOBYS, Hanna, 435; Thomas, 435; William, 435
TODD, Elis., 390; Joseph, 390
TOFFEIN, A. Magdalena, 546; Jacob, 546; Jacobi, 546
TOLLMAN, Anna Mary, 309; John Georg, 309
TOLLMANN, Anna Cath., 307, 351; Anna Marg., 307; Anna Maria, 531; Cath., 482; Joh. Georg, 531; Joh.

Mat., 351, 482, 531; Joh. Matthaeus, 307; Justina Maria, 351
TOLMANN, Cath., 323; Elis., 306; John, 306
TOLNECK, Barbara, 294; Christina, 344
TOPF, Anna Maria, 553; Mar. Barbara, 553; Zacharias, 553
TORBERG, Anna Rosina, 292; Niclaus, 292; Nicolaus, 292
TORTEL, Veronica, 370
TOSSKY, Christine, 552; Georg, 552
TOWER, Mary, 409; Peter, 409; Sarah, 409
TOWN, Sara, 409
TOY, Cath., 278, 316; John, 316; Peter, 316
TRAFINGER, Maria, 370
TRANGENSTEIN, Joh., 515; Magdalena, 515
TRANS, Anna Maria, 449
TRAPPEL, Elis., 458; Jacob, 458; Michael, 458
TRATHWEIN, Maria, 354; Sophia, 354; Wilhelm, 354
TRAUTMANN, Elis., 525
TRAUTWEIN, Anna Maria, 316; Joh. Wilhelm, 316; Maria, 540; Maria Marg., 316; Nancy, 540; Wilhelm, 540
TRAVELLER, Hnr., 451; Joh., 451; Marg., 451
TREICHEL, Elias Ludwig, 331; Maria Elis., 331
TREICKEL, Elias Ludewig, 312; Elis., 312
TREIDLE, Cath., 461; Jacob, 461; Peter, 461
TREITZ, Marg., 528; Peter, 528
TRESURE, Anna, 343; James, 344; Juliana, 344; Peter, 344
TREUER, Georg, 529; Peter, 323; Salome, 529
TREVELLER, Hnr., 485; Marg., 485
TREYER, Andreas, 553; Marg., 553
TRIESLER, Cath., 466; Michael, 466
TRION, Elis., 528, 552; Jacob, 528, 552; Maria, 528; Maria Elis., 552
TRISLER, Cath., 451; Michael, 451; Philipp, 451
TROCKENROD, Anna Christina, 323; Jacob, 323; Philip, 323
TROMBERG, Anna, 437; Anna Maria, 437; Joh., 437
TROST, Anna Maria, 301; Joh., 301; Rachel, 301
TROTTER, Benj., 401; Elis., 401; Mar. Elis., 401
TRUBY, Elis., 396; Elisha, 396, 421; Marg., 396, 421; Maria, 421
TRUCK, Mary, 395; Samuel, 395; Thomas, 395

TRUCKENMILLER, Joh. Peter, 425;
Mar. Cath., 425; Philipp, 425
TRUCKENMULLER, Anna, 473, 476,
498, 520; Anna Cath., 279; Carl, 311,
340, 473, 476, 498, 520; Carl Franz,
459; Cath., 459; Charlotta Elis., 311;
Charlotte, 520; Christina, 281; Elis.,
498; Henrietta, 520; Joh. Frdr., 281;
Joh. Philip, 279; John Ludwig, 321;
Joseph, 345; Mar. Cath., 429; Marg.
Cath., 279; Maria, 340; Maria Elis.,
281; Rachel, 321; Rahel, 345;
Susanna, 311, 340; Susanna
Charlotte, 476; Wilhelm Ludewig,
345; Wilhelm Ludwig, 321
TRUCKER, Cath., 389; Joh. Jacob, 389;
Philipp, 389
TRUMBECK, Elis., 519; Jacob, 519;
Maria, 519
TRUTLAND, Marg. Cath., 409
TUNKER, Georg, 548; Maria, 548
TURCK, Cath., 370; Joh. Gottfr., 370
TURK, Anna Elis., 363; Christian, 469;
Jacob, 469; Maria Magdal., 363;
Maria Rosina, 469; Wencesl., 363
TURNER, Georg, 316, 537; Joh., 316,
446; Mar. Marg., 412; Maria Cath.,
316; Maria Susanna, 537; Susanna,
384; William, 384
TURNIS, Conrad, 349; Georg, 279, 349,
381; Georg Philip, 279; Maria Cath.,
279, 381; Maria Christina, 349; Peter,
381
TURRINGTON, William, 409
TYDERL, Mary, 299
UBER (see also OBER), Adam, 426;
Anna, 288, 313, 325, 347, 389, 406,
420, 442, 453, 462, 512, 521; Anna
Barbara, 469; Anna Maria, 426;
Christine Doroth., 420; David, 313,
347, 389, 406, 420, 426, 442, 453,
521; Joh. Dav., 469; Joh. David, 325,
442; Joh. DAvid, 462; Joh. David,
512, 521; Joh. Frdr., 347; Lud., 288;
Ludwig, 325; Mar. Magdalena, 442;
Marg., 325, 362; Marg. Barbara, 288;
Maria, 426; Maria Magdal., 462;
Michael, 426, 442, 462
UHL, Anna Maria, 506; Christian, 429,
469, 506; Christiana, 423; Christiana
Cath., 506; Christina, 285, 469;
Christina Cath., 524; Elis., 429;
Isabella, 506; Joh., 285; Joh.
Christian, 506; Maria Elis., 452;
Reinhard, 285, 423, 524
UHLER, Andr., 414; Andreas, 357, 448,
484; Marg., 414; Marg. Barbara, 357;
Rahel, 448; Regina, 357, 414, 484;
Wilhelm, 448
ULMANN, Magdalena, 499

ULRICH, Adam, 436; An. Mar., 386;
Anna Cath., 291; Anna Maria, 331,
436; Cath., 279, 331, 358, 386, 409,
410, 436, 478, 523; ELis., 478; Ernst,
314; Eva, 291, 314, 345, 386; Frdr.,
279, 314, 331, 358, 410, 478, 523;
Jacob, 523; Joh., 386, 410; Joh. Frdr.,
291, 386, 409, 436; Joh. Nicolaus, 291;
John. Frdr., 291; Maria Madg., 358;
Maria Magdalena, 314; Nicolaus, 291,
314, 345, 358, 386; Valent., 395;
Valentin, 345
UMBACH, Elis., 477
UNANGST (see also OHNANGST), Cath.,
327, 394, 420; Cath. Marg., 313; Elis.,
327; Joh., 313, 327, 394, 420; Maria,
420
UNBEHEND, Ann. Mar., 466; Anna
Cath., 548; Anna Maria, 319, 364, 501;
Cath., 319, 364, 470; Jacob, 319, 364;
Joh., 319; Joh. Jacob, 418, 464; Maria,
418, 442, 464; Sophia, 429, 470, 501,
548; Valentin, 429, 460, 470, 501, 548;
Wilhelm, 464
UNDERWEG, Maria Marg., 511
UNFELT, George, 298
UNGAR, Christian, 509; Elis., 553; Georg,
509; Joh., 553; Maria, 335, 509;
Susanna, 553
UNGER, Anna Barbara, 335; Barbara,
403; Christian, 335, 469, 551; Elis.,
551; Marg., 379; Maria, 297, 469, 551
UNGERE, Anna Maria, 331; Georg, 331;
Joh., 331
UNGERER, Joh. Georg, 299; Maria, 299
UNSELT, Anna Marg., 332; Barbara, 283;
Georg, 332; Joh. Georg, 283
URICH, Anna Barbara, 294, 406; Hnr.,
406; Joh. Hnr., 294
URIE, Anna Barb., 433; Hnr., 433
URLEIN, Anna Maria, 413; Joh., 413
UXORER, Barbara, 534; Peter, 534
VALENTIN, Anna Cath., 485; Cath., 489;
Jacob, 489; Reinhard, 485; Rosina, 489
VAN, Anna ELis., 399
VAN LAHN, Jacob, 364; Johanna Maria,
364; Maria Marg., 364
VANDERSCHLEIS, Daniel, 486
VANOSTEN, Cath., 282
VANUPSTRAAT, Elis., 405; Eva Maria,
405
VARLEY, Elizabeth, 413; Marg., 413;
William, 413
VEGLER, Elis., 361
VEIH, Rosina, 360
VEIL, Joh. Just, 292; Joh. Ludwig, 292;
Maria Magdalena, 292
VEIT, Anna, 296; Anna Cath., 330; Elias,
331; Elis., 296; Jacob, 281, 296, 330;
Joh. Joseph, 305; Joh. Jost, 331, 370;

John Jost, 331; Maria Elis., 331;
  Maria Magd., 370; Maria Magdalena,
  305, 331
VEITS, Cath., 506; Joh., 506
VELDEBERGER, Joh., 440; Magdalene,
  440
VELDENBERGER, Joh., 411
VELTE, Antonius, 535; Christian, 551;
  Elis., 535, 546; Eva, 546; Gottfried,
  535; Hnr., 546; Maria, 551; Philip,
  546; Regina, 546
VELTENBERGER, Joh., 422;
  Magdalena, 422; Rudolph, 422 .
VERGLASS, Anna Maria, 440; Conrad,
  440; Hnr. Philipp, 440
VERNON, Philip Wilhelm, 316;
  Philippina, 316; Robert, 316
VETTER, Anna, 411; Barbara, 411;
  Cath., 306; Catharine, 306; Christian,
  484, 539; Georg, 306, 379, 411;
  George, 292; Hanna, 349, 379, 457;
  Hnr., 379; Joh., 292; Joh. Andreas,
  349; Joh. Georg, 349; Marg., 379;
  Maria, 292
VETTERER, Caspar, 422
VETTERLE, Joh., 440
VIAN, Christ., 495; Elis., 495
VIEHL, Cath., 511; Christina, 511; Jacob,
  511
VIETZ, Carl, 515
VINEMER, Hnr., 419
VISTER, Anna Maria, 331; Christoph
  Hnr., 331; Jacob, 331
VITZGERALD (see also FITZGERALD),
  John, 410
VOCKEROD, Elis., 350
VOCKINSON, Georg Michael, 514, 544;
  Joh. Georg, 544; Maria, 514, 544
VOELCKER, Anna, 509; Georg, 509;
  Hanna, 540; Hnr., 540; Joh. Ernst,
  540
VOELKER, Georg, 465; Karl Frdr., 361;
  Maria Magdalena, 361
VOGEL, Andreas, 440; Anna Maria, 530;
  Barbara, 349; Cath., 403, 419, 427,
  432, 441, 452, 467, 485, 486, 499,
  511, 527, 530, 542; Cath. Barb., 377;
  Cath. Barbara, 403; Charlotta, 538;
  Dorothea, 526; Elis., 374, 404, 414,
  425, 427, 440, 449, 453, 466, 486,
  499, 512, 529, 538; Elis. Barb., 349;
  Frdr., 349, 374, 377, 403, 404, 414,
  419, 427, 432, 441, 452, 467, 485,
  486, 511, 527, 538; Georg, 372, 374,
  414, 440, 449, 466, 499, 512, 526,
  529, 541; Georg Frdr., 530, 542; Joh.,
  313, 374; Joh. Frdr., 282, 356, 385,
  453; Joh. Georg, 357; Joh. Martin,
  377; Marg., 452; Maria Eva, 404;

Maria Marg., 414; Mary, 313; Sarah,
  485
VOLCK, Cath., 286; Josua, 286; Mat., 286
VOLCKRADT, Jacob, 494
VOLCKROTH, Barbara, 526; Philipp, 526
VOLK, Elis., 433; Joh., 433
VOLKEL, Hnr., 308; Magdalena, 308
VOLKER, Barbara, 385; Georg, 385
VOLKING, Mat., 394
VOLKROT, Barbara, 546; Elis., 546;
  Georg, 546; Joseph, 550
VOLMER, Casper, 549; Isaac, 549; Joh.,
  550; Joh. Philip, 548; Marg., 548;
  Maria, 549, 550
VONARNDT, Hnr. Leopold, 399
VONGUNDERADE, Professor, 505
VONHOLD, Conrad, 399; Elis., 399;
  Hanna, 399
VONZIEGESAR, Carl Frdr. Wilhelm, 505;
  Caroline, Henr.Mar.Sophia, 505;
  Wilhelm Carl, 505
VONZOBERN, David, 515; Hanna, 515;
  Henrica, 515; Molly, 515
VORBACH, Anna Marg., 348; Georg, 348
VORBAH, Anna Maria, 295; Benjamin,
  295; William, 295
VORSTER, Conrad, 407; Joh. Martin, 431
WAAL, Casper, 535; Elis., 535
WAALKER, Andreas, 534; Cath., 534;
  Maria, 534
WAASS, Elis., 462; Joh Georg, 462;
  Salome, 462
WACHLER, Anna Barbara, 475; Conrad,
  475; Maria, 475; Maria Rosina, 475
WACHTER, Cath., 300; Conrad, 513;
  Marg., 513; Maria, 513
WACK, Elis., 553; Joh., 553; Marg. Anna,
  444
WACKER, Andreas, 284; Cath., 284, 374;
  Elis. Rosina, 390; Hanna, 342; Joh.,
  374, 390
WACKERER, Charlotte, 409; Elis., 409;
  Joh., 409
WADE, Fr., 453
WAEGER, Hanna, 466, 532; Joh., 322,
  532; Marg., 322; Maria, 321; Peter,
  466; Philipp, 321, 466, 532; Sara, 322;
  Sarah, 532
WAESTER, Cath., 456; Joh., 456; Joh.
  Conrad, 456
WAG, Andreas, 473; Regina, 473
WAGENER, Cath., 467, 534; Conrad, 467;
  Elis., 544; Nicolaus, 550; Sara, 550;
  Susanne Louise, 550
WAGER, Anna Marg., 532; Georg, 495;
  Hanna, 495, 528, 532; Philipp, 495,
  528, 532
WAGERHORST, Hnr., 386
WAGNER, Adam, 356, 538, 545; Anna
  Cath., 335; Anna Magd., 429; Anna

Magdalena, 295, 313, 476; Anna
Magdalene, 547; Anna Maria, 442;
Balthasar, 287; Barbara, 313; Cath.,
307, 354, 356, 367, 430, 432, 492,
495, 538; Christina, 516; Conr., 492;
Conrad, 307; Dorothea, 280, 295;
Elis., 313, 367, 388, 399, 418, 447,
492, 495, 508, 516, 523, 545; Else
Cath., 344; Georg, 350; Grace, 399,
493; Hieronimus, 516; Hnr., 344; Jac.,
493; Jacob, 296, 313, 399, 411, 492,
516, 547; Joh., 290, 296, 303, 313,
340, 356, 367, 381, 418, 429, 447,
492, 508, 516, 523, 540; Joh. Adam,
430, 495; Joh. Frdr., 303; Joh. Hnr.,
290, 418; Joh. Nicol., 424, 476; Joh.
Nicolaus, 295, 329, 350, 381, 442,
471, 547; Joh. Philipp, 335; John,
354; Magdalen, 296; Magdalena, 329,
381, 399, 411, 424, 442, 471; Marg.,
303, 316, 493, 508; Maria, 290, 340,
399, 447; Maria Eva, 316; Martin,
316; Nicolaus, 296, 313, 399, 411;
Peter, 280, 287, 312, 316, 367, 388,
432, 453, 486; Rosina, 287, 316, 367,
388, 432, 453, 486; Salome, 424, 516;
Wilhelm, 471, 486, 538
WAHL, Anna Eva, 542; Caspar, 329,
343, 365, 416, 432, 443, 453, 465,
497; Cath., 329, 443; Elis., 318, 343,
365, 416, 432, 453, 465, 497; Frdr.,
527; Hnr., 527, 542; Joh. Caspar, 318;
Joh. Hnr., 485; Justina, 485, 527, 542;
Philipp, 485
WAHRLICH, Elis., 503, 536; Georg,
536; Jeremias, 503, 536; Marg., 503
WAKER, Barbara, 358; Cath., 358, 427;
Daniel, 438; Dorothea, 382, 425;
Elis., 358, 438; Georg, 358, 382, 425;
Joh., 358, 427; Maria, 427; Martin,
358
WALCK, Peggy, 438
WALCKER, Andreas, 522; Anna
Dorothea, 450; Anna Magd., 449;
Cath., 449; Christina, 451; Dorothea,
292, 493, 518; Georg, 450; George,
493; Joh., 449; Joh. Georg, 292;
Maria, 522
WALCMER, Doroth., 460
WALDERICK, Cath., 305
WALKER, Andreas, 356, 452, 501; Anna
Dorothea, 294, 328, 329, 338, 356,
418, 471; Anna Elis., 373; Anna
Marg., 371; Anna Maria, 343;
Anthonieta, 373; Barbara, 343; Cath.,
396; Dorothea, 303, 335, 344, 366,
371, 374, 534; Elis., 501; Frdr. Jacob,
341; Georg, 294, 303, 311, 328, 335,
338, 344, 356, 366, 371, 374, 418,
471; George, 329; Hanna, 396; Jacob,

371; Jane, 341; Joh. Georg, 287, 303;
Joh. Jacob, 303, 335; John, 396;
Joseph, 397; Marg., 397; Maria, 501;
Maria Dorothea, 311; Michael, 343;
Mrs., 301; Peter, 373; Philipp Jacob,
335; Sophia, 303, 335, 371
WALL, Hannah, 295; Marg., 372;
Midwife, 477
WALLACE, Elis., 504; James, 436, 504
WALLER, Jacob, 355
WALPREHT, Christoph, 303; Elis., 303;
Maria Cath., 303
WALS,·Christine, 420
WALTENBERG, Cath., 380; Joh. Dan.,
380
WALTER, Abraham, 377; Anna Maria,
528; Anna Rosina, 445, 465; Anna
Sophia, 429; Antoinette, 402;
Antonetta, 492; Antonette, 429; Barb.,
425; Barbara, 315, 360, 405, 462; Carl,
480; Cath., 315, 389, 452, 479, 539;
Christoph Joseph, 430; Dorothea, 488,
492; Elis., 360, 498; Elis. Cath., 484;
Frdr., 370, 430, 476, 517; Georg, 479,
517; Gertraut Elis., 513; Godfred, 295;
Gotfried, 377; Gottfried, 418; Hanna,
462, 480; Helena, 461, 498, 537; Isaac,
418; Jacob, 355, 389, 452, 461, 498,
526, 537; Jane, 295, 377; Jean, 418;
Joh., 528; Joh. Nicol., 364; Joh. Pet.,
492; Joh. Peter, 402, 492; Joh. Philipp,
304; Joseph, 476; Leonh., 492;
Leonhard, 446; Magdalena, 480;
Marg., 528; Maria, 461, 526; Maria
Magd., 402; Martha, 430, 517; Martin,
315, 360, 405, 462; Nicol., 379, 445;
Nicolaus, 341, 446, 465, 543; Patty,
476; Peter, 425, 427, 429, 517, 539;
Phil., 480; Philipp, 539; Philippina,
446, 492; Rosina, 354, 364, 379, 446,
543; Rosina Marg., 295; Wilhelm, 405
WALTERS, Abraham, 525; Eve Marg.,
525; Maria, 525
WALTHER, Anna Barbara, 293; Cath.,
293; Elis., 502; Frdr., 293; Helena,
502; Jacob, 502
WALTZ, Georg, 426; Maria, 426; Martin,
426
WANKAUF, Elis., 450; Hnr., 450
WANRIGHT, Cath., 511; Elis., 511;
Samuel, 511
WANS, Charles, 320; Georg, 320; John,
320; Sara, 320
WARD, Abraham, 514; Elis., 514; Isaac,
514; Joh., 514; John, 408; William,
514
WARDER, Christina, 510; Hieronimus,
510
WARDMANN, Michael, 481; Salome, 481
WARNECK, Albert, 538; Maria, 538

WARNER, Anna Magd., 372; Barbara, 297, 311; Cath. Maria, 353; Elis., 343, 388; Eva Maria, 403; Frdr., 319; Georg, 297, 311; Georg Leonard, 431; Hanna, 310; Hiskia, 310; Isaac, 396; Joh., 345; Joh. Georg, 372; Joh. Wilhelm, 297, 441; Joseph, 310, 431; Marg., 486; Maria, 319, 431; Mrs., 299; Nicolaus, 343; Peter, 377; Peter Jacob, 340; Phil., 372; Rahel, 345; . Veronica, 396; Wilhelm, 319, 345, 377, 403, 441, 486; Wilhelmina, 403, 486; Wilhelmine, 377, 441
WARTMAN, Joh., 426; Mich. Cath., 426; Sara, 426
WARTMANN, Michael, 465, 525; Sarah, 465, 525
WATENMEYER, Anna Mar., 299; Joh., 299; Maria Cath., 299
WATER, Barbara, 345; Daniel, 345; Elis., 345
WATSON, Elis., 338; Joseph, 327; Mary, 370, 407, 427; Moses, 427; Samuel, 370; Thomas, 338, 370, 407, 427; William, 338
WAXBY, Jacob, 284
WAY, Andreas, 329, 445; Cath., 330; Cath. Elis., 296; Christina, 296, 329; Elis., 445; Georg, 296, 329, 445; Georg Andreas, 329; George, 330; Regina, 445
WEALSCH, Maria Doroth., 321
WEBER, Adam, 434, 460, 541; Albert, 548; Albertus, 493; Albrecht, 514; An. Magd., 498; Andr., 458; Ann. Cath., 464; Anna, 370; Anna Barbara, 531; Anna Cath., 285, 378, 438; Anna Eva, 528; Anna Magd., 397; Anna Magdalena, 343; Bernh., 457, 493; Bernhard, 543; Cath., 302, 317, 345, 370, 378, 395, 408, 457, 493, 543; Cath. Elis., 329, 514; Christina, 292, 315, 437, 438, 458, 465, 489, 523; Conrad, 486, 551; David, 522; Elis., 280, 285, 289, 295, 299, 306, 312, 313, 319, 329, 344, 348, 356, 364, 365, 378, 383, 408, 438, 446, 464, 476, 482, 496, 506, 518, 528, 529; Eva, 458; Fanny, 490; Georg, 490, 529; Hanna, 451; Hnr., 319, 348; Jacob, 302, 319, 344, 364, 434, 543; Joh., 285, 292, 311, 312, 319, 353, 378, 424, 440, 451, 479, 490, 493, 506, 511, 514, 522, 528, 531, 541, 548; Joh. Adam, 463; Joh. Andreas, 501; Joh. Cath., 356; Joh. Jacob, 370, 464; Joh. Leon., 383; Joh. Leonard, 313; Joh. Leonh., 299; Joh. Leonhard, 329, 446; Joh. Leonhardt, 289; Joh. Ludw., 356; Joh. Michael, 299, 457;

Joh. Philip, 343; Joh. Wilhelm, 348; Joseph, 397; Magdalena, 434, 493, 514; Magdalene, 548; Marg., 292, 547, 551; Maria, 311, 316, 336, 353, 378, 412, 440, 451, 506, 511, 531, 541, 551; Maria Barbara, 501; Maria Cath., 306; Maria Elis., 289, 434, 496; Maria Magdalena, 479, 481; Martin, 493; Michael, 302, 316, 317, 383, 501; Nicol., 315, 374, 412, 438, 458, 489, 498; Nicolaus, 292, 400, 437, 465, 523, 551; Peter, 306, 343, 370, 397; Phoebe, 501; Regina, 484; Sara, 547; Sarah, 481; Sophia, 400; Veronica, 424, 451, 522; Wilh., 496; Wilhelm, 285, 295, 365, 378, 408, 438, 464, 482, 518, 529, 551; William, 280, 312, 476
WECKERLE, Cath., 485; Elis., 485; Frdr., 485; Georg, 485
WECKERLEY, Cath., 543; Elis., 439, 543; Emanuel Frdr., 543; Frdr., 439; Georg, 543; Maria Elis., 543
WEDDERSTEIN, Adam, 520; Joseph, 520; Sophia, 520
WEDELS, Cath., 298
WEDELSON, Cath., 321
WEGENER, Grace, 449; Jacob, 449
WEGER, Anna Mar., 390; Anna Marg., 446; Anna Maria, 390; Elis., 474; Hanna, 467, 521; Joh., 390, 418, 446, 474; Maria, 418; Phil., 446, 448, 521; Philip, 390, 418, 436; Philipp, 467; Sahra, 446; Sarah, 390, 418, 474
WEGERLEY, Georg, 459
WEGMANN, Christoph Frdr., 436, 457; Joh. Frdr., 482; Marg., 436, 457; Maria Magdalena, 436; Veronica, 482
WEGNER, Anna Cath., 305; Cath., 288; Joh. Philip, 305; Philip, 288
WEH, An. Marg., 375; Andr., 375; Andreas, 322, 349, 408; Cath., 305; Christina, 305; Elis., 305, 439; Georg, 305, 408; Opportuna, 333; Regina, 349, 375, 408; Wendel, 333
WEHN, Elis., 371
WEICHERT, Cath., 501; Georg, 501; Maria Cath., 501
WEICHHARD, Maria Barbara, 297; Nicolaus, 297; Susanna, 297
WEICHT, Anna Cath., 476
WEICKARD, Anna Maria, 503; Joh., 503; Mat., 503
WEICKERT, Anna Maria, 459; Dorothea, 459; Joh., 459
WEID, Cath., 296, 398; Charlotte, 517; Elis., 366; Eva, 425; Eva Marg., 366; Leonharad, 366; Leonhard, 425
WEIDBRECHT, William, 289

WHELER, Maria, 551; Wilhelm, 551
WHIG, Georg, 497; Maria, 497; Thomas, 497
WHIT, Gertr., 394; Leonard, 295; Susanna, 295
WHITAKER, Benjamin, 409; Elis., 409; Jacob Benjam., 370; John, 370, 384; Maria, 370, 384; Thomas, 409
WHITBACH, Anna, 419; Caspar, 419; Joh. Frdr., 419
WHITE, Anna Cath., 418; Peter, 515; Susanna, 515; Widow, 377
WHITEBREAD, Sara, 336
WHITEMANN, Elis., 515; Jacob, 515; Joh., 508; Marg., 508; Peter, 515
WHITVOGEL, Anna, 398; Joh. Christian, 398; Joh. Frdr., 398
WICKMANN, Adam, 322; Cath., 322
WIDDERSTEIN, Adam, 389, 390, 458, 489; Ann Elis., 389; Joh. Georg, 489; Johanna, 389; John, 389; Sophia, 389, 458, 489; Sophia Charlotte, 389, 390; Wilhelm, 458
WIDDERSTIN, Adam, 367; Sophia Charlotte, 367
WIEBECK, Christian, 427; Christina, 427
WIEG, Christian, 463; Elis., 463
WIEGAND, Peter, 304
WIEHAL, Daniel, 384; Johanna, 384; Maria Esther, 384
WIEKING, Marg., 358; William, 358
WIELAND, Elis. Barbara, 349; Joh. Mart., 377; Joh. Martin, 349
WIELER, Elis., 372; Georg, 372; Thomas, 372
WIEN, Eva, 290; Michael, 290
WILCOCKS, Cath., 363
WILD, Anna, 351; Caspar, 351; Frdr., 351
WILDBERGER, Anna Cath., 287, 356; Anna Dorothea, 356; Joh. Georg, 287; Juliana, 337; Peter, 287, 337, 356
WILDFANG, Joh., 537
WILDHAM, Ann, 371; Jane, 371; Joseph, 371
WILEY, Abigail, 346
WILHELM, Dorothea, 319; Joh. Adam, 319; Marg., 319
WILIKENS, Cath., 286; Jacob, 286; Joh., 286
WILK, Anna Maria, 319
WILKE, Christian, 411, 437, 466, 500; Elis., 411; Jacob, 466; Marg., 500; Rosina, 411, 437, 466, 500
WILKENS, Joh., 523
WILKES, John, 362
WILKINS, Marg., 408; Thomas, 372
WILKINSON, Christian, 489; Rosina, 489
WILKSON, Anna Maria, 339

WILL, Anna, 520; August, 498; Bernhard, 535; Doroth. Marg., 387; Dorothea Marg., 354; Elis., 292, 316, 354, 387, 469, 480, 491, 500, 529, 546, 547; Georg, 547; Marg., 292, 546; Maria, 535; Maria Regina, 316; Martin, 491, 500, 546; Nanette Elis., 498; Valentin, 491; Wilhelm, 292, 316, 354, 469, 480, 520, 529, 547; William, 387
WILLER, Elis., 451; Maria Magdalena, 348; Wilh., 451
WILLERICH, Elis., 320; Peter, 320
WILLIAM, Dorothea, 292; John, 292; Magdalena, 292
WILLIAMS, Anna Nancy, 400; Elis., 279; Hanna, 337; James, 279; John, 414; Marg., 414; Thomas, 337; William, 337
WILLIS, Christina, 342, 364, 396; Diana, 398; Joh., 364, 396, 398; John, 342, 396, 398; Maria, 364; Samuel, 342
WILLMAN, Elis., 409
WILPERT, Anna Barbara, 553; Christoph, 335, 388, 518, 553; Elis., 388; Geo., 345; Georg, 487; Joh. Frdr., 534; Marg., 345, 388, 487, 518, 534, 553; Maria, 518
WILSON, Cath., 488; Hanna, 488; Hetty, 436; Jane, 289; John, 488; Maria Cath., 329; Robert, 329; Ruth, 289; Ruttz, 289; Sara, 329
WILT, An. Marg., 384; Anna, 384, 466; Anna Elis., 339; Elis., 339, 384; Frdr., 339, 384, 466; Maria, 384
WIMLY, Frdr., 551; Joh., 551; Maria Magdalene, 551
WINCKLER, Cath. Magdal., 518; Frdr., 518; Ludwig, 538
WINDFIELD, Georg, 324; Rosina, 324
WINEMOR, Andreas, 511; Anna Rosina, 511
WINEY, Jacob, 419; Sus. Marg., 419
WINGARTNER, Anna Barbara, 473
WINKL, Marg., 325
WINKLER, Ludwig, 433, 546; Marg., 433, 546
WINLY, Ann, 409; Marg., 409; Samuel, 409
WINN, Elis., 332; Joseph, 332
WINRIGHT, Cath., 536; Samuel, 536; Wilhelm, 536
WINTER, Christian, 532; Conrad, 532; Maria, 532
WIRE, Elis., 527; Joh., 527; William, 527
WIRSCHON, A. Maria, 551; Casper, 551; Joh., 551
WIRSCHUM, Caspar, 286, 315, 338; Eva Maria, 286; Joh., 315; Rosina, 286, 315, 338; Sophia Susanna, 338

WORTMAN, Abraham, 533; Michael, 533; Sara, 533
WOTZER, Cath., 347; Martin, 347
WRIGHT, Cath., 340, 450, 479; Elis., 311, 479; Elis. Wilhelmina, 450; Jacob, 340; Joh., 479; John, 450; Joseph, 340
WUCHER, Elis., 456; Joh., 456
WUCHERER, Anna Maria, 495; Elis., 426, 495, 539; Esther, 539; Georg, 426; Joh., 385, 426, 495, 539
WUCKERER, Joh., 356
WUDELING, Anna Clara, 385; Joh., 385; Joh. Jac., 385
WULF, Fransciscus, 304; Marg., 304
WULLE, An. Barb., 422; Sebastian, 422, 439, 452
WULLY, Bastian, 376; Elis. Cath., 376; ELis. Cath., 478; Elis. Cath., 503
WULMANN, Maria, 546
WUNDERLICH, An. Maria, 382; Cath., 298, 318, 333, 382; Elis., 508, 545; Eva Cath., 318; Georg, 298, 318, 333, 382; Jacob, 542; Joh., 508; Michael, 298; Sophia, 542; Wilhelm, 508, 542, 545
WURM, Maria, 394; Philip, 394
WURSCHUM, Caspar, 361; Christine, 361; Rosina, 361
WURSCHUN, Caspar, 418; Regina, 418; Rosina, 418
WUSTER, Cath., 335; Georg, 283, 315, 335; Joh., 315; Joh. Peter, 283; Juliana, 283, 315, 335
WYARD, Elis., 340; John Sanders, 340; Sara Elis., 340; William, 340
WYART, Elis., 480; Marg., 480; Molly, 480; Wilhelm, 480; William, 480
WYET, Elis., 369; Martha, 369; William, 369
XERTER, Cath., 338; Elis., 338; Joh., 338
YAUST, David, 371; Lorenz, 371; Thomas, 371; Ursula, 371
YAYSER, Elis., 444, 463; Frdr., 463; Joh., 444; John, 463; Magdalena, 444; Susanna, 463
YECHTER, Dorothea, 539; Joh., 539; Maria Magdalena, 539
YEHIC, Leah, 445; Samuel, 445
YEHN, Elis. Magdalena, 462
YERGER, Anna Maria, 478; Georg, 478; Joh., 478
YESCH, Cath., 450, 502, 529; Elis., 529; Frdr., 450, 502, 529; Joh., 502
YESSERO, Elis., 516; Esther, 516; Georg, 516
YESSRAMM, Anna, 478; Georg, 478; Joh. Georg, 478

YETTER, Joh., 457; Maria, 457; Samuel, 457
YETZ, Barbara, 458; Michael, 458
YOUNG, Christopher, 343; Elis., 515; Jacob, 515; Marg., 343
ZANSINGER, Adam, 344; Joh. Hnr., 344; Susanna, 344
ZANTZINGER, Adam, 450, 475, 507, 528; Sarah, 507; Susanna, 450, 475, 507
ZANZINGER, Adam, 365, 381, 425; Cath., 365; Elis., 425; Maria, 381; Susanna, 365, 381, 425; Susanne, 418
ZEISIGER, Anna Cath., 397; Anna Maria, 397; Georg, 397
ZEISINGER, Anna Maria, 367; Daniel, 367; Joh. Georg, 367
ZEISSINGER, Anna Maria, 485; Joh. Georg, 328, 485; Marg., 328; Maria Marg., 328
ZEITZ, Georg, 536
ZELLER, Anna Marg., 521; Phil., 521
ZENDLER, Cath., 282; Clara Maria, 282; Georg Peter, 282
ZENSFELDER (see also SENSFELDER), Jacobine, 365; Joh., 365; Maria, 365
ZENT, Barbara, 487, 502; Frdr., 487, 502
ZEP, Maria Marg., 366; Philipp, 366
ZEPF, Cath., 487; Michael, 487
ZEPP, Marg., 435; Phil., 435
ZERTER, Cath., 338; Elis., 338; Joh., 338
ZESSINGER, Georg, 362
ZETT, Anna Maria, 349; Salome, 349
ZETTER, Barbara, 421; Philipp, 421
ZIEGLER, Christoph, 382, 423; David, 486; Elis., 382; Mat., 423; Susanna, 382, 423
ZIEPOLD, Maria Barbara, 539; Martin Sigismund, 539
ZIMMER, Maria Elis., 288
ZIMMERMAN, Cath., 380, 388; Christoph, 388; Elis., 480; Mar. Elis., 388
ZIMMERMANN, Anna Marg., 407; Anna Susanna, 367; Cath., 320, 359, 363; Catha., 293; Christoph, 293, 320, 346, 363; Elis., 474; Georg, 346, 359, 407; Joh. Georg, 407; Joh. Hnr., 293; Joh. Jacob, 363; Mar., 380; Marg., 474; Marg. Cath., 346; Maria Magdalena, 320
ZINCK (see also SINCK), Anna Dorothea, 290, 299; Cath., 290, 299, 328, 348, 404; Christina Barbara, 339; Christoph, 287, 303, 350; Dorothea, 339; Elis., 287; Georg, 362; Gottlieb, 348, 404; Jacob, 290, 299; Joh. Andreas, 350; Joh. Georg, 290, 299, 339; Johanna, 362; Magdalena, 287, 350; Marg., 362; Maria Magdalena, 303

Colonial Families of New Jersey, Volume 1: Middlesex and Somerset Counties

Colonial Families of Northern Neck, Virginia, Volume 1 and Volume 2
Holly G. Wright and F. Edward Wright

Colonial Families of the Eastern Shore of Maryland: Volumes 1 and 2
Robert W. Barnes and F. Edward Wright

Colonial Families of the Eastern Shore of Maryland: Volume 4
Christos Christou and F. Edward Wright

*Colonial Families of the Eastern Shore of Maryland:
Volumes 5, 6, 7, 8, 9, 11, 12, 13, 14, 16, and 19*
Henry C. Peden, Jr. and F. Edward Wright

Colonial Families of the Eastern Shore of Maryland: Volumes 15 and 17
Ralph A. Riggin and F. Edward Wright

Colonial Families of the Eastern Shore of Maryland: Volumes 10, 18, 20, and 22
Vernon L. Skinner, Jr. and F. Edward Wright

Colonial Families of the United States of America, Volume II
Holly G. Wright and F. Edward Wright

Cumberland County, Pennsylvania, Church Records of the 18th Century

Delaware Newspaper Abstracts, Volume 1: 1786–1795

Early Charles County, Maryland, Settlers, 1658–1745
Marlene Strawser Bates, F. Edward Wright

Early Church Records of Alexandria City and Fairfax County, Virginia
F. Edward Wright and Wesley E. Pippenger

Early Church Records of Bergen County, New Jersey, 1740–1800

Early Church Records of Dauphin County, Pennsylvania

Early Church Records of Lebanon County, Pennsylvania

Early Church Records of New Castle County, Delaware, Volume 1: 1701–1800

Early Church Records of Rockingham County, Virginia

Early Lists of Frederick County, Maryland, 1765–1775

Early Records of the First Reformed Church of Philadelphia, Volume 1, 1748–1780

Early Records of the First Reformed Church of Philadelphia, Volume 2, 1781–1800

Frederick County, Maryland, Militia in the War of 1812
Sallie A. Mallick and F. Edward Wright

Henrico County, Virginia, Marriage References and Family Relationships, 1654–1800

Inhabitants of Baltimore County, Maryland, 1692–1763

Judgment Records of Dorchester, Queen Anne's, and Talbot Counties [Maryland]

Kent County, Delaware, Marriage References and Family Relationships

*King George County, Virginia, Marriage References
and Family Relationships, 1721–1800*
Anne M. Watring and F. Edward Wright

Lancaster County Church Records of the 18th Century, Volumes 1–4

Lancaster County, Pennsylvania, Church Records of the 18th Century, Volume 1
F. Edward Wright and Robert L. Hess

Lancaster County, Pennsylvania, Church Records of the 18th Century, Volume 3

Lancaster County, Pennsylvania, Church Records of the 18th Century, Volume 5
Lancaster County, Pennsylvania, Church Records of the 18th Century: Volume 6
Robert L. Hess and F. Edward Wright

Lancaster County, Virginia, Marriage References
and Family Relationships, 1650–1800

Land Records of Sussex County, Delaware, 1769–1782

Land Records of Sussex County, Delaware, 1782–1789: Deed Book N No. 13
Elaine Hastings Mason and F. Edward Wright

Marriage Licenses of Washington, District of Columbia, 1811–1830

Marriage References and Family Relationships of Charles City,
Prince George, and Dinwiddie Counties, Virginia, 1634–1800

Marriages and Deaths from Eastern Shore Newspapers, 1790–1835

Marriages and Deaths from the Newspapers of Allegany
and Washington Counties, Maryland, 1820–1830

Marriages and Deaths from the York Recorder, *1821–1830*

Marriages and Deaths in the Newspapers of Frederick
and Montgomery Counties, Maryland, 1820–1830

Marriages and Deaths in the Newspapers of
Lancaster County, Pennsylvania, 1821–1830

Marriages and Deaths in the Newspapers of
Lancaster County, Pennsylvania, 1831–1840

Marriages and Deaths of Cumberland County, [Pennsylvania], 1821–1830

Marriages, Births, Deaths and Removals of New Castle County, Delaware

Maryland Calendar of Wills:
Volume 9: 1744–1749; Volume 10: 1748–1753; Volume 11: 1753–1760;
Volume 12: 1759–1764; Volume 13: 1764–1767; Volume 14: 1767–1772;
Volume 15: 1772–1774; and Volume 16: 1774–1777

Maryland Eastern Shore Newspaper Abstracts
Volume 1: 1790–1805; Volume 2: 1806–1812;
Volume 3: 1813–1818; Volume 4: 1819–1824;
Volume 5: Northern Counties, 1825–1829
F. Edward Wright and Irma Harper;
Volume 6: Southern Counties, 1825–1829;
Volume 7: Northern Counties, 1830–1834
Irma Harper and F. Edward Wright;
Volume 8: Southern Counties, 1830–1834

Maryland Eastern Shore Vital Records:
Book 1: 1648–1725, Second Edition; Book 2: 1726–1750; Book 3: 1751–1775;
Book 4: 1776–1800; and Book 5: 1801–1825

Maryland Militia in the War of 1812:
Volume 1: Eastern Shore; Volume 2: Baltimore City and County;
Volume 3: Cecil and Harford Counties; Volume 4: Anne Arundel and Calvert Counties;
Volume 5: St. Mary's and Charles Counties; Volume 6: Prince George's County;
and Volume 7: Montgomery County

Maryland Militia in the Revolutionary War
S. Eugene Clements and F. Edward Wright